Knowledge
Base

—

THE UNITED NATIONS WORLD WATER
DEVELOPMENT REPORT 4
VOLUME 2

Published in 2012 by the United Nations Educational,
Scientific and Cultural Organization
7, place de Fontenoy, 75352 Paris 07 SP, France

ISBN 978-92-3-104235-5
e-book ISBN 978-92-3-001045-4

Original title: The United Nations World Water Development
Report 4: *Managing Water under Uncertainty and Risk* (Vol. 1),
Knowledge Base (Vol. 2) and *Facing the Challenges* (Vol. 3).

Published in 2012 by the United Nations Educational,
Scientific and Cultural Organization

UNESCO Publishing: http://publishing.unesco.org/

Suggested citation:
WWAP (World Water Assessment Programme). 2012. *The United
Nations World Water Development Report 4: Managing Water under
Uncertainty and Risk*. Paris, UNESCO.

Cover and interior design and typesetting by Phoenix Design Aid
A/S, an ISO 14001 (environmental management) and a DS 49001
(corporate social responsibility) certified and approved carbon
neutral company.

Printed by Imprimerie Centrale S. A. (Imprim'Vert certified) for
UNESCO CLD, Paris.

This publication is printed with vegetable inks on FSC Mixed Sources
paper, supporting responsible use of forest reserves. This is a carbon
neutral print product. Imprimerie Centrale will contribute funds to a
project replanting trees in Panama for this publication.

Printed in Luxembourg

WWDR4 has been published on behalf of the United Nations World
Water Assessment Programme (WWAP) with the support of the
following organizations:

United Nations Funds and Programmes
United Nations Children's Fund (UNICEF)
United Nations Conference on Trade and Development (UNCTAD)
United Nations Department of Economic and Social Affairs
  (UNDESA)
United Nations Development Programme (UNDP)
United Nations Environment Programme (UNEP)
United Nations High Commissioner for Refugees (UNHCR)
United Nations Human Settlements Programme (UN-HABITAT)
United Nations University (UNU)

Specialized UN Agencies
Food and Agriculture Organization of the United Nations (FAO)
International Atomic Energy Agency (IAEA)
International Bank for Reconstruction and Development
  (World Bank)
International Fund for Agricultural Development (IFAD)
International Labour Organization (ILO)
United Nations Educational, Scientific and Cultural Organization
  (UNESCO)
United Nations Industrial Development Organization (UNIDO)
United Nations Institute for Training and Research (UNITAR)
World Health Organization (WHO)
World Meteorological Organization (WMO)
World Tourism Organization (UNWTO)

United Nations Regional Commissions
Economic and Social Commission for Asia and the Pacific
  (UNESCAP)
Economic and Social Commission for Western Asia (UNESCWA)
Economic Commission for Africa (UNECA)
Economic Commission for Europe (UNECE)
Economic Commission for Latin America and the Caribbean
  (UNECLAC)

Secretariats of United Nations Conventions and Decades
Secretariat of the Convention to Combat Desertification (UNCCD)
Secretariat of the Convention on Biological Diversity (CBD)
Secretariat of the International Strategy for Disaster Reduction
  (UNISDR)
United Nations Climate Change Secretariat (UNFCCC)

TABLE OF CONTENTS

REGIONAL REPORTS

SPECIAL REPORTS

CHAPTER 15
State of the resource: Quantity

UNESCO-IHP
—

Authors Balaji Rajagopalan and Casey Brown
Contributors Anil Mishra (Coordinator), Siegfried Demuth (Coordinator), Edith Zagona, Jose Salas, Ashish Sharma, Upmanu Lall and Austin Polebitski

||||||||||||||||||||||||||||||||||||||||||||||||||||||||||||||||||||||||||||||||||||||||||||||||||||||||||||||||||||||||||||||||||||||||||

What is the current state of the world's freshwater resources? What are the most important external drivers and their resulting pressures and impacts on these resources as well as their use and management? This chapter tries to answer these questions. It begins by describing the main issues facing the state of the resource and how these have been changing over recent years. The chapter then outlines the related principal risks, challenges, uncertainties and opportunities. Finally, geographic hotspots of particular concern are identified and examples of how some countries are dealing with the issues and challenges are provided.

15.1 Drivers of variability

15.1.1 The hydrological cycle
It is well known that a mere 2.5% of global water resources is potentially available for human, animal and plant consumption; the remaining 97.5% resides in the oceans. Adding to this limitation is the fact that freshwater is highly uneven in its spatial distribution; thus, it is not uncommon that regions habitable for human settlement find themselves with insufficient freshwater. The movement of freshwater among terrestrial parts of the earth, the oceans and the cryosphere is known as the hydrological cycle, the water cycle or the H_2O cycle.

Evaporation and evapotranspiration account for 30–70% of the losses to temperature in arid climates and groundwater recharge is about 1–30% for these regions (e.g. see table 4.1 in WWAP, 2006). A large part of the world's population lives in semi-arid and arid climates that have about 30% of precipitation available for ready use. The increase in temperature due to global warming will reduce the amount of water available for ready use in the future, and increasing temperatures will also reduce groundwater recharge, further exacerbating the water availability challenge.

Table 15.1 shows the total precipitation and renewable water available for the population in different ecosystems and regions of the world. The world's population has substantially increased while global precipitation has remained largely constant. Precipitation may be significantly reduced in the future in semi-arid and arid regions, which tend to be among the most vulnerable and poorest in the world, due to anthropogenic climate change (IPCC, 2007). Thus, a smaller fraction of global freshwater will have to satisfy an increasing population, as can be seen in Figure 15.1.

Understanding the movement of water and the spatial and temporal variability of water availability are the most important aspects of water resources that need to be understood and incorporated in planning and management for resource sustainability. Large-scale climate forcings (i.e. drivers) orchestrate the spatial and temporal movement of water. The seasonal variation of available water resources is driven by the earth's tilt and its revolution about the sun. This results in wet and dry seasons in the tropics due to the annual movement of the Intertropical Convergence Zone (ITCZ). In the tropics, annual total rainfall may be large but intra-annual variation is also large, posing a challenge to water resources management and economic

development (Brown and Lall, 2006). At high latitudes precipitation is more equally distributed, but streamflow may be influenced by the accumulation and melting of snowpack.

15.1.2 El Niño-Southern Oscillation and other oceanic oscillations
The El Niño-Southern Oscillation (ENSO), a coupled ocean-atmospheric phenomenon in the tropical Pacific Ocean, is the dominant driver of global climate at seasonal to interannual time scales. The state of the tropical Pacific triggers 'teleconnection' responses in other parts of the world – especially in Latin America, South and South-East Asia, and Africa.

The Pacific Decadal Oscillation (PDO), the North Atlantic Oscillation (NAO) and the Atlantic Multidecadal Oscillation (AMO) are drivers that operate at longer time scales (interdecadal to century); they are not robust phenomena that can easily be identified, observed and predicted like ENSO. These phenomena impact regional climates in the mid-latitudes, mainly in North America and Europe. Research in understanding these drivers and their teleconnections to regional climate and hydrology is nevertheless emerging.

All of these oscillations are drivers that impact the variability of moisture delivery in space and time around the world. Understanding and diagnosing their teleconnections to regional hydrology is a potentially powerful tool for water resources prediction and simulation, and consequently, for adaptation to climate variability and change.

15.2 Stressors on water resources
The state of water resources is constantly changing as a result of the natural variability of the earth's climate system, and the anthropogenic alteration of that climate system and the land surface through which the hydrological cycle is modulated. The state of water resources is also influenced by human activities that affect demand, such as population growth, economic development and dietary changes, as well as by the need to control the resources, such as is required for settlement in flood plains and drought-prone regions.

15.2.1 Water supply
The greatest stress on water supply comes from the variability of moisture delivery to a river basin, which predominantly reflects variability in climate – a

powerful stress on water supply around the world. The consequence of this stress is amplified by socio-economic growth, management policies, land cover and land use changes. The state of water resources is in constant change, the effects of which can be only partially anticipated. Some changes that we can anticipate are described below.

Decrease in mean flow

There is increasing evidence of substantial streamflow reduction in a number of river basins around the world in the coming decades due to global warming. While some regions, such as those in higher latitudes, could see increases in moisture and streamflow, unfortunately, in much of the populated regions of the world there is projected to be a reduction in flow (IPCC, 2007).

Increase in flood potential

The implications of climate change include acceleration of the water cycle, which could lead to an increase in the probability of heavy rainfall and consequently the flooding potential. Extreme rainfall events produce enormous volumes of water that cause loss of life and damage to property. Furthermore, without significant

TABLE 15.1

Estimates of renewable water supply, the renewable supply accessible to humans, and the population served by the renewable supply in different ecosystems and regions

System[a] or region	Area	Total precipitation (P_1)	Total renewable water supply, blue water flows (B_1)	Renewable water supply, blue water flows, accessible to humans[b] (B_2)	Population served by renewable resource[c]
Millennium Ecosystem Assessment (MA) System	(million km²)		(thousand km³ per year) [% of global runoff]	[% of B_1]	(billion) [% of world population]
Forests	41.6	49.7	22.4 [57]	16.0 [71]	4.62 [76]
Mountains	32.9	25.0	11.0 [28]	8.6 [78]	3.95 [65]
Drylands	61.6	24.7	3.2 [8]	2.8 [88]	1.90 [31]
Cultivated[d]	22.1	20.9	6.3 [16]	6.1 [97]	4.83 [80]
Islands	8.6	12.2	5.9 [15]	5.2 [87]	0.79 [13]
Coastal	7.4	8.4	3.3 [8]	3.0 [91]	1.53 [25]
Inland water	9.7	8.5	3.8 [10]	2.7 [71]	3.98 [66]
Polar	9.3	3.6	1.8 [5]	0.3 [17]	0.01 [0.2]
Urban	0.3	0.22	0.062 [0.2]	0.062 [100]	4.30 [71]
Region					
Asia	20.9	21.6	9.8 [25]	9.3 [95]	2.56 [42]
Former Soviet Union	21.9	9.2	4.0 [10]	1.8 [45]	0.27 [4]
Latin America	20.7	30.6	13.2 [33]	8.7 [66]	0.43 [7]
North Africa/ Middle East	11.8	1.8	0.25 [1]	0.24 [96]	0.22 [4]
Sub-Saharan Africa	24.3	19.9	4.4 [11]	4.1 [93]	0.57 [9]
OECD	33.8	22.4	8.1 [20]	5.6 [69]	0.87 [14]
World Total	**133**	**106**	**39.6 [100]**	**29.7 [75]**	**4.92 [81]**

a Note: double-counting for ecosystems under the MA definitions.
b Potentially available supply without downstream loss.
c Population from Vörösmarty et al. (2000).
d For cultivated systems, estimates are based on cropland extent from Ramankutty and Foley (1999) within this MA reporting unit.
Source: Hassan et al. (2005, table 7.2, p. 173). © Millennium Ecosystem Assessment. Reproduced by permission of Island Press, Washington DC.

FIGURE 15.1

Cumulative distribution of the population with respect to freshwater services, 1995–2000

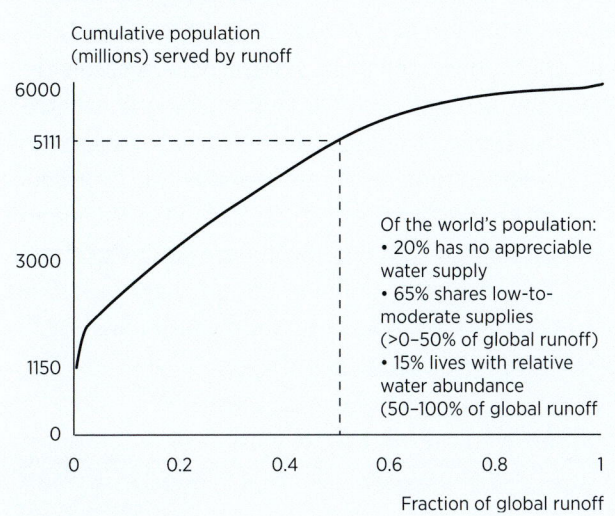

Source: Hassan et al. (2005, figure 7.7, p. 173). © Millennium Ecosystem Assessment. Reproduced by permission of Island Press, Washington DC.

storage capacity, the flood flows do not relieve periods of water shortage.

Increase in losses

It is widely believed that the mean temperature will increase in almost all parts of the world (IPCC, 2007). Climate models are much more useful in temperature projections than in those for precipitation. The consequences of increasing temperatures on water supply are direct and strong – increased evaporation, transpiration (although this is modulated to some degree by carbon fertilization) and infiltration, all of which greatly increase the losses from incoming moisture, thus severely reducing the amount of water easily available for use. The increase in evaporative demand cannot easily be countered and therefore will impact surface runoff and water availability.

Altered seasonality and timing of flow in snowmelt basins

Many river basins in the mid-latitudes (i.e. snowmelt basins) get their water in the form of snow in the winter, which then melts in the following spring to produce runoff in the rivers that is then stored in reservoirs for water supply. Snow is beneficial from a water supply perspective because it acts a reservoir. Water managers have used the timing of the melt for effective management of reservoir operations to satisfy environmental needs. In a warmer climate it is projected

that the snowmelt would occur early due to the advancement of spring and its warmer weather. This early snowmelt would reduce the snow season and increase moisture delivery in the form of rain thus increasing infiltration and evaporative losses during the melt. All of this will place a heavy stress on the amount of water available for use. This is likely to be the case over much of mid-latitude regions, but it will be especially acute in semi-arid and arid regions that depend on mountainous snowmelt.

Decrease or increase in flow due to glacier melt

Few populous places depend entirely on flow from glaciers. The Ganges and Brahmaputra rivers in India receive glacier melt during the winter and spring months (i.e. non-monsoon months) that accounts for 9–12% of their annual flow (see Eriksson et al., 2009, table 2). For India, a country with one billion people, a reduction in flow due to climate change in even one of its vital rivers could pose a serious threat to its water supply. Peru, Chile and Argentina similarly receive a substantial amount of water from glaciers in the Andes. With a warming climate there are two major impacts related to glaciers: (i) reduced snowfall in the lower elevations, resulting in a reduction in the size of the lower elevation glaciers; and (ii) increased losses during the melt season, thereby reducing the amount of flow. Projections indicate a rapid depletion of lower elevation glaciers around the world (IPCC, 2007).

Loss of the groundwater buffer

Groundwater provides a vital buffer against rainfall variability, especially in water stressed parts of the world. Almost all of the shallow groundwater reservoirs are recharged from rainfall, but recharge is greatly impacted by withdrawal, population growth and land cover change. Groundwater also plays a vital role in buffering the variability of surface water resources. With rainfall variability projected to increase in future, the groundwater buffer will become no longer available.

15.2.2 Water demand

The demand for water services involves human use of water for agriculture and industry as well as instream flow requirements for water quality and ecosystems. There is considerable uncertainty surrounding current and future global water demands. This is due in part to (a) the lack of current data describing national consumption patterns, withdrawals and sector usage; (b) large demographic changes, including population growth, economic growth and dietary changes; and (c) our limited understanding of how water demand changes dynamically in response to growing scarcity.

In many parts of the world, water demand is growing due to an increase in population, resulting in an increase in demand for agricultural and industrial products. Economic growth in developing countries often leads to an increase in water demand, for which there are at least two causes. First, direct use of water increases with economic development as access to water and household appliances improve. Second, in many countries a dietary shift occurs along with economic development – a shift from a primarily plant-based diet to one that has a higher proportion of meat. Meat production requires much greater amounts of water; for example, it takes approximately 16,000 L of water to produce 1 kg of beef compared with 3,000 L of water to produce 1 kg of rice (Water Footprint Network, n.d.). In the USA and Europe, the per capita water requirement for food is higher than in other countries, and food consumption is dominated by animal products (Figure 15.2).

Globally, agriculture is the primary water-using sector: more than 70% of water diverted from streams or renewable sources is used for agricultural purposes, and this number is even higher in developing countries.

The prevailing climate of a region is an important driver of agricultural water needs, as evapotranspiration rates are sensitive to changes in air temperature, incoming solar radiation, humidity and wind speed. Climate variability plays a large role in agricultural water needs nationally, though globally, weather-driven variability in irrigation is less than 10% (Wisser et al., 2008). The type of crops grown and the land management techniques and irrigation methods used factor strongly into regional agricultural demands. Wisser et al. (2008) noted global irrigation sensitivities to percolation rates in rice paddies: a 50% change in percolation rate creates a 10% change in global irrigation water use; therefore, about 20% of global irrigation water may be percolating from flooded rice paddies.

Countries with the largest per capita water footprints tend to have large gross domestic products (GDPs) and large durable consumption rates (see Margat and Andréassian, 2008). The consumption of durable goods increases the water footprint. The USA has the largest water footprint of any nation, with a large proportion of the per capita water footprint in industrial goods (Figure 15.3); however, the USA ranks third globally in overall water consumption (Figure 15.4). India and China have lower per capita water footprints than the USA but are overall the largest total water consumers (Figure 15.4).

FIGURE 15.2

Per capita water requirements for food (m³ per capita per year)

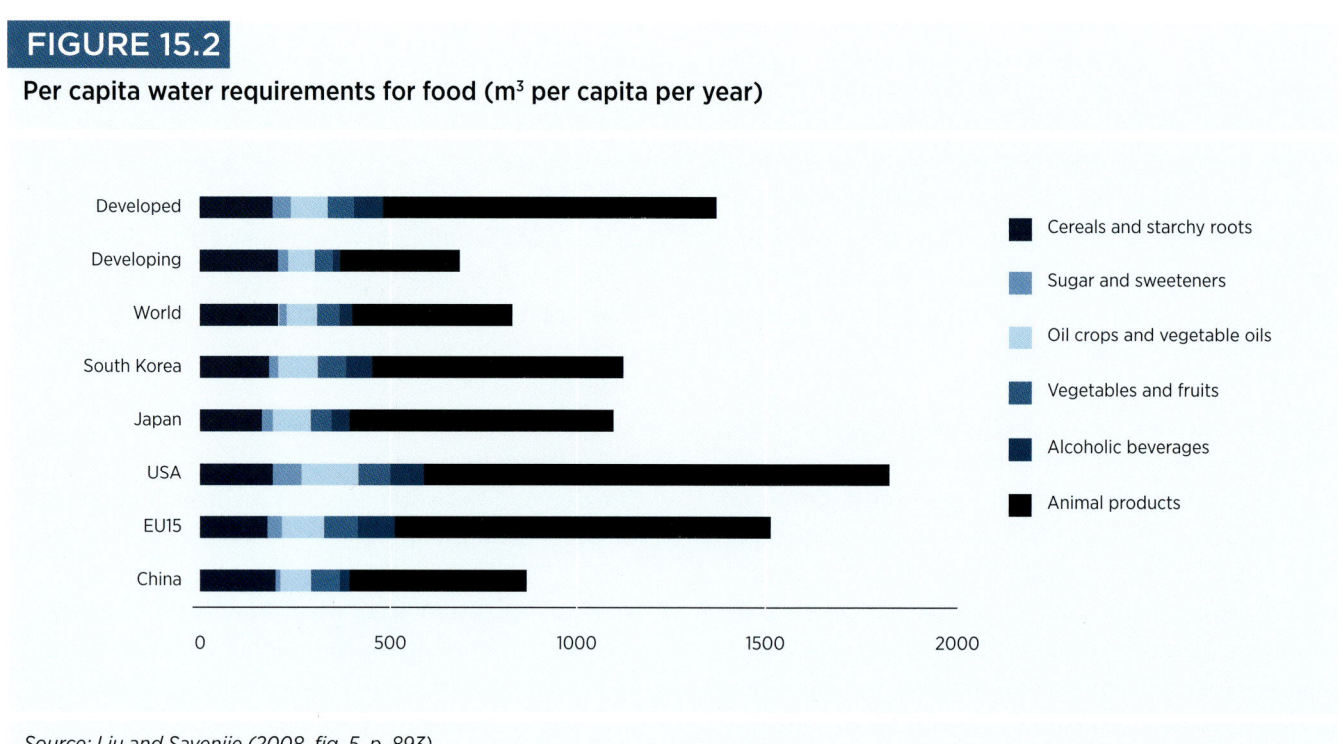

Source: Liu and Savenije (2008, fig. 5, p. 893).

Despite large water footprints, water demands in developed countries such as the USA have been on a downward trend in the past 20 years. More economically efficient water pricing and the use of water efficient technologies both domestically and in agriculture are the primary causes (Box 15.1).

Other changes in water demand are due to the evolution of human habitation from largely rural to increasingly urban. This shift offers potential advantages in terms of economies of scale for providing domestic water as well as sanitation to people. While this is a potentially helpful trend, the provision of water services in rapidly growing and economically depressed urban areas is a complex challenge that requires continuous effort. Despite domestic water use being a small proportion of total water consumed (10–20%), providing it is becoming increasingly challenging as urban populations expand.

Another major source of water demand is for sustaining flows for ecosystems, called environmental flows.

There is growing recognition of the negative impacts on ecosystems of water withdrawals and alteration of flow patterns due to human use of water. Water flows for aquatic ecosystems are now a standard part of water management objectives, and increasingly there is demand for flows that match some measure of the historical flow regime in place of minimum streamflow requirements, which are seen as insufficient.

Inevitably, the varied demand for water resources sets the scene for conflicts over allocation of water services. As the variability of water resources may increase, there is a need for more flexibility in water allocation mechanisms so that demands can be satisfied and shortfalls allocated in the most socially beneficial way. Because environmental benefits are often the most difficult to assign value to, they may be at risk of being left out or underestimated.

Demand for groundwater presents its own set of challenges. As a relatively cheap and reliable water

FIGURE 15.3

National per capita water footprint and the contribution of different consumption categories for selected countries

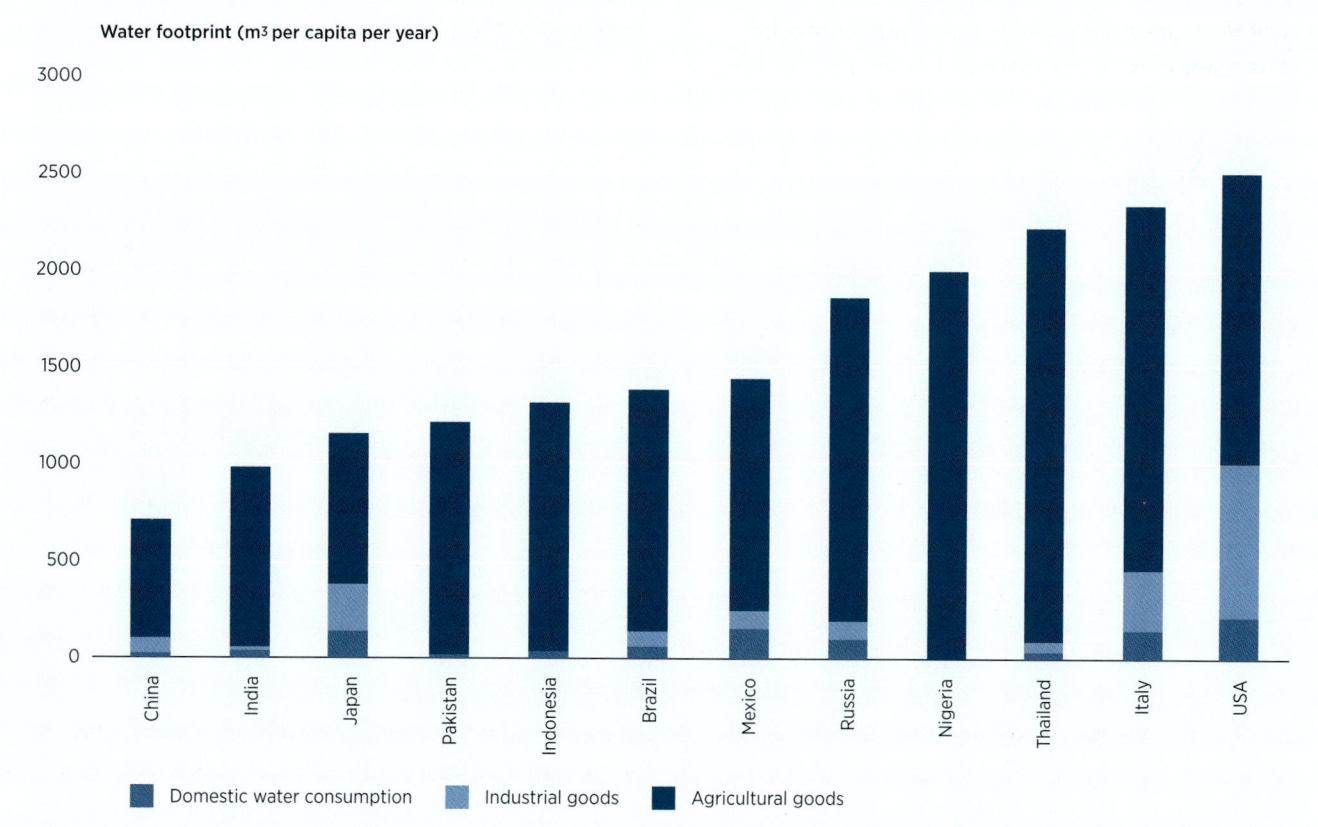

Source: Hoekstra and Chapagain (2007, fig. 5). Reproduced by permission from Springer Science+Business Media B.V.

FIGURE 15.4

Contribution of major consumers to the global water footprint

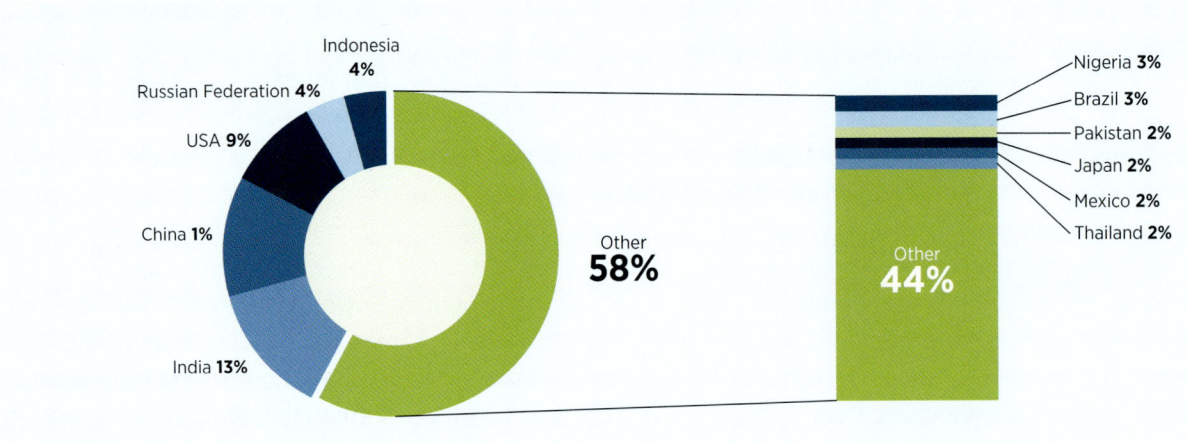

Source: Hoekstra and Chapagain (2007, fig. 4). Reproduced by permission from Springer Science+Business Media B.V.

supply, groundwater has been a boon to farmers throughout the world and a major cause of increasing food security. However, as a common property resource, groundwater is inherently prone to overuse. Many major aquifers around the world are being mined, from the High Plains of North America, to southern India, and the northern plains of China. Groundwater in these regions is being extracted at rates that far exceed recharge and often exceed the economically efficient use rate. Regulation of the common property resource is difficult due to its diffuse nature and the political issues of regulating a resource that is privately accessed.

Finally, there is demand not only for water resources but also protection from hydrological extremes. Societies around the world continue to be negatively impacted by floods and droughts, and the human toll is large. The cumulative impact of hydrological risks has a negative effect on economic development in many countries. Infrastructure and alternatives (structural and non-structural) are needed to reduce these negative impacts. Investment in storage and control structures such as dams is needed in many developing nations. Improved forecasting, early warning systems and insurance mechanisms are all important components of a strategy for addressing flood risk. Water storage at multiple scales, water markets and banks, and insurance are likely components of a strategy for addressing drought.

15.3 Risks and uncertainty in water resources management

15.3.1 Understanding the sources of uncertainty

The key sources of uncertainty related to water resources are those associated with supply, demand and the policy context. The uncertainty of water supply results originally from the natural variability of the earth's climate system and the hydrological cycle, as described earlier. However, anthropogenic influences are introducing new sources of uncertainty. These include the perturbation of the earth's climate due to the emission of greenhouse gases; the large–scale emission of aerosols that influence the physics of precipitation; and changes to the earth's surface through land use development which affect rates of runoff and evapotranspiration. Taken together, natural variability and anthropogenic forcings create a nonstationary climate and hydrological context within which water resources must be managed. This is particularly notable because the current principles for water resources management are based largely on an assumption of hydrological stationarity – the assumption that the future hydrological record can be adequately simulated with the statistics of the historical record.

Uncertainty related to water demand

The uncertainty associated with water demand is largely related to both the difficulty of anticipating demographic change and our limited understanding of how water responds to changing climate and policy conditions. Projections of water demand are

Conservation and demand hardening

Demand hardening occurs when long-term conservation practices and efficiency gains reduce the effectiveness of short-term water conservation measures within a given sector of use. Technological advancements and behavioural changes are the primary drivers of increased water use efficiency. Demand hardening increases as water availability becomes either physically or economically limiting.

The concept of 'peak water' (Gleick and Palaniappan, 2010) provides a good description of the demand hardening process. When a region extracts more water from a watershed than is naturally replenished, peak renewable water is said to be reached. Watersheds such as the Colorado River basin and the Yellow River basin are two examples approaching peak water. Ecologically, this can be unsustainable and a more appropriate metric, 'peak ecological water', may be targeted so that environmental and ecological damages are minimized. Basins that reach peak water may also be considered 'closed'; that is, all utilizable water has been allocated. Further allocation of water from the system will result in less water for other sectors or for ecological flows. It has been suggested that the USA has reached peak water, as withdrawals have remained constant or below historical peak water withdrawals reached during the late 1970s.

In response to dwindling water availability, conservation efforts such as indoor fixture retrofit programmes, outdoor watering education campaigns and technology investments have been used to extend existing supplies, thus increasing demand hardening. This by no means suggests the USA is headed for mass water shortages. Many cities in the USA use water metering coupled with water pricing policies as an effective control of outdoor water consumption. But, despite the efficiency gains from metering and pricing schemes, in much of the USA, in addition to other economically developed countries, both municipal and agricultural use remains unmetered. Metering of individual units in multifamily structures is even less common. Additional water savings can be found in the future if cities meter their residents and apply appropriate water pricing.

Gains in fixture efficiency are an important driver of indoor domestic water demands. In the USA, federal regulations made in the early 1990s continue to decrease per capita water consumption as older fixtures are replaced with newer, more efficient fixtures. In Australia, lasting drought across the continent has increased the penetration rate of efficient fixtures in domestic, agricultural and industrial sectors. National initiatives for water re-use and grey-water systems are reducing per capita consumption.

notoriously difficult to get right. Better understanding of the dynamic relationship between water demand and supply and more sophisticated means of modelling changes in demand dynamically are needed.

To model changes in demand, the underlying drivers of demand growth (or decrease) must be understood. The primary factors affecting water demand in much of the developing world are population growth and socio-economic growth. As economies grow, water use increases significantly, which typically leads to increases in water demand. The developing world is projected to have much higher growth in total water demand than the developed world. Increasing demand is projected to occur in agriculture (for irrigation), domestic and industrial sectors – all linked to economic growth. Figure 15.5 shows the global physical and economic water scarcity, the latter of which is a combination of socio-economic growth and water availability. It can be seen that both physical and economic water scarcity occurs together almost entirely in regions with high population growth and situated in the tropics. Economic water scarcity is largely a result of insufficient infrastructure and lack of management capacity.

There is considerable uncertainty in projections of water demand, especially in the projection of socio-economic factors such as population and economic growth. Without accompanying increases in the efficiency of water use, growth in water demand may be unsustainable and ultimately an impediment to continued economic growth.

Uncertainty related to water supply

Climate variations have a significant impact on the water supply and thus are an important source of uncertainty. Climate models project a decrease in precipitation and consequently in streamflow in several regions around the world. Figure 15.6 shows water availability projections for the 2050s from global climate models (taking into account climate variability, precipitation, temperature, topography and socio-economic factors that influence demand). These projections show a reduction in the future due to climate change in tropical regions. While these are projections of surface water availability, which is a major source of water for almost all human activities, the groundwater scenario is likely to be similar or worse as reduced precipitation leads to reduced recharge. With increasing exploitation from socio-economic growth, groundwater will be stressed further. The regions currently under severe stress will face severe to catastrophic stress in the future under these forces.

Projections of water supply due to climate variability come with large uncertainty. A major question that emerges is whether the uncertain climate change projections should be used to make planning and adaptation decisions. While the information used for water planning has always been uncertain, the current rate of potential change and degree of uncertainty associated with it is probably unprecedented. Managing this uncertainty is one of the great water challenges of the century.

15.3.2 Managing uncertainty and risks

Managing the irreducible uncertainties that affect water supply, demand and the policy context is a significant component of an effective water resources management strategy. Approaches to risk management offer well-developed methodologies for addressing uncertainties associated with hazardous events. There is growing recognition that many uncertainties can offer opportunities in addition to risks (e.g. de Neufville,

2002); for example, unexpectedly high flows may offer opportunities to generate additional water service benefits (such as hydropower) if water managers are prepared to address such an uncertainty.

A general framework for risk management can be described in three steps: hazard characterization, risk assessment and risk mitigation. The first step is to characterize a given event, often considered a hazard, in terms of the impacts or consequences it may have. The next step, risk assessment, involves actual calculation of the risk – defining risk as the product of the probability of an event and the consequences of that event. The final step is the development of a strategy for addressing the risks identified and quantified. Cost–benefit analysis has traditionally been used in the development of such a strategy and the process of risk quantification accommodates a quantitative cost–benefit analysis. However, if there are costs or benefits that are not easily quantified then other multi-objective decision-making methods may be needed.

FIGURE 15.5

Global physical and economic water scarcity

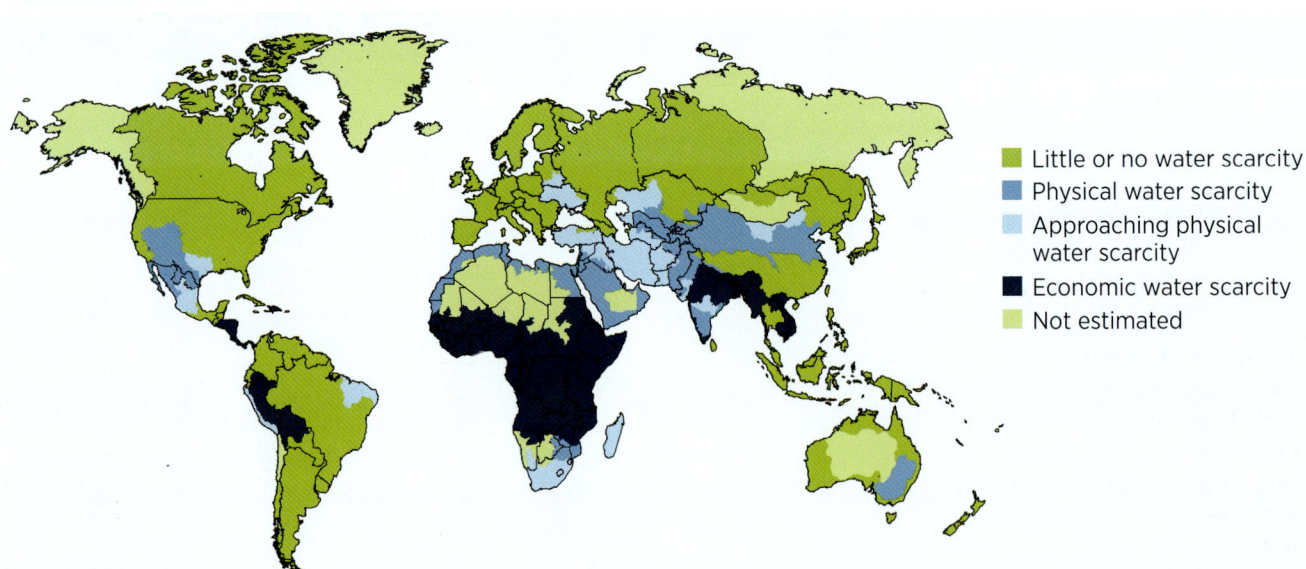

Little or no water scarcity
Physical water scarcity
Approaching physical water scarcity
Economic water scarcity
Not estimated

Definitions and indicators
- Little or no water scarcity. Abundant water resources relative to use, with less than 25% of water from rivers withdrawn for human purposes.
- Physical water scarcity (water resources development is approaching or has exceeded sustainable limits). More than 75% of river flows are withdrawn for agriculture, industry, and domestic purposes (accounting for recycling of return flows). This definition – relating water availability to water demand – implies that dry areas are not necessarily water scarce.
- Approaching physical water scarcity. More than 60% of river flows are withdrawn. These basins will experience physical water scarcity in the near future.
- Economic water scarcity (human, institutional, and financial capital limit access to water even though water in nature is available locally to meet human demands). Water resources are abundant relative to water use, with less than 25% of water from rivers withdrawn for human purposes, but malnutrition exists.

Source: Comprehensive Assessment of Water Management in Agriculture (2007, map 2.1, p. 63, © IWMI, http://www.iwmi.cgiar.org/) (from an International Water Management Institute analysis using the Watersim model).

FIGURE 15.6

Projected per capita water availability in 2050

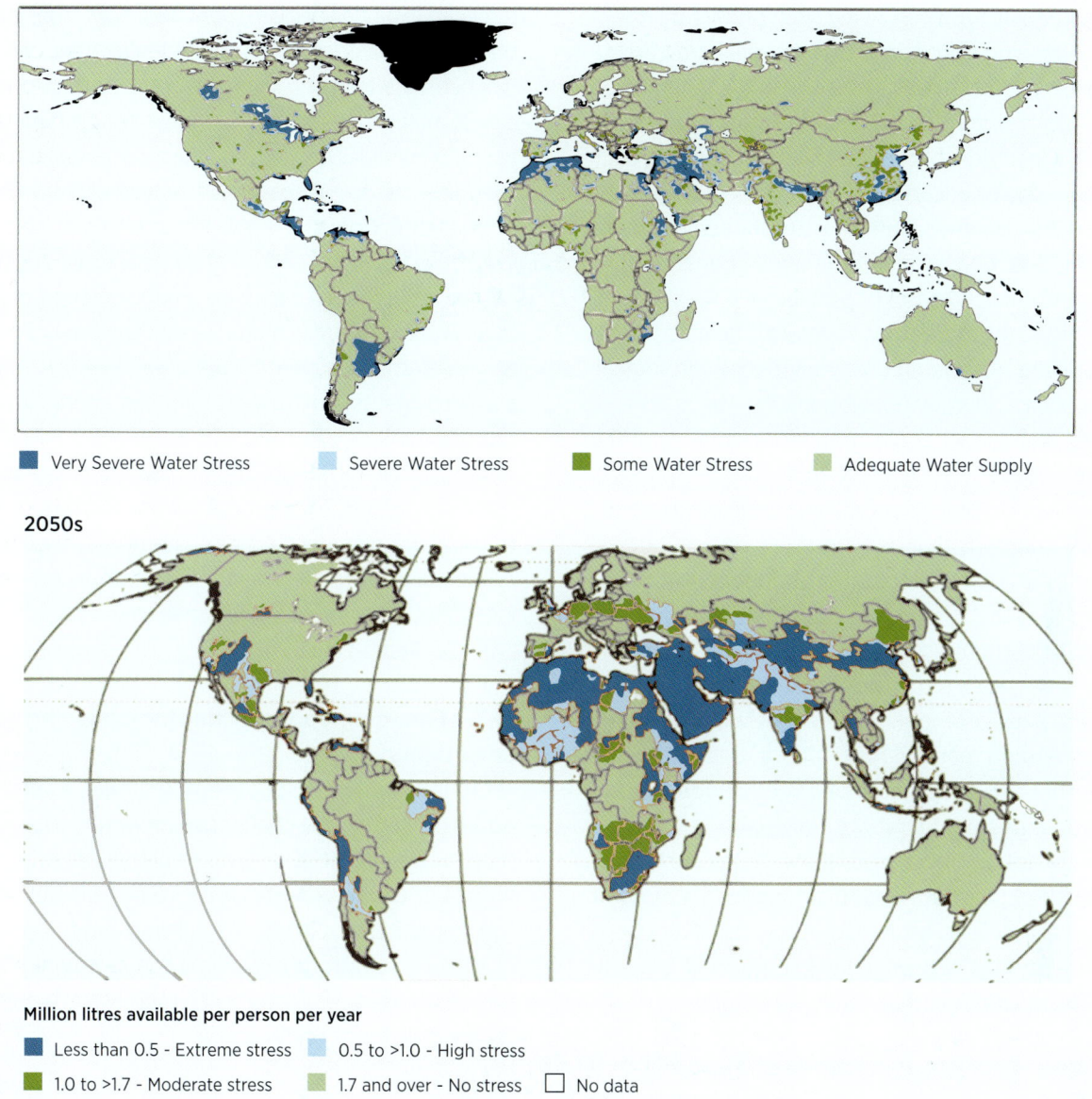

■ Very Severe Water Stress   ■ Severe Water Stress   ■ Some Water Stress   ■ Adequate Water Supply

2050s

Million litres available per person per year

■ Less than 0.5 - Extreme stress   ■ 0.5 to >1.0 - High stress
■ 1.0 to >1.7 - Moderate stress   ■ 1.7 and over - No stress   □ No data

The top panel shows a watershed basis using the most detailed digital basin boundaries available, outputs of precipitation minus evaporation (as a proxy for runoff) from the CCSM3 climate model, and population based on a combination of Global LandScan 2007 current population distribution and downscaled CIESIN country-level growth projections. 'Very severe water stress' indicates that <500 m³ per person per year of freshwater is projected for the basin; 'severe water stress', 500–1000 m³ per person per year; 'some water stress', 1000–1700 m³ per person per year; and 'adequate water supply', >1700 m³ per person per year. For further details, see http://www.ornl.gov/sci/knowledgediscovery/QDR/water/Glbdetbsn_WA2050_A2p-e_A2pop.png.

The bottom panel was prepared by Martina Floerke and colleagues at the Centre for Environmental Systems Research, University of Kassel, Germany for the BBC using the UK Met Office Hadley Centre generated projections of future temperature and rainfall along with their water resources model, waterGAP (http://www.usf.uni-kassel.de/cesr/).

Both top and bottom projections are for same assumptions of climate change mitigation strategies (A2 scenario; see Nakicenvoic et al., 2000) and aggressive population growth. These indicate there are different ways to make water availability projections (using different models and scenarios). Models are constantly improving, generating new information. Additional research efforts are required to update our knowledge concerning possible future conditions.

Climate risks are particularly relevant to water resources management and their nature warrants some discussion. Some climate risks have a degree of predictability if, for example, they are influenced by a predictable climate phenomenon such as ENSO. Any such predictability should be investigated during the hazard characterization and risk assessment steps of risk management. Climate risks may also be related to climate opportunities and a wider view of climate risk management, such as consequence or uncertainty management, should be embraced. Finally, the advent of anthropogenic climate change and the recognition of the nonstationarity of hydrological records present special challenges to traditional approaches to risk management. The calculation of probabilities associated with climate or hydrological events is confounded by nonstationarity. The historical record is no longer considered representative of the future, and projections from general circulation models (GCM) are not yet able to produce reliable predictions. As a result, methods that depend solely on accurate estimations of probability face large shortcomings.

Given the uncertainties associated with risk estimation, there is a need to consider methods for handling the potential increasing risks. One method is to identify, consider and manage residual risk. Residual risk refers to those risks that are not directly addressed by a risk management strategy. For example, low risk events may not be directly addressed because the cost of addressing them exceeds the benefits of doing so. However, because estimates of low risk events are made with unreliable probability estimates, it is possible that residual risks are actually significant.

Also relevant is the concept of surprise. A surprise is generally understood to be the occurrence of an event that has a low probability relative to other events that could occur. Such events are typically not planned for. Again, because the probability estimation may not be reliable, it is worth considering how such events would be managed if they were to occur, even if nothing is invested in directly managing their occurrence. Doing so would improve the robustness of a particular plan – a robust plan being one that works well enough under a wide range of possible futures rather than just for a best guess estimate of the future. The utility of robustness as a planning criterion reflects the growing awareness of the inability to predict the future (Brown, 2010).

Institutional complexities inhibit flexibility in planning. Large and old institutions in particular tend to have entrenched rules and stakeholders who resist change and science- and knowledge-based decision-making. Developing countries may have a comparative advantage in this regard in that as they are developing institutions they can instil flexibility in them and learn from the drawbacks of matured systems. In the Philippines, progress has been made in improving reservoir performance in the city of Manila due to the willingness of competing water users to consider new approaches to managing drought, including the use of seasonal climate forecasts (Brown et al., 2009). Progress is also possible in mature systems, especially when new information provides an opportunity for reconsideration of past assumptions. The Colorado River water resources management system is a good example. Methods such as Bayesian networks in which all the participants and their probabilistic interactions can be represented and the system performance assessed provide an excellent framework for a participatory solution (Bromley, 2005). The report from the NeWater project (http://www.newater.info) provides an excellent summary of the identification of major sources of uncertainty in integrated water resources management practice (van der Keur et al., 2006).

15.3.3 Emerging opportunities for managing uncertainty

There is a growing list of methodologies available for addressing the new challenges to water resources management. Those described below are in various stages of development but most are still nascent in their practical application. Realizing the full potential of these innovations requires a collaborative effort between the research community and the practicing water management community.

Observations, models and forecasts
The ability to monitor all aspects of the hydrological cycle has never been stronger. Remote sensing, ground-based monitoring and modelling techniques that allow real-time observations and forecasts at multiple time scales are new and potentially important tools to improve water resources management. However, gaps between the production of this information and its use in practice are wide.

Seasonal climate forecasts are increasingly skilful and there are several agencies that provide probabilistic seasonal forecasts for the entire globe. Innovative tools can translate these seasonal forecasts to hydrological and hydroclimate forecasts. For example, researchers have established connections in river basins around the globe between streamflows and large-scale climate forcings, particularly ENSO, PDO and the Pacific North American (PNA) pattern (Grantz et al., 2005; Regonda et al., 2006 and references therein). Using these connections, novel forecast methods have been developed to produce skilful streamflow forecasts at a few months lead time (e.g. Hamlet and Lettenmaier, 1999; Clark et al., 2001; Grantz et al., 2005; Regonda et al., 2006). Additionally, new stochastic simulation techniques (Rajagopalan et al., 2009) can be used to generate ensembles of hydrological scenarios in a water resources system conditional on large-scale seasonal climate forecast. The ensembles can be used in a decision tool to provide estimates of system risks at the seasonal to interannual time scales and thus enable efficient decisions. A good demonstration of these ensemble forecasts can be found in Grantz et al. (2007) and Regonda et al. (2011).

Paleo data

Historical and paleo reconstructed streamflow and climate data can be a valuable resource to quantify historical climate risk. For instance, on the Colorado River, long paleo reconstructions of streamflow indicate a much higher frequency of dry spells and low flows relative to the streamflow in the twentieth century (Figure 15.7). The paleo data provide a more realistic estimate of the drought risk than the historical observational record alone. For example, the recent prolonged drought (2000–2010) on the Colorado River appears to be highly unusual based on the observed data but quite common based on the long paleo reconstruction. There are emerging methods to combine observed and paleo information to obtain robust risk estimates (Prairie et al., 2008).

Decadal-scale patterns of variability

The paleo record affords a long view of hydrological variability that is not possible with the observed hydrological record. Recent and current research based on wavelet-based spectral analysis of paleo data reveals decadal-scale patterns of variability that correlate with large-scale multidecadal climate forcings such as the PDO and AMO described earlier. Better understanding of these modes of variability could enhance water resources management. The existence of decadal-scale variability in the historical hydrological record implies that a water resource system could benefit from flexibility to manage periods of relatively greater and less water availability.

Dynamic operational strategies

Traditional water resources management principles are based on the assumption that the probability distribution for hydrological states is the same every year; that is, the assumption of climatology that the long-term statistics are dominant in every year. For example, reservoir rule curves identify the optimal storage levels at various times of the year that best meet operating objectives, considering the time-varying hydrological conditions. Storage is drawn down before expected periods of high inflows; conservation storage is built up in anticipation of an irrigation season or a period of high hydropower demand. A typical reservoir guide curve is shown in Figure 15.8. Such curves are designed – using the probability distribution of the period of record hydrology – to provide acceptable levels of risk and reliability in meeting operational objectives and avoiding damage or catastrophe.

FIGURE 15.7

Paleo reconstruction of the Colorado River streamflow

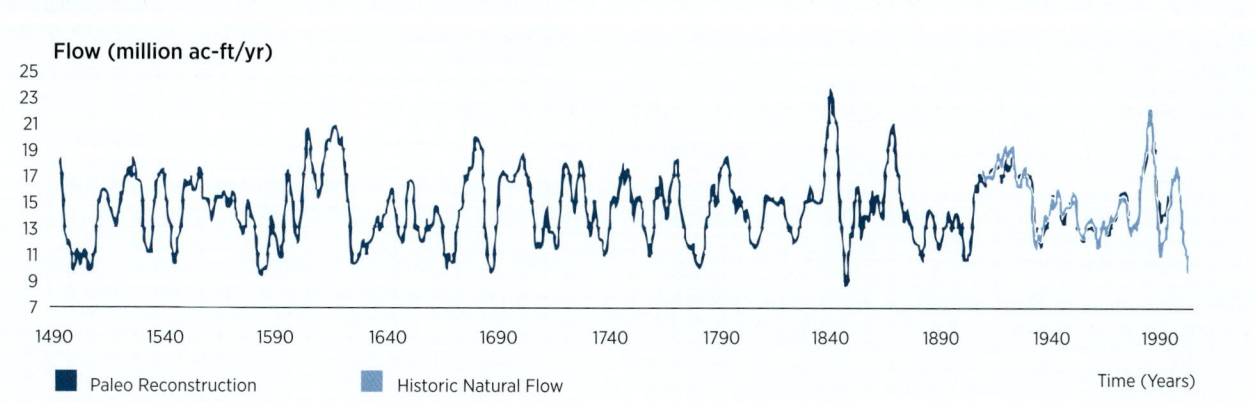

Note: One acre-foot is 1,233 m³.
Source: Based on data from Woodhouse et al. (2006) and Prairie and Callejo (2005).

Improved forecasts and understanding of multi-year variability as described above provide a refined understanding of the probability distribution seasonally and annually. A seasonal forecast may indicate a much higher than normal probability of low flows. This could be linked to ENSO or other climate signals and have multi-year effects. Similarly, the ability to forecast extended wet and dry periods may soon be possible as a result of decadal-scale forecasting research (Nowak, 2011). These scientific advances make possible the use of dynamic operational strategies such as reservoir or water system rule curves that change in response to forecasts or observations; flexible water allocation and pricing approaches, such as in response to scarcity; and the use of economic mechanisms to facilitate water exchanges. Adaptive reservoir operations, wherein rule curves are modified to produce more effective management given improved streamflow forecasts, are gaining recognition (e.g. Bayazit et al., 1990; Yao and Georgakakos, 2001).

Adaptive management

Adaptive management is a method used to address the uncertainties associated with climate change, other hydrological change, and our limited ability to correctly anticipate the future in complex water resources systems. The approach was developed in ecology. The general principle of the approach is 'learning by doing' and it emphasises monitoring and the ability to change decisions and update hypotheses on the basis of observations. It can be appropriate in cases where reversible decisions are possible, so that a decision may be changed as climate and socio-economic conditions evolve and a better understanding of the system is achieved. Sankarasubramanian et al. (2009) demonstrate that utility of climate information even of modest accuracy, when coupled with adaptive operations, can benefit water allocation projects with high demand–to–storage ratios as well as systems with multiple uses constraining the allocation process. The ability to ingrain flexibility into a system improves the opportunities for making use of adaptive management principles.

Scenarios-based approach

A common approach to dealing with the implications of climate change is the scenario-based approach. A small number of internally consistent visions of the future are created and plans are evaluated according to how well they perform under these scenarios. Projections from GCM represent internally consistent climate scenarios that are used in the planning process. The GCM projections are converted to hydrological variables through a process that includes bias correction, resolution increases and hydrological modelling, and these variables drive models of the water resources systems. Often, extreme points of the range of GCM projections are chosen to attempt to capture the range of GCM uncertainty, although the true range of climate uncertainty remains unknown. Recent examples of this approach include Traynham et al. (2011), Vano et al. (2010a, 2010b) and Vicuna et al. (2010). A downside of this approach is that water planners struggle with the very wide range of impacts represented by the scenarios, which often include negligible and severe impacts that are considered equally probable. It is difficult to design a plan that addresses all scenarios: the costs of addressing some scenarios are often exorbitant, and the analysis provides no information as to which is more likely.

Robust decision-making methodologies

Water resources planners and policy-makers have long understood that most decisions are made under considerable uncertainty related to the future. Nonetheless, anthropogenic climate change raises issues that are different from the typical uncertainty with which water planners are familiar. In particular, assumptions related to the use of the historical hydrological record are jeopardized by the prospect of changing climate. On the one hand, the water planner is informed that 'stationarity is dead' (Milly et al., 2005) and the usual use of the historical record for planning is no longer valid. On the other hand, climate change projections from general circulation models (GCM) are acknowledged to be too uncertain to be used for planning purposes and are associated with significant biases. How are decisions to be made when the future is characterized not only by uncertainty but also by two or more potentially contradictory visions of the hydrological future? A variety of approaches have emerged that attempt to address decision-making under climate uncertainty: see Box 15.2.

Information and communication technology

Advances in information and communication technologies offer great potential for improving the management of water resources. The low cost of these technologies has made them ubiquitous, including widespread use in developing countries. Potential applications include forecast transmittal, early warning systems, and crowd sourcing for data collection and monitoring.

FIGURE 15.8

Example reservoir rule curve showing drawdown for spring floods, filling as the flood season subsides, and maintenance of summer levels for water supply, recreation and hydropower production

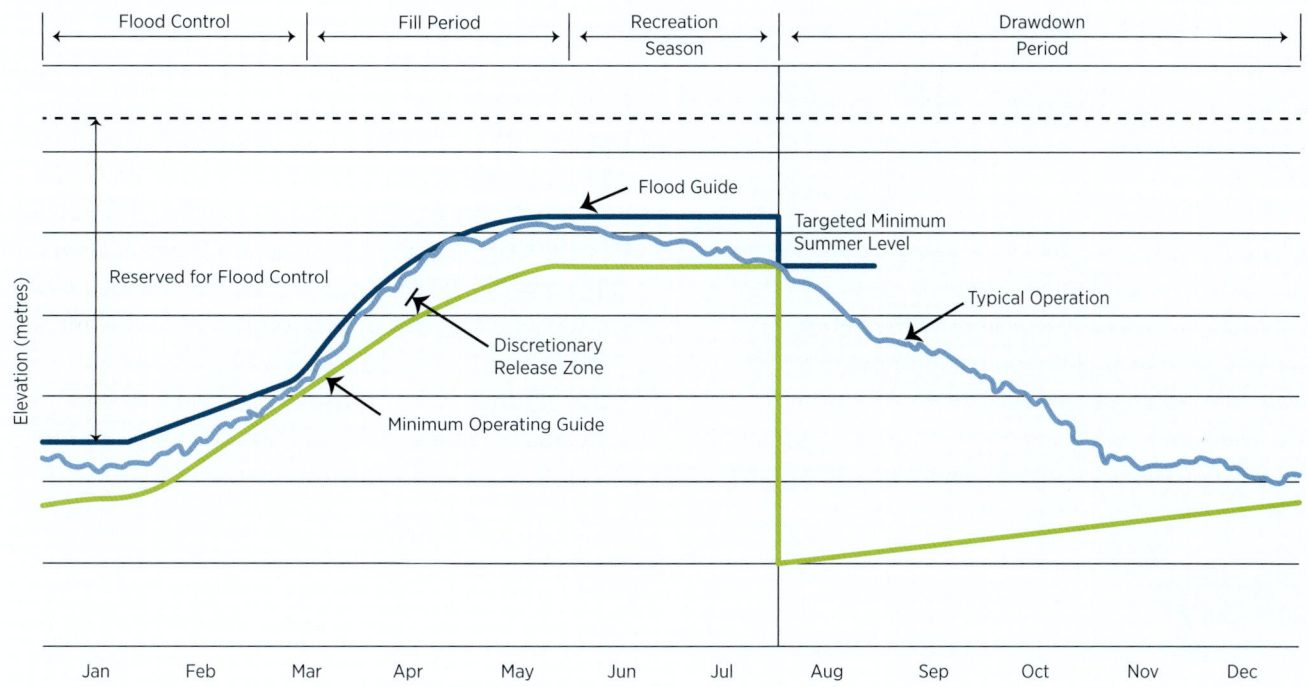

Advanced decision support systems

The application of many scientific advances, such as probabilistic forecasting, requires a decision support system in which current and future states of the hydrological system can be modelled, stochastic hydrology that reflects a wide range of assumptions as described above can be generated, and various management and infrastructure alternatives can be evaluated. Decision support tools should support the quantification of risk and reliability and offer the ability to measure performance of a management plan with respect to agreed-upon criteria such as the reliability of supply and the risk of damage to the human or ecological systems. Advanced decision support systems (ADSS) must enable the participatory involvement of a range of scientific, government and management agencies as well as various stakeholders. Such systems have been developed and applied successfully in several basins and are under development in others across the globe.

15.4 Hot spots

15.4.1 India

India faces an unprecedented crisis in the next two decades. Today, major urban areas are unable to provide a reliable and regular water supply. Industrial and energy development face water constraints. Scarcity of water for irrigation is a leading concern of farmers. This can be seen in agricultural water stress maps (Columbia Water Center, n.d.). Of particular concern is that the water stress dramatically increases with multi-year drought. This threatens the country's food and water security. Mighty rivers, such as the Ganges, are significantly depleted over much of the year, and highly polluted over much of their course. Life (biodiversity) abundant in India until as recently as the 1990s is now seriously threatened. Aquifers, the resource of choice due to subsidized energy for pumping, present variable stock and quality. Not surprisingly, aquifer depletion and inefficient water use are now endemic. Uncertainty as to what climate change portends for the water supply is a concern, but the needs for food of a growing population will likely determine the shape of the water crisis in the country. The dramatic natural climate variability (seasonal to interannual to decadal to century scale) and its spatial manifestation as floods and droughts across India poses a serious threat in this context as water stores that could normally buffer against such variations are exhausted and no infrastructure or multi-scale coordinated planning efforts are implemented.

The World Bank warns of a turbulent water future for India absent dramatic coordinated government investments in water infrastructure, governance and agricultural productivity (Briscoe, 2005). The International Water Management Institute (IWMI) talks of taming the anarchy of uncontrolled groundwater exploitation by the population as a whole, and proposes investments in groundwater recharge among policy reforms (Shah, 2008).

Despite these warnings, rather limited in-depth analyses and projections of the water resources of the country, sectoral and ecological demands, and potential solutions exist. Controlled access to the detailed data needed to reconstruct the past and project the future and a lack of institutional support for interdisciplinary research into long-range water resources planning and management are key factors contributing to the situation. Non-government organizations are active lobbyists and implementers of local solutions (e.g. rainwater harvesting, well provision, water treatment, sanitation training and water data provision) but typically do not come close to meeting the needs of a national, state and local strategic analysis.

15.4.2 Western USA

Western USA is mountainous, predominantly semi-arid and receives its water supply from snowmelt. Its population steadily increased during the latter half of the twentieth century. The large population centres are in the south-west desert, while their water is supplied by the Colorado River, which originates in the higher elevations of the Rocky Mountains far to the north. The water in the river is divided among seven basin states and two countries (USA and Mexico); thus, water management is highly contentious.

BOX 15.2

Decision-making under climate uncertainty

An emerging approach to planning under climate uncertainty focuses on providing the specific information needed to inform a decision process. These decision-based approaches typically apply decision analytics to the planning process to identify the conditions that favour a particular decision over another.

The first approach is known as identifying and implementing **'no regrets' decisions**. The idea is that there are decisions that will work well regardless of the degree of climate change or its attributes. The decision pays off for the historical record and for the anticipated climate change. Decisions such as this that are essentially insensitive to future climate are straightforward to make – the challenge is identifying them. Based on the degree to which water managers continue to struggle with the implications of climate change, no regrets decisions that adequately address these climate concerns are rare.

Robust decision-making is a decision-based approach that uses GCM projections as scenario generators that incorporate a variety of decision inputs. (Lempert et al., 2006) and addresses 'deep uncertainty' by favouring management plans that perform well over a range of possible future conditions (Brekke et al., 2009). It uses clustering techniques to identify the conditions that favour particular decisions and to assess the robustness of a decision by varying the assumptions that underlie those conditions. The objective is to identify decisions that are superior regardless of the future climate that is assumed.

Decision-scaling uses sensitivity analysis to identify the climate conditions that favour one decision over others (Brown et al., 2010). Information from multiple GCM super ensembles and historical climate analysis is tailored to estimate the relative probability of those conditions compared to the climate conditions favouring alternative decisions. Risk management strategies are then developed to address the implications of low probability outcomes. In all cases, the process begins with the identification of the key climate information that causes a particular decision to be favoured over others. The hope is that the identification of these factors may reveal that they are less uncertain than the spectrum of climate change possibilities as a whole. This allows even uncertain climate change projections to be able to offer valuable information for the planning process.

Adaptive management can be coupled with robust decision-making by continually monitoring the performance of a robust plan. At intervals in the future, if performance decreases, the plan can be modified to improve its performance. The modification would be made with improved knowledge of future possible conditions. An approach that applies decision-scaling to adaptive management is currently being adopted in the plan for the regulation of outflows from Lake Superior (Brown et al., 2011).

The river has extensive storage (almost four times the annual average flow in the river), which is managed by the United States Bureau of Reclamation (USBR), mandated to manage the water resources of the Colorado River basin in the USA and coordinate water delivery obligations with Mexico, under a complicated set of decrees and rules known as the 'law of the river'. The law of the river worked well for much of the twentieth century, when demand was much lower than supply. But a 'perfect storm' comprising economic growth, increasing population and increasing water demands, coupled with severe sustained drought in the recent decade, is stressing the physical system and the agreements. Paleo reconstructions of streamflow in the basin indicate drier epochs with regular frequency. In fact, they indicate that the twentieth century, when the law of the river was drafted, was one of the wettest. Climate change projections indicate a substantial decrease in annual average streamflow, which will only exacerbate the situation. Many studies (recently Rajagopalan et al., 2009) underscore this and also suggest that flexible and innovative management of the system and collective stakeholder participation can instil effective adaptive management practices that can help mitigate the risk. Studies indicate that the region is likely to experience severe water supply crises in the not-too-distant future if management practices are not modified (USBR, 2005).

15.4.3 West Africa: Niger basin

The Niger River basin is a transboundary basin covering significant portions of nine countries in West Africa. Approximately 100 million people are dependent in some way on the river – for livelihood, trade, transportation and food. The basin is facing complex problems of poverty and low productivity, and it is characterized by severe water constraints, including water-borne diseases and extreme weather events such as floods and droughts. Managing this river system has been challenged by the growing competition for water among urban, industrial, agricultural and ecological users, as well as by the day-to-day, intraseasonal and interannual vagaries of climate variability and climate change. Past interannual variability is large in magnitude compared to any projected climate changes. Within this context, a climate risk assessment of the infrastructure investment plan has been conducted (Brown, 2011).

Due to the great uncertainty of the future climate, a decision-scaling approach was applied that begins with an assessment of the potential impacts of hypothetical climate changes and then utilizes climate information to assess the likelihood of problematic climate changes (Brown, 2011). The resulting analysis indicated that the investment plan was largely well prepared for moderate climate changes or less. Only very large reductions (about 20%) in precipitation would pose significant impacts. The subsequent climate analysis revealed that such changes are not common in climate projections for the region and thus are considered to have a low likelihood. To enhance its preparedness for future climate variability and change, the use of seasonal hydrological forecasts is currently being investigated as an additional adaptation strategy.

15.4.4 East Africa: Nile basin

The Nile, the longest river in the world at about 6700 km, drains about 3 million km² and runs through 10 riparian African countries. The Nile comprises two main river systems: the White Nile and the Blue Nile. The White Nile has its source in the Equatorial Lakes Plateau where it originates above Lake Victoria, the second largest freshwater lake in the world, and supports populations and ecosystems of six Eastern Africa nations: Burundi, Rwanda, Tanzania, Kenya, Democratic Republic of the Congo, and Uganda. The Blue Nile originates in the Ethiopian highlands and flows west to meet the White Nile at Khartoum in Sudan. The main Nile flows north from this confluence to the High Aswan Dam in Egypt, then continues north and empties into the Mediterranean Sea through a large delta. The total population of Nile basin countries is about 300 million, and more than half of this population is dependent on the Nile. The river supports particularly large populations in Egypt, Sudan, Ethiopia and Uganda. The population in these countries is expected to increase by about 50% in the next 20 years.

The effects of climate change are not certain, although it is likely that arid countries will become warmer as more water will evaporate. Analysts expect that future stresses will be due in great part to population and development pressures, and will be aggravated by climate change. Egypt, for example, is projected to have in 2025 only about half the per capita water availability that it had in 1990.

15.4.5 Australia

Much of Australia's population is confined to a narrow strip along the coastline, which makes urban water supply a major challenge for the present and an even bigger one for the future, as climate change is projected to lead to a reduction in overall precipitation. While many studies comment on the likely reduction in rainfall across the continent in a warmer climate, it is generally accepted that the future will see an increase in evaporation (Johnson and Sharma, 2010), resulting in a significant reduction in the continent's already low water availability. Australia's farming heartland, the Murray-Darling basin, is likely to see a reduction in water supply to serve the demands for irrigation, urban use and industry along with an increase in the vulnerability of migratory birds visiting freshwater wetlands (Hennessey et al, 2007).

15.4.6 South America

South America is a large continent with a wide range of geomorphological and climatic features, such as the desert lands along the western coasts of Peru and Chile, the Andes Mountains in western South America, and the Amazon forest basin in Peru and Brazil. Thus one finds a variety of water resources problems that are typical of certain regions such as flash flooding in many high-gradient mountain rivers, large-scale floods and inundations in large rivers (e.g. the Parana and Amazon basins), and periods of low flows and droughts in many regions.

During the past few years, the economies of several South American countries have been developing significantly, making them attractive for capital investment and growth. One of the reasons for such unprecedented growth has been the mining industry. For example, many regions in Peru have important mineral stock and have attracted the attention of major mining corporations (Salas et al., 2008). While this has brought employment opportunities for thousands of Peruvian workers and has helped boost the regional and national economy, it has also brought a number of concerns related to the impact of mining operations on water resources and the environment. These impacts include effects on the water quantity and quality of nearby streams, depletion of groundwater levels and water flow from springs, and increased soil erosion. In addition, the mining boom has raised concerns about the vulnerability of inhabitants, livestock, wildlife, vegetation, soil and water to any toxic waste that may result from industrial operations and accidents.

An additional water-related problem that has become relevant in many South American countries in the past decades relates to the accelerated 'deglaciation' of the tropical Andes mountains, – due to, it has been argued, the effects of global warming. For example, Peru has lost at least 22% of its glaciers' surface since 1970, affecting some of the water supply in the Peruvian highlands. The White Cordillera, where 35% of Peruvian glaciers are located, have lost about 190 km^2 of ice surface; for example, the Broggi glacier has retreated about 950 m in the period 1948–2004 and the Pastoruri glacier about 490 m in the period 1980–2005 – the latter glacier has been closed to tourism for safety reasons (PUCP, 2008).

||||||||||||||||||||||||||||||||||||||||||||||||||||||||||||||||||||||||||||||||||||||||||

References

Bayazit, M. and Unal, N. E. 1990. Effects of hedging on reservoir performance. *Water Resources Research,* Vol. 26, No. 4, pp. 713–19.

Brekke, L. D., Kiang, J. E., Olsen, J. R., Pulwarty, R. S., Raff, D. A., Turnipseed, D. P., Webb, R. S. and White, K. D. 2009. *Climate Change and Water Resources Management – A Federal Perspective.* US Geological Survey Circular 1331. Reston, VA, USGS. http://pubs.usgs.gov/circ/1331/

Briscoe, J. 2007. *India's Water Economy: Bracing for a Turbulent Future.* Oxford, UK, Oxford University Press.

Bromley J. (ed.). 2005. *Guidelines for the Use of Bayesian Networks as a Participatory Tool for Water Resources Management.* A MERIT Report. Wallingford, UK, Centre for Ecology and Hydrology (CEH).

Brown, C. 2010. The end of reliability. *ASCE Journal of Water Resources Planning and Management,* Vol. 136, p. 143.
––––. 2011. *Decision-scaling for Robust Planning and Policy under Climate Uncertainty.* Washington DC, World Resources Report. http://www.worldresourcesreport.org

Brown, C. and Lall, U. 2006. Water and economic development: The role of variability and a framework for resilience. *Natural Resources Forum,* Vol. 30, No. 4, pp. 306–17.

Brown, C., Conrad, E., Sankarasubramanian, A. and Someshwar, S. 2009. The use of seasonal climate forecasts within a shared reservoir system: The case of Angat reservoir, Philippines. F. Ludwig, P. Kabat, H. van Schaik and M. van der Valk (eds), *Climate Change Adaptation in the Water Sector,* London, Earthscan.

Brown, C., Werick, W., Fay, D. and Leger, W. 2011. A decision analytic approach to managing climate risks – Application to the Upper Great Lakes. *Journal of the American Water Resources Association,* doi:10.1111/j.1752-1688.2011.00552.x.

Clark, M. P., Serreze, M. C. and McCabe, G. J. 2001. Historical effects of El Niño and La Niña events on the seasonal evolution of the mountain snowpack in the Columbia and Colorado River Basins. *Water Resources Research,* Vol. 37, pp. 741–57.

Columbia Water Center. n.d. Homepage. http://water.columbia.edu/?id=India&navid=india_water_stress

Comprehensive Assessment of Water Management in Agriculture. 2007. *Water for Food, Water for Life: A Comprehensive Assessment of Water Management in Agriculture.* London/Colombo, Earthscan/International Water Management Institute.

Eriksson, M., Jianchu, X., Bhakta Shrestha, A., Ananda Vaidya, R., Nepal, S. and Sandström, K. 2009. *The Changing Himalayas: Impact of Climate Change on Water Resources and Livelihoods in the Greater Himalayas.* Kathmandu, International Centre for Integrated Mountain Development (ICIMOD).

Gleick, P. H. and Palaniappan, M. 2010. Peak water limits to freshwater withdrawal and use. *Proceedings of the National Academy of Science,* Vol. 107, No. 25, pp. 11155–62.

Grantz, K., Rajagopalan, B., Clark, M. and Zagona, E. 2005. A technique for incorporating large-scale climate information in basin-scale ensemble streamflow forecasts. *Water Resources Research,* doi:10.1029/2004WR003467.

––––. 2007. Water management applications of climate-based hydrologic forecasts: Case study of the Truckee-Carson River Basin, Nevada, ASCE. *Journal of Water Resources Planning and Management,* Vol. 133, No. 4, pp. 339–50.

GreenFacts. n.d. Scientific Facts on Water Resources Web page. http://www.greenfacts.org/en/water-resources/figtableboxes/9.htm

Hamlet, A. F. and Lettenmaier, D. P. 1999. Columbia River streamflow forecasting based on ENSO and PDO climate signals. *Journal of Water Resources Planning and Management,* Vol. 125, pp. 333–41.

Hassan, R., R. Scholes and N. Ash (eds). 2005. Condition and Trends Working Group of the Millennium Ecosystem Assessment. *Ecosystems and Human Well-being: Current State and Trends, Vol. 1.* Washington DC, Island Press. http://www.eoearth.org/article/Ecosystems_and_Human_Well-Being:_Volume_1:_Current_State_and_Trends:_Freshwater_Ecosystem_Services

Hoekstra, A. Y. and Chapagain, A. K. 2007. Water footprints of nations: Water use by people as a function of their consumption pattern. *Water Resources Management,* Vol. 21, No. 1, pp. 35–48.

IPCC (Intergovernmental Panel on Climate Change). 2007. *Climate Change 2007 – The Physical Science Basis: Contribution of Working Group I to the Fourth Assessment Report of the IPCC.* Geneva, IPCC.

Johnson, F. and Sharma, A. 2010. A comparison of Australian open water body evaporation trends for current and future climates estimated from Class A evaporation pans and general circulation models. *Journal of Hydrometeorology,* doi:10.1175/2009JHM1158.1.

van der Keur, P., Henriksen, H. J., Refsgaard, J. C., Brugnach, M., Pahl-Wostl, C., Dewulf, A. and Buiteveld, H. 2006. *Identification of Major Sources of Uncertainty in Current IWRM Practice and Integration into Adaptive Management.* Report of the NeWater Project – New Approaches to Adaptive Water Management Under Uncertainty. Osnabrueck, Germany, NeWater.

Lempert, R. J., Groves, D. G., Popper, S. W. and Bankes, S. C. 2006. A general, analytic method for generating robust strategies and narrative scenarios. *Management Science,* Vol. 52, No. 4, pp. 514–28.

Liu, J. and Savenije H. H. G. 2008. Food consumption patterns and their effect on water requirement in China. *Hydrology and Earth System Sciences,* Vol. 12, pp. 887–98.

Margat, J. and Andréassian, V. 2008. *L'eau, les Idées Reçues.* Paris, Editions le Cavalier Bleu.

Milly, P. C. D., Dunne, K. A. and Vecchia, A. V. 2005. Global pattern of trends in streamflow and water availability in a changing climate. *Nature,* doi:10.1038/nature04312.

Nakicenvoic et al. 2000. *Special Report on Emissions Scenarios.* A Special Report of Working Group III of the Intergovernmental Panel on Climate Change. Cambridge, UK, Cambridge University Press.

de Neufville. 2002. *Architecting/Designing Engineering Systems Using Real Options.* ESD WP 2003-01.09. Engineering Systems Division Symposium, June 2002, http://esd.mit.edu/WPS/2003.htm

Nowak, K. 2011. Stochastic streamflow simulation at interdecadal time scales and implications to water resources management in the Colorado River Basin. PhD dissertation, University of Colorado, Boulder, CO.

Prairie, J. and Callejo, R. 2005. *Natural Flow and Salt Computation Methods,* Salt Lake City, UT, US Department of the Interior.

Prairie, J., Nowak, K., Rajagopalan, B., Lall, U. and Fulp, T. 2008. A stochastic nonparametric approach for streamflow generation combining observational and paleo reconstructed data. *Water Resources Research,* doi:10.1029/2007WR006684.

PUCP (Pontificia Universidad Católica del Perú). 2008. *Climatic Changes Website.* Lima, Peru, PUCP.

Rajagopalan, B., Nowak, K., Prairie, J., Hoerling, M., Harding, B., Barsugli, J., Ray, A. and Udall, B. 2009. Water supply risk on the Colorado River: Can management mitigate? *Water Resources Research,* doi:10.1029/2008WR007652.

Regonda, S., Rajagopalan, B., Clark, M. and Zagona, E. 2006. Multi-model ensemble forecast of spring seasonal flows in the Gunnison River basin. *Water Resources Research,* Vol. 42, 09494.

Regonda, S., Zagona, E. and Rajagopalan, B. 2011. Prototype decision support system for operations on the Gunnison basin with improved forecasts. *ASCE Journal of Water Resources Planning and Management,* Vol. 137, No. 5, pp. 428–38.

Salas, J. D., Paulet, M. and Vasconcellos, C. 2008. Feasibility study for water resources development in the Chonta and Mashcon rivers; Cajamarca, Peru. *Colorado Water,* Vol. 25, No. 5, pp. 12–13.

Sankarasubramanian, A., Lall, U., Souza Filho, F. D. and Sharma, A. 2009. Improved water allocation utilizing probabilistic climate forecasts: Short-term water contracts in a risk management framework. *Water Resources Research,* Vol. 45, W11409.

Shah, T. 2008. *Taming the Anarchy Groundwater Governance in South Asia.* London, RFF Press.

Traynham, L., Palmer, R. N. and Polebitski, A. S. 2011. Impacts of future climate conditions and forecasted population growth on water supply systems in the Puget Sound region. *Journal of Water Resources Planning and Management,* doi:10.1061/(ASCE)WR.1943-5452.0000114.

USBR (US Bureau of Reclamation). 2005. *Water 2025: Preventing Crises and Conflict in the West.* Washington, DC, USBR.

Vano, J. A, Voisin, N., Cuo, L., Hamlet, A. F., Elsner, M. M., Palmer, R. N., Polebitski, A. and Lettenmaier, D. P. 2010*a*. Climate change impacts on water management in the Puget Sound region, Washington State, USA. *Climatic Change,* doi:10.1007/s10584-010-9846-1.

Vano, J. A., Voisin, N., Scott, M., Stöckle, C. O., Hamlet, A. F., Mickelson, K. E. B., Elsner, M. M. and Lettenmaier, D. P. 2010*b*. Climate change impacts on water management and irrigated agriculture in the Yakima River Basin, Washington State, USA. *Climatic Change,* Vol. 102, No. 1–2, pp. 287–317.

Vicuna, S., Dracup, J. A., Lund, J. R., Dale, L. L. and Maurer, E. P. 2010. Basin-scale water system operations with uncertain future climate conditions: Methodology and case studies. *Water Resources Research,* doi: 10.1029/2009WR007838.

Vörösmarty, C. J., Leveque, C. and Revenga, C. 2005. Fresh water. R. Bos, C. Caudill, J. Chilton, E. M. Douglas, M. Meybeck, D. Prager, P. Balvanera, S. Barker, M. Maas, C. Nilsson, T. Oki, C. A. Reidy, *Millennium Ecosystem Assessment, Volume 1: Conditions and Trends Working Group Report.* Washington DC, Island Press, pp. 165–207.

Water Footprint Network. n.d. Homepage. http://www.waterfootprint.org

Wisser, D., Frolking, S., Douglas, E. M., Fekete, B. M., Vörösmarty, C. J. and Schumann, A. H. 2008. Global irrigation water demand: Variability and uncertainties arising from agricultural and climate data sets. *Geophysical Research Letters,* doi:10.1029/2008GL035296.

Woodhouse, C. A., Gray, S. T. and Meko, D. M. 2006. Updated streamflow reconstructions for the Upper Colorado River Basin. *Water Resources Research,* doi:10.1029/2005WR004455.

WWAP (World Water Assessment Programme). 2006. *World Water Development Report 2: Water: A Shared Responsibility.* Paris/New York, UNESCO/Berghahn Books.

Yao, H. and Georgakakos, A. 2001. Assessment of Folsom Lake response to historical and potential future climate scenarios: 2. Reservoir management. *Journal of Hydrology,* Vol. 249, No. 1–4, pp. 176–96.

CHAPTER 16
State of the resource: Quality

UNEP-DHI Centre for Water and Environment

—

Authors Mogens Dyhr-Nielsen, Gareth James Lloyd, and Paul Glennie
Contributor Peter Koefoed Bjørnsen
Acknowledgement Børge Storm

© UN Photo/Gill Fickling

A global water quality assessment framework is needed. While there are many ways to address water quality, from an international to a household scale, there is an urgent lack of water quality data to support decision-making and management processes. An assessment framework should draw on national data sources. The motivation for such a framework is to better understand the state of water quality and its causes; understand recent trends and identify hot spots; test and validate policy and management options; provide a foundation for scenarios that can be used to understand and plan for appropriate future actions; and provide much needed monitoring bench markers.

Water quality is inextricably linked with water quantity as both are key determinants of supply. Water quality degradation is not only a product of external pollutants but is also related to quantity depletion. The problem of water quality can be expected to increase as water scarcity increases. In the past, quality and quantity issues have generally been considered separately. Policy-makers must make a concerted effort to better integrate the two issues. In turn they need the support of the research community who can help to better quantify the problems, as well as the remedial solutions.

Socio-economic development is dependent on water quality. There are well-documented human and ecosystem health risks linked to poor water quality that also threaten socio-economic development. Cost-effective options for collecting, treating and disposing of human waste must still be combined with public education efforts on the environment. Efforts must be directed toward industries using or producing toxic substances. Development of clean technology and substitution processes, combined with cost-efficient treatment options, is a priority. The control of non-point sources of pollution, particularly nutrients leading to eutrophication, is an increasing global challenge. Institutional efforts are also needed to strengthen emergency responses when water sources are threatened or destroyed, and greater attention needs to be given to enforcing existing regulations.

Poor water quality is expensive. The costs of poor water quality can be significant: degradation of ecosystems, health-related costs and their impacts on economic activities, increased treatment costs and reduced property values among others. Conversely, significant savings can be can be made by improving or ensuring that water quality is maintained, such as lives saved, reduced industrial production costs and water treatment costs. More research is needed to better understand and quantify the economic costs and benefits of ecosystem services.

16.1 Introduction

> Safe drinking water and basic sanitation are intrinsic to human survival, well-being and dignity. Without a serious advance in implementing the water and sanitation agenda, there is little prospect of achieving development for all. (United Nations Secretary General Ban Ki-moon, 2008)

Good water quality is an important yet vulnerable development asset, and essential for maintaining ecosystem health. Water quality is inextricably linked with water quantity. Poor quality water that cannot be used for drinking, bathing, industry or agriculture reduces the amount of useable water (UNEP, 2010). Moreover, over-use of water may lead to quality degradation. For example, over-abstraction of groundwater can lead to saline intrusion in coastal areas, or to higher concentrations of naturally occurring toxic compounds (Stellar, 2010), whereas extraction of surface water can lead to high pollutant concentrations during low flow conditions.

The health risks related to drinking water supply and sanitation are generally acknowledged as a priority concern of global significance, as stressed in the above quote by United Nations (UN) Secretary General Ban Ki-moon (2008). Approximately 3.5 million people die each year due to inadequate water supply, sanitation, and hygiene, predominantly in developing countries (WHO, 2008a). Release of toxic wastes from waste dumps and industries is a major threat to the provision of safe water in the developed world.

Ecosystem health has historically been a concern of the richer, more developed countries. However, the increasing recognition of the many benefits of life-sustaining ecosystem goods and services, such as provision of food and fibre, has made ecosystem health and vulnerability an important socio-economic issue, even in the poorest countries.

Poor water quality can lead to significant and varied economic costs, including degradation of ecosystem services; health care; agriculture and industrial production costs; lack of tourism; increased water treatment costs; and reduced property values (UNEP, 2010). For example, the estimated costs of poor-quality water in countries in the Middle East and North Africa range between 0.5 and 2.5% of Gross Domestic Product (GDP) (World Bank, 2007). As the water resources is becoming increasingly scarce in the future, the costs associated with addressing water quality problems is

expected to increase and the consequences of not addressing such issues in a timely manner are expected to worsen.

Water quality is a global concern as risks of degradation translate directly into social and economic impacts. Improved management of vulnerability and risk must focus on the unknown and the unexpected in an era of accelerated changes. Given that the world's water quality situation is poorly understood, an important step is to develop a global water quality assessment framework to reduce the information gap and support decision-making and management processes.

16.2 Natural processes combined with social and economic drivers of water quality risks

Water quality conditions are the result of a variety of pressures created by many drivers. A causal chain links drivers to impacts on water quality and further to socio-economic concerns about human and ecosystem health. Identification of these drivers can reduce risks and vulnerabilities through appropriate management.

Drivers are the external causes of changes in water quality. In some instances they may be under the direct control of water managers (like wastewater treatment), although more typically their control is largely beyond the influence of water management. The main drivers may broadly be divided in two separate groups: social and economic. Assessment and consensus on the primary causal chains between drivers, water quality and public concerns are a precondition for developing actions to address them.

Before considering these drivers in detail, it is worth looking at the role of natural processes.

16.2.1 Natural processes
The hydrological cycle is the most important natural process influencing freshwater quality. For example, atmospheric transportation is a natural mechanism that can influence water quality by carrying and depositing atmospheric pollution from one location to another.

Sulphur emissions from fossil fuels can be transported over long distances and precipitate as acid rain. In sensitive lakes and rivers with limited buffer capacity, they may cause acidification on the ecosystems. Sulphur emission control has significantly reduced the issue of acid rain in developed countries, although many power plants still lack proper treatment methods.

Climate processes and associated climate variability and change influence the hydrological cycle. Managing risks associated with climate change is complicated by the challenges of determining the resulting impacts. It is reasonable to expect that the global temperature will rise by more than 2°C, and perhaps by more than 3°C, by the year 2050. The Intergovernmental Panel on Climate Change is predicting major risks for serious impacts, although it emphasizes that there are still major uncertainties in its forecasts (IPCC, 2008).

Many impacts may not manifest themselves for several decades, during which time promising progress could be made. Nevertheless, some issues need immediate attention in regard to risk management, as there are clear indications that climatic events are becoming increasingly erratic and violent. Major floods can destroy safe water supplies and sewage treatment plants, leaving communities with contaminated waters. Heavy rains and floods can increase erosion and sedimentation, while forest fires during droughts can also increase erosion risks.

Droughts and extreme low flows in water systems reduce ecosystem capacity to absorb and process contaminated waters. Estuaries may become affected by increasing saltwater intrusion, as in the Murray-Darling in Australia (Box 16.1), while sea level rise can increase salt intrusion, affecting major urban water supplies, as well as freshwater ecosystem stability and productivity.

BOX 16.1

Risks of salinity intrusion threaten the water supply of Adelaide, Australia

The Murray-Darling Basin (MDB) covers over 1 million km², covering four states in Australia, with the city of Adelaide at its mouth. Part of the agreement to manage the basin is to ensure the salinity at Adelaide is less than 800 electrical conductivity (EC) at least 95% of the time. In the 2000s the MDB experienced some of the lowest recorded rainfalls in the last 100 years, reducing river flows and Adelaide's water supply. The drought has highlighted the increased risks of salinity intrusion into the estuary under changing climatic conditions. Response options include ensuring more flow reaches the mouth, but this water is under high demand from upstream users, hence requiring a catchment-wide management approach.

Source: Adamson et al. (2009)

16.2.2 Social drivers

Social drivers have received little attention in water management efforts. Many emerging issues in water quality management are strongly related to social drivers causing waste discharges and associated water quality problems.

Social and political conflicts may jeopardize water management efforts, particularly in transboundary situations. Agreements frequently focus on water quantity, as it is perceived as more important, and generally easier to measure than water quality. Water quality is often neglected in agreements, although considering and improving water quality could benefit all parties (Eleftheriadou and Mylopoulos, 2008).

Community habits, preferences and consumption patterns bring additional social dimensions to uncertainties in water quality management. Cultural habits of waste disposal are difficult to change, not least in manufacturing enterprises and farming practices. Increasing needs for commodities, such as biofuels and meat products in both developed and emerging economies, put new pressures on already-intensive agricultural activities, and may increase nutrient and pesticide contamination. The production and subsequent waste deposition of an increasing number of complex chemical substances also creates new and unexpected impacts.

Population growth is a well-established driver of human wastewater loads. Demographic forecasts are well-developed, but assessment of future migrations, particularly to urban areas, where more than 50% of the world's population already live, is more uncertain. High population density may create critical pollution hot spots. An estimated 2.6 billion people worldwide live without adequate sanitation facilities (WHO and UNICEF, 2010), and the majority of wastewater in developing countries is discharged untreated into receiving water bodies (Corcoran et al., 2010).

Rudimentary control of solid waste dumping can create substantial risks of leakage of toxic chemical to both rivers and groundwater resources. Even where treatment plants exist, inefficient operation and disposal of waste sludge may contaminate soils and groundwater.

Military conflicts are also drivers that cause migration of millions of people annually, creating increasing risks for developing pollution hot spots and unsustainable pressures on the affected ecosystems.

16.2.3 Economic drivers

The importance of economic drivers is well-established in water management, and several sectors are discussed in separate challenge area reports in this edition of the *World Water Development Report*. The impacts of economic growth on urban settlements, industrial development and food production translate directly into increasing risks and emerging water quality issues. The direct economic drivers are primarily to waste discharges and construction of infrastructure such as barrages, dams and diversions.

Agriculture accounts for about 70% of global water use and the potential risk of water quality impacts of agricultural return flows is therefore significant. Agricultural practices cause nutrient contamination, and the sector is the major driver of eutrophication, except in areas with high urban concentrations. Nutrient enrichment has become one of the planet's most widespread water quality problems (WWAP, 2009). Further, pesticide application is estimated to be over two million metric tonnes per year on a global scale (UNEP, 2010). These toxic substances may carry substantial risks to the health and productivity of aquatic ecosystems, although the banning of certain substances and integrated pest management has contributed to reduced risks of pesticide pollution.

FIGURE 16.1

Hazardous waste generation in 2001 as reported by the Parties to the Basel Convention

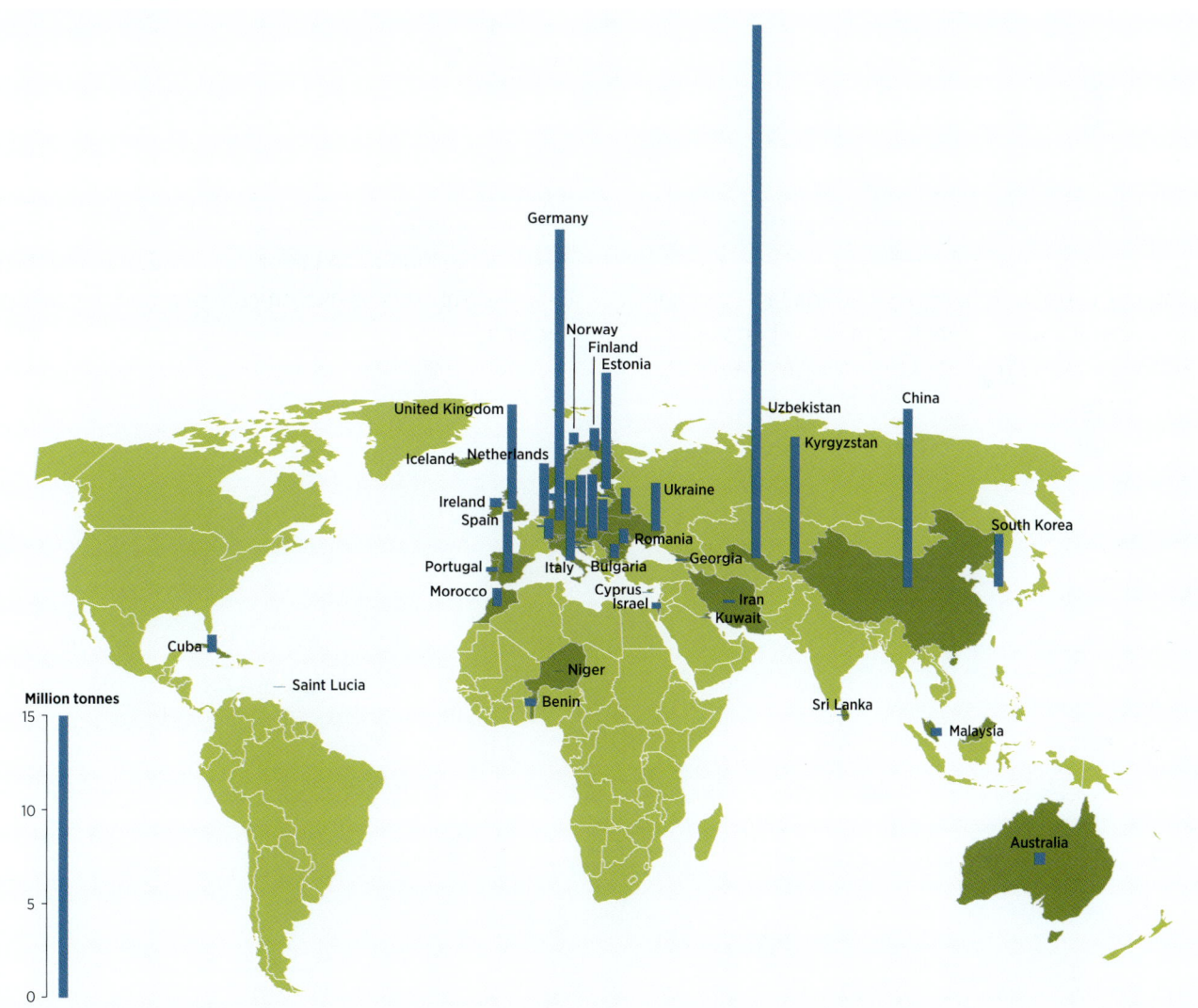

Source: UNEP/GRID-Arendal (http://maps.grida.no/go/graphic/hazardous_waste_generation_in_2001_as_reported_by_the_parties_to_the_basel_convention, a map by P. Rekacewicz, with source Basel Convention).

Intensive meat production in pig farms and feed lots may also create harmful local water contamination in the form of biological oxygen demand (BOD), ammonia, and nutrients.

Pulp and food processing industries may also create untreated BOD and nutrient rich discharges, potentially leading to oxygen deficits, eutrophication and general ecosystem degradation.

Aquaculture can also be an important source of water pollution. A particular concern is contamination of the natural environment with diseases. Such diseases have

seriously degraded large numbers of estuarine ecosystems and destroyed the potential for further aquaculture production.

Industrial development is a key driver behind the risk of hazardous substances contamination. Technological development creates more consumer goods introducing new toxic and hazardous chemicals (Figure 16.1). In the developing world, enforcement of environmental standards is challenging, making it difficult to prevent releases of untreated industrial wastes into freshwater bodies. Globalization has increased the risks of environmental dumping, both in the form of polluting

FIGURE 16.2

Hazardous industrial site, water pollution and mining hot spots in the Balkans

Source: UNEP/GRID-Arendal (http://maps.grida.no/go/graphic/balkans-hazardous-industrial-sites-water-pollution-and-mining-hot-spots, a map by UNEP/DEWA/GRID-Europe).

industries, and as direct exports of chemical wastes from developed or emerging economies to developing countries. Industrial accidents involving dangerous chemicals (not least during natural disasters) also create risks of spills to surface water and groundwater.

Energy production and distribution is a main cause of oil contamination. Hydrocarbons are biodegradable in small concentrations, but major leaks and accidents (including sabotage) create severe contamination risks. Further, shipping of hydrocarbons over the oceans as well as in inland waterways creates also risks of spills. Cooling water releases and bottom water releases from hydropower reservoirs may cause temperature shocks to ecosystems, though can generally be controlled by adequate legislation. Fossil fuel power plants emit large amounts of sulphates, which can contaminate soil and surface water through acid rain. Acid rain was a common problem in industrialized countries in the 1980s, but through legislation on emissions limits and 'cleaning' technology, the situation is vastly improved, though still present. Today, in emerging economies with rapidly expanding fossil fuel power industries, acid rain is increasing. In 2006, one-third of China was affected by acid rain, posing a major threat to soil and food safety (Zijun Li, 2006). While China has implemented programs to reduce sulphate emissions, gains are being offset by increases in nitrogen emissions (Zhao et al., 2009).

A rapidly emerging risk issue is the introduction of biofuels as a climate change mitigation strategy. Aside from the potentially detrimental impacts to food production, this activity involves intensive cultivation practices requiring high use of fertilizers and pesticides. Mining creates contamination risks from hazardous substances and acidification (Figure 16.2). Mine drainage waters can be extremely polluted by salts in the groundwater itself; metals such as lead, copper, arsenic and zinc present in the source rock; sulphur compounds leached from rock; and mercury or other materials used in extraction and processing. The pH of these drainage waters can be highly variable. Some mine drainage is extremely acidic, with a pH of 2–3; other source materials can lead to very alkaline discharges (UNEP, 2010).

Numerous small-scale and primitive mining operations are carried out in developing countries with no or limited control. Artisanal and small-scale mining is practiced in about 50 countries by people living in the poorest and most remote rural areas, with few employment alternatives. An estimated 13 million people are engaged in artisanal and small-scale mining, influencing the livelihood of additional 80–100 million people (Hentschel, 2002). These numbers are likely to increase, caused by higher prices and demands for minerals, both in Organisation for Economic Co-operation and Development (OECD) countries and emerging economies, such as China, India and Brazil.

Forest logging activities are often conducted without efficient erosion control practices jeopardizing both environmental conditions and safe water supplies. This also applies when natural forests are replaced by oil palm plantations for biofuel production.

Tourism generally provides a strong incentive to protect the environment and water quality, because a healthy environment is what attracts its trade. As such, tourism development may become a positive driver, if properly advised and facilitated, but urbanization and lack of proper waste treatment have destroyed recreational assets.

The financial sector is normally not associated with water quality risks. However, the current global financial crisis has had a potentially significant negative impact on private sector investments in clean technology, production safety and wastewater treatment. Despite increased government support to stimulus

BOX 16.2

Financing and cost recovery

Simply maintaining the current percentage of urban population with access to improved sanitation over the next 15 years will require extending access to over 800 million urban residents. However, piped wastewater systems may be too costly to apply on a wide scale, particularly in informal urban settlements, because of infrastructural and geographic cost constraints, as well as the relatively cost prohibitive hook-up expenses for individual households that lack the capacity to pay. As a result, many countries assign a lower priority for sanitation, partly as a result of the high investment costs, and partly because of the lower perceived benefits (individual and societal) of sanitation services, compared to water supply investments. Accordingly, global sanitation investment comprises only 20% of the total invested in the water and sanitation development sector.

Source: Reproduced from USAID (2010).

packages, the crisis has reduced government funds for public mitigation and adaptation responses, such as urban sewage systems and treatment plants (Box 16.2). This particularly applies to international development funding (Committee of African Finance Ministers and Central Bank Governors, 2009 and UNECA, 2009).

16.3 Relationship between water quantity and water quality

Water quality is just as important as water quantity for satisfying basic human and environmental needs, yet it has received far less investment, scientific support and public attention in recent decades, even though the two issues are closely linked (Biswas and Tortajada, 2011).

Poor water quality reduces the amount of water available for drinking, industrial and agricultural purposes (UNEP, 2010) (Box 16.3). The more polluted the water is, the greater the cost of treatment to return it to a useable standard.

Excessive pumping of groundwater can impact the water quality through increased concentrations of

naturally occurring compounds that become dangerously high as the amount of water dwindles. In India, fluorosis potentially threatens or directly affects millions of people (Box 16.4). Groundwater quality may also be affected by increasing salinity levels as a result of saltwater intrusion into their coastal aquifers, as observed in Cyprus and the Gaza Strip (Stellar, 2010).

Similarly, overuse of surface water reduces the natural flow and increases the concentration of harmful substances present in the water due to pollution. According to Stellar (2010), 'A marked example of this is the... Rio Grande River, where decreased flows in summer months coincide with large declines in water quality. During the dry season, pathogen concentrations increase by almost 100 times.'

It is important to acknowledge that there is a spectrum of quality–quantity interactions. Some water issues are purely quality related; this refers to water sources that are simply over-polluted as opposed to being overused. Other water quality problems have both quantity and quality components, for example in connection with mining activities.

16.4 Human health risks related to water quality

Reduction of human health risks are important local, national and global priorities, as expressed in the Millennium Development Goals (MDGs). Waterborne diseases are major global killers, taking millions of lives as a direct result of unsafe drinking water, and inadequate sanitation and hygiene.

Major human health risks from use of unsafe surface and groundwater are related to the presence

BOX 16.3

Water quality and quantity impacts of mining in Peru

Peru is Latin America's most water-stressed country. Water draining from the Andean highlands serves as a water tower that supports the downstream population and agricultural activities. Many mining concessions are located in headwater areas in the high Andes, and mining can adversely affect water quality downstream, with impacts potentially lasting for generations.

Source: Bebbington and Williams (2008). Photo: Paulo Tomaz at Wikimedia (http://commons.wikimedia.org/wiki/File:Antamina_Mine_Tailings_Pond.jpg)

BOX 16.4

Reduced water quantity equals reduced water quality: Fluorosis in India

Millions of people in India are threatened or directly affected by fluorosis caused by groundwater that contains excessive natural fluoride levels. India's escalating water stress is forcing people to search for water deeper underground, which is more contaminated with fluoride. Fluorosis is also a problem in countries such as Chile, Ethiopia and Uzbekistan to China, where there are an estimated 1.6 million victims.

Source: Shah and Indu (2008).

TABLE 16.1

Estimated deaths of children under the age of five (8.795 million in total)

68% (5.970 million) of deaths were from infectious diseases			
Pneumonia	18%	1.575 million	1.046–1.874 million [UR]
Diarrhoea	15%	1.336 million	0.822–2.004 million [UR]
Malaria	8%	0.732 million	0.601–0.851 million [UR]
41% (3.575 million) of deaths occurred in neonates			
PTB complications	12%	1.033 million	0.717–1.216 million [UR]
Birth asphyxia	9%	0.814 million	0.563–0.997 million [UR]
Sepsis	6%	0.521 million	0.356–0.735 million [UR]
Pneumonia	4%	0.386 million	0.264–0.545 million [UR]

Note: UR, uncertainty range.
Source: Black et al. (2010).

of pathogenic organisms and toxic substances, from municipal and industrial waste discharges as well as storm-generated non-point-source runoff. In a global context, water contamination with pathogenic substances is acknowledged as the most serious risk factor in relation to human health.

Less attention has been paid to risks of runoff from agricultural lands, where health impacts of fertilizers and pesticides may be transferred to humans through groundwater and surface water. The health impact from livestock waste, particularly from intensive farming, is of continued concern (Corcoran et al., 2010). Risks of human health impacts also arise in the food chains of fish and seafood, as noted in Section 4.1.

16.4.1 Waterborne diseases

Most waterborne diseases are related to contamination from untreated wastewater, or sewage (WSSCC, 2008). Sewage refers to liquid waste from private households as well as wastewater from non-industrial and industrial activities. In many parts of developing countries, sewage is dumped directly into local waterways. Untreated sewage contains waterborne pathogens that can cause serious human illness and even death.

Massive efforts have been made to reduce risks of waterborne contamination by establishing piped drinking water supplies in order to reach the MDGs.

Diarrhoea is typically transmitted by the consumption of food or water contaminated with faecal bacteria from an infected person. Although a global issue, it is most extreme in sub-Saharan Africa and South Asia, killing over 2 million people annually (WHO, 2008). Almost 1.5 million of these deaths are children under the age of five, accounting for 15% of all child deaths under the age of five, second only to pneumonia, and more than HIV/AIDS, measles, and malaria combined (Black et al., 2010) (Table 16.1). Less common waterborne diseases include typhoid, cholera, and hepatitis A. While the number of deaths from these diseases is relatively low, the number of cases (17 million annually for typhoid) put a high burden on communities in developing countries.

Drivers to waterborne diseases are strongly linked to population growth, combined with migration to urban centres with a high population density. Lack of finances limits the possibilities to establish costly sewer and treatment systems to handle urban wastewaters. Natural disasters (floods, storm surges, hurricanes, earthquakes) often destroy safe water supplies, leaving the population with no alternative to using contaminated water for long periods.

Response efforts may first consider public education – hand washing is the most vital component of personal hygiene (Pokhrel, 2007).This effort must be combined with appropriate, cost effective options for collecting, treating and disposing of human wastes. There is an urgent need to create more innovative solutions within the financial capabilities of municipalities in the developing world. Innovative financing of appropriate wastewater infrastructure should incorporate the full life cycle of the plants, and the valuation of non-market dividends from wastewater treatment (such as public amenity and ecosystem services) need to be better understood to enable more comprehensive cost–benefit analyses. Institutional efforts are needed to strengthen emergency responses when safe water supplies are destroyed because of natural disasters and conflicts. This will become particularly important with the emerging climate change threats.

16.4.2 Water quality degradation from toxic substances

Compared to the global importance of human waste contamination, the toxic impacts from hazardous chemicals are often of more local or regional concern. Although the number of fatalities is smaller than for waterborne pathogens, the number of people at risk is substantial (Table 16.2). Further, hazardous chemicals in developing countries are often not noticed before their toxic effects have become evident in the population. Toxic substances in water may originate from natural sources (e.g. arsenic), as well as from human sources (e.g. pesticides).

Inorganic pollutants from industrial processes include the toxic metals such as lead, mercury, and chromium. They are naturally occurring, but become a health issue due to anthropogenic contamination. When present in water, they can cause toxic effects, including damage to the brain, kidney, and lungs. They may damage neural networks and cause blood and brain disorders. Poisoning by trace metals typically arise from consumption of contaminated drinking water or food, such as irrigated crops, fish and seafood.

Arsenic in drinking water can cause human organ failure and cancer. Arsenic poisoning of groundwater from natural sources has been found in many countries and it is estimated that approximately 130 million people have been or are still consuming groundwater with arsenic concentrations above the standard set by the World Health Organization (WHO) (Royal Geographic Society with IBG, 2008) (Figure 16.3).

TABLE 16.2

Estimated impacts of toxic pollution

Top six toxic threats:	Estimated population at risk at identified sites (million people)	Estimated global impact (million people)
1. Lead	10	18–22
2. Mercury	8.6	15–19
3. Chromium	7.3	13–17
4. Arsenic	3.7	5–9
5. Pesticides	3.4	5–8
6. Radionuclides	3.3	5–8

Notes: The population estimates are preliminary and based on an ongoing global assessment of polluted sites. The estimated global impact is extrapolated from current site research and assessment coverage.
Source: Blacksmith Institute (2010, p. 7).

FIGURE 16.3

Probability of occurrence of excessively high arsenic concentrations (>0.05 mg per L) in groundwater

high
low
uncertain

Source: Brunt et al. (2004).

Nitrate is a nutrient commonly found in both surface water and groundwater as a result of fertilizer application losses. Although harmless to human health in small concentrations, nitrate may cause harm to infants at levels above 50 mg per L (WHO, 2008). Chloride from seawater intrusions may also render water unsuitable for drinking, though there is currently no guideline value for chloride (WHO, 2008).

Persistent organic pollutants (POPs) are organic compounds resistant to environmental degradation. POPs can remain in the environment for a long time and capable of bioaccumulation in human and animal tissues. POPs exposure can cause death and illness, including disruption of the endocrine, reproductive and immune systems; neurobehavioural disorders, and cancer. POPs include substances such as polychlorinated biphenyls (PCBs), many pesticides (e.g. DDT), as well as certain pharmaceuticals and body care products. PCB use has been banned in the European Union and the United States (USA).

Some of the synthetic chemicals that are found in wastewater containing pesticides and pharmaceuticals are endocrine disruptors (Colborn and vom Saal, 1993) (Box 16.5). The potentially negative effects of these chemicals on humans and human development have been documented, and studies on animals suggest

BOX 16.5

Risk of hormonal modifications in ecosystem populations

The effects of endocrine disrupting chemicals (organic chemicals that can mimic natural hormones) on wildlife include the thinning of eggshells in birds, inadequate parental behaviour, and cancerous growths (Carr and Neary, 2008). The feminization of fish and amphibians downstream of wastewater treatment plants, for example, has long been linked to estrogenic pharmaceuticals (Sumpter, 1995), and more recently to pesticides such as atrazine (Hayes et al., 2006). A WHO Global Assessment of the State-of-the-Science of Endocrine Disruptors in 2002 identified the need for better understanding of EDCs and their impacts on humans and ecosystems. However, there is still no global study on the impact of EDCs, partly due to complexities involved in identifying dose–response relationships. While many EDCs have been banned (particularly in Europe and North America), some continue to be used, such as DDT.

Source: UNEP (2010).

there is cause for concern, even at low doses. Research shows the effects may extend beyond the exposed individual, particularly affecting foetuses of exposed pregnant women and breastfed children (Diamanti-Kandarakis, 2009).

Toxic water contamination risks are primarily a function of industrial and agricultural production. Driver uncertainties are related to the particular industrial processes and practices, particularly their waste emissions, including wastewater to solid waste deposits. An important issue is the risk of accidental releases of toxic chemicals, particularly from chemical industries. Intensive agriculture practices (including the Green Revolution) are heavily dependent on pest control, with considerable risk of contaminating both surface water and groundwater. Mining enterprises represent substantial risks for toxic contamination, both from mining waste materials, as well as the mining processes themselves.

Response efforts may primarily be directed toward industries using or producing toxic substances. Development of clean technology and substitution processes, combined with cost efficient treatment options, is a priority component. However, regulations and their efficient enforcement are also needed. Risks of accidental spills must be addressed within the enterprises themselves, but supported by public alarm and response frameworks. Furthermore, handling of solid wastes from production processes must be considered from the perspective of minimizing contamination of waste dumps. Pesticide contamination can be minimized through use of low-impact substances and integrated pest management techniques (UNEP, 2010). Awareness campaigns and extension services on pesticide use are of particular importance. In 1987, the National Union of Farmers and Ranchers (UNAG) in Nicaragua founded the Programa Campesino a Campesino (PCaC), an innovative effort to promote best agricultural practices through peer-to-peer education. Producers from 817 communities are benefitting from the PCaC methodology where the producers share their knowledge and experiences with one another (UNEP, 2010).

16.5 Ecosystem health risks related to water quality

The Millennium Ecosystem Assessment (MA, 2005a,b) recognized the importance of ecosystem goods and services as an important and multifaceted asset in poverty alleviation, as well as for sustainable economic development. The report changed the focus from simply protecting endangered species to include the livelihoods and income opportunities of the poor dependent on ecosystems for their livelihoods.

16.5.1 Oxygen depletion and fish kills

A healthy aquatic environment maintains a high level of dissolved oxygen (DO), between 80 and 120% saturation. Oxygen demands by microorganisms may deplete the DO to critical levels, causing fish kills and anaerobic conditions in the water column and bottom sediments (Department of Water Affairs and Forestry, 1996). Such conditions can destroy fisheries and seriously harm the ecological structure and the recreational value of the ecosystem (Box 16.6).

Untreated sewage contains high loads of organic material, supporting the growth of microorganisms and increasing their oxygen demand as they decompose the organic matter. Oxygen deficit is related to pollution from human and industrial wastewaters. Therefore, urban centres and industries like pulp producers, abattoirs and pig farms become hot spots for DO deficits in aquatic ecosystems. Figure 16.4 shows the modelled organic loading taking into account different types of sewage treatment only. It shows hot spots in every

BOX 16.6

Bang Pakong pollution destroys valuable ecosystem assets and income opportunities

The Bang Pakong estuary has perfect conditions for the river shrimp that is one of Thailand's major delicacies. The estuary is home to endangered species (e.g. the Irawaddy dolphin) and, like many estuaries, plays an important role for both brackish and marine fisheries. However, water quality issues caused by shrimp farming within the estuary are compounded by effluents from catchment activities, including waste water discharges from all sectors. High pollution loads have been reported from different sources: domestic (nearly 6,000 kg BOD per day); industrial (nearly 9,000 kg BOD per day); and agriculture (30,000 kg BOD per day). The development of inland low salinity shrimp farms in the freshwater areas of the basin is an additional pollution threat producing up to 32 million kg BOD per year.

Although several plans have been prepared to address the situation the water quality conditions remain poor. It is recommended to adopt an ecosystems services approach to better realize the benefits of the ecosystem.

Source: UNEP (2008).

FIGURE 16.4

Modelled organic loading based on different types of sewage treatment

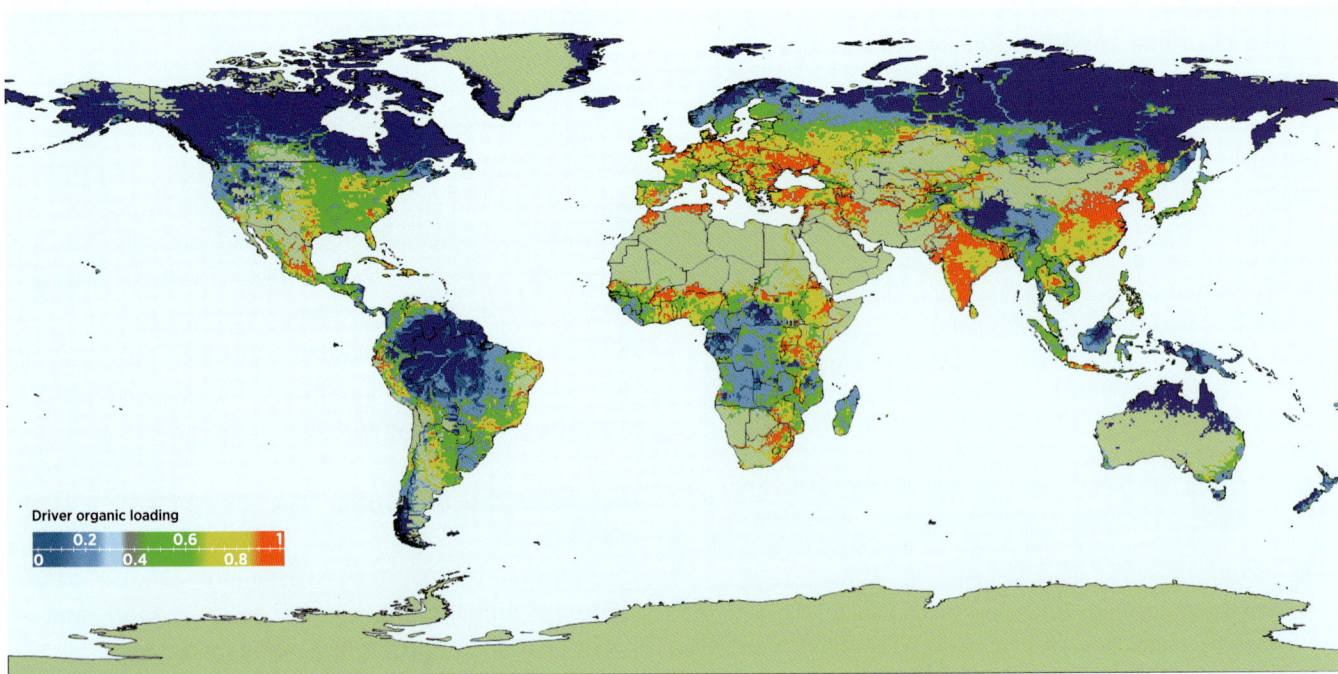

Source: Vörösmarty et al. (2010, supp. fig. 2, pp. 3–10.). Reproduced by permission from Macmillan Publishers Ltd.

Lake eutrophication in China

Taihu Lake (or Lake Tai) is the third largest freshwater lake in China, providing water to 30 million people. It has a thriving fishing industry and was previously a popular tourist destination. In May 2007 a severe algal bloom and major pollution with cyanobacteria occurred, largely driven by the high levels of industry and development in the catchment, made worse because the lake was at its lowest level in 50 years. The Chinese government called the lake a natural disaster. and banned water providers from implementing price hikes after bottled water rose to six times the normal price. It was reported that the Chinese government had shut down or given notice to over 1,300 factories around the lake by October 2007.

The State Council set a target to clean Taihu Lake by 2012, but in 2010 a fresh pollution outbreak was reported. This highlights the complexities involved in controlling pollution, often with competing political, developmental, commercial, and environmental interests.

Sources: The Economist (2010) and Wikipedia (2011).

region, with particularly large areas affected in central Asia, India, and northern China.

Eutrophication can also cause severe oxygen deficits through the microbial decomposition of dead algal cells.

High levels of nutrients like nitrate and phosphate can also destroy the normal biological structures. Often the dominating sources of nutrients are fertilizers, though domestic wastewater also contains nutrients. Agricultural losses are non-point sources, which are difficult to identify, therefore associated with considerable uncertainties and risks (Box 16.7).

Erosion caused by inappropriate land uses (e.g. deforestation) can also become critical sources of nutrients causing eutrophication. As previously noted, an emerging issue is more frequent incidences of forest fires, which may be associated with subsequent erosion.

Unfortunately, there is insufficient data to give a complete overview of eutrophication trends at the global

World hypoxic and eutrophic coastal areas

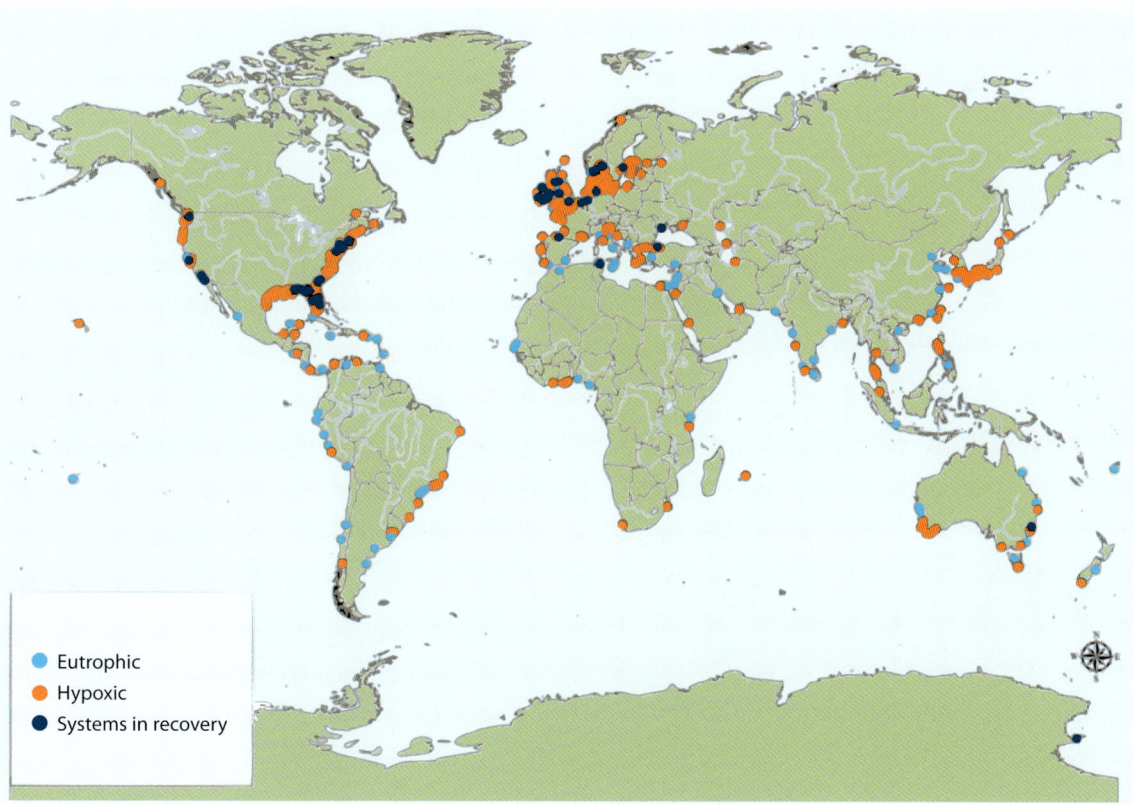

● Eutrophic
● Hypoxic
● Systems in recovery

Source: Diaz et al. (2010).

level, but it is thought that incidents of eutrophication are becoming more common and more severe. This is supported by Figure 16.5 below, which shows coastal areas suffering from eutrophic and hypoxic (insufficient oxygen) conditions.

Response efforts to urban and industrial point sources are similar to the previously described efforts. Control of non-point sources of nutrients must be conducted in close cooperation with land owners, through extension services and development of appropriate options for reducing contamination risks. The Chesapeake Bay Program, in the USA, which has run for over two decades, has shown that the control of non-point sources is a significant challenge. During this program research demonstrated that atmospheric input was a major contributor to the Bay's declining water quality. Thus, in addition to the watershed, the 'airshed' needs to be considered in an integrated management effort (GWP, 2011).

16.5.2 Ecosystem degradation from hazardous chemicals

Toxic substances that affect humans can also affect ecosystems. Fish kills and changes in biological structures are common impacts of toxic contamination, threatening the livelihood of local communities (Box 16.8).

Metals like mercury, lead and cadmium from industrial and mining wastes are characteristic ecosystem contaminants. Ammonia is a toxic waste product of the metabolism in animals which can lead to fatal poisoning of fish, often with dramatic consequences on local fisheries.

In addition to the direct poisoning of fish, seafood and vegetation, many substances (e.g. mercury, lead, POPs) accumulate in organic tissues, resulting in poisoning if eaten by humans. This bioaccumulation can also lead to toxic chemicals being transported long distances, and must be addressed by quality assurance procedures in the food sector. Irrigation with cadmium contaminated water can accumulate in crops.

Pesticides are by their very definition toxic to ecosystems. Most pesticides are soluble in water, and losses to water resulting from improper use readily translate into threats to both ecosystems and humans. Chemicals such as DDT are toxic to a wide range of

---

BOX 16.8
The Basel Convention

The Basel Convention was established to address the human health and environmental risks associated with the export of toxic wastes. With the tightening of environmental laws in developed nations in the 1970s, hazardous waste disposal costs increased dramatically. At the same time, globalization of shipping made transboundary movement of wastes more possible, and the trade in hazardous waste, particularly to developing countries, rapidly increased. The convention aims to keep waste as close to the sources as possible, and they can only be exported with prior written notification by the state of export to the states of import and transit. The vast majority of countries have ratified the treaty and it is generally seen as a success, and the Convention Secretariat now works closely with the Rotterdam and Stockholm Conventions. The Convention is legally binding, including reporting national reporting requirements on the movement of hazardous wastes.

Source: OECD (1989).

animals, in addition to insects, and are highly toxic to aquatic life. Pesticides have particularly serious impacts on fish production in rice fields, an important by-product of traditional paddy systems.

Risk mitigation of toxic contamination of ecosystems is similar to efforts focusing on human health. The drivers are the same, as are many of the response options.

16.5.3 Ecosystem modifications

Some water quality parameters may appear harmless under normal conditions, but possess significant risks when concentration levels are slightly altered.
This is particularly true for the coastal interface between fresh and marine waters. Minor changes in salinity, temperature or turbidity may catalyse significant risks of changes in the biological structures of estuaries and lagoons providing important livelihoods for coastal communities (Box 16.9).

Salinity is also an important ecological factor. Freshwater species may be evicted with increasing salinity and replaced by brackish or even marine species. Also, many plants are sensitive to salinity – an important issue for irrigation water intakes. The most critical cases of salinity changes occur in the coastal zones, where morphological changes in lagoons and

BOX 16.9

Chilika Lake: slow deterioration and rapid recovery

Chilika Lake is the largest wintering ground for migratory waterfowl on the Indian subcontinent. The highly productive lagoon ecosystem, with its rich fishery resources, sustains the livelihoods of more than 200,000 people. Threats to the lake ecosystem increased through the 1980s from pollution, intensive aquaculture, overfishing, and increased siltation from poor land management. By 1993 the situation became so severe that the lake was put on the Montreux Record (a Ramsar list signifying threats from human activities). In 1992 the State Government set up the Chilika Development Authority (CDA), which facilitated the development of an adaptive integrated management plan with stakeholder participation. Significant national funding supported activities such as catchment conservation, education campaigns, improved socio-economic conditions (e.g. improvement of services), and habitat restoration. Ten years later, Chilika Lake was awarded the Ramsar Wetland Award in recognition of significant improvements. Lessons learned included: (a) danger of unilateral decisions on established rights of stakeholders; (b) vital role of science; (c) importance of coordination and diverse funding; (d) need for long term policies; (e) stakeholder participation can lead to self–initiated good practices; and (f) links between poverty alleviation and ecosystem restoration.

Source: Ghosh and Pattanaik (2006).

estuaries can cause drastic salinity impacts. Storm surges also may raise salinity in freshwater reservoirs and soil water of low lying agricultural lands.

Many species may be temperature sensitive, particularly during spawning. Therefore, changes in the water temperature may deplete certain species. Increasing water temperature may also compound the impacts of eutrophication. Primary causes of temperature changes are cooling water releases from electricity generation and other industrial activities. However, impacts can be mitigated through legislation and enforcement. Acidity changes may also create changes in the ecosystem structures. Acid rain and acid mining wastewaters have been shown to have adverse impacts on aquatic ecosystems.

Climate change also threatens ecosystems. Sea level rise (or extended droughts) may increase salt water intrusion in estuaries and lagoons, and change the biological structure from freshwater to saltwater species.

FIGURE 16.6

Annual cost of the environmental degradation of water

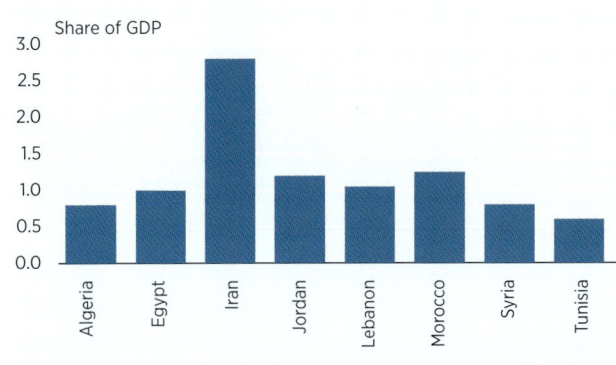

Source: World Bank (2007, fig. 4.4, p. 109), from various data sources.

A similar effect in relation to invasive species may be caused by temperature changes.

Responses to ecosystem changes depend on an in-depth understanding of the biological processes under transformation. First and foremost, an efficient and targeted monitoring system is needed to detect changes, and if trends are identified, further research must be directed towards understanding the causes.

16.6 Economic costs of poor water quality

Poor water quality may lead to significant economic costs/losses such as reduced ecosystem services; health care; increased agriculture and industrial production costs; lack of tourism; increased water treatment costs; and reduced property values (UNEP, 2010). The estimated costs of poor quality water in countries in the Middle East and North Africa range between 0.5 and 2.5% of GDP (Figure 16.6) (World Bank, 2007). With freshwater resources projected to become increasingly scarce in these and other regions, the costs associated with addressing the resulting problems can be expected to increase.

Increased health has economic benefits to governments and individuals through reduced expenditure on disease treatment and lost time in seeking treatment, and benefits to the agricultural and industrial sectors through improved productivity and fewer expenses associated with employee health care (SIWI, 2005).

Many studies on the health-related costs of poor water quality are in reference to the water and sanitation MDGs, whereby the international community is committed to halving the proportion of people without access to safe water and sanitation by 2015. If this goal is met, it is estimated that 322 million working days per year will be gained, corresponding to nearly US$750 million (SIWI, 2005). Meeting the MDGs on water and sanitation would also result in an annual savings to health sector expenses of US$7 billion. Overall, the total economic benefits of meeting the MDG target have been estimated at US$84 billion (SIWI, 2005). The benefits of wastewater treatment range between US$3–34 for every US$1 invested in sanitation and drinking water (WHO, 2004).

In terms of agriculture, salinized water can reduce crop quality or even destroy it. The use of poor quality water can also have serious consequences on human health. In 2011, several people died from an European *E. coli* outbreak, which was suspected to stem from vegetables that had come into contact with infected water. A strong consumer reaction resulting from a lack of clarity on the source led to thousands of tonnes of vegetables being dumped and an estimated cost to the European Commission of US$300 million to compensate farmers for their losses (Flynn, 2011).

TABLE 16.3

Summary of major risks and their main drivers

Risk			Main driver		Response option
Human health impact	Severity	Natural process	Social	Economic	Intervention
Waterborne disease	Millions of fatal cases Increasing waste discharge due to urbanization	Increasing flood disasters damage safe water supply	Urban migration Poverty	Shortage of investment in wastewater treatment	Urban wastewater treatment Low-cost community waste treatment
Toxic contamination	Millions of affected persons Thousands of cases of serious impacts in hot spots Lack of reliable documentation	Saltwater intrusion due to sea level rise and drought	Waste disposal attitudes Poverty	Industrial waste and spills Mining	Industrial waste treatment Clean technology Warning systems Disaster response systems
Ecosystem health impact	Severity	Natural process	Social	Economic	Intervention
Oxygen deficit and eutrophication	Thousands of km^2 Coastal fisheries decline Recreational value decline	Increasing heat waves and flood erosion events		Intensive agriculture Biofuels Urban wastewater Industrial wastewater	Sustainable agricultural practices Nutrient removal in wastewater
Poisoning	Hundreds of km^2 Fisheries destruction	Increasing flood disasters	Waste disposal attitudes Poverty	Agriculture Urban wastewater Industrial wastewater Mining	Industrial waste treatment Clean technology Integrated pest management
Ecosystem modification	Invasive species increase Invasive pest increase Turbidity increase	Seawater intrusion Heating Erosion after forest fires and floods	Poverty	Agriculture Forestry Urban wastewater Industrial wastewater Hydropower	Sustainable agricultural practices Sustainable forestry Nutrient removal in wastewater

While industrial production is foremost considered to affect water quality it can also be negatively affected by poor water quality. An indication of concern over quality and quantity is the increasing engagement of food and beverage companies, such as Nestlé and Coca Cola, in public discussions on water-related challenges. While no estimates exist on worldwide costs of poor water quality to industry, in 1992, China's industrial sector was estimated to have lost approximately US$1.7 billion as a result of water pollution (SIWI, 2005).

One of the most important services that freshwater ecosystems provide is waste treatment, although more research is required to better quantify this service. Costanza et al., (1997) estimated that the global

FIGURE 16.7

Wastewater: A global problem with differing regional issues

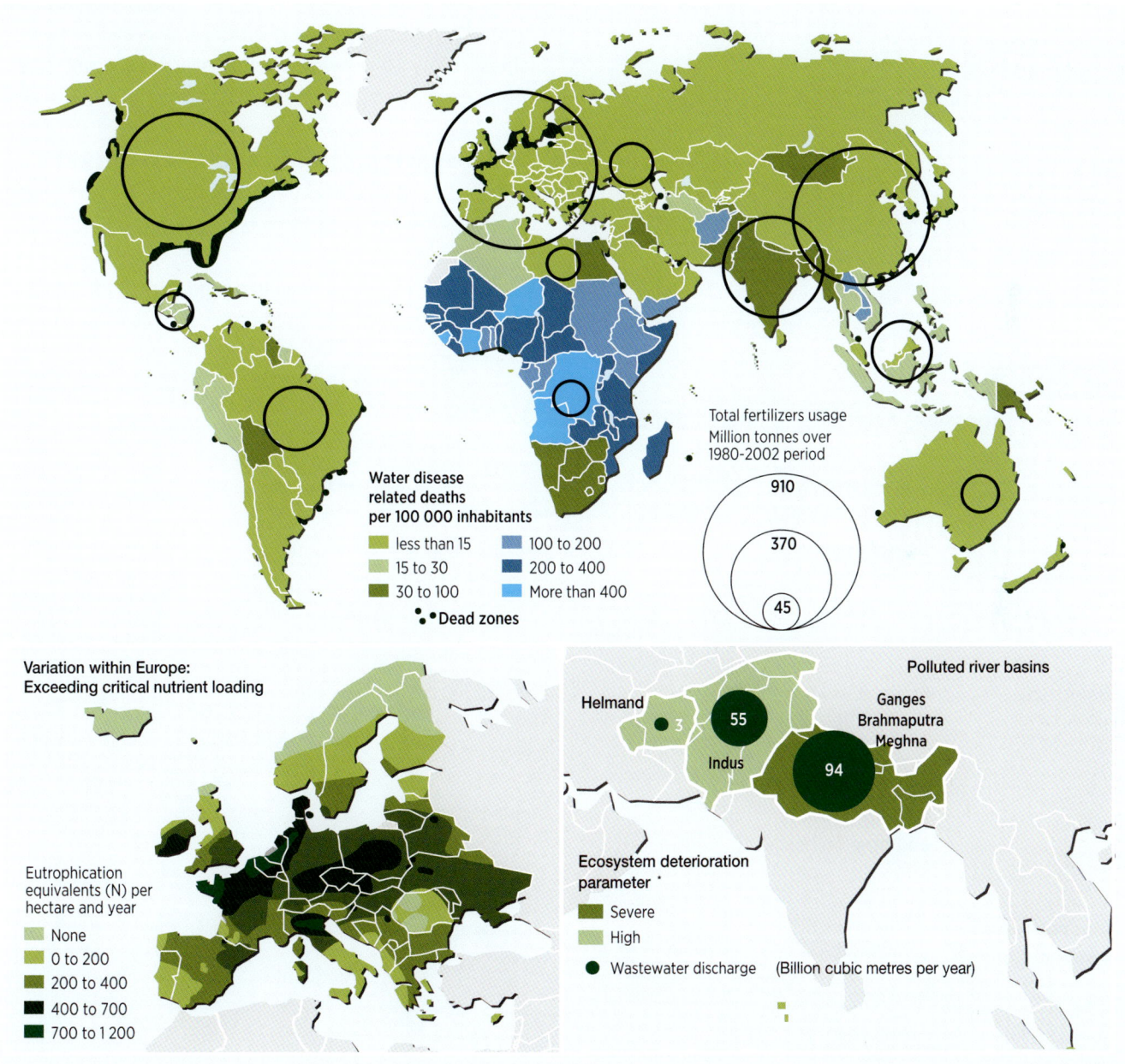

Note: The ecosystem deterioration parameter is defined as the land ratio without vegetation coverage (forest area and wetlands) used to present the contribution of an ecosystem's deterioration to the vulnerability of its water resources.
Source: UNEP/GRID-Arendal http://maps.grida.no/go/graphic/wastewater-a-global-problem-with-differing-regional-issues, a map by UNEP/GRID-Arendal with sources WHO database, data for 2002; FAO database; Babel and Walid, 2008; European Environment Agency, 2009; Diaz et al., 2008).

TABLE 16.4

Countries least likely to express satisfaction with the quality of water in their communities

Country	Risk Satisfied (%)
Chad	21
Ukraine	26
Nigeria	29
Ethiopia	29
Liberia	30
Russia	30
Tanzania	35
Lebanon	35
Sierra Leone	36
Angola*	38

*Only urban residents interviewed.

Source: Ray (2008).

services provided by lakes and rivers alone were in the region of US$133 billion per year. This figure does not take into consideration wetland biomes, some of which are coastal, which are expected to provide services of far greater value.

People have historically relied on natural processes in freshwater ecosystems to clean agricultural, municipal, and industrial wastes. Often, however, the magnitude and toxicity of these wastes has overwhelmed the capacity and resilience of such ecosystems, degrading water quality locally and regionally. Such degradations manifest themselves in impaired amenity values, declining biodiversity, and diminished ability to provide wastewater treatment and other ecosystem services (Arthington et al., 2009).

16.7 Risks, monitoring and intervention

A summary of global key risk issues, their main drivers and some response options is presented in Table 16.3.

While Table 16.3 is general in scope, it provides a useful overview of the key factors of water quality

TABLE 16.5

Summary of possible water quality interventions by scale

Scale	Education and capacity building	Policy/law/ governance	Financial/ economic	Technology/ infrastructure	Data/monitoring
International/ national	Initiate training and awareness building	Institute integrated approaches Institute pollution prevention	Institute polluter/ beneficiary pays system	Promote best practice and support capacity building	Develop monitoring framework
Watershed	Strategic level for raising awareness on impacts of water quality Establish training for practitioners and develop best practice	Create watershed-based planning units Develop water quality goals	Institute pricing systems Institute cost recovery Create incentives for efficiency	Invest in infrastructure and appropriate technologies	Build regional capacity to collect and process water quality data
Community/ household	Connect individual/ community behaviour to water quality impacts Build capacity to make improvements in sanitation/ wastewater treatment	Amend codes to allow innovative storm water treatment options Promote access to information	Encourage investments	Consider decentralized treatment technologies	Carry out and analyse household/ community surveys

Source: Adapted from UNEP (2010, table 8, p. 73).

risk. However, there is a critical lack of global water quality data upon which to make a robust assessment of trends and geographic hot spots, which means that the world's water quality situation is poorly understood. While there have been advances locally and in some regions, the overall global synthesis of water quality data has deteriorated in recent decades, making it difficult to support international decision making processes. An example of the regional differences is given in Figure 16.7. Although this Figure has been taken from a recent UN publication, much of the data is over ten years old. More up-to-date data is not available at the global scale.

An alternative to quantitative data is qualitative data, an example being the 2008 Gallup Poll on water quality satisfaction. 1000 residents from 145 countries were asked the simple question, 'In the city or area where you live, are you satisfied or dissatisfied with the quality of water?' While it might come as no surprise that the regional median rate of satisfaction was just 48% in sub-Saharan Africa (with a high of 62% in Southern Africa), the global top ten of least satisfied countries contains both Russia and Ukraine (Table 16.4).

While there can be many reasons for a country's ranking, such as the fact that Lebanon was surveyed just after the 2006 conflict with Israel, and that greater comparative emphasis is perhaps given on drinking water quality, the survey provides a simple but interesting snapshot.

Water quality issues also vary with scale, ranging from the international to the community or household level. In 2011, UNEP published its *Policy Brief on Water Quality*, which included a summary table on the possible interventions by scale in the form of education and capacity building; policy, law and governance; financial and economic; technology and infrastructure; and data and monitoring. Table 16.5 provides a summary of possible intervention measures at different scales, including increased capacity for monitoring.

A more substantial body of data on water quality is urgently required. One of the greatest challenges is to create a much needed framework for a global water quality assessment. Some possibilities for the form and value this could have are included in Table 16.5, while the motivation for such a framework would be to:

- better understand the state of water quality and its causes,
- understand recent trends and identify hot spots,
- test and validate policy and management options,
- provide a foundation for scenarios that can be used to understand and plan for appropriate future actions, and
- provide much needed monitoring bench markers (Alcamo, 2011).

The multitude of water quality parameters and uncertainties, and their impacts, makes water resources management a complex and multidimensional issue, particularly with respect to human activities. Improved management of vulnerability and risks is needed to focus on the unknown and the unexpected in an era of accelerated changes and new uncertainties.

||||||||||||||||||||||||||||||||||||||||||||||||||||||||||||||||||||||||||||||||||||

References

Adamson, D., Schrobback, P. and Quiggin, J. 2009. *Options for Managing Salinity in the Murray-Darling Basin under Reduced Rainfall.* Second International Salinity Forum. http://www.internationalsalinityforum.org/Final%20 Papers/adamson_C4.pdf

Alcamo, J. 2011. *The Global Water Quality Challenge.* Presentation at UNEP Water Strategy Meeting, 7 June 2011.

Arthington, A. H, Naiman, R. J., McClain, M. E. and Nilsson, C. 2009. Preserving the biodiversity and ecological services of rivers: New challenges and research opportunities. *Freshwater Biology,* Vol. 55, No. 1, pp. 1–16.

Ashley, R. and Cashman, A. 2006. The impacts of change on the long-term future demand for water sector infrastructure. *Infrastructure to 2030: Telecom, Land Transport, Water and Electricity,* pp. 241–349. Paris, OECD.

Ban Ki-moon. 2008. *Remarks on Sanitation and Water Supply: 'One World One Dream: Sanitation and Water for All'.* Speech given on 24 September 2008. UN News Centre. http://www.un.org/apps/news/infocus/sgspeeches/search_ full.asp?statID=330 (Accessed 28 September 2008.)

Bebbington, A. and Williams, M. 2008. Water and mining conflicts in Peru. *Mountain Research and Development,* Vol. 28, No. 3/4, pp. 190–95.

Biswas, A. and Tortajada, C. 2011. Water quality management: An introductory framework. *Water Resources Development,* Vol. 27, No. 1, pp. 5–11.

Black, R. E, Cousens S., Johnson H. L. et al. 2010. *Global Child Mortality: Status in 2008.* Presentation for the Child Health Epidemiology Reference Group of WHO and UNICEF. Global, regional, and national causes of child mortality in 2008: A systematic analysis. *The Lancet,* 5 June 2010, Vol. 375(9730), pp. 1969–87. http://cherg.org/projects/underlying_causes.html

Blacksmith Institute. 2010. *World's Worst Pollution Problems Report.* New York, Blacksmith Institute.

Brunt, R., Vasak, L. and Griffioen, J. 2004. *Arsenic in Groundwater: Probability of Occurrence of Excessive Concentration on Global Scale.* Report SP 2004-1. Utrecht, The Netherlands, International Groundwater Resource Centre (IGRAC).

Carr, G. M. and Neary, J. P. 2008. *Water Quality for Ecosystem and Human Health,* 2nd edn. Ontario, Canada, United Nations Environment Programme (UNEP) Global Environment Monitoring System.

Colborn, T., vom Saal, F. S. and Soto, A. 1993. Developmental effects of endocrine-disrupting chemicals in wildlife and humans. *Environmental Health Perspectives,* Vol. 101, No. 5, pp. 378–84.

Committee of African Finance Ministers and Central Bank Governors. 2009. *Impact of the Crisis on African Economies – Sustaining Growth and Poverty Reduction.* African Perspectives and Recommendations to the G20. A report from the Committee of African Finance Ministers and Central Bank Governors established to monitor the crisis. http://www.afdb.org

Costanza, R., d'Arge, R., de Groot, R. et al. 1997. The value of the world's ecosystem services and natural capital. *Nature,* Vol. 387, pp. 353–60.

Corcoran, E., Nellemann, C., Baker, E., Bos, R., Osborn, D. and Savelli, H. (eds). 2010. *Sick Water? The Central Role of Wastewater Management in Sustainable Development.* A Rapid Response Assessment. United Nations Environment Programme (UNEP), UN-HABITAT, GRID-Arendal. http://www.grida.no/files/publications/sickwater/poster1_SickWater.pdf

Department of Water Affairs and Forestry. 1996. South African Water Quality Guidelines. *Volume 7, Aquatic Ecosystems,* 1st edn, 1996. Republic of South Africa.

Diamanti-Kandarakis, E. et al. 2009. Endocrine-disrupting chemicals: An endocrine society scientific statement. *Endocrine Reviews,* Vol. 30, No. 4, pp. 293–342.

Diaz, R. J., Selman, M. and Chique-Canache, C. 2010. Global eutrophic and hypoxic coastal systems. *Eutrophication and Hypoxia: Nutrient Pollution in Coastal Waters.* Washington DC, World Resources Institute. http://www.wri.org/map/world-hypoxic-and-eutrophic-coastal-areas (Accessed 1 November 2011.)

The Economist. 2010. Raising a stink. Efforts to improve China's environment are having far too little effect. 5 August. http://www.economist.com/node/16744110 (Accessed 9 September 2011.)

Eleftheriadou, E. and Mylopoulos, Y. 2008. *Conflict Resolution in Transboundary Waters: Incorporating Water Quality in Negotiations.* Thessaloniki, Greece, UNESCO Chair INWEB. http://www.inweb.gr/twm4/abs/ELEFTHEIADOU%20Eleni.pdf

Flynn, D. 2011. Germany's *E. coli* outbreak most costly in history. *Food Safety News,* 16 June. http://www.foodsafetynews.com/2011/06/europes-o104-outbreak---most-costly-in-history/ (Accessed 8 September 2011.)

Ghosh, A. K. and Pattanaik, A. 2006. *Chilika Lagoon: Experience and Lessons Learned Brief.* Kusatsu-shi, Japan, Lake Basin Management Initiative, International Lake Environment Committee (ILEC).

Global Water Partnership. 2011. *Cases. USA: Chesapeake Bay (#294).* GWP Toolbox – Integrated Water Resources Management. Stockholm, Global Water Partnership (GWP). http://www.gwptoolbox.org/index.php?option=com_case&id=184&Itemid=42 (Accessed 1 November 2011.)

Hayes, T. B., Stuart, A. A., Mendoza, M., Collins, A., Noriega, N., Vonk, A., Johnston, G., Liu, R. and Kpodzo, D. 2006. Characterization of atrazine-induced gonadal malformations in African Clawed Frogs (*Xenopus laevis*) and comparisons with effects of an androgen antagonist (cyproterone acetate) and exogenous oestrogen (17β-estradiol): Support for the demasculinization/feminization hypothesis. *Environmental Health Perspectives,* Vol. 114 (S-1), pp. 134–41.

Hentschel, T., Hruschka, F. and Priester, M. 2002. *Global Report on Artisanal and Small-Scale Mining.* Mining, Minerals and Sustainable Development project, January 2002. London/Geneva, International Institute for Environment and Development (IIED)/World Business Council for Sustainable Development (WBCSD).

IPCC (Intergovernmental Panel on Climate Change) (R. K. Pachauri and A. Reisinger, eds). 2008. *Climate Change 2007: Synthesis Report. Contribution of Working Groups I, II and III to the Fourth Assessment Report of the Intergovernmental Panel on Climate Change.* IPCC, Geneva.

MA (Millennium Ecosystem Assessment). 2005a. *Ecosystems and Human Well-Being: Wetlands and Water Synthesis.* Washington DC, World Resources Institute.

––––. 2005b. *Ecosystems and Human Well-Being: Synthesis.* Washington DC, Island Press.

OECD (Organization for Economic Co-operation and Development). *Basel Convention.* 1989.

Pokhrel, A. 2007. *How to Promote Measures to Prevent Water-Borne Diseases?* The Hague, IRC International Water and Sanitation Centre. http://www.irc.nl/page/8904

Ray, J. 2008. *Water Quality an Issue Around the World: Satisfaction Lowest in Sub-Saharan Africa.* GALLUP, 19 March. http://www.gallup.com/poll/105211/water-quality-issue-around-world.aspx (Accessed 8 September 2011.)

Royal Geographic Society with IBG. 2008. *Arsenic Pollution: A Global Problem.* London, Royal Geographic Society with IBG. http://www.rgs.org/NR/rdonlyres/00D3AC7F-F6AF-48DE-B575-63ABB2F86AF8/0/ArsenicFINAL.pdf

Shah, T. and Indu, R. 2008. *Fluorosis in Gujarat: A Disaster Ahead.* Bangalore, India Water Portal. http://www.indiawaterportal.org/sites/indiawaterportal.org/files/Fluorosis_Gujarat_Tushaar%20Shah_CAREWATER_2008.pdf

SIWI (Stockholm International Water Institute). 2005. *Making Water a Part of Economic Development: The Economic Benefits of Improved Water Management and Services.* Stockholm, SIWI. http://www.siwi.org/documents/Resources/Reports/CSD_Making_water_part_of_economic_development_2005.pdf

Stellar, D. 2010. *Can We Have Our Water and Drink It, Too? Exploring the Water Quality-Quantity Nexus.* State of the Planet. Blogs from the Earth Institute. New York, Columbia University. http://blogs.ei.columbia.edu/2010/10/28/can-we-have-our-water-and-drink-it-too-exploring-the-water-quality-quantity-nexus/ (Accessed 1 September 2011.)

Sumpter, J. P. 1995. Feminized responses in fish to environmental estrogens. *Toxicology Letters,* Vol. 82–83, pp. 737–42.

UNECA (United Nations Economic Commission for Africa). 2009. *The Global Financial Crisis: Impact, Responses and Way Forward.* Addis Ababa, UNECA.

UNEP (United Nations Environment Programme). 2006. *The State of the Marine Environment: Trends and Processes.* The Hague, Coordination Office of the Global Programme of Action for the Protection of the Marine Environment from Land-based Activities (GPA), UNEP.

----. 2008. *Water Security and Ecosystem Services: The Critical Connection: Ecosystem Management Case Studies.* Nairobi, UNEP. http://www.unep.org/themes/freshwater/pdf/the_critical_connection.pdf

----. 2010. *Clearing the Waters: A Focus on Water Quality Solutions.* Nairobi, UNEP.

----. 2011. *Policy Brief on Water Quality.* Nairobi, UNEP. http://www.unwater.org/downloads/waterquality_policybrief.pdf

USAID (United States Agency for International Development). 2010. *Making Cities Work: Urban Sanitation and Wastewater Treatment.* Washington DC, USAID. http://oldmcw.zaloni.net/urbanThemes/environment/sanitation.html (Accessed 1 November 2011.)

Vörösmarty, C. J., McIntyre, P. B. and Gessner, M. O. 2010. Global threats to human water security and river biodiversity. *Nature,* Vol. 467, pp. 555–61.

WHO (World Health Organization). 2004. *Evaluation of the Costs and Benefits of Water and Sanitation Improvements at the Global Level.* Geneva, WHO.

----. 2008. *The Global Burden of Disease: 2004 Update.* Geneva, WHO.

WHO (World Health Organization) and UNICEF (United Nations Children's Fund). 2010. *Progress on Sanitation and Drinking-Water: 2010 Update.* Geneva, WHO/UNICEF Joint Monitoring Programme for Water Supply and Sanitation.

Wikipedia. 2011. Lake Tai. http://en.wikipedia.org/wiki/Taihu_Lake#Pollution (Accessed 9 September 2011.)

World Bank. 2007. *Making the Most of Scarcity: Accountability for Better Water Management Results in the Middle East and North Africa.* Washington DC, The World Bank. http://siteresources.worldbank.org/INTMENA/Resources/04-Chap04-Scarcity.pdf

WSSCC (Water Supply and Sanitation Collaborative Council). 2008. *A Guide to Investigating One of the Biggest Scandals of the Last 50 Years.* Geneva, WSSCC.

WWAP (World Water Assessment Programme). 2009. *World Water Development Report 3: Water in a Changing World.* Paris/London, UNESCO/Earthscan.

Zhao, Y., Duan, L., Xing, J., Larssen, T., Nielsen, C.P. and Hao, J. 2009. Soil acidification in China: Is controlling SO2 emissions enough? *Environmental Science and Technology,* Vol. 43, No. 21, pp. 8021–26.

Zijun, Li. 2006. *Acid Rain Affects One-Third of China: Main Pollutants Are Sulfur Dioxide and Particulate Matter.* Washington DC, Worldwatch Institute.

CHAPTER 17
Human settlements

UN-HABITAT
—

Coordinator Overall coordination was provided by Andre Dzikus (Chief Water and Sanitation, Section II, Water Sanitation and Infrastructure Branch, UN-HABITAT)

Contributors K. E. Seetharam (Director, Institute of Water Policy, Lee Kuan Yew School of Public Policy, National University of Singapore), Priyanka Anand (Research Associate, Institute of Water Policy, Lee Kuan Yew School of Public Policy, National University of Singapore), Kala Vairavamoorthy (Professor, Civil and Environmental Engineering, Executive Director, Patel School of Global Sustainability, University of South Florida), Michael Toh (Public Utilities Board Singapore), Bindeshwar Pathak (Founder, Sulabh International), Debashish Bhattacharjee (Human Settlements Officer, Water and Sanitation Section II, WSIB, UN-HABITAT), Kennedy Kamau (Research Officer, Water and Sanitation Section II, WSIB, UN-HABITAT), Bhushan Tuladhar (Regional Technical Adviser, Water for Asian Cities Programme, UN-HABITAT) and Kulwant Singh (Consultant, Water and Sanitation Section II, WSIB, UN-HABITAT)

© Philippe Bourseiller

||||||||||||||||||||||||||||||||||||||||||||||||||||||||||||||||||||||||||||||||||||||||||||||||||||||||||||||||||||||||||||||||||||||||||||||

The challenge is not to curb urbanization but to seize the opportunities it can provide, giving due consideration to environmental issues.

The very real effects of rapid urbanization and climate change on urban water and sanitation systems must be addressed, and resilience must be built in.

Particular attention must be given to the needs of women and girls.

Sustainable and ecological sanitation systems must be promoted to reduce water consumption as well as pollution; and the loop between water use, wastewater generation and wastewater treatment must be closed.

The concept of an urban continuum must be given due consideration, and the consequences for system design, institutional setup and investment needs for urban centres must be well recognized.

Planning must anticipate migration and growth so that the provision of water supply and sanitation services is not outpaced by urbanization.

17.1 The changing urban background

In 2008, for the first time ever, more people lived in urban than in rural areas. And this trend in urbanization is set to continue. In 2011, the world population crossed the 7 billion threshold – just 12 years after the 6 billion threshold was reached in 1999. Figure 17.1 shows, region by region, the proportion of total populations that live in urban areas. The graph shows a general upward trend from the 1960s up to the middle of this century.

Existing cities have been expanding rapidly while new ones are also emerging, particularly in Asia and in low income and middle income countries. In 1960, for example, seven of the world's ten largest urban conurbations were in high income, developed countries. But by 2000, just two of the ten largest were in developed countries and six were in Asia and Latin America. In 1950, only two cities, New York and Tokyo, had populations of over 10 million. By 2015, it is expected that 23 cities worldwide will have populations of over 10 million – and 19 of these will be in developing countries. In 2000, 22 cities had populations of between 5 million and 10 million; 402 cities had between 1 million and 5 million; and 433 cities were in the 0.5 million to 1 million category (UN-DESA, 2005). Projections show that this urbanization trend is set to continue in lower income and middle income countries (Table 17.1).

In 2005, the more developed regions of the world were host to 29% of the total urban population. But between 2000 and 2030, urban populations are expected to expand by 1.8% globally, and by 2.3% (from 1.9 billion to 3.9 billion) in developing countries (Cohen, 2006). And in developed countries, the urban population is expected to increase only marginally, from 0.9 billion in 2000 to 1 billion in 2030 (Brockerhoff, 2000).

While rapid urbanization, particularly in developing countries, is a major challenge, cities also bring opportunities. They generate wealth, enhance social development, provide employment and serve as incubators of innovation and creativity in an increasingly knowledge-based global economy. As for the challenges associated with urbanization, to a great extent they stem from the failure to match planning with migration and population growth. This failure has severe effects on the provision of basic services such as water supply and sanitation, and results in degraded living environments. The poor, particularly poor women, are the worst affected.

17.1.1 The growing challenge of slums
Rapidly expanding urban spheres exert increasing pressure on the resources, infrastructure and environment on which cities depend. Coupled with failure to plan for migration and demographic growth, this has resulted

FIGURE 17.1

Proportion of world population living in urban areas, 1960–2050

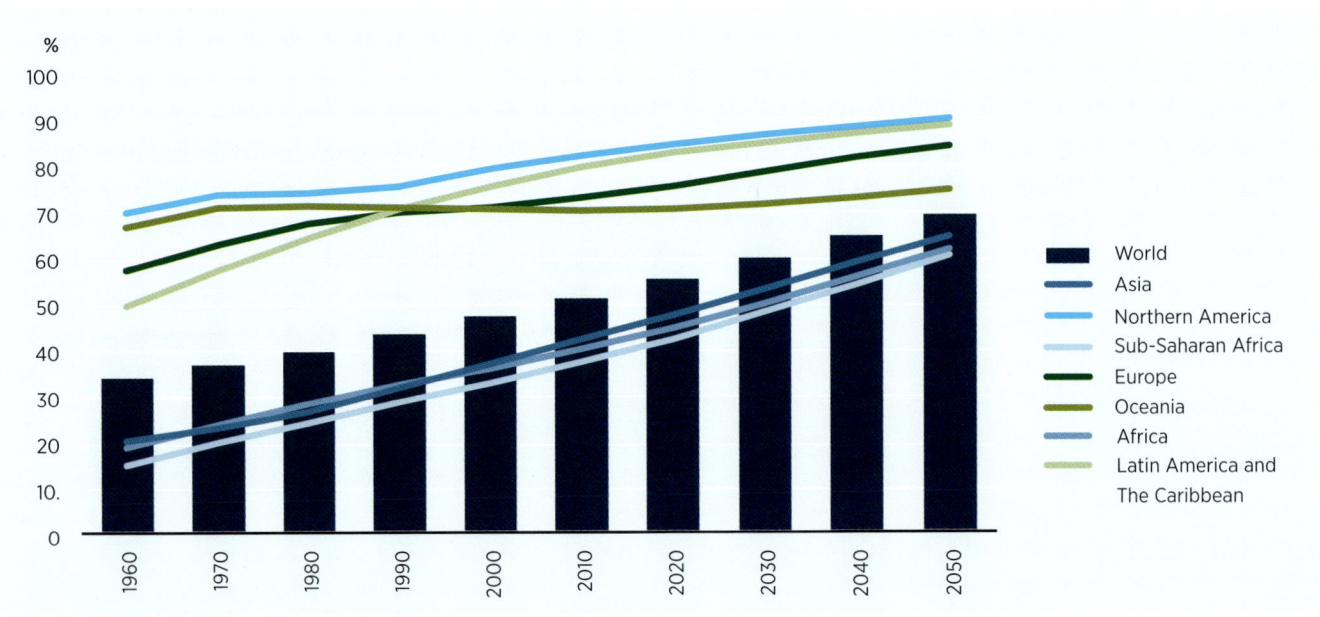

Source: Based on data from UN-DESA (2010).

TABLE 17.1

Ten largest urban conurbations, 1960–2025

By global income distribution

Income classification	Ten largest urban agglomerations								
	1960	1970	1980	1990	2000	2010	2015	2020	2025
High income economies	7	6	5	5	3	2	2	2	2
Lower middle income economies	1		2	2	4	5	5	5	5
Low income economies						1	1	1	1
Upper middle income economies	2	4	3	3	3	2	2	2	2

By geographical region

Region	Ten largest urban agglomerations								
	1960	1970	1980	1990	2000	2010	2015	2020	2025
Countries of the Commonwealth of Independent States	1	1							
Developed regions	7	6	5	4	3	2	2	2	2
Eastern Asia	1			1	1	1	1	1	1
Latin America	1	3	3	3	3	2	2	2	2
Southern Asia			2	2	3	5	5	5	5

Source: Based on data from UN-DESA (2010), '30 largest cities' data at http://esa.un.org/unpd/wup/CD-ROM_2009/WUP2009-F11a-30_Largest_Cities.xls).

in the emergence of slums, and the many problems associated with slums. These typically include poor housing, inadequate access to clean water, poor sanitation, overcrowding and insecure tenure. All these conditions have a serious effect on urban well-being (Sclar et al., 2005). Women are the worst affected. Because of bad planning and inappropriate land use policies, slums are typically located on marginal and dangerous land that is unsuitable for human settlement – locations such as on canal embankments and along railway tracks. For example, shanty towns near Buenos Aires in Argentina are built on flood-prone land, which forces residents to make a tough choice between safety and health on the one hand, and the need for shelter on the other (Davis, 2006).

The overall percentage of urban populations that live in slums is high – nearly one-third of the entire world urban population, according to some estimates (see Figure 17.2 below and Sclar et al., 2005). In some cities, such as Mumbai in India, the situation is worse with nearly 50% living in slums and shanty towns (Stecko and Barber, 2007).

UN-HABITAT's 2008 report, *State of the World Cities 2010/2011*, projected that between 2000 and 2010, 227 million people in the developing world will have moved out of slum conditions. This reflects a remarkable achievement, well beyond the 100 million target set under Millennium Development Goal (MDG) No. 7. During that period, the proportion of urban residents living in slums dropped from 39% to 33% in developing countries. However, as also pointed out in the report, these numbers do not show the whole picture. The number of slum dwellers has actually *increased* considerably during this period and this trend is predicted to continue (UN-HABITAT, 2008). The figure below shows slum population numbers in the world's major regions between 1990 and 2020.

17.1.2 Water and urbanization
Urban centres in low income countries are already facing numerous challenges such as inadequate infrastructure, a lack of basic services such as water and sanitation, and a deteriorating environment caused by pollution. Rapid urbanization and the extraction of resources to meet the demands of growing populations will put enormous stress on water resources in and

FIGURE 17.2

Slum population by region, 1990–2020 (thousands)

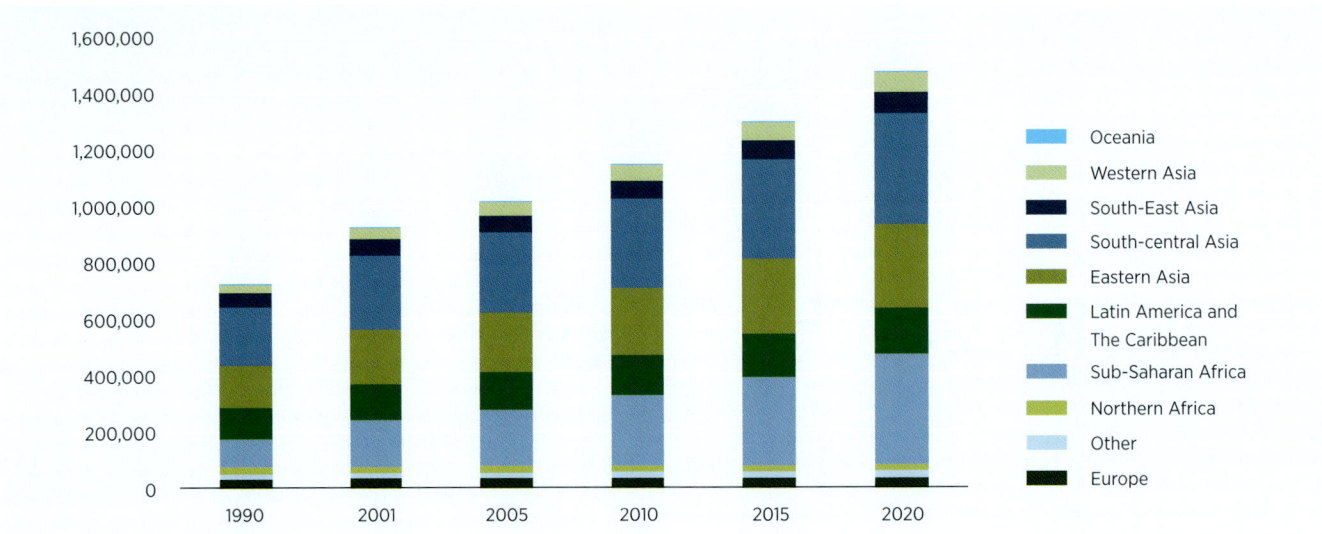

Source: Produced by UN-Habitat based on data available at http://ww2.unhabitat.org/programmes/guo/documents/Table4.pdf (published in their State of the World's Cities Report 2001).

around the cities as well as on ecosystems as a whole. Moreover, the expansion of paved and surfaced areas such as roofs, pavements and parking lots, affects the local hydrology and reduces the natural infiltration of water into the ground – which results in higher peak flows during storms.

Although the provision of water and sanitation to urban residents has improved in developing countries, it is not keeping up with the rapid pace of urbanization. According to the WHO/UNICEF Joint Monitoring Programme (JMP) on water and sanitation, the world is on track to meet the MDG on drinking water. This prediction is based on the statistic that 87% of the world population already had access to improved water sources in 2008, compared with only 77% in 1990 (WHO/UNICEF, 2010).

However, the problem is that in urban areas, the increase in access to drinking water has been only a minimal 1% during the same period. But in absolute terms, the number of urban residents with access to improved sources of drinking water has actually decreased. The case of sanitation is similar. Between 1990 and 2008, some 813 million urban residents gained first-time access to improved sanitation facilities, but during the same period, the total urban population grew by over a billion. This means that the total number of urban dwellers who do not have access to improved sanitation

actually increased by 276 million in this period (WHO/UNICEF, 2010). As urban populations keep growing, efforts to improve water supply and sanitation in Africa's and Asia's urban areas clearly must be stepped up, particularly for the poor.

Such efforts should come as part of an integrated approach that encompasses the management of upstream catchment areas and river basins, and water-related and sanitation-related infrastructure (including treatment, storage and distribution), as well as conservation of the aquatic environment in the receiving water bodies downstream. As rapid urbanization puts pressure on existing infrastructure and services, and with climate change compounding the adverse impacts on water availability and the frequency of water-related disasters, future links between water and urbanization must be analysed and managed more carefully than ever.

Achieving sustainable water supplies and improved sanitation in the cities of developing countries will require capital investment, improved governance, political will and a new ethic that values all resources and ecosystems. Figure 17.3 depicts the complex interplay between challenges, the variables that can potentially be managed, and some promising strategies that can be adopted by governments and other stakeholders. Although some broad trends, such as the scale and nature of

FIGURE 17.3

Issues and solutions related to water and urbanization

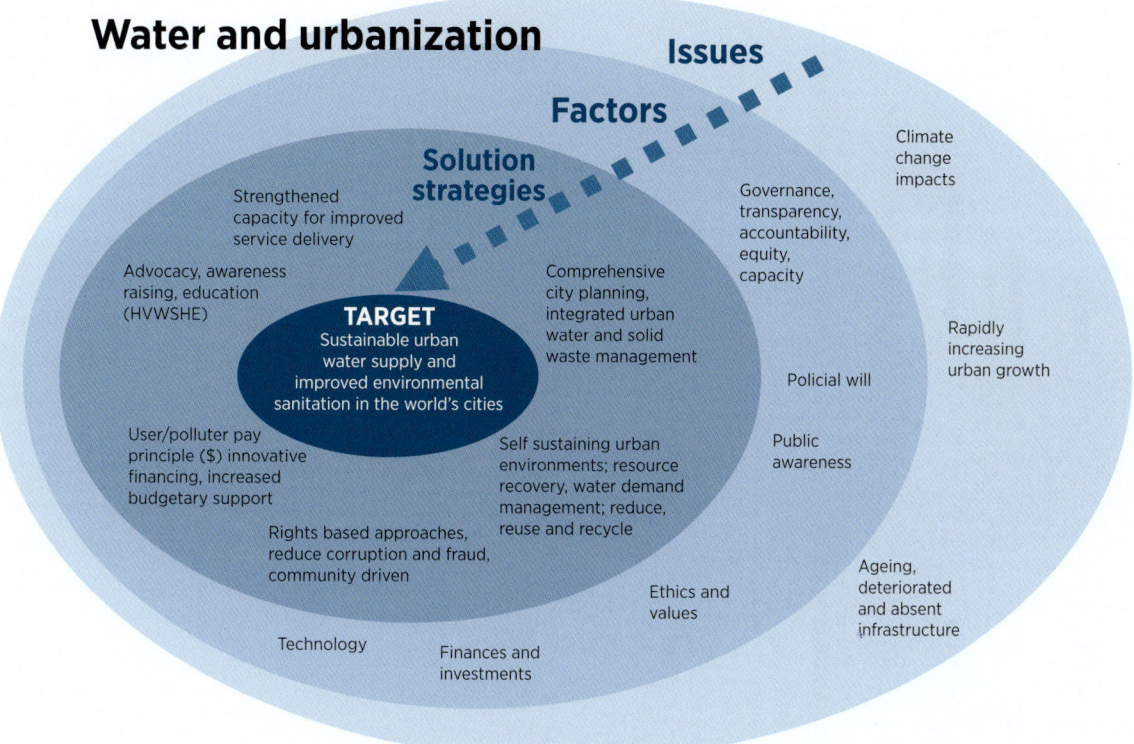

Source: WSS-II, WSIB, UN-HABITAT.

urbanization and the depletion or degradation of water resources, may be discernible, managing uncertainty and risk will be critical.

17.2 Water abstraction

The main sources of water in urban areas are surface water in upstream catchment areas, groundwater in or around the city and rainwater. These water sources, particularly the upstream catchment areas of river basins and groundwater reserves, must be preserved and used wisely to ensure long-term sustainability.

In developing countries, groundwater sources are extremely important for urban centres because they provide a relatively low-cost water supply that is usually of a high quality. However, intensive exploitation of such resources has led to major and widespread falls in aquifer levels. In conurbations such as Bangkok, Manila and the Chinese city of Tianjin, levels have fallen by as much as 20 m to 50 m, and in many others by between 10 m and 20 m. In all these cases, the drop in levels has been accompanied by either land subsidence, a deterioration in groundwater quality or, in some cases, by both. In

Mexico City, the aquifer level fell by between 5 m and 10 m between 1986 and 1992, and sections of the city have sunk by 8 m or more over the last 60 years (Foster et al., 1998; Hutton et al. 2008). In coastal areas, over-abstraction results in saltwater intrusion. In Europe, 53 out of 126 groundwater areas show saltwater intrusion. This is mostly in aquifers that are used for public and industrial water supplies (Elimelech, 2006),

Freshwater withdrawals for agriculture exceed withdrawals for other sectors (households, manufacturing, etc.). But withdrawals are expected to rise in all sectors (Fig. 17.4), and cities in developing countries will be most affected. By 2025, water withdrawals are expected to rise by 50% in developing countries as opposed to 18% rises in developed countries. In addition to high agricultural demand, pressure on water resources is compounded by the physical alteration and destruction of habitats caused by urban and industrial developments (UNEP, 2007).

FIGURE 17.4

Changes in global water use, by sector

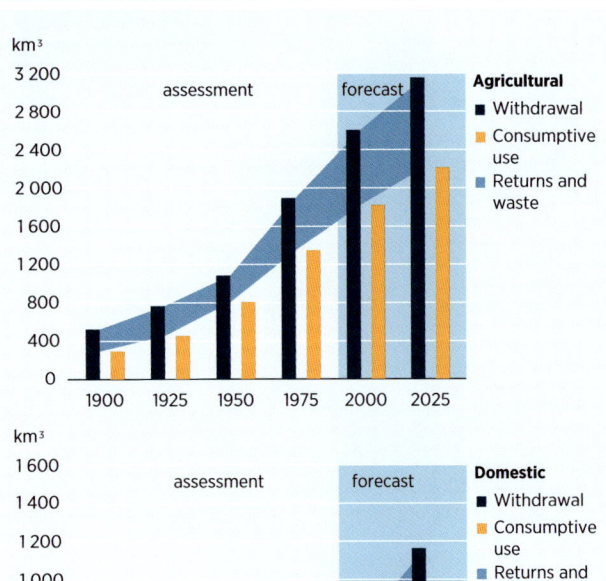

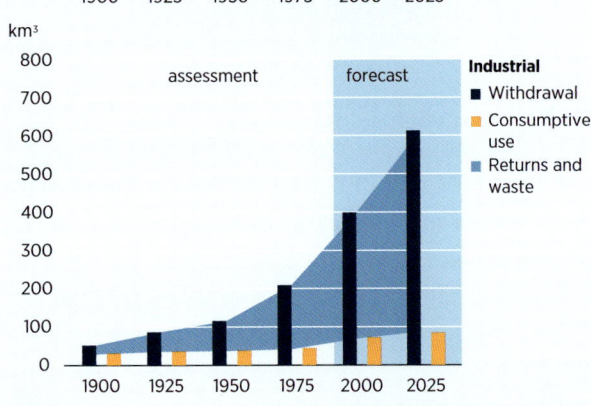

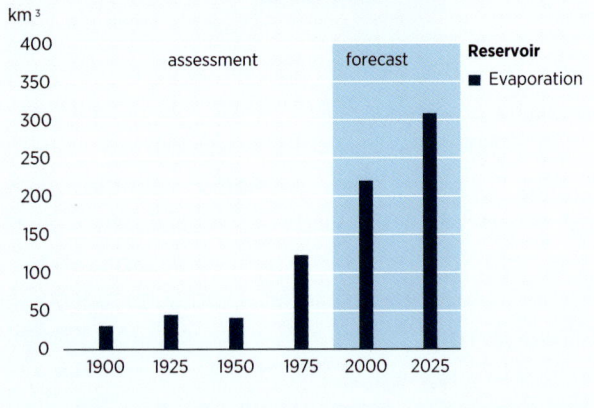

Source: UNEP/GRID-Arendal (http://maps.grida.no/go/graphic/ changes-in-global-water-use-by-sector, by Bounford.com and UNEP/ GRID-Arendal with sources UNEP/GRID-Arendal, 2002, based on Shiklomanov and UNESCO 1999).

17.2.1 Discharge of wastewater

In the course of the hydrological cycle, water sustains communities and economies throughout the watershed as it is used in agriculture, in industry and by domestic consumers (Figure 17.4). However, these users do not return the water they extract in its original condition (Corcoran et al., 2010). Across the world, the total sewage, agricultural waste and industrial effluent discharged into waterways amounts to 2 million tonnes every year (Corcoran et al., 2010). Much of this waste comes from urban areas.

Figure 17.5 depicts the ratio of treated to untreated wastewater discharged into water bodies across ten regions of the world. Urban wastewater poses a particularly serious threat when combined with untreated industrial waste. Treated urban sewage is largely limited to high income countries, while in developing countries about 90% of sewage is discharged without any treatment. In Indonesia, Jakarta's 9 million residents generate 1.3 million m^3 of sewage daily, of which less than 3% is treated. By contrast, Sydney, Australia's largest city, which has a population of over 4 million, treats nearly all its wastewater, some 1.2 million m^3 per day (Corcoran et al., 2010). Point sources such as where sewage is discharged are being controlled more and more, and the concern is now shifting to non-point pollutant loads from storm-generated runoff.

Nutrients in the wastewater discharged from municipal treatment plants and the runoff from cities and farms pose a major health problem. These nutrients have caused an increase in harmful algal blooms in freshwater and coastal systems over the last twenty years (UNEP, 2007). It is estimated that about 245,000 km^2 of marine ecosystems feature 'dead zones' caused by the discharge of untreated wastewater, which has a detrimental effect on fisheries, livelihoods and the food chain. Such discharge merely shifts problems from upstream to downstream areas.

Poor sanitation and inadequate wastewater management in developing countries results in the contamination of freshwater sources, and is a major cause of disease and death, particularly among children. It also holds serious economic and environmental consequences. For instance, World Bank research in South-East Asia found that Cambodia, Indonesia, the Philippines and Vietnam lose an estimated US$9 billion a year because of poor sanitation. This amounts to about 2% of their combined gross domestic product (GDP) (Hutton et al., 2008).

FIGURE 17.5

Urban freshwater and wastewater cycle: Water withdrawal and pollutant discharge

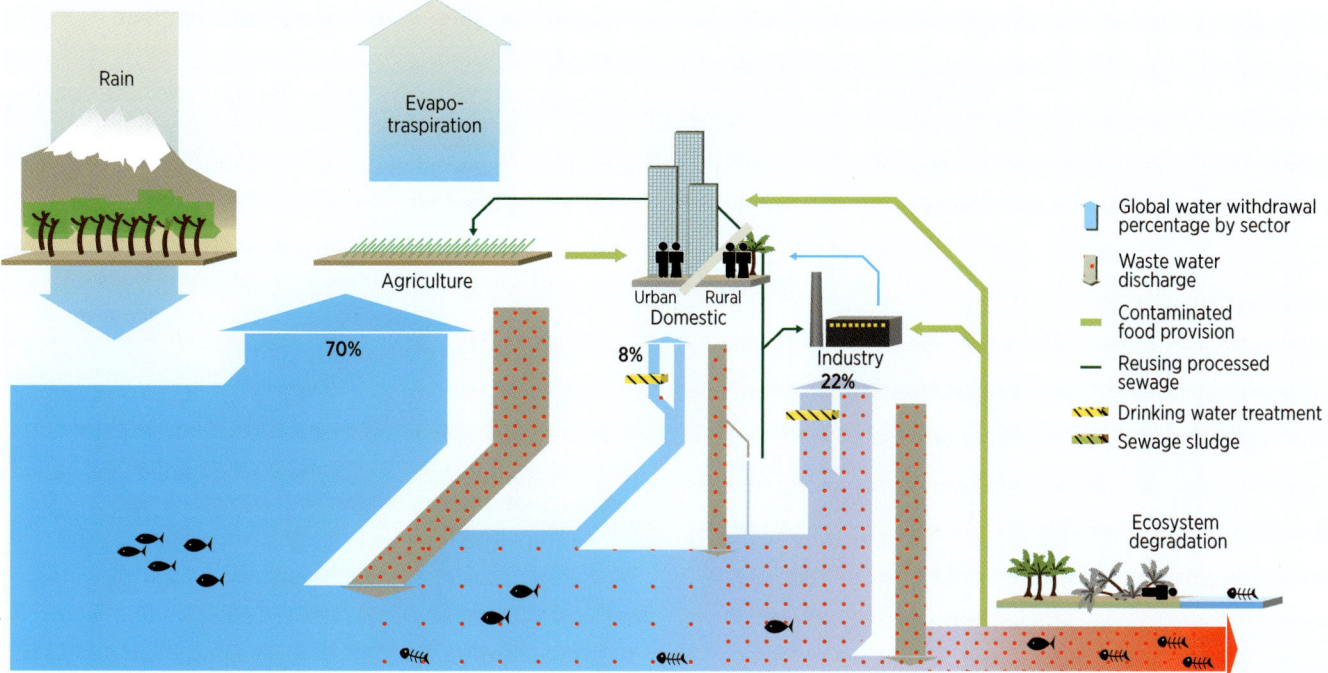

Source: UNEP/GRID-Arendal (http://maps.grida.no/go/graphic/freshwater-and-wastewater-cycle-water-withdrawal-and-pollutant-discharge, by UNEP/GRID-Arendal with sources WHO, FAO, UNESCO and IWMI).

FIGURE 17.6

Ratio of treated to untreated wastewater discharged into water bodies (March 2010)

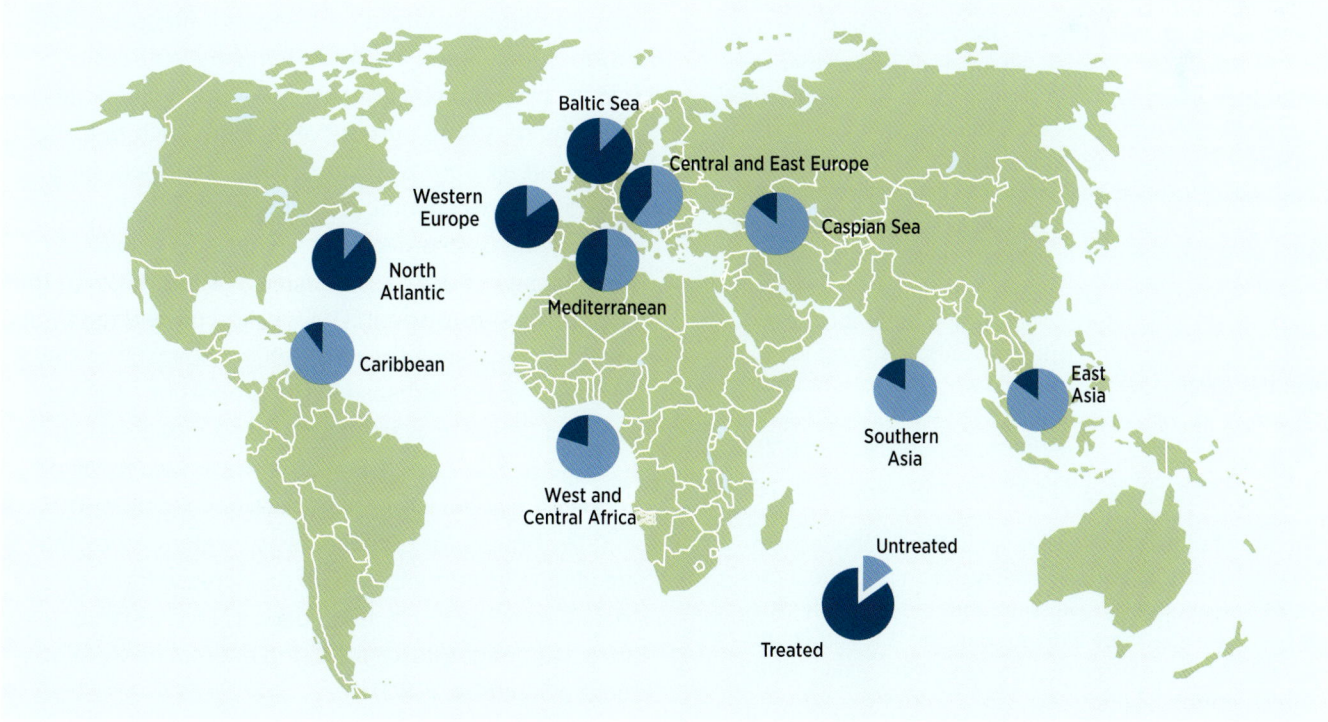

UNEP/GRID-Arendal (http://maps.grida.no/go/graphic/ratio-of-wastewater-treatment1, a map by H. Ahlenius, adapted from a map by H. Ahlenius [http://maps.grida.no/go/graphic/ratio -of-wastewater-treatment, sources UNEP-GPA, 2004]).

Even where extensive sewerage networks and treatment plants are in place, they are all too often unable to adjust to ongoing, rapid urban expansion and the associated massive capital expenditure required. In addition, they often do not have adequate capacity in the areas of planning, design, operations and maintenance. Alternatives such as off-site sanitation and decentralized wastewater treatment systems (DEWATS) are rarely explored, because of a lack of awareness among policymakers and planners, and poor capacity among utility staff. As a result, extensive sewerage systems often end up with poor, environmentally damaging sanitation services and next to no wastewater treatment.

Even in the face of growing demand, reusing and recycling water remain exceptions. Just as overlooked is the potential for recovering nutrients and energy from wastewater for use in food and fuel production. On top of these two types of technology, it must also be highlighted that other technologies exist that can reduce the

BOX 17.1

Water-saving sanitation methods: Reviewing the options

Sanitation, particularly the use of modern flush toilets, ranks among the major sources of water demand in urban areas. Conventional flushing systems use 10 L to 12 L of water per flush, wasting large amounts of water and polluting water bodies. The main alternatives to conventional toilets include the Sulabh toilet, urine-diverting dry toilets, and waterless urinals, all of which reduce water consumption while improving sanitation standards. Among these, probably the most popular is the Sulabh flush composting toilet developed by Bindeshwar Pathak and his team at Sulabh International in New Delhi. These toilets are very popular in India as well as in other developing countries.

When developing a technology, it is important to keep local culture in mind. The Sulabh toilet was designed to suit the specific needs of people who use water for anal cleansing as well as for flushing. To save water, Sulabh toilets use only 1 L to 1.5 L per flush, as opposed to the 10 L to 12 L used in conventional toilets.

On top of these significant savings, the Sulabh technology also helps to reduce global warming because it prevents greenhouse gas emissions into the atmosphere. And in public toilets where a biogas digester is linked up, the gases are burned when they are used for cooking, lighting and producing energy.

Source: B. Pathak, Sulabh International (personal communication).

amount of water that's required for sanitation – which in turn lowers the amount of wastewater that's returned to the environment untreated (see Box 17.1).

17.2.2 Urban water needs and their effects on ecosystems

Human activities have a huge effect on freshwater ecosystems across the world. Freshwater deterioration is particularly acute in cultivated systems, drylands, wetlands and urban areas. However, the effect that urban water requirements have on ecosystems is not fully or systematically researched. Cities are highly diverse, and the effects that their water needs have on ecosystems vary considerably from one to another.

When natural land surfaces are turned into impervious surfaces such as paved streets, parking lots and roofs, the percolation of rainwater and snowmelt into the soil is inhibited. The flow velocity of water over the land is increased, transferring pollutants into receiving water systems Chiramba, 2010). The reclamation of inland and coastal water systems has caused the loss of many coastal and floodplain ecosystems and services. Lost wetlands have resulted in changed flow regimes, with increased flooding in some places together with shrinking wildlife habitats (UNEP, 2007).

Healthy water ecosystems bring multiple benefits to various aspects of urban life. Wetlands provide important natural wastewater treatment functions. For instance, in Xiamen in China, municipal authorities generate revenue by imposing fines on polluters and charging fees for a number of facilities such as using marine areas. Improved wastewater treatment facilities have led to an increase in the quantity of wastewater being discharged – which has also resulted in an increase in Xiamen's revenues. This has allowed the city authorities to spend US$2 billion on sewage treatment systems since the mid-1990s. The result of this has been a huge increase in the proportion of industrial and domestic waste that's being processed. In the mid-1990s, just 20% of industrial wastewater was processed, ten years later, that figure had reached 100%. And the figures for domestic wastewater processing are almost as impressive with an increase from 28% to 85% over the much same period. Today Xiamen attracts immigrants, tourists and real-estate development (Chiramba, 2010).

In Kolkata in India, ponds provide a low cost, natural wastewater reuse and treatment system in a city that lacks conventional treatment plants. This system also provides employment for 17,000 poor fishermen and produces 20 tonnes of fish daily (Newman and Jennings, 2008; UNEP, 2002).

Every year across the world, coastal ecosystems provide an estimated US$25 billion worth of services in the form of food security, shoreline protection, tourism and carbon sequestration (Naber et al., 2008). In Zanzibar, marine ecosystem services account for 30% of GDP, 77% of investment, large amounts of foreign currency and numerous jobs (Lange and Jiddawi, 2009). Caribbean countries depend on coral reefs for tourism, fisheries and shoreline protection. Degradation of these reefs could reduce net benefits by between US$350 million and US$870 million a year. Because conventional urban management is hardly concerned with water resources management, adverse effects are expected to continue before the costs and benefits are fully recognized.

17.3 Climate change and resilient urban water systems

Alongside urbanization, climate change is a second, major, long-term and human-induced factor that affects natural and human systems alike all over the world. It has far-reaching consequences on environmental, economic and social stability (UN-HABITAT, 2011). As with urbanization, the effects of climate change are likely to be felt more sharply in developing than in developed countries.

There are close links between cities and climate change. Cities, where now half of humankind lives, are responsible for up to 70% of greenhouse gas emissions around the world; and urban populations are also vulnerable to the effects of climate change (UN-HABITAT, 2011). Cities also provide the greatest opportunities for combating climate change for two reasons: they are often centres of innovation, and action taken at city level can reach out to a large number of people.

Although vulnerability to the effects of climate change varies from place to place, in developing countries, poor people, particularly poor women, stand out as the most vulnerable. Many poor women live in risk-prone slums, along river banks for example, and their adaptive capacities are minimal (IPCC, 2007).

Water generally acts as a critical link between climate change and its effects on human and physical systems. Rising temperatures will change the hydrological cycle,

which, in turn, may alter temporal and spatial rainfall patterns and trigger extreme events such as droughts and floods. Urban water systems are likely to be very vulnerable to the effects of climate change, particularly in developing countries where they are poorly managed and ill-equipped to deal with changed conditions. Therefore, various components of urban water systems such as the protection schemes for catchment areas, water supply systems, wastewater treatment plants and drainage networks must be designed and managed in a climate-sensitive manner.

The direct effects of climate change include the destruction of infrastructure and facilities. This affects, among other things, the regular provision of water supplies, drainage and sewerage systems and solid waste management. If these systems and networks are to become sustainable, they must be more resilient to severe weather events. For instance, the capacity of water drainage or combined sewers must be a direct function of rainfall intensity (as measured in mm/hr).

On the whole, climate change adds to the uncertainty and severity of extreme water-related events. Floods and droughts are becoming increasingly unpredictable and more devastating in many 'hot spots' that are also experiencing rapid urbanization. The existing infrastructure is unable to cope, and public health is endangered because of a complex combination of factors such as the dispersal of human excreta during floods, or increased pathogen loads in freshwater supplies caused by rising water temperatures. In the face of the combined challenge of urbanization and climate change, urban water supply and sanitation infrastructure must be made 'climate proof.' What are also needed are processes that can generate optimal water management systems – processes that are robust, adaptable and sustainable under these future global change pressures (Bates et. al, 2008). Such flexible systems would be characterized by their capability to adapt to changing scenarios and associated uncertainties.

These challenges can be addressed with new techniques, including exploratory modelling that combines the best features of traditional quantitative decision analysis with those of narrative, scenario-based planning. Techniques such as risk assessment and 'real options analysis' (Zhao and Tseng, 2003) also offer opportunities in this respect. 'Real options-based decision-making' recognizes the value of flexibility, including flexibility in examining alternatives and future decision-making, and can be implemented in a flexible way as and when required to cope with uncertainty.

Some cities have begun to develop plans for vulnerability assessments and adaptation. Assisting them in this process are organizations such as UN-HABITAT, the International Council for Local Environmental Initiatives (ICLEI) and the World Mayors Council on Climate Change. Since 2008, UN-HABITAT's Cities and Climate Change Initiative has aimed to enhance the capacity of cities in developing countries to mitigate and adapt to climate change through collaboration between cities, enhanced domestic policy dialogue, risk assessment and designing pilot projects. As part of the Initiative, UN-HABITAT is supporting the preparation of Vulnerability Assessment and Adaptation Plans in 18 cities across Asia and Africa (UN-HABITAT, 2011). These plans are developed in a participatory manor, and this ensures women's involvement in processes that are properly implemented and can be monitored on an ongoing basis. Such an approach is expected to promote designs that are flexible enough to adapt to new, different or changing requirements. It is also very likely to result in 'least regret' solutions in what seems bound to remain an uncertain environment.

17.3.1 Infrastructure that is aging, deteriorated or absent

Most cities in developing countries face an urgent need to provide water and sanitation infrastructure and services to rapidly expanding populations. And many older cities, including cities in developed countries, are also faced with an aging and deteriorated water infrastructure, which is costly to rehabilitate. As well as catering for ever-expanding urban populations, poor populations in particular, these systems must be designed to adapt to and mitigate the challenges posed by global climate change.

Many cities around the world face capital expenditure backlogs for water supply systems that haven't been maintained or upgraded for a very long time. This infrastructure is likely to include source protection, water transmission lines, treatment systems, storage facilities and distribution networks. Much of this infrastructure is over 100 years old, which puts public health at increased risk because leaks, obstructions and malfunctions are more likely as equipment ages. For example, the United Kingdom is served by over 700,000 km of mains and sewer pipes, which require over 35,000 maintenance operations per month (Khatri

and Vairavamoorthy, 2007). Similarly, in Kathmandu in Nepal, some of the water pipes are over 100 years old. Here, planning has eluded the expansion of water and sewer networks for many years and about 40% of drinking water is unaccounted for, mainly as a result of leaks. High leakage rates result in increased water demand as well as greater risk of contamination and the spread of waterborne diseases (Vairavamoorthy et al., 2007).

The rehabilitation of urban water systems is becoming increasingly expensive. In Germany, for example, estimates are that over the next 15 years, €12 billion (or US$16 billion) will be required annually – that's €6.5 billion (US$9 billion) for new facilities and €5.5 billion (US$7.5 billion) for operation and maintenance. (Hiessl et al., 2001). In North America, trillions of dollars' worth of infrastructure is failing prematurely and is in need of costly repairs. The US Environmental Protection Agency anticipates a funding gap of over US$500 billion over the next 20 years in water infrastructure investment (USEPA, 2002).

As might be expected, the deterioration of urban water infrastructure is often more severe in cities in the developing world. This is the result of poor construction practices, little or no maintenance and demands that the infrastructure operates at higher capacities than it was designed for. Missing records, or a lack of data on the location and condition of water and wastewater infrastructures, combines with a lack of efficient management to make the problems even more complex (Misiunas, 2005).

17.3.2 Integrated water management and new urban planning

Because water flows in a cycle, no urban water system can be considered in isolation. No one can afford to overlook cities' links with upstream catchments and downstream areas, especially as almost all areas downstream of urban developments are left to cope with urban waste to some extent or another. Even within a given urban area, the various components of the water system – groundwater, water distribution and sewerage networks – typically interact. These interactions must be understood and taken into consideration if water supply and sanitation services are to become effective, efficient and sustainable.

Like its rural counterpart, integrated urban water management (IUWM) is based on a systems approach that looks at the hydrological cycle as a whole from catchment to consumption and treatment. Such a perspective includes any links between the various components within the system. The approach recognizes human as well as ecological demands for water, and sets out to balance environmental, economic, technical and social needs in the short term as well as the long term. In practice, this means that the planning and management of urban water systems must consider water requirements for human health, environmental protection and economic activities as well as for urban design and recreation. This approach demands an integrated and multidisciplinary approach where urban planners work closely with water engineers, landscape architects, economists and social scientists (SWITCH, 2006).

In Kathmandu, Nepal some progress has been made towards an IUWM approach. The Bagmati Action Plan was developed with support from UNEP and UN-HABITAT. The scheme identifies a range of stakeholders and corresponding actions that are needed to prevent the pollution of the Bagmati River, which serves as the city's main water source. The Plan adopts a holistic approach and sets out specific strategies and actions for five different zones within the Kathmandu Valley. The scope of the plan runs from the conservation zone in the upstream catchment area and extends all the way to the downstream zone. Under the Plan, watershed management and conservation is the main goal for upstream areas; sustainable agriculture and eco-tourism are to be promoted in the surrounding rural areas; and decentralized wastewater treatment systems are a priority for peri-urban communities (GoN/NTNC, 2009). Funds to implement the plan come from setting aside a small portion of the registration fees charged on land transactions in the Kathmandu Valley.

As urban population densities increase, the per-capita cost of providing water supply and sanitation services can be reduced (economies of scale) and can make service provision more efficient (economies of scope). This can also reduce the ecological footprint of cities. Those cities in the developing world that aim to improve services to ever-expanding populations should consider a new planning approach, and review existing density regulations, including in peri-urban areas where most of the expansion is taking place. The participation of the poor, particularly poor women, in planning will be critical. The layout of transport networks can significantly impact on growth and density and should be carefully considered, keeping in mind

the potential effect on the provision of water supply and sanitation services. New urban legislation can also promote more sustainable service provision. For example, several countries are adopting policies and regulations for the promotion of rainwater harvesting. This simple technique can reduce water stress in any city.

BOX 17.2
Singapore: A model of integrated water management

The Singapore water story is one of political determination, integrated management, continuous innovation and community partnership. In the 1960s after independence, the city-state experienced widespread water shortages cause by rapid demographic expansion and industrialization. Led by the Public Utilities Board (PUB), which is the national water agency, Singapore has turned its inherent water scarcity into growth opportunities. Taking advantage of modern technologies, the PUB has diversified water supplies under the 'Four National Taps' strategy: local catchment, imports, NEWater' (that is, treated and recycled wastewater), and desalination. Today, NEWater can meet 30% of demand, compared with only 10% for desalination. The plan is that by 2060 NEWater should meet 50% of Singapore's water demand and desalination 30%.

PUB also engages the community, encouraging wise water use, advising against the pollution of catchments and waterways, and building a closer relationship with water through leisure and entertainment activities.

Through long-term planning, Singapore has built infrastructure such as the Marina Barrage to serve the 'three-in-one' functions: water storage, flood control and leisure pursuits. The city-state also built the Deep Tunnel Sewerage System to meet Singapore's needs for the collection, treatment and disposal of used water over the next 100 years. The plans to meet water needs for the next 50 years were announced at the 2010 Singapore International Water Week (SIWW).

Through collaboration with the private sector, Singapore has created a vibrant water sector comprising 70 mutually supportive companies. Water has even been identified as one of the city-state's new economic growth engines. The equivalent of US$261 million has been committed over five years to expand the sector through research and development.

Singapore established an annual event (SIWW) and an Institute of Water Policy at the Lee Kuan Yew School of Public Policy with the intent of sharing its experiences, enhancing its capabilities and providing leadership in water governance through research and education.

Source: Public Utilities Board, Singapore.

17.3.3 Resource recovery and water demand management

The current methods of water resources management and the provision of water supply and sanitation are coming under enormous pressure from rapid urbanization. Flush toilets and waterborne sewage systems use large quantities of water, straining already depleted resources. This makes it all the more important to take a critical look into current water use and sanitation practices and to develop strategies and systems that

---

BOX 17.3

Policies and legislation on rainwater harvesting from around the world

- In India, many state governments have made rainwater harvesting mandatory in buildings. In New Delhi, the Ministry of Urban Development and Poverty Alleviation has modified the building by-laws to make rainwater harvesting mandatory in all new buildings built on plots larger than 100 m². They grant financial assistance of up to 50% or 100,000 rupees (approximately US$2,000) whichever is less. The State of Tamil Nadu has also made rainwater harvesting mandatory for all public and private buildings.
- In Nepal, the government has enacted policies and guidelines on rainwater harvesting, while cities such as Dharan are providing discounts of up to 30% on building permit fees for houses that install rainwater harvesting systems.
- In Australia, the governments of Victoria, South Australia, Sydney and New South Wales, The Gold Coast and Queensland have taken steps to ensure that energy-efficient and water-efficient measures, including rainwater harvesting, are incorporated into all new houses.
- In Germany, rainwater harvesting is encouraged by the levying of rain taxes on the amount of impervious surface a property has where runoff is directed straight to the storm sewers. So converting impervious paving into porous paved areas or harvesting rainwater from their rooftops makes property owners eligible for a reduction in rain tax.
- In the United States, several states and cities provide incentives for water conservation. Residents of Arizona were offered a one-time tax credit of 25% of the cost of water conservation systems such as grey water and rainwater recycling, up to a maximum of US$1,000. The state has allocated approximately US$250,000 annually to cover these tax credits. Similarly, the residents of San Antonio in Texas can apply for a tax rebate of up to 50% for their rainwater harvesting projects.

Source: CSE (n.d.).

---

reduce the waste, not just of water, but of other related resources such as organic matter and nutrients as well. In a conventional system, water is abstracted from surface water or groundwater sources, transported to cities, treated and distributed to households and institutions for various uses. After use, the wastewater is collected, treated if possible, and discharged into water bodies. This is a linear system where a large amount of a scarce resource is used once, contaminated and then discharged to pollute the downstream environment. In this process, water is lost – as are many other valuable resources such as organic matter and nutrients. These nutrients are valuable for agriculture, but substitutes such as chemical fertilizers (either mined or manufactured) are applied to the land instead. This may result in further deterioration of both soil and water resources. Overall, this system is unsustainable and leads to overexploitation of water bodies, the contamination of aquatic ecosystems, soil degradation and, ultimately, to food insecurity.

In traditional societies, sanitation systems were built to maximize resource recovery and reuse. In many countries in Asia, Europe, Latin America and Central America, excreta used to be collected and used in the fields as manure, thus closing the loop between resource use and recovery. For instance, in China, farmers have been aware of the benefits of human and animal excreta in crop production for more than 2,500 years. This has enabled Chinese farmers to support higher populations with the crops they produce. Some societies have also recycled excreta as fuel. For example, in Yemen's older cities, including the capital, Sana'a, separate systems for collection of excreta and urine were built into in multistorey buildings. The faeces was collected, dried and used for fuel (Lüthi et al., 2011).

Sanitation systems built around the concepts of resource recovery and reuse have been around for centuries. However, they began to disappear in the wake of the industrial revolution (and the associated urban expansion) when sewer systems and newly developed chemical fertilizers took over. By the middle of the nineteenth century, industrialized countries turned very gradually to centralized waterborne sanitation with flush toilets connected to sewer systems. Later, large sewage treatment plants were built to meet environmental standards. However, the malfunction of these treatment plants is not infrequent, leading to waste of money and environmental pollution.

Even in industrialized countries, wastewater treatment can remain a challenge for cities. In Europe, EU research found in 2001 that of 540 major cities, only 79 had tertiary sewage treatment and 223 had secondary treatment; 72 featured incomplete primary or secondary treatment, and 168 cities had no (or unspecified) treatment capacity (EU, 2001). In February 2002, the European Commission even took action against France, Greece, Germany, Ireland, Luxembourg, Belgium, Spain and the United Kingdom for alleged failure to implement the EU Urban Water Directive (SEI, 2008). Despite all these failings, the sustainability of these systems has rarely been questioned and they are still considered to be the reference for sanitation.

However, promising new approaches which use waste as a resource – such as ecological sanitation (EcoSan) – are now gaining more popularity. The waste and wastewater from households, for example, can be separated into the following streams and recycled:

- Stormwater, which can be captured and, with minimal treatment, be reused for any purpose ;
- Grey water, or wash water from kitchens and bathrooms, which can be treated and reused for flushing or irrigation;
- Blackwater or faeces, which can be used to produce energy (biogas) or compost;
- Urine or yellow water, which can be reused as liquid fertilizer; and
- Organic waste, which can be composted or used to produce biogas.

In a bid to promote sustainable sanitation systems, the Water Supply and Sanitation Collaborative Council endorsed the 'Bellagio Principles for Sustainable Sanitation' during its Fifth Global Forum in November 2000 (EAWAG, 2005). These principles consider waste as a resource and promote holistic, integrated and decentralized management.

Sustainable options based on these principles include EcoSan, rainwater harvesting and decentralized wastewater treatment systems (DEWATS). These decentralized systems focus on reducing demand for water and preventing water pollution – and they have proved effective in many communities around the world. The time has come to deploy these technologies on a larger scale, particularly in newly urbanizing areas and peri-urban areas in developing countries.

Experience gained from the projects UN-HABITAT has supported over the years proves that Water Demand Management (WDM) for utilities is effective. The method can save or defer massive amounts of capital expenditure on equipment and networks. WDM entails a 'water audit' of the supply system, the identification of areas of excessive consumption or leakage, the rehabilitation of infrastructure, and the deployment of technical and managerial controls. These measures are most effective when combined with public awareness raising and education programmes (McKenzie et al, 2003).

Promotion of sustainable sanitation and holistic water management systems will require knowledge of the water cycle as a whole and how it is affected by human

BOX 17.4

Decentralized and community-based sanitation systems

Large conventional wastewater treatment plants are often expensive to establish and difficult to operate. As a result, many cities in developing countries are unable to set up such plants and operate them properly. Transporting the wastewater through drains is the main cost of urban wastewater management. But decentralized treatment systems that are based on simple yet effective technologies and that have maximum community ownership can serve as an alternative in developing countries.

Since it was developed in the 1990s, the Decentralized Wastewater Treatment Systems (DEWATS) approach has proved to be successful in many communities, particularly in slums, peri-urban settlements and institutions in Asia and Africa. In Indonesia, for example, the Community-Based Sanitation (SANIMAS) programme (which started as a pilot project in six locations in 2003) has now been deployed on a nationwide scale covering more than 420 'clusters' all over the country. Similarly, many slum settlements in Indian cities such as Bangalore and Mumbai also enjoy community-based sanitation facilities. Some of these also generate biogas for cooking and slurry for vegetable gardening.

The DEWATS approach is based on the principles of decentralization of responsibility, simplification of technology and processes, and, where possible, the conservation and recycling of waste energy and nutrients. This modular system combines technical options such as settlers, biogas plants, anaerobic baffle reactors, constructed wetlands and ponds. All options involve community participation.

Source: Gutterer et al. (2009).

activities. In this process, water and urban managers could take advantage of the Sustainable Sanitation and Water Management Toolbox (Box 17.4).

17.4 Water education

It is increasingly recognized that improvements in water management cannot be accomplished by technical or regulatory measures alone. These must be complemented with changes in behaviour and in attitudes to the use of water in society. Following the recommendations of an International Expert Group Meeting held in Johannesburg, South Africa, in May 2001, UN-HABITAT has been promoting the Human Values-Based approach to Water, Sanitation and Hygiene promotion (HVBWSHE). This has included running many HVBWSHE training courses and the publication of the *Facilitators' and Trainers' Guidebook*. In addition to disseminating information on water, sanitation and hygiene,

BOX 17.5

The Sustainable Sanitation and Water Management Toolbox

Water resources around the world face increasing pressures from population growth, competing demands from agriculture and industry, and climate uncertainty. However, a number of solutions have been developed to address this challenge, and have been demonstrated to be effective in several parts of the world. Water managers must be aware of these solutions and be able to modify and apply them as necessary to suit their needs. This requires information to be managed effectively so that it is easily available when required. It also requires capacity-building to build confidence in the holistic approach to water resource management that is inherent to the methodology.

The Sustainable Sanitation and Water Management (SSWM) toolbox is a collection of open-source, easy-access and easy-to-use information that is available on line. It allows users to tailor it to their own needs while maintaining a holistic approach. The methodology considers the water system as a whole and focuses on human interactions with various components as water moves in a cycle from source to sea and back. In practice, simple technical and software tools and approaches are proposed for the various problems associated with the effects of human influence on the water cycle. In particular, the methodology links water resources management with sanitation and agriculture.

Source: SSWM Toolbox (n.d.).

this innovative approach inspires and motivates the public to change its behaviour in favour of the wise and sustainable use of water and sanitation. Experience has shown that a values-based approach has many benefits: it does not add to the current school curriculum because it can easily be mainstreamed into the existing curriculum, and it creates a lasting effect through character development once it is understood, appreciated and practised by children and young adults. This now proven approach has been adopted in several countries in Asia, Africa and Latin America with support from UN-HABITAT and other agencies.

17.5 Financing the water sector

Meeting wide ranging human needs as well as looking after the natural environment in a sustainable manner comes at a cost. This is often ignored or underestimated by governments and individuals, which results in dysfunctional water systems and a deterioration of critical services. Sustainable funding is required for water resources management as a whole, including providing water supply and sanitation services, and integrative functions such as policy and legislation development, capacity building, research and good governance.

Achieving the MDG targets for access to drinking water and sanitation will also require significant amounts of capital expenditure, particularly in low income countries and least developed countries. However, the benefits associated with water and sanitation, such as reductions in health costs and increases in the number of productive days, will far outweigh the cost of providing safe water and sanitation. Research has shown that every single dollar invested in drinking water and sanitation can yield a payback of US$7.40 per year. Similarly, achieving the MDG targets would result in an additional 320 million productive days every year as a result of improved health, and a time saving of 20 billion working days (Prüss-Üstün et al., 2008).

In spite of these clear benefits, capital expenditure on drinking water and sanitation has a relatively low priority for official development assistance (ODA) or domestic allocations, compared with other social development sectors such as health and education. Between 1997 and 2008, total international assistance for water-related projects (as measured by the Organisation for Economic Co-operation and Development [OECD]) *decreased* from 8% to 5% of total overseas development aid. Yet during the same period, aid for health projects increased from 7% to 12%. Furthermore, less than half of the investment made in water and sanitation by external support agencies goes to low income countries, and only a small proportion of this goes to providing those basic services which could make major contributions to the achievement of the MDGs (WHO and UN-Water, 2010). Therefore, there is a clear need for aid agencies to make greater investments in water and sanitation, particularly in low income countries where the number of urban poor continues to increase rapidly.

As well as fresh capital expenditure, the water sector also requires funding for the proper operation and maintenance of existing systems. In Nepal, for example, according to government estimates, 80% of the population have access to drinking water from improved sources – which means that, on paper, the country has met its MDG target of 73% water supply coverage. However, government data also show that only 17.9% of the water supply systems in the country are functioning properly; 38.9% need minor repairs, 11.8% need major repairs, 21% need rehabilitation, 9.1% need reconstruction and 1.6% are totally non-functional (NMIP and DWSS, 2011). Even in Kathmandu Valley, where coverage is reported to be close to 100%, actual service levels fail to meet half the water demand and the quality of the water supplied is a major concern. Therefore, even if the world is on track to meet the MDG for water supply, the operation and maintenance of water systems will continue to require financing.

17.5.1 Bridging the financing gap

A preliminary assessment by the UN Millennium Project (2005) shows that, taking all the MDGs as a whole, many low income countries, particularly in sub-Saharan Africa, face large financial gaps amounting to 20% to 30% of GDP. This is the case even when domestic resource mobilization is maximized. Consequently, these countries will require substantial external financial support to meet the MDGs, both nationwide and in smaller urban centres. Options for bridging this gap for water supply and sanitation are as follows:

- In the poorest countries, external finance and ODA should be grant based, especially for delivery to those who have no water and sanitation service and who live below the poverty line in small urban centres.
- In all low income countries, and where appropriate, substantial shares of operating costs in urban centres should be met through grants or other instruments like output-based aid.
- In middle income countries, small urban centres where people live below the poverty line may need

a variety of instruments, including lifeline tariffs (such as those used in South Africa), output-based loans buttressed by the appropriate forms of external guarantees, and internal transfers to meet the upfront costs of new infrastructure, and ultimately make charges affordable to the poor.
- Domestic resource mobilization should be maximized while ensuring that capital and operating costs are adequately funded, keeping in mind the need to provide the poor, particularly poor women, with sustainable and affordable services.
- Ensure that considerations of affordability are reconciled with the need to generate revenues from those that can afford to pay for services.
- Wherever feasible, trunk infrastructure should be funded by the public sector.

Meanwhile, at national level, strategies must be developed to enable a shift from external to domestic sources of financing, including the private sector. At international level, there should be a shift from sovereign to sub-sovereign lending, and measures such as improved financial and operational management should be put in place to improve affordability, and cost recovery. Measures are also needed to improve the performance and creditworthiness of local authorities and utilities.

All those involved must recognize the urgent need to strengthen those financial mechanisms that reduce overhead costs, and ensure that more targeted funds benefit deprived communities. Such mechanisms should also empower the communities, familiarizing them with the challenges involved, and securing their commitment to the search for common solutions. These financial mechanisms should also build national and international partnerships with appropriate financial institutions, in an effort to leverage capital expenditure.

IIIIIIIIIIIIIIIIIIIIIIIIIIIIIIIIIIIIIIIIIIIIIIIIIIIIIIIIIIIIIIIIIIIIIIIIIIIIIII

References

Bates, B. C., Kundzewicz, Z. W., Wu, S. and Palutikof, J. P. (eds). 2008. *Climate Change and Water.* Technical. Technical Paper VI. Paper of the Intergovernmental Panel on Climate Change. Geneva, IPCC.

Brockerhoff, M. 2000. An urbanising world. *Population Reference Bureau,* Washington DC, PRB. http://www.prb.org/source/acfac3f.pdf

Chiramba, T. 2010. *Ecological Impacts of Urban Water: A Contribution to World Water Day 2011.* Presentation from the 2010 World Water Week in Stockholm. Nairobi, UNEP. http://www.worldwaterweek.org/documents/WWW_PDF/2010/tuesday/T5/Chiramba_Pres_WWW_WWD2011_final.pdf

Cohen, B. 2006. Urbanization in developing countries: Current trends, future projections, and key challenges for sustainability. *Technology in Society,* Vol. 28, pp. 63–80. http://www7.nationalacademies.org/dbasse/cities_transformed_world_technologyinsociety_article.pdf

Corcoran, E., Nellemann, C., Baker, E., Bos, R., Osborn, D. and Savelli, H. (eds). 2010. *Sick Water? The Central Role of Wastewater Management in Sustainable Development.* A Rapid Response Assessment. Nairobi, UNEP/UN-HABITAT.

CSE (Centre for Science and Environment). n.d. CSE WEBNET websites. Rainwater Harvesting and International Water-harvesting and Related Financial Incentives. New Delhi, CSE. http://www.cseindia.org/node/1161 and http://www.rainwaterharvesting.org/policy/Legislation_international.htm#aus (Both accessed 5 December 2011.).

Davis, M. 2006. Slum Ecology: Inequity intensifies Earth's natural forces. *Orion Magazine.* March/April. http://www.orionmagazine.org/indexZ.php/articles/article/167 (Accessed October 2009.)

EAWAG (Swiss Federal Institute for Aquatic Science and Technology). 2005. *Household-Centred Environmental Sanitation: Implementing the Bellagio Principles in Urban Environmental Sanitation.* Provisional Guides for Decision-Makers. Dübendorf, Switzerland, EAWAG. http://www.wsscc.org/sites/default/files/publications/EAWAG_House_Centred_Environmental_Sanitation_2005.pdf

Elimelech, M. 2006. The global challenge for adequate and safe water. *Journal of Water Supply: Research and Technology–AQUA,* Vol. 55, No. 1, pp. 3–10.

EU (European Union). 2001. 2nd Forum on Implementation and Enforcement of Community Environmental Law: Intensifying Our Efforts to Clean Urban Wastewater. Brussels, EU.

Foster, S., Lawrence, A. and Morris, B. 1998. *Groundwater in Urban Development: Assessing Management Needs and Formulating Policy Strategies.* World Bank Technical Paper No. 390. Washington DC, World Bank. http://www-wds.worldbank.org/external/default/WDSContentServer/WDSP/IB/1998/03/01/000009265_3980429110739/Rendered/PDF/multi_page.pdf

GoN/NTNC (Government of Nepal/National Trust for Nature Conservation). 2009. *Bagmati Action Plan (2009–2014).* Kathmandu, NTNC.

Gutterer, B., Sasse, L., Panzerbeiter, T. and Reckerzügel, T. 2009. *Decentralised Wastewater Treatment Systems (DEWATS) and Sanitation in Developing Countries: A Practical Guide.* A. Ulrich, S. Reuter and B. Gutterer (eds). Loughborough, UK/Bremen, Germany, WEDC, Loughborough University/BORDA. http://www2.gtz.de/Dokumente/oe44/ecosan/en-sample-only-borda-dewats-2009.pdf

Hiessl, H., Walz, R. and Toussaint, D. 2001. *Design and Sustainability Assessment of Scenarios of Urban Water Infrastructure Systems.* Karlsruhe, Germany, ISI.

Hutton, G., Rodriguez, U. E., Napaitupulu L., Thang, P. and Kov, P. 2008. *Economic Impacts of Sanitation in Southeast Asia: A four-country study conducted in Cambodia, Indonesia, the Philippines and Vietnam under the Economics of Sanitation Initiative (ESI).* Jakarta and Washington DC, World Bank.

IPCC (Intergovernmental Panel on Climate Change). 2007. Climate Change 2007: Synthesis Report. Geneva, Switzerland, IPCC. http://www.ipcc.ch/pdf/assessment-report/ar4/syr/ar4_syr.pdf

Khatri, K. B. and Vairavamoorthy, K. 2007. *Challenges for Urban Water Supply and Sanitation in the Developing Countries.* Discussion Draft Paper for the session on Urbanization. Delft, the Netherlands, UNESCO-IHE.

Lange, G. M. and Jiddawi, N. 2009. Economic value of marine ecosystem services in Zanzibar: Implications for marine conservation and sustainable development. *Ocean & Coastal Management,* Vol. 52, No. 10, pp. 521–32.

Lüthi, C., Panesar, A., Schütze, T., Norström, A. McConville, J., Parkinson, J., Saywell, D. and Ingle, R. 2011. *Sustainable Sanitation in Cities: A Framework for Action.* Rijswijk, the Netherlands, Papiroz Publishing House. http://www.eawag.ch/forschung/sandec/publikationen/sesp/dl/sustainable_san.pdf

McKenzie, R. S., Wegelin, W. A. and Meyer, N. 2003. Water Demand Management Cookbook. Nairobi/Pretoria/Glenvista, South Africa, UN-HABITAT/WRP/Rand Water. http://www.google.com/url?sa=t&rct=j&q=&esrc=s&frm=1&source=web&cd=1&sqi=2&ved=0CCUQFjAA&url=http%3A%2F%2Fwww.unhabitat.org%2Fpmss%2FgetElectronicVersion.asp%3Fnr%3D1781%26alt%3D1&ei=-RvRTpSIOI6bOvDF-eoE&usg=AFQjCNEVBq__0PZZQB3tv_1Rb8NtNEINtw&sig2=zC_KmVtfz6dtR0n7VyPHxg

Misiunas, D. 2005. *Failure Monitoring and Asset Condition Assessment in Water Supply Systems.* Ph.D. Thesis, Lund University, Lund, Sweden. http://www.iea.lth.se/publications/Theses/LTH-IEA-1048.pdf

Naber, H., Lange, G.-M. and Hatziolos, M. 2008. Valuation of Marine Ecosystem Services: A Gap Analysis. Washington DC/New York, World Bank/Columbia University. http://new.cbd.int/marine/voluntary-reports/vr-mc-wb-en.pdf

Newman, P. and, Jennings, I. 2008. *Cities as Sustainable Ecosystems: Principles and Practices.* Washington DC, Island Press.

NMIP-DWSS (Nepal, National Management Information Project, Department of Water Supply and Sewerage). 2011. *Nationwide Coverage and Functionality Status of Water Supply and Sanitation in Nepal.* Kathmandu, Government of Nepal.

Prüss-Üstün, A., Bos, R., Gore, F. and Bartram, J. 2008. *Safe Water, Better Health: Costs Benefits and Sustainability of Investments to Protect and Promote Health.* Geneva, WHO (World Health Organization) . http://whqlibdoc.who.int/publications/2008/9789241596435_eng.pdf

Sclar, E. D., Garau, P. and Carolini, G. 2005. The 21st century health challenge of slums and cities. *The Lancet*, Vol. 365, No. 9462, pp. 901–3.

SEI (Stockholm Environmental Institute). 2008. The sanitation crisis. *EcoSanRes Factsheet 1*. Stockholm, SEI. http://www.ecosanres.org/pdf_files/ESR-factsheet-01.pdf

SSWM Toolbox (Sustainable Sanitation and Water Management Toolbox). n.d. Website. Basel, Switzerland, Seecon. http://www.sswm.info

Stecko, S., and Barber, N. 2007. *Exposing Vulnerabilities: Monsoon Floods in Mumbai, India.* Case study prepared for Global Report on Human Settlements 2007. Nairobi, UN-HABITAT. http://www.unhabitat.org/downloads/docs/GRHS.2007.CaseStudy.Mumbai.pdf

Sulabh International Social Service Organisation. n.d. *Avantages of Sulabh Toilets*. New Delhi, Sulabh. http://www.sulabhinternational.org/st/advantages_sulabh_toilets.php (Accessed 22 November 2011.)

SWITCH. 2006. Managing water for the city of the future. Website. Loughborough, U.K./Delft, the Netherlands, Loughborough University/UNESCO-IHE. http://www.switchurbanwater.eu (Accessed 5 December 2011.)

UN-DESA (United Nations Department of Economic and Social Affairs). 2005. *World Population Prospects: The 2004 Revision* (Analytical Report, Volume III No. ST/ESA/SER.A/246). New York, UN-DESA.

----. 2010. Website. *World Urbanization Prospects: The 2009 Revision: Percentage of Population Residing in Urban Areas by Major Area, Region and Country, 1950–2050.* New York, UN-DESA. http://esa.un.org/unpd/wup/index.htm

UNEP (United Nations Environment Programme). 2002. *Environmentally Sound Technologies for Wastewater and Stormwater Management: An International Source Book.* Nairobi, UNEP.

----. 2007. *Global Environment Outlook 4: Environment for Development.* Nairobi, UNEP.

UN-HABITAT (United Nations Agency for Human Settlements). 2001. Slum population projection 1990-2020 (based on slum annual growth rate (1990-2001)). *State of the World's Cities Report 2001.* Nairobi, UN-HABITAT. http://ww2.unhabitat.org/programmes/guo/documents/Table4.pdf

----. 2008. *State of the World's Cities 2010/2011. Cities for All: Bridging the Urban Divide.* London, Earthscan.

----. 2011. *Global Report on Human Settlements 2011: Cities and Climate Change.* London/Nairobi, Earthscan/UN-HABITAT.

USEPA (United States Environmental Protection Agency). 2002. Website: U.S. Water Infrastructure Needs & the Funding Gap. Washington DC, USEPA. http://water.epa.gov/infrastructure/sustain/infrastructureneeds.cfm (Accessed, 05 December 2011.)

Vairavamoorthy, K, Gorantiwar, S. D. and Mohan, S. 2007. Intermittent water supply under water scarcity situations. *Water International.* Vol. 32, No. 1., pp. 121–32.

WHO (World Health Organization) and UN-Water. 2010. *GLAAS 2010: UN-Water Global Annual Assessment of Sanitation and Drinking Water: Targeting Resources for Better Results.* Geneva, WHO. http://www.unwater.org/activities_GLAAS2010.html

WHO (World Health Organization) and UNICEF (United Nations Children's Fund). 2010. Progress on Sanitation and Drinking Water 2010 Update. Geneva/New York, WHO/UNICEF. http://whqlibdoc.who.int/publications/2010/9789241563956_eng_full_text.pdf

Zhao, T. and Tseng, C.-L. 2003. A note on activity floats in activity-on-arrow networks. *Journal of the Operational Research Society,* Vol. 54, pp. 1296–99.

CHAPTER 18
Managing water along the livestock value chain

FAO and IFAD

—

Lead Authors Karen Frenken and Rudolph Cleveringa
Contributing Authors Melvyn Kay and Marisha Wojciechowska
Acknowledgements Reviewers: Jacob Burke (FAO), David Coates (CBD), Theodor
Friedrich (FAO), M. Gopalakrishnan (ICID), Amir Kassam (University of Reading, UK),
Willem-Jan Laan (Unilever), Lifeng Li (WWF), Jan Lundqvist (SIWI), David Molden (IWMI),
Daniel Renault (FAO), Antonio Rota (IFAD), Pasquale Steduto (FAO), Olaf Thieme (FAO),
David Tickner (WWF), Olcay Ünver (WWAP) and Richard Connor (WWAP)

Agriculture is a valid and essential consumer of water. Water is a limited resource, and agriculture already accounts for 70% of water withdrawn by all three sectors (i.e. the agricultural, municipal and industrial), and for 90% of water consumed by these three sectors. Responsible agricultural water management will make a major contribution to future global water security.

Water is the key to food security. Globally there is enough water available for future needs, but access is uneven. Many areas of absolute water scarcity are home to the world's poor. Major changes in policy and management will be needed to make best use of available water resources.

Most least developed countries (LCDs) experience highly variable climates, which add to the uncertainties facing farmers. Climate change will make matters worse. Investment in infrastructure and strong institutions will be essential to introduce measurement and control.

Water has a vital role in all links along the agricultural value chain – from production to transformation, consumption, waste and reuse. The growing demand for water for livestock products highlights this.

We need to be more 'water smart'. We all have a responsibility to use this scarce resource wisely, efficiently, and productively.

18.1 Water: A key role in agriculture

The link between water and food is simple. Crops and livestock need water to grow, and lots of it. Producing 1 kg of rice, for example, requires about 3,500 L of water, 1 kg of beef requires some 15,000 L, and a cup of coffee requires about 140 L (Hoekstra and Chapagain, 2008). The average European diet requires about 3,500 L per person per day, and an additional 2–5 L for drinking and another 145 or so litres for cooking, cleaning, washing, and flushing. Some diets require even more water, for example, a meat-rich diet can require over 5,500 L per person per day. But all this is in stark contrast to the 1.4 billion people living in LDCs in extreme poverty (FAO, 2011e; IFAD, 2011) (Figure 18.1).[1] Despite the historic shift towards urbanization and the fact that urban poverty is increasing rapidly, poverty still largely remains a rural problem. Over 1 billion people rely on agriculture to secure their food and livelihoods on the equivalent of less than 1,000 L of water per person per day.

18.1.1 Water and food security

Food insecurity is a growing concern all over the world. However, there is too little recognition that almost 70% of the world's freshwater withdrawals are already committed to irrigated agriculture (Figure 18.2 and Table 18.1, see Table 18.2 for country groupings) and that more water will be needed as the demand for

FIGURE 18.1

Millions of rural people living in extreme poverty (less than US$1.25 per day) by region

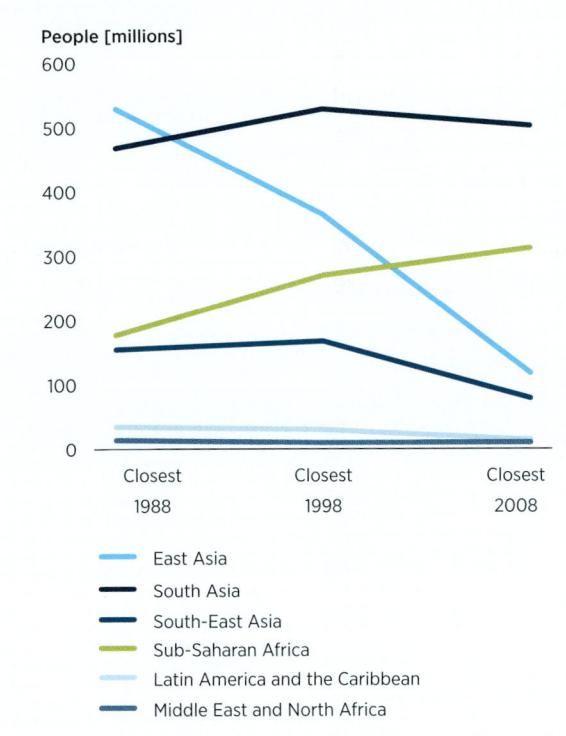

Source: IFAD (2011, fig. 4, p. 49).

FIGURE 18.2

Water withdrawal by sector by region (2005)

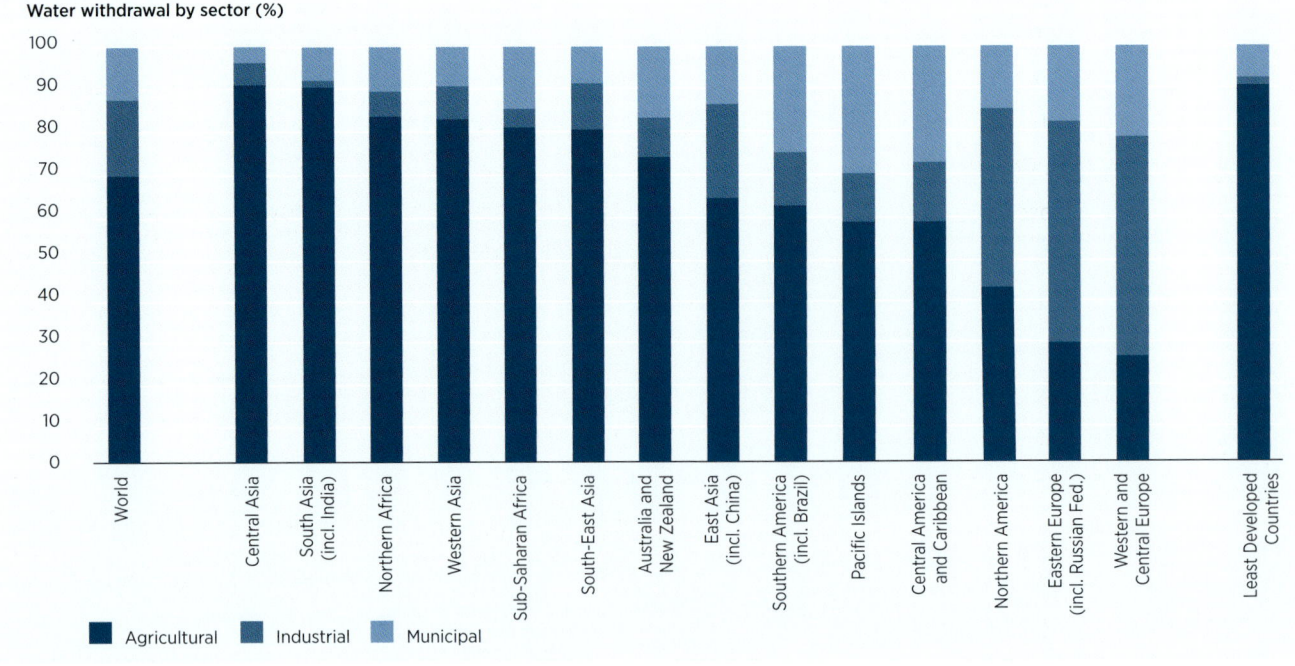

Source: FAO (2011c).

food grows. Agricultural water withdrawal accounts for 44% of total water withdrawal in Organization for Economic Co-operation and Development (OECD) countries, but this rises to more than 60% within the eight OECD countries that rely heavily on irrigated agriculture. In the BRIC countries (Brazil, Russian Federation, India and China), agriculture accounts for 74% of water withdrawals, but this ranges from a low 20% in the Russian Federation to 87% in India. In LDCs the figure is more than 90% (FAO, 2011c).

The agricultural sector as a whole has a large water footprint when compared to other sectors, particularly during the production phase (Table 18.3). The booming demand for livestock products in particular is increasing the demand for water at every stage along the livestock value chain, not just during production (see Section 18.5). It is also affecting water quality, which in turn reduces availability.

Although agriculture uses substantial volumes of water, it is time to acknowledge that is also a valid and essential user. In many countries, not just in the LDCs, water availability for agriculture is already limited and uncertain, and this is set to worsen. Several regions are already facing absolute water scarcity, where renewable

TABLE 18.1

Water withdrawal by sector and freshwater withdrawal by region (2005)

Continent	Total withdrawal by sector						Total water withdrawalw*	Total freshwater withdrawal	Freshwater withdrawal as % of IRWR**
	Municipal		Industrial		Agricultural				
Regions	km³/year	%	km³/year	%	km³/year	%	km³/year	km³/year	IRWR**
Africa	**28**	**12.5**	**11**	**5.1**	**184**	**82.4**	**224**	**224**	**5.7**
Northern Africa	9	10.0	6	6.0	80	84.0	95	95	202.2
Sub-Saharan Africa	19	1.4	6	4.5	105	81.1	129	129	3.3
Americas	**135**	**16.9**	**285**	**35.5**	**381**	**47.6**	**801**	**801**	**4.2**
Northern America	86	14.2	260	43.0	259	42.9	604	604	9.9
Central America and Caribbean	7	27.6	4	14.1	15	58.3	26	26	3.3
Southern America (incl. Brazil)	42	24.8	22	12.6	107	62.6	171	171	1.4
Asia	**227**	**9.0**	**242**	**9.6**	**2 057**	**81.4**	**2 526**	**2 521**	**21.5**
Western Asia	25	9.4	20	7.2	227	83.4	272	269	55.5
Central Asia	6	3.6	8	4.9	150	91.5	164	163	61.8
South Asia (incl. India)	70	7.0	20	2.0	913	91.0	1 004	1 004	56.9
East Asia (incl. China)	93	13.7	149	22.0	436	64.4	677	677	19.9
South-East Asia	33	8.1	46	11.2	330	80.8	409	409	7.1
Europe	**72**	**19.8**	**191**	**52.5**	**101**	**27.7**	**364**	**364**	**5.5**
Western and Central Europe	52	21.0	131	52.5	66	26.6	250	249	11.8
Eastern Europe (incl. Russian Fed.)	20	17.2	60	52.6	35	30.2	115	115	2.6
Oceania	**5**	**16.7**	**3**	**9.5**	**20**	**73.8**	**27**	**27**	**3.1**
Australia and New Zealand	5	16.6	3	9.5	20	73.9	27	27	3.3
Pacific Islands	0.03	29.8	0.01	11.3	0.05	58.9	0.08	0.08	0.1
World	**467**	**11.8**	**732**	**18.6**	**2 743**	**69.9**	**3 942**	**3 936**	**9.3**
Least Developed Countries	**15**	**7.3**	**4**	**1.8**	**186**	**90.9**	**205**	**205**	**4.4**

* Includes use of desalinated water.
** IRWR, internal renewable water resources (see Table 18.4).
Source: FAO (2011c).

TABLE 18.2

Country groupings

Africa

Northern Africa

Algeria, Egypt, Libya, Morocco, Tunisia

Sub-Saharan Africa

Angola, Benin, Botswana, Burkina Faso, Burundi, Cameroon, Cape Verde, Central African Republic, Chad, Comoros, Congo, Côte d'Ivoire, Democratic Republic of the Congo, Djibouti, Equatorial Guinea, Eritrea, Ethiopia, Gabon, Gambia, Ghana, Guinea, Guinea-Bissau, Kenya, Lesotho, Liberia, Madagascar, Malawi, Mali, Mauritania, Mauritius, Mozambique, Namibia, Niger, Nigeria, Rwanda, Sao Tome and Principe, Senegal, Seychelles, Sierra Leone, Somalia, South Africa, Sudan, Swaziland, Togo, Uganda, United Republic of Tanzania, Zambia, Zimbabwe

Americas

Northern America

Canada, Mexico, United States of America

Central America and Caribbean

Antigua and Barbuda, Bahamas, Barbados, Belize, Costa Rica, Cuba, Dominica, Dominican Republic, El Salvador, Grenada, Guatemala, Haiti, Honduras, Jamaica, Nicaragua, Panama, Puerto Rico, Saint Kitts and Nevis, Saint Lucia, Saint Vincent and the Grenadines, Trinidad and Tobago

Southern America

Argentina, Bolivia (Plurinational State of), Brazil, Chile, Colombia, Ecuador, French Guiana (France), Guyana, Paraguay, Peru, Suriname, Uruguay, Venezuela (Bolivarian Republic of)

Asia

Western Asia

Armenia, Azerbaijan, Bahrain, Georgia, Iraq, Islamic Republic of Iran, Israel, Jordan, Kuwait, Lebanon, Occupied Palestinian Territory, Oman, Qatar, Saudi Arabia, Syrian Arab Republic, Turkey, United Arab Emirates, Yemen

Central Asia

Afghanistan, Kazakhstan, Kyrgyzstan, Tajikistan, Turkmenistan, Uzbekistan

South Asia

Bangladesh, Bhutan, India, Maldives, Nepal, Pakistan, Sri Lanka

East Asia

China, Democratic People's Republic of Korea, Japan, Mongolia, Republic of Korea

South-East Asia

Brunei Darussalam, Cambodia, Indonesia, Lao People's Democratic Republic, Malaysia, Myanmar, Papua New Guinea, Philippines, Singapore, Thailand, Timor-Leste, Viet Nam

Europe

Western and Central Europe

Albania, Andorra, Austria, Belgium, Bosnia and Herzegovina, Bulgaria, Croatia, Cyprus, Czech Republic, Denmark, Faroe Islands, Finland, France, Germany, Greece, Holy See, Hungary, Iceland, Ireland, Italy, Liechtenstein, Luxembourg, Malta, Monaco, Montenegro, Netherlands, Norway, Poland, Portugal, Romania, San Marino, Serbia, Slovakia, Slovenia, Spain, Sweden, Switzerland, The former Yugoslav Republic of Macedonia, United Kingdom

Eastern Europe and Russian Federation

Belarus, Estonia, Latvia, Lithuania, Republic of Moldova, Russian Federation, Ukraine

Oceania

Australia and New Zealand

Australia, New Zealand

Pacific Islands

Cook Islands, Fiji, Kiribati, Micronesia (Federated States of), Nauru, Niue, Palau, Samoa, Solomon Islands, Tonga, Tuvalu, Vanuatu

Table 18.2 (continued from previous page)

OECD countries

Australia, Austria, Belgium, Canada, Chile, Czech Republic, Denmark, Estonia, Finland, France, Germany, Greece, Hungary, Iceland, Ireland, Israel, Italy, Japan, Luxembourg, Mexico, Netherlands, New Zealand, Norway, Poland, Portugal, Republic of Korea, Slovakia, Slovenia, Spain, Sweden, Switzerland, Turkey, United Kingdom, United States of America

BRIC countries

Brazil, Russian Federation, India, China

Least developed countries (LDCs)

Afghanistan, Angola, Bangladesh, Benin, Bhutan, Burkina Faso, Burundi, Cambodia, Central African Republic, Chad, Comoros, Democratic Republic of the Congo, Djibouti, Equatorial Guinea, Eritrea, Ethiopia, Gambia, Guinea, Guinea-Bissau, Haiti, Kiribati, Lao People's Democratic Republic, Lesotho, Liberia, Madagascar, Malawi, Maldives, Mali, Mauritania, Mozambique, Myanmar, Nepal, Niger, Rwanda, Samoa, Sao Tome and Principe, Senegal, Sierra Leone, Solomon Islands, Somalia, Sudan, Timor-Leste, Togo, Tuvalu, Uganda, United Republic of Tanzania, Vanuatu, Yemen, Zambia

TABLE 18.3

Relative water footprints of various industry sectors

	Raw material production	Suppliers	Direct operations	Product use/end of life
Apparel	●●○		○	●
High-tech/ Electronics	○		○	○
Beverage	●●		●	●
Food	●●○		●○	
Biotech/ Pharma			○	
Forest products	●		●○	
Metals/Mining	●○		●○	
Electric power/ Energy	●○		●○	

Note: Water drops indicate the value chain segments that have relatively high blue, green and grey water footprint intensities. The water footprint is an indicator of water use that looks at both direct and indirect water use of a consumer or producer. The water footprint of an individual, community or business is defined as the total volume of freshwater that is used to produce the goods and services consumed by the individual or community or produced by the business.
Source: Morrison et al. (2009, p. 20).

water resources are below 500 m³ per person per year, or are facing chronic water shortage (500–1,000 m³) or water stress (1,000–1,700 m³) (Figure 18.3 and Table 18.4) (FAO, 2011c). By 2030 food demand is predicted to increase by 50% (70% by 2050) (Bruinsma, 2009) and energy demand from hydropower and other renewable energy resources will rise by 60% (WWAP, 2009). These issues are interconnected – increasing agricultural output for example, will substantially increase both water and energy consumption, leading to increased competition for water between the different water using sectors. The main challenge facing the agricultural sector is not so much growing 70% more food in 40 years, but making 70% more food available on the plate. Reducing losses in storage and along the value chain may go a long way towards offsetting the need for more production.

Despite these challenges, there are many reasons for optimism. The world's population has already shown how resilient it can be. The large irrigation schemes built in the late nineteenth and early twentieth centuries in the Indus valley fed many millions of people who would have otherwise starved. In the second half of the twentieth century world food production more than doubled in response to a doubling of the population. Agricultural productivity rose steadily and irrigated agriculture was an important part of this success story. The 'green' revolution in the 1960s and 1970s lifted Asia out of an imminent hunger crisis although the price was heavy in terms of water use, energy consumption and environmental degradation.

In the 1990s the importance of water ecosystem services became better recognized, as did the need for a

FIGURE 18.3

Renewable water resources per person in 2008

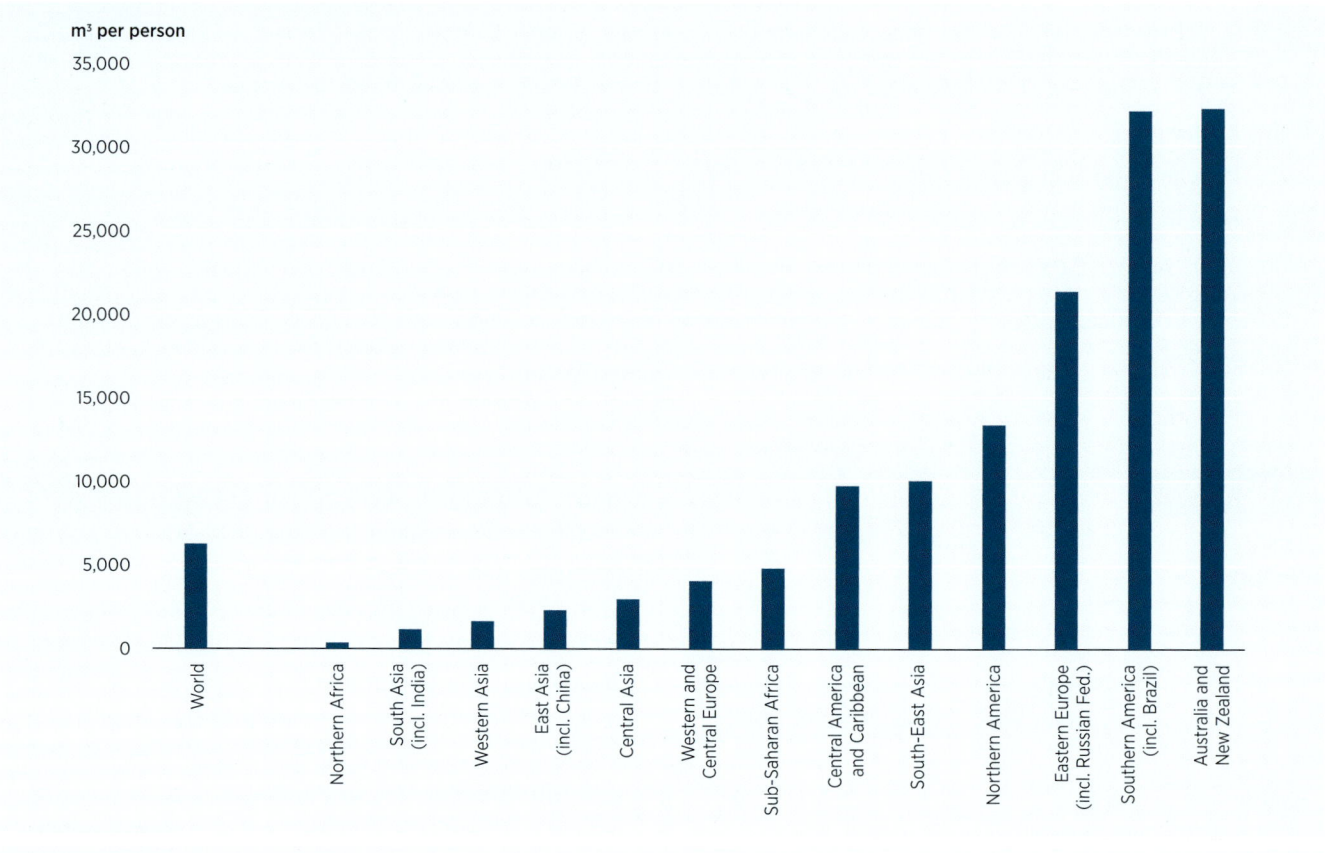

Source: FAO (2011c).

balance between water for food, people, industry and the environment. The response to this was a 'green-green' revolution founded on the principles of environmental sustainability (Conway, 1997). This revolution supported the development of 'green infrastructure' such as improving the health of rivers and their catchments to filter pollutants, mitigate floods and droughts, recharge groundwater and maintain fisheries. Technologies that maintain and enhance such services also build resilience into water delivery systems for people and for agriculture.

Although high food prices may not be popular, there are benefits. For poor farmers higher food prices can mean increased farm incomes (provided they actually receive a portion of the price increase) and for others they focus attention on food losses and wastage. In LDCs as much as half of crops produced are lost post-harvest while in OECD countries as much as 40% of food is wasted along the value chain and by consumers. Reducing these high losses would not only reduce the demand to produce more crops at the farm gate

by 2050 but also significantly reduce the demand on water resources required to grow them.

Many countries still have a large, untapped endowment of rainfall that can be harnessed using conservation farming practices, and supplementary irrigation has a significant role to play in those areas where there are sufficient water resources.

18.1.2 Agriculture's impact on water

Land use changes as a result of agriculture have produced a wide range of impacts on water quantity and quality (Scanlon et al., 2007). Wetlands in particular have been affected. Poor water quality originating from agricultural pollution is most severe in wetlands in Europe, Latin America and Asia (Figure 18.4). The status of species in freshwater and coastal wetlands has been deteriorating faster than those of other ecosystems (MEA, 2005a).

The way that water is managed in agriculture has caused wide-scale changes in ecosystems and

TABLE 18.4

Precipitation and renewable freshwater resources by region

Continent Regions	Precipitation		Internal renewable freshwater resources		
	Depth (mm/year)	Volume (km³/year)	Volume (km³/year)	% of world's freshwater resources	Per capita in year 2008 (m³)
Africa	678	20 359	3 931	9.3	4 007
Northern Africa	96	550	47	0.1	286
Sub-Saharan Africa	815	19 809	3 884	9.2	4 754
Americas	1 088	43 887	19 238	45.4	20 927
Northern America	637	13 869	6 077	14.4	13 401
Central America and Caribbean	2 012	1 510	781	1.8	9 654
Southern America (incl. Brazil)	1 602	28 507	12 380	29.2	32 165
Asia	827	26 826	11 708	27.7	2 870
Western Asia	217	1 423	484	1.1	1 632
Central Asia	273	1 270	263	0.6	3 020
South Asia (incl. India)	1 062	4 755	1 765	4.2	1 125
East Asia (incl. China)	634	7 453	3 410	8.1	2 204
South-East Asia	2 405	11 925	5 786	13.7	9 957
Europe	544	12 507	6 569	15.5	9 102
Western and Central Europe	827	4 045	2 120	5.0	4 123
Eastern Europe (incl. Russian Fed.)	467	8 462	4 449	10.5	21 430
Oceania	586	4 733	892	2.1	33 469
Australia and New Zealand	574	4 598	819	1.9	32 366
Pacific Islands	2 062	135	73	0.2	54 059
World	809	108 312	42 338	100.0	6 292

Source: FAO (2011c).

undermined the provision of a wide range of ecosystem services. Water management for agriculture has changed the physical and chemical characteristics of freshwater and coastal wetlands and the quality and quantity of water, as well as direct and indirect biological changes in terrestrial ecosystems. The external cost of the damage to people and ecosystems and clean-up processes from the agricultural sector is significant. In the United States of America (USA) for instance the estimated cost is US$9–20 billion per year (cited in Galloway et al., 2007).

Diffuse pollution from agricultural land continues to be of critical concern throughout many of the world's river basins. Eutrophication from agricultural runoff ranks among the top pollution problems in the USA, Canada, Asia and the Pacific. Australia, India, Pakistan and many parts of the arid Middle East face increasing salinization as a result of poor irrigation practices (MEA, 2005b). Nitrate is the most common chemical contaminant in the world's aquifers and mean nitrate levels have increased by about 36% in global waterways since 1990. According to data available in FAO (2011d), the USA is currently the country consuming the largest amounts of pesticides, followed by countries in Europe, especially those of Western Europe. In terms of use per unit of cultivated area, Japan is the most intensive user of pesticides. Over-abstraction of renewable groundwater resources and abstraction of fossil groundwater reserves in arid Northern Africa and the Arabian Peninsula, driven primarily by the agricultural sector, is putting irreconcilable pressures on water resources.

FIGURE 18.4

Wetlands water quality state changes by continent

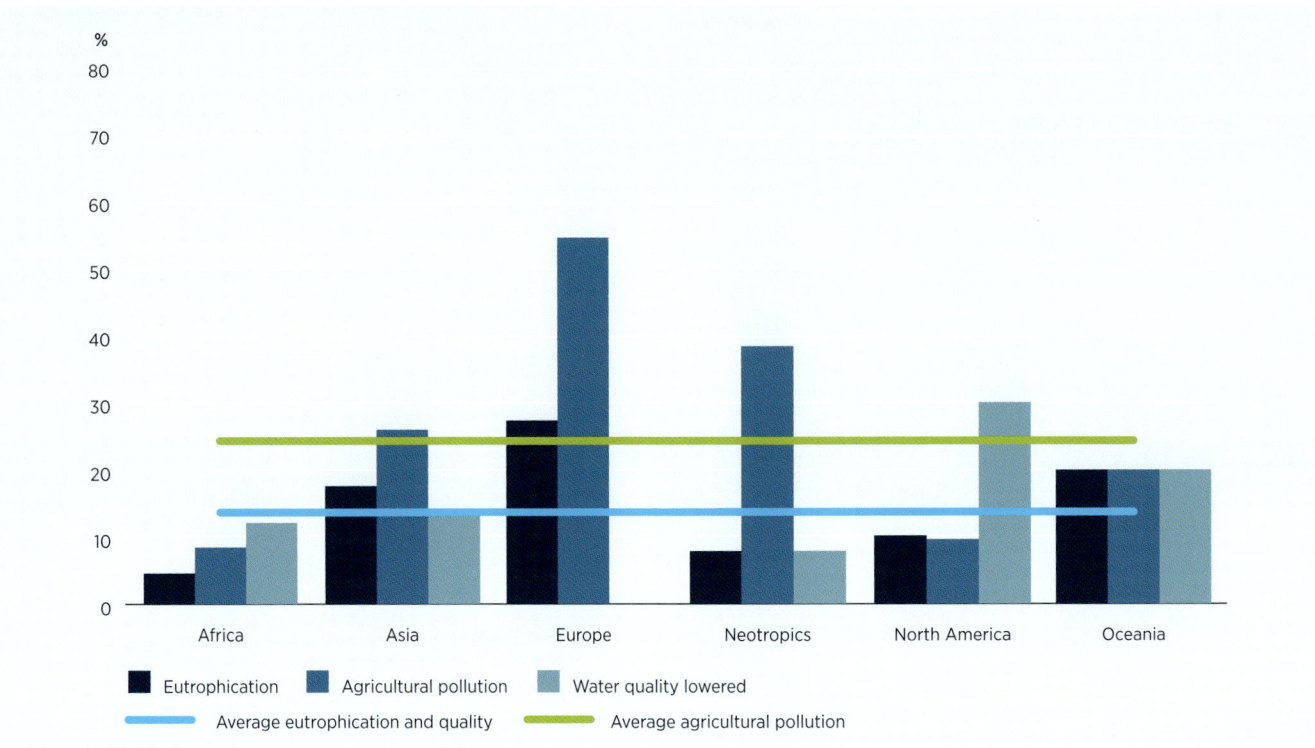

Source: FAO (2008b, p. 50).

In 2005, global conversion of forests (primarily to agricultural land) was estimated to be about 13 million ha per year, and these land cover changes also account for 20% of green house gas (GHG) emissions (Bellarby et al., 2008). South and South-East Asia and Southern and Central America have the highest net carbon flux to the atmosphere (Houghton, 2008). Such land cover changes can increase runoff, increase sediment and nutrient flows, increase floods, reduce groundwater recharge, and reduce biodiversity.

Almost 12% of the global land cover is now under cultivation with cropland covering more than 50% of the land in countries such as India and Bangladesh, and more than 30% in large parts of Europe (Table 18.6) (FAO, 2011*d*).

Between 1961 and 2008, the cultivated area increased by 12%, from 1,368 million ha to 1,527 million ha, and it is all attributable to a net increase in irrigated cropping (Table 18.5).

However, there are also many ways in which agriculture can mitigate these pollution and degradation problems. For example:

- the irrigated area can be expanded somewhat, but it is more important to increase the yield, increase cropping intensities and improve production systems, such as the system of rice intensification;
- the rainfed agriculture area can also be somewhat expanded but again it is more important to increase productivity and improve farming systems using sustainable crop production intensification technologies, such as conservation agriculture, integrated pest management and integrated plant nutrition management;
- reduce post-harvest, transformation, and consumption losses (see Section 18.5).

TABLE 18.5

Net changes in major land use (million ha)

	1961	2008	Net increase
Cultivated land	1 368	1 527	12%
Rainfed	1 229	1 223	−0.5%
Irrigated	139	304	119%

Sources: FAO (2011c, 2011d).

18.2 Managing water resources in agriculture

Do we have enough water (and land) and human capacity to produce the food for a growing population over the next 50 years? The simple answer is 'yes, there is enough' but only if we act now to improve water use in agriculture (Comprehensive Assessment of Water Management in Agriculture, 2007).

Only a small percentage of the world's freshwater is readily available for us to use. Of the 110,000 km^3 of rain falling annually on the earth's surface, 36% ends up in the sea; forestry, grazing lands, fisheries, and biodiversity consume 57%; our towns, cities, and industry consume just 0.1% (110 km^3); while agriculture, including both rainfed and irrigated cropping, consumes 7% (7,130 km^3) (Comprehensive Assessment of Water Management in Agriculture, 2007), of which only 990 km^3 per year is consumed in the OECD countries.

The annual global agricultural water consumption includes crop water consumption for food, fibre and feed production (transpiration) plus evaporation losses from

TABLE 18.6

Population, areas and gross domestic product (GDP) by region

Continent	Population			Area				GDP	
Regions	Total (2008) 1000 inh	Density inh/km²	% of economically active population active in agriculture	Total area of the country 1000 ha	Total area as % of world area %	Cultivated (2008) %	Area cultivated per person economically active in agriculture ha	Per capita (2008) US$/capita	Value added by agriculture %
Africa	**981 043**	**33**	**54**	**3 004 590**	**22**	**8**	**1.2**	**1 592**	**16**
Northern Africa	163 969	29	24	575 289	4	5	2.0	3 434	11
Sub-Saharan Africa	817 074	34	59	2 429 301	18	9	1.2	1 222	18
Americas	**919 269**	**23**	**10**	**4 032 189**	**30**	**10**	**8.8**	**21 657**	**2**
Northern America	453 480	21	5	2 178 056	16	12	23.1	36 805	1
Central America and Caribbean	80 900	108	24	75 069	1	20	1.9	3 820	7
Southern America (incl. Brazil)	384 889	22	14	1 779 064	13	7	4.9	7 574	7
Asia	**4 079 924**	**126**	**52**	**3 242 111**	**24**	**17**	**0.5**	**3 805**	**8**
Western Asia	296 556	45	21	656 650	5	10	2.9	8 242	6
Central Asia	87 214	19	31	465 513	3	8	3.5	2 272	12
South Asia (incl. India)	1 568 227	350	53	447 884	3	46	0.6	970	18
East Asia (incl. China)	1 546 824	132	56	1 176 232	9	11	0.3	6 413	6
South-East Asia	581 103	117	48	495 832	4	20	0.7	2 481	12
Europe	**721 700**	**31**	**6**	**2 300 705**	**17**	**13**	**12.8**	**29 026**	**2**
Western and Central Europe	514 081	105	5	488 872	4	26	9.7	36 777	2
Eastern Europe (incl. Russian Fed.)	207 619	11	9	1 811 833	14	9	16.8	9 434	5
Oceania	**26 659**	**3**	**7**	**807 440**	**6**	**6**	**45.8**	**41 975**	**4**
Australia and New Zealand	25 304	3	5	800 893	6	6	71.6	45 286	4
Pacific Islands	1 355	21	41	6 547	0	10	1.7	2 847	16
World	**6 728 595**	**50**	**41**	**13 387 035**	**100**	**11**	**1.2**	**8 813**	**4**
Least Developed Countries	**816 782**	**39**	**66**	**2 079 489**	**16**	**8**	**0.7**	**616**	**24**

Source: FAO (2011c, with data from UN Population Division, FAOSTAT and World Bank World Development Indicators).

the soil and from open water associated with agriculture such as rice fields, irrigation canals and reservoirs. Only about 20% of the total 7,130 km³ of agriculture's annual water consumption is 'blue water' – that is water from rivers, streams, lakes and groundwater for irrigation purposes. Although irrigation is only a modest part of agricultural water consumption, it plays a crucial role, accounting for more than 40% of the world's production on less than 20% of the cultivated land.

However, global water resource assessments hide the large differences in water availability across the world. Some regions, such as the more northern latitudes and the wet tropics, have more than enough water, whereas the drier semi-arid and arid regions have too little.

Unlike other resources, water cannot be moved across continents in any significant quantities except when it is embedded in food products.

Predicting future water demand for agriculture is fraught with uncertainty. Future demand for water in this sector is in part influenced by demand for food, which in turn depends partly on the number of people needing to be fed, and in part on what and how much they eat. This is complicated by, amongst other factors, uncertainties in seasonal climatic variations, efficiency of agriculture production processes, crop types and yields.

The world population is predicted to grow from 6.9 billion in 2010 to 8.3 billion in 2030 and 9.1 billion in 2050

TABLE 18.7

Pressure on water resources due to irrigation

Continent Regions	Precipitation (mm)	Renewable water resources (km³)	Water requirement ratio (%)	Irrigation water withdrawal (km³)	Pressure on water resources due to irrigation (%)
Year			2008	2008	2008
Africa	**678**	**3 931**	**48**	**184**	**5**
Northern Africa	96	47	69	80	170
Sub-Saharan Africa	815	3 884	30	105	3
Americas	**1 088**	**19 238**	**41**	**381**	**2**
Northern America	637	6 077	46	259	4
Central America and Caribbean	2 012	781	30	15	2
Southern America	1 602	12 380	28	107	1
Asia	**827**	**11 708**	**45**	**2 057**	**18**
Western Asia	217	484	47	227	47
Central Asia	273	263	48	150	57
South Asia	1 062	1 765	55	913	52
East Asia	634	3 410	37	436	13
South-East Asia	2 405	5 786	19	330	6
Europe	**544**	**6 569**	**48**	**101**	**2**
Western and Central Europe	827	2 120	43	56	3
Eastern Europe (incl. Russian Fed.)	467	4 449	67	35	1
Oceania	**586**	**892**	**41**	**20**	**2**
Australia and New Zealand	574	819	41	20	2
Pacific Islands	2 062	73	-	0.05	-
World	**809**	**42 338**	**44**	**2 743**	**6**

The water requirement ratio is the ratio between the irrigation requirement and irrigation water withdrawal.
*** Pressure on water resources due to irrigation is the ratio between irrigation water withdrawal and renewable water resources.*
Sources: Adapted from FAO (2011a) and FAO (2011c).

(DESA, 2009). But these figures hide the fact that the population in some countries, particularly in sub-Saharan Africa and South Asia, will continue to grow while in high income countries the population will decline. By 2050 about 7.5 billion people will be living in low and middle income countries, with 1.5 billion in sub-Saharan Africa and 2.2 billion in South Asia.

Although projections vary considerably based on different scenario assumptions and methodologies, future global agricultural water consumption (including both rainfed and irrigated agriculture) is estimated to increase by about 19% to 8,515 km^3 per year in 2050 (Comprehensive Assessment of Water Management in Agriculture, 2007). The Food and Agriculture Organization of the United Nations (FAO) estimates an 11% increase in irrigation water consumption from 2008 to 2050. This is expected to increase by about 5% the present water withdrawal for irrigation of 2,740 km^3 (Table 18.7). Although this seems a modest increase, much of it will be in regions already suffering water scarcity (FAO, 2011a).

In semi-arid environments the amount of rainfall used for cropping is relatively small. Hence in these areas, better use of rainfall is needed by integrating soil and water management – focused on soil fertility, improved rainfall infiltration and water harvesting – to reduce water losses, improve yields and raise the overall water productivity of rainfed systems. The strategy is to get 'more crop per drop'.

Globally, irrigated crop yields are about 2.7 times those of rainfed farming, hence irrigation will continue to

TABLE 18.8

Evolution of area equipped for irrigation, groundwater irrigation and percentage of cultivated land

Continent / Regions / Year	Total area equipped for irrigation (1000 ha)			By groundwater		Total irrigation as % of cultivated land		
				Area	% of total			
	1970	1990	2008	2008	2008	1970	1990	2008
Africa	8 429	10 990	13 445	2 506	19	4.6	5.4	5.4
Northern Africa	4 376	5 131	6 340	2 092	33	18.4	19.2	22.6
Sub-Saharan Africa	4 053	5 859	7 105	414	6	2.6	3.3	3.2
Americas	26 609	38 381	44 002	21 548	49	7.2	9.9	11.1
Northern America	20 004	27 218	31 826	19 147	60	6.7	9.0	12.6
Central America and Caribbean	932	1 669	1 739	683	39	8.0	12.0	11.5
Southern America (incl. Brazil)	5 673	9 494	10 437	1 717	16	6.3	8.7	8.2
Asia	116 031	168 195	222 269	80 582	36	23.3	30.3	41.0
Western Asia	11 025	19 802	23 347	10 838	46	17.2	30.0	36.3
Central Asia	7 971	13 366	14 518	1,149	8	15.2	25.9	36.8
South Asia (incl. India)	45 048	66 856	93 140	48 293	52	22.8	32.7	45.6
East Asia (incl. China)	42 894	53 299	68 491	19 331	28	38.5	37.4	51.6
South-East Asia	9 093	14 872	22 773	971	4	12.2	18.8	22.4
Europe	15 259	25 908	21 856	7 350	34	4.6	8.1	7.5
Western and Central Europe	10 844	17 635	16 221	6 857	42	7.4	12.7	13.0
Eastern Europe (incl. Russian Fed.)	4 415	8 273	5 635	493	9	2.4	4.6	3.4
Oceania	1 588	2 113	2 833	950	34	3.5	4.1	6.2
Australia and New Zealand	1 587	2 112	2 830	949	34	3.5	4.2	6.3
Pacific Islands	1	1	3	1.00	33	0.2	0.2	0.5
World	167 916	245 587	304 405	112 936	37	11.8	16.1	19.9

Sources: FAO (2011c), FAO (2011d) and Siebert et al. (2010).

play an important role in food production. The area equipped for irrigation increased from 170 million ha in 1970 to 304 million ha in 2008 (Table 18.8). There is still the potential for expansion, particularly in sub-Saharan Africa and Southern America, in places where there is sufficient water available. Pathways to improve productivity and bridge the yield gap in irrigation are: increasing the quantity, reliability and timing of water services; increasing the beneficial use of water withdrawn for irrigation; and increasing agronomic or economic productivity so that more output is obtained per unit of water consumed (FAO, 2011a).

In most LDCs, new institutional structures will be needed which enable governments to centralize responsibilities for water regulation yet decentralize water management responsibility and increase user ownership and participation. Data collection and synthesis for water resources planning will need to be strengthened, and so too will the communication between government departments which have overlapping responsibilities for water management. The need is to try and achieve integrated water resources management (IWRM).

Recognizing the local nature of water management will also be important, as will be the need to significantly increase water productivity and adjust water allocations to meet changing societal habits (FAO, 2009a). The effectiveness of existing agricultural water consumption can also be greatly improved by reducing the significant quantities of crops lost in post-harvest stores in LDCs and reducing the large amounts of food waste along the value chain in OECD and BRIC countries.

Virtual water trading may also play an increasing role in the future. This means growing food in water-rich places and exporting it (with the water embedded in its production) to water-scarce countries. This is already happening in the Middle East, although only 15% of the world's farm output in terms of embedded water is traded internationally (Allan, 2011). However, the concept of virtual water as a means of framing economic and trade policy is questioned by some (Wichelns, 2010). One of the main constraints is the low purchasing power in countries facing the largest growth in food demand and this is likely to remain so for the foreseeable future. Evidence from the recent rise in commodity prices suggests that countries are quick to raise export tariffs of staple crops as soon as national food security is threatened.

18.3 Uncertainties and risk management

There are many risks and uncertainties about future water availability for agriculture, and these are greatest in the drought prone low income countries whose GDP is dependent on agriculture. The economic performance in many LDCs is closely linked to rainfall, but there are many other issues that add to the risks and uncertainties created by climate.

18.3.1 A new 'rurality' in least developed countries

Most LDC governments look to their rural communities to produce more agricultural products but those same communities are impoverished, their productivity is low, as is their resource use efficiency. Their burden is made worse by the changing nature of rural life – known as the new 'rurality' (Rauch, 2009). Globalization is transforming the marketplace; new patterns of poverty are emerging as livelihoods adjust; reforms in governance and rural service systems are changing the nature of institutions. All these issues create uncertainty and risk and are likely to have a disproportionate impact on the rural poor and their ability to access and make good use of limited water resources.

18.3.2 Climate change

Agriculture contributes to climate change through its share of GHG emissions, which in turn is affecting the planet's water cycle and adding another layer of uncertainties and risks to food production. Climate change impacts are mainly experienced through the water regime in the form of more severe and frequent droughts and floods, with anticipated effects on the availability of water resources through changes in rainfall distribution, soil moisture, glacier and ice/snow melt, and river and groundwater flows. These climate change-induced hydrological changes are likely to affect both the extent and productivity of irrigated and rainfed agriculture worldwide, hence adaptation strategies will focus on minimizing the overall production risk (FAO, 2011b).

Agriculture is the largest contributor to global non-CO_2 GHG emissions (59% in 1990, 57% forecasted for 2020) (US-EPA, 2006). The agricultural sector contributes both directly (methane from cattle enteric fermentation, rice production, etc.) and indirectly (conversion of land to agriculture, fossil fuel use on farms, production of agro-chemicals, etc.) to GHG emissions. The sector directly contributes 14% of global annual GHG emissions and indirectly contributes an additional 4–8% (from forest clearing for rangeland and arable development) (FAO, 2011b). The most common GHGs from the agricultural sector – nitrous oxide (N_2O) and methane (CH_4) gases – emanate primarily from agricultural soils (N_2O) and livestock (CH_4 from enteric fermentation, i.e. belching) (Figures 18.5 and 18.6).

In 1990, the OECD countries, China, the Former Soviet Union countries, Latin America and Africa accounted for more than 80% of N_2O emissions from agricultural soils. By 2020, OECD countries' agricultural soil emissions are expected to decrease and contribute 23% of global emissions (compared to 32% in 1990). Expected increases in crop and livestock production elsewhere portend that Central, South and East Asia's and Eastern Europe's agricultural soil emissions will grow more than 50%, and soil emissions from Africa, Latin America and the Middle East will grow over 100%. Globally, CH_4 emissions from livestock digestion are forecasted to grow, and while most OECD countries' livestock enteric fermentation emissions are expected to decrease somewhat overall (–9%), China, Brazil, India, USA and Pakistan are predicted to be the top emitters in this category by 2020 (US-EPA, 2006).

Agriculture also offers significant mitigation potential which can be realized through a variety of site-specific options spanning from measures and practices aimed at reducing emissions, enhancing removals, and/or avoiding (or displacing) emissions. Estimates suggest that the total biophysical mitigation potential from agriculture could be 5,500–6,000 megatonnes CO_2-equivalent per year which, if fully reached, could offset about 20% of total annual CO_2 emissions (Smith et al., 2008). Specifically, crop and grazing land management, restoring the carbon content of cultivated organic soils and restoring degraded lands provide the most significant mitigation potentials in agriculture, followed by improved water and rice management, land use changes (i.e. conversion of cropland to grassland) and agro-forestry, and improved livestock and manure management (Smith et al., 2007)

In terms of the impacts, floods and droughts are increasing in incidence and severity, and this trend is predicted to continue in the future. Recent evidence

FIGURE 18.5

Sources of agricultural greenhouse gases excluding land use change

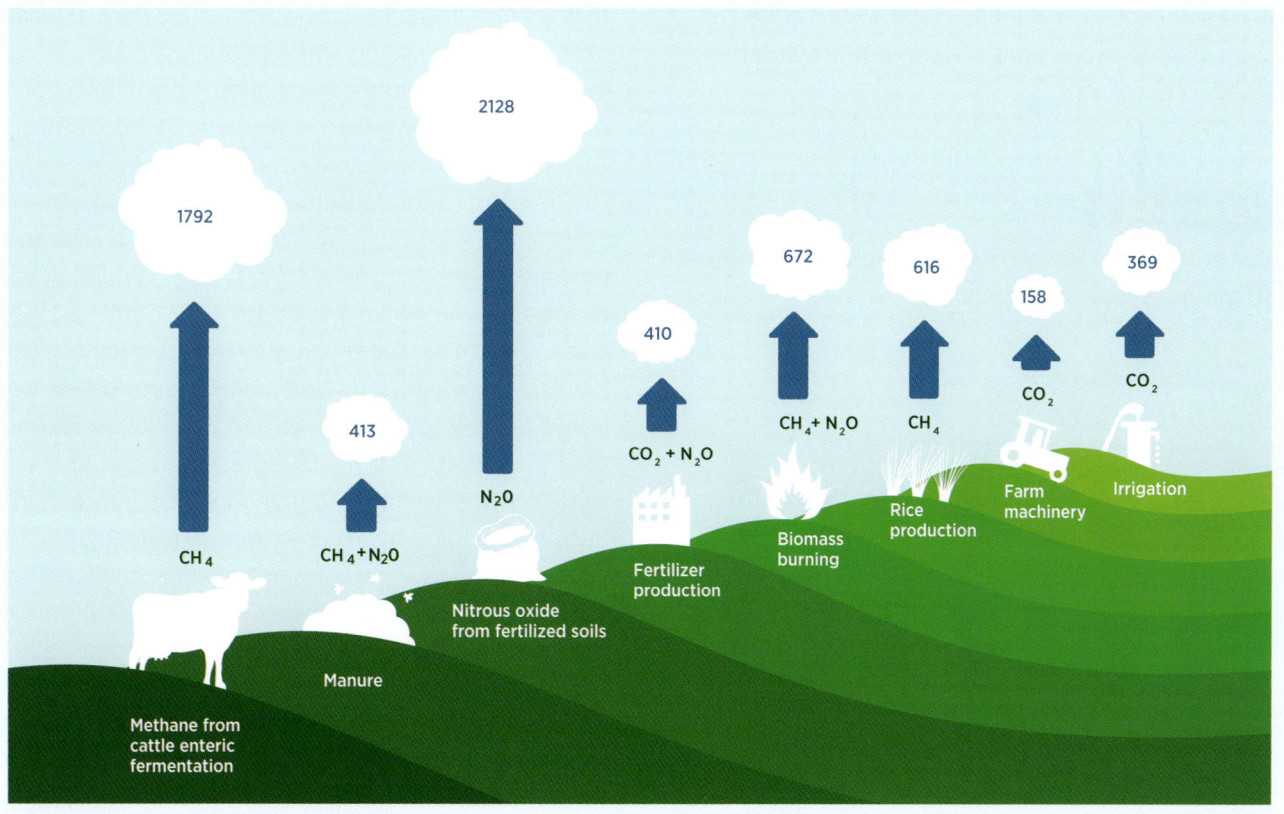

Source: Bellarby et al. (2008 fig. 2, p. 7).

forecasts that the Mediterranean basin and the semi-arid areas of the Americas, Australia, and Southern Africa will experience reductions in river runoff and aquifer recharge, affecting water availability in these already water-stressed regions. In Asia, changes in runoff patterns from snowmelt and high mountain glaciers will affect downstream dependent irrigated lands, as well as the highly populated Asian deltas, from a combination of reduced inflows, increased salinity and rising sea levels. Worldwide, the rising temperatures will increase crop water demand (FAO, 2011b).

Climate change will also affect groundwater and this in turn will affect the vulnerability of women in many countries. Since the burden of collecting water for household purposes often falls on the women, lowering groundwater levels and increasingly depleted water sources result in women having to walk longer and longer distances to fetch water, thus taking away time from agricultural activities and exposing themselves to a variety of dangers (FAO, 2010).

It is predicted that South Asia and Southern Africa will be the most vulnerable to climate change-related food shortages by 2030 (Lobell et al., 2008). Their populations are food insecure because they are highly dependent on growing crops in ecosystems that display high vulnerability and consequences to climate change projections of temperature and precipitation changes.

As climate variability has a direct impact on crop yields – mainly in terms of precipitation, temperature increases and water availability – adaptive management practices and systems need to build in flexibility which allows for adaptation in the agricultural sector. As a result, climate change research in most OECD countries for instance focuses primarily on examining the implications for agricultural production, such as forecast changes in regional rainfall and water availability, and on analysing the efficiency of farm practices under various climate change scenarios.

For water, options to adapt to the changes are a combination of improved supply management (adapting storage capacity) and demand management – to reduce groundwater overuse, promote more efficient conjunctive use and raise water productivity (FAO, 2011a).

18.3.3 Food, economy and energy crises

The food price crisis, followed shortly by the 2009 economic crisis, has had tragic consequences for world hunger. Food prices are significantly higher than they were in 2006. Although the factors which led to this increase in food prices were said to be temporary – such as drought in wheat-producing regions, low food stocks and soaring oil barrel prices that drove up the price of fertilizers – food prices in 2011 had not yet returned to their pre-2006 levels. Poor women shoulder the brunt of economic crises and women with less education tend to increase their work participation more in times of crisis in almost every region of the world (FAO, 2009b).

The demand for biofuels has soared in recent years. Substantial amounts of maize in the USA, wheat and rapeseed in the European Union (EU), oil palm in parts of sub-Saharan Africa and South and South-East Asia, and sugar in Brazil, are being raised for ethanol and biodiesel production. In 2007, biofuel production was dominated by the USA, Brazil, and to a lesser extent, the EU. Biomass and waste represented 10% of the world's primary energy demand in 2005, more than nuclear (6%) and hydro (2%) jointly (IEA, 2007).

If a projected bio-energy supply of 6,000–12,000 million tonnes of oil equivalent were to be reached in 2050, this would take up one-fifth of the world's agricultural land (IEA, 2006).[2] Biofuels are also water intensive and can add to the strain on local hydrological systems and GHG emissions. Irrigated biofuels already consume just under 2% of all irrigation water withdrawals (about 44 km^3) (FAO, 2008a) (Table 18.9). For instance, it was

FIGURE 18.6

Total greenhouse gas emissions from the agricultural sector by source

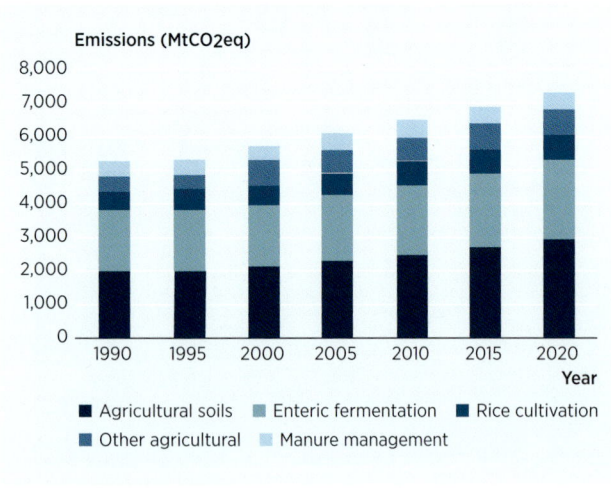

Source: US-EPA (2006).

estimated that 1 litre of ethanol produced in the irrigated south-western part of Nebraska in the USA requires about 415 L of water (Varghese, 2007). In Brazil water pollution associated with biofuel production, the application of fertilizers and agro-chemicals, soil erosion, and sugarcane washing procedures are major concerns.

18.3.4 Land acquisitions and land use changes

Land use is changing because of the rising international phenomenon of land acquisition, which will in turn impact on water use. Since 2007 some OECD and BRIC countries' sovereign funds and investment companies have bought or leased large tracts of farmland across Africa, Latin America and Asia in order to secure their fuel and food requirements. This was triggered by the fuel crisis and the demand for biofuels to replace petroleum-based products.

Although there is still potential to increase the cropped area, some 5–7 million ha (0.6%) of farmland is lost annually because of accelerating land degradation and urbanization, which takes agricultural land out of production and reduces the number of family farms as more people move to the cities. Increasing population means that the amount of cultivated land per person is declining sharply – from 0.4 ha in 1961 to 0.2 ha in 2005.

18.3.5 Policy and governance

Improving productivity of irrigated agriculture and using less water means transferring and adopting newer technologies and adapting equipment and processes to locally appropriate irrigation practices. This requires financial resources, but it also requires good policy and governance, and the links between them need to be given priority. For instance, there have been numerous efforts to link national integrated water resource and water efficiency plans to national development plans in order to access government and donor finance (GWP, 2009).

While there are established tools and instruments to better manage water assets for agriculture, there are many other seemingly unrelated issues that underpin the overall challenges of water governance such as fragile states, corruption, inequitable access to water and land tenure rights. More so, agricultural water allocations sit within increasingly competing social–economic–environmental needs and priorities that drive overall national security and development objectives, and which climate change-induced hydrological changes are set to exacerbate. Various subregional initiatives have sprouted in recent years in a bid to increase high-level political attention (hence investments) to water security issues, such as the African Ministers' Council on Water and the Asia–Pacific Water Forum. Local institutions nonetheless remain the frontline actors and here weak capacity and fragmentation of water-related institutions remain as key concerns in many regions.

18.4 A new era in food and water management?

When water is scarce it is no longer enough to just think about the amount of water we need to grow food (Lundqvist et al., 2008), we must also look at the way water is used along the entire value chain from production to consumption and beyond (Figure 18.7). This is particularly true for the more industrialized countries, and also to some extent in the towns and cities of the BRIC countries, where food increasingly comes from many different sources, often

TABLE 18.9

Water requirements for biofuel crops

Crop	Annual obtainable fuel yield	Energy yield	Evapo-transpiration equivalent	Potential crop evapo-transpiration	Rainfed crop evapo-transpiration	Irrigated crop water requirement	
	(L/ha)	(G/ha)	(L/litre fuel)	(mm/ha)	(mm/ha)	(mm/ha)*	(L/litre fuel)
Sugar cane	6 000	120	2 000	1 400	1 000	800	1 333
Maize	3 500	70	1 357	550	400	300	857
Oil palm	5 500	193	2 364	1 500	1 300	0	0
Rapeseed	1 200	42	3 333	500	400	0	0

* On the assumption of 50% irrigation efficiency.
Source: FAO (2008a).

FIGURE 18.7

Water use along the value chain, from production to recycling

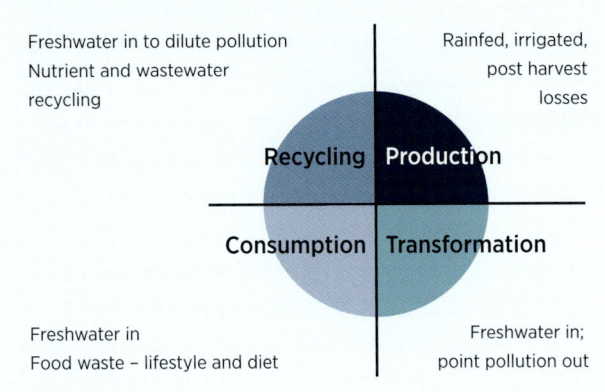

BOX 18.1

'It is distressing to note that so much time is being devoted to the culture of the plant, so much money spent on irrigation, fertilization and crop protection measures only to be wasted about a week after harvest' (FAO, 1981).

over long distances, and in some cases from many different countries. Food security is threatened by the potential for waste as agricultural products move along extensive value chains and pass through many hands – farmers, transporters, store keepers, food processors, shopkeepers and consumers – as it travels from field to fork. Food can be wasted at every step along the value chain and this means that the water used to produce it is also wasted. All this is in sharp contrast to the past when most food was produced and consumed locally, which is still the case in most LCDs.

In some countries reducing water use is no longer just about improving water productivity on the farm. Water is used for cleaning, preparing, distributing and consuming food. All these processes pollute the water which then requires recycling prior to discharge or diluting to reduce contamination.

Water management has traditionally been the responsibility of governments, but major international food companies are beginning to realize the importance of water to their businesses, particularly where their value chains are in water-short countries. Although their concern may have more to do with customer perceptions and security of profits, there are potential

knock-on benefits for everyone as water is managed with greater care. Initiatives to promote more efficient use of water along the value chain include, for example, the CEO Water Mandate and the Alliance for Water Stewardship.

We are clearly entering a new era of water management in which the links between water and other resources and the socio-economics of poor post-harvest management (Box 18.1) and food waste along the value chain are increasingly recognized.

18.5 Water use along the livestock value chain

The livestock industry, which is growing rapidly, provides a good illustration of the challenges to the water–agriculture–supply chain nexus – how water is used, consumed and polluted along the value chain as animals are produced on the farm, transformed into products, consumed, and the waste products recycled. Livestock products are also an important part of the global trade in food and so the industry also highlights the growing benefits and concerns about water footprints and the 'exporting/importing' of water and pollution as meat and dairy products are shipped from one country to another.

Livestock farming is one of the most important subsectors in agriculture, both socially and economically. It employs over 1.3 billion people across the world. It generates livelihoods for some 1 billion of the world's poorest people. However, livestock farming also contributes to the most serious environmental problems – land degradation, climate change, air pollution, water scarcity and pollution, and loss of biodiversity (FAO, 2006b).

The world food economy is being increasingly driven by the shift in diets and food consumption patterns towards livestock products (FAO, 2006a). In 2008, about 3,350 million ha were under permanent meadows and pasture – more than twice the area under arable cropping and permanent crops. Livestock provides not just meat but also dairy products, eggs, wool, hides, and so on. The livestock sector is now changing at an unprecedented pace as demand for food derived from animals has boomed in the world's most rapidly growing economies (FAO, 2006b). Livestock already contributes 40% of the global value of agricultural output. It is one of the most dynamic parts of the agricultural economy and is driven by population growth, rising affluence, and urbanization.

As the demand for livestock products grows, so too do the concerns about its impact on the environment. The expansion of land for livestock has led to deforestation in some countries (e.g. Brazil) and intensive livestock production (mainly in OECD countries) is already a major source of pollution. Livestock contributes less than 2% of global GDP and yet it produces some 18% of GHGs (FAO, 2006b). Hence critics argue that the disbenefits far outweigh the benefits that come from livestock, but others argue that this seriously underestimates the economic and social importance of livestock, particularly in low income countries. Regardless of the balance of these arguments, the increasing demand for livestock seems likely to continue. This means that resource use efficiency in livestock production is now an urgent priority, and this includes the management of water.

18.5.1 How the water flows from field to fork

Considering this global picture of livestock production – including rapid growth, the shift in world livestock output from high income to low income countries, the changing patterns of international trade, and the potential for further growth in the sector – what are the implications for water resources, now and in the future, both in terms of water consumption and the industry's impact on water through pollution?

Livestock production – on the farm

All livestock require water for drinking, cooling and cleaning, but the amount of water required differs according to the animal, the method of rearing and the location. Extensive livestock systems can increase water demand because of the additional effort needed as animals search for feed. Intensive or industrialized systems, however, require additional service water for cooling and cleaning facilities. Globally, the annual drinking water requirement for livestock is about 16 km³, and servicing requires an additional 6.5 km³ (FAO, 2006b).

The amount of water used to grow feed and fodder is much more significant in volume terms. This amount depends not just on the number and kinds of animals and amount of food they eat but also where the food is grown. It is estimated that livestock consumes about 2,000–3,000 km³ of water annually – as much as 45% of the global water embedded in food products (Comprehensive Assessment of Water Management in Agriculture, 2007; Zimmer and Renault, 2003) – although these estimates are quite imprecise. Whatever the figure, the amount involved in producing livestock products is substantial. Rainfed grasslands consume most of this water, which is generally thought to be of little environmental value. Some of the more intensively managed grazing lands and cereal and oilseed crops grown for feedstuffs may have alternative agricultural potential but they are mostly located in water abundant areas.

Irrigation water volumes are much smaller but have an important role in producing feed, fodder and grazing for livestock and have a much greater opportunity cost than rainfed cropping.[3] There is no global estimate available but the authors suggest that it could be 13% of agricultural blue water consumption (Table 18.10) – a figure which could rise in the future as the demand for livestock products increases. This figure is based on information available on irrigated feed, fodder crops and pasture for the two main animal groups – monogastrics (pigs and poultry) and ruminants (beef and dairy cows, buffalo).

Pigs and poultry are predominantly reared in intensive and industrially based production systems and rely on concentrated feedstuffs made up of four important crops – barley, maize, wheat and soybean (BMWS). Ruminants are mostly reared in extensive rainfed grazing systems though some rely on irrigated pasture and fodder. In OECD countries

TABLE 18.10

Estimated global annual water consumption of grazing, fodder and feed production for livestock

Item		Net evapotranspiration (km³ per year)
1	Global water to meet current food demand[a]	7 130
2	Rainfed agriculture[a] (green water) – % of (1)	5 855 (82%)
3	Irrigated agriculture[b] (blue water) – % of (1)	1 275 (18%)
6	Irrigated feed, fodder and grazing[b] – % of (3)	160 (13%)

Sources: [a] CA (2007); [b] FAO (2011c).

an increasing number of dairy cows rely on manu-factured compound feed, but the picture of what percentages are irrigated or rainfed is complex. Estimates are based on the FAO's global information system on water and agriculture (AQUASTAT), which can be considered as minimum values due to incom-pleteness of the information (FAO, 2011c). United States Department of Agriculture (2008) sources suggest that some 16 million ha of permanent fodder and pasture and 16 million ha of annual fodder and feed is irrigated globally, consuming about 160 km³ of water. Bringing these data together, the global irrigated evapotranspiration for livestock is estimated to be about 13% (Table 18.10 and Figure 18.8).

Transformation

The slaughterhouse is the second largest user of water in the meat processing value chain (after the produc-tion phase) and a potentially significant point source of pollution in local ecosystems and communities. The source of water entering dairies and abattoirs depends on the location. The most significant water-related issues with regards to slaughterhouse operations are the use of large amounts of water; large quantities of effluents and emissions of high organic strength liquids into the water; and energy consumption from refrigeration and water heating.

Hygiene standards in OECD countries typically re-quire large quantities of freshwater at the abattoir to be used mainly for watering and washing livestock, cleaning equipment and work areas, and for washing

carcasses (Figure 18.9). Food safety and hygiene standards have in fact been tightened in recent years following occurrences of *Salmonella, Listeria*, and the bovine spongiform encephalopathy (BSE, or mad cow disease) crisis. As a consequence, cleaning and sterilization operations using hot water have been in-tensified, most likely driving up the volume of water consumed at the slaughterhouse in many OECD coun-tries (European Commission, 2005). For example, 46% of water used in an Italian pig slaughterhouse is for cleaning, and 56% of water used at a Danish poultry slaughterhouse killing 25 million birds per year is used for washing carcasses and chilling. Together, cleaning and carcass washing can account for more than 80% of total water use and effluent volumes (European Commission, 2005).

In dairies, food safety and hygiene standards explain that the bulk of water used is for cleaning, sanitizing and pasteurization (Figure 18.10).

Water use also varies according to the type of animals being slaughtered. In Denmark and Norway poultry slaughtering requires the greatest water volumes and generates the highest nutrient loads when compared to slaughtering other animals (Table 18.11).

The floor area of the slaughterhouse also influences water use, as does the size of the animals/birds and slaughter methods, carcass dressing and cooling, and automation.

FIGURE 18.8

Global annual water consumption for livestock grazing, fodder and feed production

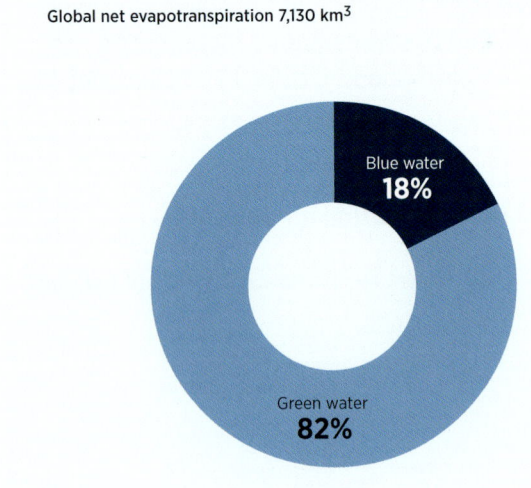

Global net evapotranspiration 7,130 km³

Blue water 18%

Green water 82%

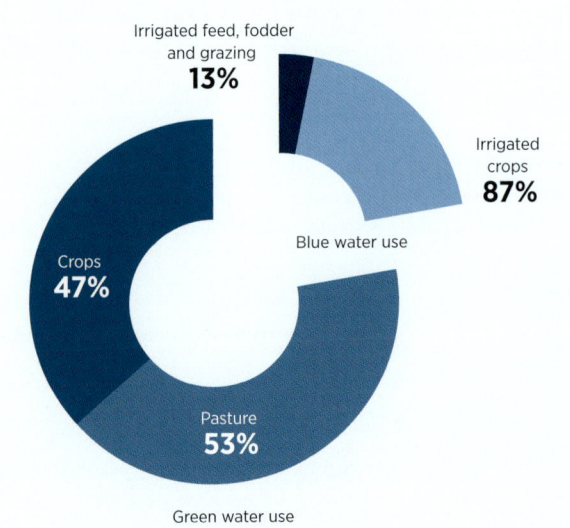

Irrigated feed, fodder and grazing 13%

Irrigated crops 87%

Blue water use

Crops 47%

Pasture 53%

Green water use

Meat processing effluents contain blood, fat, manure, undigested stomach contents and cleaning detergents. Capital and resource intensive wastewater treatment infrastructure is required to treat such effluents which, if left unchecked, will result in high biological oxygen demand (BOD), suppression of sensitive aquatic species, odours, and other problems.

Consumption

Water is used during the consumption[4] stage as food passes through retailers and is packed and prepared for eating by food processing companies and also in the home. This adds to the burden of water pollution as food is washed, cleaned and prepared.

The most serious aspect of food consumption in terms of water use is food wastage. This is particularly the case in industrialized countries where food is wasted because too much perishable food is produced and not sold, products deteriorate in storage, and food is bought and not consumed and hence thrown away. All this adds up to both a significant waste of food and also a significant waste of the water used to produce it (Lundqvist, 2010).

Recycling

Water recycling is needed at every stage of the value chain. At the production stage, the increasing numbers of livestock herds are significant sources of pollution (grey water). Livestock faeces are far more potent in nutrient loadings than human excreta. Asia generates about 35% of global annual livestock excretion of nitrogen (N) and phosphorus (P). Pig waste in Thailand, Viet Nam and Guangdong (China) contributes more to water pollution than domestic wastewater (Table 18.12). In the USA the livestock sector is responsible for about 55% of soil erosion, 32% of nitrogen loads, and 33% of potassium loads into freshwater resources. A further 37% of pesticide use and 50% of the volume of antibiotics used come from the livestock sector (FAO, 2006b), and all contribute to water pollution.

The growth in trade of livestock products is further transforming meat production and environmental relationships. Major meat importing countries get the benefit of the land and water use and nitrogen emissions in the meat producing countries. Pig and chicken meat imports into Japan, one of the world's top feed and meat importers, embody the virtual equivalent of 50% of Japan's total arable land. Furthermore, Japan's meat consumption, while annually releasing some 70,000 tonnes of nitrogen domestically, is estimated to leave 220,000 tonnes of nitrogen behind in meat exporting countries (Galloway et al., 2007). Figure 18.11 illustrates Japan's nitrogen flow in the pig and poultry trade and shows that about 1.5 times more nitrogen loss occurs

FIGURE 18.9

Data for water consumption in a typical Italian pig slaughterhouse

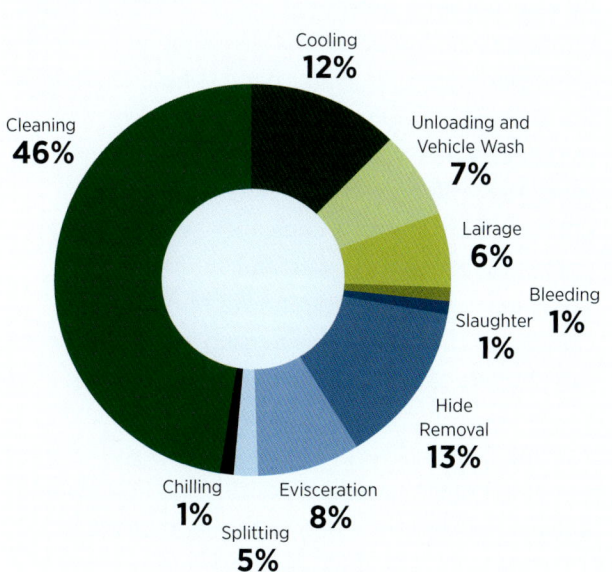

Source: European Commission (2005).

FIGURE 18.10

Typical water use by a market milk processor in Australia

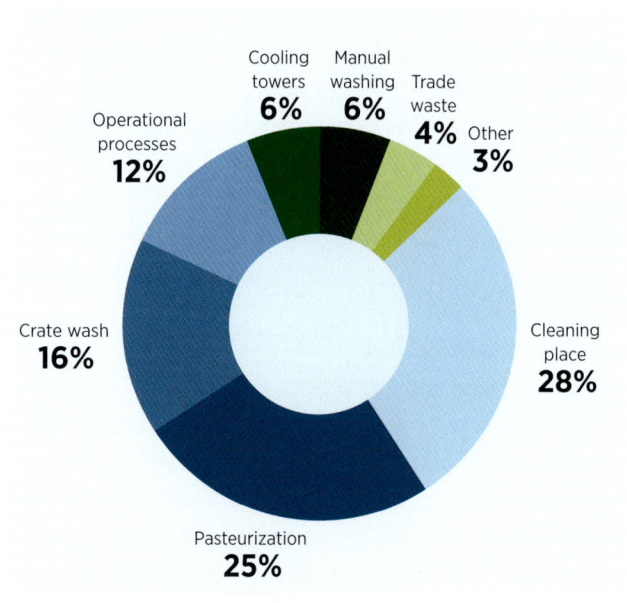

Source: UNEP (2004, p. 20).

TABLE 18.11

Water use and emission data in Danish and Norwegian slaughterhouses

All values per tonne of carcass	Water use, wastewater (L)	BOD emission (kg)	COD emission (kg)	Nitrogen emission (g)	Phosphorus emission (g)	Suspended solids emission (g)
Cattle	1 623–9 000	1.8–28	4–40	172–1 840	24.8–260	11.2–15.9
Pig	1 600–8 300	2.14–10	3.22–10	180–2 100	20–233	0.12–5.1
Sheep	5 556–8 333	8.89		1 556	500	
Poultry	5 070–67 400	2.43–43	4–41.0	560–4 652	26.2–700	48–700

Notes: Biological oxygen demand (BOD) is an indicator of water quality. Chemical oxygen demand (COD) measures the amount of organic pollutants in surface water.
Source: Water-related data extracted from European Commission (2005).

TABLE 18.12

Estimated nitrogen and phosphorous emissions in water systems

Country/Province	Nutrient	Potential load (tonnes)	Percentage contribution to nutrient emissions in water systems		
			Pig waste	Domestic wastewater	Non-point source
China-Guangdon	N	530 434	72	9	19
	P	219 824	94	1	5
Thailand	N	491 262	14	9	77
	P	52 795	61	16	23
Viet Nam	N	442 022	38	12	50
	P	212 120	92	5	3

Source: FAO (2004).

in the exporting countries (mainly the USA) than at home as a result of its large meat import volumes. Some 36% of the 220,000 tonnes of nitrogen is in the form of virtual nitrogen (nitrogen used in production but not actually embedded in the livestock product). This implies that high meat importing consumers enjoy the benefits of livestock products without paying the environmental costs of nitrogen emissions to local groundwater and surface water and the local atmosphere. In Brazil, 15% of the virtual nitrogen left behind is due to feed and meat exports to China (Galloway et al., 2007).

18.5.2 More 'protein per drop'

With an expected rise in the demand for animal products and a subsequent increase in pressure on freshwater resources, it is essential to get more protein per drop of water used, particularly for blue water. Some examples of how this can be achieved at each stage of the livestock value chain are outlined below.

- Production: raising water productivity using sustainable crop production intensification techniques for managing soil fertility (increasing crop productivity by incorporating both organic and inorganic plant nutrients which prevent soil degradation and reduces nutrient loss); rainwater harvesting and storage.
- Transformation: adopting cleaner practices that aim to reduce water volumes and capture and treat nutrient-rich effluents; better storage facilities.
- Consumption: increase consumer awareness campaigns to reduce food wastage.
- Recycling: water, nutrient and waste recycling (including cascading systems reusing treated effluents for adapted, safe uses) to close the value chain loops.

Innovative technical responses are only possible within a context of locally-adapted policies, institutions and incentives that promote productive land and water management solutions, along with investments, and the steadfast pursuit of scientific research and development.

FIGURE 18.11

Nitrogen associated with the production of pigs and chickens in Japan

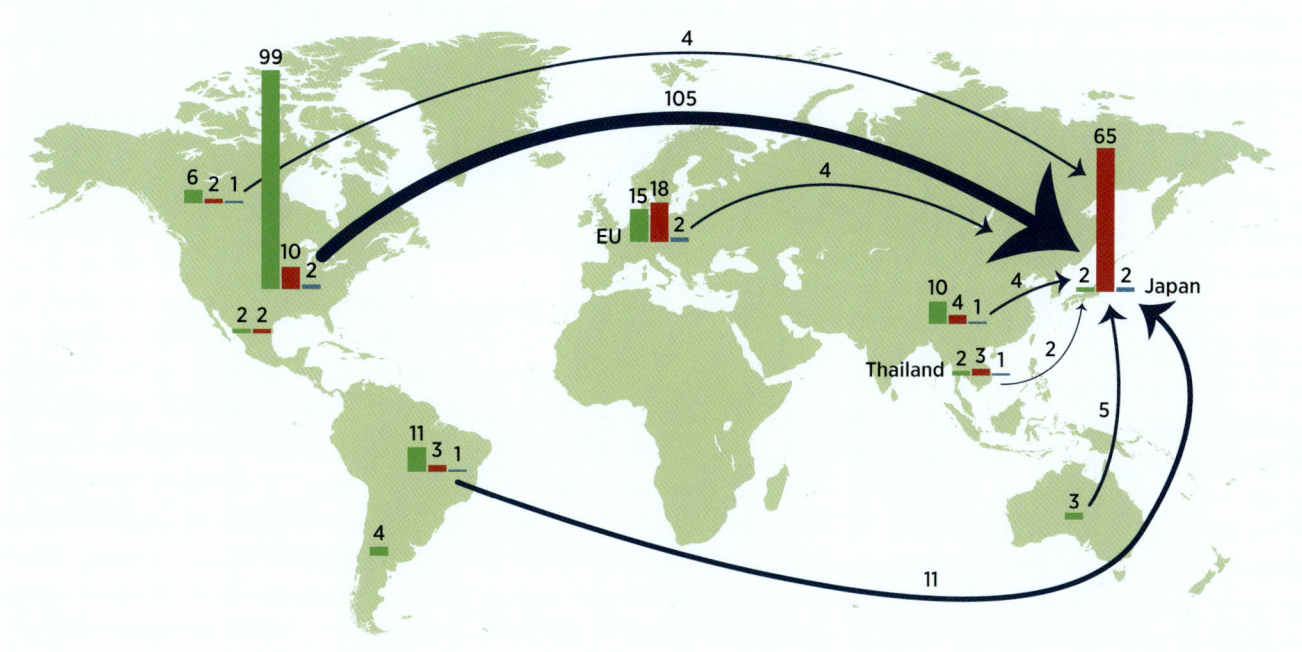

Notes: Bars refer to N left behind in the producing country during different stages of production. Green, feed; red, live animal production; blue, meat processing. Arrows represent transfer of total N embedded in shipped product. Data are annual values in thousands of tonnes, averaged over the years 2000–2002.
Source: Galloway et al. (2007, fig. 2, p. 625), reproduced with permission from the Royal Swedish Academy of Sciences.

18.6 'Water smart' food production

Some experts suggest that if everyone adopted a life style similar to that normally experienced in OECD countries then more than three 'earths' would be needed to satisfy the resource requirements. This is a bold claim but it does make the point that we cannot continue to consume natural resources at the current rate if we wish to use them sustainably for everyone's benefit both now and in the future.

Water will need to be managed so that supply and demand is balanced and shared across sectors and across regions. This may mean reducing the amount of water currently consumed to produce a reasonable and nutritious diet. Improved ratio of crop productivity to water use will be needed as will better ways to manage both green and blue water resources.

18.6.1 The role of technology

In higher income countries, science and technology have long been major drivers of global prosperity. This will undoubtedly continue in the future. Food production will need to be 'greener' and more sustainable so that it does not add to the burden of climate change and ecosystem deterioration. We will need innovative technologies that can improve crop yields and drought tolerance; produce smarter ways of using fertilizer and water; improve crop protection through new pesticides and non-chemical approaches; reduce post-harvest losses; and create more sustainable livestock and marine production. Industrialized countries are well placed to take advantage of these technologies, but they must also take responsibility to ensure that LDCs have opportunities to access them.

18.6.2 Human capacities and institutions as assets

Agricultural development in LDCs is mainly in the hands of smallholders, most of whom are women. Water technologies appropriate to their needs will play a crucial role in meeting the food security challenge. However, in many LDCs, women have only limited access to a wide range of physical assets and lack the skills to deploy them. Multiple water use schemes can provide opportunities for women to extend their influence over water allocation and management.

Most industrialized countries are have the financial resources, as well as the infrastructure, institutions and capacity, to sustain the levels of water security they now enjoy. However, perhaps they should be seeking more sustainable water use per person in the interests of other less industrialized countries. In contrast, LDCs will need to seek ways of increasing water availability per person and whether they can afford to emulate the strategies of the more industrialized countries. There is a balance to be struck between these two contrasting strategies.

Major changes in policy and management will be needed to make best possible use of available water resources. New institutional arrangements are needed which centralize the responsibility for water regulation yet decentralize water management responsibility and increase user ownership and participation. New arrangements are required for safeguarding access to water for poor and disadvantaged groups, particularly women, and ensuring they have long-term land and water security.

18.6.3 A focus on the value chain

Improvements will be needed all along the agricultural value chains. Early gains include opportunities to reduce post-harvest crop losses in LDCs and food wastage in the higher income countries, and hence saving the water embedded in them. In the medium term, innovations in climate-smart cropping are possible. In the longer term, energy-smart conversion of feed and fodder for livestock is also possible. Water recycling at all stages of the value chain will help to secure environmental water requirements when reuse of treated water is not culturally acceptable for other uses.

In the high income countries, the focus will also be on water pollution which 'reduces' freshwater availability. This includes reducing diffuse pollution (in production) and point source pollution (in transformation and consumption).

18.6.4 Managing risk creatively

Reducing vulnerability to drought will require investment in both constructed and 'green' infrastructure to improve water measurement and control and, where appropriate, increase surface water and groundwater storage in constructed reservoirs and in natural storage (both in wetlands and in the soil). Most benefit is expected to come from existing water management technologies and adapting them to new situations. 'Design for management', promoted in the 1980s to ensure infrastructure design took account of who would manage it and how it would be managed, is still highly relevant today and important for future water management.

18.6.5 Virtual water trade

Virtual water may play an increasing role as water-rich countries export water embedded in food to water-short countries that find it increasingly difficult to grow sufficient staple food crops. But the aqua-politics of exporting/importing food versus self-sufficiency will not be easy to resolve; food producing countries may not wish to export crops when food security is threatened; lower income and least developed countries may need to continue over-exploiting water resources to feed their populations.

18.6.6 Implementing 'water smart' production

A twin-track approach is needed that makes best use of available water – demand management options that increase productivity (more 'crop per drop') and supply management that makes more water available through water storage to cope with seasonality and increasingly unpredictable rainfall.

For most LDCs the biggest question, which still remains largely unanswered, is how to do it. Even once appropriate interventions for specific locations and target groups are selected, it is challenging for governments and agencies to successfully intervene in complex and changing agricultural water management (AWM) systems that have specific technical, environmental, socio-economic and institutional issues. The International Fund for Agricultural Development's learning and knowledge on innovations in water and rural poverty (InnoWat) sets out a strategy for this – the development pathway lies somewhere between the paralysis that comes from trying to take account of everything and the folly of focusing in on a single criterion solution.

Major investment in AWM will be needed, and the present-day national priorities in some countries do give cause for serious concern. In 2010, it was estimated that only US$10 billion was invested globally in irrigation systems, a surprisingly low figure given the importance of water for the agricultural sector (in comparison, the global market volume for bottled water in the same year was US$59 billion) (Wild et al., 2010). Surely it is time for the world to wake up to the fact that agriculture is a major, valid, consumer of water and investment is essential for the future of global food and water security. When water is scarce we all have a responsibility to use water wisely, efficiently and productively. Responsible AWM can make a significant contribution to future water security. Agriculture needs to be much more water-smart and must be given the right signals and incentives to make this happen.

IIIIIIIIIIIIIIIIIIIIIIIIIIIIIIIIIIIIIIIIIIIIIIIIIIIIIIIIIIIIIIIIIIII

Note

1   Least developed countries (LDCs)' is a group of countries which are identified as being particularly vulnerable, with a low income level and a low index of human assets based on nutrition, health and education (UNSD, 2006). A list of LDCs is included in Table 18.2.

2   The International Energy Agency (IEA, 2006) mentions that considering very rapid technological progress, the higher figure could be 26,200 million tonnes of oil equivalent instead of 12,000. However, IEA also indicates that a more realistic assessment based on slower yield improvements would be 6,000–12,000. A mid-range estimate of around 9,500 would require about one-fifth of the world's agricultural land to be dedicated to biomass production.

3   Opportunity cost is the cost of any activity measured in terms of the value of the best alternative that is not chosen (that is foregone).

4   No attempt is made here to closely define the word 'consumption' as food directly eaten by individuals and contributing to their nutritional requirements. Rather it is used here to describe in broad terms, the food purchased from retail outlets which may include both food eaten and food wasted.

IIIIIIIIIIIIIIIIIIIIIIIIIIIIIIIIIIIIIIIIIIIIIIIIIIIIIIIIIIIIIIIIIIIII

References

Allan, T. 2011. The water-food-trade nexus and global water resource security. *UK Irrigation*, No. 37, pp. 21–22.

Bellarby, J., Foereid, B., Hastings, A. and Smith, P. 2008. *Cool Farming: Climate Impacts of Agriculture and Mitigation Potential.* Campaigning for Sustainable Agriculture. Amsterdam, Greenpeace.

Bruinsma, J. 2009. *The Resource Outlook to 2050: By How Much do Land, Water and Crop Yields Need to Increase by 2050?* Prepared for the FAO Expert Meeting on 'How to Feed the World in 2050', 24-26 June 2009, Rome, FAO.

Comprehensive Assessment of Water Management in Agriculture. 2007. *Water for Food, Water for Life: A Comprehensive Assessment of Water Management in Agriculture.* London/Colombo, Earthscan/International Water Management Institute.

Conway, G. 1997. *The Doubly Green Revolution: Food for All in the Twenty-first Century.* New York, Cornell University Press.

DESA (Department of Economic and Social Affairs of the United Nations). 2009. *World Population Prospects: The 2008 Revision, Highlights.* Working Paper No. ESA/P/WP.210, New York, DESA Population Division.

European Commission. 2005. *Integrated Pollution Prevention and Control.* Reference document on best available techniques in the slaughterhouses and animal by-products industries.

FAO (Food and Agriculture Organization of the United Nations). 1981. Food loss prevention in perishable crops. *Agricultural Services Bulletin,* No. 43. Rome, FAO.

––––. 2004. *Livestock Waste Management in East Asia.* Project preparation report. Rome, FAO.

––––. 2006a. *World Agriculture: Towards 2030/2050 Interim Report.* FAO, Rome.

––––. 2006b. *Livestock's Long Shadow: Environmental Issues and Options.* Steinfeld, H., Gerber, P., Wassenaar, T., Castel, V., Rosales, M. and de Haan, C. Rome, FAO and LEAD.

––––. 2008a. *The State of Food and Agriculture (SOFA) 2008. Biofuels: Prospects, Risks and Opportunities.* Rome, FAO.

––––. 2008b. Scoping agriculture-wetlands interactions: towards a sustainable multi-response strategy. *FAO Water Report,* No. 33. Rome, FAO.

––––. 2009a. *The State of Food and Agriculture (SOFA) 2009: Livestock in the Balance.* Rome, FAO.

––––. 2009b.*The State of Food Insecurity in the World (SOFI) 2009: Economic Crises – Impacts and Lessons Learned.* FAO, Rome.

––––. 2010. *Farmers in a Changing Climate – Does Gender Matter? Food Security in Andhra Pradesh, India.* Y. Lambrou and S. Nelson. Rome, FAO. http://www.fao.org/docrep/013/i1721e/i1721e.pdf

––––. 2011a. *The State of the World's Land and Water Resources for Food and Agriculture: Managing Systems at Risk.* Rome/London, Land and Water Division, FAO/Earthscan.

––––. 2011b. *Climate Change, Water and Food Security. FAO Water Report,* No. 36. Rome, FAO.

––––. 2011c. *AQUASTAT online database.* http://www.fao.org/nr/aquastat (Accessed May 2011.)

––––. 2011d. *FAOSTAT online database.* http://faostat.fao.org/ (Accessed May 2011.)

––––. 2011e. *The State of Food and Agriculture (SOFA) 2010–11. Women in Agriculture: Closing the Gender Gap for Development.* Rome, FAO.

Galloway, J. N., Burke, M., Bradford, G. E., Naylor, R., Falcon, W., Chapagain, A. K., Gaskell, J. C., McCullough, J., Mooney, H. A., Oleson, K. L. L., Steinfeld, H., Wassenaar, T. and Smil, V. 2007. International trade in meat: The tip of the porkchop. *AMBIO: A Journal of the Human Environment,* Vol. 36, No. 8., pp. 622–29.

GWP (Global Water Partnership). 2009. *GWP in Action 2009: Annual Report.* Stockholm, Sweden, GWP.

Hoekstra, A. Y. and Chapagain, A. K. 2008. *Globalization of Water: Sharing the Planet's Freshwater Resources.* Oxford, UK, Blackwell Publishing Pty Ltd.

Houghton, R. A. 2008. Carbon flux to the atmosphere from land-use changes: 1850–2005. *TRENDS: A Compendium of Data on Global Change.* Oak Ridge, Tenn., Carbon Dioxide Information Analysis Center, Oak Ridge National Laboratory, U.S. Department of Energy.

IEA (International Energy Agency). 2006. *World Energy Outlook 2006.* Paris, IEA.

––––. 2007. *World Energy Outlook 2007.* Paris, IEA.

IFAD (International Fund for Agricultural Development). 2011. *Rural Poverty Report. New Realities, New Challenges: New Opportunities for Tomorrow's Generation.* Rome, IFAD.

Lobell, D. B., Burke, M. B., Tebaldi, C., Mastrandrea, M. D., Falcon, W. P., and Naylor R. L. 2008. Prioritizing climate change adaptation needs for food security in 2030. *Science,* Vol. 319, No. 5863, pp. 607–10.

Lundqvist, J. 2010. Producing more or Wasting Less. Bracing the food security challenge of unpredictable rainfall. L. Martínez-Cortina, G. Garrido and L. López-Gunn (eds), *Re-thinking Water and Food Security: Fourth Botín Foundation Water Workshop.* London, CRC Press, pp. 75–92.

Lundqvist, J., Fraiture, C. de, and Molden, D. 2008. *Saving Water: From Field to Fork – Curbing Losses and Wastage in the Food Chain.* SIWI Policy Brief. Stockholm, Stockholm International Water Institute.

MEA (Millennium Ecosystem Assessment). 2005a. *Ecosystems and Human Well-being: Synthesis.* Washington DC, World Resources Institute.

––––. 2005b. *Ecosystems and Human Well-being: Wetlands and Water.* Washington DC, World Resources Institute.

Morrison, J., Morikawa, M., Murphy, M. and Shulte, P. 2009. *Water Scarcity and Climate Change: Growing Risks for Businesses and Investors.* Boston, Mass./Oakland, Calif., Ceres/Pacific Institute.

Rauch, T. 2009. *The New Rurality – Its Implications for a New Pro-poor Agricultural Water Strategy.* InnoWat. Rome, IFAD.

Scanlon, B. R., Jolly, I., Sophocleous, M. and Zhang, L. 2007. Global impacts of conversions from natural to agricultural ecosystems on water resources: Quantity versus quality. *Water Resources Research,* Vol. 43, W03437, doi:10.1029/2006WR005486

Siebert, S., Burke, J., Faures, J. M., Frenken, K., Hoogeveen, J., Döll, P., and Portmann, F. T. 2010. Groundwater use for irrigation - a global inventory. *Hydrology and Earth System Sciences,* Vol. 14, pp. 1863–80.

Smith, P., Martino, D., Cai, Z., Gwary, D., Janzen, H., Kumar, P., McCarl, B., Ogle, S., O'Mara, F., Rice, C., Scholes, B., Sirotenko, O., Howden, M., McAllister, T., Pan, G., Romanenkov, V., Schneider, U., Towprayoon, S., Wattenbach, M. and Smith, J. 2008. Greenhouse gas mitigation in agriculture. *Philosophical Transactions of the Royal Society B: Biological Sciences.* Vol. 363, No. 1492, pp. 789–813.

Smith, P., Martino, D., Cai, Z., Gwary, D., Janzen, H., Kumar, P., McCarl, B., Ogle, S., O'Mara, F., Rice, C., Scholes, B. and Sirotenko, O. 2007. Agriculture. B. Metz, O. R. Davidson, P. R. Bosch, R. Dave, L. A. Meyer (eds), *Climate Change 2007: Mitigation. Contribution of Working Group III to the Fourth Assessment Report of the Intergovernmental Panel on Climate Change,* Cambridge, UK, Cambridge University Press, pp. 499–540

UNEP (United Nations Environment Program). 2004. *Eco-efficiency for the Dairy Processing Industry.* Melbourne, Australia, UNEP Working Group for Cleaner Production in the Food Industry/Dairy Australia.

UNSD (United Nations Statistics Division). 2006. *Note on Definition of Regions for Statistical Analysis.* Prepared by UNSD on 30 August 2006 (SA/2006/15) for the eight session of the Committee for the Coordination of Statistical Activities, Montreal, 4–5 September 2006.

USDA (United States Department of Agriculture). 2008. *Farm and Ranch Irrigation Survey (2008).* 2007 Census of Agriculture. National Agricultural Statistics Service. Issued November 2009, Updated February 2010. Washington DC, USDA.

US-EPA (United States Environmental Protection Agency). 2006. *Global Anthropogenic non-CO$_2$ Greenhouse Gas Emissions: 1990–2020.* EPA 430-R-06-003. Washington DC, US-EPA.

Varghese, S. 2007. *Biofuels and Global Water Challenges.* IATP Reports. Minneapolis, Minn., Institute for Agriculture and Trade Policy.

Wichelns, D. 2010. *An Economic Analysis of the Virtual Water Concept in Relation to the Agri-food Sector.* Paris, Organization for Economic Cooperation and Development (OECD). doi:10.1787/9789264083578-8-en

Wild, D., Buffle, M. and Hafner-Cai, J. 2010. *Water: A Market of the Future.* SAM Study 2010. Switzerland, SAM Sustainable Asset Management.

World Bank. 2011. *Online database.* http://data.worldbank.org (Accessed May 2011.)

WWAP (World Water Assessment Programme). 2009. *The United Nations World Water Development Report 3: Water in a Changing World.* World Water Assessment Programme. Paris/London, UNESCO/Earthscan.

Zimmer, D. and Renault, D. 2003. Virtual water in food production and global trade. Review of methodological issues and preliminary results. A. Hoekstra (ed.), *Proceedings of the Expert Meeting on Virtual Water Trade.* Delft, The Netherlands, UNESCO-IHE. http://www.fao.org/nr/water/docs/VirtualWater_article_DZDR.pdf

CHAPTER 19
The global nexus of energy and water

UNIDO
—

Author Michael E. Webber
Acknowledgements This chapter includes significant contributions from Carey King, Ashlynn Stillwell and Kelly Twomey. The chapter was coordinated by Igor Volodin and Carolina Gonzalez-Castro.

|||||||||||||||||||||||||||||||||||||||||||||||||||||||||||||||||||||||||||||||||||||||||||||||||||||||||||||||||||||||||||

Energy and water are inter-related; people use energy for water and water for energy.

The energy–water relationship is under strain, introducing cross-sectoral vulnerabilities (i.e. a water constraint can become an energy constraint and an energy constraint can induce a water constraint).

Trends imply that the strain will be exacerbated by:

- growth in total demand for energy and water, driven by population growth,
- growth in per capita demand for energy and water, driven by economic growth,
- global climate change, which will distort the availability of water, and
- policy choices, by which people are selecting more water-intensive energy and more energy-intensive water.

Policy options are available to decision-makers to improve energy and water supplies without compromising either resource.

19.1 Introduction

Energy and water are fundamental ingredients of modern civilization and precious resources. They are key inputs to agricultural systems, factories and buildings, and are necessary to meet human requirements for food, shelter, healthcare and education.

Energy and water are also closely interconnected and under strain. Consequently, the nexus of the two has been the subject of attention by the scientific community, popular media and governing bodies. This nexus manifests itself in society in many ways. For example, water provides electric power, is used for extraction of fuels, and plays a growing role in the irrigation of energy crops to produce biofuels such as ethanol. The thermoelectric sector is one of the largest users of water for cooling. In parallel, the water industry uses power for moving, pumping, treating and heating water. On top of this relationship, the parts of the world with high expected rates for population growth and economic expansion are also often places where water sources are scarce. Combining these trends with projections for more irrigation implies rapid growth for water demands that some localities might satisfy with desalination or wastewater treatment, both of which are very energy-intensive.

Despite the importance of energy and water, and the close relationship between the two, funding, policymaking and oversight of these resources are performed by different people in separate agencies in many governments. Integrated energy–water policymaking is rare. Energy planners often assume they will have the water they need and water planners assume they will have the energy they need – if one of these assumptions fails, consequences will be dramatic. By bringing scientific and engineering expertise into this vastly understudied problem, this scenario might be avoided.

19.1.1 Energy and water are inter-related

Energy and water are highly interconnected: people use water for energy and energy for water. Figure 19.1 shows some of these interconnections. For example, water is a direct source of energy through hydroelectric dams, which in 2007 provided about 15 per cent of global electricity generation (or approximately 2 per

FIGURE 19.1

The energy–water nexus

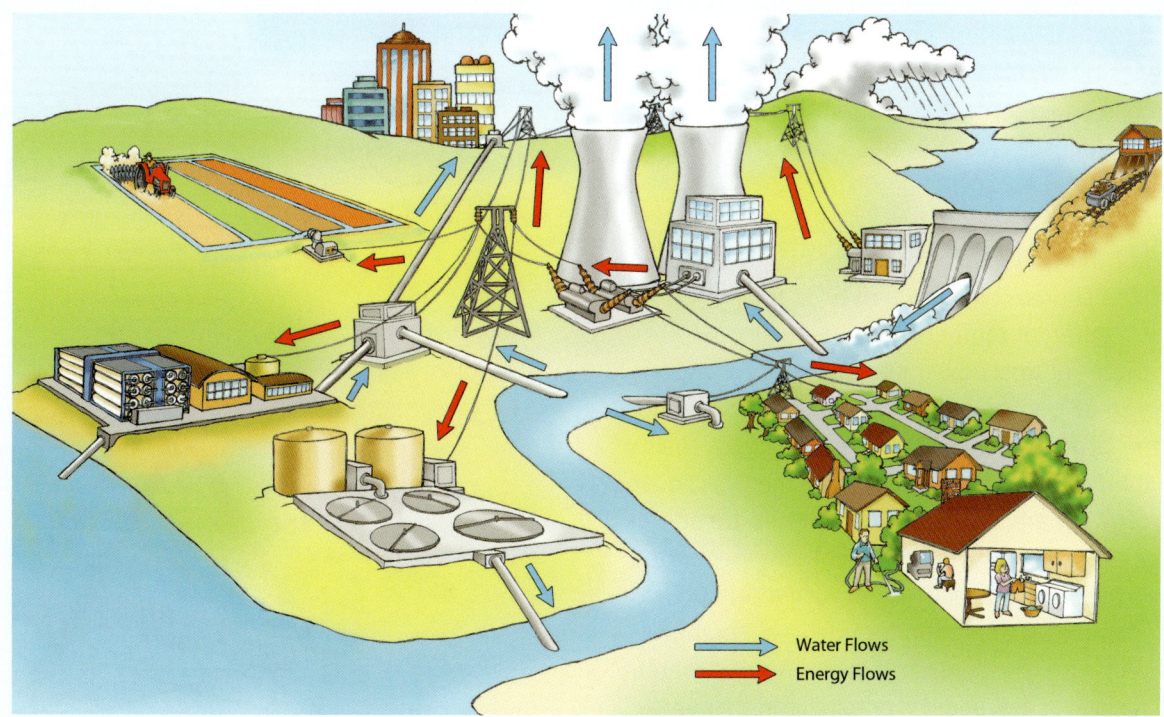

Note: Energy flows are shown in red and water flows are shown in blue. As shown in the residential community, electricity and water are both used for different purposes.
Source: Courtesy of EPRI (prepared by EPRI for a US DOE Report to Congress in 2006).

cent of total energy consumption)(IEA, 2009). Water also indirectly enables power generation through cooling thermoelectric power plants (power plants that use heat to generate power), which provide more than 75% of the electricity globally (more than 16,000 TWh) (IEA, 2009). While agriculture is the largest user of water globally, because of the large cooling needs of power plants, the thermoelectric power sector is the largest user of water (for withdrawals) in the United States (USA). In the USA the power sector is responsible for nearly half of all water withdrawals (approximately 800 billion litres per day, when including seawater), ahead of even agriculture (Hutson et al., 2004). Low– and middle– income countries use less water for power plants and more for agriculture, whereas high-income countries are the opposite (WWAP, 2003). In addition, water is used for extractive industries that produce fuels (coal, natural gas, uranium) for the power and transportation sectors.

An important feature of water use is the distinction between water *withdrawals* and *consumption*. However, this terminology is not used in a consistent manner from one country to the next. Using the terminology from King et al. (2011), water *withdrawal* refers to the volume of water removed from a water source; this water is not lost, but it cannot be allocated to other users before discharge. *Consumption* refers to the volume of water lost through evaporation, transportation, or any other means by which water is not returned to its native source in liquid form. As consumption is a subset of withdrawal, it is less than or equal to withdrawal, by definition (King et al., 2011).

Nearly all of the water used for power plants is returned to the source (typically a river or cooling pond), though at a different temperature and quality. As a result of these returns, power plants are often responsible for a small portion of national water consumption, despite the large withdrawals. Averaging across the national thermoelectric power sector in the USA[1], over 80 litres of water are withdrawn and 2 litres are consumed for every kilowatt-hour of electricity generated (Webber, 2007). Hydroelectric dams use a significant amount of water consumption for power generation primarily because the increased surface area of manufactured reservoirs beyond the nominal run-of-river accelerates the evaporation rates from river basins (Torcellini et al., 2003). Notably, the estimates for this increased evaporation depend significantly on regional location: hydroelectric reservoirs in the desert

south-west of the USA have significant evaporative losses, whereas reservoirs in cooler climates might have negligible losses. Further, whether all the evaporation should be attributed to power generation is not clear, as reservoirs serve multiple purposes, including water storage, flood control, navigation and recreation.

The amount of water withdrawn and consumed by thermal power plants is driven by (a) the type of fuel and power cycle used by a power plant (e.g. fossil fuels

FIGURE 19.2

Power plants typically use three types of cooling: open-loop (top panel), closed-loop (middle) and air-cooling (bottom)

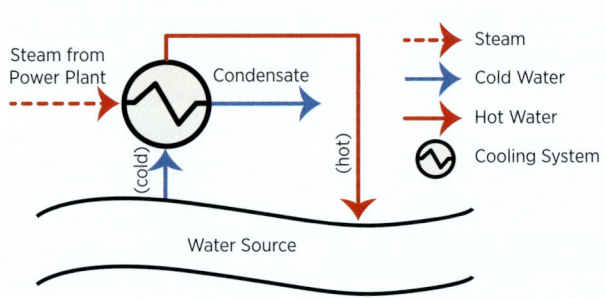

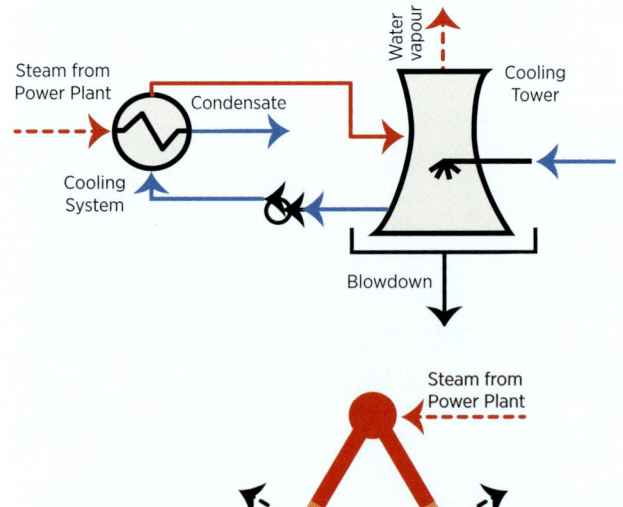

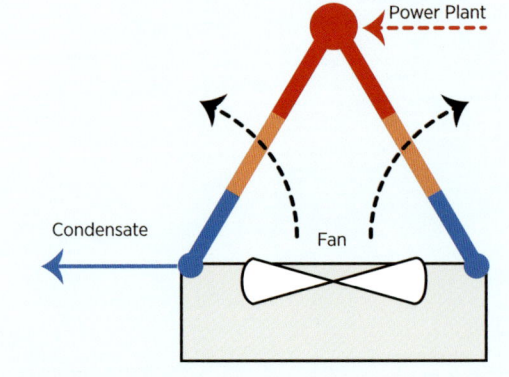

Source: Stillwell (2010), based on CEC (2002).

or nuclear fuels with steam cycles, natural gas with combined cycle) and (b) the cooling method. There are three basic cooling methods: open-loop, closed-loop, and air-cooling (Figure 19.2). For typical values on water withdrawal and consumption by power plants, see Table 19.1, which contains a breakdown by fuel and cooling type.

Open-loop, or once-through, cooling withdraws large volumes of surface water (fresh or saline), for one-time use and returns nearly all the water to the source with little of the overall water consumed due to evaporation (Stillwell et al., 2011). While open-loop cooling is energy efficient and has low infrastructure and operational costs, the discharged water is warmer than ambient water, causing thermal pollution, which can kill fish and harm aquatic ecosystems. Thus, environmental agencies regulate discharge temperatures, taking into account a water body's heat dissipation capacity. Closed-loop cooling requires less water withdrawal because the water is recirculated by cooling towers or evaporation ponds. However, as the cooling is essentially achieved through evaporation, closed-loop cooling causes higher water consumption (Table 19.1). The alternative, air-cooling, does not require water, but instead cools by use of fans that move air over a radiator, similar to that in automobiles. However, power plant efficiency for air-cooling is lower, up-front capital costs are higher and real estate requirements are sometimes larger, often making this option less attractive economically unless water resources are scarce.

Even though power plants return most of the water they withdraw, their need for large amounts of water at the right temperature for cooling subjects them to vulnerabilities. If a severe drought or heat wave reduces the availability of water or restricts its effectiveness for cooling due to heat transfer inhibitions or thermal pollution limits, the fact that the power plant consumes so little water becomes less important than the fact that it needs the water in the first place.

Significant volumes of water are also used for fuels production, such as coal, natural gas, oil, uranium and biofuels. The water requirements for fuels production for coal, natural gas and uranium, while non-trivial, are much smaller than the water requirements for their use within power plants and therefore are considered negligible by comparison. By contrast, the water requirements to produce coal, natural gas and petroleum for transportation applications is significant by comparison (because transport vehicles have no water requirements on-board), and is discussed later in this report.

All forms of energy require water at some stage of their lifecycles, including production, conversion, distribution and use. Each fuel and technology has a slightly different set of requirements.

TABLE 19.1

Water used (withdrawn and/or consumed) varies for different fuels, power cycles (combined and open cycle) and cooling methods (open-loop, closed-loop and air-cooling)

	Closed-Loop (cooling tower)		Open-Loop	
	Withdrawals (L/kWh)	Consumption (L/kWh)	Withdrawals (L/kWh)	Consumption (L/kWh)
Nuclear	3.8	2.6	160.9	1.5
Solar CSP	3.0	3.0	---	---
Coal	1.9	1.9	132.5	1.1
Natural gas (Combined cycle)	0.9	0.7	52.2	0.4
Natural gas (Combustion turbine)	Negligible	Negligible	Negligible	Negligible
Solar PV	Negligible	Negligible	Negligible	Negligible
Wind	Negligible	Negligible	Negligible	Negligible

Source: Adapted from Stillwell (2010c).

Crude oil

Crude oil is the largest primary energy source globally. Its production requires water at drilling, pumping, refinement and treatment. The average water use is estimated to be 1.058 m³ per GJ (Gerbens-Leenes et al., 2008). Unconventional oil production, which is projected to increase in North, Central and South America until 2035, consumes 2.5–4 times more water (WEC, 2010).

Coal

Coal is the second largest primary energy source globally, and its use is projected to increase by 2035. UNESCO-IHE (Gerbens-Leenes et al., 2008) estimates that approximately 0.164 m³ per GJ are used in the various processes, significantly more of which is used during underground mining operations than in open pit mining (Gleick et al., 1994).

Natural gas

Significant increases are expected in the production of natural gas by 2035. Water requirements for drilling, extraction and transportation of conventional gas sources are relatively modest, at an estimated 0.109 m³ per GJ (Gerbens-Leenes et al., 2008). However, shale gas production, which is expected to increase in Asia, Australia and North America (Pacific Energy Summit, 2011), has slightly higher water-intensity than conventional gas because its extraction method, hydraulic fracturing, injects millions of litres of water into each well.

Uranium

Uranium's share of global energy consumption is projected to increase from about 6% to 9% by 2035 (WEC, 2010). UNESCO-IHE estimates modest water requirements of 0.086 m³ per GJ for uranium mining and processing (Gerbens-Leenes et al., 2008).

Biomass and biofuel

Biomass, including wood, agro fuel, waste and municipal by-products, is an important source of fire and heating in many non-Organisation for Economic Co-operation and Development (OECD) country households (WEC, 2010). Further, bio-feedstocks are increasingly grown commercially to replace fossil fuels in OECD countries, and this trend has raised concerns about crop water requirements. However, water intensity depends on the feedstocks, where and how they are grown, and whether they are first– or second–generation crops (Gerbens-Leenes et al., 2008;

WEF, 2009). This variety in production processes makes it impractical to attribute a singular value or even a representative range of water consumption to biofuel production.

Just as significant volumes of water are used for energy, in wealthier nations a significant fraction of energy is used for water, in the form of electricity to heat, treat and move water, sometimes across vast distances (CEC 2005; Cohen et al., 2004; EIA, 2001; Stillwell et al., 2010a). Most water systems are comprised of many stages of collection, treatment, conveyance, distribution, end-use preparation, reconditioning and release Twomey and Webber (2011). The energy intensity of water is influenced by source water quality, its proximity to a water treatment facility and end-use, its intended end-use and sanitation level, as well as its conveyance to and treatment at a wastewater treatment facility. Treating water to a quality that is safe for drinking requires significant amounts of energy to pump, treat and distribute water to end-users, who are likely to heat, chill, or pressurize this water to suit their needs. After water is used in industrialized countries, much of it is collected and sent to a wastewater treatment plant where the water is reconditioned so that it can be released back into a water reservoir. In some cases, water is recycled or reclaimed, that is, it is treated to an acceptable standard for use in non-potable applications (e.g. agricultural and landscape irrigation, groundwater recharge, industrial cooling/process water, toilet flushing). Self-supplied water users, such as industrial facilities, power generators and irrigators, typically do not require water for drinking water. However, these users might utilize energy-intensive processes, such as heating, chilling and pressurizing. For the more than 1 billion people who do not have access to piped, clean drinking water, or to water-based sanitation, the availability of abundant energy, especially in the form of electricity, is a critical ingredient to enabling those services.

The energy required to produce, treat and distribute water varies depending on the source (Table 19.2 shows typical figures in the USA). Surface water (e.g. from lakes and rivers) is the easiest and least energy-intensive to treat. However, water conveyance can require anything from between zero (for gravity-fed systems) to as much as 3600 kWh per million litres for long-haul systems (CEC, 2005; Cohen et al., 2004). Groundwater (e.g. from aquifers) requires more energy for pumping water to the surface for treatment and distribution. For example, water collection alone from a depth of 40 m requires 140 kWh per ML, while a depth of 120 m requires approximately 500 kWh per ML, in addition to treatment energy use (EPRI, 2002; USDOE, 2006; Stillwell et al., 2011).

As fresh water supplies become strained, water sources once considered unusable, including brackish groundwater and seawater, are being turned to (Stillwell et al., 2010b). While use of these water sources helps mitigate constraints on drinking water supplies, treatment of brackish groundwater and seawater requires use of advanced filtration (e.g. reverse osmosis membranes), specialty materials, and high-pressure pumps for desalting. Overall, treatment of these water sources can require as much as 4400 kWh per ML (EPRI, 2002), or 10–12 times the energy use of standard water treatment. The theoretical minimum energy requirement for desalination using reverse osmosis systems is 680 kWh per ML (Shannon et al., 2008).

Wastewater treatment also requires large amounts of energy (WEF, 1997). High-income countries that have stricter discharge regulations install more energy-intensive treatment technologies. Trickling filter treatment, which uses a biologically active substrate for aerobic treatment, is a reasonably passive system, consuming on average over 250 kWh per ML (EPRI, 2002; Stillwell et al., 2011). Diffused aeration as part of activated sludge processing is a more energy-intensive form of wastewater treatment, requiring 340 kWh per ML due to blowers and gas transfer equipment

(EPRI, 2002; Stillwell et al., 2011). More advanced wastewater treatment, using filtration and the option of nitrification, requires 400–500 kWh per ML (EPRI, 2002; Stillwell et al., 2011). In fact, more advanced sludge treatment and processing can consume energy in the range of 30–80% of total wastewater plant energy use (Center for Sustainable Systems, University of Michigan, 2008). Treating wastewater sludge through anaerobic digestion can also produce energy through the creation of methane-rich biogas, a renewable fuel that can be used to generate up to 50% of the treatment plant's electricity needs (Stillwell et al., 2010b; Seiger et al., 2005).

Because systems vary significantly between regions in terms of pumping requirements, source quality, prevailing treatment practices (if any), and wastewater collection (if any), it is difficult to assess global energy inputs embedded in the water system. For the USA, where data are available, approximately 10% or more of national energy consumption is required for the entire water system (Figure 19.3) (Twomey and Webber, 2011). These figures are typical for high- income countries. For low- and middle- income countries, where large-scale water systems are rarer, the embedded energy is lower by comparison.

19.1.2 Global strain in the energy–water relationship

The interrelationship of energy and water and the strains placed on both of these resources manifests itself in tough choices at the local level. For example, low water levels in hydroelectric reservoirs can force

TABLE 19.2

Water and wastewater treatment and conveyance requires vast amounts of energy

	Source / treatment type	Energy use (kWh/million L)
Water	Surface water	60
	Groundwater	160
	Brackish groundwater	1,000–2,600
	Seawater	2,600–4,400
Wastewater	Trickling filter	250
	Activated sludge	340
	Advanced treatment without nitrification	400
	Advanced treatment with nitrification	500

Note: Average US figures for energy used for water production (not including energy used for distribution).
Sources: CEC (2005); EPRI (2002); Stillwell et al. (2010b, 2011); Stillwell (2010c).

power plants to turn off. Though hydroelectric power is attractive, it is least reliable during droughts when the need to use water for other purposes (e.g. for drinking and irrigation) may take precedence over hydroelectricity. For example, without a change in water usage patterns, lakes Mead and Powell along the Colorado River in the USA, which are used for hydroelectric power and municipal supply, are projected to have a 50% chance of running dry by 2021 (Spotts, 2008). Similarly, cities in Uruguay must choose whether they want the water in their reservoirs to be used for drinking or electricity (Proteger, 2008).

The problem is not just limited to hydroelectric reservoirs. As thermoelectric power plants require vast amounts of water, they are vulnerable to droughts or heat waves restricting their output. Heat waves in France in 2003 caused power plants to draw down their output because of limits on rejection temperatures imposed for environmental reasons (Poumadère

et al., 2005; Lagadec, 2004). Severe heat and drought killed approximately 15,000 people and created river water temperatures that were too hot for effective power plant cooling. Many nuclear power plants had to operate at much reduced capacity and an environmental exemption was enacted to allow the rejection temperatures of cooling water from power plants to exceed prior limits (Poumadère et al., 2005; Lagadec, 2004). At the same time, 20% of hydropower capacity was not available because of low river levels (Hightower and Pierce, 2008). Just as demand for electricity was spiking for air conditioning in response to the heat, supplies were being cut back. The dilemma has also shown up in other countries where drought has brought nuclear power plants within days of shutting off because the vast amounts of cooling water were at risk from diversion to other priorities, such as municipal use for drinking water.

While water limitations can restrict energy, energy limitations can restrict water. For example, power outages

FIGURE 19.3

Energy flows for the public water supply system in the USA

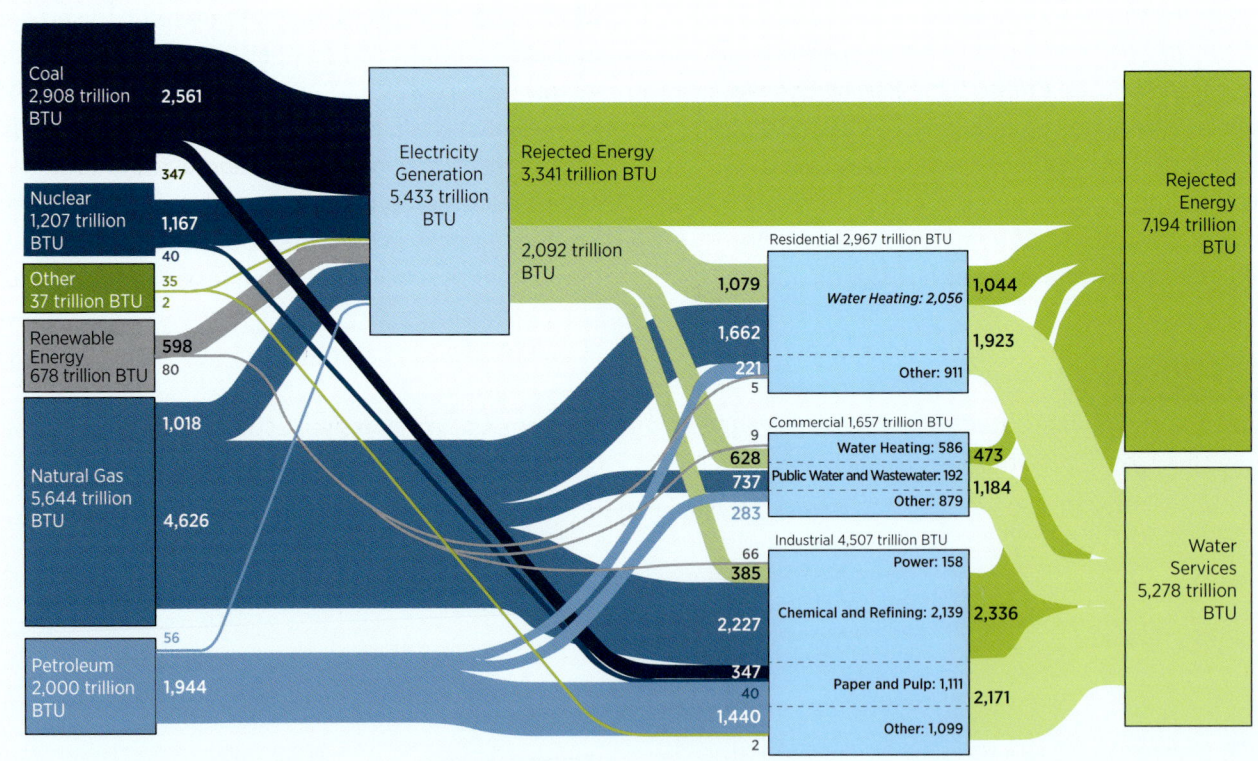

Notes: Fuels (on the left) are used directly and indirectly through electricity generation for different purposes (on the right). The thickness of the flows is proportional to the amount of energy consumed. About 60% of the total energy consumption is lost as waste heat. Only energy consumption related to the conveyance, treatment, distribution and heating (in the commercial and residential sectors) and public water and wastewater treatment distributed in the US public water supply is included. Self-supplied sectors, including agriculture and industry are not included.
Source: Courtesy of K. M. Twomey and M. E. Webber, University of Texas, Austin, USA.

(due to storms or intentional acts) at water and waste-water treatment plants put the water system at risk of disruptions due to energy shortages. This trade-off is a strategic question for some countries. Saudi Arabia uses much of its own most valuable resources (crude oil and natural gas) to obtain the resources it does not have (freshwater), facing the choice of whether it is better to sell its energy resources at high prices or have enough freshwater to maintain municipal needs (EIA, 2007; IEA, 2005).

19.2 Exacerbation of the strain in the energy–water relationship

Trends imply that the existing strain in the energy–water relationship will be exacerbated by:

- growth in total demand for energy and water, primarily driven by population growth,
- growth in per capita demand for energy and water, primarily driven by economic growth,
- global climate change, which will distort the availability of water in positive and negative ways, depending on the location, and
- policy choices, by which people are selecting more water-intensive energy and more energy-intensive water.

19.2.1 Growth in total demand for energy and water

Though the global fuel mix is diverse, fossil fuels (oil, coal and natural gas) satisfy more than 80% of the world's needs for primary energy resources. Total energy consumption, including traditional biomass, such as wood and dung, was approximately 500 exajoules in 2008. Most projections show an increase in demand for energy, predominantly driven by both population and economic growth. Based on its central scenario (New Policies Scenario), the International Energy Agency (IEA), estimates that world primary energy demand will increase by 36% between 2008 and 2035, or by 1.2% on average per year (IEA, 2010). In 2008 non-OECD countries were responsible for approximately 56% of the energy consumption (IEA, 2010) and are expected to account for 93% of the increase with China accounting for 36%. With fossil fuels accounting for 50 % of the increase from 2008–2035 and with an estimate that the demand for electricity will grow by 76% globally between 2007 and 2030 (IEA, 2009), there will be a complementary significant increase in demand for water.

The United Nations (UN) makes several projections for global population (with low–, medium– and high– growth variants), all showing population growth to at least 2050, at which time population could decrease (UN, 2005; UN, 2006). The IEA assumes for its projections that (a) global population will grow 1% per year on average from 6.4 billion in 2004 to 8.1 billion in 2030 and (b) that economic growth will take place at an average of 3.4% per year over the same period (IEA, 2009). The IEA interprets these trends to yield a growth in global primary energy demand of 70% between 2004 and 2030, without a very significant shift in the basic makeup in the fuel mix, despite policy prioritization for biofuels and other renewable sources. Similarly, this population growth should lead to increases in global water demand (Oki and Kanae, 2006).

19.2.2 Growth in per capita demand for energy and water

As the world population grows, the global demand for energy and water is increasing to meet people's subsistence and lifestyle needs. Added to this, the per capita demand for energy and water is also growing. While the developed world is looking for ways to conserve energy and water, the developing world is rapidly accumulating wealth, bringing about a desire for better transportation, a nicer lifestyle, more meat-intensive diets, and a robust economy. The combined effect is that the demand in developing countries is increasing rapidly for liquid fuels, electricity, and water (for industrial processes, higher-protein diets, and comfort). Consequently, the growth in demand for energy and water is outpacing the growth in population. For a world in which these resources are under strain, accelerating demand could have far-reaching impacts.

Despite population growth estimates of only 19–37% (UN, 2005; UN, 2006) from 2004 to 2030, the IEA projects much greater increases in energy demand, approximately 70% (IEA, 2009), indicating that the annual per capita energy use globally will increase from 1.7 to 2.1 tonnes of oil equivalent. Half of the growth in demand is projected to come from the power sector (IEA, 2009), showing that electricity is a preferred form of energy for those who can afford it. Because of the power sector's water intensity, the new demand for electricity will likely lead to increased demand for water withdrawals. The IEA also considers an alternative policy scenario, for which energy growth is lower than the nominal reference projection for energy growth. Even in this alternative, both absolute and per capita energy demands are expected to increase between

2004 and 2030 (IEA, 2009). Even in the USA, where energy-intensive manufacturing has shrunk over the last few decades, the per capita energy use is projected to increase.

One of the drivers of increasing energy use per capita is the demand for better environmental conditions as people's incomes rise (Dasgupta et al., 2002), a phenomenon that is illustrated with the case of wastewater treatment. Advanced wastewater treatment is more energy-intensive than standard wastewater treatment, so the trend towards higher treatment standards will likely increase the unit energy needs of wastewater treatment for countries moving up in income (Applebaum, 2000). However, the introduction of greater energy efficiency will possibly offset the expected increases in energy intensity for stricter treatment standards, limiting the projected growth in electricity use at treatment plants. The higher per capita energy expenditures for wastewater treatment to achieve stricter environmental standards is a scenario likely to be repeated in analogous ways throughout societies that are achieving affluence; that is, as nations get richer, they will demand more energy.

19.2.3 Intensification of cross-sectoral strain at the nexus of energy and water through global climate change

Water systems are likely to be hit hardest by climate change and will be a leading indicator of temperature changes. The effects are hard to predict, but higher temperatures could induce several consequences, including turning some snowfall into rainfall, moving the snowmelt season earlier (thereby affecting spring water flows), increasing intermittency and intensity of precipitation, affecting water quality and raising the risks of floods and droughts (Oki and Kanae, 2006; Gleick, 2000a). In addition, sea level rises could cause contamination of groundwater aquifers with saline water near the coasts, potentially affecting nearly half of the world's population (Oki and Kanae, 2006). These challenges can be fixed with greater energy expenditures for mining deeper water, moving it farther, treating water to make it drinkable, or storing it for longer periods of time. With a typical energy mix over the next few decades, these energy expenditures release greenhouse gases, which intensify the hydrological cycle further, compounding the problem in a positive feedback loop (Figure 19.4).

19.3 Policy choices towards more energy-intensive water and water-intensive energy

On top of the above-mentioned three trends is a policy-driven movement towards more energy-intensive water and water-intensive energy.

19.3.1 Growing energy-intensity of water

Many high-income societies are moving towards more energy-intensive water because of a push by municipalities for new supplies of water from sources that are farther away and of lower quality, thereby requiring more energy to get them to the required quality and location.

Because of growing environmental concerns, standards for water treatment are becoming stricter as water is expected to be cleaner, and so the amount of energy people spend per litre will increase. Unit electricity consumption for water treatment has increased at a compound rate of 0.8% per year, with no obvious expectation for the trend to stop (Applebaum, 2000). At the same time, in many industrialized societies, water or wastewater infrastructure is aging and will increase unit electricity use due to age-related losses, while other factors (e.g. replacing older equipment with more efficient new equipment and processes, and establishing larger treatment plants with higher energy economies of scale) will decrease unit energy consumption, but not enough to offset the energy needs of higher level treatment (Applebaum, 2000).

Societies are also going to greater lengths to bring freshwater from its sources to dense urban areas. These

FIGURE 19.4

The energy–climate–water cycle creates a self-reinforcing challenge

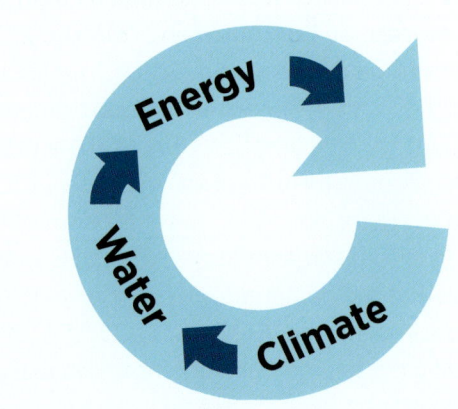

Source: Image based on suggestion of J. Long at Lawrence Livermore National Laboratory.

efforts include digging to ever-deeper underground reservoirs, or by moving water through massive long-haul projects (Stillwell et al., 2010b). For example, China is implementing the South-North Water Transfer Scheme, which is an order of magnitude larger than California's aqueduct and will move water from three river basins in the wet southern part of China to the dry northern parts (Stone and Jia, 2006). Two of these routes are more than 1000 km long (Stone and Jia, 2006), representing substantial investments in energy for transport. Similarly, in Texas, private investors are proposing a project to move groundwater from the Ogallala Aquifer (one of the world's largest) hundreds of kilometres across the state of Texas to the municipalities in the Dallas–Fort Worth Metroplex (Berfield, 2008).

On 12 April 1961, US President Kennedy said, 'If we could ever competitively – at a cheap rate – get fresh water from salt water that would be in the long-range interest of humanity, and would really dwarf any other scientific accomplishment.' (Gleick, 2000b). A few months later, he signed a bill to set the USA on a research course to seek a breakthrough in desalination (Kennedy, 1961). Since that time, global desalination capacity has seen a decades-long steep upward trend (Gleick, 2006). It is unlikely that this trend will end soon given the other trends noted above. While desalination is traditionally associated with the Middle East where energy resources are plentiful but water is scarce, cities in other locations (e.g. London, San Diego, El Paso) are considering desalination plants to get fresh water either from nearby saline aquifers or coasts. The steep market penetration rates for desalination are particularly relevant for the adoption of new membrane-based technologies (NAS, 2008). While membrane-based reverse-osmosis approaches are less energy-intensive than thermal desalination, they require much more energy than traditional freshwater production from surface sources.

19.3.2 Growing water-intensity of energy

For a variety of economic, security and environmental reasons, including the desire among high-income countries to produce a higher proportion of energy from domestic sources and to decarbonize energy systems, many of the preferred energy choices are more water-intensive. For example, nuclear energy is produced domestically, but is also more water-intensive than other forms of power generation. Carbon capture and sequestration, which is an option for decarbonizing coal combustion and other scrubber technologies, are also much more water-intensive than unscrubbed coal-fired

generation. As environmental controls are tightened on carbon and other pollutants, water use at power plants for flue gas management is likely to increase.

The move towards more water-intensive energy is especially relevant for transportation fuels, such as unconventional fossil fuels (oil shale, coal-to-liquids, gas-to-liquids, tar sands), electricity, hydrogen and biofuels, all of which can require significantly more water to produce than gasoline, depending on how they are produced. It is important to note that the push for renewable electricity also includes solar photovoltaics (PV) and wind power, which require very little water, and so not all future energy choices are worse from a water-perspective.

Almost all unconventional fossil fuels are more water-intensive than conventional fossil fuels (Figure 19.5). While gasoline might require a few litres of water for every litre of fuel that is produced (including production and refining), unconventional fossil sources are typically a factor of 2–5 more water-intensive. Electricity for plug-in hybrid electric vehicles or electric vehicles are appealing because they are clean at the vehicle's end-use and it is easier to scrub emissions at hundreds of smokestacks than millions of tailpipes. However, because most power plants use a lot of cooling water, electricity can also be about twice as water-intensive than gasoline per mile travelled if the electricity is generated from the standard grid that has high fractions of thermoelectric generation. If that electricity is generated from wind or other water-free sources, then it will be less water-consumptive than gasoline. Though unconventional fossil fuels and electricity are all potentially more water-intensive than conventional gasoline by a factor of 2–5, biofuels are particularly water-intensive. Growing biofuels consumes approximately 1000 L of water for every litre of fuel that is produced (King and Webber, 2008). Sometimes this water is provided naturally from rainfall. However, for a non-trivial and growing proportion of biofuels production, that water is provided by irrigation.

Sustained higher energy prices and emerging political consensus about climate change and energy security have brought fossil fuels into new scrutiny. Consequently, several countries are seeking an energy solution that is domestically sourced (addressing some of the national security concerns), abundant (addressing the concerns about resource depletion), and less carbon-intensive (addressing the concerns about climate change). Because significant volumes of oil are imported in many countries, and because this sector is a major contributor to carbon emissions, it is on the short-list of targets for change by policymakers, innovators and entrepreneurs.

Some energy options are unconventional fossil fuels (including compressed natural gas, coal-to-liquids, tar sands and oil shale), hydrogen, biofuels and electricity. While these options have their merits, most of their production methods are more water-intensive than conventional petroleum-based gasoline and diesel (King and Webber, 2008). The production of oil shale and tar sands is very water-intensive. For example, in situ oil shale production might use vast amounts of electric power to heat the bitumen underground, and that electric power will likely need water cooling. Tar sands production uses steam injection to reduce the viscosity of the tars. While coal production is not

particularly water-intensive, creating liquid fuels from coal using Fischer–Tropsch processes requires water as a process material. Hydrogen can also be very water-intensive if produced by electrolysis (Webber, 2007).

However, if hydrogen is produced from non-irrigated biomass resources or by reforming fossil fuels, its water-intensity is on par with conventional gasoline production and use. Notably, the biohydrogen pathway is not yet economical or scaled-up.

Biofuels are also very popular because they can be grown domestically and consume CO_2 during photosynthesis. They also hold the potential for displacing fossil fuels. The real challenge for biofuels is their water intensity (King and Webber, 2008), but there are also some

FIGURE 19.5

Water intensity of transportation

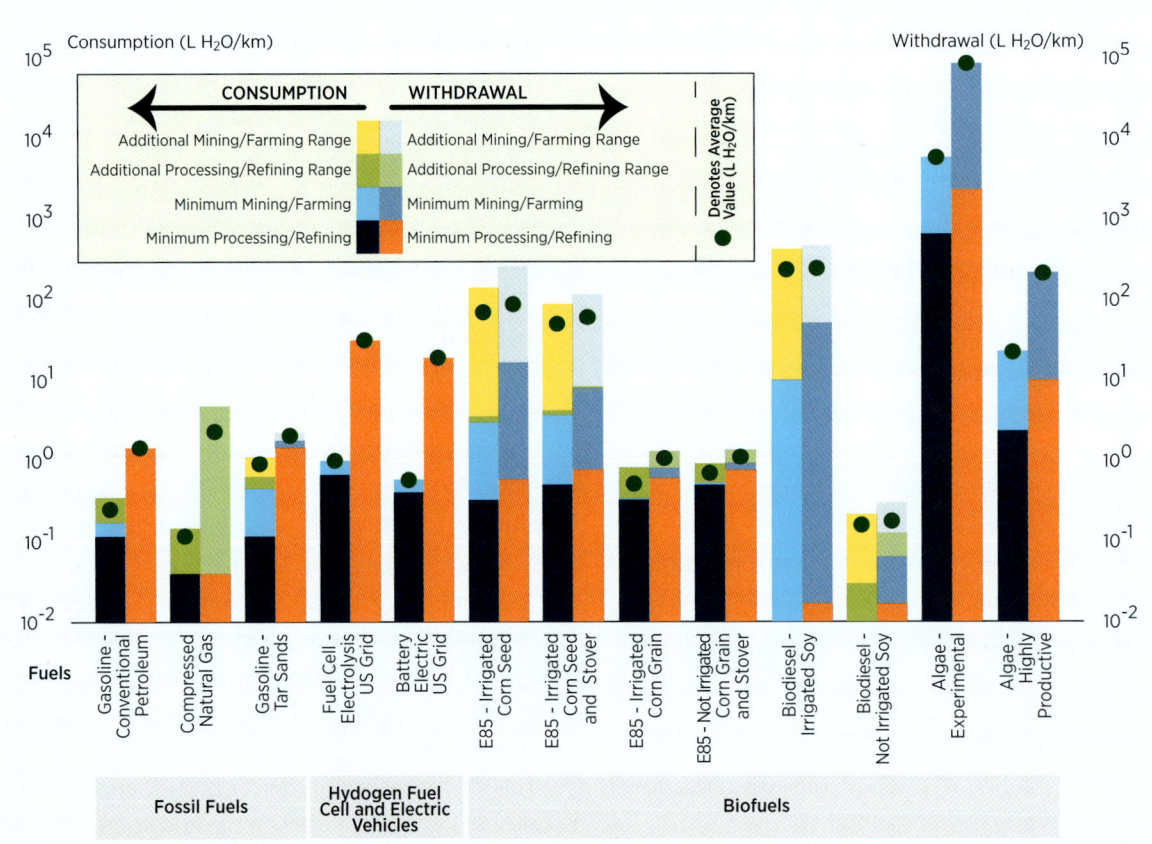

Notes: The water-intensity of different fuels in litres of water required per kilometre travelled, show great variation from irrigated biofuels (at the high end, withdrawing and consuming more than 100 L of water per km) to electricity from wind or solar resources (at the low end, requiring approximately 0 L per km). Water consumption (left stacked bars read on left axis) and withdrawal (right stacked bars read on right axis) in L per km for various fuels for light duty vehicles. Water use from mining and farming is designated differently from that used for processing and refining. Where a range of values exists (e.g. different irrigation amounts in different states), a minimum value is listed with an 'additional range'. Otherwise, the values plotted are considered average values. FT = Fischer–Tropsch; FCV = fuel cell vehicle; US Grid = electricity from average US grid mix; and Renewables = renewable electricity generated without consumption or withdrawal of water (e.g. wind and photovoltaic solar panels)
Source: Beal (2011, fig. 5-2, p. 273).

important water quality impacts (Twomey et al., 2010). Recent analysis indicates that irrigated biofuels can require over 100 litres of water for every kilometre travelled in a light-duty vehicle (King and Webber, 2008; NAS, 2007), approximately 1,000 times more water per kilometre than conventional gasoline. When scaling up this kind of production to prepare for national biofuels mandates, water can become a critical limiting factor.

Conclusions and recommendations

The nexus of water and energy is fundamental to society, is intertwined in many ways, is under strain, and that strain is projected to become worse as worldwide demand for both increases more quickly than population and the effects of climate change manifest themselves. While the energy–water relationship might appear intractable, there are many opportunities to mitigate its worst aspects through new technologies, new concepts for how to reuse water effectively, new markets that put a price on water, and recognition that conserving water and conserving energy are synonymous. Though the world's water situation appears dire for many reasons, it also presents an opportunity to address the problem and there are many tools available. In particular, policy engagement is warranted.

Because there are many rivers, watersheds, basins and aquifers that span several regions and/or countries, there is a need for national and international engagement on energy–water issues. Unfortunately, there are some policy pitfalls at the energy–water nexus. For example, energy and water policymaking are typically disaggregated. Further, the data on water quantity are sparse, error-prone and inconsistent. National databases of water use for power plants contain errors, possibly due to differences in units, formats and definitions between state and federal reporting requirements. For example, the definitions for water use, withdrawal and consumption are not always clear.

Despite the potential pitfalls, there are policy opportunities at the energy–water nexus. For example, water conservation and energy conservation are synonymous. That is, policies that promote water conservation also achieve energy conservation; and policies that promote energy conservation also achieve water conservation. Some policy actions for the energy–water nexus are to:

- Collect, maintain and make available accurate, updated and comprehensive water data. Without good data about water reserves, flows and use, it will be difficult for analysts to assess the situation and for

policymakers to respond; this hurdle remains one of the top barriers to effective action.

- Invest heavily in water-related research and development (R&D) to match recent increases in energy-related R&D. R&D investments are an excellent policy option for national and international bodies because local governments and industry usually are not in a position to adequately invest in research. Consequently, the amount of R&D in the water sector is much lower than for other sectors, such as pharmaceuticals, technology or energy. Topics for R&D include low-energy water treatment, novel approaches to desalination, remote leak detectors for water infrastructure, and air-cooling systems for power plants. In addition, R&D for biofuels should emphasize feedstocks, such as cellulosic sources or algae that do not require freshwater irrigation.

- Develop regional water plans that consider increased demands for electricity, and regional energy plans that consider increased demands for water. For example, the rise of biofuels or electricity as fuel substitutes will have very different regional impacts. Biofuels will affect water use in rural, agricultural areas, whereas electric vehicles will affect water use at power plants near major population centres.

- Encourage resource substitution to fuels that have water, emissions and security benefits. Some fuel sources, such as natural gas, wind and solar PV need much less water and reduce emissions of pollutants and carbon.

- Support the use of reclaimed water for irrigation and process cooling. Using reclaimed water for power plants, industry and agriculture can spare a significant amount of energy and cost. However, financing, regulatory and permitting hurdles restrict this option. Reuse water can also reduce the demand for freshwater, for example by using reclaimed water (e.g. treated wastewater) for power plant cooling or other industrial uses along with irrigation. There is precedent for such action, as 'nearly 80% of water used in the industrial sector in Japan is currently recycled' (Oki and Kanae, 2006, p. 1071). While most cities would refrain from using treated wastewater as a source of drinking water, this avenue is also available and has been implemented, for example, in water-scarce Singapore and the International Space Station without ill effects. Consequently, it is recommended that municipalities affected by water-scarcity should move aggressively towards the use of reclaimed water.

- Support the use of dry and hybrid wet–dry cooling at power plants. Not all power plants need wet cooling all the time. Finding ways to help plants upgrade their cooling to less water-intensive versions can spare significant volumes of water to meet public supply or in-stream flow requirements.

- Establish strict standards in building codes for water efficiency: revised standards for low-flow appliances, water-heating efficiency, purple-piping for reclaimed water, and rain barrels to reduce both water and energy consumption.
- Invest aggressively in conservation. Water conservation can be a cost-effective way to save energy, and energy conservation can be a cost-effective way to save water. Therefore, conservation has cross-cutting benefits.

Conservation is one of the easiest and most cost-effective approaches to reducing both water and energy use, especially as saving water is synonymous with saving energy, and vice-versa (Cohen et al., 2004; Hardberger, 2008). While conservation will not solve all of society's energy and water problems, it will buy some time while new solutions are developed.

IIIIIIIIIIIIIIIIIIIIIIIIIIIIIIIIIIIIIIIIIIIIIIIIIIIIIIIIIIIIIIIIIIIIIIIII

Note

1 Many numbers used in this description are for the USA because the data are available with greater fidelity and comprehensiveness than for other countries and regions. While these numbers are suitably representative for the energy–water relationship in general, there will be some variation in other regions due stage of economic development, prevailing climate and technology choices.

IIIIIIIIIIIIIIIIIIIIIIIIIIIIIIIIIIIIIIIIIIIIIIIIIIIIIIIIIIIIIIIIIIIIIIIII

References

Applebaum, B. 2000. US electricity consumption for water supply and treatment – The next half century. *Water and Sustainability*, Vol. 4. Palo Alto, CA, Electric Power Research Institute (EPRI).

Beal, C. M. 2011. *Constraints on Algal Biofuel Production*. PhD Dissertation, University of Texas, Austin.

Berfield, S. 2008. There will be water. *BusinessWeek*, 12 June.

CEC (California Energy Commission). 2002. *Comparison of Alternate Cooling Technologies for California Power Plants: Economic, Environmental and Other Tradeoffs.* Palo Alto, CA, PIER/EPRI Technical Report.

----. 2005. C*alifornia's Water-Energy Relationship: Final Staff Report.* Prepared in support of the 2005 Integrated Energy Policy Report Proceeding (04-IEPR-01E).

Center for Sustainable Systems, University of Michigan. 2008. *U.S. Wastewater Treatment Factsheet.* Pub. No. CSS04-14. http://css.snre.umich.edu/css_doc/CSS04-14.pdf (Accessed 9 March, 2008).

Cohen, R., Nelson, B. and Wolff, G. 2004. *Energy Down the Drain: The Hidden Costs of California's Water Supply.* Oakland, CA, Natural Resources Defense Council Pacific Institute.

Dasgupta, S., B. Laplante, Wang H. and Wheeler D. 2002. Confronting the environmental Kuznets Curve. *Journal of Economic Perspectives,* Vol. 16, pp. 147–68.

EIA (Energy Information Administration). 2001. *End-Use Consumption of Electricity.* Washington DC, US Department of Energy.

----. 2007. *Country Analysis Briefs: Saudi Arabia.* Washington DC, US Department of Energy.

EPRI (Electric Power Research Institute). 2002. *Water and Sustainability (Volume 4): U.S. Electricity Consumption for Water Supply and Treatment – The Next Half Century.* Technical Report. Palo Alto, CA, EPRI.

Gleick, P. H. 1994. Water and energy. *Annual Review of Energy and Environment,* Vol. 19, pp. 267–99. doi:10.1146/annurev.eg.19.110194.001411

----. 2000a. *Water: The Potential Consequences of Climate Variability and Change for the Water Resources of the United States.* Oakland, CA, United States Geological Survey and Pacific Institute.

----. 2000b. *The World's Water 2000–2001: The Biennial Report on Freshwater Resources.* WA, USA, Island Press.

Hardberger, A. 2008. *From Policy to Reality: Maximizing Urban Water Conservation in Texas.* Austin, TX, Environmental Defense Fund.

Hightower, M. and S. A. Pierce, The energy challenge. *Nature,* 2008, 452.

Hutson, S.S., Barber N. L., Kenny J. F., Linsey K. S., Lumia D. S. and Maupin M. A. 2004. *Estimated Use of Water in the United States in 2000.* USGS Circular 1268, Reston, VA, U.S. Geological Survey. (Released March 2004, revised April 2004, May 2004, February 2005.)

IEA (International Energy Agency). 2005. *World Energy Outlook 2005: Fact Sheet – Saudi Arabia.* Paris, France, IEA.

----. 2009. *World Energy Outlook 2009.* Paris, France, IEA.

----. 2010. *World Energy Outlook 2010.* Paris, France, IEA.

Kennedy, J. F. 1961. Speeches of Senator John F. Kennedy: Presidential Campaign of 1960. Washington DC, US Government Printing Office.

King, C. W., Stillwell A. S., Twomey K. M., and Webber M. E. 2011. *Coherence between Water and Energy Policies.* Paris, Organisation of Economic Co-operation and Development (OECD).

King, C. W. and Webber M. E. 2008. Water intensity of transportation. *Journal of Environmental Science and Technology ,* Vol. 42, No. 21, pp. 7866–7872. doi:10.1021/es800367m

Lagadec, P. 2004. Understanding the French 2003 heat wave experience: Beyond the heat, a multi-layered challenge. *Journal of Contingencies and Crisis Management,* Vol. 12, pp. 160–9.

National Academy of Sciences (NAS). 2007. *Water Implications of Biofuels Production in the United States,* 0-309-11360-1, Committee on Water Implications of Biofuels Production in the United States, National Research Council, National Academy of Sciences, Washington DC.

––––. 2008. *Desalination: A National Perspective,* 0-309-11924-3, Committee on Advancing Desalination Technology, Water Science and Technology Board, Division on Earth and Life Studies, National Academy of Sciences, Washington DC.

Oki, T. and Kanae S. 2006. Global hydrological cycles and world water resources. *Science,* Vol. 313, pp. 1068–72.

Pacific Energy Summit. 2011. *Unconventional Gas and Implications for the LNG Market, FACTS Global Energy.* Advance Summit paper from the 2011 Pacific Energy Summit, 21–23 February 2011, Jakarta, Indonesia. http://www.nbr.org/downloads/pdfs/eta/PES_2011_Facts_Global_Energy.pdf (Accessed 30 April 2011.)

Poumadère, M., Mays C., Mer S. L. and Blong R. 2005. Heat wave in France: Dangerous climate change here and now. *Risk Analysis,* Vol. 25, 1483–94.

Proteger, F. 2008. The Uruguay, its dams, and its people are running out of water. *International Rivers,* 1 February. http://www.internationalrivers.org/latin-america/paraguay-paraná-basin/uruguay-river-its-dams-and-its-people-are-running-out-water (Accessed 12 November 2011.)

Seiger, R. B. and Whitlock D. 2005. Session for the *CHP and Bioenergy for Landfills and Wastewater Treatment Plants* workshop, Salt Lake City, UT, 11 August 2005.

Shannon, M. S., Bohn P. W., Elimelech M., Georgiadis J. G., Marinas B. J. and Mayes A. M. 2008. Science and technology for water purification in the coming decades. Nature, Vol. 452, pp. 301–10.

Spotts, P. N. 2008. Lakes Mead and Powell could run dry by 2021. *The Christian Science Monitor,* 13 February.

Stillwell A.S. 2010. *Energy Water Nexus in Texas*, Master's Thesis, University of Texas at Austin.

Stillwell, A. S., Hoppock D. C. and Webber M. E. 2010*a*. Energy recovery from wastewater treatment plants in the United States: A case study of the energy-water nexus. *Sustainability* (special issue Energy Policy and Sustainability), Vol. 2, No. 4, pp. 945–962. doi:10.3390/su2040945

Stillwell, A. S., King C.W. and Webber M. E. 2010*b*. Desalination and long-haul water transfer as a water supply for Dallas, Texas: A case study of the energy-water nexus in Texas. *Texas Water Journal,* Vol. 1, No. 1, pp. 33–41.

Stillwell, A. S., King C. W., Webber M. E., Duncan I. J. and Hardberger A. 2011. The energy-water nexus in Texas. *Ecology and Society,* (Special Feature: The Energy-Water Nexus: Managing the Links between Energy and Water for a Sustainable Future), 16 (1): 2.

Stone, R. and Jia H. 2006. Going against the flow. *Science,* Vol. 313, 1034–37.

Torcellini, P., Long N. and Judkoff R. 2003. *Consumptive Water Use for U.S. Power Production.* NREL/TP-550-33905, Golden CO, USA, National Renewable Energy Laboratory, U.S. Department of Energy.

Twomey, K. M., Stillwell A. S. and Webber M. E. 2010. The unintended energy impacts of increased nitrate contamination from biofuels production. *Journal of Environmental Monitoring.* Issue 1. doi:10.1039/b913137j

Twomey, K. M. and Webber M. W. 2011. *Evaluating the Energy Intensity of the US Public Water System,* Proceedings of the 5th International Conference on Energy Sustainability. Washington DC.

UN (United Nations). 2005. *World Urbanization Prospects: The 2005 Revision.* New York, Population Division of the Department of Economic and Social Affairs of the United Nations Secretariat.

––––. 2006. *World Population Prospects: The 2006 Revision.* New York, Population Division of the Department of Economic and Social Affairs of the United Nations Secretariat.

Gerbens-Leenes, P.W., Hoekstra, A.Y., Van der Meer, Th. H. 2008. *Water Footprint of Bio-Energy and Other Primary Energy Carriers.* Research Report Series No. 29. Delft, The Netherlands, UNESCO-IHE. http://www.waterfootprint.org/Reports/Report29-WaterFootprintBioenergy.pdf (Accessed 30 April 2011.)

USDOE (United States Department of Energy). 2006. *Energy Demands on Water Resources:* Report to Congress on the Interdependency of Energy and Water. Washington DC, US Department of Energy.

Webber, M. E. 2007. The water intensity of the transitional hydrogen economy. *Environmental Research Letters,* 2, 034007 (7pp). doi:10.1088/1748-9326/2/3/034007

WEC (World Energy Council). 2010. *Water for Energy.* London, UK, World Energy Council. http://www.worldenergy.org/documents/water_energy_1.pdf.

WEF (Water Environment Federation). 1997. *Energy Conservation in Wastewater Treatment Facilities Manual of Practice.* No. FD-2. Alexandria, VA, WEF.

WEF (World Economic Forum). 2009. *Thirsty Energy: Water and Energy in the 21st Century.* http://www.weforum.org/reports/thirsty-energy-water-and-energy-21st-century?fo=1 (Accessed 30 April 2011.)

Wolff, G., Cooley, H., Palaniappan, M., Samulon, A., Lee, E., Morrison, J., Katz, D., Gleick, P. 2006. *The World's Water 2006–2007: The Biennial Report on Freshwater Resources.* WA, USA, Island Press.

WWAP (World Water Assessment Programme). 2003. *World Water Development Report 1: Water for People, Water for Life.* Paris/New York, UNESCO/Berghahn Books.

CHAPTER 20
Freshwater for industry

UNIDO

—

Authors John Payne (SNC-Lavalin Environment, Division of SNC-Lavalin Inc.) and
Carolina Gonzalez-Castro
Acknowledgement Igor Volodin (Coordinator)

|||||||||||||||||||||||||||||||||||||||||||||||||||||||||||||||||||||||||||||||||||||||||||||||||||||||||||||||||||||||||||||

Industry's need for water has not fundamentally changed, but it has become more critical and it is a function of water productivity in a sustainability context.

Economic forces, comprising several factors that affect the demand side, are the strongest influence on water for industry. Climate change is the main supply side driver.

Cheap, plentiful water can no longer be taken for granted. There are uncertainties with the quantity and quality of water both for industry and its supply chain.

Challenges for industry include adapting to water scarcity, changing management paradigms and minimizing environmental impacts.

Opportunities exist in proactive integrated water management using corporate water strategies that are outward looking and involve a commitment to innovation and implementation.

20.1 Key issues

Industry's need for water has not fundamentally changed, but it has become more critical over recent decades. The issues involved are the supply of and demand for water, the use and consumption of water, and wastewater discharge, all key issues for the industry to be profitable in the context of environmental sustainability.

20.1.1 Water quantity

On a global scale, industry uses relatively little water in comparison to the agriculture sector, but it does require an accessible, reliable supply of consistent and acceptable quality. Data indicate that approximately 20% of the world's freshwater withdrawals are used by industry, but this figure varies widely from region to region (UNEP, 2008) (Figure 20.1). The available data generally combine industry and energy use; it has been estimated that only about 30 to 40% of this use is for actual industry and the balance is used in various forms of power generation (Shiklomanov, 1999).

The demand for water is expected to increase in parallel with population growth and maybe even exceed it (Pacific Institute, 2004). Water management in industry is considered in terms of withdrawals and consumption. This is expressed as:

Water Withdrawal = Water Consumption + Effluent Discharge (Grobicki, 2007)

The total water withdrawal from surface water and groundwater by industry is usually much greater than the amount of water that is actually consumed (WWAP, 2006, ch. 8). Improved water management is generally reflected in overall decreased water withdrawal or use by industry. This makes obvious the connection between increased productivity and decreased consumption and effluent discharge. Indeed, if discharge becomes zero then the water component of increased water productivity is solely a function of water consumption.

20.1.2 Water quality

It is not uncommon for industry to use higher quality water than it requires, often because there is a conveniently located local supply – either a natural source (groundwater, a river or a lake) or a suitable municipal service. Water of lesser quality may be adequate for many industries, allowing the use of recycled and reclaimed water from other sources. Conversely, some industries such as food processing have requirements more demanding than those for drinking water. The pharmaceutical and high technology industries require very high quality water and further treat the water from their primary supplies.

The water quality of effluent discharges is also important to industry as pollution can affect large volumes of fresh water. While statistics show that industry, in the macro view, is not necessarily the worst polluter in terms of concentrations and loads, its effects can be very significant, particularly on regional and local scales (World Bank, 2010, fig. 3.6). Industrial contamination tends to be more concentrated, more toxic and harder to treat than other pollutants. The persistence of these contaminants with respect to their degradation and rate of movement though the environment and hydrological cycle is often lengthy.

20.1.3 Water productivity and profit

Industry needs to maximize economic output and profit yet use water efficiently and wisely. The measure of water productivity is how much dollar value can be obtained from each cubic metre of water used (Grobicki, 2007; World Bank, 2010, fig. 3.5). Figures range from well over US$100 to less than US$10 per cubic metre depending on the country (WWAP, 2009, ch. 7). As technology improves, industrial water productivity increases. Low productivity may indicate that water is undervalued or is simply abundant. High productivity is linked to high reuse as withdrawals are reduced.

The virtual water content of industrial products is another way to view how much water is being used in industry. Virtual water is the volume of fresh water consumed in all steps of the production process. It is usually considerably more than the actual water contained in the product. The global average virtual water content of industrial products is 80 L per US$ required to produce the commodity (Hoekstra and Chapagain, 2007). However, in the United States (USA) the number is 110 L; in Germany and the Netherlands it is about 50 L; and in Japan, Australia and Canada it is only 10–15 L. In large developing nations, such as China and India, the average number is 20–25 L per US$.

20.1.4 Cleaner production and sustainability

There is a need to break the paradigm of industrial growth linked to environmental damage and to decouple industrial development from environmental degradation. At a fundamental level this involves cleaner production and sustainability. Cleaner production has

FIGURE 20.1

Global freshwater use by sector at the beginning of the twenty-first century

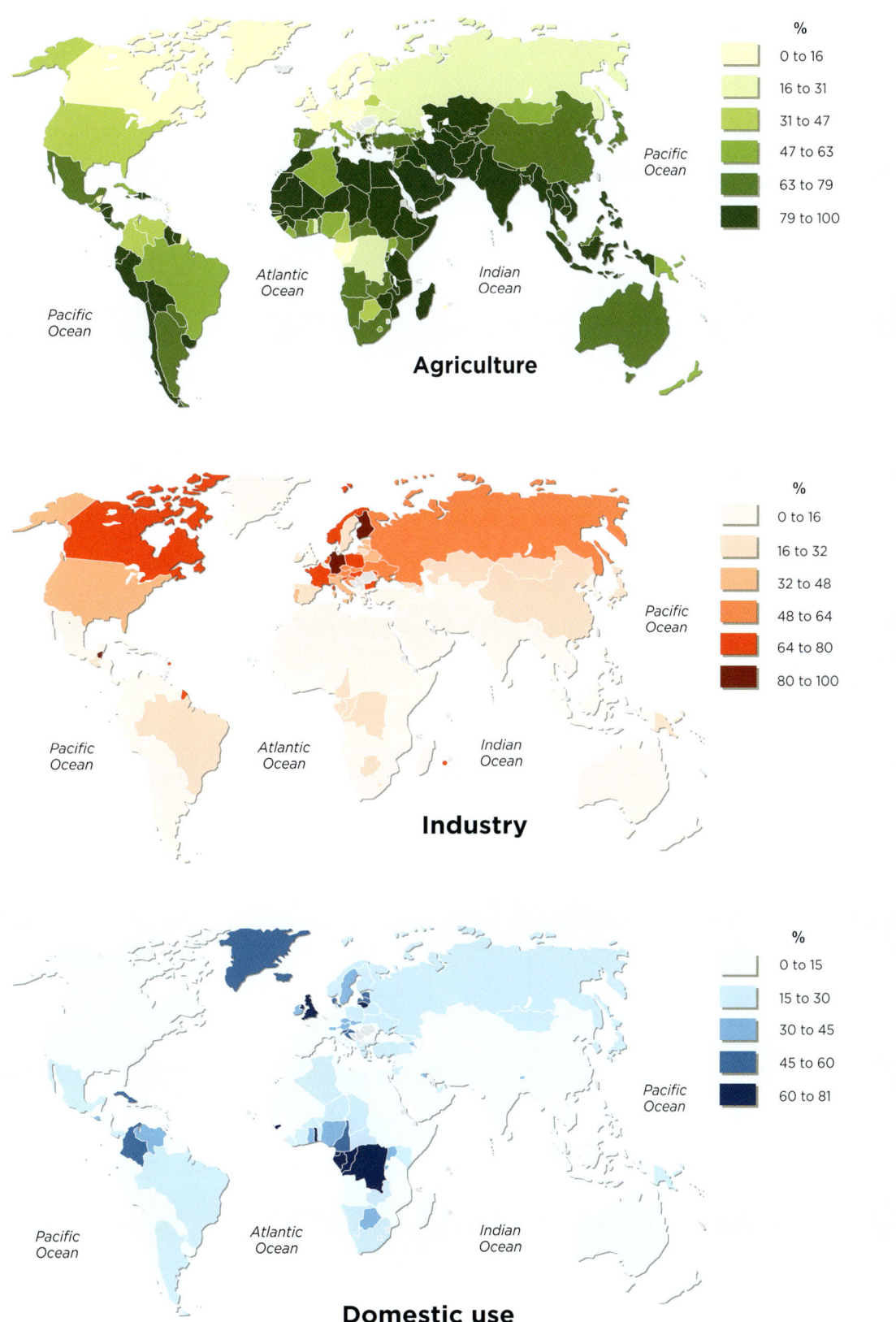

Source: UNEP/GRID-Arendal (http://maps.grida.no/go/graphic/freshwater-use-by-sector-at-the-beginning-of-the-2000s, by P. Rekacewicz, based on data from the World Resources Institute).

many facets, and one of its main objectives is to move towards zero discharge. Zero discharge changes the balance of the water productivity equation and is a key concept in matching water quality to use (WWAP, 2006). In moving towards zero discharge, an attempt is made to convert wastewater streams into useful inputs for other industries and industrial clusters. It seeks to find a use for all effluents that would otherwise be discharged by recycling them or selling them to another user. If an industry approaches this goal then its overall water consumption will equal its withdrawal. Practically, this means that withdrawal will decrease to meet consumption.

The hydrological cycle includes significant industrial intervention, such as effluent discharge into surface water bodies, the infiltration of contaminants into groundwater, and the atmospheric distribution and fallout of contaminants into water bodies (Figure 20.2). Loops of recycled and reclaimed water are included in the hydrological cycle. Recycled and reclaimed water may rejoin the cycle after much delay or perhaps never, if zero discharge becomes a reality. Zero effluent discharge is the ultimate goal for water quality (WWAP, 2006).

20.2 External drivers

The water need of industry is strongly influenced by external drivers that add a layer of uncertain complexity to corporate water management. These external drivers often act in an indirect way through a chain reaction, with many consequences. They are essentially recent phenomena and, although their impacts on water are evident, their exact effects are unpredictable. The problem is magnified because more than one factor may pressure a driver, the relationships between factors and drivers are interactive and changing, and these relationships are difficult to control. The external drivers discussed below appear to be the most influential for industry. Other drivers such as ecosystem stress, societal values, and security, while important, tend to be more local in nature.

20.2.1 Economic forces

Economic growth and development are the main drivers of the challenge to water resources (2030 Water Resources Group, 2009). Economic forces affect water, but at the same time the state of water resources influences the economy, and water is seen as both a threat and a constraint to economic growth (WWAP, 2009).

FIGURE 20.2

Water profile for the Canadian forest products industry (million m³ per year)

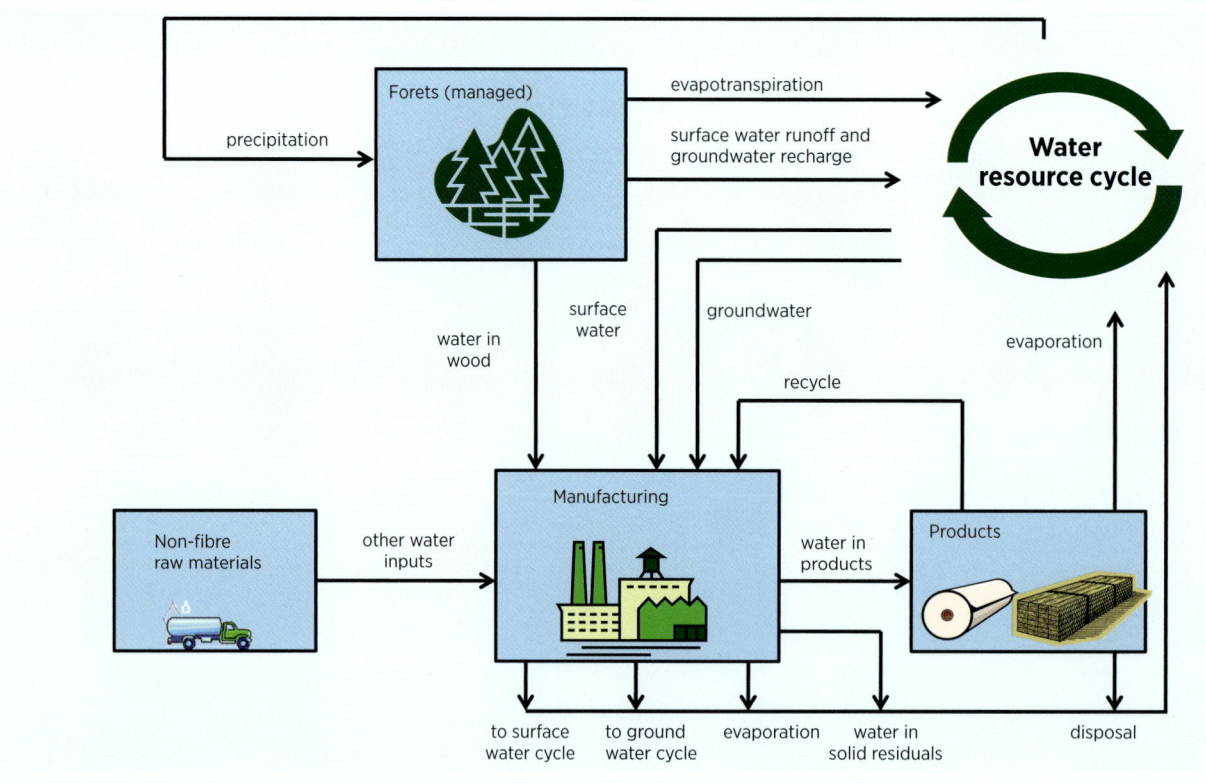

Source: NCASI (2010, fig. 2.1, p.2)

Concerns were expressed at the 2009 Davos World Economic Forum that the world is moving to 'water bankruptcy' and that this is one of the world's most pressing problems (TSG, 2009).

Competition for water resources

Industry will find itself competing more and more for limited water resources as demand and consumption increase in all areas. The Pacific Institute (2007, p. 7, referencing FAO, 2007) states, 'according to the United Nations, if present consumption patterns continue, two-thirds of the world's population will live in water-stressed conditions by the year 2025'. Lack of water is already a major constraint to industrial growth in China, India and Indonesia (Pacific Institute, 2007). Further demographic pressure is resulting from globalization, which 'with its accompanying move of labour industries from high-income to low-income countries, is creating high water demand outside of its abundant sources, often in urban areas' (WWAP, 2003, ch. 9, p. 244). Agriculture, the biggest single user of water by far, will remain the biggest competitor for this resource, potentially in conflict with industry.

The valuation of water

Underlying the competition for water is the concept that it is an 'economic good' and thus subject to market forces in terms of its cost. Figure 20.3, for example, depicts the cost components in manufacturing industries in Canada. Balanced against the economic good

FIGURE 20.3

Water costs in Canadian manufacturing industries by cost component, 2005

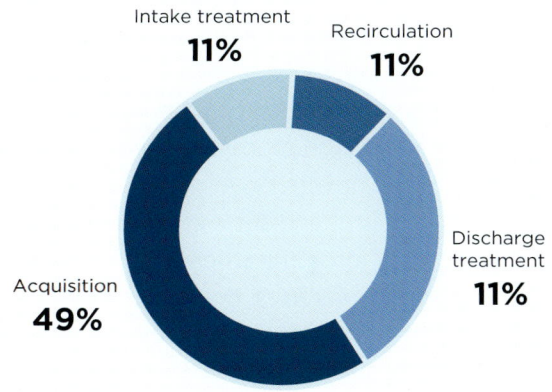

Source: Statistics Canada (2007).

notion is the belief that access to water is a human right. Therefore, there are competing trends of full-cost pricing of water versus more customary subsidies or essentially free water.

Privatization of water supply and treatment

Superimposed on the debate over the value of water is the increasing trend towards privatization of water supply and treatment – which may also include the management and ownership of water systems – particularly in high income countries (Pacific Institute, 2004).

Financial crises

The forecasts for recovery time from the 2008 global financial crisis vary greatly, as do the predictions for the success of the recovery. Financial planning in such circumstances of uncertainty is difficult and may be very short term. Moreover, as a result of the crisis, the dynamics of the world economy may change substantially. There is a growing recognition of water's value in the global financial infrastructure and it is felt that investments in water will be less affected than other investments by the current financial crisis (TSG, 2009).

In times of crisis, governments, primarily in developed countries, resort to deficit spending and much of the money goes to infrastructure. This spending may be beneficial to industry because the design and construction of infrastructure for water management and treatment that is more efficient should provide confidence in adequate supplies of good quality water. On a global scale, the pursuit of cost savings will drive industry to find more economical ways of operating; one option is the optimization of resources through the adoption of advanced technologies and practices that lead to zero discharge.

Trade

Trade is a driver for industry and water through multilateral environmental agreements (MEAs) and international standards. MEAs, such as the Basel Convention, are used to control international trade for environmental reasons and were originally devised to protect developing countries from the activities of developed countries. However, trade from developing countries now faces the hurdle of meeting the requirements of the developed countries. These requirements include ISO certifications, environmental management systems (EMS) and corporate social responsibility (CSR). These have, in turn, led to product manufacturing standards, which include energy efficiency and climate change (carbon footprint) requirements, and these affect industrial water use. Industry in developing countries is facing stricter requirements and some control by the multinational companies to which they supply their goods. A benefit for industries in these countries is the better management, including of water, such requirements necessitate, and the resulting increased efficiency.

Water trade is typically a local issue, because it is not practicable to transport water in bulk over large distances. However, the concept of virtual water puts water trade on a global scale. Virtual water trade is trade in goods and services that consume a considerable amount of water – often in their production and usually less so in their product. It is 'a tool for determining the movement of water through international trade' (WWAP, 2009, ch. 2, p. 35). Therefore, while international trade can aggravate water stress, it can also relieve it through virtual water trade. It has been estimated that virtual water accounts for 40% of total water consumption and that 20% of this virtual water is in industrial products (WWAP, 2009, box 2.1). The state of a country's water resources can be improved or made worse if goods with a large water footprint are exported or imported.

However attractive the trade of virtual water is, there are some important constraints (TSG, 2009). It has been suggested that this trade strongly reflects trade in agricultural products, which have large water footprints (GWI, 2008). Consequently, developing countries with little industry but many small farmers will export water and industrialized countries, regardless of their natural resources, will import water in food. Reversing this flow of virtual water is not practicable as 'you cannot tell peasant farmers in North Africa, India or North-East China that they should give up their land and become advertising executives or bank clerks because those professions use less water' (GWI, 2008). The situation is made more complex where an industrialized country such as the USA is also a major agricultural exporter.

20.2.2 Climate change
Climate change is a fundamental driver affecting water availability (supply side) and in turn it pressures demand side drivers for water. The resulting pressure on industry is the need to secure and maintain an adequate water supply. Fulfilling this need will become increasingly difficult with the unpredictable location and timing of climate change impacts. It could happen that many industrialized countries, which are found in the mid-latitudes and the Northern Hemisphere, will have their supplies come under stress. Competition among users will intensify in some regions when existing adequate supplies become scarce. As a result, industry may need to relocate.

Conversely, some lower income countries, which are often under water stress at present, may find their supply increases. In many cases multinational corporations have already relocated to lower income countries to take advantage of cheaper labour – with more water in these areas the trend might be expected to continue and increase, though improvements in water infrastructure will be required to take advantage of increased supply. An indirect benefit from the increased industrial presence may be improved manufacturing quality and labour conditions and better-protected ecosystems, as the markets for their products are mainly in higher income countries with demanding environmental standards and labour laws.

20.2.3 Technological innovation
Technological innovation applies to the quality of both water supply and treatment of wastewater in industry, which have a direct bearing on cleaner production and sustainability. The constraint to treatment to achieve high quality water is cost rather than technical capability. Revolutionary technological breakthroughs that will transform the treatment of water seem unlikely, but there have been many incremental technological advances and continual cost reduction (TSG, 2009). The idea is to commission the most economic system for the level of quality required.

20.2.4 Policies and governance, laws and finance
At all levels of government policies, strategies and regulations concerning water have a direct bearing on industry and are backstopped frequently by economic measures. Industry can to some extent influence government, but it is only one stakeholder in the process of devising water policy, a process that has many competing interests and drivers. Government initiatives form a variety of 'carrot and stick' approaches that will either encourage or force industries into more environmentally sustainable practices. However, well-intentioned government strategies can inhibit progress; for example, waste regulations in the USA prevent waste transfer in industrial clusters (Das, 2005).

20.2.5 Public input into water policy

Public involvement in decisions over water resources and policy is increasing (Pacific Institute, 2004, 2007). Such decisions may affect the lives of many people and thus their input is important. Protests, opposition to projects and globalization, and water controversies are becoming more common. With the media involved, bad publicity over water can affect business in a very negative way. Industry must strategically think about and plan its need for water to avoid disputes and confrontation.

20.3 Principal risks and uncertainties

In the past, water was not seen as an uncertain component of the process of the successful and profitable operation of an industry; it was taken somewhat for granted that supply would be easy and relatively cheap to secure. Discharges of wastewater presented more of a challenge but, providing standards were met, effluent was permissible. The recent number of new external drivers on water and its management has now made water use a much riskier proposition for industry (Figure 20.4). To run an industry well, water is required in the right quantity, in the right quality, at the right place, at the right time and at the right price (Payne, 2007). All these factors are now subject to greater uncertainty.

20.3.1 Reliable supply

Water scarcity is seen as an increasing business risk and the security of supply to industry is dependent on sufficient resources (2030 Water Resources Group, 2009) (Figure 20.5). This situation is compounded by geographical and seasonal variations, which are now more unpredictable, and perhaps underestimated, being subject to the risks associated with climate change, which 'challenges the traditional assumption that past hydrological experience provides a good guide to future conditions' (IPCC, 2008, p. 5).

This situation then leads into water allocation and the competing needs for water in a region, which may be beyond the control of industry. This is especially true in transboundary water situations where the needs of two or more countries may conflict.

FIGURE 20.4

Inter-relationship of water risks between business, government and society

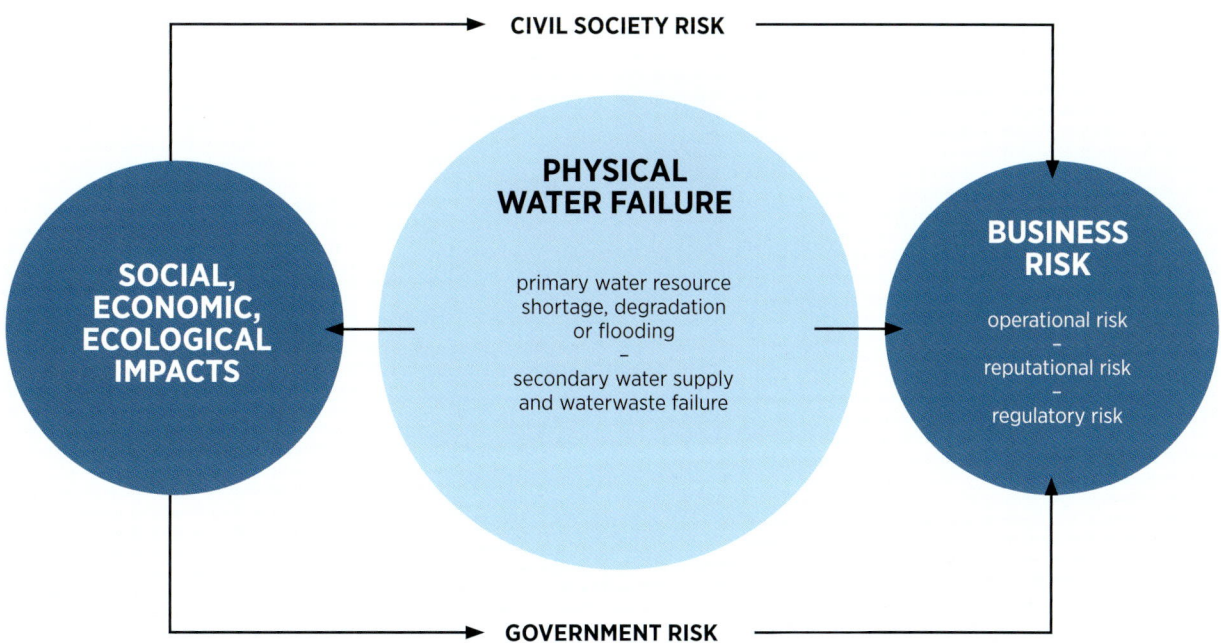

Source: SABMiller and WWF-UK (2009, fig. 2, p. 5), courtesy of SABMiller/WWF (refer to www.SABMILLER.com/water).

20.3.2 Adequate quality

Water quality risks associated with both supply and discharge affect industry. Many industries require high quality water and may use pre-treatment because natural sources of water are increasingly likely to be polluted. It is estimated that 40% of US rivers and 75% of Chinese rivers are heavily polluted, and that river water in the US may be reused up to 20 times before it reaches the sea (TSG, 2009). Groundwater is being overexploited, contamination is increasing, and saltwater intrusion is resulting from groundwater overdraft in coastal regions. Industry is exposed to these risks and the costs associated with combating them. There will be more reliance on reusing reclaimed or recycled water in the future, and in this context, there is clearly a need to improve the match between water quality and use.

Wastewater discharge regulations and standards present risks to industry. In developed countries there are pre-treatment requirements before effluent can be sent to municipal treatment plants or discharged to watercourses. In developing countries, it is estimated that 70% of industrial wastes are discharged without any treatment into usable water supply (WWAP, n.d.). Therefore, there is considerable pressure on industry to clean up its effluent and while compliance will doubtless become stricter and more onerous, the actual criteria and severity of standards will vary from jurisdiction to jurisdiction. The associated risk is that of investment in new treatment technology which may be obsolete within a few years. Industrial accidents such as uncontrolled discharges may result from economic and other drivers to move ahead quickly, possibly with unproven technology and in sensitive locations. Water quality issues therefore present restrictions on industrial expansion.

20.3.3 Supply chain disruptions

The increasing interest in water footprints highlights the importance of the supply chain in delivering the necessary raw materials and other items that an industry needs to function (Figure 20.6). The links in the supply chain are subject to external drivers and risks associated with a reliable supply of water for each industry involved in the supply chain. A significant break in this chain can result in great difficulties for an

---

FIGURE 20.5

Aggregated global gap between existing accessible, reliable supply and 2030 water withdrawals, assuming no efficiency gains

Billion m³, 154 basins/regions

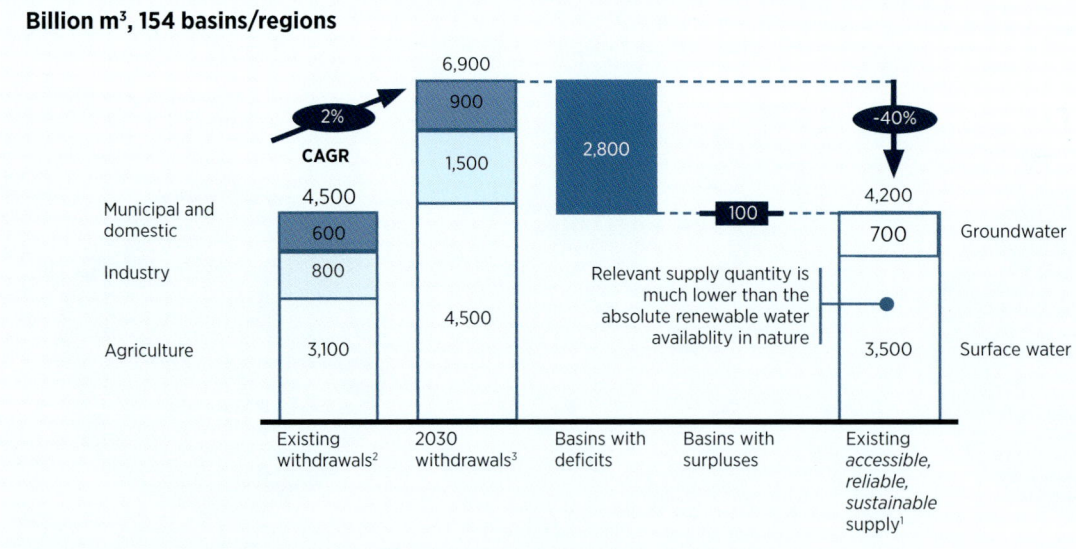

[1] Existing supply which can be provided at 90% reliabillity, based on historical hydrology and infrastructure investments scheduled through 2010; net of environmental requirements.
[2] Based on 2010 agricultural production analyses from IFPRI.
[3] Based on GPD, population projections and agricultural production projections from IFPRI; considers no water productivity gains between 2005–2030.
Source: 2030 Water Resources Group (2009, p. 6) (the Water 2030 Global Water Supply and Demand model; agricultural production based on IFPRI IMPACT-WATER base case).

industry. Such risks, with several factors coming into play, are very difficult to accommodate and make contingency plans for.

20.3.4 Government and water management

It is the practice of governments to set their own policies with respect to water, based on multifaceted agendas of particular concerns from the national to local levels. Priorities change and this variation and unpredictability makes it particularly difficult for industry, especially global companies, to locate successfully to some countries. The situation is especially difficult if regulations change after a company has started operations. As such, companies must be proactive in their efforts to anticipate these uncertain situations and take measures to address them in advance. The government perception of water risk may be at odds with industry. Poor policy and decisions may lead to overutilization of water resources in existing locations and underutilization in others. In addition, if the anti-industry bias of some governments, particularly in the light of environmental activism, is added to the new and emerging role of the public, with its own agenda in water management, the outcomes are very uncertain.

20.4 Challenge areas

The main challenge to industry is how to remain viable by properly responding to all the new water resource drivers – their unusual pressures, their heightened levels of uncertainty and their associated risks.

20.4.1 Adapting to water scarcity

Water scarcity is probably the most pressing challenge for industry. Bridging the water gap will be a

FIGURE 20.6

The production chain for cotton

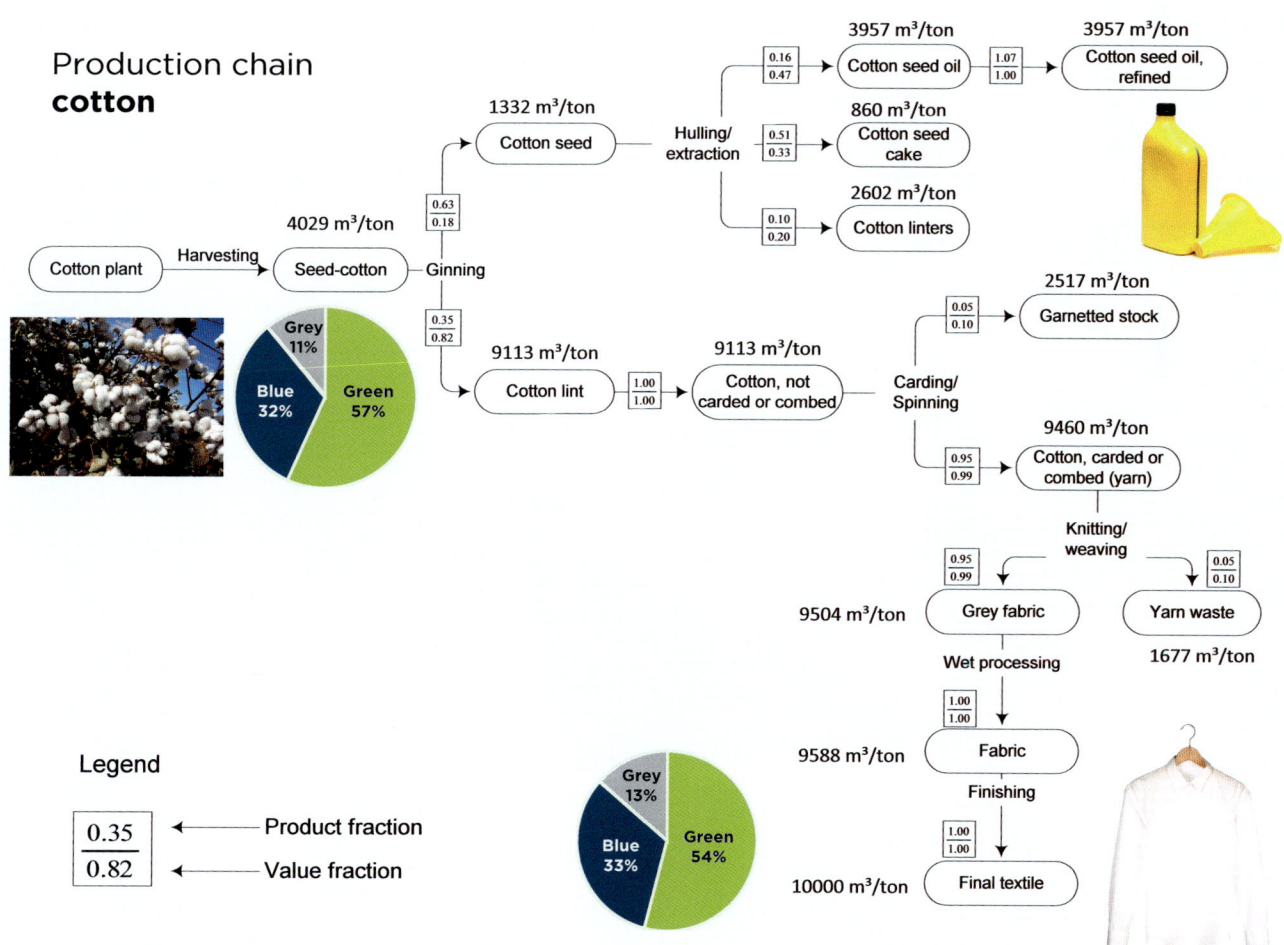

Note: The average water footprint of printed cotton (e.g. a pair of jeans weighing 1 kg) is 11,000 L per kg.
Source: Mekonnen and Hoekstra (2010).

major difficulty, and improved efficiency to meet demand and business-as-usual for supply approaches are expected to fill only approximately 40% of the gap (2030 Water Resources Group, 2009) (Figure 20.7). Scarcity may not only be simply lack of water but also inadequate delivery due to poor infrastructure or water management. Tied in to this economic shortage are ancillary challenges such as ensuring industry access in competitive situations while not coming into conflict with local communities (Pacific Institute, 2007). Resulting allocations may be constraints to find sites for sourcing, production and retail activities, particularly for those industries using large quantities of water or needing high quality water.

Meeting basic water needs

The failure of some governments in developing countries to provide basic water needs for their population places industry in a difficult position with respect to those needs on a human rights basis (Pacific Institute, 2004). The challenge is to balance public and private benefits. Many questions have been raised about the responsibilities of companies to provide or improve water for basic needs while using water for their own purposes. There are risks around this issue to a company's reputation as well as to potential financing from international agencies and institutions.

Determining water budgets

Water scarcity forces industry to understand how much water it really needs. To increase the efficiency of water use in a facility, it is necessary to know its water budget and particularly its losses. This is the baseline for water savings. Industry must know its own water balance – the ratio of the input of water to the output of water (Figure 20.8). Thus the challenge for industry is to establish its water footprint or profile to see where efficiencies may be achieved. This is dependent on good data and a consistent approach to measurement and monitoring.

The combined challenges of water scarcity and water quality generate an associated challenge: how to increase water productivity and prevent pollution. Water productivity appears to decrease with total water consumption, and economic growth usually comes through increased consumption rather than by increased productivity (WWAP, 2003). The focal point of this challenge is how to move to zero discharge. The challenge of water productivity is to do more with less; in other words, to make every drop count. If industry is to react positively to pollution prevention, particularly in tough regulatory regimes, then cleaner production and zero discharge are

---

FIGURE 20.7

Business-as-usual approaches will not meet demand for raw water

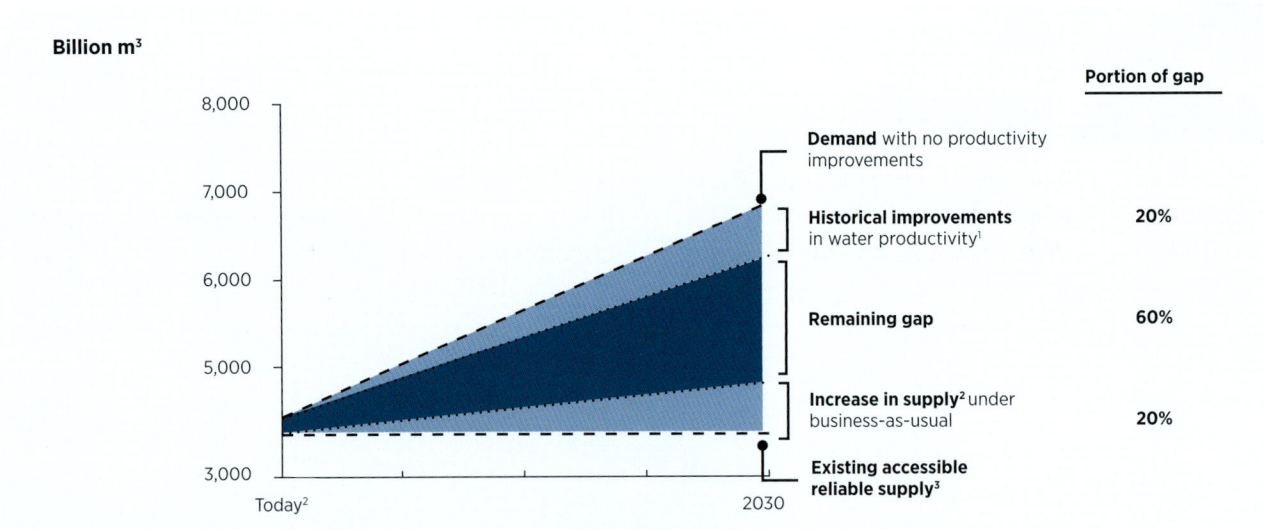

[1] Based on historical agricultural yield growth rates from 1990-2004 from FAOSTAT, agricultural and industrial efficiency improvements from IFPRI.
[2] Total increased capture of raw water through infrastructure buildout, excluding unsustainable extraction.
[3] Supply shown at 90% reliability and includes infrastructure investments scheduled and funded through 2010. Current 90%-reliable supply does not meet avarege demand.
Source: 2030 Water Resources Group (2009, p. 7) (based on the Global Water Supply and Demand model, IFPRI and FAOSTAT).

FIGURE 20.8

Rio Tinto's water balance (2009)

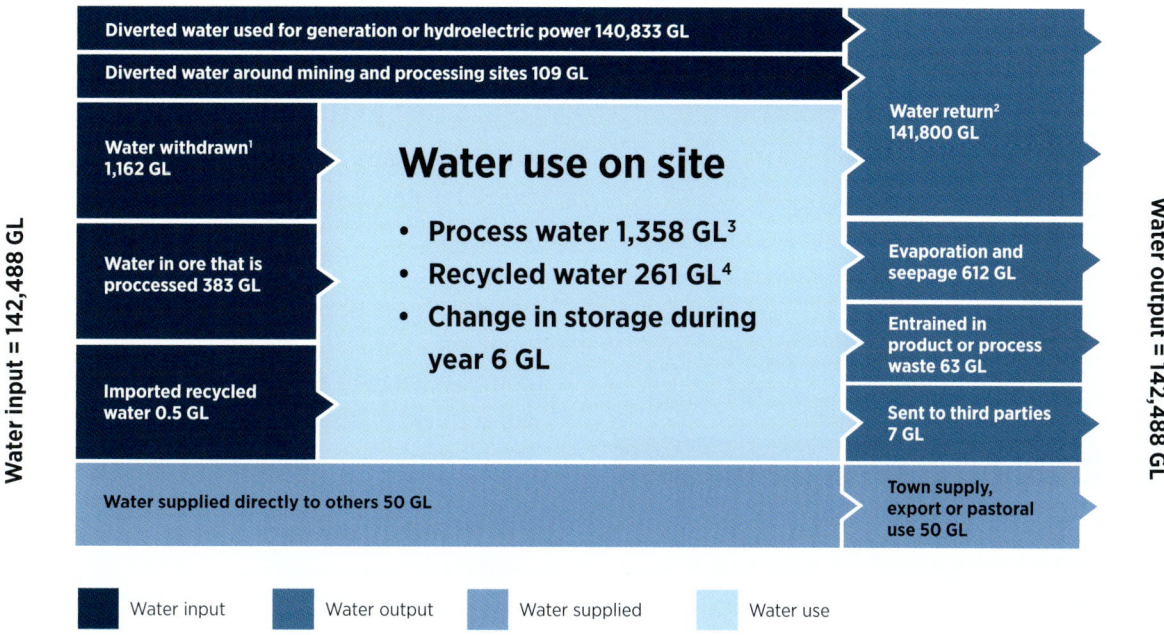

Diverted water used for generation or hydroelectric power 140,833 GL

Diverted water around mining and processing sites 109 GL

Water withdrawn[1] 1,162 GL

Water in ore that is proccessed 383 GL

Imported recycled water 0.5 GL

Water supplied directly to others 50 GL

Water use on site

- Process water 1,358 GL[3]
- Recycled water 261 GL[4]
- Change in storage during year 6 GL

Water return[2] 141,800 GL

Evaporation and seepage 612 GL

Entrained in product or process waste 63 GL

Sent to third parties 7 GL

Town supply, export or pastoral use 50 GL

Water input = 142,488 GL

Water output = 142,488 GL

Water input   Water output   Water supplied   Water use

[1] Including onsite impounded/imported surface, onsite/imported ground water (including dewatering) and marine water
[2] Including process effluent, dewatering water discharged without use and non process water
[3] Including mining (dewatering), milling, washing, power generation, dust suppression etc.
[4] Tailings, sewage or water contaminated in process that has been treated for reuse
[5] The difference between total water input and total water output is 'changed-in storage'.

1 GL = 1 gigalitre of water (1 billion litres)
Source: Rio Tinto (n.d.a).

principal objectives. Similarly, closed-loop production system can offer industries another option for pollution prevention. Individual industries can obtain economic and environmental benefits from applying this principle in their operations; however it is best achieved through industrial eco-parks, where industries from very diverse sectors can make use of by-products, traditionally considered as waste, from other industries into their production process, thereby reducing costs in raw materials and/or reducing treatment and disposal cost (Figure 20.9).

The challenges in water productivity are expressed on a geographical basis in the disparity between high and low income countries (WWAP, 2003, ch. 9). High income users have better water productivity than low income users, and while water productivity of low income users can equal that of high income users, it is generally only on a small scale. As low income countries tend to be in areas of water scarcity, and this

scarcity has become more unpredictable with climate change, the challenge of water productivity correspondingly becomes even greater.

The cost of water

Industry is conditioned to pay little for water, but increasing scarcity will result in higher charges, to which will be added higher charges for treatment and discharge. Some countries have already implemented a different price structure for industry – paying more per unit than the public and paying increasing amounts per unit as more water is used. These impacts on industry will naturally force a response towards greater efficiency of water use, as the economic realities of the cost of water will increase production costs. These effects will have repercussions in the industrialization taking place in developing countries, where water is frequently at a premium, and they may influence the location of new plants.

FIGURE 20.9

The closed-loop production system

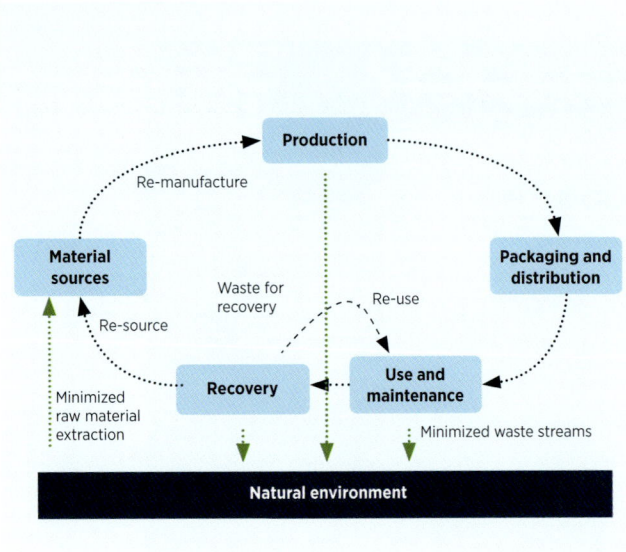

Source: OECD (2009, p. 10).

Small and medium-sized enterprises in low income countries

The economic importance of small and medium enterprises (SMEs) in low income countries is well known. However, the geographical location of the SMEs often causes additional stress on already stressed local supplies of water. The concepts of water productivity and cleaner production are either unknown or sidelined in the effort to make goods and provide jobs. However, the downside is that the markets for the SMEs' goods, which are often in high income countries, have requirements that the manufacture of goods they import be environmentally sustainable. This creates a situation where survival of these SMEs is dependent on the proper, productive and environmentally friendly use of water – a considerable challenge requiring the means and the know-how to move forwards.

20.4.2 Changing management paradigms

Notwithstanding the challenges presented by uncertain water issues, business and industry is still charged with making a profit and return on investment. Actions taken to meet this goal must be carried out in the context of corporate, social and environmental responsibility. The challenge is not to work in isolation from government, the public and other stakeholders, but to turn the situation into a win–win one. There are subchallenges such as obtaining financing, investing in new technology, and improving the reliability and

consistency of the data upon which many decisions are made. There is a need to become risk smart not risk averse.

20.4.3 Minimizing environmental impacts

Industry has impacts on its primary supplies of water and their ecosystems and therefore it has a responsibility to mitigate these impacts for the benefit of all water users and the environment. These impacts can be at a water basin or transboundary scale. Industry creates hotspots (sources) that can impact aquifers and river pathways that can cross several countries and discharge through coastal areas into large marine ecosystems. As the drivers involved become more complex, inter-related and unpredictable, effects and consequent challenges may be magnified over these large areas.

20.5 Opportunities

There are ways to address the issues, risks and challenges of water productivity, but they require implementation. Information without action is not real progress. The overarching challenge for industry is to play its role in halting the unsustainable exploitation and contamination of freshwater resources worldwide (Box 20.1). In meeting this challenge there is an opportunity to increase productivity, efficiency and competitiveness in a sustainable way. This may be summed up as integrated water management (IWM), which takes into account company requirements and the needs and interests of stakeholders and the environment. Through an IWM approach an industry identifies and manages water-related risk and opportunities that affects them either directly or indirectly, this in turn allows them to respond in time to changing trends and have a better business performance in the long run (CBSR, 2010).

20.5.1 Management and strategy

In a broad perspective, the problems surrounding water productivity in industry and the related problems surrounding water globally are inter-related, not isolated, and as such need management, a strategy, planning and action that interconnect solutions for greater effectiveness. Overarching these considerations are the concepts, ideas and visions of new and different ways of considering water and its use that provide the necessary guidance down the chain of implementation. In meeting its challenges industry must first look to management priorities and style, company values and culture to encourage positive response from within its

Water stewardship at Molson Coors

In the beer brewing process, water usage is measured as the total volume of water used for each volume unit of beer produced. Molson Coors' water use ratio is about 4.55 hL/hL. Water is used in the brewing process (the quality of beer is directly tied to the quality of the water used to produce it); for cleaning brew kettles and fermenting and ageing tanks; in the packaging lines (for rinsing bottles and cans before packaging); and for cooling machinery. Also included in the equation is water used in buildings to support the needs of the workforce. The vast majority of cleaning and rinsing water is treated to meet or exceed regulated standards, and then discharged. A small percentage is lost to evaporation.

The industry has established a working group entitled the Beverage Industry Environmental Roundtable (BIER). Formed in August 2006, the objective of this group is to bring together leading global beverage companies to define a common framework for stewardship, drive continuous improvement in industry practices and performance, and inform public policy in the areas of water conservation and resource protection, energy efficiency and climate change mitigation.

Molson Coors scores water usage at each of its breweries to identify strategic ways in which it can use less water in production, thus reducing its impact on the environment and helping enhance water's sustainability. Molson Coors has set the global target to improve water efficiency year over year by 4% (2008–2012). Water data and overall environmental performance data are verified by an independent third party before publication.

In 2009, Molson Coors committed to conducting watershed assessments at each brewery locations. In the United Kingdom (UK) and Canada, it commissioned studies of water resources, water use and water disposal at each facility to be fed into its country strategies and global policy. The study in Canada covers the entire supply chain, including the overall impact Molson has or could have in the communities where it operates.

Source: Global Compact (n.d.).

own sphere. Proactive measures by industry will not only anticipate the future but help to shape it (Pacific Institute, 2007). Innovation, investment and collaboration are key elements; they require a strategic approach rather than the ad hoc solutions more commonly found.

Water footprint

In order to develop a truly successful water strategy industry must have the necessary data available; to be able to evaluate water risks, it is necessary to know the water use in an industry. The customary approach of mass water balance is only part of the picture; water footprints or profiles are increasingly being introduced to estimate an industry's real water use. Estimation of footprints or profiles may involve using a water diagnostic tool and water scenario planning supports (WWAP, 2009, ch. 2, referencing WBCSD, 2006).

The water footprint takes into account all the obvious water content in a product as well as the less obvious inputs and uses of water in production and consumption (virtual water). Complete water footprints can be quite complex; for example, the concept of a water footprint for business adds on the indirect water use

in the producer's supply chain. Thus there is the operational water footprint and the supply chain water footprint. There are also considerations up and down the supply chain, such as the water involved in agricultural raw materials or end-use, if water is involved in utilizing the product (e.g. soap). Therefore, a water footprint reflects the true amount of water used, which may not be immediately apparent from looking at the end product. In addition, 'the ecological or social impact of a water footprint obviously depends not only on the volume of water use, but also on where and when the water is used' (Water Footprint Network, n.d.*a*). All this knowledge can direct strategy for water use to increase its productivity (output per drop) both on the supply and the demand sides (Box 20.2).

Risk assessment

In developing a water strategy a company needs to evaluate its exposure to water risks – including hydrological, economic, social and political factors in different geographical contexts – and plan for them in its decision-making.

Water strategies

Once the issues have been evaluated a company is in a realistic position to adopt a water policy, which is

BOX 20.2

The water footprint of Coca-Cola®

Researchers at the Twente University in the Netherlands in collaboration with Coca-Cola Enterprises Inc. (CCE) and Coca-Cola Europe studied the water footprint of a 0.5 L PET bottle of Coca-Cola produced at CCE's Dongen bottling plant in the Netherlands.

The accounting process began with water used in the supply chain to produce ingredients and other components (e.g. bottles, labels, packing materials). Ingredients include sugar made from sugar beets grown in the Netherlands, carbon dioxide, caramel, phosphoric acid and caffeine. The supply chain water footprint also included overheads, which account for water used to produce the energy that powers the plants and for water used for building materials, vehicles, fuel, office paper and other items not directly related to operations. Water used in operations is the water incorporated into the product as an ingredient and water used in production processes.

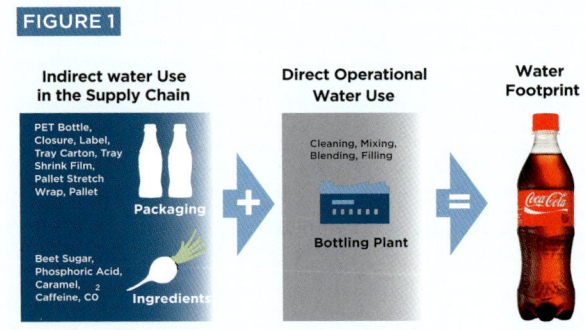

Indirect and direct water footprint components of 0.5 L of Coca-Cola in a PET bottle

The results, including all components, are shown in the second figure. The estimates are that the green water footprint of the 0.5 L Coca-Cola beverage is 15 L, the blue water footprint is 8 L and the grey water footprint is 12 L.

More than two-thirds of the total water footprint comes from green and blue water. The green and blue (consumptive) water footprints are primarily associated with sugar beet production in the supply chain. The sugar beets are largely rainfed (green water) in this water-rich temperate climate, but some external (blue) water supply is required for irrigation. Green water makes up approximately two-thirds of the consumptive water footprint and nearly half of the total water footprint. Blue water accounts for approximately one-quarter (or much less according to a subsequent study) of the total water footprint. Approximately one-third of the total water footprint is grey water, which is associated with the supply chain. A portion of the nitrogen applied as fertilizer to the sugar beet fields is released to receiving waters. Cooling water associated with PET bottle production results in a thermal load, which was considered in the grey water component.

The operational water footprint, 0.4 L, equates to only about 1% of the total water footprint. It is entirely blue water, representing water added as an ingredient. The grey water footprint associated with operations (water used for domestic purposes in the Dongen plant) was determined to be zero because all wastewater is treated to meet or exceed wastewater treatment standards in a public wastewater treatment plant and returned to the environment under The Coca-Cola Company's 'Recycle' commitment.

The supply chain overhead water footprint was calculated and found to be negligible. Before the study, there was recognition that the overhead component is a part of the overall water footprint of a product, but it was unclear how relevant it was.

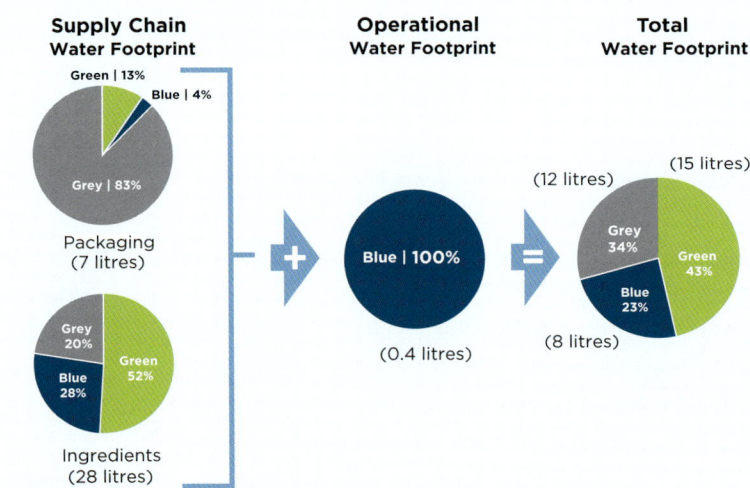

Water footprint of 0.5 L of Coca-Cola in a PET bottle produced in Dongen, the Netherlands. The green water footprint refers to the consumption of green water resources (rainwater stored in the soil as moisture); the blue water footprint refers to consumption of blue water sources (surface and groundwater); and the grey water footprint refers to pollution and is defined as the volume of freshwater that is required to assimilate the load of pollutants based on existing ambient water quality standards.

Source: The Coca-Cola Company and The Nature Conservancy (2010, pp. 11, 12 [figures, and pp. 11-15 text adapted]).

likely to embrace strategies for everything from corporate values to communication. These strategies may include:

- Promoting CSR and environmental sustainability (Figure 20.10). These principles include recognizing environmental inter-relationships such as those between water and energy and links to air emissions and climate change.
- Encouraging a paradigm shift to 'cradle-to-cradle' industrial operations – providing a service to customers to allow them to use a product and return it to the manufacturer for recycling (McDonough and Braungart, 2002; WWAP, 2006, ch. 8). Waste then has value as raw material for other production processes.
- Using the Precautionary Principle to promote action, develop options and assist decisions.
- Introducing EMS. The company culture should be such that it promotes the use of ISO 14000, best environmental practices (BEP) and best available techniques (BAT). Internal documents should reflect clarity and certainty in their application and they require regular updating with the latest science. A commitment to continuous improvement on water issues makes a strong statement, as does regularly reporting performance.
- Setting measurable goals and targets with respect to water efficiency, conservation and impacts.
- Decoupling material and energy consumption and integrating the need for energy with the requirements for water.
- Communicating frequently and effectively with the public and local stakeholders regarding the economic and environmental benefits of various industrial policies, strategies and measures to increase awareness, encourage confidence, and gain support and cooperation in issues surrounding water (Marsalek et al., 2002). Successful implementation of policies depends on a proactive, rather than a reactive, response from industry. Stakeholder engagement and direct participation can moderate conflicts.
- Collaborating with government agencies. In the attempt to implement better management and more productive ways of using water in industry, it is not the technical know-how that is the main impediment, but the framework within which to promote, encourage and accomplish increased water productivity. Alignment of corporate strategy with local, regional and national agencies is beneficial (Pacific Institute, 2007). If industrial growth and

environmental protection are seen as compatible then industry may adopt such measures for better business rather than compliance reasons (WWAP, 2003, ch. 9). Beneficial actions may then be taken at a plant or company scale, with or without regulations (Box 20.3).

- Becoming involved with organizations such as the CEO Water Mandate (UN Global Compact, 2011) the World Business Council for Sustainable Development (WBCSD, 2006), and, through the United Nations Industrial Development Organization (UNIDO)'s role in the United Nations (UN) Global Compact Inter-Agency Team, to assist particularly in the area of Supply Chain and Watershed Management (UN Global Compact, 2011), which involves:
  ○ Encouraging and engaging suppliers to improve their water conservation, quality monitoring, wastewater treatment and recycling practices
  ○ Building capacities to analyse and respond to watershed risk
  ○ Encouraging and facilitating suppliers in conducting assessments of water usage and impacts
  ○ Sharing water sustainability practices – established and emerging – with suppliers

FIGURE 20.10

The evolution of sustainable manufacturing concepts and practices

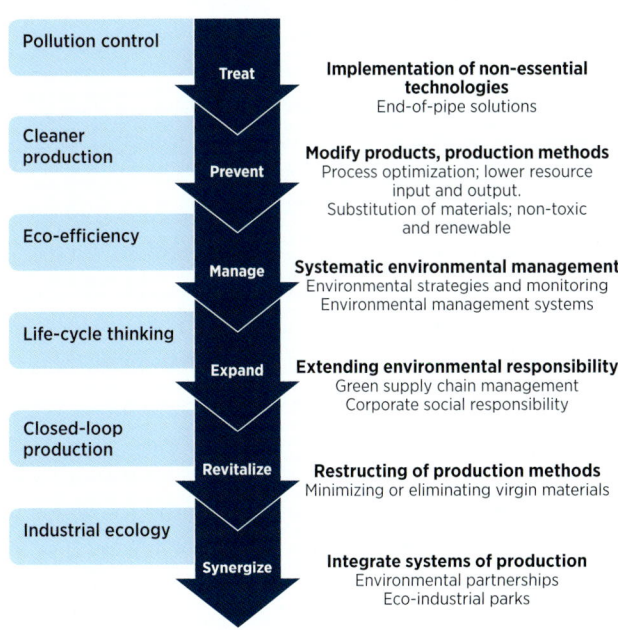

Source: OECD (2009, p. 10).

Industry–government collaboration: Rio Tinto and the Western Australian Water Corporation

The Rio Tinto HIsmelt® site is just south of Perth in Western Australia. The new iron smelting technology is more efficient than conventional methods but requires cooling water. An agreement was made with the state water utility to use treated wastewater rather than obtain potable water from the city's system, which supplies water to 1.5 million people.

The Water Corporation was considering the feasibility of building an effluent treatment plant and Rio Tinto's offer to buy the treated water for the HIsmelt facility ensured enough demand to make this plant viable. As a result, the Water Corporation was able to commission the project.

The HIsmelt facility runs on the community's recycled wastewater, which is finally evaporated. The Water Corporation has a long-term client and Rio Tinto has access to a ready supply of water, cleaned and treated to a high industrial standard. Moreover, local water supply is preserved and there is reduced effluent discharge to the ocean.

Sources: Pacific Institute (2007, p. 35); Rio Tinto (n.d.b).

○ Encouraging major suppliers to report regularly on progress achieved related to goals
• Partnering with intergovernmental organizations such as the UN to benefit regions in distress and promote advances in technology.

20.5.2 Implementation and innovation

Industry has many opportunities to address the challenges it faces and turn them into win–win situations with other major stakeholders such as governments, intergovernmental organizations, non-governmental organizations (NGOs), the private investment sector, academia and the public. In this context, the following are some of the initiatives that industry has underway and should be reinforced and others that might be brought into play.

Decreasing water use and increasing water productivity

The obvious first step for industry is to reduce water use by conservation and recycling as well as by discharge reduction and quality improvement. Measures to these ends include:
• Conducting a water audit and developing a water footprint.

• Using zero discharge and water optimization techniques to drive industrial processes (Das, 2005). This involves integrating supply side and demand side needs and considerations. Zero discharge is used to nullify water footprints by full recycling and no waste and changes the balance of the water productivity equation (Water Footprint Network, n.d.b). In moving towards zero discharge, wastewater streams are converted into useful inputs for other industries and industrial clusters. Zero discharge is a step-by-step process that industry implements through strategic corporate planning leading to design and implementation. It not only influences industry on a local scale (cleaner production and increased profits), the accumulated results also have basin, transboundary and wider impacts.
• Employing water recycling and the use of reclaimed water where possible to dovetail with zero discharge.
• Using water loss management to locate, measure and repair the sometimes huge water losses from old underground infrastructure. This might include development of surface leak detection systems, robotic and video pipeline monitoring technologies, high-precision flow monitoring and metering technologies, and pipeline rehabilitation systems (TSG, 2009).
• Providing full and consistent monitoring and reporting of the performance of applied technologies used in industry, in terms of both effectiveness and cost. Real-time monitoring of processes has distinct advantages in catching problems and contamination early and accompanying data management systems are equally important (TSG, 2009).

Introducing new technology

BAT can incur significant cost and may take time, so transition periods are necessary and implementation by regulation needs a thoughtful approach. The objective is to find the most effective technology that is technically viable, can be implemented economically and is reasonably accessible. Meeting this objective may involve:
• Adopting new green technology and incorporating natural treatment systems. It is felt by some that simpler approaches, such as sand filtration and enhanced wetland treatment, may be easier and cheaper to implement than more common traditional treatment technologies and may play a significant role in helping solve the vast majority of the world's water shortages (TSG, 2009).

UNIDO MED-TEST integrated approach

MED-TEST is a UNIDO green industry initiative supported by the Global Environment Facility (GEF) and the Italian Government to address priority hotspots of industrial pollution identified in the Mediterranean Strategic Action Plan (SAP-MED). MED-TEST is a component of the Strategic Partnership for the Mediterranean Large Marine Ecosystem (LME) of the United Nations Environment Programme (UNEP)-Mediterranean Action Plan (MAP) aiming to support governments in implementing national strategies for reducing industrial discharges. The MED-TEST project (2009–2011) targets Egypt, Morocco and Tunisia, with the potential to be extended to other countries of the MED region.

Enterprises of the South Mediterranean Region are facing numerous challenges in their effort to maintain or increase their competitiveness on the local market, access international markets with good quality products, comply with environmental standards and reduce their operational costs. The MED-TEST project has been designed to assist enterprises in dealing with these challenges and in building a long-term sustainable business strategy.

TEST (transfer of environmentally sound technology) builds on management of change within each level of the management pyramid: operational, management system and strategic. The TEST approach integrates and combines the essential elements of traditional tools such as cleaner production assessment (CPA), environmental management systems (EMS), environmental management accounting (EMA), technology transfer and corporate social responsibility (CSR), applied on the basis of a comprehensive diagnosis of enterprise needs (initial review).

The introduction of the TEST integrated approach at the enterprise level follows this sequence:
- The existing situation is improved by better management of existing processes
- The introduction of new cleaner technology (or if not sufficient, of optimized end-of-pipe solutions) is considered
- The lessons learned from each TEST project's implementation is reflected in the respective company's business strategy

Project task	Expected results
Capacity-building for national partners	National capacities built and hands-on experience gained by local experts on TEST integrated approach
Demonstration projects at pilot industries	• Existing processes optimized • Economic benefits and sustainabillity of TEST demonstrated • Reduction of polution discharges into the Mediterranean Sea • Investment portfolio for clean technology
Dissemination and replication at national and regional level	A motivated cadre of professionals from the South Mediterranean region will become engaged in commercially based TEST replication activities

Outline of the MED-TEST project

TEST tools and the management pyramid

Source: UNIDO (n.d.b).

- Continuing and expanding the use of the transfer of environmentally sound technology (TEST) methodology (UNIDO, n.d.*a*) in conjunction with environmental management accounting (EMA) (Box 20.4).
- Working with government and academia in joint research programs to develop new technology.

Employing eco-innovation

The development of industrial ecology as a part of sustainable development is a relatively recent concept used to look at the inter-relationship between industrial and economic systems and natural systems (Das, 2005). Industrial ecology connects with zero discharge in restructuring industry to eliminate waste as an alternative to end-of-pipe solutions (Figure 20.11). Some points for industry include:

- Incorporate industrial ecology and design for environment (DFE) into industrial design and overall planning (Das, 2005).
- Relocate to eco-industrial parks. This mutual grouping of industries to reuse wastewater has many apparent advantages, but there are obstacles to be overcome, such as corporate reluctance to partner with unrelated industries and the fear of dependency on a single water supplier (Das, 2005). In older areas not amenable to such groupings, the

transportation of wastewater may be a large problem. New industries with large water demands that do not require drinking water quality may need to locate near existing or new sewage treatment plants.
- Invest in environment and ecological restoration. Such programmes may include investment in upstream watershed restoration and in supply chain areas, which provides a win–win situation for business and communities and may have a more favourable cost–benefit than technological solutions (Pacific Institute, 2007).
- Adopt a life-cycle approach, whereby all stages of the products life is assessed, including raw material extraction, manufacture, distribution, use and disposal. This may be in the context of closed-loop systems. For example, the existing UNIDO programme for chemical leasing provides a big incentive to zero discharge (Chemical Leasing, n.d.*a*). It also improves the efficient use of chemicals and has economic and environmental benefits by closing the loop between the supplier and user of chemicals (Figure 20.12): the supplier sells the function of the chemicals and together with the user is involved in managing the life cycle of the material.

FIGURE 20.11

Conceptual relationships between sustainable manufacturing and eco-innovation

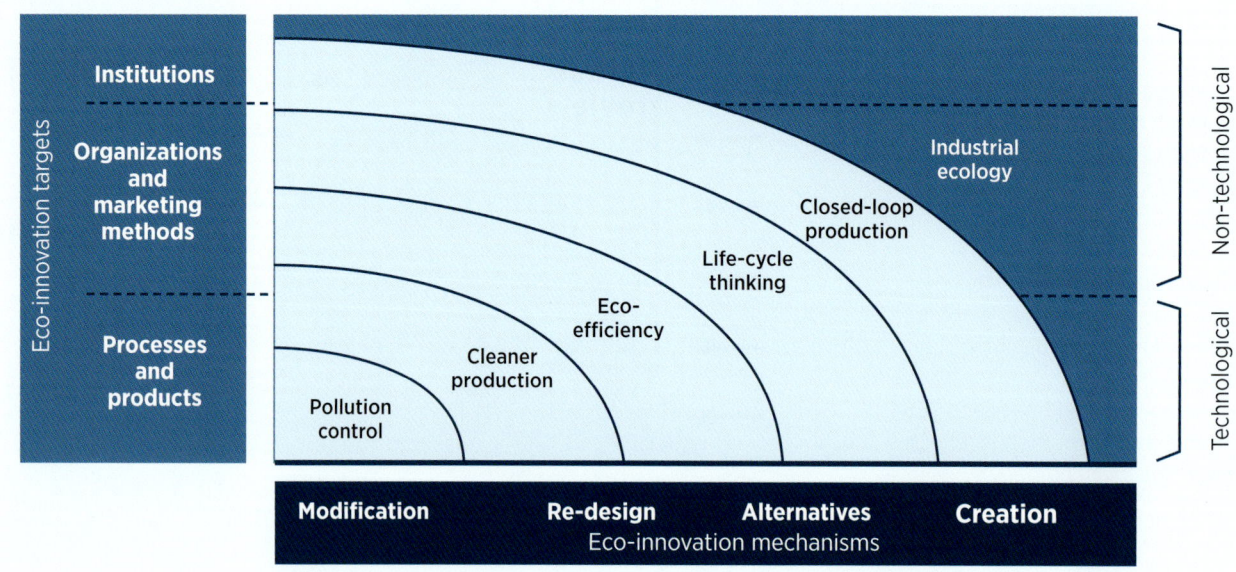

Source: OECD (2009, p. 15).

FIGURE 20.12

The concept of chemical leasing

Chemical producer

supply, no sale

Chemical user

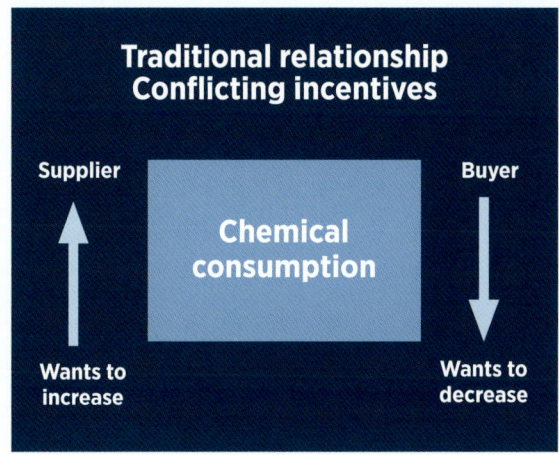

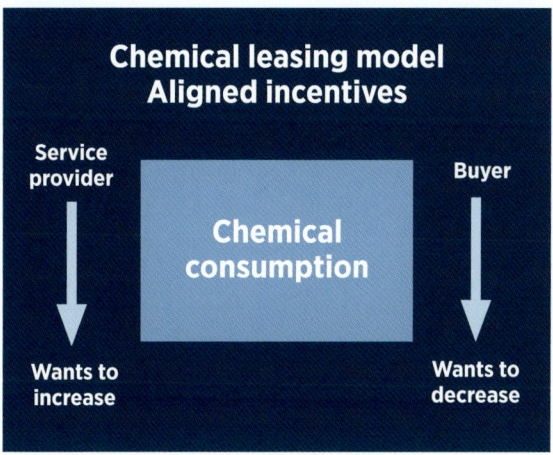

Environment:
emission reduction

Economy:
added value

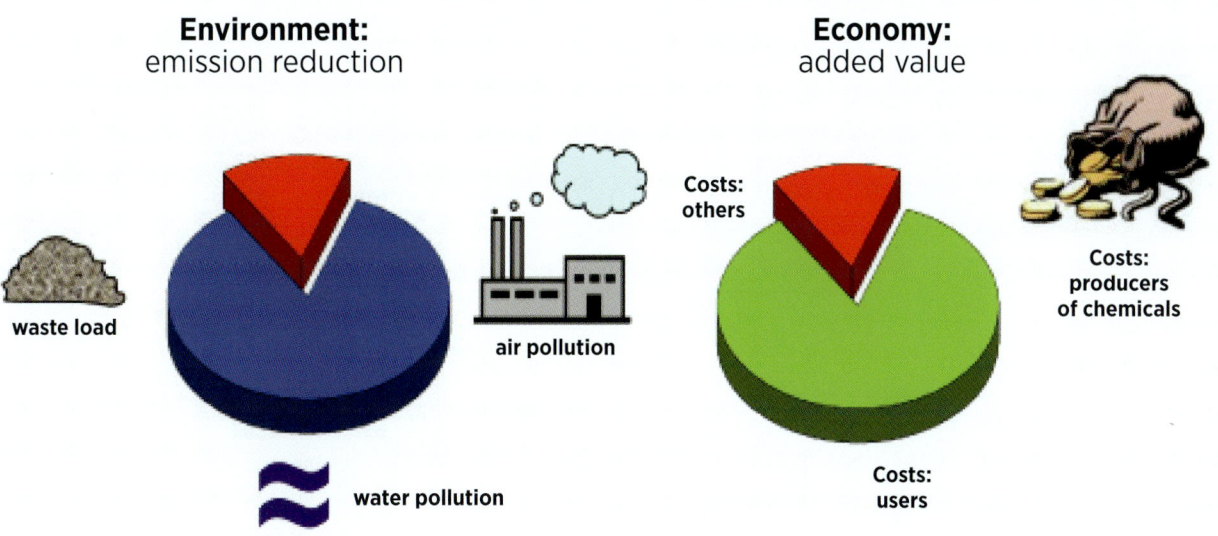

Source: Chemical Leasing (n.d.b).

II

References

2030 Water Resources Group. 2009. *Charting our Water Future: Executive Summary.* 2030 Water Resources Group. http://www.mckinsey.com/App_Media/Reports/Water/Charting_Our_Water_Future_Exec%20Summary_001.pdf

CBSR (Canadian Business for Social Responsibility). 2010. *The Business Case for an Integrated Approach to Water Management.* Vancouver, BC, CBSR. http://www.cbsr.ca/sites/default/files/file/Water%20Guide%20-%20Final%20version-v3.pdf

Chemical Leasing. n.d.*a Concept of Chemical Leasing: Involvement of UNIDO.* http://www.chemicalleasing.com/sub/concept/invunido.htm (Accessed 8 August 2011.)

----. n.d.*b Concept of Chemical Leasing.* http://www.chemicalleasing.com/sub/concept.htm (Accessed 8 August 2011.)

The Coca-Cola Company and The Nature Conservancy. 2010. *Product Water Footprint Assessments: Practical Application in Corporate Water Stewardship.* http://www.thecoca-colacompany.com/presscenter/TCCC_TNC_WaterFootprintAssessments.pdf

Das, T. K. 2005. *Towards Zero Discharge: Innovative Methodology and Technologies for Process Pollution Prevention.* New York, John Wiley & Sons.

FAO (Food and Agriculture Organization of the United Nations). 2007. *Making Every Drop Count.* Press Release, 14 February. Rome, FAO. http://www.fao.org/newsroom/en/news/2007/1000494/index.html

Grobicki, A. 2007. *The Future of Water Use in Industry.* Paper presented at the UNIDO Technology Foresight Summit, Budapest, 27–29 September 2007.

GWI (Global Water Intelligence). 2008. A *New Virtual Reality.* Vol. 9, issue 9. http://www.globalwaterintel.com/archive/9/9/analysis/a-new-virtual-reality.html

Mekonnen, M. M. and Hoekstra, A. Y. 2010. *The Green, Blue and Grey Water Footprint of Crops and Derived Crop Products.* Value of Water Research Report Series No. 47, Paris, UNESCO-IHE.

Hoekstra, A. Y. and Chapagain, A. K. 2007. Water footprints of nations: Water use by people as a function of their consumption pattern. *Water Resources Management,* Vol. 21, pp. 35–48.

IPCC (Intergovernmental Panel on Climate Change). 2008. Technical Paper on Climate Change and Water. Doc. 13. Finalized at the 370th Session of the IPCC Bureau. Geneva, IPCC.

Marsalek, J., Schaefer, K., Excall, K., Brannen, L. and Aidun, B. 2002. *Water Reuse and Recycling.* CCME Linking Water Science to Policy Workshop Series, Report No. 3. Winnipeg, Man., Canadian Council of Ministers of the Environment (CCME). http://www.ccme.ca/assets/pdf/water_reuse_wkshp_rpt_e.pdf

McDonough, W. and Braungart, M. 2002. *Cradle to Cradle: Remaking the Way We Make Things.* New York, North Point Press.

NCASI (National Council for Air and Stream Improvement). 2010. *Water Profile of the Canadian Forest Products Industry.* Technical Bulletin No. 975. Research Triangle Park, NC, NCASI. http://www.ncasi.org//Publications/Detail.aspx?id=3280

OECD (Organisation for Economic Co-operation and Development). 2009. *Sustainable Manufacturing and Eco-Innovation: Framework, Practices and Measurement* (Synthesis Report). Paris, OECD. http://www.oecd.org/dataoecd/15/58/43423689.pdf

Pacific Institute. 2004. *Freshwater Resources: Managing the Risks Facing the Private Sector.* Oakland, Calif., Pacific Institute. http://www.pacinst.org/reports/business_risks_of_water/business_risks_of_water.pdf

----. 2007. *At the Crest of a Wave: A Proactive Approach to Corporate Water Strategy.* Oakland, Calif., Pacific Institute. http://www.pacinst.org/reports/crest_of_a_wave/crest_of_a_wave.pdf

Payne, J. G. 2007. *Matching Water Quality to Use Requirements.* Paper presented at the UNIDO Technology Foresight Summit, Budapest, 27–29 September 2007.

Rio Tinto. n.d.*a Water.* http://www.riotinto.com/ourapproach/17214_water_17309.asp (Accessed 8 August 2011.)

----. n.d.*b Saving Water by Running on Recycled Waste.* http://www.riotinto.com/ourapproach/17194_features_5898.asp (Accessed 8 August 2011.)

SABMiller Plc and WWF-UK. 2009. *Water Footprinting: Identifying and Addressing Water Risks in the Value Chain.* Technical report. Woking/Surrey, UK, SABMiller Plc/World Wide Fund for Nature UK.

Shiklomanov I. A. 1999. *World Water Resources: Modern Assessment and Outlook for the 21st Century* (Summary of *World Water Resources at the Beginning of the 21st Century,* prepared in the framework of the IHP UNESCO). Saint Petersburg, Federal Service of Russia for Hydrometeorology and Environment Monitoring, State Hydrological Institute.

Statistics Canada. 2007. *EnviroStats, Fall 2007,* Vol. 1, No. 2. Ottawa, Ont., Statistics Canada. http://www.statcan.gc.ca/pub/16-002-x/16-002-x2007002-eng.pdf

TSG (TechKNOWLEDGEy Strategic Group). 2009. *The State of the Water Industry.* Boulder, CO, TSG. http://www.tech-strategy.com/index.htm

UN Global Compact. 2010. *Corporate Responsibility 2010.* New York, United Nations. http://www.unglobalcompact.org/Issues/Environment/CEO_Water_Mandate/endorsingCEOs.html

UN Global Compact. 2011. *The CEO Water Mandate.* New York, United Nations (UN) Global Compact Office. http://www.unglobalcompact.org/docs/news_events/8.1/Ceo_water_mandate.pdf

UN Global Compact. n.d. Website. http://www.unglobalcompact.org/Issues/Environment/CEO_Water_Mandate/index.html (Accessed 8 August 2011.)

UNDP (United Nations Development Programme). 2006. *Human Development Report 2006: Beyond Scarcity – Power, Poverty and the Global Water Crisis.* New York, Palgrave Macmillan.

UNEP (United Nations Environment Programme). 2008. *Vital Water Graphics: An Overview of the State of the World's Fresh and Marine Waters,* 2nd edn. Nairobi, UNEP. http://www.unep.org/dewa/vitalwater/article48.html

UNIDO (United Nations Industrial Development Organization). n.d.*a Test Approach.* http://www.unido.org/index.php?id=7677 (Accessed 8 August 2011.)

––––. n.d.*b Towards Clean Competitive Industry* (Brochure). http://www.unido.org/fileadmin/user_media/Services/Environmental_Management/Water_Management/09-84752_brochure_final.PDF (Accessed 8 August 2011.)

Water Footprint Network. n.d.*a Corporate Water Footprints.* http://www.waterfootprint.org/?page=files/CorporateWaterFootprintAccountingFramework

––––. n.d.*b Glossary.* http://www.waterfootprint.org/?page=files/Glossary (Accessed 8 August 2011.)

WBCSD (World Business Council for Sustainable Development). 2006. *Business in the World of Water: WBCSD Water Scenarios to 2025.* Washington, DC, WBCSD. http://www.wbcsd.org/Plugins/DocSearch/details.asp?DocTypeId=25&ObjectId=MTk2MzY&URLBack=%2Ftemplates%2FTemplateWBCSD2%2Flayout.asp%3Ftype%3Dp%26MenuId%3DODU%26doOpen%3D1%26ClickMenu%3DRightMenu%26CurPage%3D11%26SortOrder%3Dpubdate%2520desc

World Bank. 2010. *World Development Indicators 2010.* Washington, DC, The World Bank. http://data.worldbank.org/data-catalog/world-development-indicators/wdi-2010

WWAP (World Water Assessment Programme). 2003. *World Water Development Report 1: Water for People, Water for Life.* Paris/New York, UNESCO/Berghahn Books.

––––. 2006. *World Water Development Report 2: Water: A Shared Responsibility.* Paris/New York, UNESCO/Berghahn Books.

––––. 2009. *World Water Development Report 3: Water in A Changing World.* Paris/London, UNESCO/Earthscan.

––––. n.d. *Facts and Figures: Water and Industry.* http://www.unesco.org/water/wwap/facts_figures/water_industry.shtml (Accessed 8 August 2011.)

CHAPTER 21
Ecosystems

UNEP
—

Authors Tim Jones (DJ Environmental), Tim Davies (DJ Environmental), Thomas Chiramba (UNEP) and Elizabeth Khaka (UNEP)
Contributors Daniele Perrot-Maitre (UNEP), Renate Fleiner (UNEP), Peter Bjoernsen (UNEP-DHI Centre on Water and Environment), David Coates (Secretariat of the CBD), Anne-Leonore Boffi (WBCSD) and Sarah Davidson (The Nature Conservancy)

Ecosystems can be managed so as to sustain water availability and its quality – services provided by ecosystems – and thereby help achieve water security. The continued availability of water (of sufficient quantity and quality) depends on the continued healthy functioning of the ecosystems that supply it, while the ecosystems themselves are dependent on receiving sufficient water. This can be summed up as 'nature for water security; water security for nature', a phrase that neatly encapsulates the linkages that decision-makers have to take into account.

Ecosystems provide a wide range of services (e.g. food and fibre, nutrient recycling, climate regulation, flood and drought regulation, and tourism and recreation), all of which are underpinned by water security. Water use by all is dependent on ecosystem functioning, as are the other natural resource-based goods and services that support human society. Maintaining the ability of ecosystems to support ecosystem services is therefore critical for socio-economic well-being and sustainable development.

Managing ecosystem services is about trade-offs. Trade-offs are not necessarily about choosing one benefit over another. They are as much about sustainable multiple benefits and balanced investments to achieve an optimal outcome.

Sustainable development, including water security, is dependent on maintaining ecosystem services. Ecosystem management is therefore key.

Many ecosystem services are not generally considered in economic planning but can generate very high economic values. They are often considered as being provided free of charge by nature, but in many cases this is incorrect because they can be expensive to rehabilitate or replace artificially when degraded or lost. They are also finite and can be over-used.

There is an urgent need to incorporate ecosystem-based thinking into water governance. Water allocation needs to be based on sustainable supply, which is determined primarily by ecosystem boundaries, and not on demand.

Sustaining and restoring ecosystems is an essential response to the increased risks and uncertainty posed by climate change.

Risks and uncertainties arising from natural disasters such as floods, landslides and droughts (including those triggered by extreme storms, earthquakes and tsunamis) can be reduced by maintaining or restoring natural infrastructure. The economic benefits of reducing this vulnerability are substantial through both reducing the frequency and severity of impacts and creating more stable conditions post impact.

As a consequence of escalating pressures, ecosystems and their services continue to be degraded and lost. This increases risk. Freshwater ecosystems are the most threatened of all. The ability of ecosystems to continue providing the water resources services that we depend on is being severely compromised, with already catastrophic effects for humanity.

Sustaining or restoring ecosystems to ensure continued availability of the ecosystem services on which we depend can be a cost-effective and more sustainable solution than traditional approaches to achieving water security. Natural infrastructure solutions should be part of all options considered, alongside physical infrastructure, and assessments should factor in the co-benefits on offer, which are often high with natural solutions.

The need is to make ecosystem-based approaches mainstream under an improved and more holistic policy and management framework that capitalizes on the benefits on offer to help us achieve more sustainable solutions.

21.1 The challenges

Ecosystems are at the heart of the global water cycle. All freshwater on earth is ultimately dependent on their continued healthy functioning. Ecosystems provide a spectrum of services that benefit human society in all regions of the world, including the essential regulation of water quantity, mitigation of extremes of flooding and drought, and preservation of water quality. Ecosystems also cycle the water on which they themselves depend, thereby underpinning all terrestrial ecosystem services, such as food production, climate regulation, carbon storage and nutrient recycling. This water cycle also significantly influences the functioning of estuaries and deltas, including the significant services they provide, such as regulating land formation, coastal protection and food from fisheries.

Ecosystem loss and degradation usually results in a reduction in the delivery of these water-related services. The services previously provided by nature often have to be substituted by engineered solutions (e.g. flood control structures or water treatment facilities), usually at great economic investment and operational cost and with low sustainability. Changes in land use can significantly alter the availability of water; for example, deforestation has an impact on surface water availability and quality. Likewise, land cover depends on continued water availability; for example, forests are dependent on groundwater. Maintaining the extent and healthy functioning of ecosystems should be an integral part of dealing with water security issues. Using natural infrastructure can offer more cost effective and sustainable solutions either instead of, or in parallel with, hard engineered approaches. The challenge is to integrate ecosystem-based thinking and management approaches and water and land use planning in all sectors.

Historically, ecosystems have been treated as unproductive users of water by some groups. At the other end of the spectrum, many groups have advocated attention to them based on biodiversity, protection and conservation arguments, often articulated abstractly with regard to pressing development issues. Fortunately, perceptions are shifting towards managing human interactions with ecosystems (the environment) to support water-related development goals.

The case for ecosystem-based solutions in water policy and land and water management is supported by considerable successful local practice. The challenge is to mainstream the approach as the provider of economically and environmentally sustainable water management solutions. As recognized by the Fifth World Water Forum (Istanbul, March 2009), there needs to be a paradigm shift from 'Water for Nature' to 'Nature for Water'. This requires that decision-makers:

- understand that the availability of appropriate quantities of water of sufficient quality is a service provided by ecosystems and therefore sustaining or restoring ecosystem infrastructure is a tool to achieve water security;
- are fully aware of the direct or indirect dependence of most, if not all, socio-economic sectors, on the maintenance of sustainable ecosystem services and the nature of those services;
- understand the factors that are putting ecosystem functioning at risk;
- value ecosystem services properly, including through calculation of the economic costs of replacing them with engineered solutions;
- implement transparent and impartial policy development and management that recognizes that ecosystems can promote cost-effective solutions with the added potential to deliver multiple benefits for sustainable development; and
- implement the changes necessary to put the solutions into practice.

21.2 The role of ecosystems in regulating water quantity and quality

A simplified introduction to water ecosystems was provided in the first edition of the *World Water Development Report* (WWAP, 2003), with a focus on wetlands and freshwater components of ecosystems such as streams, rivers, lakes and marshes. This introduction needs considerable expanding to include other ecosystem components such as forests, grasslands and soils that also play a significant role in the ecosystems.

Surface vegetation (land cover) regulates runoff of water as well as soil erosion at the land surface. Plant leaves influence how rainfall reaches the ground and their roots help infiltration of water into soils. This significantly reduces erosion, stabilizes slopes (reducing land-slides), potentially reduces flood risks, and sustains soil moisture and the recharge of groundwater. Plants also take up water from the soil and release it back into the atmosphere as water vapour (transpiration), which can have a significant influence on local, regional and even global rainfall patterns. The benefits of this process are most obvious in regions where extensive tracts of original forest cover remain, such as the Amazon and Congo basins. Removal of this vegetation can reduce local, regional and global rainfall. But the relationships are complex; for example, planting of non-native tree species with high water requirements, particularly in dry areas, can lead to groundwater depletion. Proposals for extensive changes in vegetation cover should always be subject to rigorous assessment of the impacts on water cycling.

Wetlands – such as swamps, marshes, peatlands and shallow lakes – play perhaps the most obvious role in the water cycle, as they by definition permanently or intermittently store water. For example, floodplain wetlands store floodwater and slow its flow, helping reduce flood risk downstream. Wetlands also regulate nutrients, sediments and other potential pollutants, acting as an effective natural water treatment infrastructure (Box 21.1).

Mountain ecosystems comprise a complex mosaic of snowfields, glaciers, bare rock, boulder fields, screes, streams, rivers, lakes, grasslands and forests, and are the source of many of the world's major river systems. The Himalayan massif alone supplies the Brahmaputra, Ganges, Indus, Mekong and Yangtze rivers, among other major river systems in Asia, providing water, year round, to approximately one billion people (Rao et al., 2008).

BOX 21.1

Wetlands as water treatment infrastructure: Kolkata, India

Kolkata city generates some 600 million L of sewage and wastewater every day. The manmade East Kolkata Wetlands was declared a Ramsar site in 2002 for its use of this 125 km² (12,500 ha) area for sewage treatment, fish farming (4,000 ha) and irrigated agriculture (6,000 ha). Waste is pumped into the fish ponds of the East Kolkata Wetlands where biodegradation has a cumulative efficiency in reducing biological oxygen demand of more than 80% and coliform bacteria reduction exceeds 99.99% on average. The wetlands also provide about one-third (11,000 metric tons) of the city's annual fish demand and water from them is used to supply rice paddies (yielding 15,000 metric tons of rice per annum) and supports vegetable production.

Source: Department of Environment, Government of West Bengal, India (2007).

21.2.1 Ecosystems as water infrastructure

The term 'ecosystem infrastructure' has been introduced to acknowledge that ecosystems can, and do, perform similar functions to conventional engineered water infrastructure. Ecosystem infrastructure is now commonly used to address water quality needs (Box 21.2). A functioning floodplain moderates peak flows by allowing the water to spread out over a wide area, at the same time enabling sediments to settle; removing floodplains requires their benefits to be replaced by engineered flood and sediment control measures. Investment in the maintenance of 'soft' ecosystem infrastructure needs to be seen as an equally valid option to investing in 'hard' engineered infrastructure. In many cases, the former will prove to be many times more cost effective than the latter, while also providing additional benefits such as support for fisheries, tourism and biodiversity. But the interactions between landform, land cover, climate and the water cycle are complex and location-specific, and solutions for a particular situation require targeted investigation (Emerton and Bos, 2004).

21.2.2 Water allocation and environmental flows

Ecosystems are themselves dependent on receiving sufficient water for their continued functioning. Key elements for water allocation to sustain that functioning include:

- Assessments based on the economic values of water-related ecosystem services and trade-offs between users
- Adequate knowledge of how local and regional ecosystems underpin water security including water quantity, quality and timing for both ecosystem and direct human needs
- A participatory, scale appropriate approach
- Building water governance capacity
- Allocation decisions to be based upon managing and protecting *supply*, rather than simply responding to *demand*

The quantity of water needed to maintain all of the water-dependent or water-related ecosystem services that are required in a given area is often referred to as the 'environmental flow' (Dyson et al., 2008). However, current approaches to environmental flow are too often restricted to considering surface-water flows, in particular, minimum flow requirements for rivers (Box 21.3). They also need to consider groundwater, soil moisture and evapo-transpiration components necessary to sustain the water cycle.

21.2.3 Economic valuation of ecosystem services

Assigning economic values to water-related and water-dependent ecosystem services is one of the most effective means of enabling investments and operational costs to be directly compared (Box 21.4). It also is important to shed light on the gender dimensions of development because reliance on different ecosystem services varies considerably between genders (and economic classes). (See Chapter 23 for a treatment of ecosystem services within a water valuation framework.)

The fact that water underpins *all* ecosystem services generates high values when the value of water is calculated in this fashion. But amongst the full suite of ecosystem services there are those that relate more obviously and directly to water as a resource (e.g. flood mitigation and water quality). Valuing ecosystem services is sometimes regarded as difficult; but for some, it is relatively simple. The costs of flood impacts, for example, and the investments in, and operational costs of, artificial flood-control structures are frequently well known and often reflect the value of flood-mitigation services that ecosystem infrastructure previously provided. Likewise, the loss of clean water as an ecosystem service is partly reflected in costs of artificial water treatment or the economic impacts of poor water quality.

Advances in the economic valuation of ecosystem services have been made over the past 20 years and a range of techniques can now be used in practice: these are summarized by Emerton and Bos (2004), Emerton (2005) and De Groot et al. (2006). TEEB (2009a) provides a comprehensive overview of the topic, including noting the reliance of the poor on these services directly. TEEB (2009b) concluded, *inter alia*, that there is a compelling cost–benefit case for public investment in ecological infrastructure (especially restoring and conserving forests, mangroves, river basins, wetlands, etc.), particularly because of its significant potential as a means of adaptation to climate change. Even for many terrestrial ecosystems (such as forests), values related to water services outstrip more conspicuous benefits (such as timber products and carbon storage). For example, TEEB (2009b) provides examples of the water-related services provided by forests, which account for more than 44% of the total value of the forests, and exceed the combined value of climate regulation as well as food, raw materials, and recreation and tourism services. The valuation of water-related ecosystem services remains an imprecise science, and although it can provide good comparative indicators of where priorities should lie and has led to some increased national focus on relevant issues, it generally remains poorly applied. However, most reports caution that many ecosystem values, especially those relating to local benefits, are context-specific, meaning they should not necessarily be transferred from one case to another.

With attention turning to climate change risks and vulnerabilities, a greater incentive is in place for valuation studies concerning water-related ecosystem services. High values are being derived. For example, Costanza et al. (2008) value the extreme weather mitigation services (not including other services) provided by one hectare of wetland in the United States of America (USA) at US$33,000 for a single storm event. In Mexico, the value of water associated with protected areas for all human consumptive uses is estimated at US$158 million annually, with water used directly for human consumption valued at US$15 million annually (The Nature Conservancy, 2010a). Globally, between 33% and 44% of cities obtain their water from forested protected areas. These examples demonstrate an underlying convergence of interests around ecosystems although progress remains constrained by considerable diversity in the terminology in use.

The business advantage of maintaining ecosystem services is being more widely recognized and beyond just the bounds of corporate social responsibility. For example, the multibillion dollar Scottish whisky industry works closely with the Scottish Environment Protection Agency to develop and implement best practice in managing the environment to sustain the water resources upon which the industry depends. This includes the conservation of fragile peatland ecosystems and active participation in river basin management planning.

BOX 21.4

Assessing ecosystem services in the Mississippi River Delta, USA

Ecosystems of the Mississippi River Delta provide US$12–47 billion in benefits to people every year in terms of hurricane and flood protection, water supply, water quality, recreation and fisheries. If this natural capital were treated as an economic asset, the delta's minimum asset value would be US$330 billion to US$1.3 trillion (at 2007 values). However, this natural capital is being squandered through human-caused ecosystem loss and degradation. Doing nothing to invest in natural infrastructure in the coming decades would cost an estimated US$41 billion per year through lost ecosystem services, whereas protection, rehabilitation and restoration of natural infrastructure would have an estimated net benefit of US$62 billion annually.

Source: Batker et al. (2010).

The World Business Council for Sustainable Development (WBCSD), working in conjunction with the World Resources Institute, has developed the Corporate Ecosystem Services Review, which helps companies identify and measure the risks and opportunities arising from their impact and dependence on ecosystem services (WBCSD, 2010a). The WBCSD has also developed a publicly available Global Water Tool, which helps companies and organizations map their water use and assess risks relative to their global operations and supply chains (WBCSD, 2010b). Building on both tools, the WBCSD has launched the Ecosystem Valuation Initiative, which is working to develop a Guide to Corporate Ecosystem Valuation that makes the case for ecosystem valuation as an integral part of business planning and corporate decision-making (WBCSD, 2010c). WBCSD's Vision 2050 explores potential pathways by which a global population of nine billion people could be living sustainably by 2050, with particular emphasis on the role of business in relation to drivers of change (WBCSD, 2010d).

21.2.4 Payment for ecosystem services

Making payments to land owners and users can be an important tool for incentivizing land and water management practices that maximize ecosystem services (payment for ecosystem services [PES]), benefiting downstream users, where there is a clear cause-and-effect link between upstream management practices and downstream benefits. Cost recovery is likely to be easiest when certain groups already pay the consequences of lost services so that financing can be transferred from those groups to people able to reinstate a service. The clearest examples of this are with water quality (Boxes 21.2 and 21.5) and flood mitigation (e.g. compensating farmers for increased flood risks in farmland to reduce flood risk for people living in cities). PES schemes are most likely to succeed when:

- demand for ecosystem services is clear and financially valuable to one or more players;
- supply is threatened;
- specific resource management actions have the potential to address supply constraints;
- effective brokers or intermediaries exist;
- contract laws not only exist but are enforced, and resource tenure is clear; and
- clear criteria for evaluating equitable outcomes across partners are established, perhaps involving the participation of independent assessors.

Vittel, France

Nestlé S.A. produces one billion bottles of Vittel®-branded mineral water every year at Vittel in north-east France. To reduce contamination risk as far as possible, Nestlé has established a payment for ecosystem services (PES) scheme whereby farms within the protection zone for the Vittel aquifer are provided with incentives to adopt farming practices that contribute to nitrate reduction (e.g. conversion of arable land to pasture). By 2004, all farms in the area had joined the scheme. An independent study concluded that the scheme was a cost-effective means for Nestlé to virtually eliminate a significant risk to its business, while farmers were able to enter into 30-year payment agreements, benefit from debt cancellation and acquire additional land.

Source: Perrot-Maître (2006).

Further information on PES is provided by, for example, Forest Trends, The Katoomba Group, and UNEP (2008); Emerton (2005); Emerton and Bos (2004); and Smith et al. (2006).

21.3 Ecosystem status and trends

The overall negative global trend in the status of ecosystems presented in the second and third editions of the *World Water Development Report* (WWAP, 2006, 2009) as well as in the fourth *Global Environment Outlook* (UNEP, 2007) and third *Global Biodiversity Outlook* (CBD, 2010a) continues. This is also reflected in regional assessments (such as UNEP, 2008).

The Millennium Ecosystem Assessment (MA) conducted from 2000 to 2005 remains the most comprehensive overall assessment available to date. An overall synthesis report, a corresponding synthesis for wetlands and water (as well as for other specific sectors) and detailed technical reports from which these syntheses were compiled are available on the MA website (http://www.millenniumassessment.org/en/index.aspx). Referring specifically to wetlands and water, the MA found that (MA, 2005):

- Water scarcity and inadequate access to water are key factors limiting economic development in many countries. However, many water-resource development schemes have not given adequate consideration to the trade-offs with other valuable services provided by wetlands.

- Cross-sector, ecosystem-based approaches to natural resource management that consider the trade-offs between different ecosystem services are more likely to deliver sustainable development.
- Particularly important trade-offs are those between agricultural production and water quality and quantity, and between water use and biodiversity.

The third *Global Biodiversity Outlook* (CBD, 2010a) provides stark evidence that the loss and degradation of freshwater ecosystems remains the fastest of all the major biomes. This overall decay cannot be stemmed simply through declaring protected areas because of the interconnected nature of these ecosystems and in particular basin-scale interactions between land and water. For example, data from the Ramsar Convention on Wetlands national reports show that while wetland protected area is increasing, most wetland sites are degrading (CBD, 2010b). A review of the Convention on Biological Diversity (CBD's) work in this area (CBD, 2010b) concluded that the drivers of biodiversity loss remain unchanged and are all escalating and include conversion of habitat, fragmentation, the impacts of water use (particularly by agriculture), land use and other impacts on water quality and invasive alien species; excessive nutrient loading has emerged as an important direct driver of ecosystem change in inland (and coastal) waters and pollution of groundwater remains a major concern; the surface and groundwater portions of the water cycle have been subjected to massive changes by direct human use on local, regional and continental scales; and the global limit of ecological sustainability of water available for abstraction has been reached and regionally, this limit has already been exceeded for about one-third of the human population and it will rise to about half by 2030.

The Living Planet Index (LPI) measures trends in populations of more than 1,000 vertebrate species – fish, amphibians, reptiles, birds, mammals – from all around the world, providing a useful proxy for assessing ecosystem health (WWF, 2008). Taking into account different biomes, freshwater biomes continued to show a faster overall (global) rate of LPI decline than marine and fully terrestrial biomes, with a particularly rapid decline in tropical regions. Population trends in temperate (largely the developed) regions remain stable or are possibly improving, but in tropical (largely developing) regions they continue to decline (Figure 21.1). This trend is mirrored specifically for the data for freshwater dependent populations but

FIGURE 21.1

The Global Living Planet Index, all biomes (1970–2007)

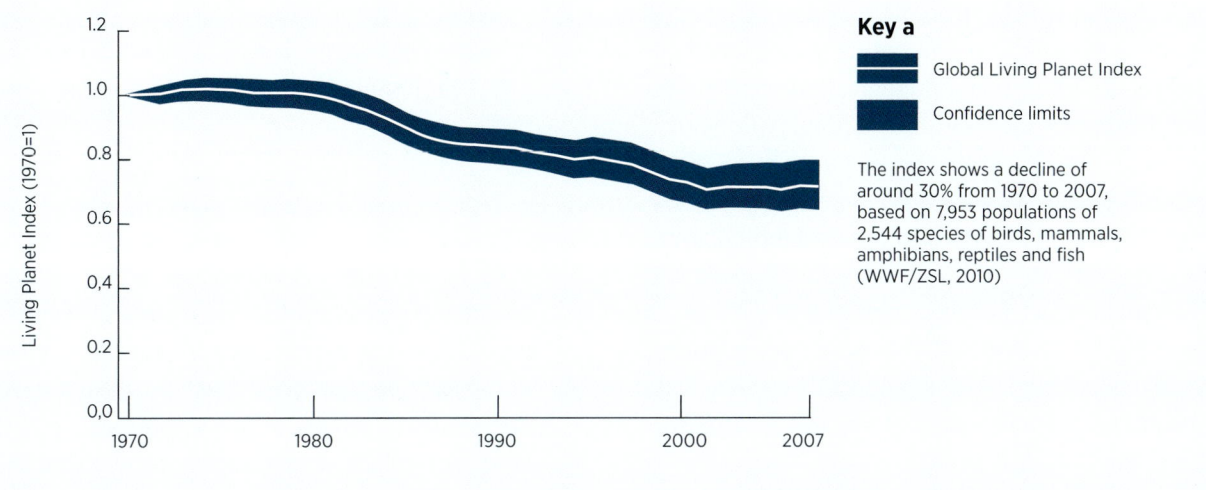

Living Planet Index (1970=1)
1.2
1.0
0.8
0.6
0,4
0.2
0,0
1970
1980
1990
2000
2007
Key a
Global Living Planet Index
Confidence limits
The index shows a decline of around 30% from 1970 to 2007, based on 7,953 populations of 2,544 species of birds, mammals, amphibians, reptiles and fish (WWF/ZSL, 2010)

Source: WWF (2010).

FIGURE 21.2

The Freshwater Living Planet Index (1970–2007)

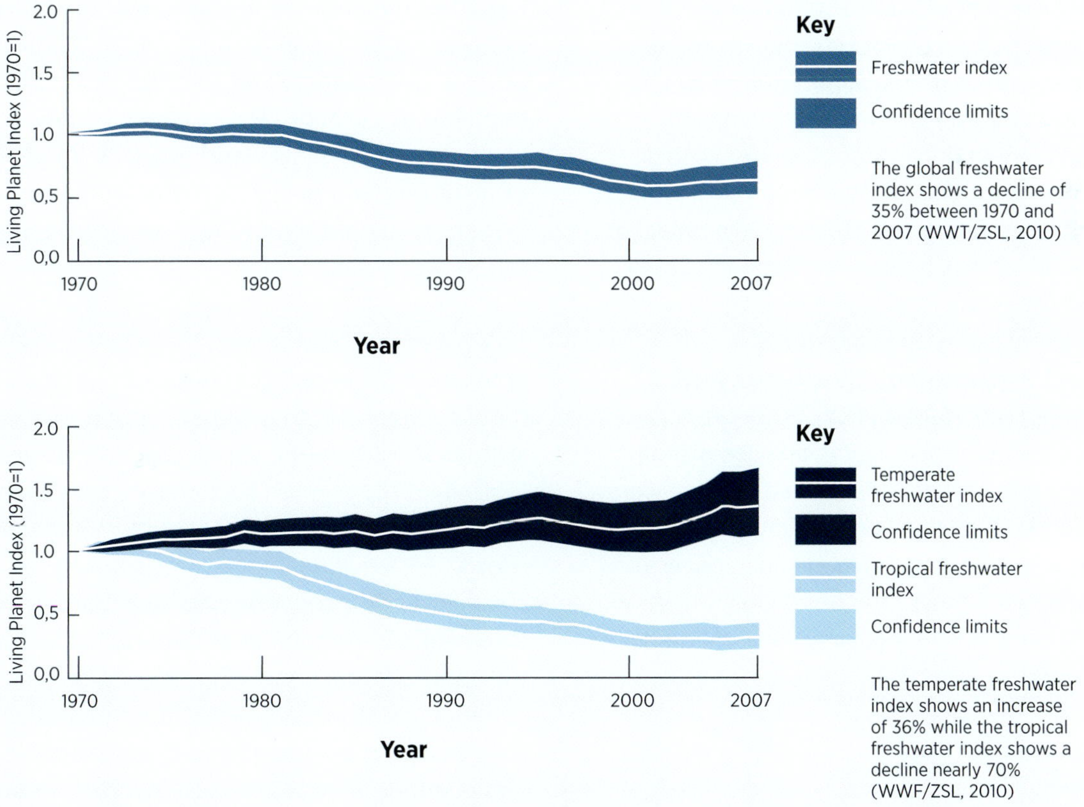

Living Planet Index (1970=1)
2.0
1.5
1.0
0,5
0,0
1970
1980
1990
2000
2007
Year
Key
Freshwater index
Confidence limits
The global freshwater index shows a decline of 35% between 1970 and 2007 (WWT/ZSL, 2010)
Living Planet Index (1970=1)
2.0
1.5
1.0
0,5
0,0
1970
1980
1990
2000
2007
Year
Key
Temperate freshwater index
Confidence limits
Tropical freshwater index
Confidence limits
The temperate freshwater index shows an increase of 36% while the tropical freshwater index shows a decline nearly 70% (WWF/ZSL, 2010)

Source: WWF (2010, p. 26).

these show more rapid decline (Figure 21.2). This is explained by biodiversity being higher in developing regions and this being where the many pressures and impacts are being felt most acutely. However, many of the drivers of ecosystem degradation in developing regions, and emerging economies, are determined – at least in part – by consumption in developed countries. While the local footprint of developed nations may appear to be stabilizing (or improving, as per Figures 21.1 and 21.2), much of their environmental footprint is now effectively being exported to the developing world and this is reflected in particular through deteriorating freshwater ecosystem conditions. The 2010 *Living Planet Report* (WWF, 2010) shows a continuation of the downward trend in the global LPI and the disproportionately adverse status of freshwater ecosystems.

21.4 Risks, vulnerabilities and uncertainties affecting ecosystems and water security

Ecosystems – and their contribution to water security – are subject to many risks, vulnerabilities and uncertainties from both natural (e.g. climate variability) and increasingly from escalating human-caused pressures at various scales, from local watershed degradation to global climate change. Ecosystems have evolved to be resilient to the impacts of extreme natural events such as floods, droughts, hurricanes, earthquakes, volcanic eruptions and tsunamis and to some extent can cope with human-induced degradation. But many consequences of ecosystem decay and catastrophic disasters are triggered or made worse through their mismanagement, leading to a reduction in their capacity to sustain the benefits humans need them to supply.

21.4.1 Principal pressures on ecosystems

The second and third editions of the *World Water Development Report* (WWAP, 2006, 2009) reviewed the principal pressures and impacts on ecosystems, focusing largely on freshwater components. These were summarized under the following headings:

- Habitat alteration (e.g. by drainage and conversion of wetlands)
- Fragmentation and flow regulation (e.g. by dams and reservoirs)
- Pollution
- Invasive species
- Climate change

Taking a wider view of ecosystem types that play a key role in achieving water security (e.g. forests, grasslands and coastal wetlands), a slightly modified approach

BOX 21.6

Net benefits of ecosystem conversion

The Millennium Ecosystem Assessment (MA, 2005) found that the net present value of intensive farmland occupying the site of a converted wetland in Canada was less than half the value of the unconverted wetland, while an intensive shrimp pond in Thailand represented less than one-quarter of the value of an unconverted mangrove.

is (a) to consider the impacts on water-related ecosystem services of three broad categories of change (ecosystem conversion, ecosystem fragmentation and ecosystem degradation) and (b) to examine the underlying indirect drivers of these changes, such as population growth, economic development and changing consumption patterns.

Ecosystem conversion

Ecosystem conversion (e.g. draining a wetland to grow a single crop) usually results in simplification of service provision and often increasing one service (e.g. food) at the expense of others (e.g. nutrient cycling and water regulation). In effect, this is trading other benefits for food production, but usually net ecosystem benefits decline (Box 21.6). There will also be parallel increases in other drivers of ecosystem change through, for example, significant decrease in water quality and quantity due to runoff of fertilizers and pesticides, abstraction of water for irrigation, and interruption or escalation of sedimentation processes.

Ecosystem fragmentation

Ecosystem fragmentation results in reduced connectivity between once contiguous tracts of a given ecosystem. Rivers are the classic example whereby ecologically disconnected sections are created by the construction of dams or floodplain drainage (Box 21.7). Similarly, blocks of forest may be clear-felled and converted to other uses, leaving disconnected fragments of the original forest. New transport corridors and urban expansion are additional common causes of ecosystem fragmentation. The remaining components will be smaller in extent, less complex in structure, and less diverse and consequently less resilient to external pressures. They will deliver fewer ecosystem services less effectively (e.g. lower capacity to regulate surface-water flow and sediment transport).

Ecosystem degradation

Ecosystem degradation occurs when the ecological functioning of an ecosystem – and therefore its capacity to deliver ecosystem services – is reduced, even if its type and extent are maintained. Diffuse or point-source pollution is one of the most serious forms of ecosystem degradation affecting water security (Box 21.8).

21.4.2 Non-linear ecosystem change: The 'tipping point' concept

The Economics of Ecosystems and Biodiversity (TEEB, 2009) underlines that ecosystem loss and degradation do not always result in an immediately detectable or proportional response in terms of lost ecosystem services. Instead, a 'tipping point' may be reached, where rapid and catastrophic collapse occurs following a period of apparent stability. CBD (2010a, p. 6) concludes that 'there is a high risk of dramatic biodiversity loss and accompanying degradation of a broad range of ecosystem services if ecosystems are pushed beyond certain thresholds or tipping points. The poor would face the earliest and most severe impacts of such changes, but ultimately all societies and communities would suffer.' A growing concern, increasingly backed by scientific evidence, relates to tipping points in forest ecosystems and their ability to support the water cycle (Box 21.9).

21.4.3 Climate change

Climate change threatens water security in many regions of the world by triggering, accelerating or intensifying (or all three) changes to the water cycle. These changes are occurring, and will continue to occur, primarily at the ecosystem level. In turn they will alter the availability (both quantity and quality) of water for ecosystems, thereby adding additional stress to ecosystem services to that resulting from other human-caused pressures on ecosystems.

The Intergovernmental Panel on Climate Change (IPCC) Fourth Assessment Report (IPCC, 2007) lists 32 examples of major projected impacts of climate change across eight regions (covering the whole earth). Twenty-five of these include primary links to hydrological changes. Of the other seven, water is implicated in four and two are general. Only one (coral bleaching) refers to major impacts not obviously linked to the hydrological cycle (being caused by the acidification effects of carbon dioxide). Notably, most of the impacts on terrestrial vegetation (and therefore also on fauna) are driven largely by hydrological shifts (changes in humidity, permafrost, snow and ice cover, rainfall patterns and groundwater).

The IPPC technical paper *Climate Change and Water* (IPCC, 2008) states that major changes in water brought about by climate change include:

- Changing precipitation patterns, intensity and extremes
- Reduced snow cover and widespread melting of ice
- Changes in soil moisture and runoff

The report (pp. 7–8) also concludes unambiguously that 'the relationship between climate change and freshwater resources is of primary concern and interest', that so far 'water resource issues have not been adequately addressed in climate change analyses and

---

BOX 21.7

Fragmentation of the Danube River basin, Central Europe

Along the Danube River more than 80% of the main river channel has been regulated by dams, while only one-fifth of the original floodplain remains functional, with significant impacts on the capacity of the river basin to deliver ecosystem services.

Source: ICDPR (2010).

BOX 21.8

Groundwater nitrate contamination in the United Kingdom

In common with many parts of Europe, intensification of UK agriculture and the over-application of nitrate fertilizers during the twentieth century led in particular to the degradation of groundwater in areas with thin or free-draining soils (or both) from which nitrates were leached rapidly by rainfall. More than 60% of nitrate pollution in the UK is attributable to agriculture. In conformity with European Union (EU) and national legislation, the UK government has designated nitrate vulnerable zones within which the application of nitrate-based fertilizers is restricted, with the aim of ensuring that groundwater nitrate levels do not exceed the permitted drinking water limits. Nevertheless, drinking water still needs to be subject to a range of expensive compensatory measures, including the mixing of groundwater from different sources (to ensure sufficient dilution of nitrates from contaminated areas) and denitrification.

Sources: Defra (2010); Tompkins (2003).

climate policy formulations' and, according to many experts, that 'water and its availability and quality will be the main pressures, and issues, on societies and the environment under climate change'.

The IPCC (p. 4) also observes that the area of land classified as very dry has already more than doubled since the 1970s and that 'many semi-arid and arid areas (e.g. the Mediterranean Basin, western USA, southern Africa and north-eastern Brazil) are particularly exposed to the impacts of climate change and are projected to suffer a decrease of water resources due to climate change'.

Global climate change compounds the vulnerability of all ecosystems, but is perhaps more noticeable, or critical, for those where water is a key variable, such as wetlands, deserts and forests, as well as those that are already suffering from the adverse impacts of conversion, fragmentation and degradation. For example, a wetland in a semi-arid region that is already stressed due to over-abstraction of water may be lost altogether if there is a regional decrease in precipitation as a consequence of climate change.

Adaptation responses to climate change can be maximized by ensuring that ecosystems are as intact and healthy as possible. For example, protecting coastal ecosystems may help prevent incursion of seawater into freshwater systems during storm

BOX 21.9

Ecosystems on the edge: the Amazon basin forests and water

Deforestation in the Amazon basin is leading to a decrease in regional rainfall because of the loss of cloud-forming evapo-transpiration from the forest. As the climate becomes drier it is less able to support rainforest vegetation. At the same time, the loss of forest cover removes the continuous supply of decaying vegetation that generates the nutrients on which the forests depend. These feedback loops mean that apparently moderate deforestation of the Amazon basin, of the order of 20% by surface area, could nevertheless reach a 'tipping point', beyond which forest ecosystems collapse across the entire Amazon basin, with devastating impacts on water security and other ecosystem services. Such impacts may have far-reaching – beyond the Amazon basin itself – effects (e.g. on regional agriculture and global carbon storage). Worryingly, deforestation is already at 18%.

Source: World Bank (2010).

events, which are predicted to become more frequent in some parts of the world. MA (2005) concluded that the adverse effects of climate change, such as sea level rise, coral bleaching, and changes in hydrology and in the temperature of water bodies, will lead to a reduction in the services provided by wetlands. Because of their intimate and direct role in hydrology, removing the existing pressures on wetlands and improving their resiliency is one of the most effective methods of coping with the adverse effects of climate change.

21.5 Ecosystem-based approaches to the management of water

The second edition of the *World Water Development Report* (WWAP, 2006) introduced the concept of ecosystem-based management (EBM), which essentially requires those making decisions about the allocation and management of water to think more holistically by including ecosystem considerations as part of water management. EBM investments and interventions are directed at sustaining or enhancing the ecosystem component of the water cycle through the use of ecosystem (natural) infrastructure.

As explained above, the ecosystem is the ultimate source of all water. Both direct human use of water and the impacts of climate change essentially involve impacts which are delivered, either directly or indirectly, through ecosystem change. The relationship between ecosystems and water implies that they are impacted by water use (and climate change). This is something that has always been known, if often articulated in different ways such as 'environmental impact', and it frames the relationship negatively (although this remains an important topic) and reinforces debate over 'development' versus 'environment'. More important, in terms of policy influence, the ecosystem–water relationship means that ecosystems can be proactively managed in ways that help humans achieve water-related development objectives. This places ecosystems as solutions (not problems) and is essentially a cornerstone of EBM.

The Ecosystem-Based Management Tools Network (2010) proposes that EBM is a process which:
- Integrates ecological, social and economic goals and recognizes humans as key components of the ecosystem
- Considers ecological – not only political and administrative – boundaries

- Addresses the complexity of natural processes and social systems and resulting uncertainties using adaptive management
- Engages multiple stakeholders in a collaborative process to define problems and find solutions
- Incorporates understanding of ecosystem processes and how ecosystems respond to environmental changes, whether natural or caused or influenced by humans
- Is concerned with the ecological integrity of ecosystems and sustainability of human uses of ecosystems and ecosystem services

When applied to water, EBM can deliver win–win solutions that contribute to poverty alleviation and economic development. They are often more cost effective than conventional engineering-based solutions, but not always so. Approaches should consider EBM solutions alongside other options (e.g. hard engineering) and proceed on the most holistic and best evidence base as possible, factoring in relevant uncertainties and risks. Assessments of all optional approaches should include benefits in terms of resilience/sustainability (risk reduction) and the co-benefits on offer, which for EBM can be considerable.

21.5.1 The role of ecosystems in enhancing water security

EBM can deliver specific and immediate water-related benefits cost effectively. Sustaining or restoring ecosystems usually also increases resilience to change, thereby mitigating present and future risks and enhancing sustainable water security. EBM approaches also apply across scales, from local interventions (e.g. wetland restoration to address localized flooding) to basin scale and beyond, and can address single or multiple water-related needs. Key areas in which EBM already has a proven track record include water quality (Box 21.2) and regulating the extremes of water, in particular flooding (Box 21.10). At all but the smallest scales, EBM is usually multifunctional and rarely a stand-alone approach but rather integrated into catchment level management and included for addressing water stress under drought conditions (Box 21.11).

21.5.2 Ecosystems and integrated water resources management

As discussed in the third edition of the *World Water Development Report,* integrated water resources management (IWRM) (considered here as homologous with integrated river basin management, IRBM) is potentially one of the most useful water resource

---

BOX 21.10

Wetland restoration as a sustainable option to address increasing flood risk: The Wash, United Kingdom

Due to the combined factors of rising sea level and land subsidence the artificial flood-protection embankment adjoining part of The Wash, an extensive estuary in eastern England, was coming under increasing pressure from wave attack during high tide. It was estimated that potential breach of the current defences would result in flood damage approaching £20 million. The cost of repairing and maintaining the embankment over a period of 50 years was estimated at £2.06 million, whereas 'managed realignment' (moving the flood bank landward and enabling the development of intertidal marshes and mudflats seaward of the realigned bank) was costed at £1.98 million, affording flood protection over a considerably longer period of time and creating significant benefits for nature conservation and recreation. An additional £150,000 was added to the local economy in the first year following restoration through increased recreational use of the area.

Source: Friess et al. (2008).

---

management tools at various scales. In principle, IWRM involves an integrated approach to land and water management which should recognize that, from an ecosystems functioning viewpoint, any distinction between the two is entirely artificial. In practice, many applications of IWRM do not fully incorporate ecosystem-level approaches. IWRM is often focused on visible (surface) water management and even where groundwater is included (which is becoming more often the case), soil moisture is often absent. In particular, IWRM rarely incorporates the management of evapo-transpiration (e.g. the impacts of land cover change). The management of wetlands, as drivers of local and often basin-scale hydrology, is likewise included irregularly. IWRM can indeed be complicated and its application is evolving based on learning by doing. But because of the intimate relationship between ecosystems and water, IWRM will not be truly integrated, or fully effective, until applied at the ecosystem scale.

Rigorous ecosystem-based thinking in IWRM requires:
- Identifying how relevant ecosystems, or their components that maintain water quantity and quality in a given area and all the ecosystem services they provide (bearing in mind they all depend on water) – including the role of terrestrial systems, especially vegetation and soil functions – support water security

BOX 21.11

Ecosystem-based management integrated into the management of the Komadugu Yobe basin, Nigeria

The Komadugu Yobe River ecosystem, supplied by a subcatchment of the vast Lake Chad basin, is part of the natural infrastructure of northern Nigeria. In the semi-arid Sahel, rainfall variability is high and severe drought a frequent hazard. The great majority of the basin's human population – which has doubled in the past three decades to more than 23 million – live in poverty. Over the same time period, flow in the river fell by 35% due to construction of two dams since the 1970s, abstraction of water for large-scale irrigation and regional reduction in rainfall.

A society already in social and economic crisis was thus confronted with ever-increasing pressure on vital water resources. The river's natural cycle of seasonal flooding and drying had been replaced by perennial low flows, causing loss of benefits (ecosystem services) that communities had historically relied on. Livelihoods dependent on fishing, farming and herding were devastated. Fish habitats were silted up, the loss of seasonal floods meant that cropland remained dry, and scarcity of water led to conflict. With growing impacts from climate change, the adaptive capacity of the Komadugu Yobe ecosystem and the communities it supports became even more fragile, just when resilience was needed most. The situation was not untypical of many river basins in Africa and elsewhere and its history typified by sector based approaches to water, lack of valuation of the full suite of benefits (services) available to be managed and the absence of any ecosystem level thinking.

However, crisis stimulated change. Restoration of the river basin's natural infrastructure, alongside existing built infrastructure, has strengthened adaptive capacity and resilience to climate change. Beginning in 2006, the federal and state governments and other stakeholders, including dam operators and farming, fishing and herding communities, came together to negotiate a plan for coordinating and investing in restoration and management of the basin. In addition to agreeing on a Catchment Management Plan, they drafted a Water Charter, spelling out the agreed principles for sustainable development of the basin and the roles and responsibilities of each stakeholder. Reform of water governance is enabling transparent co-ordination of water resource development, including remediation of degraded ecosystems and, eventually, restoration of the river's flow regime. Dialogue has reduced the number of cases of conflict to just a handful per year, and governments have pledged millions of dollars in new investment for basin restoration. This progress offers, for once, a potentially more sustainable future. Ecosystem-based management (EBM) was not a separate approach but integrated, or rather a framework for, more holistic and inclusive planning and management. Importantly, EBM delivered more sustainable water solutions and the ecosystem was not regarded as a 'user' (competing with other uses) but its management a means to deliver greater overall benefits from water.

Source: Smith and Barchiesi (2009).

- Identifying factors, including risks, vulnerabilities and uncertainties, that affect the functioning of those ecosystems and therefore services and how this impacts water security
- Taking measures to (a) manage the ecosystem so that it continues to deliver, or increases delivery, of all the benefits that are required and (b) minimizes risks, vulnerabilities and uncertainties so as to try to safeguard, as far as possible, overall ecosystem integrity and resilience (even beyond a narrow 'water' focus)

Tools for implementation can include, for example, removal of perverse incentives, including laws, regulations and financial mechanisms, that favour ecosystem degradation (such as grants for wetland drainage or conversion); payment for ecosystem services (PES); and investment in ecosystem restoration and rehabilitation (where justified through thorough and impartial analysis).

Further guidance on IWRM in practice has been provided by a number of initiatives; for example, the Global Water Partnership Toolbox (2008). The *Ramsar Wise Use Handbooks* (fourth edition: The Ramsar Convention on Wetlands, 2011) provide comprehensive guidance on integrating wetlands into IWRM – especially *River Basin Management* (Handbook 9), *Water Allocation and Management* (Handbook 10), and *Managing Groundwater* (Handbook 11).

References

Batker, D., de la Torre, I., Costanza, R., Swedeen, P., Day, J., Boumans, R. and Bagstad, K. 2010. *Gaining Ground – Wetlands, Hurricanes and the Economy: The Value of Restoring the Mississippi River Delta.* Tacoma, Wash., Earth Economics. http://www.eartheconomics.org/Page12.aspx

CBD (Secretariat of the Convention on Biological Diversity). 2010a. *Global Biodiversity Outlook 3.* Montreal, Canada, CBD. http://gbo3.cbd.int/

––––. 2010b. *In-Depth Review of the Programme of Work on the Biological Diversity of Inland Water Ecosystems.* Paper presented at the fourteenth meeting of the Subsidiary Body on Scientific, Technical and Technological Advice, Nairobi, 10–21 May 2010. http://www.cbd.int/doc/meetings/sbstta/sbstta-14/official/sbstta-14-03-en.doc

Costanza, R., Pérez-Maqueo, O., Martinez, M. L., Sutton, P., Anderson, S. J. and Mulder, K. 2008. The value of wetlands for hurricane protection. *Ambio,* Vol. 37, pp. 241–48.

Defra (Department for Environment, Food and Rural Affairs, UK). 2010. *Nitrate Vulnerable Zones in England.* London, Defra.

De Groot, R. S., Stuip, M. A. M., Finlayson, C. M. and Davidson, N. 2006. *Valuing Wetlands: Guidance for Valuing the Benefits Derived From Wetland Ecosystem Services.* Ramsar Technical Report No. 3/CBD Technical Series No. 27. Gland, Switzerland/Montreal, Canada, Ramsar Secretariat/Secretariat of the Convention on Biological Diversity (CBD).

Department of Environment, Government of West Bengal. 2007. *The Role of East Kolkata Wetlands as a Waste Recycling Region.* Kolkata, India, Government of West Bengal. http://wbenvironment.nic.in/html/wetland_files/wet_therolloff.htm (Accessed 26 January 2011.)

Dyson, M., Bergkamp, G. and Scanlon, J. (eds). 2008. *Flow – The Essentials of Environmental Flows,* 2nd edn. Gland, Switzerland, International Union for Conservation of Nature (IUCN). http://www.iucn.org/dbtw-wpd/edocs/2003-021.pdf

Ecosystem-Based Management Tools Network. 2010. *About Ecosystem-Based Management (EBM).* http://www.ebmtools.org/about_ebm.html (Accessed 26 January 2011.)

Emerton, L. 2005. *Values and Rewards: Counting and Capturing Ecosystem Water Services for Sustainable Development.* IUCN, Water, Nature and Economics Technical Paper No. 1. Gland, Switzerland, International Union for Conservation of Nature (IUCN) Ecosystems and Livelihoods Group Asia. http://iucn.org/about/work/programmes/economics/econ_resources/?347/Values-and-rewards-counting-and-capturing-ecosystem-water-services-for-sustainable-development

Emerton, L. and Bos, E. 2004. *Value: Counting Ecosystems as an Economic Part of Water Infrastructure.* Gland, Switzerland, International Union for Conservation of Nature (IUCN). http://data.iucn.org/dbtw-wpd/edocs/2004-046.pdf

Forest Trends, The Katoomba Group, and UNEP (United Nations Environment Programme). 2008. *Payments for Ecosystem Services – Getting Started: A Primer.* Washington, DC/Nairobi, Forest Trends and The Katoomba Group/UNEP. http://www.katoombagroup.org/documents/publications/GettingStarted.pdf

Forslund, A. et al. 2009. *Securing Water for Ecosystems and Human Well-Being: The Importance of Environmental Flows.* Swedish Water House Report 24. Stockholm, Stockholm International Water Institute (SIWI). http://www.siwi.org/documents/Resources/Reports/Report24_E-Flows-low-res.pdf

Friess, D., Möller, I. and Spencer, T. 2008. *Managed Realignment and the Re-establishment of Saltmarsh Habitat, Freiston Shore, Lincolnshire, United Kingdom.* Cambridge, UK, Cambridge University. http://www.proactnetwork.org/proactwebsite/en/policyresearchtoolsguidance/environmental-management-in-drr-a-cca/98

Global Water Partnership Toolbox. 2008. *IWRM – Integrated Water Resources Management.* http://www.gwptoolbox.org/index.php?option=com_content&view=article&id=8&Itemid=3 (Accessed 26 January 2011.)

ICDPR (International Commission for the Protection of the Danube River). 2010. *Dams & Structures.* http://www.icpdr.org/icpdr-pages/dams_structures.htm (Accessed 26 January 2011.)

IPCC (Intergovernmental Panel on Climate Change). 2007. *Climate Change 2007: Synthesis Report.* Contribution of Working Groups I, II and III to the Fourth Assessment Report of the Intergovernmental Panel on Climate Change. Geneva, IPCC.

––––. 2008. *Technical Paper on Climate Change and Water.* IPCCXXVIII/ Doc. 13. Geneva, IPCC. http://www.ipcc. ch/meetings/session28/doc13.pdf

MA (Millennium Ecosystem Assessment). 2005. *Ecosystems and Human Well-Being: Wetlands and Water Synthesis.* Washington, DC, World Resources Institute.

Mekong River Commission. 2010. *MRC Agreement, Procedures and Technical Guidelines.* http://www.mrcmekong.org/agreement_95/Agreement-procedures-guidelines.htm (Accessed 26 January 2011.)

The Nature Conservancy. 2010a. *Protected Areas for Freshwater Conservation.* Arlington, Va., The Nature Conservancy. http://nature.vitamininc.net/water/pdfs/water-management/protected/Freshwater_Conservation.pdf

––––. 2010b. *South America: Creating Water Funds for People and Nature.* http://www.nature.org/wherewework/southamerica/misc/art26470.html (Accessed 26 January 2011.)

Perrot-Maître, D. 2006. *The Vittel Payments for Ecosystem Services: A 'Perfect' PES Case?* London, International Institute for Environment and Development (IIED).

Ramsar Convention on Wetlands. 2011. *The Ramsar Handbooks for the Wise Use of Wetlands,* 4th edn. Gland, Switzerland, Ramsar Secretariat. http://www.ramsar.org/cda/en/ramsar-pubs-handbooks/main/ramsar/1-30-33_4000_0

Rao, P., Areendran, G. and Sareen, R. 2008. Potential impacts of climate change in the Uttarakhand Himalayas. *Mountain Forum Bulletin,* January 2008, pp. 28–9.

Revenga, C., Murray, S., Abramovitz, J. and Hammond, A. 1998. *Watersheds of the World: Ecological Value and Vulnerability.* Washington DC, World Resources Institute.

Smith, D. and Barchiesi, S. 2009. *Environment as Infrastructure – Resilience to Climate Change Impacts on Water Through Investments in Nature.* Gland, Switzerland, International Union for Conservation of Nature (IUCN). http://www.iucn.org/about/work/programmes/water/resources/wp_resources_reports/

Smith, M., de Groot, D., Perrot-Maîte, D. and Bergkamp, G. 2006. *Pay: Establishing Payments for Watershed Services.* Gland, Switzerland, International Union for Conservation of Nature (IUCN). (Reprinted 2008.) http://www.iucn.org/dbtw-wpd/edocs/2006-054.pdf

Srinetr, V. 2009. Integrated Basin Flow Management for the sustainable development of the Mekong River Basin. *eFlowNews,* Vol. 6, No. 4. http://www.eflownet.org/newsletter/viewarticle.cfm?nwaid=101&nwid=39&linkcategoryid=999&siteid=1&FuseAction=display

TEEB (The Economics of Ecosystems and Biodiversity). 2009*a*. Home page. http://www.teebweb.org (Accessed 26 January 2011.)

––––. 2009*b*. *TEEB Climate Issues Update.* Bonn, Germany, TEEB. http://www.teebweb.org/InformationMaterial/TEEBReports/tabid/1278/language/en-US/Default.aspx

Tompkins, J. 2003. *OH NO3! Nitrate Levels Are Rising.* London, Water UK. http://www.water.org.uk/home/news/comment/oh-no3-nit-140503-1

UNEP (United Nations Environment Programme). 2007. *Global Environment Outlook 4.* Nairobi, UNEP.

––––. 2008. *Africa: Atlas of Our Changing Environment.* Nairobi, UNEP. http://www.unep.org/dewa/Africa/AfricaAtlas

WBCSD (World Business Council for Sustainable Development). 2010a. *The Corporate Ecosystem Services Review – Guidelines for Identifying Business Risks and Opportunities Arising from Ecosystem Change.* Geneva, WBCSD. http://www.wbcsd.org/web/esr.htm

––––. 2010*b*. *The Global Water Tool.* http://www.wbcsd.org/web/watertool.htm (Accessed 26 January 2011.)

––––. 2010*c*. *Corporate Ecosystem Valuation – Building the Business Base.* Geneva, WBCSD. http://www.wbcsd.org/Plugins/DocSearch/details.asp?DocTypeId=25&ObjectId=MzYwMzM

––––. 2010*d*. *Vision 2050 Lays a Pathway to Sustainable Living Within Planet.* Geneva, WBCSD. http://www.wbcsd.org/Plugins/DocSearch/details.asp?DocTypeId=33&ObjectId=MzcOMDE

World Bank. 2010. *Assessment of the Risk of Amazon Dieback.* Main Report, 4 February. Washington DC, The World Bank.

WWAP (World Water Assessment Programme). 2003. *World Water Development Report 1: Water for People, Water for Life.* Paris/New York, UNESCO/Berghahn Books.

––––. 2006. *World Water Development Report 2: Water: A Shared Responsibility.* Paris/New York, UNESCO/Berghahn Books.

––––. 2009. *World Water Development Report 3: Water in A Changing World.* Paris/London, UNESCO/Earthscan.

WWF (World Wide Fund for Nature). 2008. *Global Living Planet Index (1970–2005).* Gland, Switzerland, WWF International. http://www.twentyten.net/lpi

––––. 2010. *Living Planet Report 2010: Biodiversity, Biocapacity and Development.* Gland, Switzerland, WWF International. http://wwf.panda.org/about_our_earth/all_publications/living_planet_report

CHAPTER 22
Allocating water

UNESCO-IHP and UNESCO-IHE
—

Authors Shahbaz Khan and Pieter van der Zaag
Contributors Amaury Tilmant (major contribution to Section 22.3). Case studies provided by Lucia Scodanibbio, Heather MacKay, Sharon Megdal, Léna Salamé, Philippus Wester, Akhtar Abbas and Frank Walker.

Water allocations in a majority of river systems and aquifers have already exceeded or are fast approaching water availability limits. Water diversions have to be reduced, and water re-allocated within sectors.

Water entitlements, water allocation, water distribution and water use are dynamically linked. With an increasingly variable hydrological cycle and rapid socio-economic development, there is a need for adaptive allocation mechanisms that deal with this as well as with the accompanying uncertainties.

In regions where there are large discrepancies between where the water is and where it is needed, the construction of large inter-basin transfer projects is likely to continue – despite the recognized advantages of moving the products of water rather than the water itself. Increased rainfall variability and greater pollution loads can have disastrous consequences. New reservoirs that are built to deal with increased variability in river flow may often negatively affect water quality and aquatic ecosystems, which give rise to serious governance issues.

In many cases, water re-allocation has been focusing on agriculture-to-urban water transfers where farmers are compensated by urban users for increasing the availability of water through temporary or permanent transfers. The rationale for such water transfers is often economic.

As concern over the environment grows, some water managers are investigating innovative ways of enhancing environmental water transfers by changing the operating rules of dams to improve the seasonality and availability of water for ecosystems.

Water banks have been created to improve the reliability of water markets. A public intermediary buys water from the willing sellers and sells it to buyers. Water trading markets can make more water available for high-value uses.

When making water allocation decisions, the international community is increasingly recognizing that access to water is a human right.

Water managers can benefit from the experience of other sectors that deal with the allocation of scarce resources. They can see how these sectors deal with uncertainty and risk management.

Water allocation policies need to recognize and correct racial and gender inequities in water use by addressing the expectations of all stakeholders in an equitable and transparent manner.

Building a shared vision and trusted knowledge base is crucial for individual water users to make responsible decisions when promoting integrated water resources management at the river basin level.

22.1 Allocating water

22.1.1 Introduction

A water allocation system has four main aspects, of which water allocation is one:

- *Water entitlements,* whether they are formal or informal, confer on the holder the right to draw water from a particular source (Le Quesne et al., 2007). The important point here is that the entitlement is considered legitimate by others.
- *Water allocation* describes the process of sharing the available water between legitimate claimants and distributing it to them (after Le Quesne et al., 2007).
- *Water delivery* (or *control*) is the physical act of supplying water to those who are entitled to it, in such a manner that they can use it.
- *Water use* is any deliberate application of water for a specified purpose (Perry, 2007).

Water entitlements, water allocation, water delivery and water use are dynamically linked, and are constrained by the amount of water that is available at a specific time. Using water creates expectations of similar use in future. If such use is continued over time, an entitlement emerges which may be difficult to ignore or claim back, yet the amount of water available is prone to natural and man-made fluctuations and changes (Figure 22.1).

These four linked aspects can be characterized by looking at the time scale over which they operate. Water entitlements can endure for many years, while

FIGURE 22.1

Water entitlements, water allocation, water distribution and water use are dynamically linked, and take place within the boundary of (changing) water availability

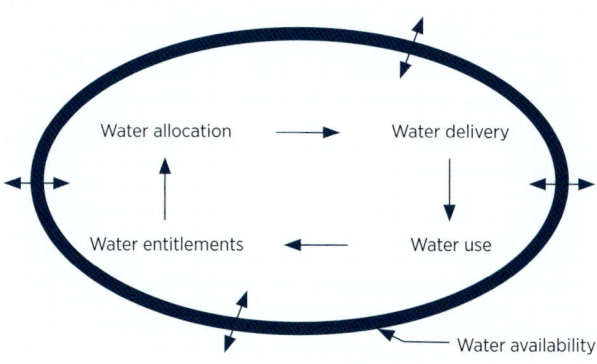

water allocation activities typically adopt a time horizon of one hydrological year, often trying to resolve issues of water scarcity by re-allocating water between sectors and between and within seasons. Water distribution and delivery are often based on weeks, days and hours, and water use is an instantaneous activity. As the hydrological cycle becomes increasingly variable, and as socio-economic development continues to change rapidly, it is important to establish what kind of allocation mechanisms can deal with change effectively and flexibly.

This challenge area chapter reviews water allocation issues and refers to a number of examples around the world where change and uncertainty were dealt with in interesting ways.

The chapter first outlines the main issues. It then reviews new water allocation paradigms that incorporate the role of markets and reallocation between sectors, and some modern computational developments that incorporate stochastic information to deal with uncertainty and risk. This chapter also highlights recent developments in the area of allocating water as a human right. Finally, it draws the conclusion that a common vision and a trusted knowledge base shared between water users is key for the individual water users to make the right decision.

22.2 Main issues

All over the world, the pressure on water resources is increasing, leading to situations where there is not always enough water to satisfy everyone's needs. Then choices have to be made about how to share, allocate and reallocate the increasingly scarce water. Water systems are 'closing', giving rise to difficult decisions about how water should be diverted, how it should be allocated within sectors and how it should be transferred between sectors. Such dilemmas throw up debates of a normative kind: what principles guide decisions on water allocation and how can the principles of equitable access, economic efficiency, sustainability and customary norms and values be reconciled in specific contexts?

Water allocation has strong *spatial and temporal dimensions.* Decisions can span decades, years, seasons, months, days, hours and even minutes. Think of the granting of water rights or permits to large irrigation schemes that are expected to last for decades or centuries; then think of hourly allocation schedules for short-term reservoir releases to cover peak demands in the electricity grid. Water allocation is generally a localized activity, but it must consider larger hydrological units and the expected inflows as well as the resulting outflows.

Many long-lasting water systems display a remarkable capacity to cope with change. In such systems, which often lack the physical capacity to fully control water flow, institutions evolved alongside specific physical design principles that were able to deal with long-term variability in supply and demand. Such institutions, which have their roots in customs and traditions, have tended to strongly embrace equity and fairness, which gives them sufficient legitimacy to enforce decisions. Examples are quoted by Leach (1961) and Martin and Yoder (1988) on two Asian cases. Several Latin American examples are referred to in Van der Zaag (1993) and Boelens and Davila (1998); while Manzungu et al. (1999) and Mohamed-Katerere and Van der Zaag (2003) refer to a number of African examples. Lankford (2004) has proposed incorporating the flexibility of these systems into the design of new smallholder irrigation systems (Figure 22.2).

But pressure on the resource is increasing everywhere, and existing as well as new water institutions face more frequent water allocation dilemmas that are increasingly complex and may be considered 'wicked' (Box 22.1). Existing rules need to be adapted and new rules, rights and duties, and organizational arrangements may need to be crafted.

There are often large spatial discrepancies between where the water is and where it is needed. So the construction of large inter-basin transfer projects is likely to continue, despite the acknowledged advantages of moving the *products* of water rather than the water itself (that is, the virtual water concept in the context of proposed transfer schemes. See, for example, Ma et al. (2006) on China and Verma et al. (2009) on India.

There is more and more demand for food, fibre, feed and biofuels. But in many river systems, large intersectoral transfers will have to be made from the agricultural to the urban and industrial sectors. The water shortage in agriculture *must* lead to enhanced water productivity, both from blue water (crops that use irrigation and supplementary irrigation) and from green water (rainfed crops).

The increasing pressure on water resources is mainly driven by four inter-related processes:
- Population growth and mobility;
- Economic growth;
- Increased demand for food, feed and biofuel; and
- Increased climate variability.

FIGURE 22.2

Designing a flexible irrigation system based on risk sharing, proportional water allocation and an adaptable irrigated area

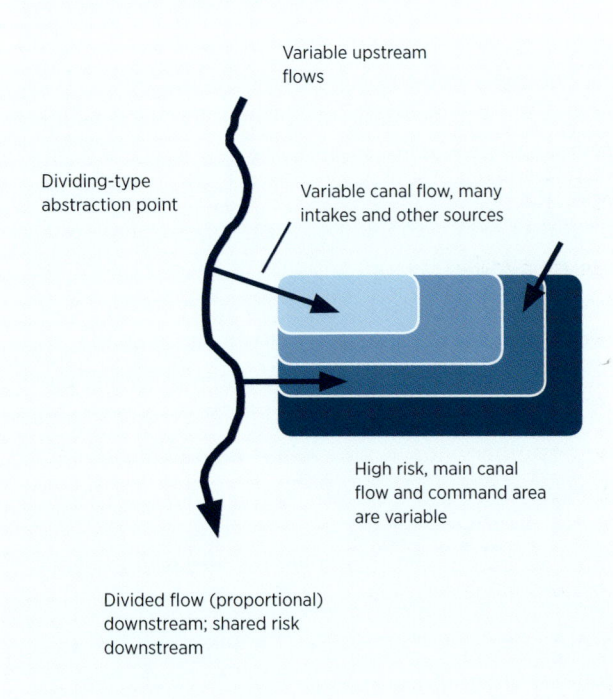

Source: Lankford (2004, fig. 1, p. 39), with permission from Elsevier.

The results often lead to unsustainable water use, which manifests in drying lakes (for example, the Lerma-Chapala case described in Box 22.7), estuaries becoming more saline, and falling groundwater levels (for example, the Deschutes case described in Box 22.4, and the Andhra Pradesh case described in Box 22.8).

Some of the external drivers interact in unexpected ways – as was seen with the policies and measures aimed at mitigating climate change through subsidies on biofuel production. The issues of water quantity and water quality are often linked. The increased variability in rainfall combined with a growing pollution can have disastrous consequences, for example in cases where dry season flows dwindle and chemical concentrations and water temperature surge to unprecedented levels. New reservoirs that are built to deal with increased variability in river flows affect water quality and aquatic ecosystems, usually negatively.

As a result of such developments in nearly every region of the world, institutions charged with water allocation face dilemmas that are difficult to solve, yet they are operating under increased scrutiny and may not have sufficient knowledge or understanding of hydro-social system dynamics. This gives rise to serious *governance issues* – water institutions are charged to make decisions, the outcomes and consequences of which are difficult to anticipate. Will water institutions be able to adapt to shifting circumstances and changing levels of uncertainty? (Box 22.2.)

22.2.1 Access to water is a human right

The allocation of water should adhere to the law and help to implement legal conventions at national and transboundary levels (see, for example, Wolf, 1999; Van der Zaag et al., 2002; Drieschova et al., 2008). The international community is increasingly recognizing water as a human right (Box 22.3). This right is referred to – both implicitly and explicitly – in many international and regional treaties and declarations. Among these are the Universal Declaration of Human Rights, the International Covenant on Civil and Political Rights (ICCPR), the International Covenant on Civil and Political Rights (ICCPR), the Geneva Convention, and the African Charter on Human and People's Rights.

After this brief overview we conclude this section by identifying four key issues in allocating water:
- How should water be allocated in times of shortage? Should certain types of use (domestic, environmental, industrial, energy and agricultural) have more priority or should the shortage be shared in an equitable manner? Should established uses and users be protected from newcomers? Is there a role

BOX 22.2

Principal uncertainties related to water allocation

Uncertainty has been defined as the lack of certainty about the nature of a phenomenon, process, system, quantity, estimate or future outcome, arising from incomplete knowledge of the relevant phenomena or processes, measurement error, model error, and imprecision associated with random factors (UNISDR, 2009).

Three types of uncertainty should be considered in water allocation decision-making:
- The *first* uncertainty relates to water availability, and the need to be able to estimate future surface and groundwater availability at different times. This uncertainty is strongly linked to climate and our lack of understanding of hydrological processes. It not only relates to the stochastic nature of these processes (which is in fact a fairly well understood uncertainty), but also to the non-stationarity of these stochastic processes, associated with long-term changes in climate and land use, and the complex feedbacks between them.
- The *second* uncertainty relates to our inability to predict future water demands and uses. The further we look into the future, the more this uncertainty increases. This uncertainty is strongly linked to uncertainties about future policies on a diverse spectrum of issues and in many sectors, which are difficult to anticipate and predict.
- The *third*, and arguably the largest uncertainty, is posed by our institutions and organizations. It relates to the risk that our institutions may not be addressing the real issues, or might take decisions that they later come to regret. This can occur if decisions are based on unreliable data that are taken as facts or on models that represent reality in biased ways, or because inadequate monitoring systems were used. This type of uncertainty increases when situations that have to be dealt with that are unique and have no historical precedent. In a changing world, these unique events will occur more frequently.

BOX 22.3

Water as a human right

In 2002, the Committee on Economic, Social and Cultural Rights (2002, articles 11 and 12) defined the right to water as the right of everyone 'to sufficient, safe, acceptable, physically accessible and affordable water for personal and domestic uses'. It further specified that signatories should ensure access to 'a minimum essential amount of water [and] adequate sanitation,' and should develop and implement a national water strategy and monitor progress made on realizing the right to water. The primary responsibility for the implementation of the right to water falls upon national governments.

On 28 July 2010, the United Nations General Assembly adopted a non-binding resolution, sponsored by Bolivia, which declared that access to clean water and sanitation is a fundamental human right. The resolution called on member states and international organizations to offer financial and technical assistance, in particular to developing countries, in order to provide clean, accessible and affordable drinking water and sanitation for everyone. The resolution invited the UN Independent Expert to report annually to the General Assembly. While 41 countries abstained, the resolution received the support of 122 of the Member States.

Source: Léna Salamé, personal communication (2010).

for markets and market transactions? If so, how can social and environmental public good values associated with water be protected?

- Water rights, permits and entitlements, as well as allocation systems, provide security and predictability. Their aim is to reduce risk. But there is a trade-off between reliability and quantity – the more secure the supply is, the smaller the flow. How can water allocation systems deal with uncertain inflows while maximizing beneficial use?
- How can water institutions be transformed into learning organizations that are forward looking, can anticipate change and adapt?
- More competition for water and tensions between users seem inevitable. These may lead to disputes and conflicts that are most likely to manifest themselves locally. How can we anticipate these rising tensions, and what strategies exist to transform them into enhanced cooperation?

The above key water allocation issues will be discussed later. First, we turn to some of the new water allocation paradigms designed to deal with uncertainty.

22.3 New water allocation paradigms in the face of uncertainty

Global change, socio-economic development, new demographics and climate change all increase competition for water. Societies face hard choices when allocating water between competing uses. Because water is a vital resource used in multiple sectors (including the environment), its allocation is inherently a political and social process – which opens it to the scrutiny of many and varied interested parties.

Because markets for this vital resource are usually absent or ineffective, allocating of water between competing demands is achieved administratively taking into account, often conflicting, social objectives such as economic efficiency, social equity and ecological integrity. Various allocation mechanisms have been developed in order to reconcile the principles of efficiency and equity (Dinar et al., 1997).

To deal with the growing demand worldwide for energy and water, societies have augmented supply by constructing more power plants and transmission lines and more hydraulic infrastructures such as dams and pumping stations. But this strategy has reached its limit in many regions. In the energy sector, for instance, rising concern about global warming and energy security have favoured conservation and the development and implementation of efficiency-promoting measures. For water, a similar trend can be observed with the 'closure' of river basins – that is, when available water resources are fully committed (Molle et al., 2010). More attention is now being given to strategies that attempt to increase the productivity of water through *temporary* reallocation, either within the same sector or across sectors. (This contrasts with permanent transfers, where water rights change hands permanently.) A temporary reallocation strategy lends itself to a water market and to market-like transactions where high-value water users would compensate low-value water users for the temporary right to use their water. Lund and Israel (1995) review types of water transfers such as permanent transfers, dry-year options, spot markets, water banks, and so forth.

Most of the studies on water reallocation reported in the literature focus on transfers from agricultural to urban use – where farmers are financially compensated by industries and/or municipalities for increasing the water available to them through either temporary or permanent transfers.

The rationale behind agriculture-to-urban water transfer is often economic. The productivity of water in urban uses is generally much higher than in agriculture. Agriculture can also cope better than other sectors with a larger variation in supply. For example, Booker and Yong (1994) analysed the efficiency gains of from intrastate and interstate water transfers in the Colorado River basin in the United States. They found that significant gains were possible, especially if both consumptive and non-consumptive use values were considered in the reallocation process.

Ward et al. (2006) investigate the effectiveness of market-based water transfers to deal with severe and sustained droughts in the Rio Grande basin, also in the United States. Using a hydro-economic model of the basin, they found drought damage could be reduced impressively if an interstate market program were enacted. This market would reallocate drought-induced water losses from higher-value water uses to lower-value uses. More specifically, farmers could reduce their losses by trading water for money whenever the income from the traded water is larger than the income that would have been produced using the same water in agriculture.

Water markets are more the exception than the rule. In fact, water markets are prone to market failure – meaning that private property and the resultant 'free' market cannot be relied on to achieve efficiency or augment supply through water reallocation. The main reasons for market failure are: the 'public good' nature of some water uses, the externalities associated with allocation decisions, and the presence of natural monopolies. Note that transaction costs must also be considered. If water markets are to serve society, water rights would have to be carefully defined and managed, and this would require continuous public sector involvement, which may lead to highly regulated water markets.

Despite these issues, incentives for water exchanges persist. The creation of water banks, such as the California Water Bank, is an attempt to improve the reliability of water markets (Jercich, 1997). Here, a public intermediary acts to create a population of buyers and sellers. The public intermediary buys water from the willing sellers and then sells it to buyers. With this system, water managers are confident they can find the water they need at a predictable price. It also means that public good services, such as environmental

BOX 22.4

Deschutes River Basin: Water banking for surface water and groundwater

This case is about reconciling water demands between different uses and users, in a situation where there are strong interconnections between groundwater and surface water. Tribal, environmental and irrigation interest groups came together in the mid-1990s to improve stream flow and water quality in Deschutes River basin in Oregon in the United States. This has materialized largely in restoring stream flow to depleted streams. It has also assisted municipalities to meet the groundwater needs of rapidly growing populations, and helped irrigation districts to improve their water delivery systems and maintain financial stability in face of changing customer bases.

Water banking tools were designed specifically to respect existing water rights, and to not jeopardize the validity of these rights when they are temporarily transferred to the water bank for use by other people for instream flow restoration. The system is flexible and offers temporary and permanent options, which builds wider support among water users and potential market participants. It also has a strong regulatory foundation which provides stability and accountability, thus meeting concerns of the regulatory agencies, especially those responsible for the administration of water rights.

Source: Heather MacKay, personal communication (2010).

flows, can in principle be protected. The case of the Deschutes River basin nicely illustrates the feasibility of this strategy (Box 22.4).

A dry-year option (Characklis et al., 2006) is an alternative to water markets and water banks. It is a contingent contract between a buyer and a seller. The dry-year option gives the buyer the right, but not the obligation, to use water owned by the seller. Usually, the contract specifies the circumstances under which the option can be exercised. For example, it could be a target flow in the river or the water level in a reservoir. One advantage of a dry-year option is that it deals with the problem of hoarding, which can be observed with water users who require a high reliability of supply.

As mentioned above, most of the water reallocation studies focus on agriculture-to-urban water transfers. However, with growing environmental concerns, some water managers are also investigating the option of environmental water transfers (see Boxes 22.4 and 22.8). For example, Hollinshead and Lund (2006) analyse the least expensive strategies for staged seasonal water purchases for an environmental water acquisition programme in California. Suen (2006) use a multi-objective model to characterize the trade-off relationship between environmental flows and human needs. Tilmant et al. (2010) determine the reservoir operating policies and the opportunity cost for power companies to restore floods in the Zambezi River basin (Box 22.5).

BOX 22.5

Modelling the benefits of jointly operated reservoirs in mitigating environmental impact in the Zambezi River basin

The Zambezi River basin is one of the largest basins in Africa. It is a largely untapped resource where water is used primarily for generating electricity. There are four main dams on the Zambezi. The Kariba Dam (1959, Zambia/Zimbabwe) and the Cahora Bassa Dam (1974; Mozambique) are both located on the main stem. They have installed capacity of 1350 MW and 2075 MW respectively. The other two are located on the Kafue River in Zambia. The Kafue Dam has an installed capacity of 900 MW, while the Itezh Itezhi Dam acts as a storage dam.

Significant work is underway to plan new reservoirs in the basin. These large storage facilities have traditionally been designed and managed to maximize revenues from energy generation. This has altered the hydrological regime by disrupting the ecosystems and their livelihood functions such as fisheries. Up to now, each of the reservoirs has operated in isolation.

Implementing hydropower–to–environment water transfers in the Zambezi requires the development of new reservoir operating policies that help to restore degraded ecosystems in the lower Zambezi without undue adverse effects on generating hydroelectricity. One way to achieve this is to coordinate reservoir releases. The coordinated operation of the reservoirs as one system could reduce the environmental impact while minimizing the benefits that had to be foregone. Preliminary findings indicate that the reduction in total energy output varies from 1.5% to 6%, depending on the type of flood to be restored in the lower Zambezi. The question is whether society wishes to incur such costs (or forego such benefits) in order to reduce negative environmental impacts.

Source: Tilmant et al. (2010).

22.3.1 Risk management and hedging

Any attempts to formulate the water resources allocation problem must be made without a perfect knowledge of future water supplies. Hydrological uncertainty exposes risk-averse water managers and users to a volume (supply) risk, which has to be managed. The traditional approach to the problem, which consists of increasing supply by constructing reservoirs and pumping stations, has reached its limit in many cases. This is because the social, environmental and economic costs have become so high that there are now incentives for non-structural measures such as water transfers to increase supply.

Where irrigated agriculture is important, this sector can absorb some of the fluctuations in climate, and thus serve as a kind of buffer by transferring risk from urban users to farmers using an option contract (see above). The idea is that one party (urban users) is willing to pay a premium for transferring the supply risk. In other words, one party seeks to secure additional water in order to reduce its exposure to hydro-climatic variability. The supplier (the farmers) must be able and willing to bear further supply risks after compensation. With such a risk-transfer mechanism, the benefits must of course exceed costs for both parties. A review of agricultural production risks and their management can be found in World Bank (2005). Gomez Ramos and Garrido (2004) design an option contract between farmers and a Spanish city. Brown and Carriquiry (2007) propose a combined option contract–insurance system to increase the reliability of supplying water to Manila in the Philippines. The idea is to transform the variability from the hydrological to the financial space where it can be levelled out using insurance products.

Risk management is also fairly common in the hydropower sector where hydropower companies are exposed to the hydrological supply risk. Water release decisions are combined with sophisticated financial products such as forward contracts and options to limit the risk exposure of the company (Mo et al., 2001, Kristiansen, 2004). With the liberalization of the electricity sector in many countries, hydropower companies now face a new source of risk: the price risk. This cannot be hedged using bilateral contracts because prices tend to increase during dry periods, which is precisely when the hydropower companies cannot rely on their own production to meet their commitments. This creates a contracting dilemma for the hydropower sector: if lightly contracted, it will be exposed during low price periods which may occur frequently and last for some time; if heavily contracted, it will be exposed to extremely high prices in the dry periods, when it may not produce enough to meet its contract (Barroso et al., 2003).

Water resources allocation problems address the issue of how water should be combined with other scarce resources to obtain the greatest return. This in turn implies that the consequences associated with the allocation decisions can, in principle, be valued. Because there usually are no markets, and even when there are they are usually absent or ineffective, allocation decisions can seldom rely on market prices. Instead, it is necessary to assess accounting or shadow prices that reflect the value of water (Young, 2005). To achieve this, economists have developed and implemented various non-market valuation techniques to address water resources management problems (Loomis, 2000).

22.4 Opportunities: How the key water allocation issues can be addressed

The water allocation challenges identified in this report are major and complex. Yet there are also opportunities that can mitigate the risks and uncertainties that we face. In this section, we address the four key water allocation issues: water shortages, uncertainty, anticipating change and dealing with conflict.

22.4.1 Dealing with water shortages

How should water be allocated when there is a shortage? Should certain types of use (domestic, environmental, industrial, energy generation or agricultural) be prioritized over others, or should the burden of shortages be shared in an equitable manner? Should established uses and users be protected from encroachments by new entrants? Is there a role for markets and market transactions? If so, how can social and environmental public good values associated with water be protected?

All the water bodies in the case studies reviewed faced periods of severe water shortage, and they all dealt with this in different ways. In the Murray–Darling basin in Australia, a maximum level of water abstraction was set and water reallocation occurred through transferring water use rights, either on a short-term basis or over the long term (Box 22.6). In the Lerma–Chapala basin in Mexico, irrigators had to decrease the amount of water they were using for irrigation and were forced

to release water stored in their reservoirs to supplement dwindling levels in Lake Chapala. This was done to ensure Guadalajara's water supply and to support environmental and tourism needs (Box 22.7). In Andhra Pradesh in India, irrigators reduced groundwater abstractions in cases where recharge rates were low as a result of low rainfall. Because they are aware that water scarcity is a recurring problem, they have shifted to crops that need less water to grow, but which fetch higher market values. As a result, farm incomes have increased over time (Box 22.9).

What we learn from these cases is that water is still being used inefficiently and wastefully. But more *can* be done with less. This requires a new attitude to water; we must become more water wise. Water demand management is central to this, and significant gains can still be made. In the domestic and industrial sectors, demand-side measures are normally more cost-effective than supply-side solutions. In irrigation, this is often not the case because a conversion to more efficient irrigation technologies tends to be capital intensive. Here, the first option is to change to growing crops that need less water, but fetch a higher price at market. Limited and temporary water transfers from agriculture to the domestic and industrial water sectors may create conditions that allow farmers to adapt.

In countries that experience 'economic water scarcity', supply-side options must not be discarded. Such countries require a greater ability to physically control water. An opportunity may present itself in the future in the form of funds being made available to help countries adapt to climate change. With these funds, new infrastructure can be provided that is better at buffering societies and water systems against increased climate variability. If properly designed and implemented, such infrastructure could give an enormous boost to poverty alleviation in many rural areas and could thus contribute to achieving the Millennium Development Goals.

These types of investment have the potential to be 'no regrets' measures; however, the challenge will be for adequate policy and design decisions to be made in the first place. There is debate about whether water buffering infrastructure should be large and centralized or small and distributed – both of which pose very different institutional requirements, governance demands and environmental impacts (Van der Zaag and Gupta, 2008). Obviously such infrastructure

BOX 22.6

Sustainable diversions limits (SDLs) in the Murray–Darling basin

The Murray–Darling River basin is the most significant river system in Australia. The basin covers 14% of Australia's mainland and covers around 1 million km^2 across large parts of Queensland, New South Wales, Victoria, South Australia and all of the Australian Capital Territory.

In accordance with the Water Act 2007, the Murray–Darling Basin Authority prepared a basin plan to manage water resources. The plan ensures that future water use is placed on a sustainable footing so that there is enough water for a healthy environment as well as for other uses. The plan sets mandatory Sustainable Diversion Limits (SDLs) for surface water and groundwater. The limits must reflect an environmentally sustainable level of water withdrawal, which is defined as the level at which water can be taken without compromising key environmental assets, key ecosystem functions, the productive base or key environmental outcomes. As well as meeting the basin's environmental requirements with the SDLs, the Water Act 2007 also requires the basin plan to optimize social, economic and environmental outcomes.

Source: Akhtar Abbas and Frank Walker, personal communication (2010).

development needs to consider issues of adaptive capacity, and robustness, as well as issues relating to the conjunctive use of groundwater and surface water (see the Deschutes and Andhra Pradesh cases). Various aspects associated with this are dealt with in detail in other chapters of this *World Water Development Report.*

22.4.2 Dealing with uncertainty

Water rights, permits and entitlements, as well as allocation systems, provide security and predictability in an uncertain world. Their aim is to reduce risk. But there is a trade-off between reliability and the amount of water one can use – the more secure the smaller the flow. How can water allocation systems better deal with uncertain inflows while maximizing beneficial use?

Such a risk-based approach needs a precise understanding of the water system –how much water is available, how much is needed, and when and where is it needed. This requires the ability to establish accurate water accounting systems (Molden and Sakthivadivel, 1999) that include quantified knowledge of water fluxes

BOX 22.7

Unresolved water allocation in the Lerma–Chapala basin

The Lerma–Chapala basin straddles five Mexican states and provides surface water and groundwater for nearly 900,000 ha of irrigation farms. It also supplements the water needs of Mexico's two largest cities, Mexico City and Guadalajara, and the touristic Chapala Lake at its downstream end. The Lerma–Chapala basin is now 'closed' as a result of increasing human pressure on its water resources, which have depleted the levels of blue water and made the basin very sensitive to climatic fluctuations. The lack of accurate water accounting in the basin, and the relatively wet period in the 1960s and 1970s, resulted in an overestimation of water availability and the 'overbuilding' of the basin. This is a common phenomenon in closing basins, and makes it very difficult to reduce water use levels once a basin has closed.

The institutional response to basin closure has focused on surface water allocation mechanisms, resulting in the 1991 surface water allocation agreement. The continued decline of Lake Chapala and Guadalajara's increasing concerns about its water supply, led to a revision of the 1989 water allocation agreement between 1999 and 2004. The negotiations were conducted at the highest political level between the basin states, Guanajuato, Jalisco, Mexico, Michoacan and Queretaro and focused on achieving an agreement on rainfall and runoff data and new formulas for water allocation.

One of the results was the transfer of water from upstream reservoirs to Lake Chapala, which alienated irrigation farmers from the negotiation process. The water challenges in the basin remain, and water crises will inevitably recur during periods of low rainfall.

What can be learned from this case is that difficult zero-sum allocation decisions need legitimacy, both scientifically and politically. Scientific legitimacy requires reliable data and information, and sound interpretation of these data; political legitimacy requires an inclusive approach that involves all those who will be affected by allocation decisions in the decision-making process.

Source: Phillippus Wester, personal communication (2010).

(inflows, outflows, abstractions, consumption, etc.) and the changes in groundwater and surface water stocks in a given basin over a given period of time.[1] Detailed monitoring of water stocks and fluxes can combine conventional ways of data collection with new ways that use remotely sensed data for rainfall, evaporation, open water levels and changes in groundwater storage.

Farmer managed groundwater systems in Andhra Pradesh

The Andhra Pradesh region of India faces severe problems with the over-exploitation of groundwater. In the 1990s, a project started to promote participatory hydrological monitoring among smallholder farmers. This was followed by the Andhra Pradesh Farmer Managed Groundwater System (APFAMGS) project, which is a community-based project that focuses on developing the capacity of groundwater users to manage their resource in a sustainable way.

The APFAMGS has a demand-side approach to groundwater management, where farmers learn about their groundwater system in such a way that they can make informed decisions about their water use. Sustainable groundwater management is feasible only if users understand the occurrence, cycle and limited availability of groundwater. And they must also accept that collective decisions taken on groundwater conservation ultimately safeguard their own interests.

Thus, the burden of controlling water extraction is transferred to individuals in communities who know the 'why and how' and act on sound information rather than because they are bound by rules and regulations. The project does not offer any incentives in the form of cash or subsidies – the assumption is that access to scientific data and knowledge will enable farmers to make the right decisions.

This has had measurable effects:
- Changing to crops that need less water and adopting new irrigation methods have led to reductions in the amount of water used.
- Farmers have consistently improved their profitability with the net value of outputs per ha nearly doubling.

A combination of the following factors appears to explain the success of this approach:
- Opportune information on groundwater availability as a key input to farmers' risk management paradigm – with relatively small monsoons usually being followed by reduced sowing in the dry season;
- The low-storage, fast-response, hard-rock aquifers that are replenished annually provide a natural limit on water over-use;
- Estimates of the available groundwater and projected demands being provided in time to inform dry planting;
- Repeating crop water planning over a number of years provides a sound framework for farmers' decisions;
- Reductions in groundwater over-use are not coming from altruistic collective action, but from many individual farmers making informed risk-management decisions – hence no authoritative leadership is required for enforcement.

Source: Garduño et al. (2009).

Much can be learned from prediction of ungauged basins (PUB) experiences.

22.4.3 Anticipating change
How can water institutions be transformed into learning organizations that are forward looking and can anticipate change?

All the case studies in this chapter highlight how important it is to understand the hydro-social system and its dynamics. The Andhra Pradesh case on groundwater management demonstrates the knowledge dimension most convincingly (Box 22.8). The most important lesson is that stakeholders themselves need to have an intimate knowledge of and appreciation for the resource on which they rely – which leads to an interest in carefully monitoring system behaviour. This creates a kind of distributed intelligence among a group of water users that may be considered a prerequisite for any organization to learn. The co-learning stakeholder management structure can be supported by appropriate access to scientific data, expertise and knowledge that can help to select alternative management choices and shared decision-making on how to use scarce water resources.

22.4.4 Dealing with conflict
It seems inevitable that there will be a rise in competition between water users as well as differences of opinion and other tensions. This may lead to disputes and conflict. How can we anticipate these rising tensions, and what strategies are there to transform them into enhanced cooperation?

Competition over water can escalate into conflict. But where decision processes are considered legitimate and fair, competition can also evolve into cooperative deals. Difficult questions are raised when making allocation decisions. Two examples:

- Which is more important, the livelihood of a fisherwoman living in a remote village near a river, or an urban middle-class person who requires internet and electricity?
- Two (hypothetical) communities live on opposite sides of a watershed divide. One is located in a relatively water-rich basin and the other in a water-scarce basin. How does the second community's right to development relate to the first community's right to live in a healthy and undisturbed environment? (Gupta and Van der Zaag, 2008)

These questions point at the normative and political dimensions of allocation decisions. Where stakeholders

BOX 22.9

Multi-stakeholder planning in the Alouette River in Canada

ity, BC Hydro, came under mounting public pressure from a number of community groups, a range of NGOs and the media to change the ways their dams operated. There were calls for the release of in-stream flows, and increased participation in decision-making processes surrounding water management in the province.
An opportunity to implement change came in 1994 when BC Hydro applied for an expansion of generating capacity at its Stave Falls power plant. Yielding to demands that flows in the contiguous Alouette River (which feeds the Stave Falls scheme) be augmented, the provincial government decided that a water use plan be conducted as a condition for going ahead with the Stave Falls upgrade. As a result, a multi-stakeholder process, which came to be known as the Alouette Water Use Plan (AWUP), was launched in 1995 to review the operating plans of the Alouette scheme.

The AWUP was an inclusive and science-based process, which had the potential to solve longstanding problems. It was based on structured decision making, which combined objective, scientific data with the values people placed on different water uses. This was crucial for its acceptance.

The process was hailed for building trust between the different parties and for gradually replacing the antagonism that had characterized previous interactions between BC Hydro and other stakeholders. As a consequence, the provincial government mandated BC Hydro to draw up water use plans for all its facilities within a five-year period. This resulted in the development of 23 WUPs, which revised the operating plans of 30 BC Hydro dams.

Source: Lucia Scodanibbio, personal communication (2010).

have been involved in decision-making and where they have been respected and receive fair treatment, then it is likely that the outcome will be sustained and enforced. This requires norms, such as the norm that a household that is to be resettled due to dam construction may not become worse off, not now but also not in the future (WCD, 2000). Multi-stakeholder planning in the Alouette River in Canada (Box 22.9) is an example of inclusive decision-making that has far-reaching consequences.

Another way of addressing water allocation's conflict potential focuses on promoting interdependency between the users of the shared water resource, while simultaneously unlocking the additional benefits that can be gained through cooperation. Examples are benefit-sharing projects and rewards for environmental services systems, which can be developed between user groups within countries but also between riparian countries. Examples of how this worked between riparian countries can be seen in the cases of the Santa Cruz River basin (Box 22.10), the Zambezi River basin (Box 22.4) and the Blue Nile River basin (Box 22.11).

BOX 22.10

Groundwater use and re-use in the transboundary Santa Cruz River basin

Climate change, hydrological variability, and rapid urban growth characterize the United States–Mexico border region and pose significant challenges for the planning and allocation of limited water resources. On the Arizona–Sonora border, the upper Santa Cruz River has only ephemeral surface flows. Meeting the water needs of 300,000 inhabitants greatly increases groundwater dependence. The basin's aquifer is shared by the sister cities, Nogales, Arizona, and Nogales, Sonora – but groundwater is allocated separately on either side of the border in accordance with prevailing national and state laws and institutions.

Adequate wastewater treatment has enlarged the water pie on both sides of the border. This was possible through joint bi-national management of urban wastewater, which is the result of years of cooperation. Two important lessons of particular relevance to bi-national groundwater management are, first, that informal collaboration based on shared trust must be strengthened through international accords, and second, that scientific data and joint studies provide the basis for operational agreements.

Source: Sharon Megdal, personal communication (2010).

Potential conflicts between water consumers and environmental water uses can be resolved through changing the operating rules of dams (Box 22.12). New approaches to dam planning and operations that optimize water allocation benefits across a range of resources and values are required to achieve more sustainable dam operations. These solutions must occur at the level of entire systems because dams are only one element of larger water management systems.

BOX 22.11

Triple win on the Blue Nile through transboundary cooperation on infrastructure development

The upper Blue Nile River Basin in Ethiopia has a huge potential for hydropower generation and irrigated agriculture. Controversies exist as to whether the numerous infrastructural development projects that are on the drawing board in Ethiopia will generate positive or negative externalities downstream in Sudan and Egypt. In order to examine the economic benefits and costs of developing reservoirs on the Blue Nile for Ethiopia, Sudan and Egypt, Goor et al. (2010) developed a basin-wide integrated hydro-economic model.

The model integrates essential hydrologic, economic and institutional components of the river basin in order to explore both the hydrologic and economic consequences of various policy options and planned infrastructural projects. Unlike most of the deterministic economic-hydrologic models reported in the literature, a stochastic programming formulation has been adopted in order to:

- Understand the effect of the hydrologic uncertainty on management decisions;
- Determine allocation policies that naturally hedge against the hydrological risk; and
- Assess the relevant risk indicators.

The study reveals that the development of four mega dams in the upper part of the Blue Nile Basin would change the drawdown refill cycle of the High Aswan Dam. Should the operation of the reservoirs be coordinated, they would enable an average saving for Egypt of at least 2.5×10^9 m^{3}a^{-1} through reduced evaporation losses from the Lake Nasser.

Moreover, the new reservoirs (Karadobi, Beko-Abo, Mandaya and Border) in Ethiopia would have significant positive impacts on hydropower generation and irrigation in Ethiopia and Sudan: at the basin scale, the annual energy generation is boosted by 38.5 TWh a^{-1} of which 14.2 TWh a^{-1} due to storage. Moreover, the regulation capacity of the above mentioned reservoirs would enable an increase of the Sudanese irrigated area by 5.5%.

Sediment fluxes poses another important dimension to these development plans, which were not considered in this study.

Source: Goor et al. (2010), with some areas of text reproduced.

BOX 22.12

Innovative approaches for improving dam planning and operations for optimized water allocation benefits

In several countries, changes in the way dams operate have been prompted by re-allocating water from consumptive to environmental uses Watts et al. (2011).

In the United States, an ongoing effort known as the Sustainable Rivers Project is changing operations at US Army Corps of Engineers' dams. The project currently involves twenty-nine dams in eight river systems as demonstration sites for national implementation.

In the Yangtze River, China, a proposal is being advanced that proposes to move flood-risk management out of hydropower reservoirs and to invest a portion of the consequent increased revenue from generating hydropower from the additional store water into flood-risk management on the floodplain and ecosystem restoration and conservation.

In South Africa, the Berg River Project is the first large instream dam that was designed according to international best practice standards, such that it can release both low and high flows that will coincide as closely as possible with natural inflows and natural flood events.

In Australia, a series of trial variable flow releases from Dartmouth Dam in the Murray-Darling Basin implemented and monitored between 2001 and 2008 demonstrate that it is possible to reduce the negative impacts of transferring consumptive water between reservoirs by altering established dam operation practices. The results from these trials were used to develop new interim operating guidelines for Dartmouth Dam.

These examples demonstrate that more sustainable approaches for dam planning and operations are possible and require close collaboration between participating organizations and stakeholders. To achieve sustainable river management at global scales will require considerably more investment in trials and demonstration sites that can illustrate new approaches, opportunities and solutions.

Source: Robyn Watts, personal communication (2010), from the results of the UNESCO Workshop 'Challenges and Solutions for Planning and Operating Dams for Optimised Benefits' held in Paris, 26–28 October 2010.

In South Africa, the National Water Act (No. 36 of 1998) introduced the Water Allocation Reform (WAR) programme to address race and gender imbalances that had been created in the water sector as a result of discriminatory legislation in the country in the past (Seetal, 2005). WAR derived its mandate from the Constitution, the National Water Policy, the National Water Act and other related legislation. The Position Paper for Water Allocation Reform in South Africa outlined the rules for allocating water to promote race and gender reform, while at the same time supporting the government's programmes for poverty eradication, job creation, economic development and nation building. This included addressing the expectations of the historically disadvantaged majority South Africans, but also dealing with the fears and uncertainty of a historically advantaged minority – primarily by minimizing the impact on existing lawful users and supporting the stability of the rural economy.

Conclusion

Water allocation lies at the heart of water management. In a world that experiences gradual and sudden changes, in terms of population, diet, land use, economic markets and climate, water allocation is an increasingly important topic.

The experiences reviewed in this chapter show that such conditions require a sound knowledge about water availability and water use, as well as the capacity to monitor infrastructure. Interactions between groundwater and surface water need to be understood, as do the effects that changes in land use have on both groundwater and surface water fluxes at different levels.

It is up to institutions to make sense of the status quo and guide decision-making. This is not trivial, as in more and more cases, allocation decisions are zero-sum. Often, a large variety of sectoral interests needs to be considered and weighted according to social, economic, ecological, cultural and political criteria. Such criteria are difficult to put under one encompassing metric, so it is not easy to reach consensus on preferences and priorities. The principles underlying allocation decisions should therefore be known, and be seen to be legitimate and just.

Finally, and importantly, a changing environment demands that institutions become learning organizations that are ready to develop and implement adaptive management practices.

Some of the cases reviewed in this chapter have shown that tools, such as water accounting and integrated hydro–economic models, can assist the water allocation process. Based on a good understanding of system interactions, optimal decisions can be reached – which allow fair compensation to be given to those who have to forego some immediate water benefits.

In some cases, market-like mechanisms can assist in finding optimal solutions, for example where uncertainty and risk can be transferred differentially between the interested sectors or parties, depending on their ability to cope.

In most cases, it was shown that building the knowledge base of water users is the essential element that the many individual water users need to be able to reach the right decisions.

There is a need for effective stakeholder engagement in decision-making in order to ensure transparency and fair treatment. The environmental sustainability, economic viability and social acceptability of water allocation decisions, rests on true stakeholder engagement, which comes from recognizing their democratic right to influence the management of water resources. A distinction must be made between the commonly practised 'cosmetic' stakeholder consultations and true empowerment where a community takes control of its water management future. True stakeholder empowerment leads to more legitimate and cost-effective solutions that have a better chance of being implemented.

It is time to rethink the operations of water infrastructure in a way that both enhances the synergy between water users, and fosters the benefits of cooperation. Systems need to be flexible, which can be achieved through a combination of investment in both infrastructure and human resources and innovative management solutions.

The water reform process also needs to recognize and correct racial and gender inequities in water use by addressing the expectations of all stakeholders in an equitable and transparent manner.

Notes

1 Such information will enable the inclusion of the state of the water resource in national accounts, viz. the United Nations Statistics Division's Standard for Environmental–Economic Accounting for Water (SEEA-W), and the UN's international recommendations for water statistics (UN, 2010); see also Brouwer et al., 2005).

References

Barroso, L. A., Granville, S., Trinkenreich, J., Pereira, M. V. and Lino, P. 2003. Managing hydrological risks in hydro-based portfolios. *Power Engineering Society General Meeting*, 2003, IEEE. doi: 10.1109/PES.2003.1270395

Boelens, R., and Dávila, G. (eds), 1998. *Searching for Equity: Conceptions of Justice and Equity in Peasant Irrigation.* Assen, the Netherlands, Van Gorcum Publishers.

Booker, J., and Young, R 1994, Modeling intrastate and interstate markets for Colorado river water resources. *Journal of Environmental Economic. Management,* Vol. 26, pp. 66–87.

Brouwer, R., Schenaub, S. and van der Veer, R. 2005. Integrated river basin accounting in the Netherlands and the European Water Framework Directive. *Statistical Journal of the United NationsEconomic Commission for Europe, ECE*, Vol. 22, No. 2, pp. 111–31.

Brown, C.and Carriquiry, M., 2007. Managing hydroclimatological risk to water supply with option contracts and reservoir index insurance. *Water Resources Research*, Vol. 43. doi:10.1029/2007WR006093

Characklis, G. W., Kirsch, B. R., Ramsey, J., Dillard, K. E. M., Kelley, C. T. 2006. Developing portfolios of water supply transfers. *Water Resources Research,* Vol. 42, No.5. doi: 10.1029/2005WR004424

Committee on Economic, Social and Cultural Rights *General Comment No. 15: The right to water (arts. 11 and 12 of the International Covenant on Economic, Social and Cultural Rights).* 2002. Twenty-ninth session, Geneva, Switzerland, UN OHCHR. http://www.unhchr.ch/tbs/doc.nsf/0/a5458d1d1bbd713fc1256cc400389e94/$FILE/G0340229.pdf

Dinar, A., Rosegrant, M. W. and Meinzen-Dick, R. S. 1997. *Water Allocation Mechanisms: Principles and Examples.* World Bank Policy Research Working Paper No. 1779. Washington DC, World Bank.

Drieschova, A., Giordano, M. and Fischhendler, I. 2008. Governance mechanisms to address flow variability in water treaties. *Global Environmental Change,* Vol. 18, pp. 285–95.

Garduño, H, Foster, S, Raj, P and van Steenbergen, F. 2009. *Addressing Groundwater Depletion Through Community-based Management Actions in the Weathered Granitic Basement Aquifer of Drought-prone Andhra Pradesh – India.* Case Profile Collection Number 19, Washington DC, World Bank. http://siteresources.worldbank.org/INTWAT/Resources/GWMATE_CP_19AndhraPradesh.pdf

Gómez Ramos, A. and Garrido, A. 2004. Formal risk-sharing mechanisms to allocate uncertain water resources: the case of option contracts. *Water Resources Research,* Vol. 40. doi: 10.1029/2004ER003340

Goor, Q., Halleux, C, Mohamed, Y and Tilmant, A. 2010. Optimal operation of a multipurpose multireservoir system in the Eastern Nile River Basin. *Hydrology and Earth System Sciences,* Vol. 14, pp. 1895–908.

Gupta, J., and van der Zaag, P. 2008. Interbasin water transfers and integrated water resources management: Where engineering, science and politics interlock. *Physics and Chemistry of the Earth.* Vol.33, pp. 28–40. doi:10.1016/j.pce.2007.04.003

Hollinshead, S., and Lund, J. 2006, Optimization of environmental water purchases with uncertainty. *Water Resources Research,* Vol. 42. doi:10.1029/2005WR004228

Jercich, S. A., 1997. California's 1995 water bank program: Purchasing water supply options. *Journal of Water Resources Planning and Management,* Vol. 123, No. 1, pp. 59–65.

Kristiansen, T. 2004. Financial risk management in the hydropower industry using stochastic optimization. *Advanced Modeling and Optimization,* Vol. 6, pp. 17–24.

Lankford, B. A., 2004. Resource-centred thinking in river basins; should we revoke the crop water requirement approach to irrigation planning? *Agricultural Water Management,* Vol. 68, pp. 33–46.

Le Quesne, T, Pegram, G. and von der Heyden, C. 2007. *Allocating Scarce Water: A Primer on Water Allocation, Water Rights and Water Markets.* WWF Water Security Series 1. Godalming, UK, WWF-UK.

Leach, E. R. 1961. *Pul Eliya, a village in Ceylon: a study of land tenure and kinship.* New York, Cambridge University Press.

Loomis, J. 2000, Environmental valuation techniques in water resources decision making. *Journal of Water Resources Planning and Management,* Vol. 126, pp. 339–44.

Lund, J. R. and Israel, M., 1995. Water transfers in water resource systems. *Journal of Water Resources Planning and Management,* Vol. 121, No. 2, pp. 193–204.

Ma, J., Hoekstra, A. Y., Wang, H., Chapagain, A. K. and Wang, D. 2006. Virtual versus real water transfers within China. *Philosophical Transactions of the Royal Society, Biological Science,* Vol. 361, pp. 835–842. http://www.waterfootprint.org/Reports/Ma_et_al_2006.pdf

Manzungu, E., Senzanje, A. and van der Zaag, P. (eds.). 1999. *Water for Agriculture in Zimbabwe: Policy and Management Options for the Smallholder Sector.* Harare, University of Zimbabwe Publications.

Martin, E. D., and Yoder, R. 1988. A comparative description of two farmer-managed irrigation systems in Nepal. *Irrigation and Drainage Systems,* Vol. 2, No. 2, pp. 147–172.

Mo, B., Gjelsvik, A. and Grundt, A. 2001. Integrated risk management of hydropower scheduling and contract management. *IEEE Transactions on Power Systems,* Vol. 16, pp. 216–21. doi:10.1109/59.918289

Mohamed-Katerere, J. and van der Zaag, P. 2003. Untying the 'Knot of Silence': Making water policy and law responsive to local normative systems. Hassan, F. A., Reuss, M., Trottier, J., Bernhardt, C., Wolf, A. T., Mohamed-Katerere, J. and van der Zaag, P. (eds), *History and Future of Shared Water Resources. IHP Technical Documents in Hydrology, PCCP series No. 6.* Paris, UNESCO Publishing.

Molden, D. and Sakthivadivel, R. 1999. Water accounting to assess use and productivity of water. *Water Resources Development,* Vol. 15, pp. 55–71.

Molle, F., Wester, P. and Hirsch, P. 2010 River basin closure: Processes, implications and responses. *Agricultural Water Management,* Vol. 97, pp. 569–77.

Perry, C. 2007. Efficient irrigation; inefficient communication; flawed recommendations. *Irrigation and Drainage,* Vol. 56, pp. 367–78.

Rittel, H. J. W. and Webber, M. M. 1973. Dilemmas in a general theory of planning. *Policy Sciences,* Vol. 4, pp. 155–69.

Seetal, A. R. 2005. Progress with water allocation reform in South Africa. *OECD Workshop on Agriculture and Water: Sustainability, Markets and Policies, Session 5.* Adelaide, South Australia 14–18 November.

Suen J.-P. and Eheart, J. W. 2006. Reservoir management to balance ecosystem and human needs: Incorporating the paradigm of the ecological flow regime. *Water Resources Research 42,* Vol. 3. doi:10.1029/2005WR004314

Tilmant, A., Beevers, L. and Muyunda, B. 2010. Restoring a flow regime through the coordinated operation of a multireservoir system: The case of the Zambezi River basin. *Water Resources Research,* Vol. 46.

UN (United Nations) 2010. *International Recommendations for Water Statistics.* New York, UN Department of Economic and Social Affairs, Statistics Division. http://unstats.un.org/unsd/envaccounting/irws/irwswebversion.pdf

UNISDR (United Nations International Strategy for Disaster Reduction), 2009. *UNISDR Terminology for Disaster Risk Reduction.* http://unisdr.org/files/7817_UNISDRTerminologyEnglish.pdf

Van der Zaag, P. 1993. Factors influencing the operational flexibility of three farmer-managed irrigation systems in Mexico. Proceedings of the 15th International Congress on Irrigation and Drainage, The Hague, ICID, pp. 65–661.

Van der Zaag, P., and Gupta, J. 2008. Scale issues in the governance of water storage projects. *Water Resources. Research*, Vol. 44. doi:10.1029/2007WR006364

Van der Zaag, P., Seyam, I. M. and Savenije, H. H. G. 2002. Towards measurable criteria for the equitable sharing of international water resources. *Water Policy,* Vol. 4, pp. 19–32.

Verma, S., Kampman, D. A., van der Zaag, P. and Hoekstra, A. Y. 2009. Going against the flow: A critical analysis of virtual water trade in the context of India's National River Linking Program. *Physics and Chemistry of the Earth,* Vol. 34, pp. 261–69.

Ward, F. A., Booker, J. F., and Michelsen, A. M., 2006. Integrated economic, hydrologic, and institutional analysis of policy responses to mitigate drought impacts in Rio Grande Basin, *Journal of Water Resources Planning and Management,* Vol. 132, pp. 488–502.

Watts, R., Richter, B., Oppermann, J. J. and Bowmer, K. 2011 Dam reoperation in an era of climate change. *Marine and Freshwater Research,* Vol. 62, No. 3, pp. 321–27.

WCD. 2000. Dams and Development: *A New Framework for Decision-making.* The report of the World Commission on Dams. London, Earthscan.

Wester, P., Vargas-Velazquez, S., Mollard, E. and Silva-Ochoa, P. 2008. Negotiating surface water allocations to achieve a soft landing in the closed Lerma–Chapala basin, Mexico. *Water Resources Development,* Vol. 24, No. 2, pp. 275–88.

Wolf, A. T. 1999. Criteria for equitable allocations: The heart of international water conflict. *Natural Resources Forum,* Vol. 23, No. 1, pp. 3–30.

World Bank, 2005. *Managing Agricultural Production Risk: Innovations in Developing Countries.* Washington DC, World Bank, Agricultural and Rural Development Department.

Young, R. A., 2005. *Determining the Economic Value of Water – Concepts and Methods.* Washington DC, Resources for the Future.

UN DESA
—

Authors Josefina Maestu (UN DESA, UNW–DPAC) and Carlos Mario Gómez (University of Alcalá and IMDEA)

Acknowledgements With the support of Jack Moss (AquaFed), David Coates (UN CBD), Peter Borkey and Roberto Martinez-Hurtado (OECD), and Diego Rodriguez (World Bank). Thanks to Jake Burke (FAO), Rudolph Cleveringa (IFAD), Claudio Caponi (WMO), Ti Le-Huu (UNESCAP), Nikhil Chandavarkar (UN DESA), Thomas Chiramba (UNEP), and William Cosgrove and Richard Connor (WWAP) for comments and materials provided and to Maria Mercedes Sanchez (UN DESA) for proofreading.

© Shutterstock/TonyV3112

Failure to properly recognize the full value of water, including its benefits and costs, is one of the root causes of water resources mismanagement and the political neglect of water issues.

A valuation of the benefits of water is essential in order to improve the decisions of governments, international organizations, the donor community and other stakeholders.

Valuation is a powerful instrument for making the public aware of water's many benefits. Without a doubt, it brings the less-visible benefits of water into the public arena.

Providing reliable information on the benefits of water development and water resources conservation will help to convince governments and stakeholders that water needs to be given priority in national policies. Having the right information will help to target investment, make real differences to economies and societies – and so help to eradicate poverty.

Water valuation is central to the water-related decisions of public and private agents. It can help water managers and stakeholders to choose between water supply and demand alternatives and to recognize the options that will improve welfare while simultaneously sustaining ecosystem services. Water valuation also helps water managers to design subsidies, public incentives and economic instruments that respond to current water challenges.

Water valuation is a tool that can be used to shape cooperative agreements to protect and share the benefits of water resources conservation.

More efforts need to be made to analyse the costs and benefits of water and to incorporate this analysis into decision-making. This helps in the move towards more integrated and holistic socio-economic approaches. Ways of looking at the valuation of water have been shifting from a rather limited focus on the economic benefits, to a more comprehensive focus that also takes into account social, cultural and non-market values. Valuation methods need to be chosen and adapted so that they respond better to policy questions and management needs.

23.1 Introducing the issues

Water is essential for human life. It is used in the production of food, the generation of energy and the manufacture of goods. It is vital to the economy and for preserving the structure and functioning of ecosystems and all the environmental services they provide (Box 23.1). The importance of these benefits makes the provision of water services crucially and intimately linked with development, both as an integral part of a strategy for socio-economic progress and as a precondition for holding on to the advances that have already been made.

However, decisions about how water is used and managed and about how scarce resources should be conserved are still being taken using only part of the information on its multiple benefits. The 'non-visible', external and indirect benefits (and costs) of using water are mostly ignored by end users when they decide how much water to use and what to use it for. This is often true of businesses when they make decisions about what to invest in and produce; of farmers when they decide what crops to grow; and of governments and institutions when they make decisions about priorities for water investment, management and allocation.

This lack of understanding of the multiple benefits of water results in water issues being given a low political priority. It also causes fragmentation of resources and underinvestment, or overinvestment, in water infrastructure. Ultimately, this results in water being given a low priority in national development programmes and in strategies for reducing poverty. It also leads to inefficiencies in how water is used in the many areas of the economy where it is an essential production input.

Valuation, or 'valuing', is a process that judges the importance of water for human welfare. It refers to all the ways that can be used to identify, assess, measure and eventually assign a value to the importance that each benefit, and potential benefit, has for human welfare. Bringing this knowledge to the policy arena can improve water management in many significant ways. Valuations of the economic and social development benefits of water will push water management issues up the political agenda and will help decision-makers to make informed judgements about development opportunities and challenges. Valuation is also important because there are trade-offs to be considered when examining the various management options. Sometimes using available water for one purpose means forgoing the benefits that another use would bring. Valuation results in information that allows economic efficiency and political and social priorities to be addressed more transparently. It might also have a role in resolving water conflicts by indicating the potential shared benefits that come from cooperating to preserve critical water assets (such as transboundary river basins or common pool underground waters) rather than competing for their use.

23.1.1 Valuing the benefits of water so that it can be made a priority in the political agenda

Water is important for development. But if this is so, why do so many poor countries still lack water infrastructures, have difficulty benefiting from water's productive uses and suffer from poor access to basic sanitation and water supply services?

Part of the answer lies in the fact that most of the benefits obtained from (and the costs incurred by) investing in water and water management are external to the agencies and firms making the investments. Valuation shows that the benefits that countries derive from having water exceed the benefits obtained from the direct productive uses of water. In order to understand this, it is necessary to analyse how the overall productivity of all sectors is constrained by the availability and quality of water facilities (Kemp, 2005).

BOX 23.1

Categories of economic values

Direct use values: The direct uses of water resources for consumption include inputs to agriculture, manufacturing and domestic households. Non-consumption uses include hydroelectricity generation, recreation, navigation and cultural activities.

Indirect use values: The indirect environmental services provided by water include waste assimilation and the protection of habitats, biodiversity and hydrological functions.

Option values: These refer to the value of having the option to use water directly or indirectly in the future.

Non-use values: These include water's bequest value (passing on this natural resource to future generations) and the intrinsic value of water and water ecosystems, including biodiversity, the value people place simply on knowing that a wild river, for example, exists.

Source: UNSD (2007).

Better access to and more widespread availability of water expands the productive capacity of the economy by, for example, increasing the productivity of land or labour, and improving the quality of crops, energy and other products. Valuation also shows the

BOX 23.2

Valuing water's indirect benefits to support investment decisions

The Bhakra multipurpose dam system in northern India generated indirect benefits in two ways. First, the inter-industry links that were forged resulted in increases in the demand for inputs from other sectors. Second, the direct outputs of the dam led to higher levels of income, increased wages and generally higher levels of economic prosperity. For every rupee of direct benefit in terms of electricity generated, farms irrigated, water supplied, floods controlled and drought prevented, the indirect benefits amounted to an additional 0.9 rupee. The gains perceived by rural workers were also higher than the gains for other rural and urban households. This showed that one of the benefits of the project was that it led to a more equal distribution of income (Bhatia et al., 2007).

'The multiplier for the Sobradinho Dam in Brazil was estimated at between 2.0 and 2.4 depending on what assumptions are applied to the supply of labour and capital. This means that for every US$1 invested, there was a total economic return of US$2 to US$2.4.'

Source: SIWI, WHO and NORAD (2005, p. 22).

important benefits that improved water infrastructures and services bring to production – having access to water is a cost-effective and safe way of reducing production costs. Farmers' incomes increase substantially when they shift from rain-fed to irrigated agriculture. Hydroelectricity provides energy for production and reduces reliance on expensive fossil fuels. Deliberation on the importance of these direct benefits has supported decisions to invest in multipurpose infrastructures as an effective way of fostering productivity and saving costs in all the activities to which water contributes as a production input (Box 23.2).

Valuation also highlights the importance of the intangible health benefits of improving basic sanitation and access to safe drinking water. Improved health means fewer lost working days – and increased productivity. The effects of better health can be seen in people living longer and having a better quality of life. Better services contribute to human development by allowing people to look and plan further into the future. They also enhance capacity so that people see the benefits of spending time acquiring an education, in the knowledge that they will have the better health conditions that will allow them to benefit from it into the future.

The World Health Organization believes that half the consequences of malnutrition are caused by

TABLE 23.1

Overall benefits of achieving the MDGs for water and sanitation

Types of benefit	Breakdown	Monetized benefits (in US$)
Time saved by improving water and sanitation services	• 20 billion working days a year	US$63 billion a year
Productivity savings	• 320 million productive days gained in the 15–59 age group • 272 million school attendance days a year • 1.5 billion healthy days for children under five	US$9.9 billion a year
Health-care savings		• US$7 billion a year for health agencies • US$340 million for individuals
Value of deaths averted, based on discounted future earnings		US$3.6 billion a year
Total benefits		**US$84 billion a year**

Sources: OECD (2010); Prüss-Üstün et al. (2008); Hutton and Haller (2004).

inadequate water, sanitation and hygiene. Providing access to safe drinking water in poor societies is one of the most effective labour-saving measures. For governments to consider just the financial value of healthcare savings in their budget decisions, would be to overlook the importance of less visible, but in many cases more significant, economic values (Table 23.1). In poor countries, this is a concern because when the financial benefits are lower than the economic ones, the effort made to improve water services is usually less than what is required for economic development.

Information about the macroeconomic performance of poor countries – measured in gross domestic product (GDP), employment and productivity – has helped to confirm the vital correlation between water and economic development, and the potential that water development has to boost economic growth: Countries without improved water management and access to water and sanitation services, with per capita annual income below US$750 grew on average at only 0.1% per year, which is equivalent to being trapped in the same level of income, while countries in the same range of income but with better access to water services grew at 3.7%, a rate that, if sustained in the long term, might guarantee their escape from poverty and help them converge to middle income economies (SIWI, WHO and NORAD, 2005).

23.1.2 Valuing the benefits of water can support pro-poor strategies and better targeting

The benefits of water, when properly valued, show that projects aimed at improving access to basic sanitation and safe drinking water make economic sense. And what is more important, they show that they are effective in promoting equity, in stimulating gender fairness and in opening new windows of opportunity for the poor and for future generations. Valuing the many non-financial benefits of water is essential to enable societies to take advantage of development opportunities, to focus on poverty alleviation and to avoid unsustainable trends in water policy (Box 23.3 and Figure 23.1).

Valuation of the health benefits of investing in water and improving water management shows that providing basic water and sanitation services is essential to halt the poverty spiral of low income, low savings and low investment in human and physical capital. 'Poor people in Africa spend at least a third of their incomes on the treatment of water-related diseases like malaria and diarrhoea. … The cost of the productive time lost due to these diseases as well as widespread human

BOX 23.3

Valuing the effects that water-related diseases have on productivity can improve investment targeting

In a study in 2008, the World Bank presented an estimate of the economic effects of mortality from malaria, pneumonia and acute lower respiratory illnesses in Ghana and Pakistan. The same study also looked at the prevalence of diarrhoea and malnutrition. A human capital approach was applied to quantify lost wages that resulted from environmental factors. The long-term direct and indirect costs in Ghana and Pakistan were estimated at 9.3% and 8.8%, of their respective GDPs. At least half of this impact is attributed to water-related environmental risks.

The 1991 cholera epidemic in Peru was treated at a cost of US$1 billion, but could have been prevented by expending US$100 million.

Source: Moss et al. (2003).

BOX 23.4

Valuing the benefits of water can define international priorities and target support at the poor

The Copenhagen Consensus sought to compare the costs and benefits of a broad range of development interventions in order to help define international priorities. It did this by evaluating benefit–cost ratios (BCRs) using standardized methodologies across a number of sectors. In 2008, Whittington et al. carried out an exercise on a range of low-cost water and sanitation sector interventions. Not all water and sanitation projects would pass a benefit–cost analysis, especially because of the substantial upfront capital investment required, which yields benefits over a long period. As a result, it is vital to evaluate the costs as well as the benefits of alternative investments, given that different service levels may yield comparable benefits at very different costs.

The Whittington study (2008, p. 3) concluded by stating: 'the key to successful water and sanitation investments is to discover forms of service and payment mechanisms that will render the improvements worthwhile for those who must pay for them. In many cases, the conventional network technologies of water supply will fail this test and poor households need alternative, non-networked technologies'.

FIGURE 23.1

Access to water and potential gains in terms of gender, equity and education opportunities for children.
Left panel, distribution of those who usually collect drinking water; right panel, proportion of the population using drinking water piped on premises, other improved drinking water source or an unimproved source, by wealth quintile, sub-Saharan Africa.

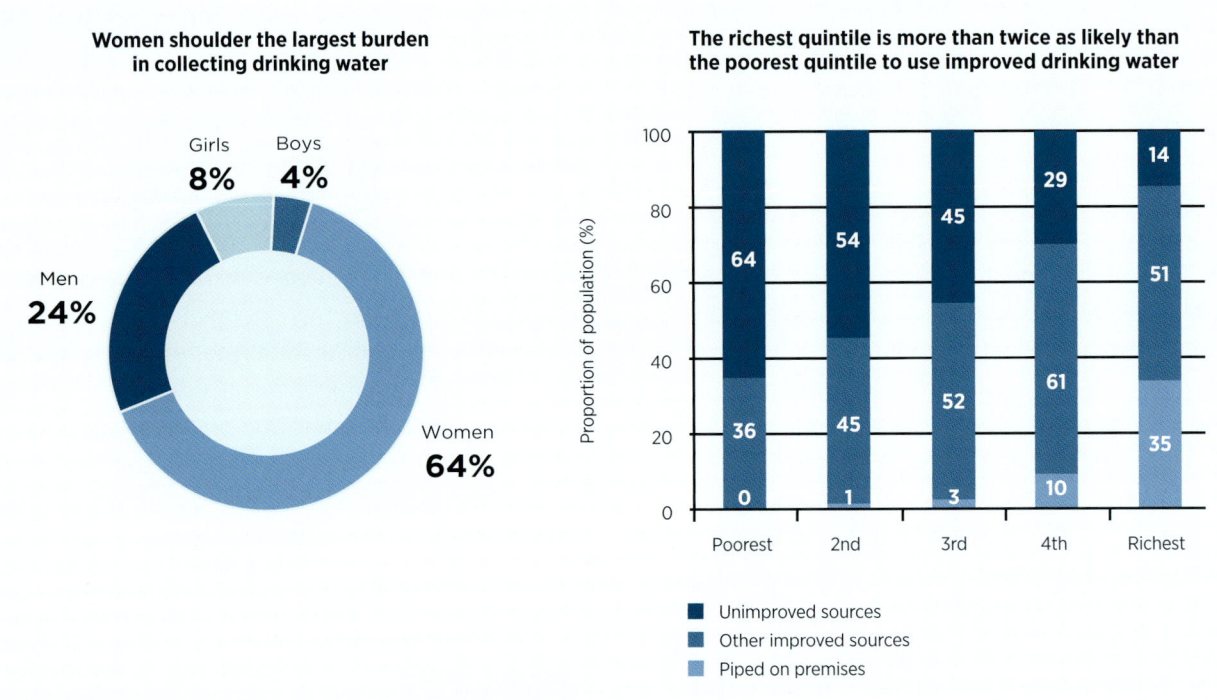

Women shoulder the largest burden in collecting drinking water

Girls **8%** Boys **4%** Men **24%** Women **64%**

The richest quintile is more than twice as likely than the poorest quintile to use improved drinking water

Proportion of population (%)

	Poorest	2nd	3rd	4th	Richest
Unimproved sources	64	54	45	29	14
Other improved sources	36	45	52	61	51
Piped on premises	0	1	3	10	35

- Unimproved sources
- Other improved sources
- Piped on premises

Note: For families without a drinking water source on the premises it is usually women who go to the source to collect drinking water. Surveys from 45 developing countries show that this is the case in almost two-thirds of households, while in almost a quarter of households, it is men who usually collect the water. In 12% of households, however, children carry the main responsibility for collecting water, with girls under 15 years of age being twice as likely to carry this responsibility as boys under the age of 15 years. The real burden on children is likely to be higher because, in many households the water collection burden is shared, and children – though not the main person responsible – often make several roundtrips carrying water.
Sources: WHO and UNICEF (2010).

suffering must also be added to this' (SIWI, WHO and NORAD, 2005, p. 13).

People who do not have access to water from a safe facility that is located nearby pay a high opportunity cost for collecting the minimum amount they need to satisfy their basic needs. Although this cost is not measured in monetary terms, it is effectively paid in terms of lost time, lost school days and lost working days. Making water available to the poor is a means of freeing up human capital that can then be put to creating wealth. A valuation of these benefits justifies the collective provision of water because self-provision for household consumption is proportionally more expensive for the poor than for the rich and represents a heavier burden for women and children. But it is important to understand which interventions will bring

about the greatest benefits, based on levels of service and ability of poor households to pay.

Halting the poverty spiral is generally possible if income earning opportunities for the poor are increased. Improving water supply for productive uses, particularly for food production, would facilitate this (Box 23.5). Agriculture is still the main livelihood and the engine of growth for three-quarters of the world's poor, who still predominantly live in rural areas. Strategies to reduce poverty need to focus on improving farmers' incomes and building resilience in this sector. Valuing the impacts of higher yields and the effects of growing a greater variety of crops can help to bring about better poverty reduction strategies relating to the agricultural use of water. Knowledge of the value of higher incomes and the impact of lower food prices

Valuing the benefits of sanitation can foster government action and redouble the focus on sanitation

- 2008 was the International Year of Sanitation. This helped to put the neglected sanitation crisis onto the agendas of government leaders, the donor community, and civil society.
- The Sanitation and Water for All initiative aims to encourage donor governments and recipient countries' finance ministers to increase the efforts being made in the area of sanitation.
- Sustainable Sanitation: The Five-Year Drive to 2015 is an advocacy vehicle committed to keeping sanitation high on the political agenda, promoting national coordination and inspiring actors in the sanitation and health fields.

All these efforts are built, to a large extent, on the results of valuation analysis that show the links that sanitation and health have with economic development and environmental sustainability. The crucial information came from the work of the World Health Organization (WHO) (which highlights the important economic benefits of appropriate sanitation actions), and the UN-Water GLAAS analysis of existing drinking water and sanitation financing and its recommendations. Recommendation 1 says: 'Developing countries and external support agencies to demonstrate greater political commitment to sanitation and drinking water, given their central role in human and economic development.'

helps to measure those effects and target strategies appropriately.

23.1.3 Valuing the benefits of water can inform water management choices

Water valuation makes a real contribution by providing relevant information on the value of the different types of benefits and costs attached to the different courses of action open to water managers. Some of these courses of action complement other water and sanitation initiatives, while others are mutually exclusive (Table 23.2).

Each alternative considered on its own can be assessed as an individual project. Nevertheless this information, while useful, is not enough to make a decision. It requires comparing the value of its opportunity costs with the best available alternative. Dams, for example, are used to store water for drinking, irrigation, and

hydroelectricity generation as well as flood management. All these uses provide considerable benefits to society. However, dams have negative effects on the hydromorphological conditions of rivers by modifying aquatic habitats and influencing other valuable ecosystem services downstream. The impact of the value, or the cost, of losing these services must be considered when assessing the overall economic benefits of a dam. It is perhaps even more important to consider the alternative options for storing water, as was done in the case of New York when the city needed to plan a new water supply system (Box 6). Alternatives can include using natural infrastructure such as wetlands, soil or groundwater to store water. Each of these, along with other options, will provide co-benefits such as fisheries, water purification or flood mitigation. In the case of desalinated water, it may be more expensive to produce but its provision is more dependable. The cost of provision, however, needs to be compared with the full cost of using alternative sources of water. This comparison should include environmental costs that would not occur if the overuse of resources were prevented.

The relevant comparison of opportunity costs and benefits that are either obtained or foregone with each management option in the decision-making process are varied and context specific – for example, when considering how new infrastructure projects may (or may not) be more beneficial than demand-management options for ensuring water security. Demand management may be the most cost-effective way of increasing available water, but existing arrangements may make it financially unviable for water distribution managers. Managers will 'sell' fewer services, and so get a reduced income. With price caps on water services and no support from governments, this may affect the funding that is available for the operation, maintenance and replacement of infrastructures – and the viability of the services themselves.

When assessing alternative courses of action, it is also important to consider that the market price cannot capture the full range of benefits that water brings to people and economies. Benefits and costs that affect peoples' welfare through, for example, water pollution and exhaustion, are often absent in the balance of costs and benefits that individuals and firms take into account when making decisions. For example, when judged on the basis of their own interest, using groundwater may be financially cost effective for farmers. But it can exhaust water supplies and transfer the

TABLE 23.2

Types of benefit attached to different water and sanitation interventions

Investments options	Types of benefit
Providing access to safe water and sanitation	
Providing access to safe water near the home • Building water access point • Building and operating water treatment plants • Providing point-of-use water treatment methods **Providing access to sanitation and hygiene** • Building sanitation facilities • Promoting the adoption of hygienic practices **Wastewater collection and transport** • Collecting wastewater via sewerage networks • Collecting and transporting pit sludge outside the home	**Health benefits** • Reduced incidence of waterborne diseases (e.g. diarrhoea) and of water-washed diseases **Non-health benefits/economic benefits** • Time saved for productive activities • Reduced coping costs **Economic benefits** • Increase in productivity • Use of urine and faeces as economic input • Impact on tourism from improved amenity **Other benefits** • Increases in overall cleanliness, dignity and pride • Increased school attendance, especially for girls
– downstream, in wastewater treatment for safe disposal	
• Building and operating wastewater treatment plants • Ensuring safe disposal of residual sludge • Relying on natural treatment processes	**Health benefits** • Reduced incidence of waterborne diseases (e.g. diarrhoea) and of water-washed diseases • Benefits from improved recreational waters **Environmental benefits** • Reduced eutrophication **Economic benefits** • Reduced pre-treatment costs downstream (for drinking water and industrial purposes) • Protection of commercial fish stocks and aquaculture • Enhanced tourism activities • Increased water supply for irrigation • Saving of fertilizers through use of sludge **Other benefits** • Recreational benefits • Increased property values
– upstream, in managing the supply/demand balance sustainably	
Protecting water resources • Establishing catchment protection zones • Establishing voluntary agreements • Establishing regulations **Increasing and ensuring supply** • Building storage capacity • Building abstraction capacity • Developing alternative sources, such as aquifer recharge, desalination, re-use of treated effluent • Adopting drought management plans **Managing demand** • Reducing leakage (on the network and within customers' premises) • Introducing incentive pricing • Installing water-saving devices • Raising awareness and educating the public	**Environmental benefits** • Reducing pressure on available resources (especially groundwater) and improving river flows • Economic impact on use of water for economic activities (agriculture, hydropower) **Economic benefits** • Reduction in water pre-treatment costs • Uninterrupted supply for production processes • Downsizing of facilities • Reduced need for desalination (energy savings) **Other benefits** • Increased quality of life due to reliable water supply • Indirect benefits (e.g. linked to recreational activities on dams)

Source: OECD (2011).

costs to other water users. Where short-term profits are higher than real economic costs, boom and bust outcomes result, and sustainable development may be undermined. There are many examples of much effort having been put into building water infrastructures that eventually became useless when water resources were exhausted.

The external costs incurred by the overuse and degradation of water resources often remain ignored until a crisis is reached – by which time the value of the infrastructure itself is usually reduced and is compromising the sustainability of services. If institutions governing water fail to properly manage its use, there is a danger of market incentives favouring short-term financial benefits at the expense of the integrity of the resource base and its long-term economic value. Worldwide evidence of the overexploitation of surface water and groundwater unveils this fact. It is expected that by 2025, 1.8 billion people will live in countries or regions with absolute water scarcity and two-thirds of the world population could be affected by water stress conditions (UNESCO–WWAP, 2006). In many places, society has been willing and able to go further with investment opportunities where the short-term financial returns for water users are transparently inferior to the economic benefits that will be available as a result of long-term sustainability.

23.1.4 Valuing non-market benefits can prevent critical ecosystem services from being neglected

Ecosystem services are the benefits, or services, that ecosystems bring to people. Drinking water, water

BOX 23.6

Balancing benefits and costs when assessing water management options: New filtration infrastructures versus water catchment protection in New York

'Presented with a choice between provision of clean water through building a filtration plant or managing the watershed, New York City easily concluded that the latter was more cost effective. It was estimated that a filtration plant would cost between $6 billion and $8 billion to build. By contrast, watershed protection efforts, which would include not only the acquisition of critical watershed lands but also a variety of other programs designed to reduce contamination sources in the watershed, would cost only about $1.5 billion.'

Source: Daily and Ellison (2003).

for food production and the generation of hydroelectricity are all ecosystem services – as are other often neglected services such as nutrient recycling, climate regulation, cultural and recreational benefits and flood mitigation. Most of the decisions that have to be taken are actually about maximizing one particular service, often at the expense of others. In this way, water decisions nearly always involve trade-offs. The objective should be to optimize the delivery of multiple inter-related ecosystem services. The purpose of effective valuation is two-fold. First, to identify and recognize what services are involved in the trade-off (even if they can't be valued). And second, to quantify values as much as possible in order to assist in calculating trade-offs.

Some of the non-market services provided by ecosystems can be relatively easily quantified and generate substantial values. Examples include the value of ecosystems such as wetlands in flood mitigation, and forests in sustaining drinking water quality. It is the growing recognition of these values that is motivating greater interest in the restoration of these services. Valuation has often shown that conserving ecosystems, or reversing their degradation, is not only a sustainable ecological alternative (very often with multiple benefits), but is also economically beneficial.

Valuation essentially provides evidence that economic benefits are relinquished when policy, management and investment cause avoidable environmental degradation. For producers of goods and services who use water directly, water prices and costs are the basic criteria for water-use decisions. But prices often do not reflect the real production costs or economic value of water. In particular, prices often do not reflect the decline in the natural capital stocks that support the production of all ecosystem services. Therefore, decisions taken on infrastructure investments are disconnected from what is efficient and sustainable for the economy and the environment as a whole.

Better awareness of the issues and more sharing of information on the economic benefits of maintaining or restoring natural capital is also important when trying to reach collective agreements and when trying to design financial incentives that align individual behaviour with the common good. Valuation and better communication of the costs and benefits are crucial for taking better individual and collective decisions on the use of water.

Valuing non-market ecosystem services in the European Union can inform decisions on environmental objectives in planning processes

In the European Water Framework Directive, valuing the costs and benefits provides the information required to assess whether the opportunity cost of improving water bodies – is disproportionate compared with the potential socio-economic and environmental benefits, and to then decide on the precise objectives and timing of measures to improve water status in the river basin management plans. It is widely accepted that in many water bodies there are more welfare gains to be obtained by improving the ecological status than by allowing their further degradation.

There are now a number of examples that demonstrate the benefits of environmental improvements and influence water planning and decision-making (Box 23.7).

23.1.5 Valuing to assess trade-offs in water allocation decisions

Water ecosystems have only a limited ability to continue to provide water services to the economy. So it is important for economic growth that water is used well and allocated to its various uses efficiently. Competition can be managed and degradation prevented by having sufficient accurate information about the economic, social and environmental value of water in its various uses. This will also help with re-allocating water so that it provides greater benefits to the economy and to society. There will be trade-offs to be considered too and decisions to be taken about which benefits to forgo when using water for one purpose instead of another.

In a world of scarcity, the valuation of water productivity in agriculture also needs to be considered. Information needed by governments so that they can assess whether water is being used for low-yield crops in water-scarce areas – and if so, determine alternative crops or uses that would make the greatest contribution to the economy. Such a valuation provides a database that farmers can use to make informed decisions about investing in improved infrastructure and crop varieties, and that governments can use to target their investment and to formulate incentives for improving efficiency in water use.

Legal frameworks and institutions need to be set up and better ways of allocating water need to be found. These need to be done using principles – such as equity and efficiency – that may be politically difficult to implement in practice. There is also a need to improve the mechanisms that deliver desired objectives to a range of diverse stakeholder interests (Box 23.8). If there are institutional arrangements that allow water to be allocated to where its use is most valuable, this may help in drawing up mutually beneficial allocation agreements. Establishing legal frameworks for decentralized water management is the type of institutional arrangement that has become important in many water scarce countries. These can be used to implement economic instruments such as water trading, licences and rights to use water. Water trading has developed in countries such as Australia, the United States, India, Chile and Spain (Box 23.9).

Stakeholder-oriented valuation can support allocation decisions water management in Tanzania

In the United Republic of Tanzania, some areas face severe water scarcity. Demand for water has been growing and there is conflict between the energy and irrigation sectors, between these sectors and conservationists, and between upstream and downstream users. In 2005, the government established a legal framework that decentralizes water management and increases stakeholder involvement by including local catchment area committees, river basin associations and water-users associations. A participatory approach to water valuation – through surveys, data collections and workshops to analyse data and results – was implemented to enable local stakeholders to engage in implementing IWRM.

Indicators for economic, social and environmental values were considered including crop water productivity in different zones, value across all water sectors, income from water-related production activities, food security (including the nutritional value of crops), access to drinking water, conflict over water, environmental base flows and environmental changes. The valuing process supported decisions to change to crops that use less water, to improve capacities to increase water productivity, to review existing water rights and the training of water-users associations, and to coordinate farmers' own marketing of agricultural products in order to increase income and improve stability.

Source: Hermans et al. (2006).

23.1.6 Valuing water can help to contain water conflicts and promote cooperation in preserving water resources

In the context of access to critical transboundary water resources, valuing can inform governments about the advantages of cooperation instead of competition or conflict. Working towards a common vision of the value of shared water resources is a powerful instrument for finding a way in which agreements in international disputes over water can be self-enforced.

Countries are more likely to cooperate when the net benefits of cooperating are perceived to be greater than those of non-cooperation – and this is even more likely when the sharing arrangement is perceived to be fair. The advantages of cooperation and collective action are easier to see when the benefits can be made visible to each one of the parties (Box 23.10).

Valuing provides key information that allows stakeholders to move towards cooperative agreements. It also enables the creation of benefits for all those involved in providing solutions. For example, valuing the benefits that water catchment protection can have in securing adequate supplies of quality water can open up solutions that were not envisaged. This can include cost saved by reducing the need for downstream treatment. Protecting watersheds also leads to a broad range of positive environmental effects on the quality of water in water bodies, in groundwater resources, in soil resources and the quality of water available for vegetation and for native flora and fauna.

23.1.7 Valuing water to design appropriate subsidies and targeted financing

Despite the substantial economic returns involved in providing water services to households, to industry and for food production, the basic water needs of people in many poor countries are still not being met. This is a result of a combination of the inability of individuals and business to pay and too few financial incentives to invest in the required facilities. These are key reasons why decisions should be taken to give water operators and community service providers better access to loans and well-targeted subsidies (Box 23.11).

BOX 23.9

Valuation of scarcity in water markets

Values associated with water can be observed directly through market activity in arid regions where there is trading, where water is fully allocated and where irrigation is under pressure from municipal, industrial and, in some cases, environmental, demands. There are some basins where rights to use water are defined, enforced and tradable. Market prices in examples in the United States (in California's Central Valley, Colorado's South Platte basin and Nevada's Truckee River basin), and in Australia (in the Murray-Darling basin) confirm that the value of water use varies considerably and that it is driven by variations in market conditions and supply.

Data suggest that in many river basins, market transfers are happening in line with the agricultural value of water, but at a rate that's below the value of water to the domestic consumer or industrial user. Markets that don't have significant urban demand see prices that reflect the agricultural production value of water, which is calculated as the difference in the price of irrigated versus dry land. Where there is significant urban demand, prices are driven by this and shaped by the cost of transferring the water to urban use through conveyances and so forth.

Market values for permanent water rights acquisitions are roughly one order of magnitude greater than the prices for temporary allocations. From this it can be deduced that capitalization rates will be roughly on the order of magnitude expected given current costs of credit. The market value of water is intrinsically regional, or even local, because physical limitations constrain the scope of cost-effective trade. As a result, price observations from one context may have little relevance in another.

Source: Aylward et al. (2010).

BOX 23.10

Valuing benefits supports cooperation in international river basins

Benefit-sharing agreements exist for various international rivers, including the Danube, the Niger, the Okavango and many others. The Organization for the Development of the Senegal River was created in 1972. Disagreement about the competing rights of Mali, Senegal, Guinea and Mauritania was no impediment to the four countries reaching an agreement to share the benefits of various river projects. A common knowledge of the benefits was essential for building an institutional framework: 'the development of multi-purpose water resources infrastructure is expected to yield expanded opportunities for growth, reduced immigration and poverty, and improved health and livelihoods of the population while also preserving the environment' (World Bank, 2009, p. 12).

Valuation can help to identify when it is justifiable to charge water fees that are lower than full cost of recovering the investment.

Valuation can also give society crucial information that can be used to find practical solutions that ease the transition from the subsidized tariffs that are designed to stop poverty spirals, to a set of self-financed services that make water services financially sustainable.

In many poor countries, only a small portion of the benefits of water services can be funded entirely by the public or by private organizations. On purely financial grounds, providing water is not an attractive opportunity for private businesses. This can lead to poor maintenance and the deterioration of privately run water infrastructure and basic services. The consequence of this is a vicious downward spiral of underinvestment leading to poor service that undermines the ability to capture adequate revenue to operate, maintain and invest in systems (Figure 23.2).

BOX 23.11

Valuation can support the design of subsidies and targeted financing

There are economic benefits to be had from improving access to basic sanitation and safe drinking water. The benefits of irrigation have been estimated by the World Bank to yield average rates of return of 20%. However, financial problems and mismanagement can lead to the downfall of many irrigation systems. The prices of agricultural products have been falling and some investments are now less financially viable. There may be a need to stabilize the income of poor farmers who are subsisting below a certain income level and who are exposed to regular drought and crop insecurity.

Valuing the social and environmental consequences of abandoning financially unsustainable systems has found that there should be support for the implementation of financial packages and other capacity building programmes (such as record keeping and the collection of fees) by international donors. Donor resources that are already in place are being redesigned to help attract other resources and investment. They are also focusing in providing funding to bridge the gap between investment in infrastructure and income generation. This supports the development of local capital and financial markets including microcredit initiatives and local banks and is consistent with the aims of output-based aid.

Source: Grimm and Richter (2006).

Changes in the provision and management of water from being mostly self-collected to being a communally provided set of water provision services might mean that people have more time and better health. But they still won't have enough money to pay the financial cost of the services they get. In the first stage of this, even if the valuation exercise shows that the expected economic benefits are undeniable (particularly for the poor) people cannot afford to pay the full financial cost of the service. So in the absence of a collective action, they will continue without access to basic sanitation and safe water.

But improvements in water access might not be sustainable in the medium term if society and water institutions are not able to manage the transition from the initial stage (where the priority is to improve access to basic services) to an advanced stage where the financial sustainability of providing water needs to be ensured. New ways have to be found to transform the new opportunity of improved access to water into effective education, crop diversification or earning prospects for the poor.

Valuation is useful for determining what economic incentives are required to align individual behaviour with collective targets and objectives. For example, valuing less-visible non-market ecosystem services can provide clearer indications of the value of preserving or restoring ecosystems. Such valuation can be simpler than is often thought. For example, the loss of an ecosystem's ability to deliver clean water can be estimated from the point of view of the cost of rectifying the problem artificially (for example, the cost of artificial water treatment) or from the point of view of the economic cost of living the consequences of poor quality water (for example, a fall-off in productivity, higher health-care expenses, etc.). In many instances, the absence of an ecosystem service is already generating an economic, and often direct, financial cost. Identifying where benefits arise and costs are incurred helps to ascertain how costs can be transformed into incentives that will bring more efficient economic outcomes (Box 23. 12).

23.1.8 Valuing can support decisions on what measures to take to improve water security

There are increasing demands on water and less-predictable rainfall patterns and water flows (including a higher frequency and intensity of extreme events such as floods and droughts). So better water security and more-resilient management options have an increasingly higher value. Valuation approaches should factor in and provide information on the benefits, or risks, of increased or decreased water security. When done effectively, they should shed light on the costs and benefits of more resilient management options. The information that a valuation approach provides about the changing values of water in its various uses can be vital for implementing adaptive planning and management. It can also help to prevent inappropriate uncontrolled individual responses to risk and uncertainty.

Management that makes water supplies secure has a critical role in making the benefits of development more predictable. Poor and water-scarce societies that are now trying to establish systems to supply water and basic sanitation services are faced with the potential adverse effects of climate change (World Bank, 2010; Danilenko et al., 2010; Box 23.13).

Collective decisions on measures that will increase water security and facilitate the financial resources to do so cannot be properly informed without a proper valuation of the benefits and costs. Valuation can

improve the accuracy of the information that private and public agents use to take better-informed decisions with full knowledge of the costs involved. Water storage schemes and infrastructure, water conservation programmes and improvements in efficiency are all examples of the kinds of measure that are already considered beneficial, but which are even more valuable in a climate stress context. Other measures, which need only be considered in the face of uncertainty, may include the diversification of water sources (such as desalination and non-conventional sources), the upgrading of storm water systems, the reversal of coastal developments to reduce exposure, the recovery of floodplains for flood protection and the recovery of aquifers for buffering security stocks.

Valuing can provide valuable information on the capital and maintenance cost of these various options. And it can also give an insight into the benefits and opportunity costs involved in water security and other ecosystems services.

Economic incentives can have a role in enhancing adaptive capacities. When water supply and quality

FIGURE 23.2

The vicious spiral of low funding

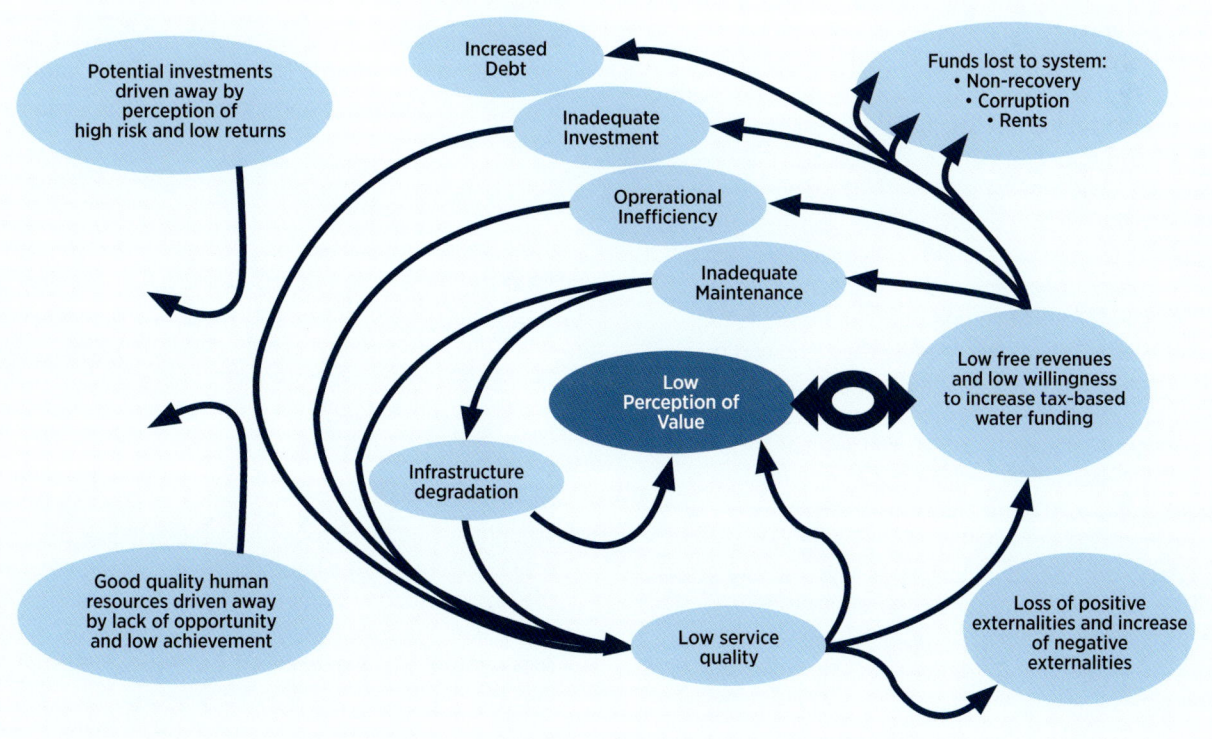

Source: Adapted from Moss et al. (2003, fig. 4, p. 13) by J. M. Moss.

vary unpredictably over time and from location to location, stakeholders and water users might be more efficient than public authorities in finding the most cost-effective and appropriate answers. For example, valuation can support water trading and the design

BOX 23.12

Valuing compensation payments for environmental services in China

China's ecological compensation mechanisms are a modern variant of traditional government payments to providers of ecological services. The government transfers money and compensates land owners (or land users) for specific actions that produce environmental benefits. There are various applications of the eco-compensation approach. These include compensation paid to residents living near water sources or reservoirs to migrate to other areas, subsidies paid to sewage treatment plants, compensation to support the forestry sector in upstream areas and payments to farmers to compensate for lost production caused by reducing the use of fertilizers and pesticides.

At the central government level, China has developed and implemented some of the largest public payment schemes for ecosystem conservation in the world. These schemes include the Sloping Land Conversion Program (SLCP), the Natural Forest Protection Project (NFPP), and the Forest Ecosystem Compensation Fund (FECF). The SLCP (also called the 'Grain for Green' program) was initiated in 1999 to restore natural ecosystems and mitigate the adverse impacts of farming in previously forested areas or marginal land. Farming these lands resulted in flooding, the sedimentation of reservoirs, and dust storms. Farmers who enrol in the scheme receive payments for seeds, seedlings, and management expenses. It is one of the largest public transfer schemes in the world, reaching some 30 million farms spread over 7 million hectares (ha) of cropland. It disburses around US$8 billion per year. The FECF programme targets the management of privately owned forests. It compensates land owners for the ecosystem services provided by their land and for the land and resource use restrictions that are subject to when they participate in the programme. The scheme currently covers 26 million ha in 11 provinces, and costs the government about RMB 2 billion ($253 million) annually – of which about 70% goes to farmers, who are paid an average of US$9 per hectare. Local governments are encouraged to provide additional funds. In December 2004, the FECF was extended to the entire country. It covers key state-owned non-commercial forests, as well as woodlands in areas that are at risk from desertification and soil erosion.

Source: Jian (2009).

and implementation of a weather-based insurance scheme that may provide incentives to invest in water saving and make water allocation and reallocation decisions acceptable, and adaptable. Such a scheme may be contingent on changes in water supply and the stabilization of income and economic output.

The extent to which some of these measures need to be taken depends on how individuals and governments value the increased security they provide. It also depends on how they value the benefits that have to be foregone in each case. A higher aversion to uncertain events means a higher risk premium – that is to say, the more people fear exposure to extreme events, and the more likely these events are seen to be, the more people will be willing to pay for insurance. Valuing the private willingness to pay to increase security is an important step in judging the extent to which available measures would be financially viable.

Valuing provides reliable evidence of the potential damage and reduction in welfare that may result from leaving risk responses to spontaneous individual answers instead of implementing collective and more comprehensive anticipatory responses to water variability and climate change. Leaving risk response to individual efforts to defend and maintain production

BOX 23.13

Valuing the economic loses of droughts and the effects of climate change can make the case for political action

In Kenya, droughts occur on average once every seven years. Their economic cost (as was the case on the 1999–2000 drought) was equivalent to one-sixth of the gross domestic product (GDP). This figure suggest that if the country could decouple its economy from rainfall variability, its annual economic growth could increase by 3.5% (SIWI and WHO, 2005).

Nicholas Stern's review, *The Economics of Climate Change* found that climate change had a significant impact on economic output. In a baseline climate-change scenario, the review estimated that climate change would be responsible for a 2.5% loss in GDP in India and South East Asia by 2100, and would cause a 1.9% loss in GDP in Africa and the Middle East over the same period.

Source: Stern (2007).

activities could lead to the extension or intensification of existing vulnerabilities. Spontaneous answers from people, businesses, and farmers in rural communities depend on their perception of value and risk, the options available to them and their individual economic incentives. The lack of a planned and coordinated response to increased scarcity and risk will favour individual answers that do not necessarily produce the best or most sustainable outcomes. For example, they may add more pressure to cultivate marginal land or adopt unsustainable cultivation practices because erratic rainfall has made yields drop. All of these possibilities could reinforce water scarcity and land degradation and endanger the biodiversity of both wild and domestic species. They might also increasing vulnerability and jeopardize the ability to respond to climate and other risks later on.

Showing the difference between the financial and economic costs and benefits of alternative actions is a useful way of underlining the importance of a planned, anticipatory and coordinated response to water management challenges. Collective actions instead of spontaneous individual responses are required as well as implementing risk management options instead of coping with the consequences of extreme events and adapting to negative trends. Valuation may play a critical role in showing the advantages of cooperation, leading to better responses and higher security, instead of individual actions.

23.2 Challenges for Valuing water

Many valuation methods already exist and, have been tested in a variety of situations and contexts that are relevant for policy decisions. Water valuation methods vary according to how they obtain information about the importance that people give to water benefits.

In spite of its relevance to policy and in spite of the growing number of successful examples, valuation is still controversial. Among the issues most commonly discussed are: the usefulness of the various valuation approaches for any specific decision problem; the robustness of the results provided by valuation exercises; the comparability of costs and benefits when both are obtained from different sources, at different geographical scales and with different valuation methods (UNSD, 2007 and Chapter 8).

Water valuation is still challenging because data is often not available and is expensive to collect and because assumptions sometimes need to be made to overcome the absence of relevant information. Water

TABLE 23.3
Valuation techniques for water

Valuation techniques	Comments
1. Water as an intermediate input to production: agriculture, manufacturing Residual value Change in net income Production function approach Mathematical programming models Sales and rentals of water rights Hedonic pricing Demand functions from water utility sales	Techniques provide average or marginal value of water based on observed market behaviour.
2. Water as a final consumer good Sales and rentals of water rights Demand functions from water utility sales Mathematical programming models Alternative cost Contingent valuation	All techniques execpt contingent valuation provide average or marginal value of water based on observed market behaviour. Contingent valuation measures total economic value based on hypothetical purchases.
3. Environmental services of water: waste assimilation Costs of actions to prevent damage Benefits from damage averted	Both techniques provide information on average or marginal values

Source: UNSD (2007, table 8.1, p. 120).

benefits are usually site-specific and cannot be easily transferred from context to context. Methods and assumptions are not standardized and uncertainty in the numerical results obtained may be quite high. Valuation methods have been developed in response to these limitations and the results are validated by extensive scientific research. However, the assumptions, the numerical results, and the limitations on how valuation results can be used to assess policy options, are still difficult to communicate to stakeholders.

Decision-making contexts have favoured valuation methods and results that are less controversial in that they do not involve sensitive value judgments and are easier to communicate to stakeholders (Table 23.3). These are methods where, in the main, results are initially obtained from directly observed behaviour in existing markets – rather than from laboratory tests or chosen experiments in implicit markets and artificially created decision environments. They are also methods that can make the best possible use of the information that is already contained in existing market prices to derive the value of other water benefits. Examples of contexts where these methods have been used are welfare measures such as averted costs (for example measures to value the costs that were avoided when clean, safe drinking was obtained); averted damage (methods to value the flood mitigation services provided by the environment); the residual value (methods to show how crop yields and farmers' incomes increased when irrigation was made possible); and avoided treatment cost (from the water purification services provided by the natural water course instead of by manufactured systems). These methods provide useful information about three important categories of water benefits: water as an intermediate input to produce other goods, water as a final consumer good and the environmental services of water.

Considering values and specially value perspectives is of great importance in implementing measures – especially measures related to adapting to climate change because these will necessarily mean a change to the status quo. Managing participatory decision-making is becoming increasingly important. In practice, valuation and the consideration of value perspectives are fundamental when balancing trade-offs. They also support decision-making processes where compromises need to be reached between different stakeholders – especially when managing water demands and allocation decisions (Hermans et al., 2006).

There is a need to develop valuation frameworks that can be used in information gathering and policy-making. The links between ecosystems and human well-being are complex. A basic conceptual framework has been developed by the Millennium Ecosystem Assessment that provides a logical structure for the analysis and valuation of ecosystem services (Millennium Ecosystem Assessment, 2005). Including information on the value of water in water accounting frameworks would be an important step forward. The UN Statistics SEEAW framework (System of Environmental-Economic Accounts for Water) provides such an integrated information system to study the interactions between the environment and the economy (UNSD, 2007). It can provide the basis for progress, specifically because it covers the stocks and flows associated with water. There is also a need for further adaptation of valuation methods so that they can better respond to policy questions and management needs.

IIIIIIIIIIIIIIIIIIIIIIIIIIIIIIIIIIIIIIIIIIIIIIIIIIIIIIIIIIIIIIIIIIIIIIIIIIIIIIIIIIIIII

References

Aylward, B., Seely, H., Hartwell, R. and Dengel, J. 2010. *The Economic Value of Water for Agricultural, Domestic and Industrial uses: A Global Compilation of Economic Studies and Market Prices.* Rome, Italy, Food and Agriculture Organization of the United Nations (FAO).

Bhatia, R., Malik, R. P. S. and Bhatia, M. 2007. Direct and indirect economic impacts of the Bhakra multipurpose dam, India. *Irrigation and Drainage*, Vol. 56, Issue 2–3, pp. 195–206. doi:10.1002/ird.315.

Daly, G. and Ellison, K. 2003. *The New Economy of Nature: The Quest to Make Conservation Profitable. Washington DC*, Island Press.

Danilenko, A., Dickson, E. and Jacobsen, M. 2010. Climate Change and Urban Water Utilities: Challenges & Opportunities. *Water Working Notes. Note No. 24.* Washington DC, World Bank.

Grimm, J. and Richter, M. 2006. *Financing Small-Scale Irrigation in Sub-Saharan Africa.* Desk Study commissioned by the World Bank. Eschborn, Germany, ETZ.

Hermans, L., Renault, D., Emerton, L., Perrot-Maître, D., Nguyen-Khoa, S. and Smith, L. 2006. Stakeholder-oriented valuation to support water resources management processes: Confronting concepts with local practice. *FAO Water Reports,* 30. Rome, Italy, Food and Agriculture Organization of the United Nations (FAO).

Hutton, G. and Haller, L. 2004. *Evaluation of the Costs and Benefits of Water and Sanitation Improvements at the Global Level.* Geneva, Switzerland, World Health Organization (WHO).

Jian, X. 2009. *Addressing China's Water Scarcity Recommendations for Selected Water Management Issues.* Water, P-Notes, Issue 37, No.48725. Washington DC, World Bank.

Kemp, R. 2005. America on the Road to Ruin? *Public Works Management & Policy* Vol. 10, Issue 1, pp. 77–82. doi:10.1177/1087724X05280384.

Moss, J., Wolff, G., Gladden, G. and Gutierrez, E. 2003. *Valuing Water for Better Governance, How to Promote Dialogue to Balance Social, Environmental and Economic Values?* Business and Industry CEO Panel for Water.

OECD (Organisation for Economic Co-operation and Development). 2011. *Benefits of Investing in Water and Sanitation: An OECD Perspective.* Paris, France, OECD. doi:10.1787/9789264100817-en.

Prüss-Üstün, A., Bos, R., Gore, F. and Bartram, J. 2008. *Safer Water, Better Health: Costs, Benefits and Sustainability of Interventions to Protect and Promote Health.* Geneva, Switzerland, World Health Organization (WHO).

Sachs, J. D. 2001. *Macroeconomics and Health: Investing in Health for Economic Development.* Report of the Commission on Macroeconomics and Health. Geneva, Switzerland, World Health Organization (WHO).

SIWI (Stockholm International Water Institute), WHO (World Health Organization) and NORAD (The Norwegian Agency for Development Cooperation). 2005. *Making Water a Part of Development: The Economic Benefit of Improved Water Management and Services.* Stockholm, SIWI.

Stern, N. 2007. *The Economics of Climate Change: The Stern Review.* Cambridge, U. K., Cambridge University Press.

UNSD (United Nations Statistics Division). 2007. *System of Environmental-Economic Accounting for Water.* Background Document. New York, UNSD.

Whittington, D., Hanemann, W. M., Sadoff, C. and Jeuland, M. 2008. The challenge of improving water and sanitation services in less developed countries. *Foundations and Trends in Microeconomics.* Vol. 4, Issue 6–7. Hanover, Germany, Now Publishers Inc. DOA:10.1561/0700000030.

WHO (World Health Organization) and UNICEF (United Nations Children's Fund). 2010. *Progress on Sanitation and Drinking-Water: 2010 Update.* Geneva, WHO/UNICEF Joint Monitoring Programme for Water Supply and Sanitation.

World Bank. 2008. *Environmental Health and Child Survival: Epidemiology, Economics, Experiences.* Washington DC, World Bank.

––––. 2009. *IDA at Work: Water Resources – Improving Services for the Poor.* Washington, D. C., World Bank.

––––. 2010. *World Development Report 2010: Development and Climate Change.* Washington DC, World Bank.

WWAP (World Water Assessment Programme). 2006. *World Water Development Report 2: Water: A Shared Responsibility.* Paris/New York, UNESCO/Berghahn Books

CHAPTER 24

Investing in water infrastructure, its operation and its maintenance

The World Bank
—

Authors Diego J. Rodriguez, Caroline van den Berg and Amanda McMahon
Acknowledgements Research assistance was provided by Olusola Ikuforiji. This work is a product of the staff of The World Bank with external contributions. The findings, interpretations, and conclusions expressed in this work do not necessarily reflect the views of The World Bank, its Board of Executive Directors, or the governments they represent.

© Shutterstock/Andrey Kekyalyaynen

Developing countries face a growing funding gap as they try to keep up with the rehabilitation, operation, and maintenance of aging water infrastructures. New water systems must also be built to cope with growing populations, increasing demands for water, changing consumption patterns and climate change.

More than 80% of water investment comes from public funds. While the international private sector has brought vital efficiency improvements, their appetite for risk in developing countries is low and diminishing. Public or private, availability of resources for water infrastructure is becoming more uncertain.

This gap can only be filled by an optimal mix of funds that is different for each country. But regardless of the formula, all countries can improve the use of money in the water sector and all actors have a role to play.

When service providers are able to recover more costs, they can stop the vicious cycle of degraded services, making them better equipped to mitigate the risks associated with climate change and the volatility of financial markets.

By improving the way funds are allocated, transferred, and used, governments can do more with scarce resources and reach a level of governance that enables them to benefit from private sector innovation and long-term financial sustainability.

In the meantime, development institutions can provide stopgap assistance and promote the consideration of greener infrastructure strategies. Assessment of tradeoffs at the national level can yield demand-side interventions that are more cost-effective than large scale systems and decrease the fiscal burden on poor countries.

24.1 Water, risk and uncertainty

24.1.1 Background

Economies will not grow and poverty will not be reduced without sufficient investment in water services and water resource infrastructure. Poor quality water and limited access have substantial implications for the poor, ranging from ill health caused by unsafe water and sanitation to reduced productivity (Fay et al., 2005). But adequate and well-managed infrastructure underpins water's role as a driver of socio-economic development.

The 10th Millennium Developments Goal (MDG) aims to halve the number of people worldwide who do not have access to improved drinking water and sanitation. This is a necessary condition for other 2015 MDGs, including the goal of reducing poverty. According to the World Health Organization (WHO), 80% of diseases in the developing world are caused by unsafe water, poor sanitation and a lack of hygiene education. Women and girls in developing countries benefit immensely from well-sustained water supply and sanitation services. The enrolment of girls in school rises when latrines are provided, and the improvement of safe water sources frees women from spending hours every day drawing water and carrying it home (WaterAid, 2005).

The 2011 MDG report reveals that between 1990 and 2008, more than 1.8 billion people gained access to improved sources of drinking water. This raises the proportion of the population with access from 77% to 87%. Progress, however, is uneven. The ratio of rural to urban inhabitants who don't have access to improved drinking water is 5:1. And meeting the sanitation target has proved daunting. Although the number of people with improved access to sanitation rose from 43% in 1990 to 52% in 2008, over half of the world's developing nations are still without access to adequate sanitation (UN, 2011). And the food, energy and financial crises have exacerbated matters.

24.1.2 Global crises

Water is a critical input in production and services, which means that it is directly affected by the global financial, energy and food crises (Winpenny et al., 2009). To guarantee water security, it is necessary to address how these crises affect water.

According to the *Global Monitoring Report 2010: The MDGs after the Crisis,* the financial crisis left some 50 million more people in extreme poverty in 2009 and 64 million more likely to fall into that category by the end of 2010. The report also projects that an additional 100 million people may lose access to drinking water by 2015 (Box 24.1).

The water sector is vulnerable to economic vagaries. Levels of investment in water were already low before the crisis in most developing countries – and these levels are now even lower, with private sector participation in particular falling sharply. An analysis of the World Bank's Private Participation in Infrastructure (PPI) project database shows that by the end of the first few months of full-scale financial crisis, the number of projects had fallen by 45% and associated investments by 29% compared with the same period in 2007 (World Bank and PPIAF, PPI Project Database).

Winpenny et al. (2009) highlights other impacts that the crisis had on financial flows to the water sector. In a financial crisis, public funding is more limited and tariff revenues fall as poverty deepens. This, in turn, reduces the ability of service providers to access private finance (i.e. loans, bonds and equity). However, international aid agencies and multilateral development banks have made a renewed commitment to increase assistance to the water sector to offset these changes.

The food crisis is being driven by population growth and a surge in energy prices. This has led to higher food prices and brought more people below the poverty line. With the global population expected to increase to nine billion by 2050, Hanjra and Qureshi (2010) estimate a 3,300 km^3 per year water gap for food production. Agricultural productivity – which accounts for over 70% of worldwide water consumption – has to be increased to meet these demands.

Food security depends on a sustainable and efficient water management system. Rosegrant et al. (2002) predicts a severe food crisis by 2025 unless fundamental policy changes are made to change future water use. New investments in irrigation infrastructure and water productivity can minimize the impact of water scarcity and partially meet the water demands for food production (Falkenmark and Molden, 2008).

Climate change will impose an additional cost on achieving and sustaining water security. An analysis of the impact that climate change may have on water resources was conducted by the Intergovernmental Panel on Climate Change (IPCC). The analysis expects serious shortages of water in semi-arid regions, which

BOX 24.1

The impact that the financial crisis has had on access to improved water supply sources: Three alternative scenarios

The Global Monitoring Report 2010 created three possible scenarios to analyse the effects that the financial crisis would have on Gross Domestic Product (GDP) growth in developing countries: the post-crisis trend, the pre-crisis (high growth) trend and the low-growth scenario. These were used in projecting the percentage of the population in developing countries who would not have access to improved water sources.

- The post-crisis scenario shows the effects on GDP assuming a relatively rapid economic recovery starting in 2010. This is the report's base case forecast.
- The pre-crisis (high growth) scenario shows what the effects on GDP would have been had developing countries continued the impressive growth pattern that occurred between 2000 and 2007. The impact that the crisis had on the MDGs can thus be measured by comparing the post-crisis trend with the pre-crisis trend.
- The low growth scenario assumes that the things that got worse because of the financial crisis will continue to adversely affect GDP in the medium-term, resulting in little or no growth for about five years, followed by a slow recovery.

(Percentage of the population without improved water source)				2015		
Region	2015 Target	1990	2006	Post crisis	Pre crisis/ High growth	Low growth
East Asia and Pacific	16	32	13	3.3	0.6	4.1
Europe and Central Asia	5	10	5	0	0	1.8
Latin America and the Caribbean	8	16	9	5.4	4.5	7.1
Middle East and North Africa	6	11	12	8.3	7.4	10.0
South Asia	13	27	13	9.3	5.1	10.2
Sub-Saharan Africa	26	51	42	39.1	38.8	39.8
All developing countries	12	24	14	10.1	9.6	11

Source: World Bank (2010a, table 4.2, p. 105).

will result in an increase in the frequency of droughts (Bates et al., 2008).

Extreme water situations affect almost everyone, but the poor will suffer most because of where they live, their low incomes, their deficient infrastructure, and the great reliance they have on climate-sensitive sectors such as agriculture. For example, over a three-year period, Kenya was hit by extreme floods that cost its economy 16% of its GDP and by an extreme drought that cost 11% of its GDP. Poor water management will only exacerbate these problems (World Bank, 2004). Zambia's economy too is prone to hydrological variability that will cost it US$4.3 billion in lost GDP over ten years and lower its agricultural growth by one percentage point each year (World Bank, 2008a). Because the dominant livelihood is rain-fed subsistence farming, droughts and floods significantly affect food security in these regions.

Between US$13 billion and US$17 billion is needed annually to help developing countries' water resources sectors to adapt to climate change (World Bank, 2010b) – and that's just the cost of adapting the hard infrastructure.

24.2 Investment needs in the water sector

24.2.1 Global estimates

Water infrastructure in any country requires huge investment. And water services generally do not recover their basic operation and maintenance costs. In developing countries, where funds for anything are scarce and where systems are already under tremendous pressure, funding for water represents an enormous financial burden. Data on water investments are sparse and incomplete because estimating actual needs is difficult and fraught with uncertainty. This stems from the lack of reliable data on public spending on infrastructure, current stocks, lack of a systematic way of monitoring spending and difficulty in tracking the flow of investments. Fay et al. (2010) asserts that a thorough analysis of investment needs requires four distinct steps:

- Understand how much is being spent and how that relates to the current quantity of infrastructure and its quality.
- Set a target and have it priced. The infrastructure gap is the difference between current spending and the target.
- Determine how much of the gap can be bridged through improved efficiency.
- Calculate what additional spending is needed once the improved efficiencies are in place (financing gap).

There are difficulties at every step. Countries and financial institutions do not account for infrastructure investment in a clear way in national accounts, and inefficiencies in the system are difficult to estimate.

Yepes (2008) estimates that investment requirements for water, sanitation and wastewater treatment in low and middle income countries will amount to US$103 billion between 2008 and 2015.[1] This is in line with the $72 billion estimated by WHO for meeting the water supply and sanitation (WSS) MDGs (OECD, 2010a).

On a regional level, the Africa Infrastructure Country Diagnostic (AICD) estimates the investment needed for water, sanitation and irrigation (Foster and Briceño-Garmendia, 2010). To close the infrastructure gap in WSS, meet the MDGs and achieve national targets in sub-Saharan Africa within ten years, an annual investment of approximately US$22 billion is needed. US$3.4 billion is needed to double Africa's irrigated area.

24.2.2 Public contributions to water

A snapshot of the current flow of public funding to the water sector

The lack of centralized and reliable information makes estimating current public spending in the water sector challenging. It is hard to imagine such a deficiency given that the public sector contributes approximately 80% of all WSS infrastructure costs (Winpenny, 2003, from Prynn and Sunman (2000).[2]

Most of the limited information on public spending stems from the OECD's Development Assistance Committee (DAC). Aid flows, known as Official Development Assistance (ODA), has become the main source of statistics, although it includes only aid from government sources. Aid from private sources, including from non-governmental organizations (NGOs), is not captured.

Official development assistance (ODA) for water and sanitation has been rising sharply. According to DAC, average annual commitments rose from US$3.3 billion in 2002–2003 to US$8.2 billion in 2008–2009.

24.2.3 Investment and risk

Private contributions in water

The main source of reliable information on private investment in infrastructure is the Private Participation in Infrastructure (PPI) database. This provides information on more than 4,800 infrastructure projects dating from 1984 to 2010, which are owned or managed by private energy, telecommunications, transport and water companies.

In its last reporting period (July 2011), PPI reported that in 2010, seven low- or middle-income countries implemented 25 water projects that involved private investment of US$2.3 billion (Figure 24.1).[3] The number of new projects with private participation that started in 2010 was 34% lower than 2009 and was the lowest annual number since 1995. Despite fewer new projects starting, annual investment commitments in 2010 were 17% higher than in 2009.

New private activity in 2010 included twenty-five projects, with the three largest comprising 76% of the investment volume. Two countries (China and Brazil) accounted for twenty of the projects and 36% of the investment. Fifteen of the projects were in China and fourteen of these were small to medium sized wastewater treatment plants. Overall, private activity in 2010 focused on water and sewage treatment plants, accounting for seventeen of the projects and US$1.4 billion in investment (Figure 24.2).

Analysis of investment commitments to all sectors (energy, telecom, transport and water) reveals water represents 1% of total private participation in developing countries (World Bank, 2011). And the financial crisis is imposing new challenges for financing. Public resources are scarcer than ever and the private sector is reluctant to engage in new undertakings that could involve additional risks. International investments bring the added risk of fluctuating exchange rates, which domestic lenders do not face. Between 1995 and 2005,

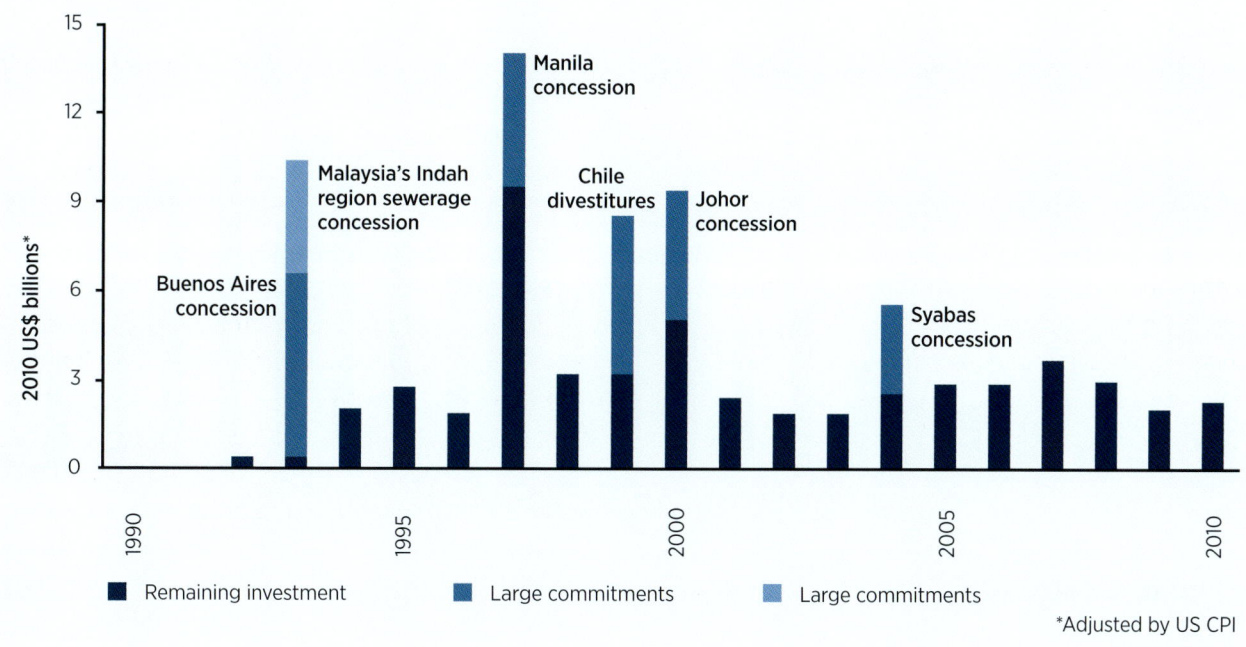

FIGURE 24.1

Investment in water projects with private participation (1990–2010)

Source: Perard (2011, fig. 1, p. 1) (PPI Project database).

the portion of private international flows to WSS fell by 6%, while local private flows rose by 10% (Jimenez and Perez Foguet, 2009).

Investment risk in the face of uncertainty

Even in the developed world, robust utilities are vulnerable to climate-induced risks such as drought, interstate disputes over water, and regulatory changes. A 2010 study by New York-based global equity investors, Water Asset Management and non-profit organization, Ceres, looked at six water utilities in the United States to assess their vulnerability to changes in water availability up to 2030 (Leurig, 2010). The study informs investors buying public utility bonds about the potential risks associated with changes in hydrological variability – risks which aren't currently reflected in the bond ratings issued by the three largest ratings agencies. Ceres reports that ratings agencies endorse the over-use of water by rewarding utilities that sell more of it, despite very real supply constraints in the medium term.

Cities in Arizona and Nevada rely on Lake Mead as a primary water source, but a decade-long drought is reducing available supplies. On the other side of the country, the City of Atlanta may have to reduce supplies by 40% on foot of a new judicial order to make more water

available for environmental services. While each utility has a different capacity to manage such risks, their ability to attract financing remains more or less unscathed because these issues go unreported. The Water Asset Management–Ceres' analysis sheds light on the real need to factor climate risks and uncertainty into long-term planning, financing and tariff adjustments, in addition to developing sound adaptation plans. For developing countries, failure to address the uncertainty of water supplies today will only exacerbate risks and curtail effective long-term strategic financial planning.

24.2.4 Opportunities in green growth and green economy agendas

The challenges of population growth, food and energy security, urbanization, volatile international financial flows, and climate change call for sustainable solutions that reduce reliance on natural resources. The 'green economy' agenda is being promoted across developed and developing countries alike in an effort to transform business, including the planning and design of new infrastructure. Fay et al. (2010) argue that when planning sustainable development, it is necessary to consider the significant environmental implications of expanding infrastructure and to assess the interactions between infrastructure policy and environment policy.

FIGURE 24.2

Water projects with private participation, by subsector (1990–2010)

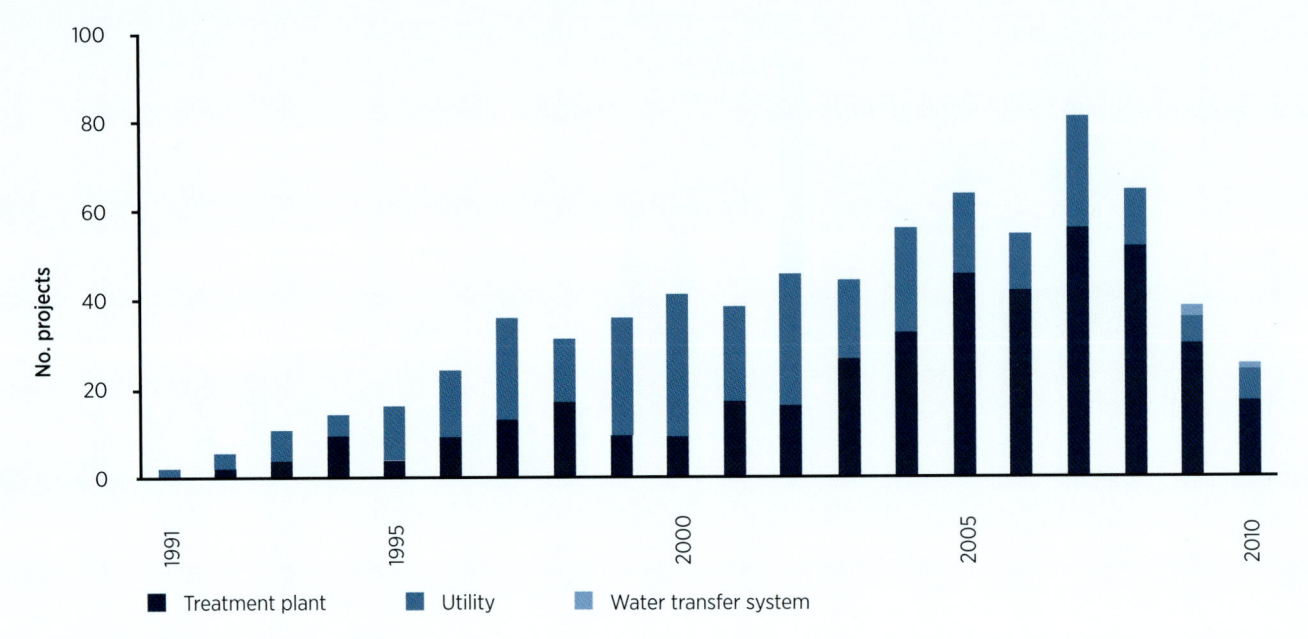

Source: Perard (2011, fig. 2, p. 1) (PPI Project database).

The green economy challenges policy-makers to improve the design of our water infrastructure, and offers an opportunity to reverse the trend of over-consumption. But green infrastructure comes at a cost. In Korea, the National Strategy for Green Growth and the Five Year Plan (2009–2013) is expected to cost 2% of GDP (OECD, 2011*b*). For developing countries, such a price will prove even more difficult to bear. Fostering green investment in these countries will require solid incentives such as expanding funding, enhancing political will, establishing a well-defined institutional framework – and, most importantly, initiating policy reforms that reduce harmful subsidies and promote an enabling investment climate. In addition to formulating polices to increase economic productivity without damaging the environment, it is also imperative to intensify global environmental research and ease technology transfer for clean technologies.

24.3 Financing the gap

24.3.1 A Linear reform agenda

Developing countries alone need to invest US$72 billion a year to meet water sector demands. This is on top of the estimated US$15 billion needed for climate change adaptation measures. While investment needs are growing exponentially, developing countries are coming out of the financial crises with fewer available resources. Given the already low capacity of utilities

to recover costs, what's required is a more efficient combination of tools that will finance the gap between demand and supply.

Narrowing the financing gap involves a four-step reform agenda. First, service providers must reduce a range of inefficiencies to increase revenues and lower costs. Second, providers should tap available public funding (including ODA and subsidies), while governments improve the efficiency and efficacy of funds. Third, having improved profitability and the quality of the service they provide, utilities can begin raising tariffs to reflect the real costs of the service. Finally, once they have the necessary political will and institutional capacity, providers should form public-private partnerships and apply for commercial loans.

24.3.2 Providing a more sustainable service

Inefficiencies as implicit subsidies

Inefficiencies in water provision come in many different guises. Low water productivity, high rates of drinking water consumption and the subsequent flows of wastewater that need to be collected and treated are all the by-products of inefficiency.

In Africa alone, water utilities loose approximately US$1 billion a year as a result of operating inefficiencies associated with poor maintenance, overstaffing, high distribution losses and under-collection of revenues (Foster and Briceño-Garmendia, 2010). The AICD suggests that Africa's water supply resources would go considerably further if various inefficiencies – amounting to US$2.7 billion a year – could be addressed. In seventeen countries, these inefficiencies – consisting of mispricing (where tariffs are below the cost of the services), collection inefficiencies and water losses, are in the order of 0.6% of GDP. Reducing inefficiencies will not entirely close the existing finance gaps, but it will reduce them considerably and enable systems to operate better. It may also postpone the need for certain investments and will certainly boost the financial health of utilities and pave the way to private financial resources by improving creditworthiness.

Examining hidden costs shows that policy decisions are being made that are not cost-effective. Among the main causes of losses in water agencies are tariff regimes that don't allow for cost recovery, an official tolerance of arrears and low collection rates and a tolerance of pilferage. All of these mean that there is not enough money to carry out maintenance or to invest in new infrastructure – which is implicit borrowing from future taxpayers or future water users.

Efficiency improvements

Governments need to consider eliminating the technical and managerial inefficiencies associated with delivering water services. They also need to concentrate on creating a policy and regulatory and environment that will attract investment – and this should be done before looking for public and private finance (Beato and Vives, 2008).

Non-revenue water (NRW) is a major source of inefficiency in water utilities (Box 24.2). Kingdom et al. (2006) shows that unaccounted-for water is responsible for losses of almost US$14 billion each year. This includes an estimated 45 million m^3 of treated water that leaks from urban water supply systems every day and another 30 million m^3 delivered to consumers but not billed for as a result of pilferage, corruption, and poor metering. It is estimated that about 70% of these losses are incurred in developing countries, where utilities urgently need additional revenues in order to expand, and where many connected customers have to deal with intermittent supply and poor water quality. The benefits of reducing the amount of NRW are

obvious, but programmes aimed at this require strong institutional capacity and substantial financial resources. Reducing NRW is not only a technical issue. If water tariffs are too low, the cost of reducing NRW may exceed the monies saved.

Billing and collection

Experience has shown that improving billing goes beyond simply delivering invoices and bills. Transferring management to an organization that has financial autonomy will reassure users that their payments are going to the service provider. Autonomous organizations that have strong user participation and are transparent in the way they set water charges are more likely to achieve high collection rates. Water user associations can play an important role in this (Box 24.3). Incentive systems that encourage the prompt collection of fees can also contribute to improvements in cost recovery.

The role of technology choice

Choosing the right technology is important in reducing service costs. This affects initial investment costs as well as operation and maintenance costs. And lower capital costs don't necessarily mean low running costs (Box 24.4).

BOX 24.2

Reducing the amount of non-revenue water

Inaccurate metering, unauthorized consumption and leakages all results in non-revenue water (NRW). NRW should be considered within the broader context of utility reform in order to ensure that appropriate funds and resources are allocated. The full scope of the problem should be identified at the onset by characterizing the sources of NRW through a baseline assessment.

The private sector has much to offer here. Under a performance-based services contract, a private firm's remuneration is based on enforced operational performance measures. This strategy was adopted by the Companhia de Saneamento Básico do Estado de São Paulo (SABEP) water utility that serves the São Paulo metropolitan region in Brazil. Under a three-year contract, a private contractor assisted the utility to improve the production and delivery of water through such activities as better micro metering. This increased revenue and reduced the city's debt. The outcome led to a 45 million m^3 increase in the volume of metered consumption and increased revenues of US$72 million.

Source: Kingdom et al. (2006).

Assumptions about technology choices can make significant differences in total investment requirements. The cost of supplying water and sanitation services varies widely with the level of service provided – especially in rural areas because of lower population densities and higher transport costs. In view of such large cost differentials, coupled with the fact that an expensive, high-quality service is likely to be used only by richer consumers – there is a rationale for providing a minimum level of service to consumers. Then higher levels of services can be added on and financed by households themselves.

It is also important to standardize the technologies used in any country. Using multiple technologies makes spare parts harder to find (and therefore more expensive), and there is not always the local knowledge to deal with many different technologies. A Water Aid Study conducted in seventeen districts in Tanzania found a negative correlation between the number of different technologies used in these districts, and the functionality rate of rural water points.

Technology can also be transformational in filling the water gap for a green economy (Figure 24.3). While new treatment systems and dams can supply more water, there are a variety of lower-cost, and often greener, options for managing demand. For example, large quantities of water can be saved in India through the use of better and more drip irrigation technologies so that new raw water sources don't have to be exploited. In China, industrial water reuse systems can save water and reduce the need to build expensive transfer systems. Many of the technologies that can make a difference already exist and are in use in developing countries. Further application needs to be supported by institutions and promoted by sector leaders.

24.3.3 The real cost of water
Water as an economic good
Pricing water to recover investment, operation, and maintenance costs has been a contentious issue for decades. The Dublin principles confirmed that water is a scarce resource and an economic good – so economic principles and incentives need to be used to improve allocation and enhance quality. Yet including more economic incentives in water pricing has proved difficult. Historically, WSS and irrigation charges have been systematically under-priced. So achieving full cost recovery through tariffs and user charges alone will require price hikes that are difficult to manage politically, and may make water services unaffordable. Full cost recovery through tariffs has proved elusive even in many developed countries.

What is cost recovery?
Water fees are collected from users for two main objectives, to cover costs and to encourage efficient water use (Box 24.5). The first objective is to cover the direct financial costs in order to guarantee a sustainable service. These direct costs cover the basic operation and maintenance of the service, the renewal of existing infrastructure, and the possible capital expansion of water services. In many countries, utilities and irrigation agencies pass only a fraction of these direct costs on to users. Utilities in developing countries barely cover their basic operation and maintenance costs – in 2008, operating revenues covered 105% of operation and maintenance costs (IBNET, 2010). Yet large differences exist between utilities in terms of achieving cost recovery (Table 24.1).

BOX 24.3

Water users associations as an essential component in improving cost recovery: An irrigation systems example from the Kyrgyz Republic

An on-farm irrigation project was implemented in the Kyrgyz Republic between 2000 and 2008. Its aim was to increase crop production through reliable and sustainable water distribution across seven administrative regions. Farm infrastructure was also rehabilitated under the management of water users associations (WUAs). The targeted WUAs represented 166,000 members, who managed some 710,000 hectares, or 70% of the country's irrigated land.

Members from each participating WUA signed an agreement to repay 25% of the farm rehabilitation costs, raise irrigation fees to support their WUA, and pay the water supplier an irrigation service fee for water delivered to the WUA's headgate.

Considerable success was achieved:
- The performance of the WUA members was improved.
- Infrastructure that fed 120,000 hectares was rehabilitated, and irrigation water delivered to farmers in 80% of the rehabilitated systems now closely matches demand.
- Three agricultural seasons later, irrigation service fees have doubled on average and collection rates by WUAs are close to 100%.
- Overall cost recovery rose from about 20% to 60%, and at least 80% of water users were satisfied with the performance of WUA management.

Source: World Bank (2008b).

The proportion of utilities that were not able to cover their basic operation and maintenance costs increased from 35% in 2000 to 43% in 2008 – with most of that increase occurring since the fuel crisis hit the sector and increased operating costs substantially. The effect is especially noticeable in low-income countries, where there was a sharper increase in the number of utilities that could not cover basic operation and maintenance costs. In irrigation, overall cost recovery rates tend to be even lower. Easter and Liu (2005) show that federal irrigation projects in the United States generally do not recover more than 20% of costs from farmers. In developing countries, the picture is even grimmer.

The second objective for charging for water involves pricing to provide incentives to use water more efficiently. Not charging for water often results in unsustainable levels of consumption that result in early depletion of water resources – which ultimately increases the costs of production.

Improving water use efficiency requires increasing the value of each unit of water consumed. This is already politically difficult, but it will become more important as water scarcity increases. To guarantee economic sustainability, users should be charged the full supply costs, plus the costs created by any externalities.[5] Externalities

BOX 24.4

The cost of agricultural water demand

The 2009 report, *Charting our Water Future: Economic Frameworks to Inform Decision-Making*, is a study carried out by the 2030 Water Resources Group and led by the International Finance Corporation and McKinsey & Company. It provides an evaluation of the scale of the water challenge, estimating that by 2030, global water requirements may grow by over 40% from 4,500 billion m³ to 6,900 billion m³.

Demand for agricultural water, which currently accounts for 71% of water used, is projected to be most significant in the poorest regions - India (1,195 billion m³), sub-Saharan Africa (820 billion m³), and China (420 billion m³). In India, closing the 2030 gap could cost between US$0.10 per m³ and US$0.50 per m³. Meeting new demand by building large infrastructure (right side of the curve) will be costly. However, many of the demand-side interventions (left side of the curve) are not only more cost effective, but support a green economy by focusing on resource savings over increased exploitation. By assessing the trade-offs between new infrastructure and demand-side measures, countries can define the appropriate mix of interventions for filling the gap between future water demand and supply.

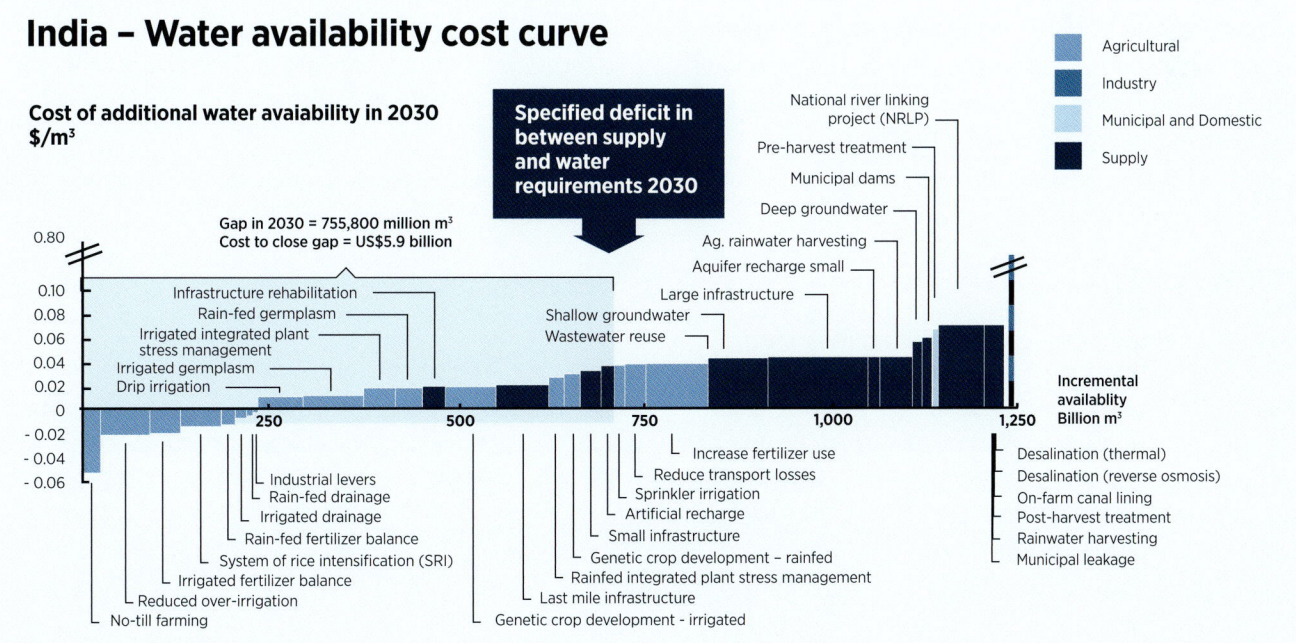

India – Water availability cost curve

The report proposes that future demand for water could be met through cost-effective measures using existing technologies.

Source: 2030 Water Resources Group (2009, p. 12).

include the cost to producers and consumers (economic externalities) and to public health and ecosystems (environmental externalities). Including externalities is likely to substantially increase the total cost of many water services, which is why few pricing systems in the world include them in their pricing structures.

Inadequate cost recovery is a function not only of low tariff levels, but also of low collection rates, unaccounted-for water and other operational efficiencies. The 2009, evaluation of water sector projects conducted by the Independent Evaluation Group of the World Bank concluded that for WSS projects, the factor that contributed most to successfully meeting cost recovery targets was improving collection rates (IEG, 2009). Most often this involved increasing the capacity and willingness of water institutions to collect fees from beneficiaries. Increasing water tariffs also had a discernible impact on overall project results (World Bank, 2010c).

24.3.4 Improving the use of public funds
Subsidies revisited
When consumers do not pay the full cost of the service, someone else has to bridge the finance gap. This is either future consumers, current or future taxpayers or a combination of these.

Most of the financing gap is paid for by government subsidies (taxes). Subsidies are ubiquitous in the sector for funding both capital outlay and operations and maintenance costs. There are various instruments through which subsidies are channelled. These include capital and operating subsidies, social safety nets, consumption subsidies, and cross-subsidies.

In developed countries, capital subsidies are relatively common. In the United States, capital investments are often funded through tax-free municipal bonds. This

BOX 24.5
What the European Union Water Framework Directive says about water pricing

Article 9 of the European Union Water Framework Directive (WFD) required Member States to adopt water pricing policies by 2010 that provided adequate incentives for the efficient use of water resources.

Water service costs include environmental costs, and are based on the *polluter pays* principle – whether that user is industry, agriculture or individual households. The rationale behind the polluter pays principle is to mitigate environmental problems through reliance on economic efficiency.

The WFD's concept of cost recovery is based on two levels of recovery, financial recovery and environmental and resource recovery.
• Financial costs or the full cost of supply: This includes the costs of providing and administering water services. It includes all operation and maintenance costs, capital costs (including initial outlay and interest payments), and any return on equity.
• Resource costs: These represent opportunities lost to other uses as a result of the depletion of the resource beyond its natural rate of recharge or recovery (for example, costs linked to the over-abstraction of groundwater).
• Environmental costs: These refer to the cost of damage that water use imposes on the environment and ecosystems (for example, the ecological quality of aquatic ecosystems can be damaged and productive soils can become saliferous and degraded).

Sources: Garrido and Calatrava (2010); Francois et al.(2010); Commission of the European Communities (2000).

TABLE 24.1
Median operating cost coverage in utilities

Year	2000	2001	2002	2003	2004	2005	2006	2007	2008
Operating cost coverage (ratio of operating revenues over operation and maintenance costs)	1.11	1.13	1.10	1.11	1.08	1.07	1.07	1.08	1.05
Standard deviation	0.55	0.56	0.58	0.61	0.57	0.56	0.55	0.54	0.50
Number of utilities reporting	579	615	723	999	1 151	1 173	1 379	1 229	930

Note: The 2008 data collection cycle is not yet complete.
Source: Van den Berg and Danilenko (2011, table 3.6, p. 23).

means that utilities are provided with an implicit subsidy. Similarly, in the European Union, utilities receive generous capital investment grants to aid compliance with stringent wastewater standards. In developing countries, water sector subsidies are provided in the form of capital grants and also often in the form of operating subsidies, which creates severe distortions in the production and consumption of services. Operating subsidies have considerable drawbacks because they distort incentives for more efficient use of water. Highly inefficient systems that receive operating subsidies do not have any incentives to improve services.

In water supply and sewerage systems, where coverage is far from universal, subsidies tend to benefit those already connected to the piped system – which tends to be better-off households. A 2007 evaluation of thirty-two water subsidy programs showed that quantity-based subsidies, the most common type of subsidy, do not reach the poor customers they target (Komives et al., 2007). Connection subsidies, as well as consumption subsidies that are means-tested or geographically targeted, have a better record of reaching the poor than quantity-based subsidies.

The AICD also showed that in Africa, around 90% of beneficiaries with access to piped water are the richest 60% of the population. In such a context, any subsidy for piped water is largely captured by better-off households. In irrigation, wealthier farmers tend to benefit more proportionally from subsidies than poorer farmers.

The World Panel for Financing Water Infrastructure calls for a greater assurance that resources for subsidies are budgeted in advance, as part of a trend towards a more 'sustainable cost recovery' (Winpenny 2003). When large government subsidies are not provided directly and on a regular basis, water agencies tend to postpone maintenance, which shortens the life-span of the assets and means that infrastructure needs to be replaced more often. Irregular and inadequate subsidies can also result in investments not being made and untreated wastewater being discharged into water bodies, groundwater resources being overexploited, and higher pollution levels.

Cross subsidies, whereby industrial users pay more to support the cost of residential use, are quite common in WSS, and the direct fiscal repercussions are small. Whether this instrument can work depends largely on the tariff structure. Maxing out cross-subsidies can be problematic. If costs become too expensive for non-residential water users, they may opt out of the piped water supply system, thereby undermining utilities' revenue base. The International Benchmarking Network for Water and Sanitation Utilities (IBNET) database[4] shows that in 2008, the average water company charged non-residential users up to 1.35 times more per cubic meter than they charged residential users. High levels of cross-subsidies tend to be more common in low-income countries than in middle-income countries.

Because subsidies distort incentives, some basic principles should be set in place. Subsidies should:
- be predictable to ensure longer-term planning and budgeting;
- be transparent, and reviewed continuously to ensure that they provide incentives to improve performance;
- be reduced over time to allow charges to take over; and
- take affordability into consideration.

Management of government transfers
Although there is sufficient scope for full cost recovery in the short-to-medium term, the role of government transfers is an essential element in ensuring the long-term sustainability of the sector. Although no global data exist on the size of government transfers in the sector, anecdotal evidence suggest that they are large. The prevalence of capital and operating subsidies is high. A significant portion of these hidden costs is used to support operation and maintenance of existing systems. These implicit subsidies tend to be regressive, benefiting a relatively small, well-off, group of consumers. In Africa, 40% of government transfers are used for operation and maintenance, resulting in capital investment being crowded out and limiting the capacity of countries to invest (Foster and Briceño-Garmendia, 2010).

Larger government transfers, however, will not necessarily result in improved access to sustainable water services. When large flows of resources in the sector are managed by the government, the efficiency and effectiveness with which they are managed becomes critical to the sustainability of the services. Countries must look at the incentives and potential bottlenecks in fiscal and public finance policies, and not only at the way that financial resources are managed.

A new tool that is proving instrumental in understanding the flow of public funds in water is the Public

Expenditure Review (PER). A PER is concerned with public-based (not always government) revenues and expenditure as expressions of public policy and public involvement in the economy (World Bank, 2009). It entails a careful examination and analysis of the fundamental drivers of public finance. The recommendations provide guidance to governments on critical reform processes that can be taken to ensure efficiency, efficacy and transparency in the use of public monies flowing to one or many sectors.

Since 2003, the World Bank has funded 40 PERs in which the water sector featured in some capacity. A quick assessment of some of the water sector PERs suggests that the efficiency and effectiveness of how governments allocate, disburse and use resources in the sector can be improved. A number of countries that have undertaken these exercises have adopted comprehensive budget legislation, reduced waste in public expenditure, given greater budget autonomy to local governments, and attempted to open budgets to public scrutiny (Deolalikar, 2008).

The efficiency (is the money spent on the right things?) and effectiveness (is the money spent well in light of the allocation decisions?) of expenditure can be affected by many factors. The World Bank is compiling a report based on findings from 15 PERs in sub-Saharan Africa (World Bank, 2012). It documents regional trends and provides opportunities for the more efficient use of public funds. For example, adequate regulations and institutions generally exist in the region, but capacity is weak. By bringing line ministries into the budgeting process, investments will be more realistic, appropriate, and responsive to needs. Countries can also improve adherence to procurement plans, create more bylaws to aid implementation of reforms, and reconcentrate utility staff to local levels to realize decentralization.

As demonstrated in many PERs, sector-specific issues play a major role in explaining the performance of translating funds into actual outcomes. Three ways in which efficiency can be enhanced are (i) by improving sector and investment planning; (ii) by improving the capacity to procure, disburse, audit and monitor resources; and (iii) maintain a sharper focus on incentives in the allocation of funds.

First, although its use has declined in recent years, cost-benefit analysis must be used to improve investment planning and prioritization. Water variability should be a key concern for long-term planning in both developed and developing countries. Sensitivity and risk analysis can help to determine how robust various investments are to changes in circumstance. Sector planning should be combined with multi-year budgeting to ensure that short-, medium- and long-term investments can be implemented properly.

Second, governments must improve disbursement functions, often a major source of the inefficiencies that cause higher procurement costs. For example, late funds result in budgets not being fully carried out, which may have implications for future access to funds. Many developing countries have inefficient mechanisms to transfer resources from central, to regional, and then to local authorities. Yearly budget cycles often entail that capital works must be contracted and completed within the cycle. Lack of capacity in procurement curtails and delays investment in the sector.

Third, by using results-based incentives, water agencies can access funds on the basis of their performance, as long as tangible and verifiable results are accomplished. Results-based financing (RBF) encompasses a range of mechanisms that are designed to enhance the delivery of infrastructure and social services through the use of performance-based incentives, rewards, and subsidies. A funding entity (typically a government or sub-governmental agency) provides a financial incentive, on condition that the recipient undertakes pre-determined actions or achieves particular outputs. Resources are disbursed not against individual expenditures or contracts on the input side (as is traditionally done), but against demonstrated and independently verified results that are largely within the control of the recipient.

RBFs can be structured in several ways depending on the objectives and goals set by the government. There are several types of RBF mechanism, including carbon finance strategies, conditional cash transfers, output-based disbursements, and advance market commitments. The application of RBFs in the water sector is quite limited, but in recent years some projects have been financed through the Global Partnership on Output-Based Aid (GPOBA). This is a donor trust fund managed by the World Bank. OBA in the water sector is generally a payment of a subsidy to cover pro-poor access. Service delivery is contracted out to a service provider (private or public utility or an NGO), with payment tied to the achievement of specified performance or outputs. OBA subsidies can either buy down the capital cost or cover the difference between an affordable user fee and a cost-recovery user fee, such as a consumption subsidy.

GPOBA has approved close to US$4 billion in grants. Of these, US$137 million is for WSS. There are currently 22 projects with World Bank participation with approximately US$140 million allocated to subsidies: 15 are water supply schemes, 3 are sanitation schemes, and 4 provide both water and sanitation (Kumar and Mugabi, 2010). Many of these projects are already showing promising results. Within less than a year, 6,700 connections were made in Cameroon (project target is 40,000); in India, 77,000 connections were completed in rural communities in Andhra Pradesh. There are, however, criticisms of OBA, including high costs and low leverage of commercial funds. Kumar and Mugabi argue that countries with sound regulatory frameworks, good capacity for implementing programmes, and experience with private sector provision have more success than others.

The role of external and internal governance in the sector
Good governance is part and parcel of the successful implementation of finance reforms. Good governance has several dimensions, from political stability, rule of law, government effectiveness, and regulatory quality, to voice and accountability and corruption control. Improving governance structures requires identifying the main actors and clarifying their exact mandate with regard to the key functions of: (i) policy formulation; (ii) asset management and infrastructure development; (iii) service provision; (iv) financing the sector and the development of water infrastructure; and (v) regulation of the service. Clarifying the contractual arrangement that allows the actors to interact with each other, and assessing the adequacy of the instruments used by the actors to fulfil their mandates are critical steps in understanding governance frameworks. Official policies are often not fully carried out in countries that have weak governance regimes. It is important to look at the de facto functioning of institutions rather than at the paper policy framework (Locussol and van Ginneken, 2010).

Improved sector governance, better management of public funds, and efficiency improvements at the utility level can improve water services for the end user. Providers can then consider increasing tariff levels to achieve greater (or full) cost recovery. At this stage,

providers will be able to justify increases in tariff levels, enabling them to better save for future investments and achieve the creditworthiness needed to access domestic and international commercial finance in the long-run.

24.3.5 Translating reforms into revenue
Increasing tariffs
When users pay a larger share of the actual cost of water services, there is more rational use of water. However, raising tariffs when service quality is low is a difficult task. In many countries, water tariff increases are lower than inflation – which results in cheaper water over time. Keeping up with inflation is not a trivial factor. Prices must be determined not only to guard against further erosion of a water agency's revenue base, but also to ensure that no perverse incentive to consume more water is established.

Since 2000, the average revenue per cubic meter of water sold has more than doubled to US$0.71 in the utilities participating in IBNET (See Table 24.2). The variation in the revenues generated per m³ water sold between utilities also levelled off – suggesting that more utilities are moving in the same direction.

Such reform is helping to reduce consumption. In low-income countries between 2000 and 2008, consumption fell sharply from 138 L per capita per day (lpcd) to 75 lpcd (Van den Berg and Danilenko, 2011).

Despite the incentive to conserve water, many countries still face significant challenges to increasing water tariffs. Even in OECD countries, keeping to real, rather than nominal, levels of tariffs has been tricky (OECD 2010), with several countries showing a decreasing average annual rate of change in tariff levels over the last decade when adjusted for inflation.

The role of public–private partnerships
PPPs were established in most developing countries to bridge gaps in financing, expertise and management in order to improve the performance of public utilities. These objectives can be achieved under various contractual schemes through collaborative efforts of the private operators and contracting government.

Marin (2009) analysed more than sixty-five water projects with PPPs in the urban water sector in developing countries over a fifteen-year period. Results suggest that though some projects performed better than others, the overall performance of water PPPs has been satisfactory. The urban population serviced by private operators in the developing world rose steadily from 94 million in 2000 to more than 160 million by the end of 2007 (Marin, 2009). PPP projects have provided to piped water to more than 24 million people in developing countries since 1990. Some of the major findings of the study include:

- *The largest contribution of private operators was through improved service quality and operational efficiency.* Improvements achieved through operational efficiency and quality service depends on the allocation of responsibilities and risks, which is based on multiple factors such as the incentive structure and the nature of the arrangement.
- *Efficient private operators have a positive, although mostly indirect, financial contribution.* They do this by improving the creditworthiness of the utility and allowing it to secure investment funding more easily and at better terms. A better service increases customers' willingness to pay, and this improves collection rates and makes raising tariffs easier. Experiences from Cote d'Ivoire and Gabon show that operating efficiently enabled investments to be funded through cash flows for more than a decade without needing to incur new debt.
- *Successful water PPPs have to be implemented within a well-conceived, broader sectoral reform.* Successful experiences in countries such as, Colombia, Cote d'Ivoire, and Morocco show that introducing PPPs was part of a wider reform to establish a sector framework that supported financial viability and accountability for performance. These countries had clear policies in place to move to cost recovery tariffs in a sustainable and socially acceptable manner.
- *Establishing a good partnership that achieves tangible results takes time.* It took a decade to achieve the desired results in Senegal. The outcome of a PPP depends heavily on solid collaboration, and government officials need to move away from old habits of interfering in the operation of water utilities.
- *Traditional classification of PPP projects as management contracts, lease-affermages, and concessions have become obsolete.* The most sustainable projects observed in the study did not fit into any of the traditional categories.

The study is the most comprehensive analysis to date in the sector and its recommendations are instrumental in ensuring the proper design of the next generation of PPP arrangements particularly given the fact that local private operators are entering the market more and more.

Conclusions and recommendations: The way forward

Global financial volatility and water stress have combined to bring a new set of challenges to the developing world. In the context of growing risk, more frequent floods and droughts, and uncertainty about the availability of capital and raw water supplies for drinking, sanitation and production, countries must analyse the trade-offs and make difficult decisions about how to finance vital water services.

Closing the financing gap in the water sector requires the application of a range of instruments including higher collection rates, more efficient service provision with lower costs, more targeted subsidies, and higher user charges. It is likely to be a longer-term process in which the appropriate mix of instruments will change over time. Such efficiencies, even in the absence of full cost recovery, will improve the ability of utilities to adapt to future risk, and will make them less dependent on external funding.

TABLE 24.2

Average revenues per m³ water sold (in US$) – median values

	2000	2001	2002	2003	2004	2005	2006	2007	2008
Average revenues	0.37	0.34	0.28	0.32	0.37	0.43	0.50	0.63	0.71
Standard deviation	0.34	0.34	0.37	0.42	0.47	0.50	0.53	0.59	0.51
Number of utilities reporting	567	632	725	982	1 137	1 154	1 188	1 203	878

Note: The 2008 data collection cycle is not yet complete.
Source: Van den Berg and Danilenko (2011, table 3.8, p. 26).

Decisions about how to allocate the cost of water services depends on political preferences, but it also depends on the structure of the local water market. It is important that an explicit agreement is reached on who pays for the uncovered portion of the costs. Without such an arrangement, the real costs of water services may be deferred into the future, seriously hampering short-term and medium-term sustainability. Any allocation of costs through stakeholders must take into consideration social equity and affordability. Subsidies play a critical social function in the distribution of equity.

Because the majority of funds in the sector are public monies, more attention should be paid to the efficiency and efficacy of public transfers and subsides. The political costs of removing subsidies is usually very high, particularly given that better-off users are usually the main beneficiaries. Tariffs that reflect the cost of inflation can assist in maintaining the trend toward lower per capita consumption, while those that account for environmental externalities can go one step further by addressing water scarcity and supporting a green economy.

Trade-offs will need to be made as financial sustainability is likely to be only one of several objectives that form part of a government's agenda to improve the performance of the water sector. Making these trade-offs more explicit will improve accountability and transparency. They may also incentivize much-needed reform, such as strategies for a green economy and improved conservation.

Public Expenditure Reviews and results-based financing are tools that can improve the functionality of a resource-constrained, inefficient sector. Similarly, public-private partnerships have some success in the sector and offer opportunities for risk-sharing in today's uncertain environment. Ensuring that institutional capacities are strengthened to implement some of the new methods and tools should be a priority.

||||||||||||||||||||||||||||||||||||||||||||||||||||||||||||||||||||||||||||

Notes

1   Includes low income and low to middle income countries. Analysis is based on a 'top-down approach using data on infrastructure services and parameters for construction and maintenance costs to model investment needs'. (Yepes, 2008).

2   The sector's financial sources were estimated, in the mid-1990s, to be: domestic public sector 65–70%, domestic private sector 5%, international donors 10–15% and international private companies 10–15%.

3   Includes a second partial divestiture of a utility in China. Chongqing Water Affairs Company sold 6% of its capital (US$516 million) via an initial public offering on the Shanghai Stock Exchange.

4   The International Benchmarking Network for Water and Sanitation Utilities (IBNET) is the world largest database of performance data for water and sanitation utilities.

5   Externalities can be positive (benefits) or negative (costs). When externalities are positive, the economic costs of the water service are lower than the financial costs; the opposite is true when the externalities are negative.

||||||||||||||||||||||||||||||||||||||||||||||||||||||||||||||||||||||||||||

References

2030 Water Resources Group. 2009. *Charting Our Water Future: Economic Frameworks to Inform Decision-making.* The Barilla Group, The Coca-Cola Company, The International Finance Corporation, McKinsey & Company, Nestlé S.A., New Holland Agriculture, SABMiller plc, Standard Chartered Bank, and Syngenta AG. http://www.mckinsey.com/App_Media/Reports/Water/Charting_Our_Water_Future_Full_Report_001.pdf

Agrawal, P. C. 2009. *Enhancing Water Services through Performance Agreements.* World Bank Water and Sanitation Program (WSP). New Delhi, WSP. http://www.wsp.org/wsp/sites/wsp.org/files/publications/PIP5_Press.pdf

Bates, B. C. et al. 2008. *Climate Change and Water.* IPCC (Intergovernmental Panel on Climate Change) Technical Paper. Geneva, IPCC.

Beato, P. and Vives, A. 2008. *A Primer for Water Economics and Financing for Developing Countries.* Paper prepared for EXPO 2008 in Zaragoza. Washington DC, World Bank.

Commission of the European Communities. 2000. Pricing policies for enhancing the sustainability of water resources. A Communication from the Commission to the Council, the European Parliament and the Economic and Social Committee. COM (2000) 477, Brussels, EC.

Deolalikar, A. B. 2008. Lessons from the World Bank's Public Expenditure Reviews, 2000–2007, for improving the effectiveness of public spending. Transparency and Accountability Project. Washington, DC, The Brookings Institute.

Easter, K. W and Liu, Y. 2005. Cost recovery and water pricing for irrigation and drainage projects Agriculture and Rural Development Discussion Paper 26. Washington DC, World Bank. http://siteresources.worldbank.org/INTARD/Resources/Cost_Recovery_final.pdf

Falkenmark, M. and Molden, D. 2008. Wake up to realities of river basin closure. Water Resources Development Vol. 24, No. 2, pp. 201–15.

Fay, M. et al. 2005. Achieving child-health-related Millennium Development Goals: The role of infrastructure. *World Development*, Vol. 33, pp. 1267–284.

Fay, M. et al. 2010. *Infrastructure and Sustainable Development in Post Crisis Growth and Development.* Washington DC, World Bank.

Foster, V. and Briceño-Garmendia, C., (eds). 2010. *Africa's Infrastructure: A Time for Transformation.* Washington DC, World Bank.

François, D. et al. 2010. Cost recovery in the water supply and sanitation sector: A case of competing policy objectives? *Utilities Policy,* Vol. 3, pp. 135–41.

Garrido, A. and Calatrava, J. 2010. *Agricultural Water Pricing: EU and Mexico.* Background report for OECD study, Sustainable Management of Water Resources in Agriculture. Paris, Organisation for Economic Co-operation and Development (OECD).

Hanjra, M. A and Qureshi, M. E. 2010. Global Water Crisis and Future Food Security in an era of Climate Change. *Food Policy*, Vol.35, pp. 365–77

IBNET (International Benchmarking Network for Water and Sanitation Utilities). http://www.ib-net.org

IEG (Independent Evaluation Group). 2009. *Water and Development: An Evaluation of World Bank Support 1997–2007 (Vol.1).* Washington DC, World Bank.

Izaguirre, A. K. and Perard, E. 2010. Private activity in water and sewerage declines for second consecutive year. PPI data update brief. Washington DC, World Bank.

Jimenez A., and Perez-Foguet, A. 2009. International Investments in the Water Sector. *International Journal of Water Resources Development,* Vol. 25, pp. 1–14.

Kingdom, W. et al. 2006. *The Challenge of Reducing Non-Revenue Water (NRW) in Developing Countries. How the Private Sector can Help – A Look at Performance Based Contracting.* Washington DC, World Bank.

Komives, K. et al. 2007. Subsidies as social transfers: an empirical evaluation of targeting performances *Development Policy Review,* Vol. 25, pp. 659–79.

Kumar, G. and Mugabi, J. 2010. Output-based aid in water and sanitation: the experience so far *OBA Approaches,* Note Number 36. Washington DC, World Bank.

Leurig, S. 2010. *The Ripple Effect: Water Risk in the Municipal Bond Market.* Boston, Mass. and New York, Ceres and Water Asset Management.

Locussol, A. and Van Ginneken, M. 2010. *Template for Assessing the Governance of Public Water Supply and Sanitation Service Providers.* Water Working Notes No. 23. Washington DC, World Bank.

Marin, P. 2009. *Public-Private Partnerships for Urban Water Utilities: A Review of Experiences in Developing Countries.* Washington, DC, PPIAF, World Bank.

OECD (Organisation for Economic Co-operation and Development). 2010. *Pricing Water Resources and Water and Sanitation Services.* Paris, OECD.

––––. 2011a. *Financing Water and Sanitation in Developing Countries: The Contribution of External Aid.* Paris, OECD Publishing. http://webnet.oecd.org/dcdgraphs/water/

––––. 2011b. *Towards Green Growth: A Summary for Policy Makers.* Paris, OECD. http://www.oecd.org/dataoecd/32/49/48012345.pdf

Perard, E. 2011. Private activity in water and sewerage remains subdued. Private Participation in Infrastructure Database (PPI), Data Update Note 49. Washington, DC,

PPIAF–World Bank. http://ppi.worldbank.org/features/July2011/2010-Water-note-final.pdf

Prynn, P. and Sunman, H. 2000. Getting the water to where it is needed and getting the tariff right. Paper prepared for the FT Energy Conference, Dublin, November 2000.

Rosegrant, M. W., Cai, X. and Cline, S. A. 2002. *World Water and Food to 2025: Dealing with Scarcity.* Washington DC, International Food Policy Research Institute (IFPRI).

UN (United Nations). 2011. *The Millennium Development Goals Report.* New York, UN.

Van den Berg, C. and Danilenko, A. 2011. *The IBNET Water Supply and Sanitation Performance Blue Book: The International Benchmarking Network for Water and Sanitation Utilities Databook.* Washington DC. World Bank and Water and Sanitation Program.

WaterAid. 2005. Problems for women. http://www.wateraid.org/uk/what_we_do/the_need/206.asp

Winpenny, J. 2003. *Financing Water for All.* Report of the World Panel on Financing Water Infrastructure. World Water Council and Global Water Partnership. http://www.worldwatercouncil.org/fileadmin/wwc/Library/Publications_and_reports/CamdessusSummary.pdf

Winpenny, J et al. 2009. *The Global Financial and Economic Crisis and the Water Sector.* Report for the Stockholm International Water Institute. Stockholm, SIWI.

World Bank. 2004. *Towards a Water-Secure Kenya*: *Water Resources Sector Memorandum.* Washington DC, The World Bank.

––––. 2008a. *Zambia – Managing Water for Sustainable Growth and Poverty Reduction: A Country Water Resources Assistance Strategy for Zambia.* Washington DC, World Bank.

––––. 2008b. *Kyrgyz Republic: On-Farm Irrigation Project.* Implementation Completion and Results Report. Washington DC, World Bank.

––––. 2009. *Preparing PERs for Human Development: Core Guidance.* Washington DC, World Bank.

––––. 2010a. *Global Monitoring Report 2010: The MDGs after the Crisis.* A Joint Report of the Staffs of the World Bank and the International Monetary Fund. Washington DC, World Bank.

––––. 2010b. *The Cost to Developing Countries of Adapting to Climate Change.* The Global Report of the Economics of Adaptation to Climate Change Study. Consultation Draft. Washington DC, World Bank.

––––. 2010c. Cost recovery in the water sector. Project Concept Note. Unpublished.

––––. 2011. Private activity in infrastructure remained at peak levels and highly selective in 2010. Private Participation in Infrastructure Database (PPI) data update note 55. Washington DC, PPIAG-World Bank. http://ppi/features/September-2011/2010-Global-update-note-final-08-31-2011.pdf

––––. 2012, Forthcoming. *Trends in Public Expenditure on Water and Sanitation in Sub-Saharan Africa.* Washington DC, World Bank.

Yepes, T. 2008. Investment needs in infrastructure in developing countries: 2008–2015. Unpublished. Commissioned by World Bank, Washington DC.

CHAPTER 25

Water and institutional change: Responding to present and future uncertainty

UNDP Water Governance Facility at SIWI
—

Authors Håkan Tropp and John Joyce
Contributors Rose Osinde and Maja Schlüter

A mounting water challenge is how to manage uncertainty of present and future variability in precipitation, evaporation, and water uses and demands. Policy-makers and water managers around the world grapple with water availability, water supply and water demand uncertainties, magnified by pressures such as climate change, economic growth, and population growth and mobility. These pressures impact on the spatial and temporal distribution of water resources. Uncertainty appears in technical, social and natural systems (Brugnach et al., 2009). Natural systems include for example climate change impacts.

Technical systems include human interventions that affect the supply of water, such as dams and irrigation canals. Social systems have cultural, political, economic, legal, demographic, administrative and organizational dimensions that add to the complexities of managing water resources. Growing populations and urbanization coupled with changing consumption preferences contribute to uncertainty in water demands. Various and often conflicting water demands have to be satisfied with varying levels of political will, scarce financial resources, and a deficit of effective institutions and management approaches.

An example of the impacts of complexities and uncertainty in water-related decision-making is illustrated by the Australian farmers who in 2007, swayed by a favourable rainfall forecast after a multi-year drought, took out loans or sold their expected crops on futures markets. Unfortunately, the rainfall that actually occurred was much lower than predicted, so many farmers were unable to repay their loans or were forced to buy crops at much higher prices than the prices at which they sold them to fulfil their contractual obligations (Brugnach et al., 2009).

One important aspect of managing uncertainty is the role of institutions. Institutions provide 'the rules of the game' and can provide incentives and disincentives for how well society can expect to adapt to uncertainty (North, 1990). In response to increasing water supply and demand challenges, water-related institutions are undergoing far-reaching changes worldwide. As well as the redefinition of roles and responsibilities, institutional arrangements and frameworks have provided direction on what is needed in terms of building and strengthening human, technological, information, knowledge and delivery capacities.

Uncertainty can be understood as a range of reasonably expectable future conditions that need to be taken into account for decision-making at all levels, from the individual farmer to international water and environmental negotiations (Brugnach et al., 2009). For example, the uncertainty in assessing the probability of a once-in-fifty-years flood needs to be offset by appropriate sensitivity analysis and the design of an adequate safety margin. The size of the margin depends on the available financial resources to invest in management and mitigation measures as well as on the risk propensity of the decision-maker and the population of concern. Despite some countries facing similar risks, their capacity to deal with it can differ considerably. For example, the Netherlands and Bangladesh both face recurrent flood risks, but the Netherlands is in a stronger economic position and can afford to invest heavily in infrastructure development and human capacity to reduce uncertainties in water management. The purpose of this chapter is to illustrate the growing need to strengthen water-related institutions, particularly with increasing water supply and demand uncertainties due to growing pressures such as climate change, economic growth and population growth. The chapter discusses what institutions are in relation to sustainable water development, and why they matter. It looks at some current challenges in water institutional reform. Finally, institutional responses and adaptive capacities to growing uncertainties are discussed and examples of attributes required for effective institutional change and implementation are provided.

25.1 Institutions: Form and function

25.1.1 Defining institutions

A broad definition of institutions provided by Ostrom (2005) is the prescription that humans use to organize all forms of repetitive and structured interactions including those within families, neighbourhoods, markets, firms, sports leagues, religious associations, private associations, and governments at all scales. Individuals and groups interacting within rule-structured situations face choices regarding the actions and strategies they take, leading to consequences for themselves and for others. Importantly, these systems are constructed by humans and are a complex mix of norms, conventions, rules and behavioural characteristics (North, 2000); that is, 'the rules of the game' with organizations as 'the players of the game'. Institutions involve rules that define roles and procedures for people; have a degree of permanency and are relatively stable; determine what is appropriate, legitimate and proper; and are cognitive and normative structures defining perceptions, interpretations and sanctions.

While formal and informal water institutions are part of overall institutional architecture, they affect social, economic and political life in different ways and a distinction is made between them.[1] Formal institutions are generally created by government policy, laws, rules and regulations, and they have the resources and authority to coordinate large numbers of users and areas. They are involved in the processes of extracting, distributing and using water. Such institutions are under the purview and responsibility of the political regime (e.g. parliament, government, courts, districts and municipalities) and agencies are set in place to perform functions such as water resources management, distribution of water services, regulatory monitoring and water quality protection. Non-governmental organizations (NGOs) such as water user associations and private water service providers can be part of the formal institutional set-up in addition to having watch-dog functions.

Informal institutions are part of traditional and contemporary social rules applied to water use and allocation. The 'players-of-the game', that is, those who define 'the rules of the game', can be community-based organizations, the local private sector, religious associations and so forth. Informal water-related institutions are usually equated with norms and traditions of how to allocate, distribute and use water resources. But informal water rights systems are not just 'customary' or 'archaic' – on the contrary, they can comprise a dynamic mixture of principles and organizational forms of different origins (Boelens, 2008). They can combine local, national and global rules and they often mix indigenous, colonial and contemporary rights. Important sources of local rights systems tend to be state laws, religious laws (formal or indigenous), ancestral laws, market laws, and the rights frameworks generated or imposed by water project interventions, each of which often sets its own regulations. Therefore, local water rights exist under legal pluralism, where rules and principles of different origin and legitimization co-exist and interact in the same water territory.

From the perspective of local water users in many parts of the world, legitimate water rights and authority are not only those laid down in legislation (Boelens, 2008). One example of such a water rights system is *Aflaj*, prevalent in many Middle Eastern countries. *Aflaj* are traditional and well-recognized (sometimes by legislation) systems of water allocation and distribution. Over the years *Aflaj* have set traditional practices for inter-temporal water resources allocation and established user rights on an ownership or a rent basis.

Informal institutions also include clientelism and corruption. Such discretionary practices can distort legitimate institutions and result in unpredictable and ineffective decision-making processes and outcomes in allocation of water resources and services between sectors and groups (see for example Stålgren, 2006 and Plummer, 2007). In the Central Asian Former Soviet Union countries Tajikistan, Kyrgyzstan and Uzbekistan, for example, local actors combine newly established rules of local water management (water user associations) with informal institutions that often originate from institutionalized Soviet and pre-Soviet patterns of behaviour (Sehring, 2009; Schlüter and Herrfahrdt-Pähle, 2011). This mixing of different institutional logics changes their meaning and can significantly limit proper implementation of the reforms. Because informal institutions can support, disrupt and replace formal institutions, it is important that informal institutions are incorporated into analyses of risks and uncertainties in the context of institutional design (or change) and implementation. For example, in Paraguay, informal private water supply systems were recognized and agreements were developed between local government entities and small-scale private water vendors. The outcome was easier control and monitoring of pricing and quality of service (Phumpiu and Gustafsson, 2009).

25.1.2 Institutions matter

Current institutional systems and how they function impose considerable constraints for doing business, according to a survey by Kaufmann (2005). Figure 25.1 illustrates business constraints and the importance of well-functioning institutions for effective regulation, corruption control and so forth. Conventional wisdom holds that insufficient infrastructure constitutes the major market access constraint. It is therefore striking that institutional and governance issues, such as performance of bureaucracy and corruption control, rank higher than infrastructure in regions such as sub-Saharan Africa, South Asia, Latin America, and transition economies in the survey.[2] Interestingly, the results show the importance of combining so-called 'soft' and 'hard' measures to improved water development and that institutional (soft) measures should have a higher priority than they typically have had.

Institutions are also shaped by larger social, political and economic contexts, and inevitably countries show great variation in institutional design. For example, in many countries in the Middle East and North Africa (MENA) region and in China, water institutions are characterized by strong government steering, top-down management and control. In contrast, many other countries around the world have moved towards institutions with increasing power diffusion across government, civil society and markets, and with a strengthening of institutional process features such as transparency, multi-stakeholder participation and accountability.

The effective performance of institutional functions can reduce natural, technical and social uncertainties. For example, if tensions and conflicts over shared water are successfully negotiated within a particular institutional framework, uncertainties in stakeholder behaviour will be reduced and this in turn will promote more predictable outcomes in water allocation and use. In performing its functions it is important for any institution to do the following.

Define roles, rights and responsibilities of stakeholders at all levels

Institutional arrangements define who controls a resource and how it is used. In this sense, institutions

---

FIGURE 25.1

Key constraints to doing business in several geographic and economic regions

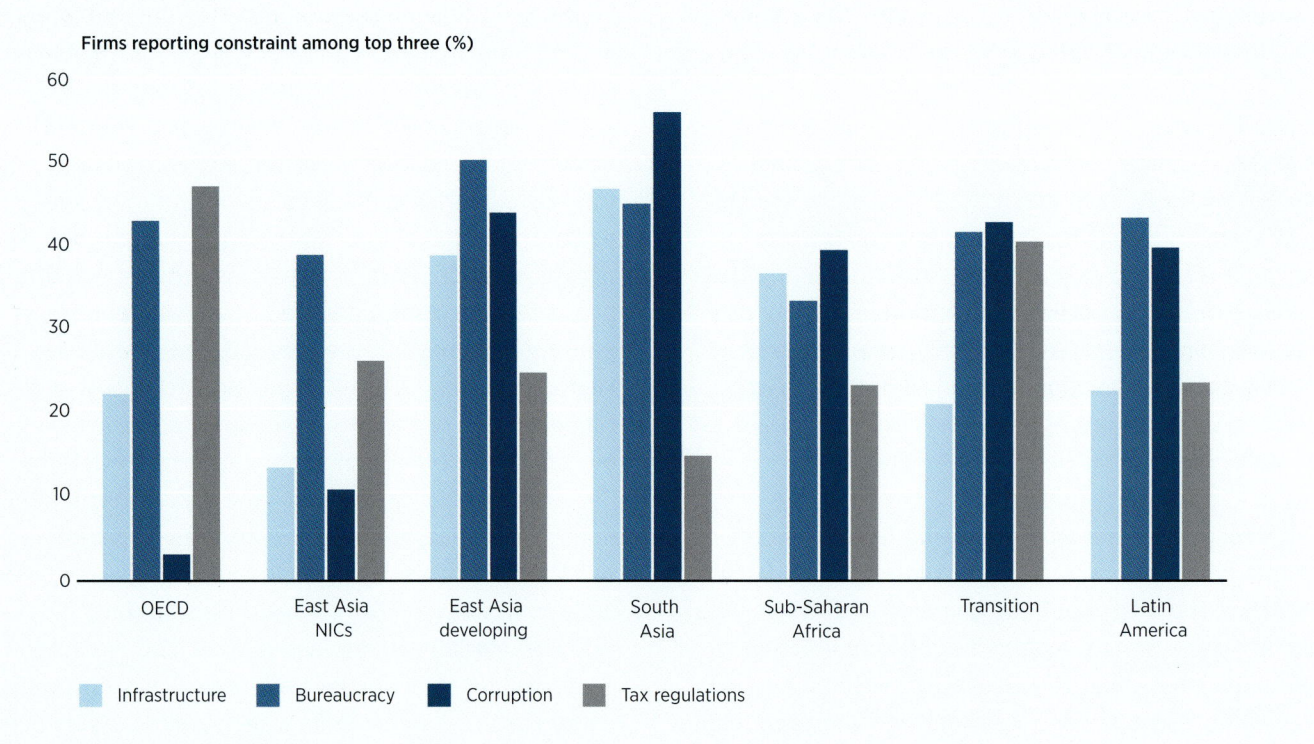

Note: The question posed to the firm was 'Select among the above 14 constraints the five most problematic factors for doing business in your country'.
Source: Kaufmann (2005, fig. 2, p. 85).

are vital in establishing the working rules of rights and duties, and in characterizing the relationship of two or more users to one another and to a specific natural resource. For example, property *rights* can determine rights and *restrictions* to a resource. The efficiency and productivity of water use can also determine rights. In Kenya, water sector reforms have clearly delineated institutional arrangements, highlighting the roles and responsibilities of subsectors at both the service delivery level and the river basin management level. One outcome of these reforms is the facilitation of institutional set-ups such as the sector-wide approach to planning (SWAP), which provides for the delivery of institutional mechanisms such as partnership principles, codes of conduct and investment plans as well as coordination, monitoring and decision-making mechanisms – all of which are geared towards enhancing service delivery and accountability for the sector. Some other Kenyan reform features include the separation of the management of water resources from the provision of water services; the separation of policy-making from day-to-day administration and regulation; the decentralization of functions to lower level government agencies; and increased involvement of non-government entities in the management of water resources and in the provision of water services. Kenya has made progress in its water reform but has faced serious challenges in funding and capacity and thus has not yet been able to implement all introduced institutional reforms (MWI, 2005, 2009).

Determine restrictions on use and mechanisms for conflict mediation

Institutions set individual and collective restrictions on water use – who can use which water, how much of it, when, and for what purpose. Increasing the water supply–demand gap intensifies competition and conflict between water users, regions and economic sectors – such a situation can demonstrate limitations in existing resource allocation and management institutions, but importantly, these institutions can develop mechanisms to deal with such conflicting interests. In transboundary river contexts, water-related tensions may have been historically contained but given current water scarcity trends caused by both environmental and developmental changes, these tensions could escalate. A water scarcity–water conflict dynamic often constitutes a justification for institutional water reform and for the development of clearly defined regulatory and allocation mechanisms. The reforms of water institutions and the legal instruments governing transboundary water are, however, complex and often take a long

time to debate and introduce; tensions could accelerate in the meantime. However, in some instances water tensions have accelerated institutional change. In Australia, long-standing water use tensions between environmentalists and farmers in the Murray–Darling Basin provide backdrop to the Landcare movement and to developing multi-stakeholder fora for managing water in its basin context. The competing water demands of states have served as the basis for institutional development of the Murray-Darling Basin water management framework. Conflicting visions of catchment management, such as the degree of stakeholder participation, have shaped institutional approaches in the state of New South Wales. Conflict avoidance can itself be a driver of innovation in the area of water governance. In South-East Asia, the spectre of resource-based conflict between the countries sharing the Mekong River has been a strong driver for cooperation through the Mekong River Commission (MRC) and an important justification of official assistance to the Commission (Boesen and Munk Ranvborg, 2004).

Reduce transaction costs and stimulate investment

The development of institutions and their effective enforcement contributes to, among other things, lowering the transaction costs of organizations and investors. Put simply, a transaction cost is a cost incurred in making an economic exchange; that is, the cost of participating in a market, such as in fee-based systems of provision of water and water-related services. Costs involved can include the search for information, bargaining for and deciding on proper fees, and policing and enforcement. From an economic perspective, effective institutional change takes place when transaction costs are less than the corresponding opportunity costs. Transaction cost analysis is seen by many as the core of institutional economics analysis but is seldom used in developing new water institutions. In Kenya, for example, some stakeholders see institutional changes such as the introduction of SWAP as potentially increasing the bureaucracy and level of complexity of the institution and removing decision-making further from the grass roots level. There is some concern that transaction costs could rise with SWAP and some NGOs fear that SWAP could result in reduced funding for them. This institutional reform is thus seen by some stakeholders as requiring high levels of transparency and high capacity of government monitoring systems, which would increase the probability of failure as these are weak points in the sector.

25.2 Institutional responses to uncertainty

Conventional water planning tends to be rigid and challenges remain regarding how to develop adaptive governance frameworks and institutions with increasingly uncertain and changing water futures. There are calls for more attention to be paid to resilient and adaptive institutions and approaches (GWP, 2009). The *World Water Development Report* 2 (WWAP, 2006) notes that insufficient access to water resources and services is not necessarily driven by water shortages but by the 'institutional resistance to change' that emanates from 'lack of appropriate institutions' to manage and secure resources for developing human capacity, management approaches, and provision of technical and physical infrastructure.

Without institutions capable of accommodating to uncertainty and shifting water supplies to where they are needed most, climate change and other drivers will impose significant impacts on water users and water-dependent communities. Yet much work remains to effectively integrate climate-related policies with water policies. This is problematic because many of the measures to adapt to climate change will have to be water-related (Björklund et al., 2009).

Institutional change or policy reform will be less effective unless it is coupled with enforcement of legislation to guarantee integrity and accountability in decision-making at all levels. Mismanagement, corruption, bureaucratic inertia and 'red tapism' all affect water management in detrimental ways. They increase transaction costs, discourage investments and can provide strong disincentives for water reform implementation and amplify risks and uncertainties for users. At the core they are symptoms of governance crisis. Recent studies confirm that for example petty corruption at the provider–consumer interface is one key area of risk that water projects and programmes must consider (Butterworth and de la Harpe, 2009). This calls for, among other things, more effective enforcement of regulatory institutions to monitor performance and expenditures of service providers.

In this section, some examples of response to uncertainty in decision-making are highlighted and analysed to provide snapshots of adaptive capacity of institutions; that is, to what extent are they flexible and robust to change as the social, political and ecological environment changes. Adaptive capacity has been defined as the potential or capability of a system to adjust, via changes in its characteristics or behaviours, so as to cope better with existing and future stresses. More specifically, adaptive capacity refers to the 'ability of a socio-ecological system to cope with novelty without losing options for the future' (Folke et al., 2002) and in a way 'that reflects learning, flexibility to experiment and adopt novel solutions, and development of generalized responses to broad classes of challenges' (Walker et al., 2002). In some cases new institutions might need to be created to deal with specific water challenges, as for example in the recent development of water quality trading for diffuse pollution and eutrophication management (van Bochove, et al. , 2011; Joyce et al., 2011).

Box 25.1 provides a detailed discussion of institutional change and adaptation in the context of water supply and sanitation services.

25.2.1 Evolving institutions

During the past decades many developing countries have been facing increasing challenges of water pollution such as those common in Western Europe and North America. This has led to the establishment of environment ministries, but much work remains to fully develop and implement pollution monitoring, legislation and regulation. It also seems likely that politically and financially weak ministries will face increasing tensions with water agencies responsible for water resources development projects. How governments will resolve these disputes is a challenge; there seems to be very limited institutions that can mediate water-related disputes between urban, rural and environmental interests.

Some interesting examples of how such disputes can be institutionally managed are found in so-called watershed markets. Put simply, watershed services are provided by upstream water users to downstream beneficiaries making some kind of payment or other compensations to those upstream. The 1998 New York City watershed agreement is well known (WWAP, 2009): in response to conflict with upstream water users over new land use restrictions and to protect New York City's water supply, a model was negotiated between farmers and the City that was built on financial compensation to farmers and guarantees that the City could acquire land only from willing farmers at fair market price. Similar agreements are emerging in other places in the USA; for example, the Cuyahoga River basin in Ohio identifies trading systems for stream, wetland and

Institutional change in water supply and sanitation services

Urban water supply services have traditionally been provided by state-owned and managed water utilities. A common trait in much reform around the world in the past decades has been that governments have attempted to turn state-owned water utilities into effective and viable organizations – with mixed success. The World Bank looked at 11 case studies (from Europe, Africa, Latin and North America, and Asia) of utilities that were well functioning and asked the question: Why have some public utilities become more efficient service providers while others have not been able to break the vicious cycle of low performance and low cost recovery? It presents a framework of attributes of well-functioning utilities and describes how these utilities have introduced key institutional measures.

The report concludes that water utilities are a part of the overall institutional landscape with its trends of change, which offers opportunities. The major transition of most utilities in the past decades has not been from public to private operation but from centralized to decentralized public provision. Fiscal squeeze has hit utilities hard: as public budgets decreased in the 1990s, infrastructure investments dropped disproportionally because governments have few discretionary spending categories. Under budgetary pressure, many public institutions have adopted new management tools, often borrowed from the private sector, to complement more traditional bureaucratic tools. Many countries have democratized, and an emerging civil society – including a consumer movement – has put pressure on utilities to deliver better services.

Institutional attributes

There is no perfect model for public utilities that guarantees good performance. But well-functioning utilities share these attributes:
- Autonomy: being independent to manage professionally without arbitrary interference by others. However, autonomy requires transparent processes so that regulators, consumers and others can exercise accountability and consumer orientation more easily.
- Accountability: being answerable to other parties for policy decisions, for the use of resources and for performance. Accountability extends to many different groups, such as regulators and the public (consumers).
- Consumer orientation: reporting on performance and listening to clients, and working to better meet their needs.

These attributes apply to the relationship between the utility and the environment in which it operates as well as to the internal functioning of the utility.

There are still noticeable obstacles to many utilities performing independently. Politicians can see utilities as a 'cash cow' if, for example, cost recovery rates increase. Many times staff is not held to account and practices of corruption and mismanagement are poorly addressed. Many sector reforms are currently underway, but meaningful consumer participation is often overlooked. In this respect, the launch of separate regulatory bodies has helped to some extent; for instance, Ofwat and its WaterVoice Committees in the United Kingdom (UK); the National Water Supply and Sanitation Council (NWASCO) and the Water Watch Group in Zambia; and the Consumer Consultative Council to be set up by the water and power regulatory body in Tanzania.

Institutional measures

The tools to achieve the above attributes can vary from case to case, but certain patterns of governance practices are emerging as being critical. Institutional measures to make public utilities more effective include corporatization, performance agreements, transparency and consumer accountability tools, and capacity-building.

Source: Baietti et al. (2006).

habitat mitigation banks as well as for water quality and carbon. The next step will be to quantify watershed services to establish who provides particular services and for what payment. An enabling feature for the Cuyahoga River basin system as well as in many other parts of the country is the existence of conservancy districts. These districts are organized along watershed borders and have the authority to tax and control land use (Flows, 2006).

25.2.2 Communication, coordination and integration among institutions of all scales

Institutions of all scales, local to global, need to respond to uncertainties. For an individual farm, droughts and floods are devastating events that threaten immediate income and future livelihood. There are increasing efforts to manage risk through insurance and other financial risk transfer instruments for smallholder rainfed agriculture in developing countries.

Basing insurance payouts on an objectively measured index (e.g. rainfall amount, modelled water stress, area-averaged production) that is correlated to loss instead of actual losses overcomes problems with moral hazard (the incentive for farmers to let crops fail), adverse selection (when less skilled farmers preferentially purchase insurance) and high transaction costs that have generally made traditional insurance unviable for smallholder farmers in developing countries (Brown and Hansen, 2008). As discussed in Box 25.2, some farmers in Kenya are now using financial risk transfer to lower crop yield risks related to rainfall variability. Another example is the World Bank's Commodity Risk Management Group that works with partners in several African and Latin American countries to implement bundled index-based insurance, credit and production packages that can overcome barriers to adoption of more profitable, intensified production technology by targeting the risk aversion of lenders (Brown and Hansen, 2008).

Local customary institutions can take a holistic approach to reduce uncertainties by accessing multiple water sources for multiple purposes (Sullivan et al., 2008). Five case studies undertaken by the International Centre for Integrated Mountain Development (ICIMOD) look at situations where people are responding to too much water (floods, water logging) or too little water (drought, water stress) across the greater Himalayan region: the dry mountain valleys of Chitral in Pakistan; the middle hills in Nepal; the Koshi basin floodplains in Bihar, India; the Brahmaputra floodplains in Assam, India; and the hill areas of Yunnan, China. Some of the key adaptation strategies were livelihood diversification and making use of and strengthening local institutions and social networks. Cultural norms and rules affect people's adaptive behaviour but importantly these are dynamic and can shift over time in response to needs. It was acknowledged that national institutions and policies strongly affect people's ability to adapt at the local level, but institutions and policies at the national level are rarely informed by adaptation concerns and priorities (ICIMOD, 2009).

Moving higher up the scale, institutions are required to regulate upstream and downstream water use and allocation at the watershed or river basin level. River basin management is not a new idea; it was applied,

BOX 25.2

Institutional adaptation at the local scale: Responding to climate uncertainties through farmer micro-insurance schemes

Many farmers are held back from investing to increase their yields due to many factors, such as unsecure land tenure and difficulties in accessing traditional credit markets. An increasingly important factor is the risks and uncertainties associated with flooding and drought. After a one-year drought a farmer runs the risk of not being able to repay an investment loan and therefore of losing his or her farm. One solution is to develop insurance schemes that use new information and communication technologies to protect farmers' investments from weather fluctuations.

For example, a micro-insurance scheme is emerging in Kenya that is supported by a national insurance company, a mobile phone network operator and an agribusiness. Farmers pay an extra 5% to insure a bag of seed, fertilizer or herbicide against crop failure. The agribusiness involved hopes to benefit from higher sales of its products and matches the farmers' investment to meet the full 10% cost of the insurance premium. Administration costs are kept to a minimum and the system is supposed to be self-financing. Local agents register a policy with the insurance company by using a camera phone to scan a bar code on each bag sold. A text message is then sent to the farmer's mobile phone that confirms the insurance policy. Farmers are registered at the nearest (solar-powered) weather station, which transmits data over the mobile phone network. If weather conditions worsen, a panel of experts uses an index system to decide if crops will no longer be viable. If they will not be, at this point payouts are made directly to farmers' mobile phones using the M-PESA mobile-money service. The system comes with minimal transaction costs because it has eliminated field surveys, most paperwork and the middleman.

During the trial, one area was hit with severe drought. This triggered compensation payments of 80% of farmers' investments. Without this insurance, farmers would have had severe financial difficulties to ensure seeds, fertilizers and so forth for the next cropping season. After a successful trial of 200 farmers, the initiative is now targeting 5,000 farmers in western and central Kenya.

Source: The Economist (2010).

for example, in Niger in the 1970s. The drought of the Sahel in the 1970s spurred the creation of river basin development authorities (RBDAs), which soon increased their responsibilities to encompass water management for the country as a whole. Their purpose in addition to general water resources management was to assure systematic use of groundwater and surface water, develop water for multiple purposes, supply irrigation water, control floods and control erosion. In some countries, such as Spain and Portugal, river basin organizations have been around for more than 100 years (Delli Priscoli, 2008). A recent Cap-Net study of river basin organizations points to some positive aspects of coordination among government agencies and water stakeholders. It also acknowledges, however, many cases where river basin organizations have a long way to go to manage water in equitable, sustainable and efficient manner (Cap-Net, 2008).

BOX 25.3

Time-bound multilateral institutions: An EU common water implementation strategy

A Common Implementation Strategy (CIS) was developed in May 2001 at the European level to support European Union Member States in addressing the scientific, technical and practical challenges of implementation of the EU Water Framework Directive. Most of the challenges and difficulties that arise during implementation will inevitably be common to all Member States, and indeed many of the European river basins are shared – crossing administrative and territorial borders – so a common understanding and approach is crucial to successful and effective implementation of the directive. A common strategy could limit the risks of the Directive being poorly applied and disputes subsequent to that scenario.

The focus of the CIS is to clarify and develop, where appropriate, technical and scientific information to assist in the practical implementation of the Directive. Such documents have an informal and non-legally binding character and are be placed at the disposal of Member States on a voluntary basis. The CIS is an example of a multilateral institution that is time-bound and subject-specific, designed to address the challenges faced by Member States in a cooperative and coordinated way; they are normally chaired by one Member State and funding is generally pooled by the Member States who manage the working groups.

Source: Common Implementation Strategy for the Water Framework Directive (2000/60/EC) 2001.

Moving on to regional scales, the European Union (EU) has developed a multilateral Common Implementation Strategy to support the implementation (and limit the risks and disputes related to implementation) of the Water Framework Directive (see Box 25.3). Water-related responses should be integrative and supportive of each other in a particular country or river basin. The EU's Common Implementation Strategy is an example of the supranational institutional level guiding country processes. The integrated water resources management concept provides guidance on horizontal and vertical coordination and integration of decision-making. Meaningful communication, built on an open flow of relevant data and information, is critical for unlocking the potential of integrative approaches.

25.3 Implementation of acceptable and workable institutions

In the earlier sections of this chapter, examples were provided of institutional development in relation to water resources access, use and allocation as well as to performance and distribution of water services. But why do some institutions work better than others? The development of institutions should be seen as path-dependent. For example, in a context where markets and regulatory functions are faced with severe constraints, it is not likely that water privatization will be effective; in a context where communities have limited resources and capacities, it is not likely that delegation of water management will work effectively. Institutional reform will have a greater chance of success if it has economic rationality; political willingness and sensitivity; and pays attention to social factors and stakeholders.

Robertson and Nielsen-Pincus (2009) suggest criteria that increase the chances of success of institutional reform: leadership and political will; social capital and inter-personal trust among participants; committed and cooperative participants; adequate and sustainable financing; participation and inclusiveness; adequate time; well-defined process rules; effective enforcement mechanisms; effective communication; adequate scientific and technical information; adequate monitoring; low or medium levels of conflict; limited (manageable) temporal and geographical scope of activities; training in collaborative skills; and adequate human capacities. Importantly, blueprints cannot be applied: what works in one context may not work in another. The factors for successful delegation of water governance in Canada capture some of the political, economic and social mechanisms essential for effective institutional change (Box 25.4).

25.3.1 Lowering transaction costs and avoiding free-riders

Water resource institutions determine who can use which water, how much of it, when, and for what purpose as well as set management responsibilities, fees and fee collection processes and so forth. Community-based water supply projects in rural areas have frequently proved untenable, with many communities being unable to raise sufficient funds to meet operation and maintenance costs of common water resources. Typical costs of community water projects include payment of electricity bills or for diesel to operate pumps; purchases of spare parts and maintenance; stationery for bookkeeping; staff transportation costs; telephone bills; and payment or compensation for bookkeepers and committee members. To keep the system operational, the members need to pay their fees.

'Free-riding' – when legitimate water users take more than their allocated share of water – can impose up-stream and downstream disputes of water allocation. Free-riding also occurs when water resources are extracted by illegitimate users; that is, users who are not part of the institution. In sum, the free-rider is a water user who does not stick to commonly agreed rules. If too many free-riders operate in an institution, it will collapse because the transaction costs for monitoring and policing water users will be so high they outweigh the benefits, particularly in rural areas where water users can be dispersed over large areas and may lack shared community goals of fairness in water allocation and sharing of costs. In many places, social sanctioning serves as an effective way to minimize the number of free-riders. Social norms can generate costly punishment of community members breaking the rules – free-riders may run the risk of social exclusion or disrespect. Other ways to overcome the free-rider problem are community mobilization, social intermediation and institution building (Breier and Visser, 2006; Ostrom, 2000).

BOX 25.4

Water governance reform: Successful delegation of water governance in Canada

Water governance has undergone dramatic changes in Canada over the past decade, characterized by three key trends:
1. The introduction of new watershed-based delegated governance management models in a number of provinces.
2. Legislative and policy reform that has set higher standards for drinking water supply in a number of jurisdictions.
3. Greater citizen involvement in environmental policy-making and environmental management.

These trends have emerged due to several reasons: a shift in the view of the role and mandate of governments; new legal requirements (particularly with respect to First Nations, and also mandated by a new generation of environmental laws); awareness of the expertise available outside government, particularly in the context of decreased government resources; new approaches to citizen participation; increased emphasis on integrated management of environmental issues and watershed-based management; and concern over the implications of climate change for both water resources and supply.

In the context of overall water reform in Canada, the approach of delegated water governance is considered successful through the following factors:
• Effective leadership: clear structuring of processes, sustainable financing, adequate human resource support and the ability to implement recommendations.
• Inter-personal trust: transparency and respect for the rule of law.
• Committed participants: open or closed participation and an adequate range of participants.
• Sufficient scientific information: necessary for sound decision-making, this needs to be accessible to participants.
• Sufficient and sustainable funding: necessary to support collaborative bodies.
• Manageable scope of activities: it is important to limit scope and set targets.
• Policy feedback: a formal mechanism is needed to deal with recommendations from delegated water governance bodies.

Whereas the shift from state or centralized water management to community management and the increased participation of marginalized groups has in some instances provided new opportunities and benefits, such a shift might in some cases increase the burden on community resources and on women's labour and time.

Source: Nowlan and Bakker (2007).

Free-riders receive benefits without actually contributing anything, thus creating an unfair balance in the distribution of revenues or other resources. The social, political and economic dilemmas of free-riding occur not only in rural water supply but in any area and at any scale. Take for example urban drinking water supply around the world: some consumers – often in collusion with public officials – avoid paying fees by manipulating water metres or by other means. It has been noted that drivers of change, such as water scarcity, macroeconomic developments and natural calamities, interact to raise the opportunity cost of institutional change and reduce the corresponding transaction cost. This creates a conducive environment for institutional change.

25.3.2 Moving from inertia or resistance to political will

United Nations Secretary-General Ban Ki-moon's message on World Water Day, 22 March, in 2008 pointed to the lack of political will as the biggest problem in institutional reform: 'progress is hampered by population growth, widespread poverty, insufficient investments to address the problem and the biggest culprit: a lack of political will' (Ban Ki-moon, 2008). Institutional water reform needs to be firmly anchored among stakeholders and their leadership. If institutions are considered as unacceptable in their set-up and produce undesired outcomes, they will not receive support and stakeholders are more likely to keep the status quo or even develop their own informal rules rather than adhere to existing rules.

Because reforms change status quo, one can expect both support for and opposition to institutional reform agendas by affected groups. In some cases, the implementing agency may not have a reform agenda that coincides with that of the government initiating the reform. For example, an analysis of the parties involved in a proposed water fee reform for the capital of Honduras, Tegucigalpa, revealed that the public agency in charge of water supply was a major opponent to the reform. Support for institutional reform was driven by external international development agencies, but in this case, the support was not sufficient for reform to take place – for the reform to go forward it had to be supported by national power centres. In Pakistan for example, some government ministries and agencies opposed reform – part of which was to transfer power and financial resources from the irrigation ministry and its regional offices to area boards – because they felt it would affect them negatively (WWAP, 2006).

It has also been observed that bureaucratic behaviour can cause disincentives for effective institutional reform to deal with new challenges. For example, in efforts for decentralizing water decision-making and management, bureaucratic behaviour can lead to a pre-occupation of roles, hierarchies and procedures that protect the affected department from having to respond to institutional change. On an individual basis, staff members are concerned about employment security and station location. Clearly, the combination of organizational inertia or resistance to change coupled with staff concerns makes change hard unless pressure and/or incentives are applied by higher political and administrative levels (Holmes, 2003).

The importance of political will can be illustrated by water reform in some countries. In Canada, effective leadership is considered one of the required factors for institutional change in delegating water governance (Box 25.4). In Scotland, the transition from old to new regulatory approaches is not without tensions and inconsistencies, particularly at the legal and operational levels. Water disputes in Scotland are associated with the redesign of national administrative responsibilities and the re-establishment of a devolved parliament. There is still a gap in understanding the effective possibilities and tensions associated with the new regulatory regime based on the EU Water Framework Directive. For example, the income from new water charges was expected to cover 50% of the operational costs incurred by the Scottish Environment Protection Agency (SEPA), while the other 50% was to come from the government in the form of general taxation. It has been argued that despite a discursive construction and sustainability as well as stakeholder participation, the new institutional landscape has so far failed to improve long-term patterns of water use and conservation. Whereas formal changes in the legislation created a positive space for institutional reforms, the effective improvement of water policy and catchment management has been curtailed by political inertia and the hidden balance of power. The farming sector in Scotland through the National Farmers Union (NFUS) stated that new charges for regulating farms that abstract water have generated a lot of heat and debate with SEPA and the Scottish Executive (Loris, 2009; NFUS, 2006).

25.3.3 Building trust, integrity and accountability

Several studies on institutions bring up inter-organizational trust, inter-personal trust and networks as important for effective institutional development and implementation. In the case of local adaptation to climate change in the greater Himalayan region, social networks were seen as important to enhance adaptive capacities. Similarly, inter-personal trust was critical for effective delegation of water governance in Canada (Box 25.4). Recent case studies (Ross, 2009) suggest that trust – social trust within a community or trust between communities and public authorities – is more important the higher the risks and uncertainties involved. One case study area, Toowoomba in Queensland, Australia, was set in a high perceived risk context for a proposed water re-use scheme for potable water. Perceptions of risk had a very strong direct effect on acceptance of the scheme, and the trust, risk and acceptance relationship was stronger than it was for other case study areas. Moreover, the relational variables of procedural fairness, identification with one's community, in-group membership of the water authority, and shared values with the water authority were all found to affect trust, directly or indirectly. The credibility of the authority – measured as technical competence and a lack of vested interests – was found to have a significant impact on trust. In sum, the results highlight the need for water authorities and policymakers to build trust among stakeholders through procedural fairness, developing a sense of the water authority as a member of the community, and demonstrating technical competence and concern for the interests of the public (Ross, 2009).

A formidable problem in many water institutions is corruption (Transparency International, 2008; WWAP, 2009). In too many cases corrupt behaviour has become the norm and ironically, corruption can constitute an institution in its own right. Corruption not only undercuts development and raises the stakes regarding risks and uncertainties of water availability and allocation, it also undermines critical foundations of trust, the rule of law, fairness, and efficiency of water institutions. Well-functioning institutions have developed systems of accountability. Considering the frequency of corruption in water, formal systems of accountability are often deterred and replaced by discretionary decision-making, characterized by exclusiveness and limited transparency. This renders water institutions less effective and less prone to adapt to new challenges as the status quo is preferred to protect vested interests.

There is a growing knowledge base on measures to strengthen accountability and integrity and hence reduce corruption. The simplification of procedures, increased transparency and participation will go a long way in reducing corruption: this was illustrated in the World Bank-supported Kecamatan Development Project (KDP). This project has a scope of more than 34,000 villages across Indonesia and has supported the country's water sector by building 7,178 clean water supply units, 2,904 sanitation units and 7,326 irrigation systems. Corruption was initially involved: officials being bribed to award projects, funding cuts by upper levels of government, illicit fees being charged to users, and under-delivery of materials and services by suppliers. As a result the KDP built anti-corruption measures into its projects that emphasized simplification of procedures, transparency and information-sharing throughout the project cycle (WIN, 2009).

25.4 Opportunities for improving water institutions

Uncertainty in natural, technical and social systems is relevant to institutional responses because it can distort decision-making. Decisions made under conditions of uncertainty may underestimate or overestimate the challenges to which they respond, resulting in too-costly or non-required measures, or conversely, insufficient measures that can threaten investments and progress already made. Institutional responses are crafted and implemented by social systems, which can be as hard to predict as climate change and its impacts. An institutional response measure based on an acceptable degree of certainty how natural systems will behave in the near future may not go far if there are different perceptions on what is fair as well as disparate objectives and interest among water users in the social system. It is important that risk and uncertainty associated with climate change be put into context relative to other risks that water institutions face. Changes in water demand may be more important for some countries than changes in actual supply.

Uncertainty can partly be overcome by better data, information and knowledge(see Chapter 26, 'Knowledge and capacity development') but even so, the future will always be unpredictable and requires flexibility, hence the imperative to develop responsive institutions that can deal with at least some of the uncertainties. Situations of high natural, technical or social uncertainty can create disincentives for cooperation and stakeholder participation. The probability of institutional failure and thus the ability to deal with situations of uncertainty is higher the more actors who break the rules of the game without appropriate sanctions. For example, new water regulatory institutions in corrupt environments may not provide sufficient incentive for fairer and more effective water reallocation and improved accountability. Knowledge on how institutions can develop to better respond to present and future risks and uncertainties is rudimentary and there needs to be a lot more research into practical application of institutional measures to determine what works, and under what conditions it works. Long-term investment to build water institutions is needed; in particular, investment for monitoring in relation to governance and institutional performance is severely lacking.

This chapter has indicated some of the factors required for successful water institutions and highlighted that these vary considerably according to context. Effective institutional change and to what degree it can deal with uncertainty is closely related to path dependence as well as to context specific conditions. It is important that water decision-makers intensify their efforts to provide incentives for meaningful institutional change to better cope with uncertainty. Among other actions, the following should be taken into account.

Implementation challenges remain a big obstacle to effective water reform and management and should be more coherently addressed as part of institutional reform processes. Challenges such as vested political interests and accountability systems should be more carefully analysed and addressed as part of water related institutional reform. Many countries are plagued with implementation problems, driven by for example limited capacities and funding, elite capture of policy processes, and institutional gaps and fragmentation. As a part of overcoming some of these challenges this it is important to:

- Seek continuous alignment and implementation of water, energy, ecosystem and land policies within formal and informal institutions and processes that effectively guide actions for these areas. Currently many institutions tend to be fragmented, over-lapping and sometimes even conflictive. There is thus a lot of room for continuing to develop institutional linkages as a strategy to strengthen adaptive management. Hence, this also means increased policy synergies between issues related to water, food, energy and ecosystems.

- Address fundamental governance challenges – such as limited transparency, accountability and stakeholder involvement – that provide reform implementation disincentives. It is less likely that water institutions can perform their intended functions (e.g. fair and efficient water allocation or water services provision) in governance systems characterized by clientelism, corruption and vested political interests. In such cases decision-making gets more unpredictable and increases uncertainty in for example social systems for those that lack political and economic influence.

- Target particular capacity development, data and information needs and promote learning-oriented institutional processes. Experience suggests that institutional reform is an iterative learning process where institutional change is negotiated between different groups. There are no perfect solutions; there are only solutions that work in a particular context. Others have expressed this as 'look for the best fit, not the best practice' (Baietti et al., 2006).

- Go beyond formal regulation and incorporate informal institutions into analyses of risk and uncertainty. Water resources in many parts of the world are allocated by informal local institutions and formal regulatory systems may have only limited influence. To fully understand institutional drivers and implement effective water reform it is critical to look at the dynamics between formal and informal institutions. Meeting the challenge of reaching poor and marginalized groups of society – who normally depend on informal systems of water allocation and water services – will rely on water decision-makers providing incentives to strengthen local informal institutions and making water policies and regulations more supportive of them.

- Underline that financing remains an important challenge to cope with present and future uncertainties in social, natural and technical systems. Acceptable and functioning institutions underpin increased and more effective investments in water development. Poor institutions constitute amplified investment risk and affect the competitiveness of countries in global markets, the attraction of foreign direct investment, as well as impacting on firms in national and local markets. While the need for additional investment in water is acknowledged, much more focus has to be put on how to make most effective use of present funding for more informed investment decision-making to reduce risks and cope with uncertainties. There is thus a need to develop better cost–benefit analyses of various investments options on how public and private sectors best should use their funding, capacities and knowledge.

||||||||||||||||||||||||||||||||||||||||||||||||||||||||||||||||||||||||

Notes

1   Sociological studies suggest that informal institutions at local levels can be perceived as formal. Sometimes a distinction is made by using statutory and customary institutions.

2   It is acknowledged that there can be big variations between countries within a region. The results of the survey should be perceived as relative and not suitable for regional comparison.

||||||||||||||||||||||||||||||||||||||||||||||||||||||||||||||||||||||||

References

Baietti, A., Kingdom, W. and Van Ginneken, M. 2006. *Characteristics of Well-Performing Public Water Utilities.* Water Supply and Sanitation Working Notes No. 9, May. Washington DC, World Bank.

Ban Ki-moon. 2008. Secretary-General, in message for World Water Day, calls lack of political will biggest culprit in failure to achieve basic sanitation goal. Press Release. New York, United Nations. http://www.un.org/News/Press/docs/2008/sgsm11451.doc.htm

Björklund, G., Tropp, H., Harlin, J., Morrison, A. and Hudson, A. 2009. *Water Adaptation in National Adaptation Programmes for Action: Freshwater in Climate Adaptation Planning and Climate Adaptation in Freshwater Planning.* Dialogue Paper for the United Nations World Water Assessment Programme (WWAP). Paris, UNESCO.

van Bochove, E., Vanrolleghem, P. A., Chambers, P. A., Thériault, G., Novotná, B. and Burkart, M. R. (eds). 2011. *Issues and Solutions to Diffuse Pollution:* Selected Papers from the 14th International Conference of the IWA Diffuse Pollution Specialist Group, DIPCON 2010, Québec, Canada.

Boelens, R. A. 2008. The rules of the game and the game of the rules. Dissertation, Wageningen University, the Netherlands.

Boesen, J. and Munk Ranvborg, H. (eds). 2004. *From Water Wars to Water Riots? Lessons from Transboundary Water Management.* Danish Institute for International Studies (DIIS) Working Paper No. 2004/6. Copenhagen, DIIS.

Breier, M. and Visser, M. 2006. *The Free Rider Problem in Community-based Rural Water Supply: A Game Theoretic Analysis.* SALDRU Working Paper No. 06/05. Cape Town, Southern Africa Labour and Development Research Unit (SALDRU), University of Cape Town.

Brown, C. and Hansen, J. W. 2008. *Agricultural Water Management and Climate Risk.* Report to the Bill and Melinda Gates Foundation. IRI Technical Report No. 08-01. Palisades. New York, The International Research Institute for Climate and Society (IRI).

Brugnach, M., van der Keur, P., Henriksen, H. J. and Myšiak, J. (eds). 2009. *Uncertainty and Adaptive Water Management Concepts and Guidelines.* Osnabrück, Germany, Institute of Environmental Systems Research, University of Osnabrück.

Butterworth, J. and de la Harpe, J. 2009. *Not So Petty: Corruption Risks in Payment and Licensing Systems of Water.* Brief No. 26. Bergen, Norway, U4 Anti-Corruption Resource Centre.

Cap-Net. 2008. *Performance and Capacity of River Basin Organizations: Cross-Case Comparison of Four RBOs.* Pretoria, South Africa, Cap-Net.

Common Implementation Strategy for the Water Framework Directive (2000/60/EC) 2001. Strategic document. As agreed by the Water Directors under the Swedish EU Presidency. May 2001. http://ec.europa.eu/environment/water/water-framework/objectives/pdf/strategy.pdf

Delli Priscoli, J. 2008. *Case Study of River Basin Organizations.* Corvallis, Oreg., Institute for Water and Watersheds, Oregon State University. http://www.transboundarywaters.orst.edu/research/case_studies/River_Basin_Organization_New.htm

The Economist. 2010. Security for shillings: Insuring crops with a mobile phone, 11 March, pp. 13–19.

Flows. 2006. Review: Creating 21st century institutions for watershed markets. *Flows Bulletin,* No. 23.

Folke, C., Carpenter, S., Elmqvist, T., Gunderson, L., Holling, C. S. and Walker, B. 2002. Resilience and sustainable development: Building adaptive capacity in a world of transformations. *Ambio,* Vol. 31, No. 5, 437–40.

GWP (Global Water Partnership). 2009. *Institutional Arrangements for IWRM in Eastern Africa.* Policy Brief 1. Stockholm, GWP.

Holmes, P. R. 2003. On Risky Ground: The Water Professional in Politics. Paper presented at the Stockholm Water Symposium, Stockholm, 11–14 August 2003.

ICIMOD (International Centre for Integrated Mountain Development). 2009. *Local Responses to Too Much and Too Little Water in the Greater Himalayan Region.* Kathmandu, ICIMOD.

Joyce, J., Collentine, D. and Blacklocke, S. 2011. Conducting cost-effectiveness analysis to identify potential buyers and sellers of water pollution control credits to initiate water quality trades. E. van Bochove, P. A. Vanrolleghem, P. A. Chambers, G. Thériault, B. Novotná and M. R. Burkart (eds), *Issues and Solutions to Diffuse Pollution:* Selected Papers from the 14th International Conference of the IWA Diffuse Pollution Specialist Group, DIPCON 2010, Québec, Canada.

Kaufmann, D. 2005. Myths and realities of governance and corruption. *Global Competitiveness Report 2005– 20 06.* pp. 81–98. Cologney/Geneva, World Economic Forum.

Loris, A. 2009. Water institutional reforms in Scotland: Contested objectives and hidden disputes. *Water Alternatives,* Vol. 1, No. 2, pp. 253–70.

MWI (Ministry of Water and Irrigation). 2005. *Human Resource Management Strategy and Capacity Building for the Ministry of Water and Irrigation.* Final Draft, November. Nairobi, MWI, Government of Kenya.

-. 2009. *Annual Water Sector Review 2009: Water Sector Financial Turnout.* Nairobi, MWI, Government of Kenya.

NFUS (National Farmers Union, Scotland). 2006. *Annual Report.* Newbridge, Scotland, NFUS.

North, D. C. 1990. *Institutions, Institutional Change and Economic Performance.* Cambridge, UK, Cambridge University Press.

––––. 2000. Understanding institutions. C. Menard (ed.), *Institutions, Contracts and Organizations: Perspectives from New Institutional Economics.* Cheltenham, UK, Edward Elgar, pp. 7–11.

Nowlan, L. and Bakker, K. 2007. *Delegating Water Governance: Issues and Challenges in the British Columbia (BC) Context.* Report for the BC Water Governance Project. Vancouver, BC, Program on Water Governance, University of British Columbia. http://www.watergovernance.ca/Institute2/PDF/FBCwatergovernancefinal2.pdf

Ostrom, E. 2000. Collective action and the evolution of social norms. *Journal of Economic Perspectives,* Vol. 14, No. 3, pp. 137–58.

––––. 2005. *Understanding Institutional Diversity.* Princeton, NJ, Princeton University Press.

Phumpiu, P. and Gustafsson, J. E. 2009. When are partnerships a viable tool for development? Institutions and partnerships for water and sanitation service in Latin America. *Water Resources Management,* Vol. 23, No. 1, pp. 19–38.

Plummer, J. 2007. *Making Anti-corruption Approaches Work for the Poor: Issues for Consideration in the Development of Pro-poor Anti-corruption Strategies in Water Services and Irrigation.* WIN/Swedish Water House Report No. 22. Stockholm, Stockholm International Water Institute (SIWI).

Robertson, S. and Nielsen-Pincus, M. 2009. *Keys to Success for Watershed Management Organizations.* EWP Working Paper No. 21. Corvallis, Oreg., Ecosystem Workforce Program (EWP), University of Oregon.

Ross, V. 2009. The role of trust in community acceptance of urban water management schemes: A social-psychological model of the characteristics and determinants of trust and acceptance. Dissertation, School of Psychology, The University of Queensland.

Schlüter, M. and Herrfahrdt-Pähle, E. 2011. Exploring resilience and transformability of a river basin in the face of socio-economic and ecological crisis: An example from the Amudarya river basin, Central Asia. *Ecology and Society,* Vol. 16, No. 1, p. 32.

Sehring, J. 2009. Path dependence and institutional bricolage in post-Soviet water governance. *Water Alternatives,* Vol. 2, pp. 61–81.

Stålgren, P. 2006. *Corruption in the Water Sector: Causes, Consequences and Potential Reform.* Swedish Water House Policy Brief No. 4. Stockholm, Stockholm International Water Institute (SIWI).

Sullivan, C. A., Bonjean, M., Anton, B., Cox, D., Smits, S., Chonguica, E., Monggae, F., Nyagwambo, L., Pule, R. and Berraondo, M. 2008. *Making Water Work for Local Governments and Helping Local Governments Work for Water: Ten Top Tips for Integration in Water Management.* Cape Town, South Africa, ICLEI Africa.

Transparency International. 2008. *Global Corruption Report 2008: Corruption in the Water Sector.* Cambridge, UK, Cambridge University Press.

Walker, B., Carpenter, S., Anderies, J., Abel, N., Cummings, G., Janssen, M., Lebel, L., Norberg, J., Peterson, G.D. and Pritchard, R. 2002. Resilience management in social-ecological systems: A working hypothesis for a participatory approach. *Conservation Ecology,* Vol. 6, No. 1, p. 14.

WIN (Water Integrity Network). 2009. *Advocacy Guide: A Toolbox for Water Integrity Action.* Berlin, WIN. http://www.waterintegritynetwork.net/home/learn/library/all_documents

WWAP (World Water Assessment Programme). 2006. *World Water Development Report 2: Water: A Shared Responsibility.* Paris/New York, UNESCO/Berghahn Books.

––––. 2009. *World Water Development Report 3: Water in A Changing World.* Paris/London, UNESCO/Earthscan.

CHAPTER 26

Developing knowledge and capacity

UNW-DPC and UNESCO-IHE

—

Authors Hani Sewilam (UNW-DPC) and Guy Alaerts (UNESCO–IHE/Delft University of Technology)

|||||||||||||||||||||||||||||||||||||||||||||||||||||||||||||||||||||||||||||||||||||||||||||||||||||||||||||||||||||||||||||||||||||||||||||||||||||||||||||||

The water sector will increasingly be subject to externally driven changes, yet societies will at the same time expect more reliable water services and less risk. Our understanding of natural and social phenomena has gaps, and, therefore, knowledge and capacity development is a top priority on the international agenda.

To deal with the new and dynamic challenges, the adaptive capacity of individuals, society and institutions is to be enhanced.

Knowledge sharing and collaborative tools will become prominent. ICT will be a powerful instrument to disseminate information and involve stakeholders in decision-making.
The existing gaps in our knowledge about how global change is going to affect us and how all societies should continuously adjust their water sectors to new external changes and evolving internal demands put developing knowledge and capacity as a top priority on the international agenda.

Developing the adaptive capacity of individuals, society and institutions is needed to face the new and dynamic challenges caused by global change.

There is a need for an increased use of knowledge sharing and collaborative tools. The power of ICT should be used to accelerate the dissemination of information and impose social learning within water institutions.

26.1 A changing agenda

Sustainable water management is one of humanity's most important challenges – today and in the future. Rapid changes in the hydrological cycle, and increased incidence of hazards such as extreme weather events, are further complicating the processes of decision-making for stakeholders and water managers by increasing risk and uncertainty. For example, uncertainties in water management are associated with various hydrological, hydraulic, structural and economic aspects. Risks are also present at different levels of water systems including the risk of natural disasters, risks involved in the operation of water infrastructures, drought, and risks associated with investing in water projects. The resulting adverse impacts are neither uniform across time, space and sectors, nor fair to all groups. Box 26.1 illustrates the impact that natural disasters have on women as a result of their intensive involvement in water management and their weak adaptive capacities.

The knowledge to address many of these challenges does exist. However, there are still considerable gaps in what we know. For example there are gaps in our

---

BOX 26.1

Gender challenges

In developing countries, women are generally responsible for producing food. This makes them the first to face the risks that come with drought and uncertain rainfall. Climate change often means that women and young girls have to walk ever further to collect water. For instance, women in sub-Saharan Africa spend 40 billion hours per year collecting water – equivalent to a year's labour by the entire workforce in France. The following are some examples that show that women are the first to suffer from the risk and uncertainty of climate change:

- Women, boys and girls are 14 times more likely than men to die during a disaster (Peterson, 2007).
- In Bangladesh, during the cyclone disasters in 1991, 90% of the 140,000 fatalities were women (Zeitlin, 2007).
- During the emergency caused by hurricane Katrina in the United States, most of the victims trapped in New Orleans were the poor African–American women with their children (Gault et. al., 2005; Williams et al., 2006).
- In Sri Lanka, it was easier for men to survive during the tsunami because boys are generally taught how to swim and climb trees while girls are not (Oxfam, 2005).

Source: UNDP (2009).

---

knowledge about how global change is going to affect us and what our responses should be. There are gaps in our understanding of how water services should be delivered, and of how to manage the resource of water more effectively and sustainably. This represents the first key challenge. But what is equally important is that even when the appropriate knowledge is available, it does not always get readily disseminated and shared – and translated into proper planning or effective action.

On the one hand, the time-lapse between research findings and widespread local actions is still too long. On the other hand, institutions are weak in certain developing nations, especially at local-government level and in many communities. While this constraining effect is especially noticeable in countries that are developing into modern economies, it is a challenge for all societies as they continuously adjust their water sectors to new external changes and evolving internal demands. Therefore, it is the weak capacity in the water sector institutions that is the key obstacle to enhanced performance, and not the shortfall in financial support, as was the case in the 1970s and 1980s.

The international development banks report ongoing problems in identifying feasible and well-prepared investment projects. For instance, in Asia, both the Asian Development Bank and the World Bank have been experiencing constraints over the past decade in their attempts to increase investment in the water sector. The European Union reports a similar situation; only a portion of the 2002–2010 structural funding for water infrastructure in the new member states in central and southern Europe was absorbed effectively. The European Commission assessed that this was caused *inter alia* by factors related to weak capacities in the sector's agencies – capacities in terms of the number of civil servants and specialists; of the skills and experience available; and of the prevailing managerial and policy environment in the public sector.

26.2 Developing capacity

26.2.1 Basic understanding

Capacity is an attribute of individuals, organizations and other forms of institutions. It is not something external to these individuals and bodies. In 2005, the OECD defined capacity as the 'ability of people, organizations, and society as whole to manage their affairs successfully'. Capacity development (CD) furnishes the frameworks, approaches and tools needed to carry out institutional development. By its very nature,

CD is relevant only in the context of change, and it is part and parcel of change management (Alaerts, 1999; EuropeAid, 2005).

Capacity development and knowledge management are two sides of the same coin. This definition allows a measurable, operational interpretation to be given to capacity. It also emphasizes the link between capacity and a verifiable, on-the-ground impact after CD interventions have taken place. Seeing CD and knowledge management in this way also makes the case for developing critical 'extra' capacity to generate fresh knowledge to prepare for the future. Knowledge management has become a mainstream strategy used by private businesses to remain competitive, and therefore profitable, but most governments and sector agencies, and non-governmental organizations for that matter, still lack the structural provisions that would allow this learning to take place.

The application domain of CD is broad. However, there are a number of common situations where CD initiatives are having an effect.

- *Improving technical competence* Such an objective is generally readily appreciated and accepted because it can often be addressed by targeting the individual technical competences of staff and the skills mix in the organization. Generally, such programmes do not lead to structural change and reform.
- *Improving overall performance and results* To enable staff and other agents to build capacity and use it, improved incentives may have to be offered – for instance better career opportunities, higher remuneration, and education opportunities. It is often assumed that working on an organization's technical competence is enough to develop capacity. But a CD effort may also involve changes in legal and regulatory frameworks. Examples of such change process are the Uganda Water and Drainage Board (Mugisha, 2009; WWAP, 2009, p. 263) and the Netherlands Ministry of Transport, Public Works and Water Management – now the Ministry of Infrastructure and the Environment (Box 26.2).
- *Strengthening accountability and making the local voice heard* Sometimes there is a need to build the capacities of local groups and local councils to help them update their skills and build resilience (Box 26.3)
- *Improving decision-making* Increasingly, the aim of decision-makers is to help sectoral agencies and

society at large to become better able to deal with uncertainty in the future. This is of special relevance when discussing geopolitical situations such as international river basin conflicts, health epidemics, climate change, etc. and calls for the establishment of a communications and information platform where

BOX 26.2

Changing tides: Change management at the Netherlands Ministry of Transport, Public Works and Water Management

All nations are regularly searching for better and more effective public administration systems. This is illustrated by changes that have taken place in the Netherlands' Ministry of Transport, Public Works and Water Management – which in 2010 became the Ministry of Infrastructure and the Environment. Institutional reform was implemented in a series of phases through capacity development and knowledge management processes.

Phase 1: Readiness for change In the 1970s, public pressure had forced the ministry to change to integrated water resources management and to acquire ecological expertise. But in the late 1990s, the ministry's decentralized structure with its regional directorates and dominant engineering services was deemed to be unable to cope with the new generation of national-scale projects and demands for tighter budget discipline.

Phase 2: Developing the new capacity The new institutional structure took shape between 2004 and 2007. The supportive capacity development included the following:
- Workshops, brainstorming sessions, leadership training and other interactive events.
- A new skills mix. Many experts became redundant, while personnel with new skills in the areas of contract management, budget control and communications were taken on.
- A communications strategy to keep the public and politicians informed about progress.

Phase 3: Lessons learned After the reform, the ministry and the executive agency were deemed to be better prepared for the new decade. The phased CD process allowed them to pilot new ideas and generate solutions, thus creating a fertile learning ground for learning-by-doing. At the same time, early retirement and release of seasoned senior experts severely eroded the ministry's knowledge base and its capacity to train new staff.

Source: Various reports including Metze (2009).

project initiators and government can adapt their initiatives and build a broader political consensus.[1]

- Education, research and innovation In its most traditional form, capacity development focuses on a country's educational, research and innovation systems. Such programmes can be narrow and specific or broad and general.

26.2.2 Developing adaptive capacity

As discussed in Section 26.2.1, ignoring uncertainty increases the risk of inappropriate water management decisions. adaptive water management (AWM) is designed to address increased uncertainty and risk by making them fundamental parts of the management approach. AWM uses the lessons learnt from the outcomes of management strategies. It considers changes in external factors in a proactive manner to develop

BOX 26.3

Women's participation in the adaptation and mitigation processes

In many societies, women have unique climate change related skills, experiences and capacities that have been acquired over centuries of active participation in water management activities. Capacity development activities can add even more value to this knowledge and allow them to contribute positively to the identification of appropriate adaptation and mitigation techniques. The following are three real examples:

- In 1998, the Honduran community of La Masica was given gender-sensitive community training about early warning and risk systems. During Hurricane Mitch a few months later, not a single death was reported in La Masica because the municipal government had been able to evacuate the population in time (Sánchez del Valle, 2000).
- During a drought on the small islands of the Federated States of Micronesia, the women's ancestral knowledge of the islands' hydrology allowed them to identify places to dig wells for drinking water. (Anderson, 2002).
- The floods in Bangladesh in 2004 left 280 dead, around four million evacuees, and thousands of others without food or housing. Recently, in the district of Gaibandha, a woman named Sahena has organized a committee to prepare the women for floods. The committee trains the women to make portable clay ovens, raise their houses, and use radios to hear floods warnings and news of climate change. Efforts such as Sahena's save many lives and empower women (Oxfam, 2008).

Source: UNDP (2009).

a systemic process for improving management policies and practices. It maintains as its central objective to improve the adaptive capacity of the management regime in general (Pahl-Wostl et al., 2010) and particularly the actors involved. As noted by Bormann et al. (1993), 'Adaptive management is learning to manage by managing to learn.'

While traditional technical knowledge and the capacity to manage water resources (as described in Section 26.2.1) remains important in the context of AWM, the ability of water institutions and management actors to absorb, adopt and implement new forms of management is dependent on additional knowledge and capacities. In AWM, capacity development refers to the development of the knowledge, skills and attitudes that are necessary for managers and professional organizations to increase their adaptive capacity and create institutions that are flexible and responsive enough to cope with risk and uncertainty (Van Scheltinga et al., 2010).

People's adaptive capacity needs to be analysed and quantified to face the risk and uncertainty caused by such sources as climate change. Therefore, the African Climate Change Resilience Alliance (ACCRA) has identified five characteristics of adaptive capacity. These can be used to analyse people's own adaptive capacity in the face of a combination of risk and stress. These characteristics also help to analyse how different programming approaches either support or hinder adaptive capacity. The five characteristics are summarized as follows (ACCRA, 2010):

- **The asset base:** These are the various financial, physical, natural, social, political and human capitals necessary to best prepare a system to respond to a changing climate.
- **Institutions and entitlements:** The ability of system to guarantee equitable access and entitlement to key resources and assets is a fundamental characteristic of adaptive capacity.
- **Knowledge and information:** Successful adaptation requires information about and understanding of future change, knowledge about adaptation options and the ability to assess them, and the capacity to implement the most suitable interventions.
- **Innovation:** A key characteristic of adaptive capacity relates to a system's ability to support innovation and risk taking.
- **Flexible forward-thinking decision-making and governance:** Informed decision-making, transparency, and prioritization each form key elements of

adaptive capacity.

There are different approaches to improving the adaptive capacities of individuals and institutions. For example, the Institute of Development Studies proposed an approach to develop adaptive capacity as one of three pillars of a new approach to Climate Smart Disaster Risk Management CSDRM (Mitchell et al., 2010). This approach involved over five hundred researchers, community leaders, non-governmental organization (NGO) workers and government officials from ten disaster-prone countries. The approach is outlined as follows:

- To strengthen the ability of people, organizations and networks to experiment and innovate.
- To promote regular learning and reflection to improve the implementation of policies and practices.
- To ensure that policies and practices to tackle changing disaster risk are flexible, integrated across sectors and scale, and have regular feedback loops.
- To use tools and methods to plan for uncertainty and unexpected events.

BOX 26.4

Enhancing adaptive capacity in the Mekong basin

In 2000, the Mekong delta faced the worst floods in 40 years. More than 800 people died, nine million were affected, and the costs of damages exceeded US$455 million. Since then, a range of initiatives have been implemented under the Flood Mitigation and Management Programme (FMMP). These included flood forecasting capacities, best practice guidelines for integrated flood risk management, guidelines for integration of flood preparedness plans, flood probability mapping and land use zoning, and an annual Mekong flood forum.

The FMMP's 2009 flood report highlighted how climate change specifically influenced flood risk. Climate change was also a key theme at the FMMP annual Mekong Flood Forum in 2010. The forum promotes learning across the Mekong basin. It provides governments and others involved in the programme an opportunity to gather data and to explore implications and responses by sharing their experiences. For example, the Asian Disaster Preparedness Centre (ADPC) is giving lessons on integrating flood risk management at district and provincial levels to countries facing similar challenges.

Source: Mitchell et al. (2010).

In 2009, CARE International proposed four related strategies to form an integrated approach that combines traditional knowledge with innovative strategies. The aim was to build adaptive capacity in order to face the new and dynamic challenges caused by climate change. (Table 26.1):

- Climate-resilient livelihood strategies in combination with income diversification and capacity building for planning and improved risk management;
- Disaster risk reduction strategies to reduce the impact of hazards, particularly on vulnerable households and individuals;
- Capacity development strategies for local civil society and government institutions so that they can provide better support to communities, households and individuals in their adaptation efforts; and
- Advocacy and social mobilization strategies to address the underlying causes of vulnerability; causes such as poor governance, lack of control over resources, or limited access to basic services.

26.3 Preparing a capacity development strategy

26.3.1 A rational comprehensive framework for analysis

Figure 26.1 illustrates the elements of capacity development. It also provides a comprehensive analytical framework that helps to guide assessments of CD needs and define appropriate, case-specific CD programmes (Alaerts and Kaspersma, 2009). The diagram identifies four levels of attention: the individual, the organization, the enabling environment, and civil society. It specifies, in broad terms, what capacity and knowledge imply, how CD can take place, what the potential outcomes are, and how the CD can be assessed after interventions.

Capacity, or the lack of it, can best be assessed through practical and narrowly defined proxies and checklists that are tailored to suit various situations and purposes (Lusthaus et al., 2002; Alaerts and Kaspersma, 2009).

The performance of the water sector and all its sub-sectors is the result of the effective action of individuals with the proper knowledge and capacity, who function in larger organizations such as ministries, local governments, water user associations and civil society organizations. Effectiveness depends both on the effectiveness of individuals and on the features that shape the capacity of the organization itself – its skills mix, its internal operational and administrative procedures, incentives, etc. Organizations with the right capacity and procedures still need an enabling environment to put the facilitating factors in place. Such an environment includes an enabling legal and regulatory framework, fiscal rules that stimulate action, and a broadly supportive parliament, electorate and consumer base. The scope and depth of the desired CD process will depend on the outcomes of the above analysis and the extent of the political support for change. The analytical frame is exhaustive and can

TABLE 26.1

CARE's framework for community-based adaptation

	Climate-resilient livelihoods	Disaster risk reduction	Capacity development	Addressing underlying causes of vulnerability
National level	- Government is monitoring, analysing and disseminating current and future climate information related to livelihoods - Climate change is integrated into relevant sectoral policies - Climate change is integrated into poverty reduction strategies and/or other development policies	- Government is monitoring, analysing and disseminating disaster risk information - Government is engaged in planning and implementing disaster risk management (prevention, preparedness, response and recovery) - Functional early warning systems are in place - Government has the capacity to respond to disasters	- Government has the capacity to monitor, analyse and disseminate information on current and future climate risks - Government has a mandate to integrate climate change into policies - National policies are rolled out at regional and local levels - Resources are allocated for the implementation of adaptation related policies	- Government recognizes the specific vulnerability of women and marginalized groups to climate change - Policy and implementation is focused on reducing these vulnerabilities - Civil society is involved in planning and implementation of adaptation activities
Local government and community level	- Local institutions have access to climate information - Local plans and policies support climate-resilient livelihoods - Local government and NGO extension workers understand climate risks and are promoting adaptation strategies	- Local institutions have access to disaster risk information - Local disaster risk management plans are being implemented - Functional early warning systems are in place - Local government has the capacity to respond to disasters	- Local institutions have the capacity to monitor, analyse and disseminate information on current and future climate risks - Local institutions have the capacity and resources to plan and implement adaptation activities	- Local planning processes are participatory - Women and marginalized groups have a voice in local planning processes - Local policies provide access to and control over critical livelihoods resources for all
Household and individual level	- People are generating and using climate information for planning - Households are employing climate-resilient agricultural practices - Households have diversified livelihoods, including non-agricultural strategies - People are managing risk by planning for and investing in the future	- Households have protected reserves of food and agricultural inputs - Households have secure shelter - Key assets are protected - People have access to early warnings for climate hazards - People have the mobility to escape danger in the event of climate hazards	- Social and economic safety nets are available to households - Financial services are available to households - People have knowledge and skills to employ adaptation strategies - People have access to seasonal forecasts and other climate information	- Men and women are working together to address challenges - Households have control over critical livelihood resources - Women and marginalized groups have equal access to information, skills and services - Women and marginalized groups have equal rights and access to critical livelihood resources

Source: CARE (2009), reproduced with permission of the CARE International Poverty, Environment and Climate Change Network (PECCN).

help to identify the sub-set of institutions where demand, readiness and likely impact may be highest. Knowledge, understanding and skills are generally developed through knowledge transfer instruments such as training and education. However, whether the desired capacity or knowledge is explicit or tacit dictates which instrument should be chosen. Tacit knowledge is eventually far more important because it shapes skills and deeper attitudes. This is best transferred through one-on-one interaction between junior and senior, apprentice and teacher. Organizational capacity is enhanced by educating staff and by helping the organization to learn from experiences. Technical assistance, management advice, learning experiences, comparison with peers, and benchmarking, are important instruments. Networks and information communication systems (ICSs) have an increasingly important role for improving knowledge and capacity and opening up new avenues for disseminating knowledge.

At the level of the enabling environment, governments and other actors also learn and become able to develop more supportive environments. Policymakers, government departments, and politicians also learn lessons from 'best practices' in other countries. Finally, the role of society is of course critically important as it shapes the nation's consensus for the future by electing politicians and holding its government accountable.

Eventually, 'capable' individuals and organizations possess aggregate competences to act. There are four types of aggregate competences (Baser, 2009; Alaerts and Kaspersma, 2009):

FIGURE 26.1

Schematic of capacity development at different levels, showing inputs, outcomes and methods of measurement

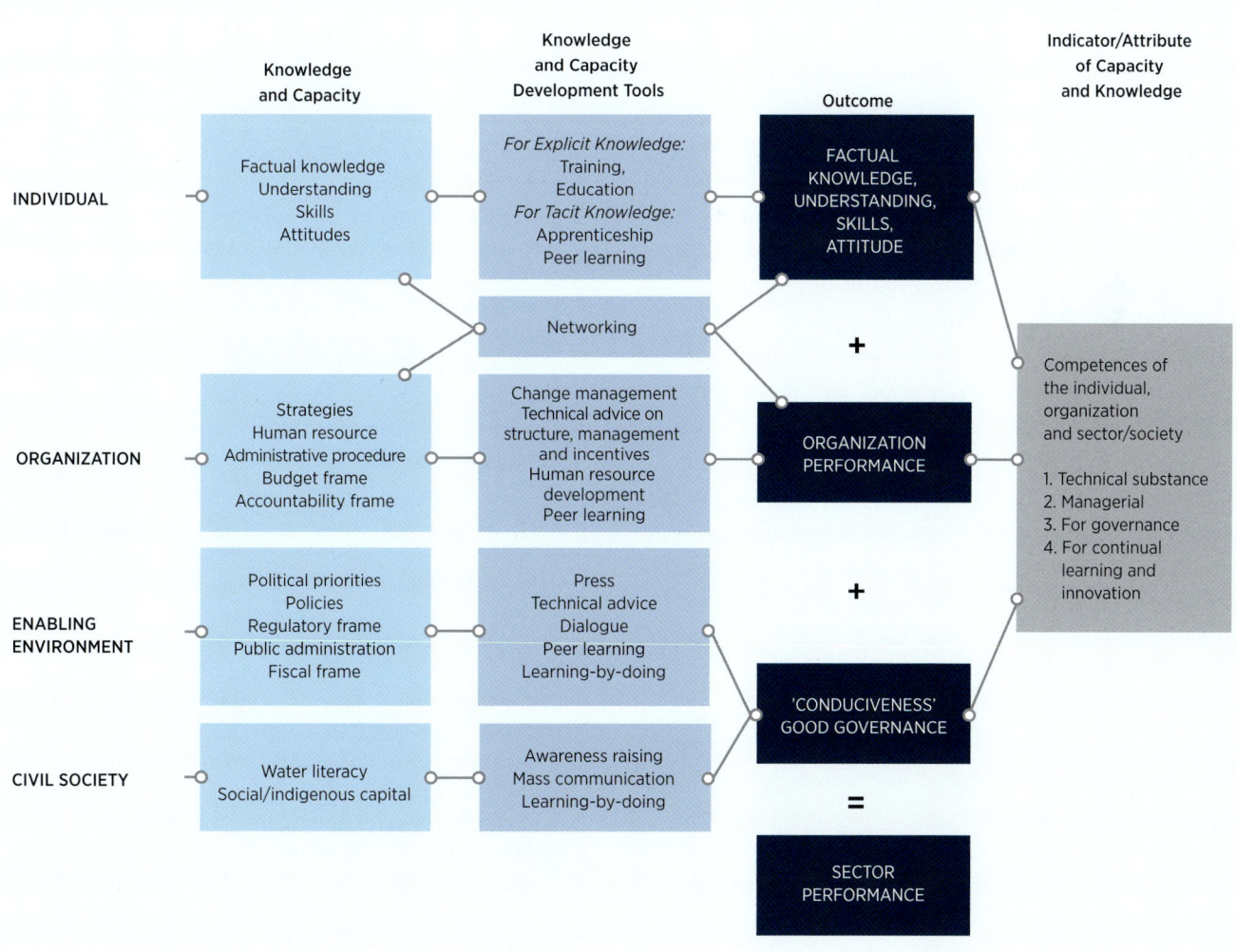

Source: Alaerts et al. (2010), reproduced with permission from Taylor & Francis.

- Technical or substantive competence is required to analyse and solve technical problems in a range of areas from construction to financial accounting.
- Organizations need a pool of leadership and management competences embodied in their senior staff. In many developing countries, agencies may score well on technical and civil engineering aspects skills, but may be less effective in managing personnel and administration. Management competences ensure that 'things get done'.
- An effective and sustainable water sector requires organizations that are able to foster and apply the principles of good governance – dialogue and communication with stakeholders, resource allocation within policy frameworks that aim for equity and poverty alleviation, sensitivity to vulnerable groups and transparency and accountability.
- Capable individuals and organizations are those who continuously learn and innovate. Learning and innovation do not come naturally; they require financial resources, personnel and managerial procedures.

26.3.2 Assessment of capacity and needs

As a first step, decision-makers should assess the institutional performance of the water sector or sub-sector. This should include all the institutions that are involved with it. A number of organizations and UN agencies are offering guidance and checklists for use in such assessments. Box 26.5 describes a number of relevant sources of information and further guidance is available in the second *World Water Development Report* (WWAP, 2006, p. 454–8).

In 2007, the United Nations Development Programme (UNDP) compiled a collection of CD assessment experiences and it offers a framework for assessing capacity. The core issues it lists are institutional development, leadership, knowledge, and mutual accountability. Some of the critical functional capacities it includes are the capacity to engage in multi-stakeholder dialogue, situational analysis, vision creation, policy and strategy formulation, budgeting, and monitoring and evaluation.

Once a CD assessment has been completed, a strategy and action plan can be derived. Such strategy should be shaped contextually through dialogue with stakeholders because there is no 'one size fits all' strategy. Addressing weak institutional environments is not a straightforward or linear process. It often works best through 'strategic incrementalism' where practical steps and incremental reforms are adopted, even if

they don't fully address all the performance problems at once (Nelson and Tejasvi, 2009).

In 2008, the World Bank developed its own Development Results Framework to Assess Capacity. It did this by measuring capacity through the actual impact and performance in the field. The World Bank and UNDP frameworks derive partly from Lopes and Theison (2003), who suggest a checklist with key questions that should be considered in assessments (see also WWAP, 2006, p. 456).

BOX 26.5
Sources for capacity development

- **The UNDP capacity development website** (www.capacity.undp.org) includes key sources for generic information on how to perform capacity assessments. It includes initiatives, networks, resources and tools. It offers access to the Capacity 2015 initiative developed to operationalize the MDGs.
- **The South African Capacity Initiative** (SACI) (www.undp-saci.co.za) developed a Capacity Mobilization Toolkit for southern African countries, which takes into consideration the particularly complex human capacity challenges associated with the impact of HIV/Aids, poverty and recurring disasters.
- **The World Bank** provides an online Capacity Development Resource Centre (www.worldbank.org/capacity), which provides an overview of case studies, lessons learned, 'how to' approaches and good practices pertaining to capacity development.
- **The Canadian International Development Agency** (CIDA) has developed a CD toolkit (www.acdi-cida.gc.ca) that includes reference documents for capacity development.
- **The European Centre for Development Policy Management's** capacity development website (www.capacity.org) aims to look at policy and practice of capacity development within international development cooperation and provides a newsletter and a comprehensive material related to capacity development in all sectors.
- **The International Development Research Centre** (IDRC), the **International Institute of Rural Reconstruction** (IIRR) and the **International Service for National Agricultural Research** (ISNAR) implemented a project to better understand how CD takes place and how its results can be evaluated.
- A team from the **German Agency for Technical Cooperation** (GTZ) supported the Indonesian Government in preparing guidelines on how to organize and manage a needs assessment process. This resulted in a medium-term regional CD action plan.

The Asian Development Bank (ADB, 2008) provides a practical guide to CD at the sector level. According to this, three pre-conditions must be fulfilled for a successful CD process: there must be dissatisfaction with the current situation; a credible change process must have been proposed; and a vision of the future should be shared by stakeholders (Box 26.2). Again, it appears essential that the key stakeholders, particularly the government, need to own the change process.

At the sectoral level, many water management ministries and departments face staffing constraints and are seeking advice on building competencies. Two initiatives are currently mapping the water sector's human resources needs. UNESCO-IHP and UNESCO-IHE have been assessing water education needs in several regions. Together, the International Water Association (IWA) and the UK Department for International Development (DFID) in association with UNESCO-IHE are assessing the human resources development requirements for achieving the Millennium Development Goals (MDGs) for water supply and sanitation (WSS). A standardized methodological framework is being developed based on five country-based pilot studies.

26. 3.3 Assessment of adaptive capacity

Capacity development activities should seek to enhance the ability to cope with uncertainty and risk. The following are just some examples of abilities and functions that should be available at each CD level to ensure adaptive capacity:

- Individuals should have information on current problems, sources of risk and the desired direction of change. Behaviour should be proactive, and individuals should able to learn flexibly in a variety of ways, (Fazey et al., 2007).
- Organizations should have the ability to learn, to challenge their own established ways of thinking and acting, to react to unpredictable internal and external changes, and to produce social change and achieve mission impact.
- An enabling environment requires the freedom to adjust policies to the new reality of climate change

TABLE 26.2

Indicators for assessing adaptive capacity

Level	Indicators
Individual	• Are people generating and using climate information for planning? • Are people managing risk by planning for and investing in the future? • Do people have the knowledge and skills to employ adaptation strategies? • Are men and women working together to address challenges? • Do women and other marginalized groups have equal access to information, skills and services?
Organization	• Is the organization aware of which areas and groups are at risk? • Can the organization identify and assess the risks to the services being provided? • Is the organization addressing these risks in the local community strategy or community plan? • Have disaster risk management policies and practices been changed as a result of reflection and learning-by-doing? • Is there a process in place for information and learning to flow from communities to the organization and vice versa?
Enabling Environment	• Are the institutional frameworks adapted to the new reality of risks? • Are policies reviewed using the global change 'lens'? • Is the environment supporting the implementation of local disaster risk management plans? • What is the level of participatory planning processes at local levels? • Is there a mechanism for the communication of climate information? • Are the voices of women and other marginalized groups supported in local planning processes?
Civil Society	• Are civil society entities able to mobilize awareness and resources to manage the process? • Can the society learn from change? • Does the society seek creative solutions to change? • How long does it take the society to respond to changes? • Are there strong communication channels within the society?

Sources: CARE (2009); Maguire and Cartwright (2008); Urban and Mitchell (2011).

and other sources of uncertainty and risk. It is no longer realistic to have stable long-term policies for dealing with extreme weather events, flood, and drought; policies should acknowledge the new conditions where the baseline is inherently unstable and changing (UNDP, 2007).

- Civil society organizations and networks should be entities that mobilize and raise awareness. They should have the resources to manage processes, have strong communications links with organizations and individuals, and be able to innovate and create adaptive solutions using available resources and technologies.

Table 26.2 provides selected indicators from CARE's handbook (CARE, 2009) for assessing adaptive capacity to risks and hazards caused by climate change at the four levels of action.

26.4 Capacity development strategies and approaches

26.4.1 Education and training

Capacity development, and in a more general sense, the generation and dissemination of knowledge, can take place through formal, non-formal and informal education and training. The objectives of a CD initiative and the choice of processes and instruments used depend on the context because the institutions they focus on are the exponents of a particular set of economic, social and cultural factors.

As the global demand for managing water under conditions of risk and uncertainty increases, the lag between the demand for and the supply of qualified staff is becoming significant, especially in developing countries. The needs of the water sector in terms of the development of individual capacities can only be adequately addressed through the close collaboration of water and education professionals. The importance of primary and secondary education levels should not be underestimated as most of the people working on the water sector are formally educated only at these levels and most of the decisions affecting water resources are taken by people who have very limited formal water resources education. New water-oriented education, training programmes and approaches are needed to bridge the ever-widening knowledge and skills gap between developed and developing countries. A number of principal recommendations for action, made by 50 experts who participated in the workshop 'Education for Water

Sustainability: Where Decades meet'[2] are summarized as follows.

At school

- Students should become aware of how precious water is and learn about water-related global challenges.
- To foster positive attitudes and behaviour teachers should promote the social, economic and environmental values of water through cross-curricula development and values education.
- Governments, together with other stakeholders, should develop databases of existing teaching and learning materials. Teachers should be trained to use these materials. Cooperation between governments and public enterprises can provide incentives to motivate teachers.

Vocational education and training

- Demonstration projects for integrating vocational education and training approaches into the water supply and sanitation (WSS) sector should be set up with the support of UNESCO. Occupational competencies regarding WSS should be developed and

BOX 26.6

How to save water in Palestine

The King Talal Secondary School in Nablus is a member of the UNESCO Associated Schools Project Network (ASPnet). It organized a series of excursions to enable students to examine water resources under the guidance of experts and to learn more about this precious commodity. The students then reported their experiences and ideas to the local media so that they could share what they had learned with the rest of the community. The school also introduced new and creative teaching methods and students were invited to translate their ideas and views through drawing, singing and putting on plays.

The main impact of the project is that it enhanced students' understanding of the significance of the water shortage facing the Palestinian Territories, and made them more aware of possible solutions. Students came to realize that access to water is a basic human right, as well as an individual and collective responsibility. The project also raised the students' awareness of the power of peaceful dialogue and generated cooperation between teachers and students and helped them to respect other points of view.

Source: UNESCO (2009).

introduced for the water workforce (especially in developing countries).
- Investment in infrastructure should be complemented by training technical staff and policy-makers to maintain and manage investments.

BOX 26.7

Adaptive water management (AWM) training helps groups to face uncertainty and risk

Example 1: Training educators how to teach AWM
The UN Water Decade Programme on Capacity Development (UNW–DPC) and the European Union Integrated Project, New Approaches to Adaptive Water Management under Uncertainty, ran a workshop in New Delhi in 2008 to train educators to disseminate the NeWater–GWSP (New Approaches to Uncertainty in Water Management–Global Water System Project) curriculum on AWM. The aim was to encourage the water managers and policy-makers of tomorrow to adopt an AWM approach to climate-proofing WSS strategies in the face of increasing climate-related uncertainty. By the end of the workshop, participants had drafted designs for adapting their water and environmental management studies curricula.

Lecturers and educators from developing countries in Latin America, Africa and Asia were trained by trainers from UNW–DPC, the University of Osnabrück in Germany, and Alterra Wageningen University and Research Centre in the Netherlands in the didactics of passing on the skills, knowledge and attitudes required for AWM.

Example 2: IWRM as a Tool for adapting to climate change
The Institute of Water Education (UNESCO–IHE) offers an online course for professionals actively involved in the water and climate sectors. Such professionals include local, regional and national policy-makers; NGO staff and representatives of the private sector dealing with adaptation; and junior university lecturers and scientists. The course objectives are to promote:
- Understanding of the concept of Integrated Water Resources Management (IWRM) in relation to climate change;
- Understanding of the climate system and the hydrological cycle;
- Awareness of the impact of climate change on society;
- Understanding of how to deal with risk and uncertainty; and
- Understanding of how to adapt to water changes and climate change.

Source: UNESCO (http://www.unesco-ihe.org/Education/Short-courses/Online-courses/IWRM-as-a-Tool-for-Adaptation-to-Climate-Change).

- Training should be developed with the help of educators to bridge the gap between theory and practice.

Higher Education
- Universities should open a window to the world by offering action research, problem-based learning and experiential learning. They should cooperate with society, and engage with the community in teaching and research.
- Universities need to develop mechanisms that ensure that teaching materials on basic water knowledge and on state-of-the-art of water management are freely available to all practitioners.
- The higher education sector should develop an academically recognized peer-review process for advanced and innovative teaching materials.
- Changes in academic structures should reflect the efficacy of successful university interventions in improving best practices in communities. We should emphasise effective action programmes.

There is no single body of knowledge about the way water should be managed. Universities must take measures to ensure that the existing variety of paradigmatic approaches is made available to the public.

26.4.2 Networking and sharing knowledge
Knowledge sharing is a fragile process because it requires individuals to share their personal beliefs with others, without physical or psychological impediment,

BOX 26.8

Adaptive river basin management: The NeWater online teaching curriculum

A curriculum for adaptive river basin management was developed as part of the training and education activities of the New Approaches to Uncertainty in Water Management (NeWater) project. NeWater's explicit aim is to provide an effective outreach mechanism for scientific results, methodologies and tools to stakeholders in the water sector, including university educators, water management practitioners and policy-makers. The curriculum has been implemented by the Institute of Environmental Systems Research at the University of Osnabrück, in Germany, at Alterra Wageningen University and Research Centre in the Netherlands and as part of the Global Water System Project. Details on the programme can be found at www.newatereducation.nl

Source: NeWater (n.d.).

to facilitate justification, explanation, persuasion and connectedness among peers. (Schenk et al., 2006). A useful indicator for knowledge facilitation in the water sector is the presence of formal and informal networks among sector specialists and peers. Such networks are of great importance when it comes to exchanging knowledge between government and other actors in the sector (Luijendijk and Lincklaen-Arriëns, 2009). Networks can take many forms, for example:

- Professional, formal associations of people with a specific technical background or expertise – for example, associations of water experts, social scientists or economists such as the International Water Association and the International Water Resources Association.

- Loosely organized networks of individual specialists who are often centred around a publication or newsletter – for example, journals such as the IRC's *Waterlines*.

- Communities-of-practice (CoPs) that are organized for a specified task. These usually operate within given time frames, have internal work agendas and agreed outputs such as publications or policy notes. The World Bank–UNDP Water and Sanitation Programme has managed CoPs on topics ranging from hand washing to low-cost sewage disposal.

- Networks of government, semi-government and non-governmental organizations that cooperate on a declared subject and that often receive funding for meetings, research, publications, workshops, and operational costs. Examples are Cap-Net, which is a UNDP initiative that connects about 25 educational and capacity building institutions; PoWER, UNESCO-IHE's partnership for water education and research, is a global network of about 30 research and education institutions ; Informal and social networks that are driven by cultural or social considerations but that may often be instrumental in bringing together people who can share both explicit and tacit knowledge.

26.4.3 Ownership as a key to effectiveness

Water management agencies close the door on opportunities for effective integrated water management when they don't give a voice to relatively powerless groups, such as women and indigenous people. Efforts to ensure the ownership of local stakeholders are often absent. The lack of broad commitment is systematically identified as a main reason why investments and programmes fail. For example, many WSS programmes in developing countries throughout the

1980s and 1990s proved ineffectual because the beneficiaries could not or did not want to use or maintain the new water supply systems and latrines. Numerous projects arranged for experts to assist in project preparation, but such experts were generally never mainstreamed into the engineering organizations.

International development aid too often proved ineffective because programmes were not well embedded locally. After the Paris Declaration in 2005 and the Third High Level Forum on Aid Effectiveness in Accra in 2008, it is now the norm for aid recipients to forge their own national development strategies, which ensure the broader ownership of policies and programmes (OECD 2005, 2008). The IWRM concept emphasizes that effective and sustainable water management requires the explicit involvement of stakeholders in planning and decision-making (see the Global Water Partnership Toolbox at www.gwptoolbox.org). The

BOX 26.9
Strengthening local ownership: The Lake Victoria Region Water and Sanitation Initiative

Twenty-seven capacity development interventions support the UN-HABITAT Lake Victoria Region Water and Sanitation Initiative (LVWATSANI). This initiative, which is helping Kenya, Tanzania and Uganda to achieve their MDGs for WSS, is an example of the modern integrated approach.

The Lake Victoria catchment provides livelihoods for about one-third of the combined populations of the three countries (30 million people). Most of the region's rapidly growing urban centres are experiencing unplanned growth, poor infrastructure, and a fragile ecosystem. Piped water leakage and low billing rates are usual and sanitation and solid waste collection are poor.

Progress to date. Initial investments have been completed: key water infrastructure has been rehabilitated or expanded, public latrines have been built, micro-credit for household latrines has been provided, and solid-waste removal equipment has been supplied – all resulting in better performance by the water utilities in the project towns. The CD design responds to the on-the-ground issues. Multi-disciplinary teams conducted in-depth interviews with the stakeholders and designed 27 tailor-made CD interventions. These included interventions on environmental services, pro-poor governance, equity and local economic development. All concluded with a personal action plan that requires each participant or group to identify the activities that are within their authority and capability and that will contribute to improving water environmental services.

European Union's Water Framework Directive mandates that river basin management plans in which the role of the informed and empowered stakeholders are treated as critical, should be developed for all river basins. Targeted CD programmes may then be required to approach and prepare these groups (Box 26.9).

In a rapidly changing world, our economies and well-being increasingly depend on accurate forecasting of future events and trends. There is a growing need to shape policies that best reflect the courses of action that are most appropriate technologically as well as representing the preferences of society. Challenges of broad social significance such as responses to climate change and public health threats require that society is informed and 'educated'. Consultation with an informed society can lead to policies that are owned by society – and diligently implemented by everybody in that society.

26.4.4 Information and communications technology (ICT)

The generation, manipulation and communication of information are essential parts of the decision-making process for organizations involved in water management. ICT is recognized as a strategic enabler in the process of developing innovative solutions to address problems such as water scarcity. ICT also facilitates the analysis of environmental data so that researchers and climatologists can build more accurate models for weather forecasting (ITU, 2010). The main areas in which ICT could play a pivotal role in water management are shown in Figure 26.2.

The cost of traditional face-to-face training courses and the time they consume significantly restrict CD plans. The rapid advance of ICT has made access to knowledge through eLearning easier, much more readily available and cheaper: eLearning, or preferably *blended learning*,[3] has helped to develop the capacity of water management stakeholders. It does this through its use of online training, online university courses, multimedia materials for public awareness, etc. The UN–Water Decade Programme on Capacity Development has developed an online system called UNWAIS+ (UN Water Activity Information System) which includes an eTraining pool (www.ais.unwater.org).

Mobile and wireless technologies are also providing a chance for users to learn remotely. This makes mobile-learning (mLearning) even more attractive than eLearning. Mobile technology applied to CD activities offers cost-effective learning opportunities. Mobile devices with expanding capabilities are now available at significantly reduced prices (UN DESA, 2007).

The department of Engineering Hydrology at the RWTH Aachen University in Germany is offering several online courses covering different water management

FIGURE 26.2

Major areas for information and communications technology in water management

Mapping of water resources and weather forecasting

- Remote sensing from satellites
- In-situ terrestrial sensing system
- Geographical information system
- Sensor networks and Internet

Asset management for the water distribution network

- Buried asset identification and electronic tagging
- Smart pipes
- Just-in-time repairs/real time risk assessment

Setting up early warning systems and meeting water demand in cities of the future

- Rain/storm water harvesting
- Flood management
- Managed aquifer recharge
- Smart metering
- Process knowledge systems

Just in time irrigation in agriculture and landscaping

- Geographical information system
- Sensor networks and Internet

Source: ITU (2010).

related topics (Box 26.10) as well as water exercises and mobile phone app quizzes.

26.4.5 Social learning: 'Learning together to manage together'

Social learning has been described as an alternative to transmissive expert-based teaching. It is a form of community-based learning (Capra, 2007) that takes place in networks or CoPs that are influenced by the governance structure in which they are embedded. Social learning requires relatively stable institutional settings which are not rigid or inflexible. Such conditions are developed through continued processes of social learning in which multi-level stakeholders are connected through networks that allow them to develop the capacity and trust necessary to collaborate in a variety of relationships both formal and informal (Pahl-Wostl, 2007).

Social learning supports the capacity development of managers to address uncertainty and risk more effectively. Successful social learning (learning in and with social groups through interaction) leads to new knowledge, shared understanding, trust and, ultimately, collective action. Learning may take place at different levels from *incremental improvements* (single-loop) through to *reframing* where assumptions are revisited (double-loop) and *transforming* where underlying values and world views may be changed (triple-loop) (Pahl-Wostl, 2007). Box 26.11 presents a good practice

BOX 26.10

The Online Training System for Water Professionals (TOTWAT)

TOTWAT is an EU-funded project under the umbrella of the TEMPUS programme coordinated by the RWTH Aachen University in Germany. The project aims to develop an eLearning system for water professionals in Egypt. More than ten training courses have been developed in the fields of modelling, water management, socio-economics, environmental engineering and interdisciplinary water management. The electronic contents of the courses are suitable for use by other water institutions in the Middle East and North Africa region. User feedback shows that such online training courses have a significant impact on the performance of water engineers, and more than 90% of users indicated that it helped them to share knowledge and learn from each other.

Source: TOTWAT project (2011).

case for social learning implementation that enhanced adaptive water management.

26.5 The way forward

- There is a lack of best practice at all levels in analysing and assessing adaptive capacity for risk. There is a need to conduct regular capacity assessments including assessing the capacities of the workforce, the institutions, the key agencies, the policy and

BOX 26.11

Social learning and AWM in the South Indian Lower Bhavani

The Lower Bhavani Project (LBP) has an 84,000-hectare catchment area in the South Indian state of Tamil Nadu. One of the most significant uncertainty factors here is rainfall variability. Farmers frequently have to cope with unpredictable supplies of water and seasons without rainfall. The large-scale development of wells in the area shows how farmers have successfully managed to increase water availability during seasons when there is no supply. They have also learned to swiftly adjust their cropping patterns in line with the highly unpredictable variability of seasonal canal water supply, and have even adapted what they grow to cope with entirely rain-fed conditions.

The entire chain of system changes shows that social learning is taking place within the LBP system. The various actors have learned how to optimize the system within the limits of the technical infrastructure, the capacity of the reservoir, the discharge capacity of the canal and the unpredictable supply of water dictated the by erratic rainfall. The way farmers have learned from and been inspired by each other are examples of social learning between actors. From a long-term perspective, all the actors in the LBP system have learned from the environmental responses and from each other's behaviour. Together they have contributed to the alteration of governance structures and have developed new practices without being bound by the original technical infrastructure. All actors, thus, live with change, but few appear to remember what caused the change in the system and why it changed. The AWM analysis shows that the LBP system has fulfilled the criteria of a complex adaptive system again and again. Several changes have taken place and earlier mistakes and failures have been addressed step-by-step to reach the present complex human–environmental–technological system. Social learning takes place at both system level and with individual farmers. The uncertainty factors have been considered one at a time during the system change cycles and have been included in the system design.

Source: Lannerstad and Molden (2009).

regulatory frameworks, and the main stakeholders. There is a need to identify realistic capacity development priorities that can be implemented within a practical time frame and which focus on ownership.

- There is a need to assess the capability of education systems and prepare adequate numbers of sector professionals who have the appropriate skills mix. This is particularly important for managerial and governance skills so that there is the ability to prepare and carry out investments. In this process, it is necessary to promote collaboration and cooperation between organizations and water and education experts.

- The water sector needs to engage in dialogue with society about investment initiatives and major policies. This ensures that decisions reflect actual expectations and foster ownership. The media needs to be taught about water issues so that their capacity to report on such issues is improved.

- Social learning should be promoted to build the adaptability of all stakeholders involved in making decisions about water management. This helps to increase flexibility and responsiveness when dealing with risk and uncertainty.

- ICT should be used more to reduce costs and offer more flexible learning opportunities. Investments made in high quality learning materials for adaptive water management can be used by water professionals and students across a wide area.

Notes

1. For example, Thorkilsen and Dynesen (2001) describe how an internet-based interactive facility was at the core of a broad knowledge sharing and communication effort to muster the support of politicians and the community and attract funding for one of Europe's largest and most controversial infrastructure projects, the rail and road bridge and tunnel across the Øresund Strait linking Denmark to Sweden.

2. This workshop was jointly run during the UNESCO World ESD Conference in Bonn, Germany in 2009 by the UNESCO International Hydrological Programme (IHP); the German Federal Ministry for the Environment, Nature Conservation and Nuclear Safety (BMU); and the UN Water Decade Programme on Capacity Development (UNW–DPC). Its purpose was to promote exchange between water and education stakeholders by linking the two UN Decades – the UN Decade of Education for Sustainable Development (UN DESD) and the UN International Decade for Action, 'Water for Life'.

3. Blended learning is a mix of different leaning environments, e.g. eLearning and face-to-face learning.

References

ADB (Asian Development Bank). 2008. *Practical Guide to Capacity Development in a Sector Context.* Manila, ADB.

Alaerts, G. J. 1999. Capacity Building as knowledge management: purpose, definition and instruments. G. J. Alaerts, F. J. A. Hartvelt and F.-M. Patorni (eds), *Water Sector Capacity Building: Concepts and Instruments.* Rotterdam, the Netherlands, A. A. Balkema Publishers.

––––. 2009. Knowledge and capacity development (KCD) as tool for institutional strengthening and change, Alaerts, G. J. and Dickinson N. (eds), *Water for a Changing World: Developing Local Knowledge and Capacity. Boca Raton/ London, CRC Press/Taylor & Francis.*

Alaerts, G. J. and Kaspersma, J. 2009. Progress and challenges in knowledge and capacity development, M. W. Blokland, G. J. Alaerts, J. M. Kaspersma and M. Hare (eds), *Capacity Development for Improved Water Management.* Boca Raton and London, CRC Press and Taylor & Francis.

Anderson, C. L. 2002. Gender matters: implications for climate variability and climate change and disaster management in the Pacific Islands. *InterCoast Newsletter,* Winter 2002, No. 41. Narragansett, RI, Coastal Resources Center, University of Rhode Island.

Baser, H. 2009. Capacity and capacity development: Breaking down the concepts and analysing the processes. Alaerts, G. J., and Dickinson, N. (eds), *Water for a Changing World: Developing Local Knowledge and Capacity. Boca Raton/London, CRC Press/Taylor & Francis.*

Bates, B. C., Kundzewicz, Z. W., Wu, S. and Palutikof, J. 2010. Consultation document, The ACCRA (Africa Climate Change Resilience Alliance) Local Adaptive Capacity framework (LAC).

Bormann, B. T., Cunningham, P. G., Brookes, M. H., Manning, V. W. and Collopy, M. W. 1993. *Adaptive Ecosystem Management in the Pacific Northwest: A Case Study from Coastal Oregon.* General Technical Report PNW-GTR-341. U.S. Portland, Oreg., Forest Service Pacific Northwest Research Station.

Capra, F. 2007. Foreword. Wals, A. (ed.), *Social Learning: Towards a Sustainable World.* Wageningen, the Netherlands, Wageningen Academic Publishers.

CARE. 2009. *Climate Vulnerability and Capacity Analysis.* A handbook prepared by Angie Dazé, Kaia Ambrose and Charles Ehrhart. Atlanta, Ga., CARE.

EuropeAid. 2005. *Institutional Assessment and Capacity Development: Why, What and How?* Tools and Methods Series. Luxemburg, Office for Official Publications of the European Communities.

Fazey, I., Fazey, J. A. Fischer, J., Sherren, K., Warren, J., Noss, R. F. and Dovers, S. R. 2007. Adaptive capacity and learning to learn as leverage for social–ecological resilience. *Frontiers in Ecology and the Environment,* Vol. 5, pp. 375–80. DOI:10.1890/1540-9295(2007)5[375:ACALTL]2.0.CO;2.

Gault, B. et al. 2005. The women of New Orleans and the Gulf Coast: multiple disadvantages and key assets for recovery. Part I: Poverty, Race, Gender, and Class. Washington DC, *The Gender and Disaster Sourcebook*. Institute for Women's Policy Research.

ITU (International Telecommunication Union). 2010. *ICT as an Enabler for Smart Water Management.* Technology Watch Report, ITU.

Lannerstad, M. and Molden, D. 2009. *Adaptive Water Resource Management in the South Indian Lower Bhavani Project Command Area.* Colombo, Sri Lanka, International Water Management Institute. (IWMI Research Report 129). http://www.iwmi.cgiar.org/assessment/files_new/research_projects/RR129.pdf

Lopes, C. and Theisohn, T. 2003. *Ownership, Leadership and Transformation: Can We Do Better for Capacity Development?* London and Sterling, Va., Earthscan publications.

Luijendijk J. and Lincklaen-Arriëns, W. F. 2009. Bridging the knowledge gap: the value of knowledge networks. Blokland, M. W., Alaerts, G. J., Kaspersma, J. M., & Hare, M. (eds), *Capacity Development for Improved Water Management.* Boca Raton/London, CRC Press/Taylor & Francis.

Lusthaus, C., Adrien, M.-H., Anderson, G., Carden, F. and Montalvan, G. P. 2002. *Organizational Assessment: A Framework for Improving Performance.* Washington DC/Ottawa, IDB/IDRC.

Maguire, B. and Cartwright, S. 2008. *Assessing a Community's Capacity to Manage Change: A Resilience Approach to Social Assessment.* Canberra, Commonwealth of Australia.

Metze, M. 2009. *Changing Tides: The Ministry of Transport and Water Management in Crisis.* (In Dutch.) Amsterdam, Uitgeverij Balans.

Mitchell, T., Ibrahim, M., Harris K., Hedger, M., Polack, E., Ahmed, A., Hall, N., Hawrylyshyn, K., Nightingale, K., Onyango, M., Adow, M. and Sajjad Mohammed, S. 2010. *Climate Smart Disaster Risk Management, Strengthening Climate Resilience.* Brighton, UK, Institute of Development Studies. http://community.eldis.org/.59e0d267/SCR%20DRM.pdf

Mugisha, S. 2009 Capacity building and optimization of Infrastructure operations: a case of national water and sewerage corporation. Uganda, Blokland, M. W., Alaerts, G. J., Kaspersma, J. M., and Hare, M. (eds), *Capacity Development for Improved Water Management.* Boca Raton/London, CRC Press/Taylor & Francis.

Nelson, M. and Tejasvi, A. 2009. Capacity development in Africa: lessons of the past decade. Blokland, M. W., Alaerts, G. J., Kaspersma, J. M. and Hare, M. (eds), *Capacity Development for Improved Water Management.* Boca Raton/London, CRC Press/Taylor & Francis.

NeWater. n.d. NeWater *New Approaches to Adaptive Water Management Under Uncertainty.* Integrated Project in the 6th EU Framework Programme. Brussels, EC. http://www.newater.info/index.php?pid=1021

OECD (Organisation for Economic Co-operation and Development). 2005. *The Paris Declaration*. Paris, OECD–DAC.

————. 2006. *The Challenge of Capacity Development: Working Towards Good Practice.* Paris, OECD–DAC.

————. 2008. *The Accra Agenda for Action.* Paris, OECD–DAC.

Oxfam (The Oxford Committee for Famine Relief). 2005. *The Tsunami's Impact on Women.* Oxfam International Briefing Note. http://www.oxfam.uk/applications/blogs/campaigners/2008/03/sahena_the_voice_of_climate_ch.html

Pahl-Wostl, C. 2007. Requirements for Adaptive Water Management. Pahl-Wostl, C., Kabat, P. and Möltgen, J. (eds), *Adaptive and Integrated Water Management Coping with Complexity and Uncertainty,* pp. 1–22. Berlin, Springer Verlag.

Pahl-Wostl, C., Holtz, G., Kastens, B. and Knieper, C. 2010. Analysing complex water governance regimes: the management and transition framework. *Environmental Science & Policy,* Special issue: Water governance in times of change, Vol. 13, No. 7, pp. 571–81.

Peterson, K. 2007. *Reaching Out to Women When Disaster Strikes.* Soroptimist White Paper. http://www.soroptimist.org/whitepapers/wp_disaster.html

Sánchez del Valle, R. 2000. Local risk management in Central America: lessons learnt from the FEMID project. http://www.crid.or.cr/digitalizacion/pdf/spa/doc12912/doc12912-9.pdf

Schenk, M., Callahan, S. and Rixon, S. 2006. Our take on how to talk about knowledge management. http://www.anecdote.com.au/whitepapers.php?wpid=6

Sveiby, K. E. 1997. *The New Organizational Wealth. Managing and Measuring Knowledge-based Assets.* San Francisco, Berrett-Koehler.

TERI (The Energy and Resources Institute). 2010.*Water and climate change adaptation in South Asia.* New Delhi, Regional Knowledge Hub for Water and Climate Change adaptation in South Asia. www.waterknowledgehub.org

Thorkilsen, M, and Dynesen, C. 2001. An owner's view of hydroinformatics: its role in realising the bridge and tunnel connection between Denmark and Sweden. *Journal of Hydroinformatics,* Vol.3, pp. 105–35.

TOTWAT Project. 2011. Training-of-Trainers Program in Interdisciplinary Water Management. Aachen, Germany, RWTH Aachen University. http://totwat.lfi.rwth-aachen.de

UN DESA (United Nations Department of Economic and Social Affairs). 2007. *Compendium of ICT Applications on Electronic Government: Volume I, Mobile Applications on Health and Learning.* New York, UNDESA. http://unpan1.un.org/intradoc/groups/public/documents/un/unpan030003.pdf

UNDP (United Nations Development Programme) 1997. *Capacity Development: Technical Advisory Paper 2.* New York, UNDP.

————. 2007. Capacity assessment methodology: user's guide. Capacity Development Group. New York, Bureau for Development Policy, UNDP.

————. 2009. *Resources Guide on Gender and Climate Change.* New York, UNDP. http://www.uneca.org/acpc/about_acpc/

docs/UNDP-GENDER-CLIMATE-CHANGE-RESOURCE-GUIDE.pdf

UNEP (The United Nations Environment Programme). 2009. *Resources Guide on Gender and Climate Change.* UNEP.

UNESCO. 2009. *Second Collection of Good Practices Education for Sustainable Development.* Paris, UNESCO.

Urban, F. and Mitchell, T. 2011. *Climate Change, Disasters and Electricity Generation: Strengthening Climate Resilience.* Discussion Paper 8. Brighton, UK, Institute of Development Studies. http://community.eldis.org/.59d5ba58/LatestClimate%20change%20disasters%20and%20electricity%20generation.pdf

Van Scheltinga, T. C., Van Bers, C. and Hare, M. 2009. Learning systems for adaptive water management: experiences with the development of opencourseware and training of trainers. Blokland, M. W, Alaerts, M. G., Kaspersma, J. M. and Hare, M. (eds). *Capacity Development for Improved Water Management. Boca Raton/London, CRC Press/Taylor & Francis*, pp. 45–60.

Williams, E. et al. 2006. *The Women of New Orleans and the Gulf Coast: Multiple Disadvantages and Key Assets for Recovery.* Part II: Poverty, Race, Gender, and Class in the Labor Market. Institute for Women's Policy Research.

WWAP (World Water Assessment Programme). 2006. *World Water Development Report 2: Water: A Shared Responsibility.* Paris/New York, UNESCO/Berghahn Books.

––––. 2009. *World Water Development Report 3: Water in A Changing World.* Paris/London, UNESCO/Earthscan.

Zeitlin, J. 2007. Statement at the Informal Thematic Debate: Climate Change as a Global Challenge. http://www.wedo.org/learn/library/media-type/pdf/june-zeitlins-statement-on-climate-change-as-a-global-challenge

UNISDR
—

Authors and contributors Bina Desai (Programme Officer), John Harding (Head, Policy) and Justin Ginnetti (Associate Programme Officer)

© UN Photo/Marco Dormino

Countries in all regions have been successful in strengthening their capacities to address the mortality risk associated with major weather-related hazards such as floods. Despite the increasing number of people living in floodplains, mortality risk relative to population size is now trending down. In East Asia and the Pacific mortality risk is now at a third of its 1980 level (UNISDR, 2011).

In contrast, countries have had a far more difficult time addressing successfully other risks. Economic loss risk due to tropical cyclones and floods is trending up because the rapidly increasing exposure of economic assets is outstripping reductions in vulnerability.

Water management should actively engage in shaping national agendas that reduce the risk from natural hazards and assist adaptation to climate change, in support of a coherent planning process that targets national and local sustainable development plans.

Disaster risk reduction needs to be an integral part of integrated water resources management (IWRM) to enhance and effectively protect water investments and to contribute to reducing risks. Reducing the risk of floods and drought, and in particular, promoting development practices that reduce the risk of floods and drought, will contribute to governments' efforts to adapt to climate change. One of the key challenges faced by decision-makers today is the need to increase understanding of which forms of investment are effective in reducing the risk of floods and drought – in the water management as well as in the broader development arena.

27.1 Introduction

This chapter addresses the risks associated with water-related disasters, in particular, floods and drought, and contributes to the broader topics of risk and uncertainty. It also addresses climate change issues by examining the impacts of climate change on extreme event trends, in particular, natural hazards (again focusing on floods and drought), as well as adaptation approaches based upon the reduction of risk related to water-related hazards. It focuses on policy responses and actions and their effectiveness, describing solutions, their applicability and their relation to risk. This component, along with the monitoring of risk trends for floods and drought, will be built up more systematically in future reports.

27.1.1 Disaster impacts

The most significant water-related disasters, such as floods, include flash floods, tropical cyclones and other storms, and ocean storm surges (Box 27.1). Other related events, including those triggered by earthquakes, comprise tsunamis, landslides that dam rivers, breakage of levees and dams, glacial lake outbursts, coastal flooding associated with abnormal or rising sea levels, and epidemics and pest outbreaks associated with too little or too much water.

One water-related disaster that seldom makes it into the impacts statistics is drought. Since 1900, more than 11 million people have been killed and more than 2 billion affected by drought, more than any other physical hazard (UNISDR, 2011). However, these figures are probably lower than the real total as few countries systematically report and record drought losses and impacts (Box 27.2), while those that do, such as the United States of America, report only insured losses (Figure 27.1).

BOX 27.1

Extreme water-related disasters in 2010

Water-related disasters account for 90% of all natural hazards, and their frequency and intensity is generally rising. Some 373 natural disasters killed over 296,800 people in 2010, affected nearly 208 million others, and cost nearly US$110 billion.

In 2010, extreme disasters included storm Xynthia in Western Europe (February) and the spate of heavy flooding in France (June). Unusually, Asia experienced fewer disaster deaths that year than the Americas and Europe, accounting for just 4.7% of total mortality. However, it remains the most greatly affected continent: some 89% of all people affected by disasters in 2010 lived in Asia, according to the Centre for Research on the Epidemiology of Disasters (CRED).

Of the list of top ten disasters with the highest death counts, five occurred in Asia. In Indonesia from May to August, floods killed 1,691 people and a further 1,765 were killed by mudslides, landslides or rock falls triggered by heavy rains and floods in August. In Pakistan, massive floods caused by heavy rains in the north-west from July to August covered one-fifth of the country's landmass, and caused the deaths of nearly 2,000 people.

In China, floods and landslides during the summer are estimated to have cost US$18 billion, while the Pakistan floods cost US$9.5 billion. Yet economic losses in 2010 still do not surpass those of 2005, when damage from hurricanes Katrina, Rita and Wilma alone amounted to US$139 billion.

Summary of flood disasters, 1980–2008	
Number of events	2 887
Number of people killed	195 843
Average number of people killed per year	6 753
Number of people affected	2 809 481 489
Average number of people affected per year	96 878 672
Economic damage (US$ × 1 000)	397 333 885
Economic damage per year (US$ × 1 000)	13 701 168

Source: EM-DAT (2010).

Source: CRED (2011).

BOX 27.2

Data from a systematic registration of disaster in Mozambique

Mozambique is one of the few countries with a disaster database that systematically records drought losses (INGC, 2010). Here, the real scale of drought impacts becomes visible: since 1990, 8 million ha of crops have been damaged (of which half were destroyed) during drought events, 1,040 people have been killed, and an additional 11.5 million have been affected.

Source: UNISDR (2011).

FIGURE 27.1

Recorded drought fatalities per year, 1990–2009

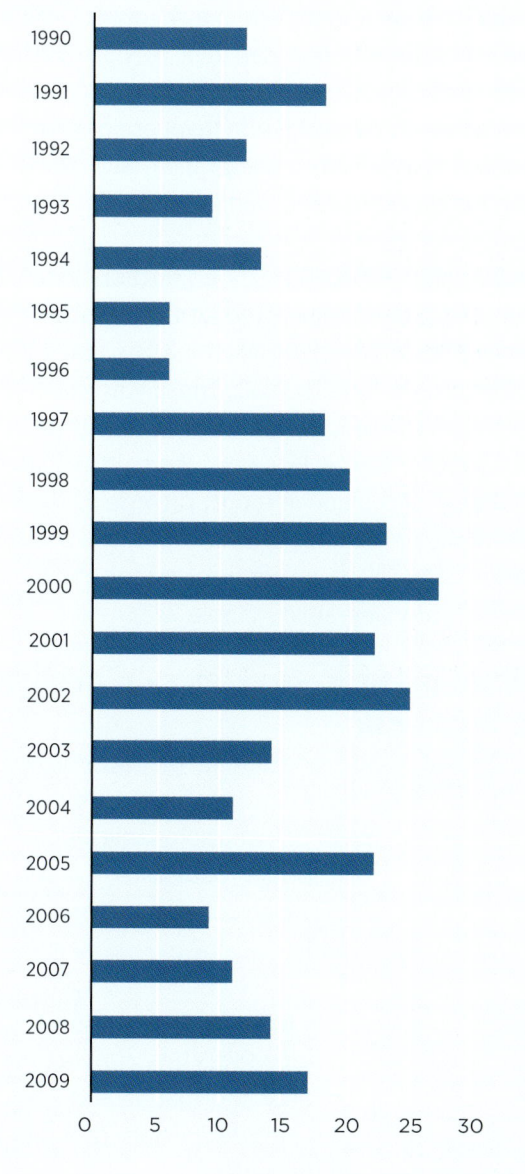

Number of fatalities (thousands)

27.1.2 Water-related disasters impact on development

Water hazards may be a natural part of our earth system, but the disasters that sometimes arise from them should be recognized as strongly interlinked with particular human vulnerabilities of our own making. Key factors that increase both the intensity of the hazard as well as the related vulnerability include environmental degradation; settlements in marginal hazard-prone lands; inadequate buildings and water management systems; lack of risk awareness and information; poverty and low capacities for prevention, preparedness and early warning; and lack of political and institutional commitment to reducing risks.

Disaster risk manifests itself as high impact catastrophes, as well as an increasing number of high frequency, lower relative severity losses, almost all of which are associated with water-related hazards. The risk of losses from these hazards is a factor of social and economic development (WWAP, 2009).

These impacts are an impediment to achieving the Millennium Development Goals (MDGs), because disasters regularly destroy accumulated development gains, in terms of damage and losses to infrastructure and other assets. In developing countries, these losses are generally not insured and imply a constant leakage of resources from development budgets to deal with relief and reconstruction, as well as the steady erosion of livelihoods, rendering vulnerable countries even more vulnerable.

For example, annual average disaster losses in Mexico, in the built environment alone, have been estimated at US$2.9 billion per year (ERN-AL, 2010). Current analysis of MDG monitoring suggests that incremental international aid of US$35 billion will be required annually from 2010 until 2015 to raise the standard of living of the nearly 1 billion people who live below the US$1.25 per capita income line, as well as to achieve the other MDGs (UNDP, 2010). Nearly US$8 billion is required to provide access to safe drinking water to those without access. While the current financial crisis is constraining abilities to increase aid flows, billions of US$ of development funding are being re-directed every year to restore development assets damaged or destroyed by disasters.

Losses in agricultural production are particularly significant (Box 27.3). The United Nations Economic Commission for Latin America and the Caribbean

(ECLAC) estimates that annual losses of US$1.3 billion have been associated with drought and other climate related hazards in Central America since 1975 (ECLAC, 2002). This represents more than 10% of the region's average annual Gross Domestic Product (GDP) and nearly 30% of its gross capital formation (Zapata and Madrigal, 2009).

27.1.3 Reducing the risk of disasters is intrinsic to development practices

The *Global Assessment Reports* (GARs) (UNISDR, 2009, 2011) demonstrate that exposure of people and assets to floods and drought is largely determined by

BOX 27.3

Example of drought impacts

Global data on drought impacts remains uncertain. However, local and regional examples provide a better understanding of the impacts of drought:

- In the Caribbean, during the 2009–2010 drought, the banana harvest on Dominica decreased from 2010 to 2009 by 43%, agricultural production in St Vincent and the Grenadines was 20% below historic averages, while in Antigua and Barbuda, onion and tomato crop yields declined by 25% and 30%, respectively (UNISDR, 2011).
- Australia experienced losses of US$2.34 billion during the 2002–2003 drought, reducing national GDP by 1.6%; two-thirds of the losses were agricultural, while the remaining one-third was attributed to knock-on impacts in other economic sectors (Horridge et al., 2005).
- During the 2002 drought, India's food grain production declined by 29 million tonnes, from 212 million tonnes in 2001 to 183 million tonnes in 2002 (Shaw et al., 2010).
- Due to a severe drought in Syria during the 2007–2008 growing season, 75% of the country's farmers experienced total crop failure (Erian et al., 2010); and more than a year after the drought ended, Syria's livestock population was estimated to be 50% below the pre-drought level (Erian et al., 2010).
- In Ceará, Brazil, agricultural drought risk is concentrated among smallholder farmers who do not hold water rights or have access to Ceará's irrigation and water-storage infrastructure, and whose livelihoods depend entirely on rainfed, dryland agriculture. As a result, GDP per capita of the rural communities is approximately one-third that of the urban settlements situated along the coast, and Human Development Index values of the rural districts are below 0.65, compared to 0.699 for Brazil as a whole (Sávio Martins, 2010; UNDP, 2010).

Source: UNISDR (2011).

historical and ongoing investments in infrastructure and in urban and economic development. In the case of small islands, often the entire territory is exposed.

Levels of disaster-related risk are socially constructed, often over long periods, by layers of decisions and investments by individuals, households, communities, private businesses and governments. Physical hazards may be modified. For example, a decision to drain wetlands may increase flood hazard in a city downstream. Similarly, the amount of people and assets exposed may increase due to decisions to locate economic and urban development in hazard-prone areas. However, choosing to live in hazard-prone areas may be the lesser evil for poor households. Older people and women are particularly vulnerable to these factors.

While public investment usually represents only a small proportion of total investment in any country – 14% on average and seldom more than 20% (UNISDR, 2009) – governments play a key role in shaping risk construction processes, through the effectiveness of planning and regulation as well as through their own investments in infrastructure and public services.

The GAR (UNISDR, 2009) provided further evidence that the poor are more exposed and vulnerable to natural hazards. In some countries, the areas that experience most disasters are actually those with the most dynamic economic and urban growth, or with prosperous rural economies. However, the studies initiated in the context of the above report provide evidence to show that communities in poor areas lose a higher proportion of their assets, confirming that they have higher levels of vulnerability (Table 27.1).

27.2 Anatomy of disasters: Trends in flood and drought risk

Observation of flood and drought risk patterns and trends at the global level permits visualization of the major concentrations of risk. It also enables identification of geographic distribution of disaster risk across countries, trends over time and the major drivers of these patterns and trends.

The analysis presented in this chapter was developed by UNEP/GRID Europe PREVIEW (Project for Risk Evaluation Vulnerability Information and Early Warning), assisted by an interdisciplinary group of researchers from around the world.

Figure 27.2 shows the updated global distribution of mortality risk for three weather–related hazards: tropical cyclones, floods, and landslides provoked by rains UNEP, 2010). The areas of highest risk visible correspond to areas where concentrations of vulnerable people are exposed to severe and frequent major hazards. Flood mortality risk is highest in rural areas with a denser and rapidly growing population in countries with weak governance.

TABLE 27.1

Summary of case study findings on the social distribution of disaster loss

Country	Findings
Burkino Faso	The 1984–1985 drought affected the poorest third of a sample of rural households by 10% more than the wealthier third: the former experienced crop-income losses of 69% versus a 58% drop for the latter.
Madagascar	Tropical cyclone impacts led to a reduction of 11% in the volume of agricultural production of the poorest 20% households, compared to a 6% reduction in the case of the richest 20%.
Mexico	Municipalities with the highest number of loss reports also had large percentages of their population with high or very high levels of marginality, according to an Index of Municipal Marginality developed by the National Population Council; for example, Acapulco (54.4%), Coatzocoalcos (54.1%), Juarez (45%), Tapachula (54.1%), Tijuana (31.3%) or Veracruz (31%). Municipalities with high or very high levels of marginality had high proportions of damaged and destroyed housing. In one-third of these municipalities, between 10% and 25% of the housing stock was damaged or destroyed, while in another third this proportion was more than 25%. Over 20% had more than 50% of their housing stock affected. In contrast, only 8% of the housing stock was affected in municipalities with low or very low levels of marginality.
Nepal	Areas affected by floods tended to have lower poverty rates and higher per capita expenditures. Flooding incidence and impacts are concentrated in the highly productive lowland agricultural plains of the Terai belt in south-eastern Nepal. As flooding contributes to the soil fertility of the region, it also contributes to the wealth of the area. Areas affected by landslides tend to have higher poverty and mortality rates. Landslide impacts are heavily concentrated in districts in mountainous western Nepal with marginal rainfed agriculture, where the country's rural poverty is concentrated.
Orissa, India	A statistically significant relationship was found between families living in houses with earth walls and thatch roofs (typically the housing of the poor) and those most affected by tropical cyclone, flood, fire and lightning. The incidence of extensive risk loss reports was higher in the central-eastern coastal region, where there are higher levels of urbanization and relatively affluent agricultural areas on floodplains and deltas. Mortality in extensive risk disasters was concentrated in the districts of Bolangir, Kalahandi and Koraput in southern Orissa, which are characterized by repeated droughts, floods, food insecurity, chronic income poverty and localized near-famine conditions.
Peru	Rural households that reported a disaster impact in 2002 had on average less access to public services, were less well integrated into the market, and had a higher proportion of agricultural income.
Sri Lanka	A very strong correlation was found between the proportion of the population living below the poverty line and the number of houses damaged due to floods; a less strong but significant correlation was found between this population group and houses damaged due to landslides. This reinforces the case that exposed human settlements and unsafe, vulnerable housing are poverty factors that increase the likelihood of suffering greater loss due to natural hazard.
Tamil Nadu, India	Mortality in areas with manifestations of extensive flood risk was higher in areas with vulnerable housing. Similarly, tropical cyclone housing damage was inversely related to the literacy rate. If literacy is taken to be a proxy for poverty, again this indicates that the poor were more likely to suffer housing damage typically because their houses are more vulnerable or situated in more exposed locations. Mortality among the socially and economically excluded scheduled castes was also higher in blocks with a high proportion of vulnerable housing.

Source: UNISDR (2009, table 3.5, p. 80).

Across all weather–related hazards, countries with low GDP and weak governance tend to feature drastically higher mortality risk than wealthier countries with strong governance.

27.2.1 Flood risk trends

Disaster risk for floods has been calculated for large rural flood events, although the risk calculations do not include flash floods or urban flooding from inadequate drainage. The geographical distribution of flood mortality risk mirrors that for exposure (exposed assets). It is heavily concentrated in Asia, especially in Bangladesh, China and India. Between them these countries concentrate 75% of the modelled annual global mortality. Viet Nam also has high absolute and relative flood risks. The top ten countries at risk of floods (based on number of lives lost) are India, Bangladesh, China, Viet Nam, Cambodia, Myanmar, Sudan, Democratic People's Republic of Korea, Afghanistan and Pakistan (UNEP, 2010).

Between 1970 and 2010 the world's population increased by 87% (from 3.7 billion to 6.9 billion). In the same period, the annual average population exposed to flood increased by 112% (from 33.3 to 70.4 million per year) (UN-Habitat, 2010). Relatively speaking, more and more people are living in floodplains, meaning that the economic advantages of flood-prone areas for intensive agriculture, for example, outweigh the perceived risks. Within income regions, relatively more people are concentrated in flood-prone areas in lower middle-income countries and, in terms of geographic regions, in East Asia and the Pacific (Figure 27.3).

As Table 27.2 shows, more than 90% of the global population exposed to floods lives in South Asia and East Asia and in the Pacific. Exposure is growing most rapidly in the Middle East and in North Africa and sub-Saharan Africa. In contrast, exposure is stable in countries of the Organisation for Economic Co-operation and Development (OECD), while it is starting to trend downwards in eastern and south-eastern Europe and Central Asia, reflecting a broader trend of demographic decline.

Global vulnerability to flood hazard was stable in the 1990s, but has subsequently decreased (UNISDR, 2011). Vulnerability has declined in all regions except Europe and Central Asia and the OECD countries, where it has remained stable. As these are regional averages, there may be countries with increasing vulnerability. But in general the statistics reflect how improved development conditions have reduced vulnerability and led to strengthened disaster management capacities.

FIGURE 27.2

Hazard mortality risk (floods, tropical cyclones and precipitation-triggered landslides)

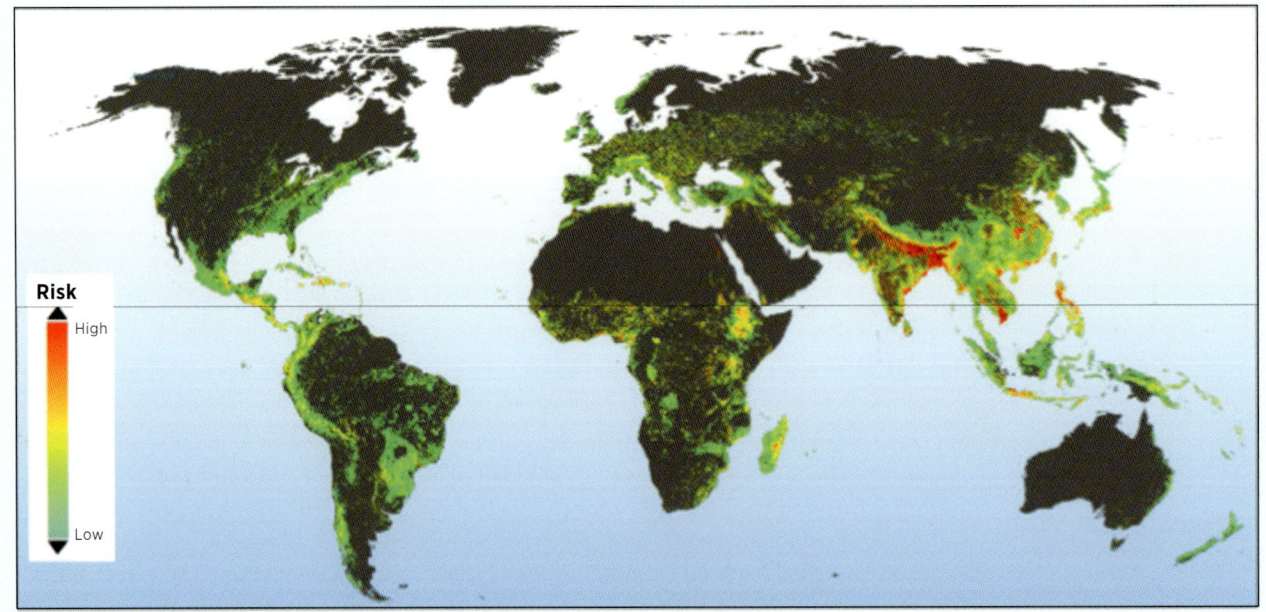

Source: Developed by the GAR team at UNISDR.

Flood mortality risk (Box 27.4) has decreased in all regions since 1990, with the exception of South Asia. In East Asia and Pacific, in particular, it has decreased by about two-thirds (UNISDR, 2011).

This growing vulnerability is reflected in the challenges faced by South Asia to reduce the impact of the August 2010 floods in Pakistan. These floods killed approximately 1,700 people and caused US$9.7 billion in damage to infrastructure, farms and homes, as well as other direct and indirect losses (ADB/World Bank,

2010). The map in Figure 27.4 contrasts modelled flood hazard and observed flooded areas in Pakistan. As with any flood event, some areas at risk of flooding did not flood in August 2010. The model did not highlight other areas that did flood.

27.2.2 Drought risk trends

Drought risks are only partly associated with deficient or erratic rainfall. Instead, they are primarily triggered by a range of drivers that include poverty and rural vulnerability; increasing water demand due to

FIGURE 27.3

People exposed to floods

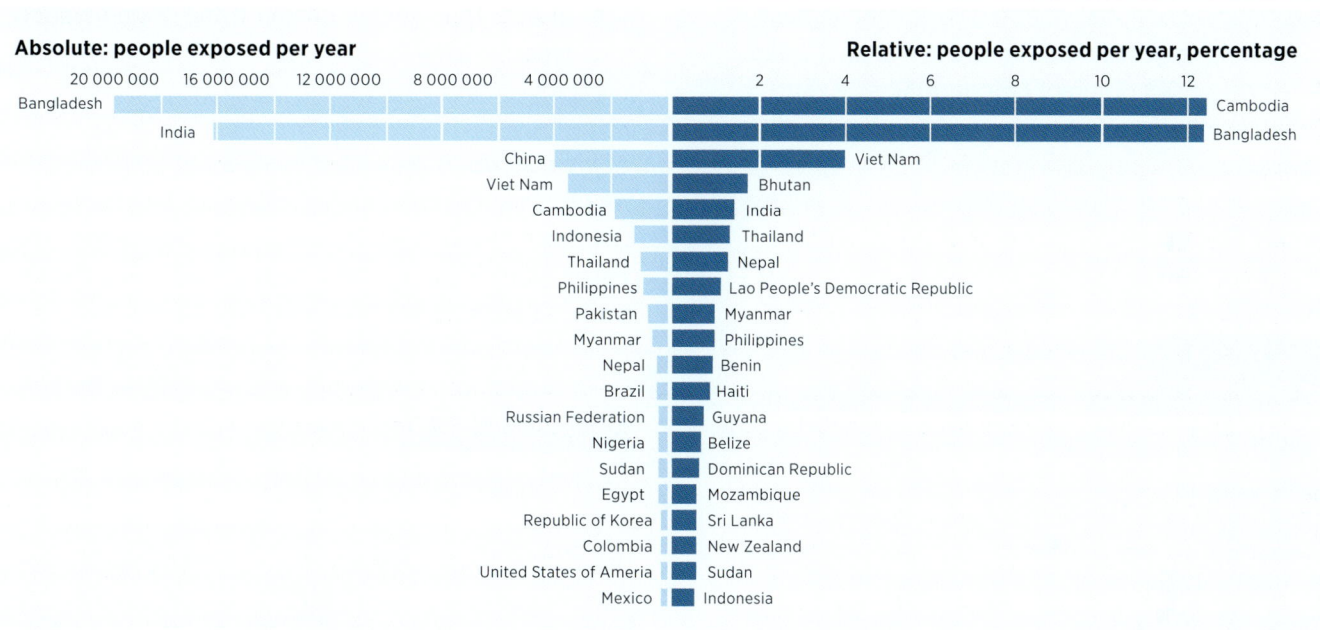

Source: UNISDR (2009, fig. 2.14, p. 36).

TABLE 27.2

Flood exposure by region (in millions of people per year)

Region	1970	1980	1990	2000	2010
East Asia and Pacific	9.4	11.4	13.9	16.2	18.0
Europe and Central Asia	1.0	1.1	1.2	1.2	1.2
Latin America and the Caribbean	0.6	0.8	1.0	1.2	1.3
Middle East and North Africa	0.2	0.3	0.4	0.5	0.5
OECD countries	1.4	1.5	1.6	1.8	1.9
South Asia	19.3	24.8	31.4	38.2	44.7
Sub–Saharan Africa	0.5	0.7	1.0	1.4	1.8
World	32.5	40.6	50.5	60.3	69.4

Sources: Data from PREVIEW flood global model: Landscan 2008 (extrapolated between 1970 to 2010 using UN world population data).

urbanization, industrialization and the growth of agro-business; poor water and soil management; weak or ineffective governance; and climate change. Unlike the risks associated with tropical cyclones and floods, drought risks remain poorly understood. Drought losses and impacts are not systematically captured, standards for measuring drought hazard have only recently being introduced, and data collection constraints make it difficult to accurately model risk in many locations.

Meteorological droughts are usually defined as deficiencies in rainfall, from periods ranging from a few months to several years. Long droughts often change in intensity over time and undergo geographic shifts, thereby affecting different areas. Until recently, there was no agreed global standard for identifying and measuring meteorological drought. National weather services used different criteria, making it difficult to establish exactly when and where droughts occur. Consequently, drought has often been confused with other climate conditions such as aridity or desertification.

BOX 27.4

From the Disaster Risk Index to the Mortality Risk Index

The second *World Water Development Report* used the Disaster Risk Index (DRI) as the main indicator for monitoring flood and drought risk. This approach was subsequently reviewed and several institutions joined their efforts over a two-year period to develop a new methodology for the global modelling of hazards: the Mortality Risk Index (MRI).

The improved estimates of global disaster risk were made possible thanks to higher model resolutions and more complete data on geographic and physical hazard event characteristics, especially for floods, tropical cyclones and earthquakes. They also benefited from higher resolution exposure data on population and economic assets (sub-national GDP). The main improvement came from the 'event per event analysis'. Previous global studies such as the DRI used a 21-year returning period on average. This prevented the computation of specific event intensity. By analysing individual events and linking a hazard event outcome (i.e. losses) with the geographic, physical and socio-economical characteristics of the event, the model can incorporate more adequately the contextual conditions in which each disaster occurred.

Source: Peduzzi et al. (2009); UNISDR (2011).

The World Meteorological Organization (WMO) has recently adopted the Standardized Precipitation Index (SPI) as a global standard to measure meteorological droughts, and is encouraging its use by national meteorological and hydrological services (NMHSs), in addition to other indices currently being utilized in each region.

The SPI (McKee et al., 1993, 1995) is a tool based on rainfall data, which can identify wet periods/cycles as well as dry periods/cycles. The SPI compares rainfall at a given location and during a desired period, normally from one to twenty-four months (Guttman, 1994), with long–term mean precipitation at the same location (Edwards and McKee, 1997). Positive SPI values indicate greater than normal rainfall in the chosen period and negative SPI values indicate less than normal rainfall (Figure 27.5).

At least 20 to 30 years (optimally 50 to 60 years) of monthly rainfall data is needed to calculate the SPI (Guttman, 1994). Given the lack of complete data series in many locations, and the fact that many drought-prone regions do not have sufficient rainfall stations,

FIGURE 27.4

Extent of flooding in Pakistan on 30 August 2010

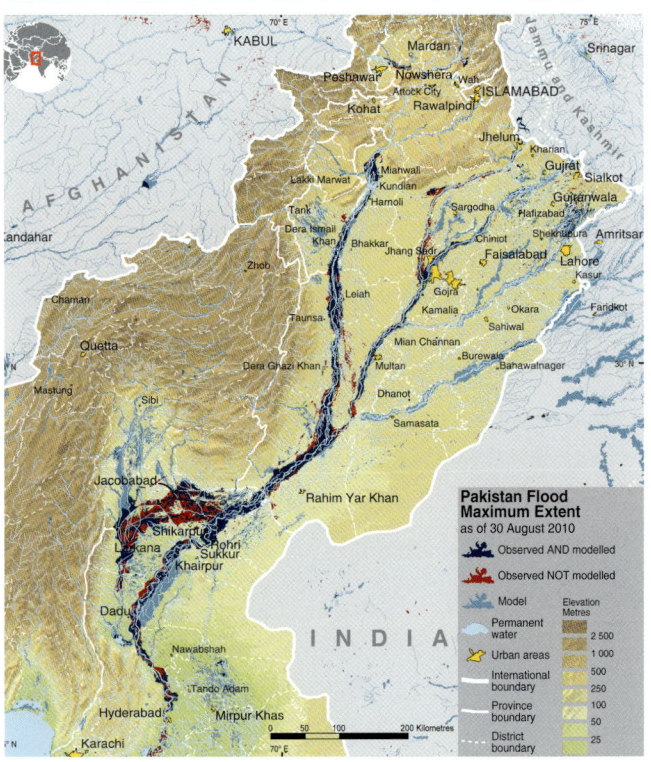

Source: UNISDR (2011, fig. 2.13, p. 30).

many users have to apply interpolation techniques to fill in temporal and geographic gaps in the data.

The application of SPI will strengthen the capacity of countries to monitor and assess meteorological drought. Despite its simplicity, however, many countries are challenged by the low density of rainfall stations in some areas and their decline in number, given the low priority given to hazard monitoring in government budgets. Since the mid–1970s, for example, the number of rainfall stations maintained by Spain's national meteorological agency, AEMET, has declined from 4,800 to approximately 2,600 (Mestre, 2010).

Global drought risk models were developed in the context of earlier assessments of disaster risk (Dilley et al., 2005; UNDP, 2004). But the mortality drought risk index proposed by the United Nations Development Programme (UNDP) was unsuccessful because most droughts do not produce fatalities and most major recorded mortality, in sub-Saharan Africa for example, is concentrated in countries experiencing conflict or political crisis. Only weak correlations were found between the population exposed to meteorological drought and attributed mortality (UNDP, 2004). Drought impacts on human development provide a much more satisfactory metric than mortality for calculating human risk. But while these impacts are captured in locally specific micro-studies (de la Fuente and Dercon, 2008), systematic data is not available to calibrate a global risk model.

27.3 Water-related disaster risk drivers

Understanding the underlying drivers of risk for floods and droughts is the cornerstone of any effort to reduce risk and future impacts. The examples provided below show that climate change, increasing poverty and inequality, and badly planned and managed urban and regional development all contribute to increasing the risk of natural hazards.

27.3.1 Climate change

As the reports of the Intergovernmental Panel on Climate Change (IPCC) have made clear, climate change leads to gradual changes in variables such as

FIGURE 27.5

Interpolated global map product for the six-month Standardized Precipitation Index (SPI) (April–September 2010)

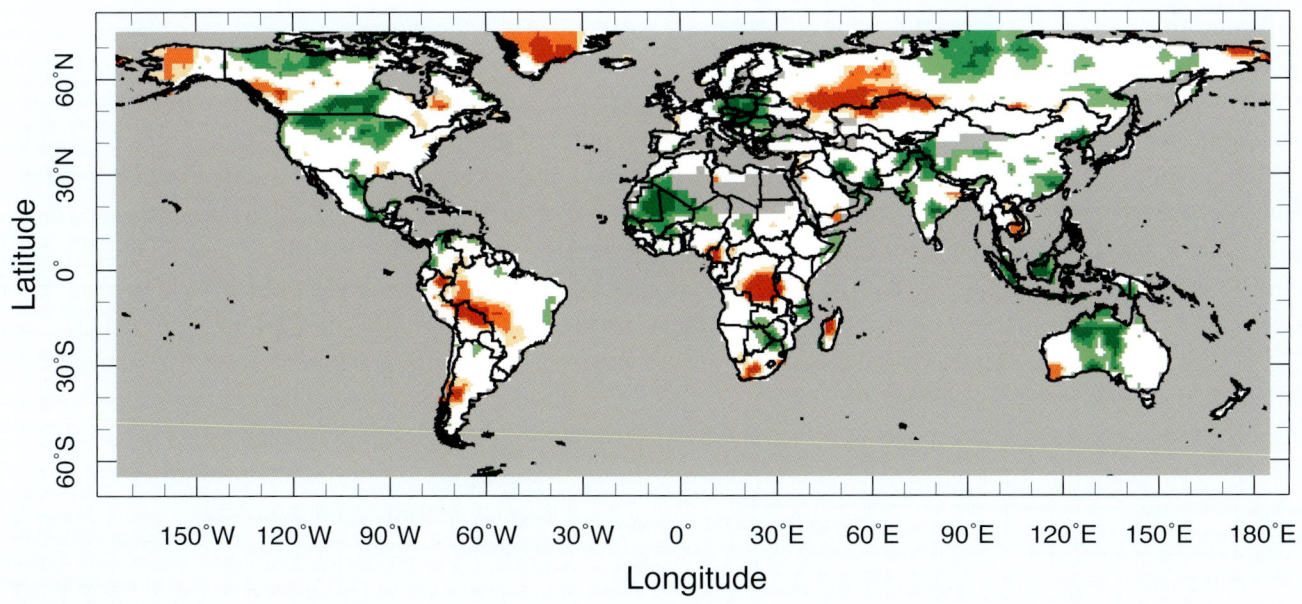

Note: The map shows the global distribution of meteorological drought at the end of September 2010 using a six–month SPI. It highlights the drought in Russia associated with wildfires, as well as droughts in western Brazil, a normally humid climate, and southern Africa.
The green shading, from light green to dark green, shows increasing SPI values from 1.0 to 3.0 (moderately wet to extremely wet). The red shading, from light red to dark red, shows SPI values from –1.0 to –3.0 (moderately dry to extremely dry).

Source: International Research Institute for Climate and Society Data Library, Columbia University (see http://iridl.ldeo.columbia.edu/maproom/. Global/.Precipitation/SPI.html).

average temperature, sea level, and the timing and amount of precipitation. Climate change also contributes to more frequent, severe and unpredictable hazards such as cyclones, floods and heatwaves – 'extreme weather events' (IPCC, 2007). Other climate phenomena such as La Niña are thought to be linked to the floods and landslides that occurred from April to December 2010 in Colombia, and the floods in Queensland, Australia, which were triggered by rains that began in December 2010.

Economies that rely on primary resources and climate-sensitive sectors like agriculture are more vulnerable to greater climate variability and changes in average precipitation and temperature (OECD, 2010). For example, a warming of 2°C could result in a 4%–5% permanent reduction in annual per capita income in Africa and South Asia, compared with minimal losses (approximately 1%) in developed and larger developing countries (World Bank, 2010). These economies are ill prepared to absorb such decreases in income.

27.3.2 Weak risk governance capacities

Despite increased global awareness of disaster risk and climate change, and greater political commitment (as reflected in regional ministerial declarations in Africa [Declaration of the Second African Ministerial Conference on Disaster Risk Reduction, Nairobi, 14–16 April 2010] and Asia [Third Asian Ministerial Conference on Disaster Risk Reduction, Kuala Lumpur, 2–4 December 2008]), disaster risk reduction and management has been only timidly incorporated into development planning, and the institutional mechanisms required for such integration are still emerging (UNISDR, 2009). In addition, many bilateral and multilateral country assistance strategies for countries facing well-known risks are not planned with a risk sensitive lens. The outcome is that the exposure of people and assets to climate-related hazards is increasing faster than many low-income countries are able to reduce their vulnerabilities. Such countries often have difficulties in addressing underlying risk drivers such as ecosystem decline, poverty and badly planned and managed urbanization. The outcome is a rapid increase in the number of and loss of assets in disasters.

27.3.3 Badly planned and managed urban development

Informal settlements, inadequate housing, non-existent services and poor health are reflections of poverty. However, they are also reflections of weaknesses in the way urban growth is planned and managed. One example of an informal settlement called '9 October' in Lima, Peru, shows the relationship between poverty, poor planning and disaster impact. This particular hillside was urbanized informally from the bottom upwards by nearby agricultural workers. Multi-storey concrete and brick houses soon replaced early constructions of bamboo matting. By the 1990s,

> 9 October had a population of more than 1,300, as well as domestic electricity, water and telephone connections, and property titles. In 1999, a local development plan classified the area as a zone of environmental risk and social vulnerability due to high salinity in the soil which was eroding foundations and containing walls; two and three-storey houses occupying unstable sites without load-bearing capacity; and leaks from a deteriorated water and sanitation network, which were causing subterranean erosion. In June 2003, part of the hillside subsided and collapsed, damaging 280 houses of which 70 were destroyed. (UNISDR, 2009, p. 100)

Disaster risk may be increasing fastest in rapidly growing small and medium-sized urban centres than in either rural areas or larger cities. Large and megacities generally have stronger risk governance and investment capacities than small and medium cities. This finding is supported by the fact that in most Latin American countries, the number of disasters reported is increasing at a faster rate than in large urban centres and megacities (Mansilla, 2010). More than 80% of all reports of disaster loss in Latin America occur in urban areas. While each country has a different urban structure, between 40% and 70% of all nationally reported disasters occur in urban centres of less than 100,000 inhabitants, and between 14% and 36% take place in small urban centres. This proportion is growing. In Mexico, for example, small and medium urban centres accounted for 45.5% of total disaster municipal loss reports in the 1980s, but 54% since 2000.

27.3.4 Poverty and rural vulnerability

Within countries, poorer areas tend to have higher disaster risk, mirroring global patterns and illustrating the complex interactions between poverty and disaster risk analysed in detail in the *Global Assessment Report* 2009, as presented previously in the summary of case study findings on the social distribution of disaster loss. An exercise in Colombia showed that those municipalities with a greater proportion of unsatisfied basic needs and lower GDP per capita were more likely to experience a higher number of people affected and more houses damaged in floods (OSSO, 2011).

Rural poverty is both a cause and a symptom of drought risk in Kenya's Mwingi district. Between 70% and 80% of Mwingi's population depends on rainfed agriculture and livestock production for both food and income, and 60% of the population subsists on US$1 per day or less (Galu et al., 2010). Therefore, when drought occurs it can wipe out income and investments, leaving communities with limited means to buffer losses. During the 2008–2009 drought, for example, 70% of the population depended on food aid (Galu et al., 2010). While this massive relief successfully averted a food security crisis, it reveals the extreme vulnerability of many rural agricultural and agro-pastoral livelihoods.

Poor rural households, whose livelihoods depend on rainfed subsistence agriculture, are almost always the social group most exposed and vulnerable to drought. In many countries, they have been historically forced to occupy marginal drought-exposed land. And they often lack the resources to access irrigation technology or drought-resistant seeds, which could reduce their vulnerability. For example, sub-Saharan Africa's water storage facilities are severely under-developed, with a per capita storage capacity of 200 m³ per year on average (as compared to 1,277 m³ for Thailand and 5,961 m³ for North America) (Foster and Briceno–Garmendia, 2010; Grey and Sadoff, 2006).

Groups of countries with small and vulnerable economies, such as many small island developing states (SIDS), land-locked developing countries (LLDCs) and least developed countries (LDCs), would appear to have particular difficulties in absorbing and recovering from disaster impacts (Corrales and Miquelena, 2008; Noy, 2009). SIDS, for example, often have higher relative disaster risk than larger countries because almost all of their population and assets are exposed to hazards such as tropical cyclones (Kelman, 2010; UNISDR, 2009), while their economies may be concentrated around a single vulnerable sector, such as tourism.

The expansion of intensive market agriculture and urbanization can lead to the sale of water rights, pushing the rural poor to farm marginal lands more intensively, and thereby increasing their drought risk further still (Fitzhugh and Richter, 2004). For example, Mexico's

water management and land tenure policies date back to the 1910 revolution, and are based on communal ownership of land and water by smallholder farmers known as *ejido* – 25% of whom live in abject poverty. Nowadays, the *ejido* cannot compete with large farmers and agribusinesses. In the state of Sonora, nearly 75% of irrigation water is allocated to this sector, increasing the agricultural drought risk of the *ejido* (Neri and Briones, 2010).

27.3.5 Ecosystem degradation

Many ecosystems have been intentionally or unintentionally modified to increase the supply of certain categories of services, and institutions have been developed to govern access to, and use of, these services. However, because ecosystems produce many services simultaneously, an increase in the supply of one service, such as food, can frequently lead to declines in other services, such as flood protection. The Millennium Ecosystem Assessment identified modifications to ecosystems that have unintentionally led to the decline of regulating ecosystem services, including those responsible for reducing people's exposure to hazards, such as fires and floods.

Water management also affects the provision of ecosystem services in ways that modify levels of disaster risk. For example, the increasing demand on rivers for irrigation, as well as extraction of water for industrial and domestic use, reduces the sedimentation that

BOX 27.5
The Mississippi wetlands

The drainage of approximately 4,800 km² of wetlands in the Mississippi Delta in the United States of America was one of the underlying factors behind the scale of the flooding associated with hurricane Katrina. Many areas formerly above sea level lay below sea level at the time of Katrina as a result of wetland drainage, while the capacity of the wetlands to dissipate storm surge and absorb floodwaters had diminished. The forested riparian wetlands adjacent to the Mississippi River during pre-settlement times had the capacity to store about sixty days of river discharge. Today, the few remaining wetlands have a reduced storage capacity of less than twelve days discharge, implying an 80% reduction in flood storage capacity. This loss of wetlands also contributed substantially to the severity and damage experienced in the 1993 Mississippi Basin flood.

reaches the coast. This can affect downstream agricultural yields and fish productivity, damage the health of coastal wetlands, and increase coastal flood hazard levels. Excessive groundwater extraction is leading to a potentially irreversible degradation of aquifers, again with compound effects on rural livelihoods. Coastal and inland wetlands have a critical influence on both livelihoods and the regulation of flood and drought (Box 27.5).

27.4 Methodologies and tools for reducing water-related hazard risk

The elements that constitute effective methods and tools to reduce water-related hazard risk are context specific, as well as dependant on the perspective of the respective experts and institutions engaged.

During the analytical work undertaken for this chapter it became apparent that the identification of the most appropriate and effective methods and tools is seldom based on a sufficiently broad understanding of the underlying problem. For the meteorological community, the best approach to floods lies in better forecasting and issuing of early warnings, while for a ministry of infrastructure, the optimal approach will be structural in nature, such as the dams and levees required for both water storage and flood control. Of course, experience shows that a combination of different approaches is most effective. The cost–benefit of preventive investment against post-disaster financing mechanisms is also insufficiently taken into account. Post-disaster approaches include catastrophic risk financing and other insurance mechanisms, and the disbursement of response funds.

The World Conference on Disaster Reduction in Kobe, Japan in 2005 concluded a ground-breaking agreement that provides a clear mandate for action to reduce disaster risks; namely, the Hyogo Framework for Action 2005–2015: Building the Resilience of Nations and Communities to Disasters. The over-riding expected outcome of the Hyogo Framework for Action is the *'substantial reduction of disaster losses, in lives and in the social, economic and environmental assets of communities and states'*.

The Hyogo Framework emphasizes that disaster risk reduction is a central issue for development policies, as well as being of interest to various scientific, humanitarian and environmental fields, stressing that without concerted efforts to address disaster losses, disasters will become an increasingly evident obstacle to the achievement of the MDGs.

While the Hyogo Framework for Action provides a comprehensive set of actions that a country can take to strengthen its risk governance capacities, it does not provide a set of tools and methods from which national and local authorities can establish the most socially, environmentally and economical approaches to reduce risk.

Methods and tools are required to correct existing risk levels through actions such as retrofitting buildings, relocating settlements and restoring ecosystems. This, however, is more expensive than avoiding such risks in the first place. Given the high level of recurrent losses, it is usually cost-effective to correct the risks related to frequent recurrent disasters, but increasingly less so for very high intensity but less frequent events, given the costs involved and long periods before benefits are potentially realized. However, investments to protect critical facilities, such as schools and health facilities, against more extreme risks may be justified, for both economic and political reasons. For example, if a city government invests to relocate squatter settlements subject to recurrent flooding along a cyclone-prone coastline, this relocation programme will not only lead to a short-term reduction in high-frequency, low-severity losses associated with the floods, but would also reduce the periodic cyclone losses. In contrast, in other contexts, protecting an area against 100-year floods may encourage greater investment in the area, leading to increased losses in the event of a 500-year flood. Ultimately, all investments in risk reduction involve trade-offs between different social and economic objectives.

For certain intensive risks that cannot be reduced cost-effectively, risk transfer measures such as insurance and catastrophe risk pools/bonds can mitigate disaster impacts on physical assets and enhance the ability of governments to respond. One model that has demonstrated some success is the Caribbean Catastrophe Risk Insurance Facility (CCRIF). This risk-pooling facility is operated in the Caribbean for Caribbean governments. It is designed to limit the financial impact of catastrophic hurricanes and earthquakes on Caribbean governments by quickly providing short-term liquidity when a policy is triggered. Since 2007, 16 Caribbean governments have included CCRIF parametric insurance policies against hurricanes and earthquakes as part of their countries' disaster risk management portfolios. An example of the kind of payout provided by CCRIF is the US$6.3 million paid to the Turks and Caicos Islands after hurricane Ike made a direct hit in September 2008 (World Bank, 2010). However, the limited scale of the payouts in the context of growing levels of risk is becoming a concern for governments. The payout for Haiti following the 12 January 2010 earthquake was only US$7.75 million.

Traditional disaster management, including effective early warning, preparedness and response, is essential to strengthening resilience to and facilitating recovery

from all manifestations of risk. A number of developing countries have made significant progress in this area, resulting in saved lives. Almost all households (98%) have access to radio and TV in Cuba; consequently, these comprise the main communication channels used by the national meteorological service (with government authority) to issue tropical cyclone and related flood warnings. In Bangladesh, far fewer people have televisions and radios, so the Bangladesh Meteorological Department conveys cyclone and storm surge warnings through multiple channels (fax, Internet, radio and TV). But the centralized warning centre of the Bangladesh Cyclone Preparedness Programme ensures that the warnings reach coastal communities. The centre alerts a network of volunteers through HF/VHF radio broadcasts, and they in turn fan out into the communities to warn the people (WMO, 2009).

There are likely to be greater incentives for reducing risks associated with water-related hazards when such instruments address the needs of a number of stakeholders and competing priorities simultaneously; for example, if better water management not only addresses drought risk, but also increases hydro-energy generation, water-storage capacity for agricultural use, and the availability of domestic drinking water. In general, these incentives are stronger when reduction in risk to water-related hazards contributes visibly to improved economic and social well-being and choice for each citizen.

A number of countries, however, are now innovating and building approaches to reducing risk related to water-related hazards into existing development instruments – in areas such as public investment planning, ecosystem management, urban development and social protection (Box 27.6). While many of these innovations are still in their early stages, they hold the promise of exponentially increasing the impact of reducing risk related to water-related hazards. Importantly they also contribute to other social and economic development goals, which in turn feed back into reduced risk. The upgrading of inefficient, ageing water and drainage infrastructure, if planned from a risk reduction perspective, can reduce vulnerability to drought and floods, while improving the quality of water and sanitation.

This section of the report has presented different methods and tools to address water-related hazard risk and will be augmented in future with more systematic measures of effectiveness.

27.5 Emerging approaches to reduce flood and drought hazard risk

27.5.1 Land-use planning and building

The ways in which land is used in cities and how buildings, infrastructure and networks are designed and constructed have a decisive impact on exposure, and whether a country's accumulated risk increases or decreases. As such, land-use planning is a prime instrument for reducing risk related to water-related hazards. If existing and potential hazards are taken into account in land-use decisions, new risks could be avoided and existing risks reduced over time. Decisions on land use underpin most risk construction, given that once investments in infrastructure, housing and other facilities have been made in hazardous locations, the risk is locked in place for decades or more.

In a number of cities in Colombia, disaster risk reduction has been incorporated as an integral part of improvements in urban and local governance. In Manizales, an innovative cross-subsidized insurance scheme called Predio Seguro, supported by the city government, has enabled poor households to obtain catastrophe insurance cover. The city government, in partnership with women's groups in informal settlements, also invests in stabilizing slopes in landslide prone informal settlements (Cardona, 2009).

27.5.2 Ecosystem management

Protecting ecosystems that will, in turn, reduce the risk of natural hazards such as floods and drought, requires actions at different scales, the participation of a wide array of stakeholders, and different bodies of knowledge – scientific, technical, local and traditional.

Dense vegetation cover within upper watershed areas increases infiltration of rainfall as opposed to surface runoff, reducing peak flow rates except in the most extreme conditions when soils are already fully saturated. Vegetation also protects against erosion, thereby reducing soil loss and the transport of mud and rock that greatly increase the destructive power of floodwaters. Dense vegetation also protects riverbanks and adjacent land structures from erosion by floodwaters. Wetlands and floodplain soils absorb water, reducing peak flow rates downstream (World Bank, 2010).

A study around Mantadia National Park, Madagascar, concluded that conversion from primary forest to swidden (area cleared for temporary cultivation by cutting and burning the vegetation) can increase downstream storm flow by as much as 4.5 times (Stolton et al., 2008).

In the case of ecosystem restoration, the avoided costs may significantly exceed the restoration costs (Box 27.7). In Viet Nam, for example, the International Federation of Red Cross and Red Crescent societies (IFRC) planted and protected 12,000 ha of mangroves, an action that cost approximately US$1 million, but reduced the costs of sea dyke maintenance by US$7.3 million per year. Moreover, the co-benefits may also greatly exceed the opportunity costs. For example, the Millennium Ecosystem Assessment estimated that the value of healthy coastal mangroves as nurseries, pollution filters and coastal defences is US$1,000 to US$36,000 for mangrove value versus US$200 per ha for shrimp farming (MA, 2005). 'In Malaysia, the

---

BOX 27.7

Examples showing the value of ecosystem services to reducing disaster risk

- As coastal defences, mangrove forests in Malaysia have been estimated to have an economic value of US$300,000 per km based on comparison with engineered alternatives (ProAct, 2008).
- Since 1994, communities have been planting and protecting mangrove forests in northern Viet Nam to buffer against storms. An initial investment of US$1.1 million saved an estimated US$7.3 million a year in sea dyke maintenance and appeared to significantly reduce losses of life and property from typhoon Wukong in 2000, compared with other areas (WWF, 2008).
- In the Lužnice floodplain – one of the last floodplains in the Czech Republic with an unaltered hydrological regime – 470 ha have monetary values per hectare of US$11,788 for flood mitigation (water retention), US$15,000 for biodiversity, US$144 for carbon sequestration, US$78 for hay production, US$37 for fish production and US$21 for wood production (ProAct, 2008).
- The economic value of forests for preventing avalanches is estimated at around US$100 per ha per year in open expanses of land in the Swiss Alps, and up to more than US$170,000 per ha per year in areas with valuable assets (ProAct, 2008).
- A recent study on the role of wetlands in reducing flooding associated with hurricanes in the United States of America calculated an average value of US$8,240 per ha per year, with coastal wetlands estimated to provide US$23.2 billion per year in storm protection services (Costanza et al., 2008).

Source: World Bank (2010).

economic value of mangroves as coastal defences has been estimated at US$300,000 per km, taking into account the costs of hard engineering work to achieve the same protective effect' (UNISDR, 2009). In Switzerland, the economic value of forests in preventing avalanches is valued at US$100 per ha per year in open areas, but up to US$170,000 in areas with high-value assets (World Bank, 2010).

At the same time, ecosystems often provide important co-benefits if properly managed. Some of the most fertile agricultural land on the planet depends on regular flooding to recharge the soil with nutrients. Flooding can also recharge aquifers in semi-arid areas or transport vital sediments and nutrients to sustain coastal fisheries in other areas.

27.5.3 Social protection: Increasing resilience to disasters

There are two compelling reasons why social protection can be a strategic mechanism for the management of water hazards. First, social protection instruments (community cohesion, healthcare facilities, accommodation insurance, etc.) can be adapted to enhance the disaster resilience of individuals and households, as well as providing important benefits in terms of poverty reduction and human capital development. Second, many of these instruments are already being delivered on a large scale, which make them a powerful tool for reducing the risk associated with floods and drought. Existing mechanisms for social protection can thus usually be used to encompass large numbers of disaster-prone households and communities through relatively minor adaptations of targeting criteria and timeframes, and often with relatively low additional costs.

The countries best able to develop effective social protection for risk–prone households and individuals are those that already have requisite social policies backed up by a wide range of legislative provisions (ERD, 2010). They include labour market laws (including the regulation of unemployment benefits), health and safety regulations in the work place, basic entitlements and welfare payments, and the stipulation of affirmative action for marginal groups. Countries that have strongly developed social legislation, corresponding regulation, and up–to–date public registries find it easier to embed both targeted and universal social protection as an instrument for reducing water-related hazard risks.

27.5.4 Adapting to climate change

Climate change adaptation can be understood in terms of both (a) adapting development to gradual changes in average temperature, sea level and precipitation; and (b) reducing and managing the risks associated with more frequent, severe and unpredictable extreme weather events.

There is evidence that the momentum to develop country-level adaptation programming owes more to the perceived opportunity to access climate change funding mechanisms than to social demand for adaptation. But given that in practice most adaptation measures address disaster risks, adaptation provides an additional set of instruments and mechanisms for reducing water-related hazard risk.

As with disaster risk reduction, adaptation measures can generate benefits at the appropriate scale only when they are integrated into mainstream development planning and public investment decisions (ECA, 2009). Unfortunately, many climate change adaptation initiatives are still conceived of and implemented as stand–alone projects. Governments' failure to integrate efforts to reduce water-related hazard risk and climate change adaptation into national and sector development planning and investment perpetuates the misconception that climate change adaptation is predominantly an environmental issue, rather than a core component of development, and that reducing water-related hazard risk is limited to early warning insurance and disaster preparedness and response (Mercer, 2010).

The inability to recognize the links between adaptation, disaster risk reduction and development processes leads to an inaccurate understanding of climate-related risks. As a result, there is a tendency to emphasize the use of risk transfer measures for managing extreme events, rather than adopting a more comprehensive approach that also reduces the extensive risks upon which climate change will have the greatest impact in the short term.

27.6 Conclusions and required actions

27.6.1 Disaster trends

The exponential increase in the damage associated with highly localized flash and urban flooding, landslides, fires, storms and torrential rains in many low and middle-income countries provide a real-time indicator of the accumulation of risk (Box 27.1). Most of these losses disproportionately affect low-income households and communities and go largely unaccounted for. In other words, there is a social distribution of disaster loss.

In most of the world, the risk of being killed by a tropical cyclone or a major river flood is lower than in 1990. Countries are successfully strengthening their capacities for early warning, preparedness and disaster response. However, drought impact still goes largely unaccounted for and falls on poor rural households. As a result there may be little political or economic incentive to address it.

In most countries drought risk management is remedial, emphasizing early warning, response and insurance rather than policies that address the underlying risk drivers. Institutionally, drought risk reduction and management are rarely integrated into either national disaster risk reduction or other policy frameworks such as water management (e.g. IWRM). But given the evidence of rapidly increasing impacts and climate projections through the end of this century, the need to address drought risk and its underlying drivers will be fundamental to the sustainability of many countries and localities over the coming decades.

27.6.2 Integrated measures

A balanced portfolio of measures and investments that reduce flood and drought risk is likely to improve social and economic development. Such measures include development and land-use planning; targeted investments, for example, through retrofitting critical facilities such as schools and hospitals; risk transfer schemes to protect against the most intensive risks; and investment in social protection and disaster management. Thus, if on the one hand disaster risk reduction programmes improve development, on the other hand development programmes should integrate a disaster risk reduction aspect, including it into their portfolio. Perhaps the most strategic of these instruments is a country's national planning and public investment system (see Section 27.1.3).

Mainstreaming disaster risk reduction in national planning and public investment system decisions is a potentially very high impact strategy, particularly considering the scale and volume of public investment, infrastructure and public asset, particularly in middle-income countries. This include the incorporation of water-related disaster risk reduction into IWRM through the adoption of regulatory and other legal measures, institutional reform, improved analytical and methodological capabilities, appropriate technologies, capacity-building, financial planning, public education, community involvement and awareness-raising. This approach would also provide a cost-effective and first barrier against climate change impacts.

||||||||||||||||||||||||||||||||||||||||||||||||||||||||||||||||||||||||||||

References

ADB (Asian Development Bank)/World Bank. 2010. *Preliminary Floods Damage and Needs Assessment.* Islamabad, Pakistan, ADB/World Bank.

Cardona, O. D. 2009. *La gestión financiera del riesgo de desastres: Instrumentos financieros de retención y transferencia para la comunidad andina.* Lima, PREDECAN, Comunidad Andina.

Corrales, W. and Miquelena, T. 2008. *Disasters in Developing Countries' Sustainable Development: A Conceptual Framework for Strategic Action.* Background paper for the 2009 Global Assessment Report on Disaster Risk Reduction. Geneva, UNISDR.

Costanza, R., Perez-Maqueo, O., Martinez, M. L., Sutton, P., Anderson, S. J. and Mulder, K. 2008. The value of coastal wetlands for hurricane protection. *AMBIO: A Journal of the Human Environment*, Vol. 37, No. 4, pp. 241–8.

CRED (Centre for Research on the Epidemiology for Disasters). 2011. *Annual Disaster Statistical Review 2010: The Numbers and Trends.* Brussels, Université Catholique de Louvain. http://www.cred.be/sites/default/files/ADSR_2010.pdf

de la Fuente, A. and Dercon, S. 2008. *Disasters, Growth and Poverty in Africa: Revisiting the Microeconomic Evidence.* Background for the 2009 Global Assessment Report on Disaster Risk Reduction. Geneva, UNISDR.

Dilley, M., Chen, R., Deichmann, W., Lerner-Lam, A. L. and Arnold, M. 2005. *Natural Disaster Hotspots.* Washington DC, The World Bank.

ECA (Economics of Climate Adaptation). 2009. *Shaping Climate Adaptation: A Framework for Decision-making.* New York, McKinsey & Company.

ECLAC (United Nations Economic Commission for Latin America and the Caribbean). 2002. *Handbook for Estimating the Socio-economic and Environmental Effects of Disasters.* Report LC/MEX/L.519. Mexico City, ECLAC.

Edwards, D. and McKee, T. 1997. *Characteristics of 20th Century Drought in the United States at Multiple Time Scales.* Climatology Report No. 97-2. Fort Collins, Colo., Colorado State University.

EM-DAT (OFDA/CRED International Disaster Database). 2010. *Global 'Number Killed' and 'Number Affected' by Drought Between 1900–2009.* Brussels, Université Catholique de Louvain.

Erian, W., Katlan, B. and Babah, O. 2010. *Drought Vulnerability in the Arab Region: Special Case Study: Syria.* Background paper for the 2011 Global Assessment Report on Disaster Risk Reduction. Geneva, UNISDR.

ERD (European Report on Development). 2010. *Social Protection for Inclusive Development – A New Perspective on EU Cooperation with Africa.* The 2010 European report on development. Draft. Florence, Italy, Robert Schuman Centre for Advanced Studies, European University Institute.

ERN-AL (Evaluacion de Riescos Naturales-America Latina). 2010. *Probabilistic Modelling of Natural Risks at the Global Level.* Background paper for the 2011 United Nations Global Assessment Report on Disaster Risk Reduction. Geneva, UNISDR.

Fitzhugh, T. and Richter, B. 2004. Quenching urban thirst: Growing cities and their impacts on freshwater ecosystems. *BioScience,* Vol. 54, No. 8, pp. 741–54.

Foster, V. and Briceno-Garmendia, C. 2010. *Africa's Infrastructure. A Time for Transformation.* Washington DC, International Bank for Reconstruction and Development (IBRD)/The World Bank.

Galu, G., Kere, J., Funk, C. and Husak, G. 2010. *Case Study on Understanding Food Security Trends and Development of Decision-support Tools and their Impact on Vulnerable Livelihoods in East Africa.* Background paper for the 2011 Global Assessment Report on Disaster Risk Reduction. Geneva, UNISDR.

Grey, D. and Sadoff, C. 2006. *Water for Growth and Development.* Thematic documents of the 4th World Water Forum. Mexico City, Comision Nacional del Agua.

Guttman, N. 1994. On the sensitivity of sample L moments to sample size. *Journal of Climatology,* Vol. 7, pp. 1026–9.

Horridge, M., Madden, J. and Wittwer, G. 2005. The impacts of the 2002–2003 drought on Australia. *Journal of Policy Modeling,* Vol. 27, No. 3, pp. 285–308.

IISD (International Institute for Sustainable Development). 2003. *Livelihoods and Climate Change: Combining Disaster Risk Reduction, Natural Resource Management and Climate Change Adaptation in a New Approach to the Reduction of Vulnerability and Poverty.* Winnipeg, Canada, IISD.

IPCC (Intergovernmental Panel on Climate Change). 2007. Summary for policymakers. M. L. Parry, O. F. Canziani, J. P. Palutikof, P. J. van der Linden and C. E. Hanson (eds) *Climate Change 2007: Impacts, Adaptation and Vulnerability.* Contribution of Working Group II to the Fourth Assessment Report of the IPCC. Cambridge, UK, Cambridge University Press, pp. 7–22.

Kelman, I. 2010. Policy arena: Introduction to climate, disasters and international development. *Journal of International Development,* Vol. 22, pp. 208–17.

MA (Millennium Ecosystem Assessment). 2005. *Ecosystems and Human Well-Being: Synthesis.* Washington DC, World Resources Institute.

Mansilla, E. 2010. *Riesgo urbano y políticas públicas en America Latina: La irregularidad y el acceso al suelo.* Background paper for the 2011 Global Assessment Report on Disaster Risk Reduction. Geneva, UNISDR.

McKee, T. B., Doesken, N. J. and Kleist, J., 1993. The relationship of drought frequency and duration to time scales. Proceedings of the Eighth Conference on Applied Climatology, Anaheim, Calif., 17–22 January, pp. 179–84.

––––. 1995. *Drought Monitoring with Multiple Time Scales.* Proceedings of the Ninth Conference on Applied Climatology. Boston, USA, American Meteorological Society.

Mercer, J. 2010. Disaster risk reduction or climate change adaptation: Are we reinventing the wheel? *Journal of International Development* Vol. 22, No. 2, 247–64.

Mestre, A. 2010. *Drought Monitoring and Drought Management in Spain.* Background paper for the 2011 Global Assessment Report on Disaster Risk Reduction. Geneva, UNISDR.

Ministerial Declaration. 2008. *Third Asian Ministerial Conference on Disaster Risk Reduction.* Kuala Lumpur, 2–4 December 2008.

––––. 2010. *Declaration of the Second African Ministerial Conference on Disaster Risk Reduction.* Nairobi, 14–16 April 2010.

Neri, C. and Briones, F. 2010. *Assessing Drought Risk and Identifying Policy Alternatives for Drought Risk Management. Risks, Impacts and Social Meaning of Drought: Characterization of the Vulnerability in Sonora, Mexico.* Background paper for the 2011 Global Assessment Report on Disaster Risk Reduction. Geneva, UNISDR.

Noy, I. 2009. The macroeconomic consequences of disasters. *Journal of Development Economics,* Vol. 88, No. 2, pp. 221–31.

OECD (Organisation for Economic Co operation and Development). 2010. *Development Co-operation Report 2010.* Paris, OECD Publishing.

OSSO (Observatorio Sismológico del Sur-Occidente). 2011. *Extensive risk analysis for the 2011 Global Assessment Report on Disaster Risk Reduction: Análisis de manifestaciones de riesgo en America Latina: Patrones y tendencias de las manifestaciones intensivas y extensivas de riesgo.* Background paper for the 2011 Global Assessment Report on Disaster Risk Reduction. Geneva, UNISDR.

Peduzzi, P., Chatenoux, B., Dao, H., De Bono, A., Deichmann, U., Giuliani, G., Herold, C., Kalsnesm, B., Kluser, S., Løvholt, F., Lyon, B., Maskrey, A., Mouton, F., Nadim, F. and Smebye, H. 2009. Global Risk Analysis. 2009 *Global Assessment Report on Disaster Risk Reduction: Risk and Poverty in a Changing Climate.* Geneva, UNISDR.

ProAct. 2008. *The Role of Environmental Management and Eco-Engineering in Disaster Risk Reduction and Climate Change Adaptation.* http://proactnetwork.org/proactwebsite/media/download/CCA_DRR_reports/em_ecoeng_in_drr_cca.pdf

Sávio Martins, E. 2010. *Assessing Drought Risk and Identifying Policy Alternatives for Drought Risk Management: Ceará, Brazil.* Background paper for the 2011 Global Assessment Report on Disaster Risk Reduction. Geneva, UNISDR.

Shaw, R., Nguyen, H., Habiba, U. and Takeuchi, Y. 2010. *Drought in Asian Monsoon Region.* Background Paper for the 2011 Global Assessment Report on Disaster Risk Reduction. Geneva, UNISDR.

Stolton, S., Dudley, N. and Randall, J. 2008. *Arguments for Protection: Natural Security: Protected Areas and Hazard Mitigation.* A research report by WWF and Equilibrium. Gland, Switzerland, World Wide Fund for Nature (WFF). http://www.wwf.de/fileadmin/fm-wwf/pdf_neu/natural_security___protected_areas___hazard_mitigation.pdf

UNDP (United Nations Development Programme). 2004. *Reducing Disaster Risk: A Challenge for Development.* Geneva, UNDP, Bureau for Crisis Prevention and Recovery.

----. 2010. *Human Development Report 2010. The Real Wealth of Nations: Pathways to Human Development.* New York, UNDP.

UNEP (United Nations Environment Programme). 2010. *Linking Ecosystems to Risk and Vulnerability Reduction: The Case of Jamaica. Risk and Vulnerability Assessment Methodology Development Project (RIVAMP). Results of the Pilot Assessment.* Geneva, UNEP/GRID-Europe.

UN-Habitat. 2010. *The State of the World's Cities 2010/2011: Cities for All: Bridging the Urban Divide.* Nairobi, UN-Habitat.

UNISDR (United Nations International Strategy for Disaster Reduction Secretariat). 2009. *Global Assessment Report on Disaster Risk Reduction: Risk and Poverty in a Changing Climate.* Geneva, UNISDR.

----. 2011. *Global Assessment Report on Disaster Risk Reduction.* Geneva, UNISDR.

WMO (World Meteorological Organization). 2009. *Thematic Progress Review Sub-component on Early Warning Systems.* Background paper for the 2009 Global Assessment Report on Disaster Risk Reduction. Geneva, UNISDR.

World Bank. 2010. *Natural Hazards, Unnatural Disasters: The Economics of Effective Prevention.* Washington DC, The World Bank/International Bank for Reconstruction and Development (IBRD).

WWAP (World Water Assessment Programme). 2009. *World Water Development Report 3: Water in a Changing World.* Paris/London, UNESCO/Earthscan.

WWF (World Wide Fund for Nature). 2008. *Natural Security: Protected Areas and Hazard Mitigation.* Gland, Switzerland, WWF. http://assets.panda.org/downloads/natural_security_final.pdf

Zapata, R. and Madrigal, B. 2009. *Economic Impact of Disasters: Evidence from DALA assessments by ECLAC in Latin America and the Caribbean.* Mexico City, ECLAC. http://www.eclac.cl/publicaciones/xml/1/38101/2009-S117EyP-MEX-L941.PDF_parte_1.pdf

CHAPTER 28

Desertification, land degradation and drought and their impacts on water resources in the drylands

UNCCD and UNU
—
Author Juliane Zeidler and Asellah David (IECN)
Contributors Sergio Zelaya Bonilla and Emmanuel Chinyamakobvu (UNCCD)
Acknowledgements Peer review was carried out by Zafar Adeel and Fabrice Renaud (UNU).

Water degradation in drylands will have detrimental effects for the people and the economy of dryland countries.

Although it is clear by definition that drylands are water-scarce, human drivers and climate change pose serious threats to water resources in drylands.

The impacts of desertification, land degradation and drought (DLDD) on water resources negatively affect development potentials in drylands.

Urgent and dedicated responses to protect drylands resources including water are needed to support sustainable development in dryland countries.

28.1 Introduction

The key challenges: desertification, land degradation and drought (DLDD) are specifically, but not exclusively, related to drylands. Drylands are by definition water limited environments. Water is a key resource that is under high pressure from increasing demand and decreasing quality. Productivity of drylands is determined by water availability and quality. Any further degradation of this essential resource will have detrimental effects for the people and the economy of dryland countries.

Drivers: DLDD are caused and exacerbated by different drivers, including (a) natural drivers, which are often related to the geographical situation and associated environmental and climatic settings of a site; (b) human drivers, related to unsustainable human development aspirations, which are often economic in nature and not attuned to the environmental frame conditions, and (c) climate change, which is a new, partially natural and partially human-induced driver.

Risks and uncertainties: There are various DLDD-related impacts on water, including: lower recharge of groundwater and runoff; water degradation, for example through pollutants, and changes in turbidity, sedimentation and siltation; and salinity. All these DLDD-related impacts have severe implications for the development potential in drylands. They negatively affect agricultural production, ecosystem health and the sustainability of industrial and energy projects and infrastructure. A major concern for sustainable development in drylands is the increasing threat of water scarcity (Figure 28.1). Water availability and quality are existing challenges to potential dryland development that are expected to be exacerbated by the impacts of climate change.

Hotspots: Geographic hotspots of intensified DLDD expand across the drylands of the world – countries with a low Gross Domestic Product (GDP) and a low Human Development Index (HDI) are particularly vulnerable, as interventions are costly. Dryland areas with high human populations or connected high density areas 'downstream' are prone to land degradation and associated negative water impacts.

Responses: A range of specific examples of strategic responses to the challenges exists and each has been tested and implemented on a pilot basis. However, these successes need to be scaled up in dryland areas, which often requires support actions (such as policy, financial and, structural and) and material resources. Generally three main areas of response are considered:

Innovations in water management and technology to cope with water scarcity, including concepts such as cost of and payment for water; investments for sustainable ecosystem services; investment in appropriate techniques, technologies and infrastructure; development of new water resources; and investments in water research, management and policy-making capacities.

Promoting water use efficiency by reducing water wastage and prioritizing water uses in the drylands.

Supporting policy changes needed in and for dryland countries, including policy changes in water demand management and food self-sufficiency versus food security, as well as global investments in long-term food security in water-restricted drylands.

A dedicated international framework to act upon the pressing issue of water scarcity in drylands as well as DLDD-related water and land issues is urgently required. The establishment of a 'Water Compact for Drylands' has been proposed as one such international priority action. Existing United Nations (UN) instruments – such as the UN Convention to Combat Desertification in those Countries Experiencing Serious Drought and/or Desertification, Particularly in Africa (UNCCD), the UN-Water and UN-Land initiatives, and the priority outcomes from the seventeenth session

© UNCCD photo award 2005/Kushal Gangopadhyay

of the UN Commission on Sustainable Development – should be positioned to support and drive such work.

28.2 The challenge: Water as a key resource under pressure in the drylands

The growth in the use of this water resources has tended to be much greater than the growth in the number of people. For example, in the twentieth century, the world's population increased fourfold, whereas freshwater usage increased nine times over (Lean, 2009). In addition to this increased usage, DLDD means that natural recharge is reduced as the soil loses its water retention capacity (DG Environment – European Commission, 2007). and Rainfall is also reduced in times of drought. Consequently, a number of countries in the drylands are increasingly faced with water scarcity.

Water scarcity is the imbalance between available water resources and demands (UNCCD, 2010), occurring when water resources are insufficient to satisfy long-term average requirements. This long-term water imbalance is caused by a combination of low water availability and a level of water demand exceeding the natural recharge. Water scarcity frequently appears in areas with low rainfall but also in areas affected by DLDD, as well as in areas with high population density and intensive agriculture and/or industrial activity, particularly in the drylands. Large spatial and temporal differences in the amount of water available are observed across the drylands. Dryland problems of DLDD and water scarcity, among others, put immense pressure on the management of water resources.

Water scarcity, whether natural or human-induced, serves to trigger and exacerbate the effects of desertification through direct, long-term impacts on land and soil quality, soil structure, organic matter content, and ultimately on soil moisture levels. The direct physical effects of land degradation include the drying up of freshwater resources, an increased frequency of drought and sand and dust storms, and a greater occurrence of flooding due to inadequate drainage or poor irrigation practices. Should these trends continue,

FIGURE 28.2

The extent of dryland systems worldwide

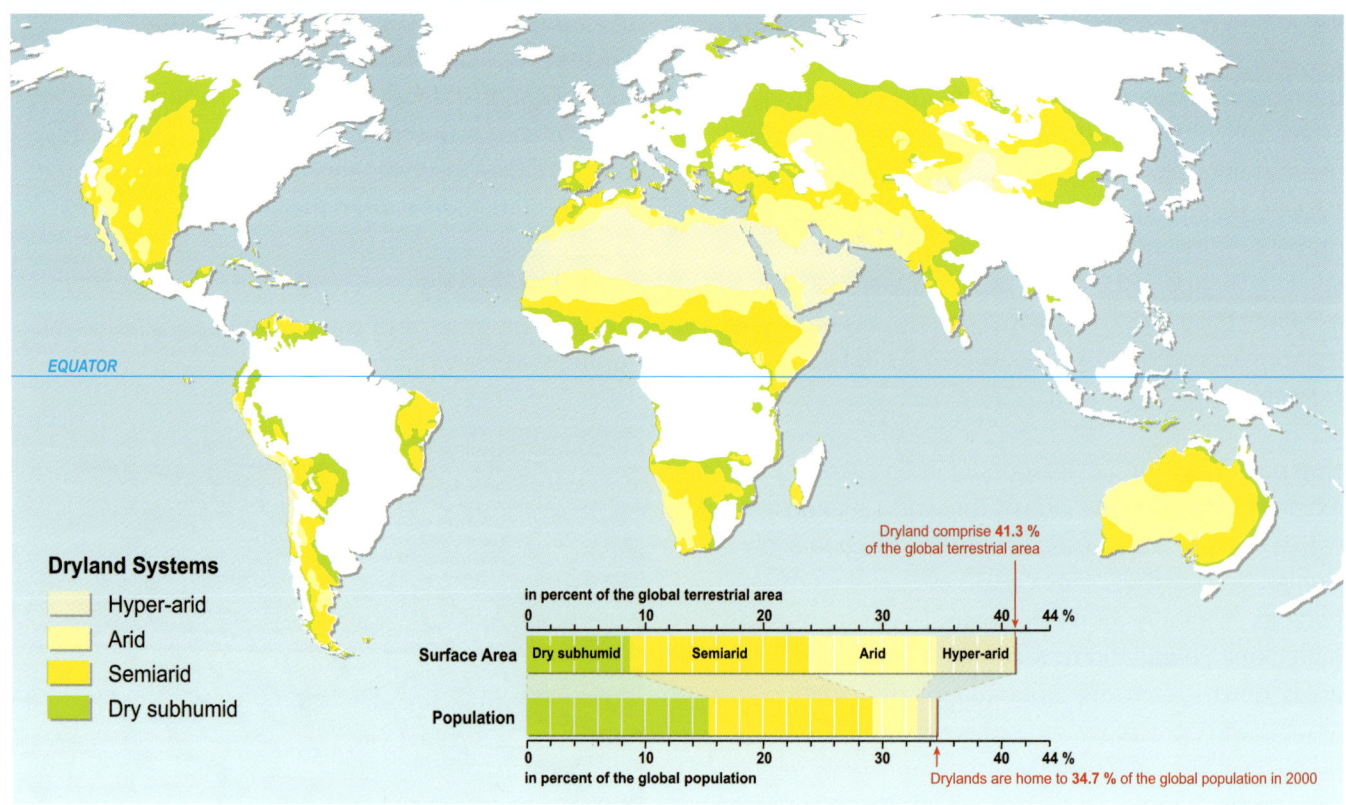

Notes: Overall 41.3% of the global terrestrial areas are categorized as drylands and 34.7% of the global population lived in drylands in 2000.
The long-term mean of the ratio of an area's average annual precipitation to its average annual potential evapotranspiration is the Aridity Index (AI).
Source: Millennium Ecosystem Assessment (2005, appendix A, p. 23, from data sources cited therein).

it would bring about a sharp decline in soil nutrients, accelerating the loss of vegetation cover. This in turn leads to further land and water degradation, such as pollution of surface and groundwater, siltation, and the salinization and alkalization of soils.

28.2.1 An introduction to drylands of the world

Desertification is land degradation, resulting from various factors including climatic variations and human activities. DLDD are concepts mainly associated with, but not exclusive to, dryland areas around the world. Over 60 countries are characterized by dryland ecosystems (Table 28.1) – with prevailing hyper-arid, arid and dry subhumid climatic conditions. They are categorized using the Aridity Index (AI) which is the long-term mean of the ratio of an area's average annual precipitation to its mean annual potential evapotranspiration. For 17 of these countries, drylands account for more than 90% of their land area. Overall, 41.3% of the global terrestrial area is categorized as drylands and 34.7% of the global population lived in drylands in 2000 (Figure 28.2) (Millennium Ecosystem Assessment, 2005).

In drylands, water is usually the most important limiting resource – for both ecosystems and human and economic development. Poor management of drylands ecosystems leads to desertification and land degradation, and to increasing and long-term loss of productivity (UNCCD, 1994). Linkages with natural water limitation, unsuitable water management practices and negative feedback loops, as well as interconnectivity between land degradation and water resources, often exacerbate unsustainable use of water.

Although several dryland countries are counted as among the wealthiest globally, endowed as they are with non-renewable natural resources such as oil, diamonds and uranium, most dryland countries have a low GDP, and rank poorly in terms of their HDI (Table 28.1). The high dependence of drylands inhabitants on the natural resource base means that they are vulnerable to land degradation.

28.2.2 Water sources and their sustainability in the drylands

Sources of water in the drylands usually consist of surface water, groundwater (including fossil groundwater) and rainfall. Average annual rainfall in the drylands is relatively low in dry subhumid areas and is even lower for other drylands types. In hot arid climates, much of the precipitation is lost to evapotranspiration due to

extremely high temperatures. For example, data collected in southern Africa suggest that less than 3% of precipitation actually contributes to ground or surface water recharge, less than 1% of precipitation contributes to aquifer and groundwater recharge, and approximately 2% contributes to surface water (perennial and ephemeral rivers, wetlands and dams) through runoff. Hence only a small percentage (approximately 17%) is productively used for ecosystem maintenance and rain-fed production systems (Heyns et al., 1998; Schlesinger, 1997).

As water demand in drylands usually exceeds water availability, local inhabitants depend largely on groundwater, obtaining their water supply through boreholes and wells, although small-scale rainwater harvesting also takes place. In areas where larger settlements and cities (with associated industries) are situated, water demand frequently exceeds availability. In such cases, groundwater availability determines whether local water supply is accessible and sustainable. In many instances excessive water mining has already taken place and existing sources of water have been depleted without replenishment. In certain countries, alternative water sources are sought from other areas, by pipeline, or through the desalination of sea water.

Water resources in various watersheds in drylands are already considered highly over utilized. An analysis projecting water supply data for the year 2025 in water catchments in drylands worldwide presents a disturbing picture. According to the analysis, seven major basins in the drylands – mostly in Asia, and one large basin in Africa and another in North America – are expected to experience water scarcity by 2025 (Figure 28.3) and fourteen major watersheds are projected to be water stressed by 2025. In total, half of the major watersheds investigated in the drylands are predicted to experience some type of water shortage in the coming years (White and Nackoney, 2003) exacerbated by the anticipated climatic changes in dryland areas around the world.

28.2.3 Primary human water requirement activities and limitations in drylands

The importance of access to safe water was confirmed in the 64th UN General Assembly resolution (UN, 2010), which explicitly recognized access to safe and clean water and sanitation as a human right. The primary human water requirement activities are for drinking water,

TABLE 28.1

Gross Domestic Product (GDP) per capita and Human Development Indices of countries with drylands areas

#	Country with dryland areas	Total land area (km²)	Percentage of total dryland surface area (if exceeding 90%)[a]	GDP (PPP) per capita (US$)	HDI	Population
1	Afghanistan	647 500	94.0	$800	0.352	28 395 716
2	Albania	27 398		$6 300	0.818	3 639 453
3	Algeria	2 381 740		$7 000	0.754	34 178 188
4	Angola	1 220 000		$8 900	0.564	12 799 293
5	Argentina	2 736 690		$13 800	0.866	40 913 584
6	Armenia	28 454	98.1	$5 900	0.798	2 967 004
7	Australia	7 617 930		$38 911	0.970	21 262 641
8	Azerbaijan	86 100		$10 400	0.787	8 238 672
9	Botswana	585 370	100.0	$13 100	0.694	1 990 876
10	Bulgaria	110 550		$12 600	0.840	7 204 687
11	Burkina Faso	273 800	100.0	$1 200	0.389	15 746 232
12	Chad	1 259 200		$1 600	0.392	10 329 208
13	China	9 326 410		$6 600	0.772	1 338 612 968
14	Egypt	995 450		$6 000	0.703	78 866 635
15	El Salvador	20 720		$7 100	0.747	7 185 218
16	Eritrea	121 320		$700	0.472	5 647 168
17	Ethiopia	1 119 683		$900	0.414	85 237 338
18	Gambia	100 000	97.2	$1 400	0.456	1 778 081
19	Greece	130 800		$32 100	0.942	10 737 428
20	India	2 973 190		$3 100	0.612	1 156 897 766
21	Iran	1 636 000	90.2	$12 900	0.782	66 429 284
22	Iraq	432 162	99.9	$3 600	0.583	28 945 569
23	Israel	20 330		$28 400	0.935	7 233 701
24	Jordan	91 971		$5 300	0.770	6 269 285
25	Kazakhstan	2 669 800	99.1	$11 800	0.804	15 399 437
26	Kenya	569 250		$1 600	0.541	39 002 772
27	Kuwait	17 820	92.9	$54 100	0.916	2 692 526
28	Kyrgyzstan	191 300		$2 100	0.710	5 431 747
29	Lebanon	10 230		$13 100	0.803	4 017 095
30	Libya	1 759 540		$15 200	0.847	6 324 357
31	Macedonia	24 856		$9 000	0.817	2 066 718
32	Madagascar	581 540		$1 000	0.543	20 653 556
33	Malawi	94 080		$900	0.493	15 028 757
34	Mali	1 220 000		$1 200	0.371	13 443 225

#	Country with dryland areas	Total land area (km²)	Percentage of total dryland surface area (if exceeding 90%)[a]	GDP (PPP) per capita (US$)	HDI	Population
35	Mauritania	1 030 400		$2 100	0.520	3 129 486
36	Mexico	1 923 040		$13 500	0.854	111 211 789
37	Moldova	33 371	99.9	$2 300	0.720	4 320 748
38	Mongolia	1 554 731		$3 200	0.727	3 041 142
39	Morocco	446 300	92.2	$4 600	0.654	31 285 174
40	Mozambique	784 090		$900	0.402	21 669 278
41	Namibia	825 418	90.8	$6 400	0.686	2 108 665
42	Niger	1 266 700		$700	0.340	15 306 252
43	Nigeria	910 768		$2 400	0.511	149 229 090
44	Oman	212 460		$23 900	0.846	3 418 085
45	Pakistan	778 720		$2 600	0.572	174 578 558
46	Romania	230 340		$11 500	0.837	22 215 421
47	Russia	16 995 800		$15 100	0.817	140 041 247
48	Saudi Arabia	2 149 690		$20 400	0.843	28 686 633
49	Senegal	192 000	94.1	$1 600	0.464	13 711 597
50	Somalia	627 337		$600	0.284	9 832 017
51	South Africa	1 219 912		$10 100	0.683	49 052 489
52	Spain	499 542		$33 700	0.955	40 525 002
53	Sudan	2 376 000		$2 300	0.531	41 087 825
54	Syria	184 050	98.0	$4 600	0.742	21 762 978
55	Tajikistan	142 700		$1 800	0.688	7 349 145
56	Tunisia	155 360	93.7	$8 000	0.769	10 486 339
57	Turkey	770 760		$11 200	0.806	76 805 524
58	Turkmenistan	488 100	100.0	$6 900	0.739	4 884 887
59	Ukraine	603 700		$6 400	0.796	45 700 395
60	Uzbekistan	425 400	99.2	$2 800	0.710	27 606 007
61	Venezuela	882 050		$13 100	0.844	26 814 843
62	Yemen	527 970		$2 500	0.575	22 858 238
63	Zimbabwe	386 670		$100	0.513	11 392 629

Note: Three countries have been added to the original listing: Senegal, Gambia and Tunisia.
[a] Data not available for countries with less than 90% dryland areas.
Sources: Updated and revised after Harrison and Pearce (2000) and White and Nackoney (2003). Updated and additional information: HDI (2007) from UNDP (HDI indices provided on Wikipedia); GDP per capita (2009 estimate) from CIA (n.d.); and population (2009 estimate) from CIA (n.d.).

agriculture (food production), industry and domestic use. Where water is a limiting resource, priorities need to be set among competing uses to meet the essential requirements. can be met. The following key requirement activities can be specified.

Drinking water

Water is required for humans, livestock and wildlife, and plant life (excluding crops and agricultural production). Livestock production is common in the drylands, where rangelands tend to support large herds of herbivores if there is sufficient drinking water.

Domestic water requirements

Basic human needs include clean and safe water for washing and sanitation. The health of people is directly linked to the availability of clean and safe water. Water scarcity in the drylands is a major limiting factor for human habitation and its unavailability leads to dehydration and ultimately the death of the affected people.

Agricultural water demand

In most drylands regions, food production for local consumption or trade at a household level depends largely on rainfed agriculture or small-scale irrigation based on rainwater harvesting technologies. Large-scale irrigation systems tend to be unsustainable in most drylands, depending on the source and management of water. Rainfed agriculture often performs poorly, with high production variability as determined by the highly variable rainfall patterns.

Industrial demand

In general, water-dependent industries are not appropriate for the drylands, and this can have severe negative impacts on national economies. Given the prevalence of water scarcity in the drylands, promoting water-dependent industries becomes difficult, unless sustainable alternative sources of water can be accessed and managed in an efficient way without compromising domestic and agricultural water needs.

28.2.4 Global and regional water management policies in drylands

Water management is a critical aspect of dryland development. As the local and regional water cycles are extremely sensitive, the balance between demand and supply has often been disturbed and severe

FIGURE 28.3

Projected water supply in major watersheds in drylands by 2025: water scarcity will be exacerbated in many key dryland areas worldwide

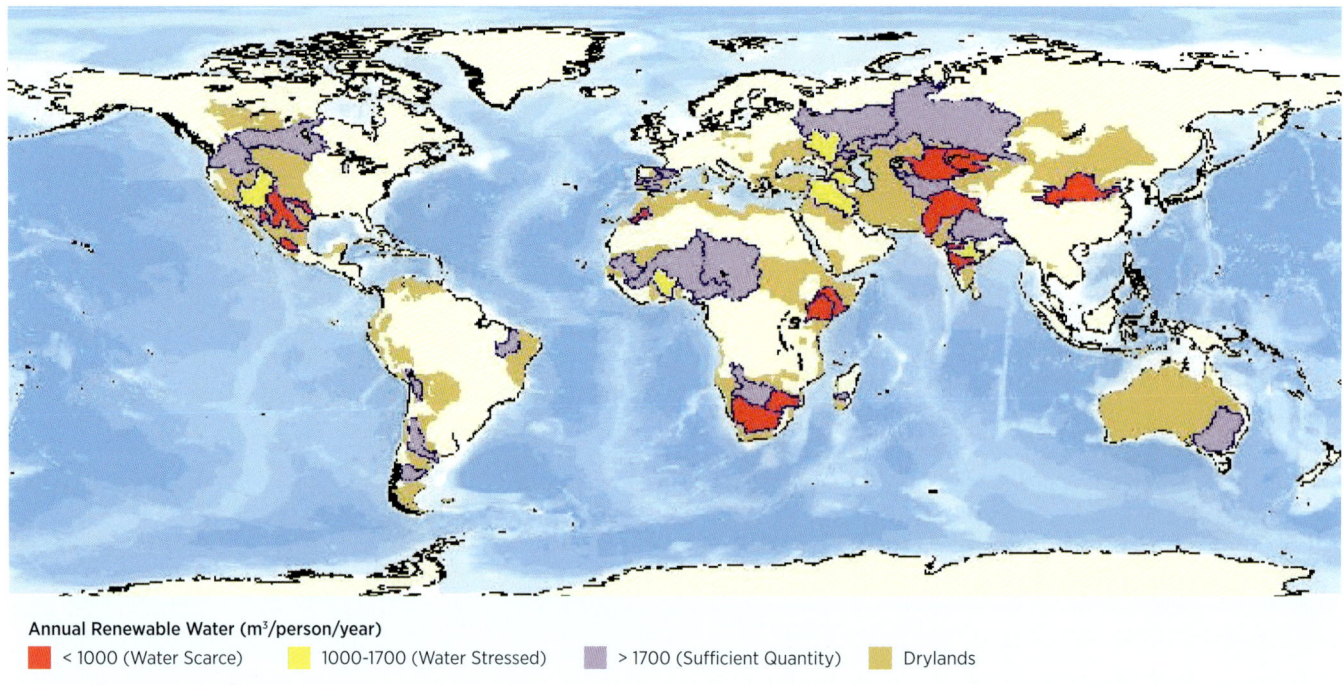

Annual Renewable Water (m³/person/year)
■ < 1000 (Water Scarce)   ■ 1000-1700 (Water Stressed)   ■ > 1700 (Sufficient Quantity)   ■ Drylands

Source: White and Nackoney (2003).

depletion of the water resources have occurred. Land and water use conflicts often arise. Where transboundary disagreements occur, capacity development in collaborative management of the scarce water resources is needed in order to avoid the potential escalation of these disagreements into major political crises.

Migration related to DLDD and water has already been observed and could potentially accelerate in the future. Water management must start at the local level. In drylands, priority should be given to strong investment in locally adapted technical and technological solutions, along with appropriate policy-making at national and international levels, to ensure improved water use efficiency. Water policies must be based on the availability of the resource, which has to be properly and economically valued. (See a more detailed overview of relevant policy instruments and examples of responses that help to reduce the impacts of DLDD on water resources and address water scarcity later in this chapter.)

Currently there are numerous regional and global water management policies in place. These policies often relate to transboundary agreements where watersheds reach across national borders (Figure 28.4). Also, projects such as 'Every River has its People' (KCS, n.d.) work with local communities on establishing basin management committees that also promote sustainable land management practices along the river to curb impacts of DLDD and its drivers (see Section 28.2 for further details).

28.3 Desertification, land degradation and drought: Drivers, risks and uncertainties, and hotspots

28.3.1 Drivers of desertification, land degradation and drought and water linkages

DLDD are caused and exacerbated by different drivers, relating to natural phenomena, human activities and climate change. The combined effects of desertification, land degradation and drought result in reduced water resources availability and accessibility. Both ground and surface water systems are affected.

Natural phenomena
It is important to recognize that certain geographic areas are naturally arid. It is normal for these areas to be exposed to highly variable and extreme climates,

FIGURE 28.4
World's major watersheds

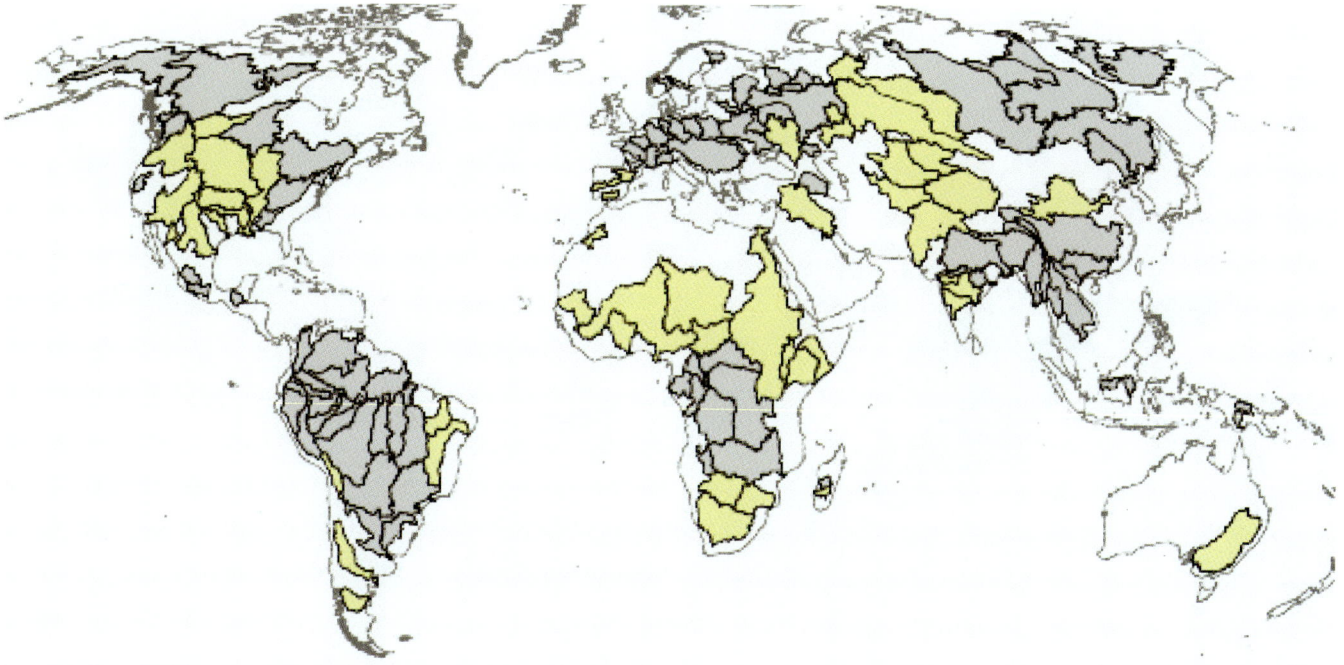

Note: Watersheds that are situated in key dryland areas are indicated in yellow. Most of these watersheds are transboundary.
Source: World Resources Institute (http://earthtrends.wri.org/images/maps/P1_22_LG.GIF).

and droughts are a common phenomenon that results in water scarcity being experienced. Such dryland areas are limited in their production potential and have developed specific adaptive characteristics shaped by long-term climatic conditions, geomorphological circumstances and earth history, resulting in strong variations and shifts in the evolvement and geographic position of drylands being observed through the millennia.

Human activities

Many drylands have been characterized by a culture of human activities being in harmony with nature. However, high human-related pressure on natural resources has increasingly led to desertification and land degradation symptoms, which may be irreversible or may lead to the long-term loss of productive potential and increased water scarcity. Poor and inadequate land management practices, that are insensitive to the natural limitations and ecological processes of dryland ecosystems, coupled with frequent and often severe droughts, frequently lead to severe desertification and land degradation and hence water scarcity as the land loses its water retention capacity. This phenomenon also holds true for non-arid systems. Increased demands on the productivity of drylands – related to the development aspirations of local people and governments and increased populations who are dependent on the limited natural resource base – and the application of inefficient land management practices have led to drylands that are less and less inhabitable.

FIGURE 28.5

Projected impacts of climate change on perennial drainage density

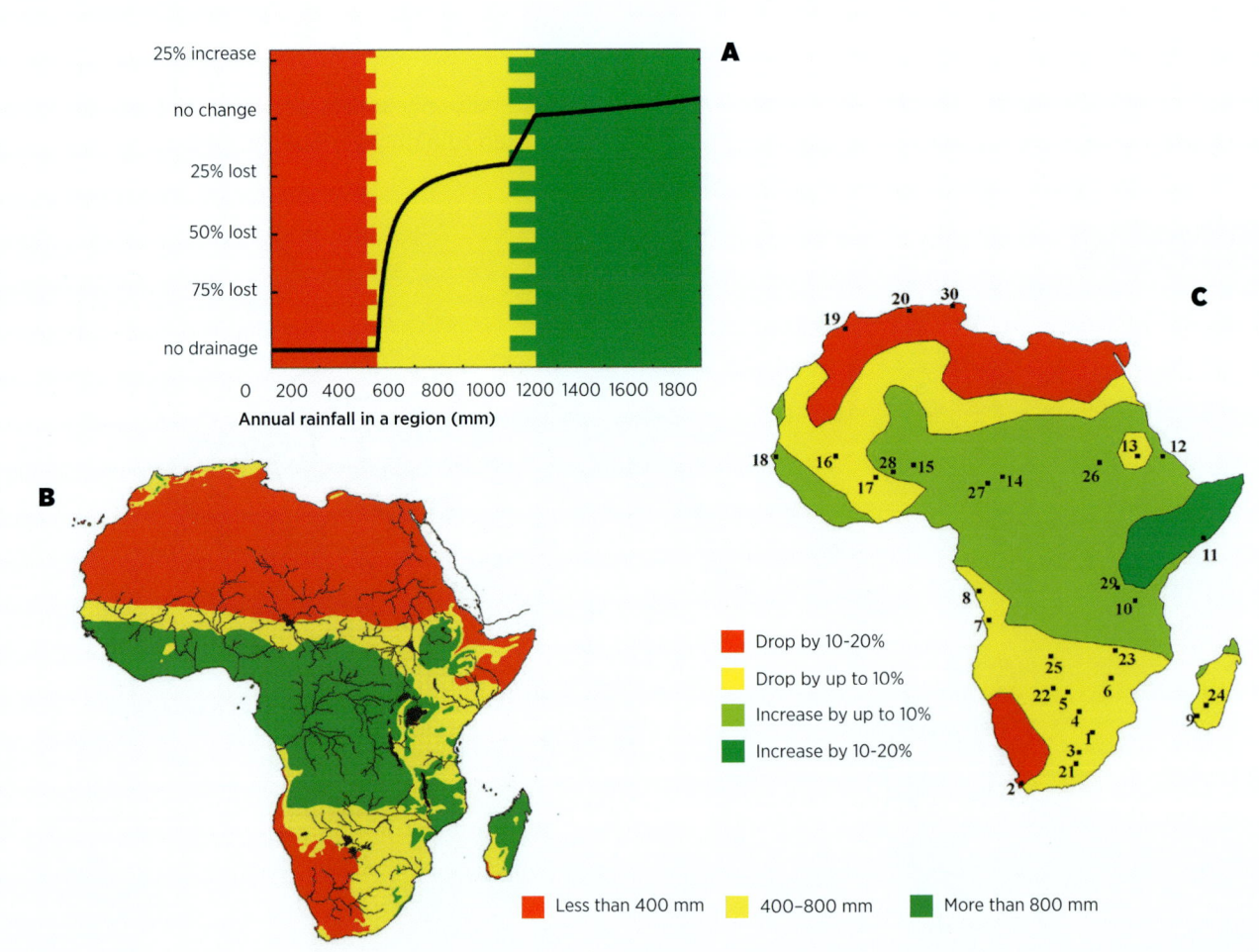

Notes: Effects of a 10% reduction in rainfall on perennial drainage density by 2070–2099. (A) Rainfall regimes at the end of the twentieth century; (B) map of Africa showing predicted change in precipitation; and (C) numbers indicate selected locations for which the effect on perennial drainage density has been calculated.
Source: de Wit and Stankiewicz (2006), reproduced with permission from AAAS.

Climate change

Globally predicted climatic changes will pose differing risks and opportunities in different dryland regions of the world. In broad categories, climatic change will lead to either/and/or increases/decreases in temperatures and precipitation, affecting evaporation rates, water availability and tolerance levels of specific livestock, crop plants, and other elements of the natural ecosystems. The occurrence of more extreme weather events – such as prolonged and more severe droughts, unprecedented extreme flooding events in normally arid areas, and seasonal shifts of known weather patterns (for example changes to the onset of rainy seasons and shortening of growing seasons) – pose enormous challenges to ecosystems. Essential ecosystem services are affected by climate change, leading to DLDD. The difficulty of coping and adapting to climatic changes often worsens desertification and land degradation and poses a major management challenge. The impacts of climate change on water – that is, changes in groundwater recharge and runoff in catchment areas – are expected to be significant and lead to both the drying up of aquifers and/or flash floods and flooding in other areas. Major changes are predicted in the dynamics of perennial rivers in Africa (Figure 28.5), where major flooding disasters are already occurring more frequently, while elsewhere river courses are drying up.

28.3.2 Risks and uncertainties: The impact of desertification, land degradation and drought on water resources availability, quality and accessibility

DLDD directly affects and worsens already critical water resources, especially in drylands. Overuse and depletion of limited water resources are already an issue, but the direct effects of DLDD further negatively impact on the resource – bringing with it the risks and uncertainties described below.

Lower recharge of groundwater and changed runoff

Soil compaction and changes in soil, vegetation and soil faunal parameters directly affect the recharge rate of groundwater and water dynamics in ecosystems (FAO, 2002). It is well known that deforestation in catchment areas leads to altered runoff regimes, disturbing the natural water recharge and storage in ecosystems. On a smaller scale, water infiltration rates are disturbed by unsustainable land use practices, which have altered soil faunal associations and the balance of incorporating soil organic matter (SOM) back into soils, negatively affecting soil water holding capacities (Box 28.1).

The degradation of land by physical compaction of soils – for example through trampling by livestock, sealing of soil surfaces by buildings or industrial activities, or movements of tractors – all have negative effects on the percolation of water into the ground. Soil compaction creates more impervious surfaces that do not allow percolation of the water down through the soil into the aquifer. If the infiltration capacity of the soil is reduced or if vegetation has been removed on a large scale then peak flows or floods increase (Calder, 1998).

This reduction in soil infiltration capacity increases surface runoff. Surface runoff causes erosion of the earth's surface, including splash, gully, sheet or stream bed erosion. With increased runoff, water is instead forced directly into streams or storm-water runoff drains, reducing groundwater recharge, thus lowering the water table and making droughts worse,

BOX 28.1

Role of soil fauna in maintaining soil water holding capacities

DLDD often leads to a destruction of healthy soil biological properties, which in turn negatively affects the soil's water holding capacities. Water percolation and holding capacities of soils are essential for allowing rainwater to infiltrate into the ground and eventually contribute to groundwater recharge. The loss of biodiversity in soil fauna, through the occurrences of desertification and land degradation, leads to the disturbance of critical biogeochemical and physical soil processes such as soil water infiltration and holding capacity. Soil fauna improves physical soil properties such as macroporosity, thus increasing soil water infiltration capacity (Leonard and Rajot, 2001; Mando et al., 1999). For example, termites and ants, which dominate dryland soil macrofaunal invertebrates, translocate organic material such as pieces of grass stalks, leaves and wood into the soil, where these materials are broken down by various soil organisms into soil organic matter (SOM). SOM is critical for enhancing the water holding capacity of soils. Soil fauna modify the soil and litter environment playing a key role in SOM transformations and nutrient dynamics at different spatial and temporal scales thus affecting the soil's physical properties, nutrient cycling, water retention capacity and plant growth (Bhadauria and Saxena, 2010). If soil faunal assemblages are disturbed through DLDD-related impacts (e.g. overstocking, inappropriate use of insecticides) the soil's physical and chemical properties will be negatively affected resulting in negative impacts on water balances.

especially for farmers and others who depend on the water wells.

Degradation of water resources and the environment

DLDD can create important impacts on water quality, which in turn may have negative effects on downstream uses of water (FAO, 1993, 2002). These impacts can include changes in sediment load and the concentration of nutrients, salts, metals and agrochemicals; the influx of pathogens; and a change in the temperature regime. Where poor land management practices prevail, increased loads of nitrogen, phosphorus and related nitrate and phosphate concentrations result in severe eutrophication of water sources. Pathogenic bacteria in surface waters will increase as a consequence of riparian grazing or waste influx from livestock production. Pesticides and persistent organic pollutants may find their way into water courses in areas where DLDD effects are high, for example through soil erosion and increased runoff.

Turbidity, sedimentation and siltation

Soil erosion is a major manifestation of desertification and land degradation. Soil is transported by runoff or wind into water sources, such as rivers and the sea, causing the loss of valuable topsoil and adding sediment that can produce turbidity in surface waters. This soil loss and sedimentation, and the effects of turbidity such as limited penetration of sunlight, destroys the natural habitat of fauna and flora in the rivers (FAO, 2002), changing biodiversity patterns and leading to a loss of freshwater fish stocks. In extreme cases of changed climatic conditions combined with poor management of water resources and DLDD, the complete siltation and drying up of entire catchments and river systems has been observed.

Salinity

Salinization of soils and water resources is a major problem related to desertification and land degradation. An increase in salinity of surface and groundwater tends to have detrimental effects on downstream water uses such as irrigation or domestic water supply. Irrigation and drainage activities can lead to increased salinity of surface and groundwater as a consequence of evaporation and the leaching of salts from soils. This is of special concern in arid areas, where subsurface drainage water always has higher salt concentrations and higher sodium absorption rates than supply water for irrigation. Irrigation consequently leads to a surfacing and concentration of salts.

Water scarcity

Water scarcity poses a major threat to drylands. Drylands are water-constrained ecosystems where maintaining the balance between water demand and supply can be very challenging. When abstracting water for human use it is always important to allow for an ecological reserve – to retain sufficient water resources that are needed for maintaining underlying ecosystem services. In the event of water scarcity and the subsequent failure of water scarcity management plans, agriculture, which is often the largest consumer of water, is the most affected, translating into millions of dollars in lost income, particularly in economies that have a strong agriculture base. Simultaneously, with the failure of agricultural production, food security is threatened and hunger and malnutrition become inevitable in poor dryland countries.

28.3.3 Desertification, land degradation and drought hotspots and degradation of water resources in drylands

Geographic hotspots of DLDD are prevalent across the drylands of the world (Figure 28.2). Countries with low GDP and HDIs (Table 28.1) are particularly vulnerable because interventions are often costly. Dryland areas with high populations, or which are connected to high population density areas downstream, are prone to land degradation and the associated negative water impacts. Figure 28.4 displays major watersheds situated in dryland areas. According to White and Nackoney (2003), several of these major watersheds are already facing water scarcity (central and east Asia, southern and eastern Africa, central North America) and it is projected that in the future several of them will be further negatively affected by the impacts of climate change. For example, Figure 28.5 projects climate change induced impacts on drainage in Africa, negatively affecting at least 65% of the continent. Such projections overlay areas of DLDD in Africa, where severe interlinked impacts on ecosystems and ecosystem services, populations and economies can be foreseen.

It must be highlighted that, in addition to its scarcity, naturally available water resources in most drylands are often mismanaged. Exorbitant development expectations in such areas lead to unsustainable exploitation of existing water sources. Inappropriate land uses lead to DLDD and degradation of natural resources including water. Improving water use efficiency is a serious challenge. Seeking alternative water provision (e.g. large-scale desalination of sea water, long-distance transportation of water via canals and pipelines) has also led to an exacerbation of DLDD issues, promoting incompatible land uses such as overstocking of livestock leading to a change in vegetation cover and degradation of soils.

28.4 Potential responses to save the drylands and their populations

Current major drylands challenges include (a) poverty, (b) food crises (food insecurity and famine), (c) drought and water scarcity, (d) climate change, (e) loss of biodiversity, (f) deforestation, (g) energy challenges, and (h) environmentally forced human migration. In light of these challenges, one cannot fail to see that the need to address desertification and land degradation in the drylands is imperative. Indeed, where economic, social, political and geographic assets have become highly virtual, mobile and dynamic, it is easy to lose sight of the human interconnectedness of socio-economic assets such as land and water resources. Water scarcity in the drylands has an inevitable negative impact on sustainable development, hampers local governance and exacerbates social conflicts.

The future productivity and development options of the drylands are dramatically affected by both the low and further diminishing water resources in drylands and the DLDD impacts exacerbating water scarcity and quality. These effects are discernible on the environment, social systems and economies of the drylands. Although expected climate change impacts may improve water balances in some regions, other dryland areas will certainly have to deal with worsening water situations, and all regions will have to be able to manage change through numerous strategic response options to the water challenges. Some of these options are outlined in the following sections.

28.4.1 Strategic approaches

Securing water resources in the drylands requires an integrated approach to the management of the natural environment and associated natural resources, which takes into account all factors influencing decisions on land and water resources use at local, national and regional levels. It requires partnership building between different sectors of governments and societies, international agencies, scientific communities, non-governmental organizations, bilateral agencies, and others to tackle the complexity of securing water resources. In

tandem, a number of policies and technological measures and innovations should be employed to mitigate water scarcity in the drylands.

Innovations in water management and technology to cope with water scarcity

Cost of and payment for water
The tradition of having free or heavily subsidized water for livestock, irrigation and domestic use has wrongly created the impression that water is plentiful and of low value. This brings about a need to reduce the excessive demand and improve water use efficiency through promoting efficient water use practices and proper resource use planning and management, and through the proper costing and valuation of this limited resource. Paying for water is an increasingly accepted concept, even in rural communities (see Chapter 23, 'Valuing water'). Costs usually cover the delivery and supply of water. External costs, such as costs associated with the sustainability of the resource, are often not fully incorporated into existing pricing systems. Opportunity costs, a third category of costs, refers to the fact that we have conflicting water use demands and certain people/industries may lose the opportunity to do something because the limited water has been used in other ways.

Development of new water resources
Innovation in terms of developing and negotiating new water resources is important for the dryland countries. Whilst investments in desalination plants and improved transfers from other areas (e.g. by pipelines) are one avenue, others include improved recycling and improved transboundary management of existing resources. Some impressive examples of technological solutions come from the Middle East, and models of collaboration and application of new technologies are available from elsewhere, for example Germany and other EU-countries.

Desertification, land degradation and drought – investing in sustainable ecosystem services
Valuation of ecosystem services has proven to be a reasonable concept although it is not yet fully embraced by most water providers and users (Box 28.2; see also Chapter 21, 'Ecosystems'). Placing an adequate value/price on ecosystem services is critical to ensuring long-term sustainable use and management of finite resources such as water (Emerton and Bos, 2004; Smith et al., 2006). In the DLDD context, maintenance of critical ecosystem services such as

those provided by watersheds and associated vegetation and soil interactions must be fully considered. Relevant investments to curb the negative effects of DLDD on water resources need to be made and fully incorporated into such valuations. Ecosystem values then need to be translated into water management decision-making. For example, economic valuation (of ecosystem services) is best applied to an incremental change and within a policy context such as DLDD. To date there is mainly access to case study materials that illustrate methods and actual values. Investment in policy-relevant research is needed in most countries to inform decision-making.

BOX 28.2

Approaches to introducing payment for ecosystem services – examples from Kenya

According to Engel et al. (2007), payment for environmental services (PES) is an innovative market-based mechanism. It is based on twin principles that those benefiting from environmental services should pay for their provision and that those who provide environmental services should be compensated for doing so. The Pro-poor Rewards for Environmental Services in Africa initiative supported by the World Bank (www.worldbank.org) with the World Agroforestry Centre (ICRAF) and partners is working with communities and governments on introducing PES approaches including for watershed management and conservation. Various examples of projects in their early stages exist. In Kenya, Nairobi relies on distant forested catchments for its water supplies, like other major cities in Africa. One such catchment is the Sasumua watershed, which supplies 15% of Nairobi's water demand. Land use changes in upstream areas of the Sasumua watershed have led to increased sedimentation and water contamination (Porras et al., 2008). Ensuring proper hydrological functioning of the watershed is of critical importance to the future water supply of Nairobi. Baseline studies have recently been undertaken that will guide decision-making and the establishment of the PES mechanism in the watershed (Vågen, 2007). Learning from experiences in other countries such as Costa Rica and Columbia, which have already established very advanced PES mechanisms for water systems, is essential (Porras et al., 2008).

One PES mechanism that has been tried is the green water credits (GWC) concept. GWC offer a tried and tested means of providing Kenya with food, water and power security. GWC are payments or rewards for water and land management services provided by farmers, which in turn benefit downstream users by providing them with better-quality water and a more reliable supply.

Investing in appropriate innovations, technologies and infrastructure

Enhancing environmental flow and thus curbing the negative impacts of DLDD on water availability is one aspect of new technology and infrastructure development. For example, South Africa introduced the Working for Water programme (http://www.dwaf.gov.za/wfw/), where scientists and field workers use a range of methods to control aquatic invasive alien plants. This programme is one example a technological intervention. Another example is the construction of dams, either for water storage or energy generation. A wide range of innovations are available today that reduce water use and/or loss, as well as improve the soil's moisture balance due to their improved designs. Drylands countries experiencing water scarcity need to invest in water use reduction techniques, technologies and infrastructures. These include household appliances such as sanitation installations that should be researched, developed and preferentially marketed. Incentive measures that promote the development and use of such innovations must be rigorously supported.

Apart from investment in water-use-reduction technologies, investments in innovations that curb DLDD, particularly in drylands, must be made to reduce negative impacts on the water base. Regularly cited examples are the development of agricultural systems, such as improved irrigation systems, and improved water and soil management technologies at the farm level. The appropriate management of water disposal and sanitation is another important issue, which can also lead to efficient use of water through highly advanced recycling technologies.

Investing in water and production system research, management and policy-making capacities and addressing the linkages to desertification, land degradation and drought

Many dryland countries are developing nations where capacity development is a critical issue – as is strongly reflected in the UNCCD ten-year strategy. In addition to the need for technical capacities, which promote advances in technical and technological development, capacities should be developed at all levels to implement and act on water and DLDD-related issues. There is a need to build or strengthen national water and other related institutions with adequate support and decentralizing. There is also a need for local level institutions to act on immediate water management requirements on the ground (Iza and Stein, 2009). Many countries are devolving water management structures and institutions – structures that are charged with managing demand, maintaining infrastructure, and coordinating payment schedules (see chapters 25, 'Water and institutional change: Responding to present and future uncertainty' and 26, 'Developing knowledge and capacity'). These structures should also address land management and DLDD-related water issues. For example, village societies in India often address integrated agendas and more recently have also dealt with climate change risk and possible adaptation measures (Box 28.3). It is clear that similar capacities need to be built in other related sectors and production systems, such as agriculture and forestry. Crop research, for example, needs to shift from conventional agriculture to a more conservation-effective agriculture, such as adopting an eco-agriculture or agro-ecosystems approach.

Irrespective of the measures, it is critical to recognize that outreach and engagement of the local farmers and natural resource managers is imperative for the success of any intervention (see Box 28.3). Adoption

BOX 28.3

Participatory watershed management: A case from India

A watershed can be defined as a catchment area from which all water drains into a common area, making it a suitable target for technical efforts to manage water and soil resources (Shiferaw et al., 2008). A watershed connects various communities sharing a specific water resource depending on their specific position within the catchment. In the long run this creates interdependency in both the watershed resources and user communities.

Water scarcity and land degradation resulting from overgrazing was already a problem in Sukhomajri village in India in the 1970s. Local villagers, with institutional support, established a village society that was responsible for planning and implementing conservation activities in the village and later in surrounding areas, leading to the rehabilitation and more effective use of the farmland. Participatory decision-making and the establishment of formal governance structures in the village and later in the greater watershed area have been identified as key instruments for success. Evidence and information-based decision-making is promoted and villagers are directly involved in adaptive management. In this village, sustainable land management (SLM) practices were integrated with water management practices from the beginning.

Source: Centre for Science and Environment (1998); Porras and Neves (2006); and Porras et al. (2008).

pathways for technologies as well as implementation of policies depend on the end user, and sufficient effort must be made to include such users in the design and development of solutions. It is clear that such outreach is resource-intense, however without this extra effort, limited progress can be made.

Water use efficiency

Water use efficiency in drylands should consider rehabilitation of degraded lands and conservation of water catchment areas, including reducing losses by lining channels, avoiding direct evaporation and avoiding runoff and percolation losses due to over-irrigation. Evaporation from the bare soil should be reduced by appropriate practices, such as mulching and applying weed control measures. Enhancement of crop growth by implementing sustainable land management practices is also important, such as choosing suitable and marketable crops, considering optimal timing for planting and harvesting, applying optimal tillage and green manures, and appropriate drainage systems.

Reducing water wastage

A vital contribution to managing water wisely is the reduction of water losses. At all levels of governance it is important that leakages are reduced or prevented. This includes support and know-how for local communities to implement integrated strategies and for using water resources efficiently and maintaining wells, taps and water points in good working conditions. On a larger scale, national water carriers, storage dams and other infrastructure need to be well maintained, and systems that help detect unaccounted-for water losses must be established. Innovative recycling and integrated multiple use systems especially for larger industries need to be designed and implemented.

Sustainable land management practices in the drylands

Poor and unsustainable land management techniques tend to worsen land and water resources degradation. Recent estimates indicate that nearly 2 billion hectares of land worldwide – an area twice the size of China – is already seriously degraded, some of it irreversibly (FAO, 2008). Over-cultivation, overgrazing and deforestation put great strain on water resources by reducing fertile topsoil and vegetation cover, and lead to greater dependence on irrigated cropping. Observed effects include siltation and reduced flow in rivers that feed large lakes such as the Aral Sea and Lake Chad, leading to the alarmingly fast retreat of the shorelines of these natural reservoirs in central Asia and northern Africa, respectively.

It is fundamental therefore to promote soil, water and vegetation conservation and to enhance measures that rehabilitate, conserve and protect the natural environment. Sustainable land management is one of the few options for sustaining livelihoods and generating income without destroying the quality of the land and the water resources which are the basis of production (Figure 28.6).

The essence of a sustainable land management approach finds expression in the coordination of the sectoral planning and management activities concerned with the various aspects of land, land use and water

Sub-Saharan Africa is predicted to be highly affected by drought and water scarcity in the face of climate change. Existing environmental problems – such as desertification, land degradation, floods and droughts – are expected to worsen with climate change. This will be a challenge to farmers and communities to adjust their production systems. Sustainable land management (SLM) strategies and practices enable farmers and communities to become more resilient to drought and water scarcity by increasing food production, conserving soil and water, enhancing food security, and restoring productive natural resources. Integrated land and water resources management tend to prevent land degradation, restore degraded lands, and reduce the need for further conversion of natural forests and grasslands to agricultural production (Woodfine, 2009), as well as enhancing the soil water retention capacity.

Other SLM practices that are relevant to mitigating drought and water scarcity include: crop diversification/intercropping; conservation tillage and conservation agriculture; organic agriculture; integrated plant nutrient management; and integrated plan and pest management, zero tillage farming, crop rotation, mulching and crop residues utilization and fallowing.

Sustainable land management makes it possible to minimize conflicts and make the most efficient trade-offs, and to link social and economic development with environmental protection and enhancement, thus helping to achieve the objectives of sustainable development.

resources (UNEP, 2007). Initiatives for sustainable land management are particularly significant for dryland ecosystems, where the majority of people are still engaged in primary agriculture, livestock production, forestry and fishery, and their livelihood and options for economic development are directly linked to the availability and quality of the land and water resources.

Examples of sustainable land management practices for drought and water scarcity mitigation and adaptation are presented in Box 28.4.

Prioritizing the use of water in drylands

The careful prioritization of water use is more important in the drylands than in any other ecosystems. Different land uses place different demands on water and other natural resources and ecosystem services. Based on the valuation of these resources, in-country policy decisions for water allocation, provision and pricing have to be made. Examples from Israel and Namibia calculate water use efficiency in terms of economic output per cubic metre of water consumed. It is clear in both countries that irrigated agriculture consumes the majority of water supplied (in Namibia 44%, in Israel 70%), while the economic returns measured in contribution to the gross national product or income generated are extremely low (Heyns et al., 1998). It is

FIGURE 28.6

The sustainable land management virtuous circle of improvement starts with land condition improvement

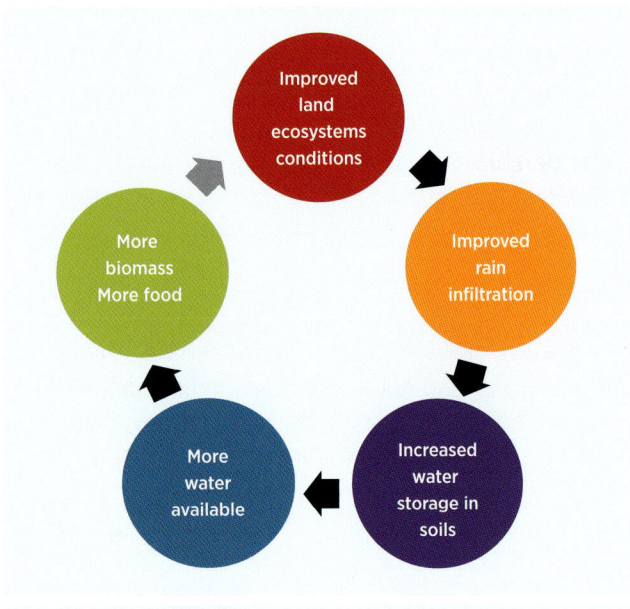

Source: UNCCD (2010).

notable that Israel is regarded as having one of the most efficient irrigation systems in the world and yet does not reap significant economic returns on water investments.

Policy changes needed in and for dryland countries

A variety of solutions and strategies have been developed to mitigate the impacts of water scarcity. These include empowering of existing institutions cooperating on transboundary river basins with the required authority to address water scarcity impacts, through opening consultations, pooling knowledge and initiating joint action. For years the integrated land and water resources management (ILWRM) principles have been promoted to enhance sustainable management of water resources. Management of the full cycle of water, where groundwater and surface water are linked with land management, has also come into the fold, with decentralization and the full participation of all stakeholders in the water sector considered imperative.

The major goal is to ensure the delivery of enough water to all communities. Therefore, sets of policy tools are needed to help decision-makers design tailored programmes to deal with water scarcity. For example, in countries where demand is driven largely by growth in the agricultural sector in the face of population growth, the most cost-effective policy solutions should be dominated by agricultural measures, both in irrigated and rainfed crop production. In countries where agriculture is expected to account for less water demand however, while household and industry demand account for higher consumption, the most cost-effective policy solutions will include some agricultural policy measures, but also a range of industrial efficiency measures and common household measures.

Water demand management

Water demand management is part of an integrated approach towards the sustainable development and use of water resources. This involves planning and establishing policies for efficient use of water, economic efficiency and environmental sustainability. Managing water demand can reduce water consumption, delay the implementation of additional water supplies and infrastructure, and conserve scarce water resources.

A special dryland debate: Food self-sufficiency versus food security

As food and water needs continue to rise, it is becoming increasingly difficult to supply more water to farmers. The supply of easily accessible freshwater resources is limited both locally and globally. In arid and semi-arid regions, in densely populated countries and in most of the industrialized world, competition for water resources has set in. In major food-producing regions, scarcity of water is spreading as a result of climate change and increased climate variability. In the light of demographic and economic projections, the freshwater resources not yet committed are a strategic asset for development, food security, the health of the aquatic environment and, in some cases, national security (Koohafkan and Steward, 2008).

Many dryland countries still pursue national policies for food self-sufficiency. Developing dryland countries in particular are exposed to great difficulties when it comes to assuring food-security, especially for rural communities threatened by frequent droughts and the impacts of DLDD. Although these communities live largely traditional lifestyles, which are often very well adapted to the prevailing climatic conditions (including nomadic/migratory lifestyles), modern aspirations and sometimes controversial government policies (e.g. forced settlement policies) have left such communities extremely vulnerable. Relevant alternatives and tools for planning are needed to assist with the prioritization and selection of the most appropriate and sustainable water and resource allocations. Under the projected medium and long-term climate change risks for dryland areas around the world, debates on food self-sufficiency or food security are gaining new significance and must be addressed more analytically to avoid entire nations facing aggravated DLDD and eventually famine, deteriorating development potential and increasing poverty.

Global investments in long-term food security in drylands with water scarcity

How to address food security in drylands experiencing water scarcity is a complex issue, and countries are confronted with difficult policy and development options. However as water availability, quality and accessibility are at the heart of local food production potential – and DLDD threats – it becomes imperative to explore and support promising alternatives. Many countries have been advised to promote and develop secondary and tertiary industries, a process that is often a very difficult undertaking in already marginalized and poor countries. While it is difficult enough to build up alternative production industries in developing countries with low human capacities, it is also difficult to secure reliable and equitable international food and commodity trade conditions that are conducive to the requirements of developing nations. Relevant in-country and international responses should be promoted to assist dryland countries in developing long-term food security strategies – at the same time curbing the threats of DLDD and worsening water scarcity conditions.

In tandem, meeting food security targets in the drylands requires the implementation of sustainable agricultural policies from which local populations would benefit most. As current irrigated cropping systems require the greatest share of water in most countries and demand is expected to rise 14% in the next 30 years (UNCCD, 2010), adaptation to this increase is vital and will require variability and flexibility. Changes to land use and cropping patterns are one option for adaptation. Less water-demanding and drought tolerant crops could also be an alternative. No-tillage, which is the practice of leaving residue of the previous season's crops on farmland, can increase water infiltration while reducing evaporation as well as controlling wind and water erosion. The use of other soil fertilization and techniques such as biochar – which simultaneously increases retention of soil moisture associated with carbon sequestration – is also promising.

Switching from annual to permanent or semi-permanent crops could be another option. The advantages of such farming include reducing tillage energy requirements, limited topsoil disturbance and soil erosion prevention. Multi-annual crops also bring the benefits of easy access to water and soil nutrients in deep soil layers. Land use changes should be considered where current agricultural patterns are no longer sustainable in terms of water consumption. Rehabilitation and conversion of marginal agricultural lands into suitable alternatives, such as forests or grassland, can prevent further land degradation and enhance soil water retention capacity and regeneration of the long-term farming potential of the land.

28.4.2 An international framework on land and water

The need to address pressing dryland-specific water issues is urgent. The impact of DLDD on water resources is a major problem and the associated water scarcity in the drylands is of overriding concern, especially in the context of the projected changes in climatic conditions. While a number of expert institutions within the UN are dealing with relevant individual issues (water, land, food security, etc.), there is a pressing need for

cooperation and agreements at the international level to address the problems of water scarcity specifically in the drylands. Addressing and coordinating such specific needs through establishing, for example, a water compact for drylands and a related multi-stakeholder dialogue can be useful.

The importance of multi-stakeholder coordination has been recognized within the UN system, both for effective agenda setting and for the coordination of interconnected issues such as effective water and land management for sustainable development.

Several relevant coordination mechanisms have been launched over the past years including UN-Water (www.unwater.org), which was established in 2003. UN-Water strengthens coordination and coherence among UN entities dealing with issues related to all aspects of fresh water and sanitation. Similar to the UN-Water approach, member governments called for a coherent UN system-wide response to the land challenges (UN-Land). A UN Issue Management Group (IMG) on land was established in September 2009 for a period of two years. The IMG proposed options for a coherent UN system-wide contribution to land challenges, including the implementation of the ten year strategic plan of the UNCCD. The IMG also prepared a UN system-wide rapid response report on drylands highlighting the importance of key emerging issues on the global agenda, including climate change, food security and human settlements. In addition, the IMG presented options for follow-up action on all issues that were included as priorities in the outcomes of the 17th session of the UN Commission on Sustainable Development.

Conclusions and recommendations

Water scarcity in the drylands is an increasingly pressing issue that needs to be recognized and addressed on the international agenda. It is exacerbated by the negative impacts of DLDD on the availability, quantity and quality of water resources. As DLDD imperatives take their toll, water crises and scarcity are expected to continue raising ethnic and political tensions, contributing to conflicts where water resources straddle or delineate country borders. In some countries, desertification, land degradation and the associated water scarcity inevitably exacerbates internal migrations, forcing whole villages to flee their farms and move to already overcrowded cities. In the next ten years, 50 million people are at risk of displacement if desertification is not checked. Implementing sustainable land and water management policies would help to overcome the challenge of these increasingly extreme situations.

The impact of water scarcity varies from region to region and from country to country. Countries that have the technical and financial capacity to deal with the effects of water scarcity tend to experience less severe impacts compared to poorer countries. The impacts of water scarcity are also experienced differently depending on whether the scarcity is chronic and long-term, periodic and unpredictable, or regional and local. Clear support mechanisms are required to aid the drylands countries, especially those with already vulnerable economies and development challenges, to address and invest in measures that can alleviate water scarcity in the future. Projected climate change impacts will pose an increasingly serious threat to human beings and development prospects in certain drylands areas. Hotspots in which worsening climatic conditions are expected to affect already vulnerable water resources must be identified and recognized, and urgent support measures must be put into place to address the water crises in such regions.

DLDD impacts on water resources are evident and must be addressed in an integrated manner with ongoing SLM activities. ILWRM is a key to achieving longer-lasting development advancements. The UN system can play a major role in establishing and coordinating multilateral action on the water crises in the drylands. The UNCCD is proposing establishing a 'Water Compact for Drylands', which could be a suitable tool to generate the necessary support for addressing this priority issue – water scarcity.

|||||||||||||||||||||||||||||||||||||||||||||||||||||||||||||||||||||||||||||||||||

References

Bhadauria, T. and Saxena, G. K. 2010. Role of earthworms in soil fertility maintenance through the production of biogenic structures. *Applied and Environmental Soil Science.* doi:10.1155/2010/816073.

Calder, I. R. 1998. *Water Resource and Land Use Issues.* SWIM Paper 3. Colombo, Sri Lanka, International Water Management Institute.

Centre for Science and Environment. 1998. Sukhomajri at the crossroads. *Down to Earth,* Vol. 7, No. 19981215. http://www. indiaenvironmentportal.org.in/node/302 (Accessed April 2010.)

CIA (Central Intelligence Agency). n.d. *The World Fact Book.* https://www.cia.gov/library/publications/the-world-factbook (Accessed April 2010)

Emerton, L. and Bos, E. 2004. *Value: Counting Ecosystems as an Economic Part of Water Infrastructures.* Gland, Switzerland/Cambridge, UK, International Union for Conservation of Nature and Natural Resources (IUCN).

Engel, S., Pagiola, S., and Wander, S. 2008. Designing payments for environmental services in theory and practice: an overview of the issues. *Ecological Economics,* Vol. 65, No. 4, pp. 663–74.

DG Environment – European Commission. 2007. *Water Scarcity and Droughts Second Interim Report June 2007.* DG Environment – European Commission. http://ec.europa. eu/environment/water/quantity/pdf/comm_droughts/2nd_ int_report.pdf

FAO (Food and Agriculture Organization). 1993. Prevention of water pollution by agriculture and related activities. Proceedings of FAO Expert Consultation, Santiago, Chile, 20–23 October 1992. *FAO Water Reports,* No. 1. Rome, FAO.

----. 2002. *Land Water Linkages in Rural Watersheds.* Proceedings of the electronic workshop organized by the FAO Land and Water Development Division 18 September–27 October 2000. *FAO Land and Water Bulletin,* No. 9. Rome, FAO.

----. 2008. *Sustainable Land Management.* NR factsheet, produced by Natural Resources Management and Environment Department. ftp://ftp.fao.org/docrep/ fao/010/ai559e/ai559e00.pdf

Harrison, P. and Pearce, F. 2000. *AAAS Atlas of Population and Environment.* Berkeley, CA, University of California Press.

Heyns, P., Montgomery, S., Pallett, J. and Seely, M. 1998. *Namibia's Water: A Decision Makers' Guide.* Windhoek, Namibia, Water and Rural Development, Department of Water Affairs, Ministry of Agriculture.

Iza, A. and Stein, R. (eds). 2009. *Rule – Reforming Water Governance.* Gland, Switzerland, International Union for Conservation of Nature and Natural Resources (IUCN).

KCS (Kalahari Conservation Society). n.d. *Every River has its People.* http://www.kcs.org.bw/Page.aspx?PID=58 (Accessed April 2010.)

Koohafkan, P. and Steward, B. 2008. *Water and Cereals in Drylands.* Rome/London, FAO/Earthscan.

Lean, G. 2009. Water scarcity 'now bigger threat than financial crisis'. *The Independent,* 16 March 2009. http:// www.independent.co.uk/environment/climate-change/ water-scarcity-now-bigger-threat-than-financial-crisis-1645358.html (Accessed April 2010.)

Leonard, J. and Rajot, J. L. 2001. Influence of termites on runoff and infiltration: Quantification and analysis. *Geoderma,* Vol. 104, No. 1, pp. 17–40.

Mando, A., Brussaard, L. and Stroosnijder, L. 1999. Termite and mulch-mediated rehabilitation of vegetation on crusted soil in West Africa. *Restoration Ecology,* Vol. 7, No. 1, pp. 33–41.

Millennium Ecosystem Assessment. 2005. *Ecosystems and Human Well-being: Desertification Synthesis.* World Resources Institute, Washington, DC.

Porras, I., Grieg-Gran, M. and Neves, N. 2008. All that glitters: A review of payments for watershed services in developing countries. *Natural Resource Issues* No. 11. London, International Institute for Environment and Development (IIED).

Porras, I. and Neves, N. 2006. Markets for watershed services – country profile. *Watershed Markets.* London, UK, International Institute for Environment and Development (IIED).

Schlesinger, W. 1997. *Biogeochemistry an Analysis of Global Change.* London, Academic Press.

Shiferaw, B. et al. 2008. *Community Watershed Management in Semi-arid India – The State of Collective Action and its Effects on Natural Resources and Rural Livelihoods.* CAPRI Working Paper No. 85. Washington, DC, CGIAR Systemwide Program on Collective Action and Property Rights (CAPRi), International Food Policy Research Institute.

Smith, M., de Groot, D., Perrot-Maître, D. and Bergkamp, G. (eds.). 2006. *Pay: Establishing Payments for Watershed Services.* Gland, Switzerland, International Union for Conservation of Nature and Natural Resources (IUCN).

UN (United Nations). 1948. *The Universal Declaration of Human Rights.* New York, General Assembly of the United Nations. http://www.un.org/Overview/rights.html

––––. 2010. *Resolution Recognizing Access to Clean Water, Sanitation as Human Right.* Sixty-fourth General Assembly Plenary, 108th Meeting, New York. http://www.un.org/News/Press/docs/2010/ga10967.doc.htm

UNCCD (United Nations Convention to Combat Desertification). 1994. *United Nations Convention to Combat Desertification in Countries Experiencing Serious Drought and/or Desertification, Particularly in Africa.* Bonn, Germany, UNCCD. http://www.unccd.int/convention/text/pdf/conv-eng.pdf (Accessed 12 September 2011.)

––––. 2010. *Water Scarcity and Desertification.* Thematic Fact Sheet Series No. 2. http://www.unccd.int/documents/Desertificationandwater.pdf (Accessed on 16 August 2011.)

UNEP (United Nations Environment Programme). 2007. Chapter 10: Integrated approach to the planning and management of land resources. *Agenda 21.* http://www.unep.org/Documents.Multilingual/Default.asp?DocumentID=52&ArticleID=58&l=en (Accessed April 2010.)

Vågen, Tor-G. 2007. *Assessment of Land Degradation in the Sasumua Watershed: Baseline Report.* Technical report conducted by KAPSLM and Sasumua Local Farmers Association. Nairobi, World Agroforestry Centre.

de Wit, M. and Stankiewicz, J. 2006. Changes in surface water supply across Africa with predicted climate change. *Science,* Vol. 311, No. 5769, pp. 1917–1921.

Woodfine, A. 2009. *Using Sustainable Land Management Practices to Adapt to and Mitigate Climate Change in Sub-Saharan Africa.* TERRAFRICA Regional Sustainable Land Management. www.terrafrica.org

White, R. P and Nackoney, J. 2003. *Drylands, People, and Ecosystem Goods and Services: A Web-based Geospatial Analysis.* Washington, DC, World Resources Institute. http://www.wri.org/publication/drylands-people-and-ecosystem-goods-and-services

Wikipedia. n.d. List of countries by Human Development Index. http://en.wikipedia.org/wiki/List_of_countries_by_Human_Development_Index (Accessed April 2010)

CHAPTER 29
Africa

WWAP, in consultation with UN Water/Africa, AMCOW and UNECA
—

Authors Albert Wright, Kodwo Andah and Michael Mutale
Acknowledgements Daniel Adom, Roberto Chionne, Christine Young Adjei and Stephen Max Donkor (review)

After decades of poor economic growth, Africa is now experiencing prospects of robust growth. But without innovative and concerted efforts, this will not be able to be sustained.

As a result of natural and man-made challenges, the region's water resources are vastly underdeveloped.

Although sub-Saharan Africa uses barely 5% of its annual renewable freshwater, access to improved water supply in both urban and rural contexts is still the lowest in the world. Lack of sanitation facilities is an even greater challenge to water management in Africa. If MDG Target 7c on drinking water and sanitation is to be achieved, the number of people served must more than double, from 350 million in 2000 to 720 million in 2015.

If governments do not take immediate and radical action, the urban slum population in sub-Saharan African countries is expected to double, from 200 million in 2005, by 2020.

The lack of access to adequate and safe drinking water and food security is not necessarily tied to the availability of water itself but rather to low adaptive capacity, lack of effective development strategies, lack of effective regional and subregional institutional frameworks, and economic and financial constraints.

Transboundary river basin management must find ways of turning potential conflicts into constructive cooperation and 'zero-sum predicaments' – in which one party's gain is another's loss – into win–win situations.

29.1 Regional issues and recent developments

Africa is home to 54 countries. It is a region characterized by transboundary waters, with international river basins covering about 62% of its land area. The region is also endowed with precious industrial and strategic minerals. Yet these resources remain largely under-exploited, leaving Africa as one of the poorest and least developed regions of the world. In fact, economic performance from the mid-1970s to the early 1990s was so poor the period was dubbed the 'lost decade'.

However, in recent years this situation has changed for the better. Analysis by *The Economist* (2011) reveals that in the first decade of the new millennium, leading up to 2010, ten of the fastest growing economies in the world were in Africa. There are also positive indicators showing that far-reaching economic reforms adopted across the region have begun to yield positive results in many of its countries. Negative GDP growths have given way to progressively increasing growth across the region, averaging around the mean figures for developing countries (Figure 29.1). In terms of per capita GDP growth, however, Africa is still far behind all other regions (Figure 29.2).

Hence, in its Outlook for Africa document *Africa's Pulse*, the World Bank (2011) reports that, prior to the present worldwide economic crisis, more than a decade of steady growth and debt relief had strengthened African countries' fiscal balances. By 2008, 72% of African countries had positive primary fiscal balances compared with 28% in the early 1990s. Figure 29.3 shows the dynamics of economic growth in the region, and, as depicted in Figure 29.4, among the 15 fastest growing economies of the world, 12 are in Africa. All this shows that in spite of the perturbations in the global economy, as well as drought in the eastern parts of the continent, Africa's growth prospects for the forecast horizon remain robust.

> Africa appears to be endowed with abundant water resources. It has 17 rivers with a total estimated catchment area of over 100,000 km², 160 lakes larger than 27 km². It has vast wetlands and a limited but widespread groundwater resource. In addition, it has a huge potential for energy production through hydropower production... [However], there are natural and man-made challenges that make it difficult to capture the inherent benefits and the full potential in Africa's water resources to support sustainable developments in Africa. (SARPN, 2002, p. 13)

As is the case with other natural resources in the region, the water resources of Africa are vastly underdeveloped; however, it is now generally recognized

FIGURE 29.1

Annual GDP growth rate

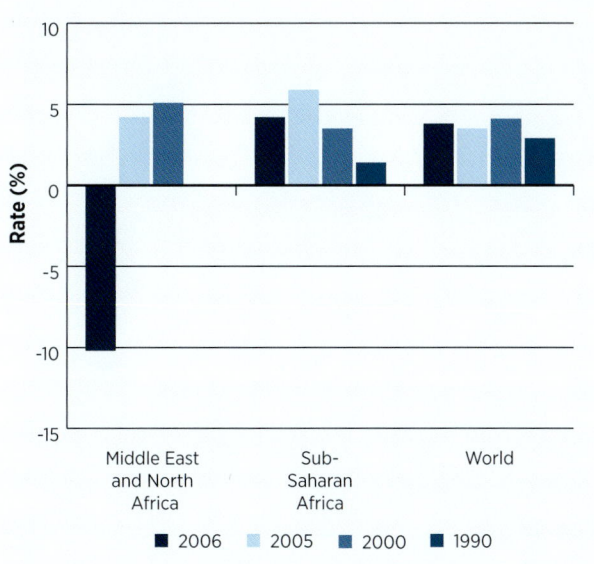

Sources: Prepared by K. Andah from data from World Bank (2008) and the EarthTrends database (no longer active) from the World Resources Institute.

FIGURE 29.2

Per capita GDP (constant $US)

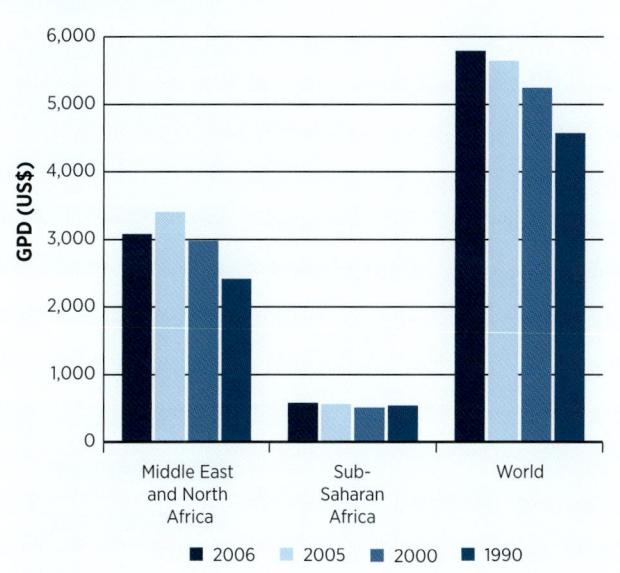

Sources: Prepared by K. Andah from data from World Bank (2008) and the EarthTrends database (no longer active) from the World Resources Institute.

FIGURE 29.3

Dynamics of sub-Saharan Africa economic growth

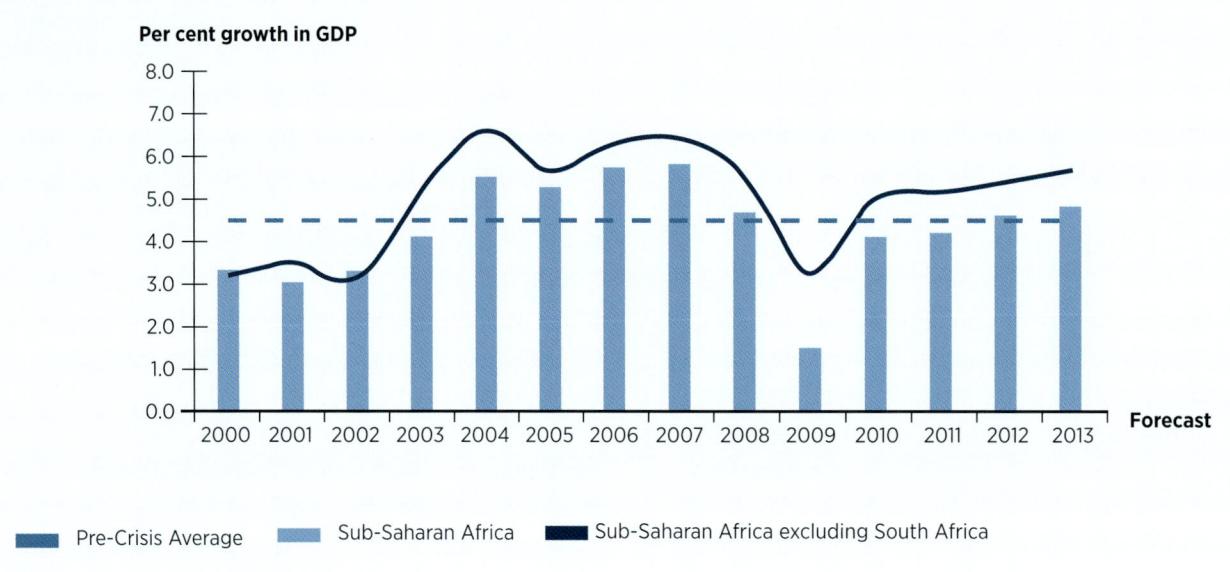

Per cent growth in GDP

| Pre-Crisis Average | Sub-Saharan Africa | Sub-Saharan Africa excluding South Africa |

Source: World Bank (2011, fig. 2, p.3).

FIGURE 29.4

Fastest growing economies of sub-Saharan Africa

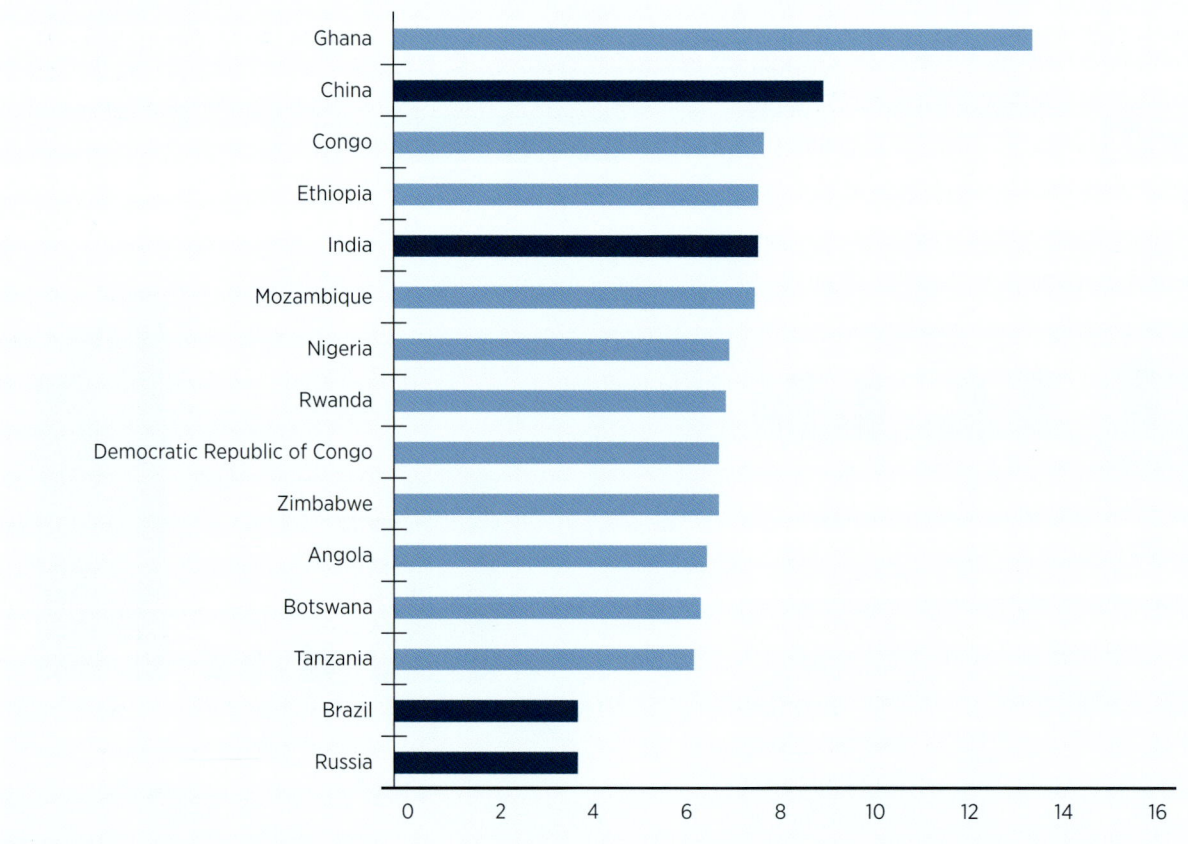

Source: World Bank (2011, fig, 3, p. 3).

that water has a vital role to play in the development agenda for the region. It is understood that although water can become an instrument for sustainable development, it can also become a constraint, 'capable of wiping away the gains of development either progressively or overnight, as happened in Mozambique in the floods of 2000' (SARPN, 2002, p. 2). Its improper management can result in degradation of productive soils, as has been happening in the Sahel region; or in the loss of valuable ecosystem use, as is occurring in the Lake Chad basin. In addition, unless appropriate approaches are followed, economic and social development could negatively impact on the availability and quality of water resources, thereby limiting their value for future development. There is therefore a concerted effort to address challenges that may hamper the effective development and management of the region's water resources. These efforts are enshrined in the African Water Vision 2025, which was endorsed by the African Union in 2004 and serves as the basis for water development and management by the African Ministers' Council on Water (AMCOW), the African Development Bank (AfDB) and the UN system organized as UN Water/Africa.

This chapter reviews some of the drivers and challenges being encountered in water resources management in the region. It reviews the risks and uncertainties they pose, and presents some of the response measures being followed.

29.2 External drivers
29.2.1 Climate change

Africa is characterized by extreme climatic zones; from humid equatorial and tropical zones through the semi-arid to the arid North, creating about seven distinct hydro-climatic zones. The distribution of rainfall over Africa therefore exhibits extreme unevenness, both spatially and temporally. (UNECA, 2001, p. 1)

On a continental basis, Africa has a relatively plentiful supply of rainwater: a total of 20,359 km³ per year or 678 mm per year (FAO, 2005). The variation in precipitation is determined by climate variability, which is in turn driven by the movement of the Inter-Tropical Convergence Zone (ITCZ). Average precipitation is distributed over the continent from the equator towards the northern and southern fringes in a diminishing manner. Risks due to uncertainties inherent in

movement of the ITCZ are manifested in high seasonality in rainfall, uncertain timing of the onset and duration of the rainfall season, and frequent hydrometeorological extremes of floods and droughts.

Rainfall anomalies, both positive and negative, are very frequent over the continent. Most freshwater comes from seasonal rains, which vary with the climatic zone. The greatest rainfall occurs along the equator, especially the area from the Niger Delta to the Congo River Basin. The Sahara Desert has virtually no rain … Southern Africa receive[s] 12% … of the region's rainfall (FAO, 1995). In Western and Central Africa, rainfall is exceptionally variable and unpredictable. (UNECA, 2001, p. 3)

Several factors influence climate variability in the region. The most dominant is the El Niño-Southern Oscillation (ENSO), which is responsible for inter-annual climate variability over eastern and southern Africa. The 1997–1998 ENSO event resulted in extreme weather conditions over eastern Africa; and the 1999–2000 La Niña is suspected to have caused the devastating floods in Mozambique. In the Sahel, ENSO appears to influence annual variation and reduces rainfall. Rainfall variability in the area is also influenced by factors like sea surface temperature (SST) and atmospheric dynamics. Across western Africa, the Atlantic Ocean plays a key role in year-to-year changes in seasonal climatic variations.

The climate in the region also displays high interdecadal variability. It appears that aerosols and dust may also play important roles in modulating climate variability in the region, indicating the presence of extremely dense and deep dust layers in the Sahel/Sudan area (reaching several kilometres) during the main Harmattan or dust season from November to April.

29.2.2 Transboundary water basins
Transboundary water basins cover two-thirds of the total land area in the region. They are 'home to three-quarters of the entire African population and account for a staggering 93% of the total surface water resource base of the continent' (Turton et al., 2006, p. 23). Some of them are shared by as many as ten countries.

The continent has over 80 major river/lake basins, some of which are among the largest in the world. About 55 of the world's 200 major international rivers are in Africa – a number greater than in any other continent. ...The political boundaries of four-teen African countries almost entirely fall within the catchment areas of one or more transboundary river systems. (UNECA, 2006, p. 201)

Ten major river basins are shared by more than four African countries:

The Nile Basin, for instance, has 10 riparian coun-tries [9 within sub-Saharan Africa]; the Congo has 9, the Niger has 11, and the Zambezi has 9. The Volta has 6 and the Chad has 8. Then there are countries through which several international rivers pass. One extreme case is Guinea, which has 12 such rivers.

Water interdependency is accentuated by the fact that high percentages of total flows in downstream countries originate from outside their borders. For example, ... in Mauritania and Botswana, the cor-responding figures are 95% and 94%, respectively; in the Gambia it is 86% and in the Sudan it is 77%. (Mwanza, 2005, p. 99)

Of great importance is the transboundary Nubian Sandstone Aquifer System beneath the north-eastern Sahara, with a total extension of over 2.2 million km^2.

This is shared between four countries: Chad, Egypt, Libya and Sudan. It is the world's biggest repository of fossil water with a volume estimated from 150,000 km^3 to 457,550 km^3. The most important sub-basins are the western Kufra Basin and the eastern Dahkla Basin. Actual withdrawal rates by the main riparian countries have been estimated (Bakhbakhi, 2004) as:

- Egypt: 1,029 mm^3 per year
- Libya: 857 mm^3 per year
- Sudan: 407 mm^3 per year
- Chad: very low rate

29.2.3 Demographic pressures

Pressures emanating from the region's population dynamics, especially rapid rural migration into peri-urban areas, constitute a major challenge to the pro-vision of water and sanitation services, coupled with fast growing urban centres. An estimated 61% of the region's population lives in rural areas, exceeding the world average of 50%, and the average population density is 29 inhabitants per km^2, with very high vari-ations at national and subregional levels. The region's urban population grew at 3.4% between 2005 and 2010, which is 1.1% faster than the rural population growth rate (UNEP, 2010). The urban slum popula-tion in African countries is expected to double by 2020, from 200 million in 2005, if governments do

FIGURE 29.5

Population distribution in Africa

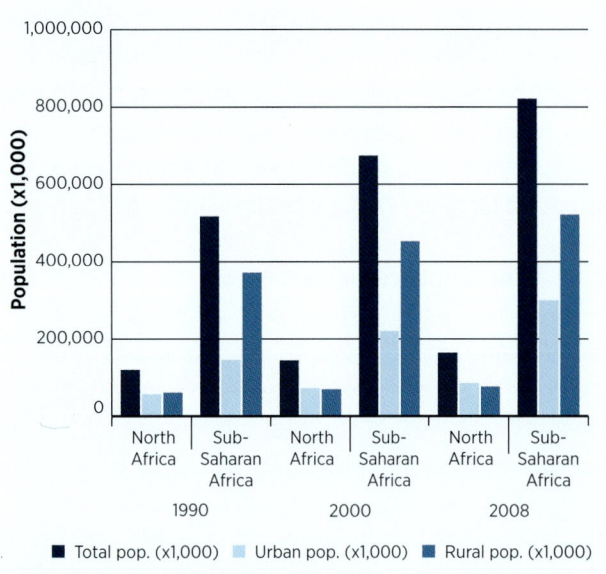

Sources: Prepared by K. Andah from data from WHO/UNICEF (2010), UNDESA (2007), and the EarthTrends database (no longer active) from the World Resources Institute.

FIGURE 29.6

Comparative population growth rate

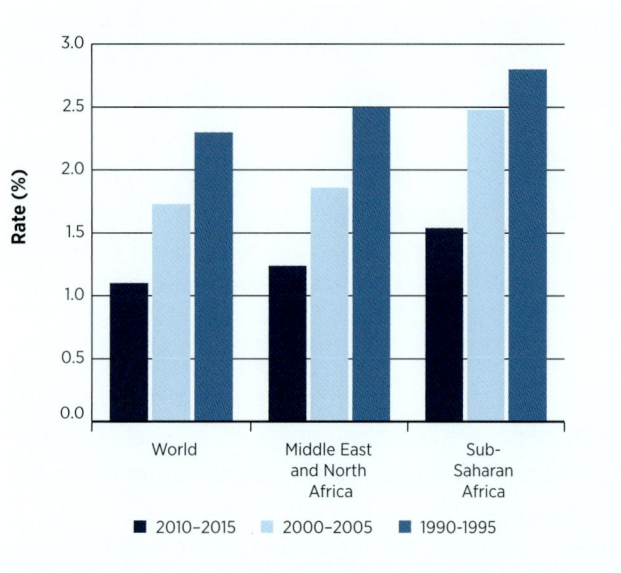

Sources: Prepared by K. Andah from data from UNDESA (2007) and the EarthTrends database (no longer active) from the World Resources Institute.

not take immediate and radical action (UN-Habitat, 2005). However, urban slum populations are highly mobile and the numbers are difficult to assess. It is clear, though, that improvements are not keeping pace with the rapid urbanization of slum populations (UN-Habitat, 2010). This rapid and poorly managed growth of urban areas, especially in peri-urban slums, has overwhelmed most municipal water services and constitutes a major challenge to water and sanitation development.

In 2004, Africa's population was estimated at 868 million inhabitants, representing about 14% of the world's population. At the time that total population growth in Africa appeared to be stabilizing (Figure 29.5), the global population growth rate was progressively decreasing, from about 2.8% in 1990–1995 to a projected value of about 2.3% in 2010–2015 (Figure 29.6). This trend, coupled with an increasing trend of economic growth, is likely to contribute to increased prospects for socioeconomic development.

29.3 Principal risks, uncertainties and opportunities

29.3.1 Principal risks
Principal risks in Africa include water scarcity, extreme hydrological events, water quality degradation, and loss of water-related ecosystems.

Water scarcity
Although blessed with an abundant water supply, Africa is the second driest continent in the world, after Australia. It is estimated that around 200 million people in sub-Saharan Africa face serious water shortages, and that by 2025 nearly 230 million will face water scarcity (UNEP, 2008). One of the consequences of this is the prevalence of aridity and drought conditions. About 16% of the population in the region lives in semi-arid areas. In Niger, severe drought resulted in famine in 2005, causing food insecurity for 2.5 million people (WFP, 2005). According to Sharma et al. (1996) eight countries in sub-Saharan Africa were suffering from water stress or water scarcity in 1990, and the World Bank estimates that by 2025, the number of countries experiencing water stress will rise to 18, affecting 600 million people.

There are many contributing factors to the increase in water scarcity in the region. Climate change is a major factor. In the case of the long-term drought that afflicted the Sahel from the 1960s to the 1990s, and caused widespread disasters, sea surface temperature changes were implicated. Other likely contributing factors were under-investment in water storage infrastructure, use of inefficient systems, rapid population growth, expanding urbanization, and increased economic and industrial development. Additional factors include changes in lifestyles, as well as poor and unsustainable land management practices like over-grazing, over-cultivation and deforestation.

In addition to drought and aridity, risks from water scarcity include conflict between sectors and between countries, land and water quality degradation, eutrophication, siltation, salination, alkalinization of soils, reduced flows in rivers and adverse impacts on business.

29.3.2 Uncertainty
The two basic sources of uncertainty in water resources management in Africa are natural variability in physical phenomena and incomplete knowledge.

An example of natural variability is the distribution of rainfall, which exhibits extreme unevenness, both spatially and temporally over the region (see Section 29.2.1). As regards incomplete knowledge, the major cause in the region is two-fold, namely inadequate historical hydrometeorological data, and lack of scientific understanding of the nature of the physical phenomena and processes. Inadequate past investment in hydrometeorological data collection and analysis has led to hydrological, hydraulic and structural uncertainties. This, combined with the lack of scientific understanding of the systems and processes taking place, has resulted in inadequate knowledge about the present and past states of the resource being managed. There is also a lack of knowledge about how the water resource systems will change over time. In effect, it is impossible to adequately model current situations and predict future conditions, or to construct appropriate probabilities necessary to understand the nature of the hazards facing vulnerable groups so that appropriate strategies for addressing the risks they face can be developed. As a result of the complexity of the physical phenomena, both types of uncertainties are expected to remain in the foreseeable future. This highlights a need for water resources management, including integrated water resources management (IWRM) practices, to adapt to reflect these uncertainties.

29.3.3 Opportunities

Some of these transboundary water basins in the region hold tremendous potential for mutually beneficial uses, including cross-boundary hydropower generation, large-scale multi-country irrigation schemes, inter- and intra-country navigation, joint inland fisheries development, joint water supply projects, environmental protection, wildlife conservation, recreation and eco-tourism development. The Congo River Basin alone holds almost 30% of Africa's total fresh surface water reserves and the world's largest hydropower potential in any one single river basin [an estimated 100,000 MW of power production capacity] …

The main thrust of the management of transboundary river basins is to find ways of turning potential conflicts into constructive cooperation, and to turn what is often perceived as a zero-sum predicament – in which one party's gain is another's loss – into a win-win situation. (UNECA, 2006, pp. 201–4)

The challenge is to adopt a paradigm shift from water sharing to benefits sharing.

Integrated development of these transboundary natural resources will not only contribute significantly to the socio-economic development of the Riparian countries sharing these rivers and lakes, they will also promote and enhance sub regional and regional cooperation for economic integration in Africa. However, integrated development of these resources on the basis of win-win principles needs enhanced and concerted cooperation among the Riparian countries sharing these resources. (UNECA, 2006, pp. 202)

The SADC example

As a vivid example, under the auspices of the Southern African Development Community (SADC), falling within the framework of the Revised Protocol on Shared Water Courses in SADC, South Africa has entered into various cooperation agreements on multilateral projects with relevant riparian countries on subregional integration, including the following (Turton et al., 2006):

- The Lesotho Highlands Water Project, comprising dams, tunnels and pipelines for transferring water from rivers in Lesotho, through the divide onto the Vaal river catchment in South Africa
- The Komati River Development Project, consisting currently of the Maguga and Driekoppies Dams for

storing water mainly for irrigation development in Swaziland and South Africa
- The Noord-Oewer Irrigation Project, which uses South African infrastructure for a development in Namibia
- The Barberton Water Supply Project, which draws water from the Lomati River in Swaziland for use in South Africa
- The Phongolo Poort Dam where Swaziland has granted South Africa a storage servitude
- The Gaberone Water Supply Project, which transfers water from South Africa to the capital of Botswana

The most pressing challenge is the lack of complete, reliable and consistent data about the transboundary water resources, especially groundwater; followed by weak institutional frameworks. Thus, there is the potential for conflicts over these waters. Nevertheless, there are also over 90 international water agreements to help manage shared water basins on the African continent (UNEP, 2010).

Inter-basin water transfer schemes

The Lesotho Highlands Water Project (LHWP), listed above, is an example of an inter-basin water-transfer scheme. The Congo Cross-Border Water Pipeline Project (CWPP) is another such example. As envisaged, the latter project will involve diverting water from one of the river's southern tributaries by pumping it over the Angolan highlands to boost the flow of a tributary of the Kavango River. The CWPP is expected to be the biggest water project in sub-Saharan Africa. It is estimated to cost US$6 billion and will generate thousands of jobs for local economies in Angola, Botswana, Central African Republic, the Democratic Republic of the Congo (DRC), Namibia and the Sudan. It will also generate huge business opportunities such as electricity and communications supplies resulting from the fibre optics that will be positioned along the pipelines.

Namibia sees the water from Congo as an ideal opportunity to have 'irrigation schemes in the Namib Desert, modelled on similar projects undertaken by Sahara desert countries'. To do that, however, Namibia will pump the water from the Kavango River (250 km) to deliver it to the capital, Windhoek. Botswana, on the other hand, intends to pump the water from the Kavango Delta (300 km) to the nearest agricultural area, or a further 700 km to its capital, Gaborone. (Ngurare, 2001; Tennyson, n.d.)

29.4 Geographical hotspots

29.4.1 The Sahel

One of the hotspots in Africa is the Sahel. The term refers both to an eco-climatic zone and to a geopolitical entity. The eco-climatic zone refers to the semi-arid transition region between the Sahara desert and the wetter regions of equatorial Africa. It extends from the Atlantic to the Indian Ocean, and it is characterized by dryness, intense heat and sporadic irregular rainfall, as well as periodic flooding and prolonged droughts that are often accompanied by widespread famine and large-scale deaths as well as the displacement of people and livestock.

Rainfall records, archaeological and other forms of evidence suggest that drought and floods, as well as consequent famines and other forms of widespread devastation that are characteristic of the Sahel in our time, are not a recent phenomenon. On the contrary, they have been a recurring feature in the region from time immemorial; what is more, they seem to be recurring with increasing intensity and frequency.

A major drought occurred in the Sahel from June to August 2010. There was also a major drought during the early 1970s, which caught the world unprepared and resulted in disasters of major proportions and resulted in costly international interventions. The nature of this experience raised questions about how best to coordinate the multitude of assistance efforts by donors and recipients. It also raised questions about the optimal balance between relief, recovery and development.

Consideration of these questions led to the establishment of a new organization in 1973 by heads of state and governments of countries in West Africa that have parts of their territories falling within the Sahel region. This organization is known as the Permanent Inter-State Committee for Drought Control in the Sahel (CILSS). The part of the broader eco-climatic Sahel zone that falls within the territorial boundaries of member states of the CILSS is what constitutes the geopolitical 'Sahel' region of West Africa.

There are nine Member States in the CILSS of which four are coastal countries (The Gambia, Guinea Bissau, Mauritania and Senegal), four are landlocked countries (Burkina Faso, Chad, Mali and Niger), and one is an island state (Cape Verde).

There are approximately 58 million people in the CILSS countries, which cover an area of 5.7 million km^2. In addition to having similar climatic conditions – the Sahel climate – the people of these countries:

> have a lot in common in terms of cultures and livelihood systems. These livelihood systems include agriculture, livestock herding, fishing, short and long-distance trading, and a variety of urban occupations. Dryland crops such as millet, sorghum and cowpeas constitute the staple foods of the populations while groundnut and cotton are the major cash crops. Farming in this region is almost entirely reliant on three to four months of summer rainfall, except along the banks of the major rivers, lakes, and other seasonal water courses, where some irrigation activities are undertaken. Livestock herding is a very important aspect of life in the region, and constitutes the major source of income in some areas. (UNEP, 2006, p. 2)

The mandate of CILSS is to invest in research in food security and in the fight against the effects of drought and desertification. Recognizing the crucial role water plays in its mandate, the members of CILLS have decided to form a complementary global coalition on water to address specific problems at a local level.

29.4.2 Lake Chad

Lake Chad is the fourth largest lake in Africa, after lakes Victoria, Tangayika and Nyasa. It is a very shallow freshwater lake, averaging about 1.5 m deep even in normal years. Its four riparian countries are Cameroon, Chad, Niger and Nigeria, who collectively comprise the original members of the Lake Chad Basin Commission (LCBC). The Central African Republic (CAR) became a member in 1994, Libya joined in 2008, and Sudan and the Republic of Congo were accepted as observer countries. The basin extends over an area of 2,397,423 km^2 distributed over eight countries as follows: Chad (46.3% of the basin), Niger (28%), CAR (9.1%), Nigeria (7.5%), Algeria (3.7%), Sudan (3.4%), Cameroon (1.9%) and Libya (0.1%).

The lake, first surveyed in 1823, is believed to be a remnant of a former inland sea that has grown and shrunk with changes in climate over the past 13,000 years. In 1964, when the LCBC was established, the lake covered an area of 25,000 km^2. Today, it covers an area of less than 1000 km^2 during the annual lowest water levels in the region.

The shrinkage has been attributed to many causes such as overgrazing in the area surrounding the lake, which triggers a process of desertification and the decline of vegetation. Some have placed the blame on human water use such as irrigation; others highlight climate change as a key factor.

The shrinkage is also reported to have given rise to disputes between countries over rights to the remaining water. Violence is also emerging between farmers and herders over the use of water.

> [The lake is] fringed by a zone of swampy vegetation dominated by reeds (*Phragmites spp.*), papyrus (*Cyperus papyrus*) and cattail (*Typha australis*) ... There are many small islands formed by the invasion of moving sand dunes near the northeastern coast; some of them are inhabited or utilized as bases for fishing. Besides the products of agriculture, livestock grazing and fishery, the drainage basin of L. Chad is known for its yield of natural soda, an activity that contributes to keeping the lake water fresh. (ILEC, n.d.)

The lake is home to many flora and fauna including over 44 species of algae, and has large areas of swamp and reed beds covered with *Yaere* grassland of *Echinoclora pyramidalis*, *Vetiveria nigritana*, *Oryza longistminata* and *Hyparrhenia rufa* varieties. Its floating islands host a wide variety of wildlife and large communities of migratory and near endemic birds. It is feared that the shrinking of the lake is threatening nesting sites of the Black Crowned Crane (*Bolearica pavonia pavonina*). The lake is also a good source of fish.

Environmental problems

A transboundary diagnostic analysis conducted in 1989 and 2007 by LCBC identified the following seven regional environmental problems (LCBC, 2008):
- Variability of the hydrological regime and availability of freshwater
- Water pollution
- Low variability of biological resources
- Loss of biodiversity
- Destruction and modification of ecosystems
- Sedimentation of rivers and water courses
- Invading species

They were all determined to be products of the combined effects of global climate change and the use of unsustainable practices and resources by the ever-growing basin populations.

Saving the lake and its basin

The LCBC has launched a programme to save the lake. A key feature of this effort is the Inter-Basin-Water Transfer Project (IBWT). This entails the transfer of water from the Congo/Oubangui Rivers into Lake Chad. Member States of the LCBC have already contributed the US$6.07 needed for the project's feasibility study. A complementary effort includes the following:
- The 2008 adoption by the LCBC Council of Ministers of a Strategic Action Plan developed within the framework of a GEF project. The aim of this Action Plan is to reverse the general ecosystem degradation trends in the area.
- The development of national action plans to meet the priorities of the national portions of the lake.

The proposed inter-basin water transfer project is envisaged as the solution to the problems of underdevelopment, food insecurity and poverty in the West and Central African subregion.

29.4.3 The Horn of Africa: Macroeconomic effects of drought

In addition to the turmoil in the global economy, parts of Africa are facing specific challenges, the most severe of which is the drought in the Horn of Africa – the worst in over 50 years. The most affected economy is Somalia, but parts of Ethiopia, Eritrea, Kenya and Tanzania are also suffering from poor rains and dry weather conditions. An estimated 13.3 million people are in need of humanitarian assistance across the Horn. With agriculture accounting for about 20% to 40% of GDP in most African countries, and with about 93% dependent on good rains, the impact of poor rains on GDP growth in sub-Saharan African economies can be significant.

Initial estimates suggest that in the average sub-Saharan African economy, every percentage decline in growth in the agricultural sector cuts GDP growth by 0.26 percentage points. However, the decline in GDP will differ by country, depending on the size of the agricultural sector in the country's economy and the strength of the agricultural sector's linkages with the rest of the economy. First quarter 2011 GDP figures for Kenya already show that growth in the agriculture sector slowed down to 2.2% compared to 5.7% over the same quarter in 2010. Coffee delivery fell by some 28%

in the first quarter of 2011 in Kenya and, for the first half of 2011, tea production fell by 16% (year-on-year) on account of the unseasonal hot and dry weather conditions and poorly distributed rainfall in tea-growing areas.

A simulated 10% reduction in crop and livestock production in the pastoralist areas in Ethiopia – the areas most affected by the current drought – shows agricultural growth declining by 0.6 percentage points and industry and services sectors by about 0.2 percentage points (for 2010–2011). The overall effect would be to dampen GDP growth by 0.4 percentage points. Households directly impacted by drought-related production shocks are likely to be severely affected as they lose income and livelihoods. To the extent that these shocks are reflected in prices at the local and national level, net consumers of food in both rural and urban areas lose. Persistence of drought or worsening of the severity of the drought would have more adverse effects. For example, a shock simulating three years of drought (i.e. through 2012–2013) would shave 0.3 percentage points off GDP growth in 2012 and 2013. Poor rains would reduce hydroelectric power generation in an environment where lack of adequate power supply is already a binding constraint on economic activity. Tanzania has carried out extensive power rationing in 2011. Some 90% of large firms in the country have their own generators which, being much more expensive, significantly reduce the profit margins of firms. In Tanzania, growth forecasts have already been lowered by some 0.3% on account of the lower rains, power outages and higher inflation rates.

There has also been some power rationing in Kenya. The Kenya Manufacturers Association estimates that generator power costs alone could account for some 40% of overall costs. The estimated impact of the drought and high food and fuel prices, combined with below normal rainfall, is a 1 percentage point reduction in GDP growth in Kenya. The GDP impact of the drought does not adequately capture the effects on households. In general, droughts affect poorer households disproportionately. For instance, in Kenya where some 3.8 million people are estimated to have been affected, the poverty head count in the drought-affected areas averages 70% compared with a national poverty rate of 47%. Similarly, in Ethiopia the majority of the 4.8 million people affected by the drought live below the poverty line. In both countries, cereal prices have risen sharply, significantly reducing the purchasing power of poor households, who spend 60–70% of their incomes on food (World Bank, 2011).

29.5 Response measures

Using the Africa Water Vision 2025 as the regional policy framework, a number of initiatives have been undertaken since 2000 to respond to these regional challenges. They include initiatives at regional level (by such organizations as the African Union, the UN Economic Commission for Africa, AfDB, UN Water/Africa, AMCOW, the Africa Water Task Force, the New Partnership for Africa's Development [NEPAD] and the Africa Water Facility); initiatives at basin level (by various water basin authorities) and actions at country level. Other responses include collaborations between regional and international water resources agencies like the Global Water Partnership (GWP)/AMCOW programme to support climate change adaptation in Africa region. In addition, a number of special and regular meetings on water have been introduced. These include the annual Africa Water Week series, AfricaSan meetings, and the Sharm el-Sheikh and Sirte Summits of the African Union, dedicated to discussion of water and agriculture, respectively.

29.5.1 Concerted African response to regional and international commitments

Political and institutional perspectives increasingly acknowledge that regional and subregional concerted efforts can go a long way to ensure that African countries can face the challenging task of mobilizing their water resources for sustainable development in the face of climate variability and change and other uncertainties. It is therefore important to pool all human and institutional resources at local, national, subregional and continental scales to tackle the common challenges by improving:
- Understanding and quantitative knowledge of the various sources of uncertainty
- The way in which this is communicated to water resource managers and other stakeholders
- The way in which uncertainty is incorporated into water resource management decision-making (Hughes, 2008)

The challenges include the need for early warning systems for the prediction of:
- Onset and duration of rainfall seasons
- Intra seasonal dry spells
- Rainfall anomalies based on inter-hemispherical teleconnections
- Lead time of impacts of El Niño and La Niña

African Union initiatives, AMCOW, the African Water Facility and the increasing role of the AfDB in water resources development and management, with special reference to the rural water and sanitation sector, all testify to ongoing high commitments to water resources development and management. The meetings of the 2nd Extraordinary Session of Heads of State and Governments of the African Union, in Sirte, Libya in 2004 dedicated to agriculture, and the African Union Summit of Heads of State on Water and Sanitation held at Sharm el-Sheikh, Egypt in 2008, in particular, reflect political support at the highest level. The annual Africa Water Week series, held under the auspices of AMCOW and launched in 2007, have added further impetus to the platform for information sharing and awareness on water resources development and management. There is now an urgent need for wider international cooperation to augment regional and subregional efforts. This can be through collaborative efforts such as the EU-Africa Strategic Initiative and others to be developed with other development partners, such as the growing relationships with developing Asian partners, in particular Japan.

These continental and subregional institutional frameworks are necessary for 'strengthening specialized institutional capacities in order to provide useful and reliable data-information-knowledge and services in support of more effective development policies, economic plans, socio-economic activities and investments across the African continent' (UNECA, 2010, p. 2), which take into account the uncertainties in climate change. For example:

> African climate institutions like the African Centre for Meteorological Applications for Development (ACMAD), the IGAD Climate Prediction and Applications Centre (ICPAC), the SADC Drought Monitoring Centre (SADC-DMC) have worked on the CRM [Climate Risk Management] approach in conjunction with the International Research Institute for Climate and Society (IRI) and are building capacities for its smooth integration within sectoral decision-making processes, such as agricultural production, food security, water resource management, health protection and disaster risk management. (UNECA, 2010, p. 3)

They can also facilitate the harmonization of legal frameworks at the regional level for protecting shared water resources and for making their use sustainable through a benefit-sharing paradigm. Feasible arrangements can also be made for inter-basin water transfer schemes that involve saving dying water ecosystems such as Lake Chad, and initiating transfers from water-rich basins to drier zones like the Sahel. Many such projects are being studied across the continent (UN Water/Africa, 2007).

29.5.2 Implementation of targets under the African Water Vision and the MDGs

During 1999–2000, the Organisation of African Unity (OAU) (now the African Union), together with the United Nations Economic Commission for Africa (UNECA), GWP branches in Africa and the AfDB mobilized human and material resources for the drafting and adoption of the African Water Vision 2025 along with its Framework for Action, and towards Africa's full participation in the 2nd World Water Forum in The Hague in 2000. Financed by the secretariat of the 2nd World Water Forum, the final document was published by UNECA. Implementation of the provisions of the Vision include: the Accra conference on Sustainable Development in 2002, the first Pan African Water Conference in 2003 (Box 29.1), the development of the Africa Water Facility in 2004, and the publication in 2006 of the first edition of the *African Water Development Report* (Box 29.2).

The Accra Conference on Sustainable Development
The first, most significant activity to flow from the Africa Water Vision was the Accra Conference on Water and Sustainable Development, held in April 2002. The conference was organized by the Africa Water Task Force (AWTF) with financial support from the Government of the Netherlands. Its success was followed by the organization of the Water Dome event by the AWTF during the World Conference on Sustainable Development, held in Johannesburg later in 2002. The Water Dome enabled all water-related activities to be conducted at a single venue during the conference.

African Water Facility
The African Water Facility (AWF) is an initiative developed by AWTF, and developed under the leadership of AMCOW and AfDB. It is hosted by AfDB, at the request of AMCOW, and is designed to mobilize resources to finance water resources development activities in Africa within the framework of building African capacity for effective water resources project development, preparation and implementation.

Within this context it has been estimated 'that on aggregate, US$20 billion per year will be required to achieve the targets of the African Water Vision 2025' (NEPAD, 2006). Out of this amount, it is estimated that about US$10 billion is required to meet urgent water needs. The AWF therefore focuses its operational support on the attainment of the following main strategic objectives:

- Strengthen water governance
- Mobilize and apply resources to meet urgent water and sanitation needs
- Strengthen the financial base
- Improve water knowledge

Since it became operational in 2006, the AWF has approved 66 projects at a total investment of €79 million.

The African Water Information Clearing House (AWICH)
UNECA has been entrusted by UN Water/Africa with setting up an information clearing house for water-related issues in Africa. A technical group was created to discuss in detail the modalities and technicalities of the clearing house. The African Water Information Clearing House was finally established in 2005 as part of the UNECA website, and covers the following water and environmental components:

- Rainfall and climatic data
- Environment
- Rivers
- Lakes
- Groundwater
- Seas/oceans
- Water quality

BOX 29.1

The Pan African Water Conference

The first Pan African Implementation and Partnership Conference on Water was convened by AMCOW, UN-Water/Africa and the AfDB and was held at the United Nations Conference Centre in Addis Ababa from 8–13 December 2003. The second was held in November 2009 at Addis Ababa.

'The [first] Conference attracted more than 1400 delegates and 45 ministers in charge of water, environment and housing. The participants included national delegates, key stakeholders, intergovernmental organizations, co-operation development partners and non-governmental organizations (NGOs)' (UNECA, 2006, p. 293). The Conference confirmed the determination of African countries in 'confronting issues of integrated water resources management (IWRM) and in meeting the targets of the Millennium Development Goals (MDGs), both at national and subregional levels, and also through partnerships at the international level, by placing water and sanitation at the centre of their strategies for socio-economic development. ... The Conference provided a platform for African countries, the international community and UN agencies to reaffirm their commitment to solving Africa's water crisis and to collectively implement the actions envisaged in the African Water Vision 2025, the Water Agenda of the New Partnership for Africa's Development (NEPAD), the World Summit on Sustainable Development (WSSD) targets and the MDGs on water.... The thematic sessions were dedicated to the challenge areas, including: water, sanitation and human settlements; water and food security; protecting ecosystems and livelihoods; water and climate; financing water infrastructure; integrated water resources management (IWRM); water allocation; water wisdom; and water governance. Each session came out with recommendations, which were discussed at a joint ministerial and stakeholders plenary sessions. One of the main outcomes of the Conference was the presentation and adoption of subregional project portfolios to the ministerial segment. These projects have been prepared through national and subregional consultations and meetings, addressing the implication of the outcomes of the WSSD on regional water initiatives and setting up a concrete agenda in implementing the targets of the African Water Vision and the MDGs, with special emphasis on water supply and sanitation and the strategic application of IWRM.' (UNECA, 2006, pp. 293–4)

BOX 29.2

The African Water Development Report (AWDR)

Due to the particular problems of water resources development and management in Africa, the Inter-Agency Group on Water in Africa (now referred to as UN Water/Africa), decided in April 2001 in Niamey to develop an *African Water Development Report* (AWDR). It was conceived along the framework of the *World Water Development Report* (WWDR), and is intended to serve as an input to the preparation of the WWDRs. The first edition was published in 2006 and launched at the 4th World Water Forum in Mexico under the aegis of AMCOW. The aim of the AWDR is to afford African countries and other stakeholders the necessary tools and skills to monitor the goals and targets of the African Water Vision. The World Water Assessment Programme (WWAP), UN Water/Africa and AMCOW initiated contact in 2011 to revitalize this report as a part of a broader monitoring and assessment effort.

UN Water/Africa

In 1992, the United Nations (UN) family organizations operating in the water and environmental sectors in Africa decided to pool resources together under the name Inter Agency Group on Water (IGWA), with the objective of placing Africa at the forefront of international water concerns. The Secretariat is provided by UNECA in Addis Ababa, Ethiopia. Other strategic partners do participate in meetings of UN Water/Africa, and take part in some of its initiatives. These include: AMCOW, the NEPAD Secretariat, inter-governmental bodies such as subregional economic groupings (ECOWAS, IGAD, SADC, etc.), and reputable research institutions, centres and networks.

The principal objective of UN Water/Africa is to contribute to the UN system-wide response to the challenges and opportunities connected with pursuing the MDGs, and participation in the World Summit on Sustainable Development (WSSD) and other major inter-governmental conferences and summits through technical support to the African Union. Specifically, UN Water/Africa seeks to facilitate:

(i) The adoption of effective national and regional policies and institutional frameworks based on the principle of integrated water resources management (IWRM); (ii) the establishment of collaborative framework on agreements to facilitate the management and development of shared water resources; (iii) capacity building; and the urgent need for improved water wisdom. (NEPAD, 2006, p. 4)

Conclusion

Africa has made significant progress in mobilizing its vast water resources potential. The nature of these resources is influenced by natural and human external drivers that are complex and characterized by inherent uncertainties. The uncertainties arise from both natural variability and lack of knowledge. Good progress has been made in resolving the current uncertainties. New ones are likely to emerge so coping strategies should

---

BOX 29.3

Financing water: The role of AfDB

The African Development Bank has placed high priority on the water sector as a way of assisting Regional Member Countries (RMCs) to achieve the objectives of poverty reduction and economic growth because of the unique potential of this sector to contribute to achieving the other MDGs on poverty, health, education and gender. The Bank's portfolio of interventions in the water and sanitation sector spans drinking water supply, water resources management, sanitation and hygiene, capacity building and policy reform among others. The Bank is currently financing more than 50 active projects in 29 countries amounting to about US$2 billion.

The Bank aims at significantly increasing its interventions in rural water supply and sanitation while continuing to support urban and peri-urban water supply and sanitation, and promoting integrated management of water resources. In summary, the strategy seeks to:
- Increase water supply and sanitation financing
- Focus primarily on poorest 65% of population living in rural areas
- Provide some support for peri-urban areas, small and medium towns; and specifically for urban sanitation
- Promote transboundary water resources management
- Support the enabling environment to attract more resources

Moreover, the AfDB is also hosting a number of complementary initiatives which together enhance the effectiveness of the Bank's work and provides vital resources for scaling up and for promoting innovation and supporting knowledge management activities. The four main initiatives underpinning the Bank strategy in the water sector are the:
- Rural Water Supply and Sanitation Initiative (RWSSI)
- African Water Facility (AWF)
- NEPAD Water and Sanitation Programme
- Multi-donor Water Partnership Programme (MDWPP)

Source: Reproduced from AfDB (2011).

be flexible and adaptive in design, and approaches need to be modified to benefit from adaptive strategies. At present much action is taking place to address the problems in the water resources management area and in meeting the urgent needs defined in the African Water Vision 2025. To be fruitful, coping strategies should emphasize the importance of addressing knowledge gaps but most importantly the mobilization of sustainable financing to achieve the target of the African Water Vision 2025.

||||||||||||||||||||||||||||||||||||||||||||||||||||||||||||||||||||||||

References

AfDB (African Development Bank Group). 2011. *Water Supply and Sanitation*. (Webpage). Tunis, AfDB http://www.afdb.org/en/topics-and-sectors/sectors/water-supply-sanitation/angola/

Bakhbakhi, M. 2004. Hydrogeological framework of the Nubian Sandstone Aquifer System. B. Appelgren (ed.) *Managing Shared Aquifer Resources in Africa*. IHP-VI, Series on Groundwater No. 8, UNESCO. http://unesdoc.unesco.org/images/0013/001385/138581m.pdf (Accessed 16 December 2011.)

The Economist. 2011. Africa's impressive growth. *The Economist online,* January 2011. http://www.economist.com/blogs/dailychart/2011/01/daily_chart.

FAO (Food and Agriculture Organization of the United Nations). 1995. *Irrigation in Africa in Figures: Water Reports.* Rome, FAO.

––––. 2005. *Irrigation in Africa in Figures: AQUASTAT Survey.* Rome, FAO.

––––. 2007. *The State of Food and Agriculture.* Rome, FAO.

Hughes, D. 2008. *Water Resource Assessment Uncertainty Analysis: Project Inception Report.* Water Research Commission Project (K5/1838). Grahamstown, South Africa, Rhodes University.

ILEC (International Lake Environment Committee). n.d. *Lake Chad.* (Web Page). Shiga, Japan, ILEC.

LCBC (Lake Chad Basin Commission). 2008. *Roundtable to Save Lake Chad. Background Paper.* Prepared for the 'High-level Conference on Water for Agriculture and Energy in Africa: The Challenges of Climate', Sirte, Libyan Arab Jamahiriya, 15–17 December 2008. Chad, LCBC.

Mwanza, D. 2005. Water for Sustainable Development in Africa. L Hens and B. Nath (eds) *The World Summit on Sustainable Development: The Johannesburg Conference.* Dordrecht, Netherlands, Springer, pp. 91–111.

NEPAD (New Partnership for Africa's Development). 2006. *Water in Africa: Management Options to Enhance Survival and Growth.* Johannesburg, NEPAD. http://www.uneca.org/awich/nepadwater.pdf.

Ngurare, T. E. 2001. *Legal and Institutional Implications of Cross-Border Water Pipelines in International Law: The Congo Cross-Border Water Pipeline Project (CWPP) Case Study.* Centre for Energy, Petroleum and Mineral Law and Policy (CEPMLP) Annual Review 2001, Article 10. Dundee, CEPMLP. http://www.dundee.ac.uk/cepmlp/car/html/car5arti10.htm

SARPN (South African Regional Poverty Network). 2002. *Water and Sustainable Development in Africa: An African Position Paper.* World Summit on Sustainable Development in Johannesburg, South Africa, 26 August – 4 September 2002. Pretoria, SARPN. http://www.sarpn.org/wssd/may2002/water/position_paper.pdf

Sharma, N. P., Dambaug, T., Gilgan-Hunt, E., Grey, D. and Rothberg, D. 1996. *African Water Resources: Challenges and Opportunities for Sustainable Development.* World Bank Technical Paper No. 331. Washington DC, The World Bank.

Tennyson, R. n.d, *Trans Africa Pipeline: Sustainable Water for Sub-Saharan Africa.* Trans-Africa Pipeline Inc. http://transafricapipeline.org/PDFs/SustainableWaterAcademyPaper.pdf

Turton, A. R., W.R., Patrick, M. J. and Julien, F. 2006. Transboundary water resources in Southern Africa: conflict or cooperation? *Development,* Vol. 49, No. 3, pp. 22–31.

UNDESA (United Nations Department of Economic and Social Affairs, Population Division). 2007. *World Population Prospects.* New York, UN.

UNECA (United Nations Economic Commission for Africa). 2000. *African Water Vision 2025.* Addis Ababa, UN Water/Africa and UNECA.

––––. 2001. *Freshwater Resources in Africa.* Addis Ababa, UNECA.

––––. 2006. *African Water Development Report* (AWDR). Addis Ababa, UN Water/Africa and UNECA.

––––. 2010. *Climate Risk Management: Monitoring, Assessment, Early Warning and Response;* Issues Paper 4. Seventh African Development Forum: Acting on Climate Change for Sustainable Development in Africa. ADF VII, 10–15 October 2010, United Nations Conference Centre, Addis Ababa.

UNEP. 2006. *Climate Change and Variability in the Sahel Region: Impacts and Adaptation Strategies in the Agricultural Sector.* Nairobi, UNEP.

––––. 2008. *Vital Water Graphics: An Overview of the State of the World's Fresh Water and Marine Water* (2nd edn). Nairobi, UNEP.

––––. 2010. *Africa Water Atlas.* Nairobi, UNEP. http://na.unep.net/atlas/africaWater/book.php.

UN-Habitat. 2005. *Habitat Debate,* Vol. 11, No. 3.

----. 2010. *The State of African Cities 2010: Governance, Inequality and Urban Land Markets.* Nairobi, UN-Habitat.

UN Water/Africa. 2007. *Guidelines On Inter-Basin Water Transfers (IBWTs) In Africa.* Report of the Regional Workshop on 'Developing Guidelines for Inter-Basin Water Transfers for Policy Makers In Africa', held in Accra, Ghana, 25-29 September 2006. UNECA, Addis Ababa

WHO/UNICEF. 2010. *Joint Monitoring Programme (JMP) for Water and Sanitation.* Geneva, WHO.

World Bank. 2008. The 2008 World Development Indicators Online. Washington DC, Development Data Group, The World Bank. http://go.worldbank.org/U0FSM7AQ40.

World Bank. 2011. *Africa's Pulse: An Analysis of Issues Shaping Africa's Economic Future.* Washington DC, The World Bank. http://www.worldbank.org/africaspulse

WFP (United Nations World Food Programme). 2005. *WPF's Niger Appeal Triples to Help 2.5 million People Facing Extreme Hunger.* Rome, WFP. http://reliefweb.int/sites/reliefweb.int/files/reliefweb_pdf/node-180661.pdf

CHAPTER 30
Europe and North America

UNECE

—

Authors Francesca Bernardini, Rainer Enderlein, Sonja Koeppel and Annukka Lipponen
in consultation with EEA and GWP/CACENA

Specific water quality and quantity problems arise from pressures placed on water resources by agriculture, manufacturing industries, and sewerage and wastewaters. Climate change and economic development aggravate these pressures. Distinct subregional water problems (e.g. in Central Asia, Western Europe and North America) need tailor-made solutions. Although many issues are yet to be solved, over the last two decades the status of water resources has been improved and integrated water resources management plans have been developed at local, national and transboundary levels.

The region's surface waters and groundwaters contain pollutants, such as nutrients, metals, pesticides, microbes, industrial chemicals and pharmaceutical products. These have adverse effects on freshwater ecosystems. Prevention, control and reduction of water pollution are of utmost priority. Pollution sources are extremely diverse and vary considerably over river basins. Agriculture and urban sources (e.g. industries, urban wastewaters) contribute most of the freshwater pollution.

Climate change is projected to increase the risks of floods and droughts in many areas of the region. Costly water infrastructures designed to serve for decades in stationary climatic conditions are vulnerable to climate change. Concern over water scarcity is also increasing. Citizens and economic sectors are directly affected by abstraction pressures to satisfy urban needs and needs for irrigated agriculture, and especially in arid and semi-arid areas by diminishing water availability due to climate change.

Re-naturalization of watercourses is a challenge. Past structural measures (e.g. building dams and reservoirs for hydropower generation and irrigational water supply, constructing dykes, straightening waterways and enforcing river banks) have caused significant hydro-morphological changes in river basins in Europe and North America.

Insufficient wastewater treatment and its adverse effects on sources of drinking water and recreational waters are further priorities for action. The health impact of floods and heat waves add to the burden of water-related diseases.

Due the large numbers of transboundary rivers, lakes and groundwaters in the region, there is an understanding that transboundary cooperation for their management is necessary. This has led to strengthened bilateral and multilateral cooperation on shared waters, supported by bilateral and multilateral agreements, in many cases underpinned by UNECE Water Convention.

National and international response measures have been agreed upon, including European Union (EU) environmental legislation and United Nations Economic Commission for Europe (UNECE) conventions and protocols, supplemented by recommendations and guidelines for action. EU assistance programmes and bilateral assistance programmes for countries in Eastern Europe, the Caucasus and Central Asia are important for putting in place legal and other response measures, and contribute to strengthening water management.

30.1 Introduction

More than 1.2 billion people live in the 56 countries of the UNECE region (Table 30.1).[1] Western and Central Europe is one of the most densely populated areas of the world, with an average of nearly 110 people per km^2. This is in contrast to the relatively small populations in other parts of the world, where the average density is below 20 people per km^2. Between 1960 and 2000, Central Asia (more than 120% population increase) and the Caucasus (60% increase) have experienced considerably higher growth rates than other countries. For most countries in Western and Central Europe and in North America, there is a trend towards stable or even declining populations.

Migration of people has been increasing since the 1990s, including migration along gradients of political stability or economic prospects, in-country migration from rural to urban areas and seasonal migration of workers and retirees. These are among the reasons for increased abstraction pressure to satisfy water needs in major Western cities. Migration along gradients of economic prospects also gives rise to a mostly unconsidered effect on data about domestic water consumption and sanitation figures: the water statistics in some countries is based on the number of people officially registered to apartments and not the number of people actually living there – as in Armenia, Georgia, Kyrgyzstan and the Republic of Moldova, many residents of which work for most of their time abroad.

Economic development is also highly diverse in the region. Some of the countries are among the richest in the world, while others, particularly those whose

TABLE 30.1

Grouping of the 56 United Nations Economic Commission for Europe (UNECE) Member States

Group	Subgroup	Countries
EU countries		Austria, Belgium, Denmark, Finland, France, Germany, Greece, Ireland, Italy, Luxembourg, Netherlands, Portugal, Spain, Sweden, United Kingdom, Bulgaria, Cyprus, Czech Republic, Estonia, Hungary, Latvia, Lithuania, Malta, Poland, Romania, Slovakia, Slovenia
Western Europe		Andorra, Austria, Belgium, Denmark, Finland, France, Germany, Greece, Iceland, Ireland, Italy, Liechtenstein, Luxembourg, Monaco, Netherlands, Norway, Portugal, San Marino, Spain, Sweden, Switzerland, United Kingdom
	EU-15 countries	Austria, Belgium, Denmark, Finland, France, Germany, Greece, Ireland, Italy, Luxembourg, Netherlands, Portugal, Spain, Sweden, United Kingdom
Central and Eastern Europe		Albania, Bosnia and Herzegovina, Bulgaria, Czech Republic, Croatia, Cyprus, Estonia, Hungary, Latvia, Lithuania, Malta, Montenegro, Poland, Romania, Serbia, Slovakia, Slovenia, The former Yugoslav Republic of Macedonia, Turkey
	Countries that became EU Member States in the course of the EU enlargement process	Bulgaria, Cyprus, Czech Republic, Estonia, Hungary, Latvia, Lithuania, Malta, Poland, Romania, Slovakia, Slovenia
Eastern Europe, Caucasus and Central Asia		Armenia, Azerbaijan, Belarus, Georgia, Kazakhstan, Kyrgyzstan, Republic of Moldova, Russian Federation, Tajikistan, Turkmenistan, Ukraine and Uzbekistan
	Caucasus	Armenia, Azerbaijan, Georgia
	Central Asia	Kazakhstan, Kyrgyzstan, Tajikistan, Turkmenistan, Uzbekistan
Pan-European region		UNECE countries, except Canada, Israel and the United States
North America		Canada, United States

economies have been in transition since the 1990s, are still catching up. Per capita levels of gross domestic product (GDP) vary widely, from well over US$20,000 reported in EU-15, the United States, Canada, Norway, Switzerland and other countries, to less than one-eighth of this figure in the Caucasus and Central Asia. By 2009, two decades after the transition period began, some countries in Eastern Europe, the Caucasus and Central Asia had increased their per capita incomes approximately 50% above their 1989 levels, most had only returned to something similar to their 1989 level, while a few economies (Georgia, the Republic of Moldova, Serbia, Tajikistan, and Ukraine) remained 30% or more below this earlier level (UNECE, 2010).

Demographic patterns and migration, economic development and – as analysed further below – climate change are key external drivers in the UNECE region (EEA, 2007; EEA, 2010a; EEA, 2010b; UNECE, 2011b). National legislation (e.g. the US Clean Water Act), EU legislation and UNECE environmental conventions and protocols are designed to counteract the many adverse effects of external driving forces, prevent water pollution and the degradation of ecosystems, and mitigate climate change. A large number of states are bound by UNECE environmental conventions and protocols, and half of the Member States are under the obligations of the EU legislation. International assistances rendered under national and EU assistance programmes are decisive for achieving response measures and contribute to strengthening water governance.

A particular challenge stems from the large number of transboundary waters, whose status is comprehensively assessed on a regular basis by UNECE in collaboration with governments and international organizations (UNECE, 2007a; UNECE 2011b). More than 100 first-order transboundary rivers, with a basin area of over 1,000 km² and many of their tributaries run along or cross the border between two and more states. One of these rivers, the Danube, has 19 countries in its basin. Around 40 large lakes are shared by two countries (e.g. Lake Geneva, Lake Peipsi, the Great Lakes) or even three countries (e.g. Lake Constance), and over 100 transboundary groundwater aquifers have been identified. This has led to strengthened cooperation, supported by bilateral and multilateral agreements in Europe and North America.

30.2 Water management and response measures

The key external drivers in the region lead to pressures on water resources, influence in a multifaceted way the status of water bodies, impact on human health and call for response measures. Tables 30.2 and 30.3 summarize the relative importance of pressures on water resources over typical subregions and provide response measures depending on external drivers (UNECE, 2007a; UNECE 2011b). With the revival of economy in Eastern Europe, the Caucasus and in Central Asia, a shift in the relative importance of some pressure factors might occur.

TABLE 30.2

Main pressures on water resources in order of priority (from high to low)

Countries in Eastern Europe, Caucasus and Central Asia	EU-15 countries and North America
Pressures on water quality	
Municipal sewage treatment, non-sewered population, old industrial installations, illegal wastewater discharges, illegal disposal of household and industrial wastes in river basins, tailing dams and dangerous landfills	Agriculture and urban sources
Abstraction pressures	
Agricultural water use	Agricultural water use (particularly in Southern Europe), major urban centres
Hydromorphological alterations	
Hydropower dams, irrigation channels, river alterations	Hydropower dams, river alterations
Other pressures	
Agriculture (with a trend to become more severe), mining and quarrying	Selected industries discharging hazardous substances, mining and quarrying

30.2.1 Water and agriculture

Agricultural practice in the region has changed considerably over the past four decades: mechanization, increased use of fertilizers and pesticides, farm specialization, growth of farm size, land drainage and developments in animal husbandry have led to adverse impacts on the aquatic environment with some specific subregional differentiation of water use and water pollution. Water use for crop and animal production, for example, in Central Asia, Greece, Italy, Portugal and Spain accounts for 50–60% of the total use. In other countries, agriculture only accounts for around 20%, while the bulk is used by manufacturing industries and for cooling purposes.

In many river basins, nitrogen and phosphorus from fertilizers as well as pesticides are often detected at excessive levels and give rise to detrimental impacts on the aquatic environment (e.g. eutrophication) and human health (UNECE, 2011b). *Campylobacter* and *Cryptosporidium* excreted by livestock grazing next to waterways make waters unfit for recreation or contaminate sources of drinking water. Certain features of the rural landscape, such as small ponds, brooks and wetlands, have disappeared, thus one of their important roles in the water cycle – attenuation of pollutants – has been lost because of intensified agricultural production. In some basins, particularly in Central Asia, the predominant consumptive water use (i.e. irrigation) has also led to problems, such as salinization of soils and high mineral salt contents in water bodies.

The legal framework to cut down pollution from agriculture was established in the 1990s (e.g. EU Nitrates

TABLE 30.3

Selected water management issues and responses

Main issues	Possible water management responses[a]
Pressures by nutrients and pesticides from agriculture with economic development as main driver	Coordination of objectives, coordination of measures and combined approach for pollution control from agriculture (e.g. good agricultural practice, payments for ecosystem services)
Pressures by specific substances from manufacturing industries with economic development as main driver	Inventory of existing and potential polluters, coordination of objectives, coordination of measures and combined approach for pollution control from industrial installations (e.g. best available technology for hazardous substances, pollution reduction through installation of closed water systems)
Pressures by organic matter and bacteriological pollution with economic development, demographic patterns, and migration as main drivers	Inventory of existing and potential polluters, coordination of objectives, coordination of measures and combined approach for pollution control from municipal wastewater treatment plants (at least biological treatment or equivalent processes)
Flooding with climate change and economic development as main drivers	Climate change adaptation, holistic approach to flood management (combination of non-structural and structural measures)
Pressures due to hydromorphological alterations with economic development as main driver	Re-naturalization of small and medium-sized rivers, payment for ecosystem services
Water scarcity and/or abstraction pressures with economic development, demographic patterns, migration and climate change as main drivers	Climate change adaptation, conjunctive management of surface waters and groundwaters, licensing groundwater use
Water management in a transboundary context with political transitions and security concerns, economic development, demographic patterns, migration and climate change as main drivers	Transboundary cooperation as stipulated by applicable bilateral and multilateral agreements, implementation of the UNECE Water Convention (UNECE, 1992) and its Protocols

[a] Terminology according to the Water Framework Directive (European Commission, 2000) and UNECE (2007a, 2007b, 2009d).

Directive and national legislation in EU countries, Norway and Switzerland, Canada and the USA) and good practice guidance to control water pollution by fertilizers and pesticides in agriculture is broadly available and applied. However, agriculture remains a major concern as the relative importance of agricultural pollution over industrial pollution grew, mainly from cutting down of pollution by industrial enterprises in many countries over the last three decades. In EU countries located in the drainage basins of the Mediterranean Sea, the East Atlantic Ocean, the Baltic Sea and the Black Sea, the impact of agriculture on the quality of water resources is still striking, mostly because the implementation of the above-mentioned pieces of legislation and recommended practices as well as the recovery of water bodies takes more time than expected (UNECE, 2011b). Experience has also shown that 'command and control' approaches promulgated through legislation need to be supplemented by voluntary measures and innovative financing schemes, such as payments for ecosystem services (UNECE, 2007b).

In Eastern Europe, the Caucasus and Central Asia, if diffuse pressures from the use of pesticides and fertilizers in agriculture increase in the future alongside the revival of countries' economies, their use will be much higher than in the last decade and will cause growing negative effects on national and transboundary waters and human health.

Apart from the implementation of legal–regulatory, institutional and management measures, it is important to focus on education, training and advice to promote understanding of good agricultural practice and respect for existing legislation by various economic entities. The establishment of Nitrate Vulnerable Zones and the implementation of action programmes in areas where agricultural sources of nitrates have led to excessive concentrations in freshwater are other positive examples from Western Europe. The idea of conservation agriculture, developed under the auspices of Food and Agriculture Organization (FAO) is another example that should be taken up in the agricultural practices of Central Asia and other countries.

BOX 30.1

Water quality of rivers and lakes in the United States

In the United States, the National Water Quality Inventory Report to Congress (USEPA, 2009a; the next report was due in 2011) covers 16% of the total river length and 39% of the lakes areas (with the exception of the Great Lakes). In general, the inventory shows an improvement of the water quality: the waters were generally suitable for irrigation, supplying drinking water, and domestic and recreational uses. However, the report also stated that about half of the assessed stream miles and 64% of assessed lake acres (see the first table) were still not clean enough to support uses such as fishing and swimming, and require enforcement of existing legal requirements and improvement of management practices, awareness raising and training.

Leading causes of impairment in assessed watercourses	
Rivers	Lakes and reservoirs
Pathogens	Mercury
Habitat alterations	PCBs
Organic enrichment	Nutrients

Leading causes of impairment included pathogens, mercury, nutrients, and organic enrichment/low dissolved oxygen. The main pressure factors were agriculture and hydromorphological modifications. In areas with significant agricultural and urban development, the quality of surface waters and groundwaters has been degraded by contaminants such as pesticides (insecticides in urban areas, herbicides in agricultural areas), nutrients, metals, and gasoline-related compounds. However, concentrations of contaminants in water samples from wells were almost always lower than current Environment Protection Authority drinking water standards.

Water body	Assessed	Conditions (% of assessed water bodies)		
		Good	Good but threatened	Impaired
Rivers	16%	53	3	44
Lakes	39%	35	1	64

30.2.2 Industries and municipal wastewater treatment

Most water pollution problems in the region seem to originate from the great number of small and medium-sized industries, and small municipal wastewater treatment plants, rather than big undertakings, mostly equipped with modern pollution abatement technologies.

The biggest area of concern is Eastern Europe, the Caucasus and Central Asia. The aftermath of the economic decline in the 1990s, which often caused a breakdown of essential infrastructure, is still visible, despite many assistance programmes from Western European countries. Apart from some major enterprises, wastewaters are usually discharged into collective sanitation systems for treatment at municipal wastewater treatment plants, which do not operate according to standards, as the infrastructure is worn out. In addition to pollution by heavy metals, phosphorus and nitrogen, a few watercourses show increased levels of pollution by oil products, specifically discharges from oil refineries and surface runoff from refinery sites. Accidental pollution from industrial installations and unauthorized discharges of hazardous substances (mostly at night and during holidays) are still major concerns. Illegal waste disposal along rivers, as well as old and uncontrolled waste disposal sites in many transboundary river basins are additional pollution sources.

Regarding pressures from industries in basins in Western Europe and North America (Box 30.1), a particular challenge that needs proper response measures is the control and reduction of pollution by new substances produced by the chemical industry, including new pharmaceuticals – which are difficult to eliminate in wastewater treatment processes – as well as the control of pollution by priority substances given provisions of the Water Framework Directive and other applicable directives of the EU (EEA, 2010b) and other relevant regulation.

In most of the countries that became EU Member States in the course of the enlargement process (e.g. Bulgaria, Poland, Romania, Slovakia) as well as in transboundary and national rivers draining to the East Atlantic Ocean, untreated or insufficiently treated industrial wastewater remains a concern and breakdowns of municipal wastewater treatment systems result in significant discharges of polluted waters into rivers (UNECE, 2007a; UNECE 2011b).

30.2.3 Abstraction pressures, water scarcity and droughts

Over-abstraction, water scarcity and drought have a direct impact on citizens and economic sectors, and large areas of the UNECE region are already affected. There are three principal areas of concern in the region: abstraction pressures to satisfy urban needs (Box 30.2); growing abstraction pressures from irrigated agriculture in many Southern European countries, Ukraine, Russia, in Central Asia and parts of Canada and the United States; and reduced water availability and increased pressure on water resources because of anticipated climate change. A particular challenge for countries in Eastern Europe and Central Asia is water use efficiency in irrigated agriculture (Box 30.3). Abstraction of water for industrial use has largely decreased over the last three decades in parts of the region, partly from a general decline in water-intensive heavy industry in Western Europe and North America, partly from an increase in water use efficiency.

BOX 30.2

Abstraction pressure to satisfy water needs in major cities

In the past, with growing populations and increasing demand for water, Europe's larger cities have relied on the surrounding region for water. Athens, Paris and Istanbul have all developed wide water networks for transporting water, often over more than 100–200 km. Growing urban populations, improved lifestyles, reduced water availability due to climate change and the introduction of drinking water quality standards (the water around large cities is often polluted and cannot be used for drinking water) are all factors that should be taken into account when seeking to reduce the vulnerability of large cities to water stress.

In dry years, there have been problems supplying sufficient water to the 12 million people living in Istanbul and the four million Ankara, and water supplies have been rationed. During the 2008 drought, Barcelona turned off civic fountains and beachside showers, brought in hosepipe bans, and banned the filling of swimming pools. In the same year, Cyprus applied emergency measures that included cutting water supply by 30%; and households were supplied with water for around 12 hours a day, 3 times a week (EEA, 2007; EEA, 2010b).

In a growing number of cases, such severe restrictions in emergency situations became part of a consultative process with stakeholders; this was also influenced by the requirements of the Aarhus Convention (UNECE, 1998).

Abstraction for cooling water has also decreased, given advanced cooling technologies.

A comparison of the impacts of droughts in the EU area between 1976–1990 and 1991–2006 has both shown a doubling in the affected area and a doubling in the number of affected people. For example, an intense drought throughout the Iberian Peninsula in the hydrological year 2004–2005 led to a 40% average decrease of cereals production and hydroelectric power production was heavily impacted. During summer 2006, rainfall in Lithuania was only half the long-term average and agricultural production fell by 30% with an estimated loss of around €200 million. Increasing water scarcity also limits access to water for sanitation purposes and hygiene, which may result in increased adverse health impacts, and water scarcity is reducing the self-purification capacities of water bodies (EEA, 2010b).

BOX 30.3

Agriculture in Central Asia

In Central Asia, the agricultural sector ensures livelihoods of half of Central Asia's population. Agriculture consumes more than 90% of surface water and 43% of groundwater. It produces US$13.54 billion of the annual domestic product and plays a critical role in the generation of Central Asia's total gross domestic product of US$58.5 billion (Stulina, 2009).

Despite what was learned from the Aral Sea disaster, the use of water resources is still geared to meet the water requirements of agriculture and hydropower generation without paying proper attention to the needs of other sectors and nature. As a result, drinking water quality and health of local population are deteriorating; land productivity and crop yields are decreasing; and poverty, unemployment, migration, and risks of conflicts are rising (GWP/CACENA, 2006).

Measures are being progressively implemented to reduce water losses by redesigning irrigation systems, improving irrigation techniques, and applying technologies for the reuse of drainage water. However, scarce financial means often delay the implementation of measures. Therefore it was recognized that in addition to the implementation of technical measures, a major objectiveshould be the involvement of stakeholders and relevant sectors in negotiations (coordinating water allocation) and development of acceptable for all rules for water allocation. The Interstate Commission for Water Coordination (ICWC) of Central Asia is the regional institution responsible for water allocation between the countries.

Drought management has become an essential element of water resource policy and strategies, and drought management plans (European Commission, 2009) were already drawn up or are under preparationin, for example, Spain, Portugal, England and Wales, Finland and the USA to mitigate the consequences of droughts and water scarcity. To address the impact of drought and water scarcity on human health, UNECE and WHO/EURO have developed specific guidance and recommendations, which include adaptation measures for drainage, sewerage and wastewater treatment (WHO, 2010).

30.2.4 Hydromorphological alterations

Structural measures (e.g. building dams and reservoirs for hydropower and irrigational agriculture, constructing dykes, straightening waterways and enforcing river banks) have caused significant hydromorphological changes in the UNECE region. This includes changes in the hydrological regime of many rivers, interruption of river and habitat continuity, disconnection of rivers from adjacent wetlands and floodplains, and change of the erosion process and sediment transport. For many rivers, restoring former floodplains and wetlands would both reduce flood risk and improve their ecological status (Box 30.4). At the same time, however, many European countries are still developing plans and studies for new dams, reservoirs and small hydropower projects.

30.2.5 Floods

Since the beginning of this century, more than three million people have been affected in the UNECE region by floods – almost two million in Eastern Europe alone – exposing people to various health hazards and causing deaths, displacement of people and large economic losses. Major floods have included those along the Danube in spring 2006 and in summer 2009 in rivers shared between Romania and Ukraine, and the Republic of Moldova and Ukraine; and in 2010 in the Oder basin, Southern France, and the Prut River (Romania and the Republic of Moldova). In the USA, significant flood events during the twentieth century were comprehensively documented (Perry, 2000). The recent floods include those in 2008 in Nebraska, Indiana and Illinois and the June 2010 flood in Arkansas.

In the region, the costs of floods have increased rapidly. Flood damage is mostly attributed to socio-economic factors, such as an increase in population, urbanization in flood-prone areas, and to unfavourable changes in land use such as deforestation and loss of wetlands.

BOX 30.4

Hydromorphological alterations in the Danube Basin

Like many other European rivers, the Danube is heavily influenced by human activities, such as intensive navigation and hydraulic engineering. On many stretches the natural structure of the river has been changed, including its depth and width, flow regime, natural sediment transport and fish migration routes. Dams have been built in mountain areas and some lowland regions of the Danube basin; and navigation channels, dykes and irrigation networks are widespread along the middle and lower reaches of the Danube:

- More than four-fifths of the Danube is regulated for flood protection, and about 30% of its length is impounded for hydropower generation.
- About half of the Danube tributaries are used to generate hydropower of around 30,000 MW.
- More than 700 dams and weirs have been built along the main tributaries of the Danube.

The Danube River Basin Management Plan addresses hydromorphological alterations. Basin-wide objectives by 2015 include the construction of fish migration aids and other measures to achieve and improve river continuity in the Danube River and in respective tributaries to ensure reproducing and self-sustaining of sturgeon species and specified other migratory species, as well as the restoration, conservation and improvement of habitats and their continuity for sturgeon species and specified other migratory species in the Danube River and its tributaries (ICPDR, 2007).

In Western Europe, initiatives to enhance the natural environment and improve its capacity to perform ecosystem services have been brought forward under the Water Framework Directive (e.g. the Dutch 'Room for the River' programme, the Spanish 'National Strategy for Restoring Rivers') or under national legislation (e.g. the Swiss 'Guiding Principles for Sustainable Water Management'). An innovative approach in the UNECE region is 'payment for ecosystem services' (PES), which is widely used in Latin America (Wunder, 2005) and explored in the UNECE region (UNECE, 2005). Prominent examples from the UNECE region (UNECE, 2007b) include the water supply of New York City (Catskill/Delaware basin management programme), the nitrate strategy of Switzerland, agro-environmental measures as part of the EU Common Agricultural Policy, and the management of natural mineral water springs in France (Nestlé/Vittel). Under the UNECE Water Convention, pilot projects on payments for ecosystem services have been carried out in Kyrgyzstan (Lake Issyk Kul basin) and in Armenia.

However, floods are natural phenomena that can also bring benefits: seasonal floodplain inundation is essential to maintaining healthy rivers, creating new habitats, depositing silts and fertile organic material, and sustaining wetlands. Therefore, an integrated approach to flood management – one that recognizes both the opportunities provided by floodplains for socio-economic activities and that manages the associated risks – is being implemented in many countries (e.g. Austria, Czech Republic, Germany, France, the Netherlands, Slovakia and Switzerland). The lessons learned from these events, particularly related to transboundary watercourses, have recently been summarized by UNECE and the World Meteorological Organization (UNECE, 2009e) and are now in pilot applications in in transboundary river basins such as the Dniester, shared by Ukraine and the Republic of Moldova.

30.2.6 Impact on human health

In parts of the region, inadequate sanitation, improper wastewater treatment, unsafe disposal methods for chemicals, and fertilizers and pesticides that leak into sources of water supply threaten human health. Microbial contamination of the sources of drinking water and water used for recreational purposes is one of the consequences as it is the case with man-made chemical pollution of the sources of drinking water supply; in some cases the natural background pollution causes immense problems, for example, in Hungary (naturally occurring arsenic) and the Caucasus (relatively high background concentration of some metals due to the weathering of rocks).

One hundred and twenty million people[2] in the European region do not have access to safe drinking water. Even more lack access to sanitation, resulting in water-related diseases like diarrhoea, typhoid fever (170,000 reported cases in 2006, which is probably an underestimate) and hepatitis A. In Eastern and Southeastern Europe, the Caucasus and Central Asia, access to improved sources of drinking water and improved sanitation is particularly inadequate in rural areas. In Western Europe and North America, outbreaks of water-related diseases occur occasionally despite state-of-the-art of water purification and wastewater treatment technology. For example, the USA reported that chemicals (16%), viruses (6%), bacteria (18%), and parasitic protozoa (21%) were identified as causes of outbreaks whereas in the remaining 39% of cases, it was not possible to identify the exact source (Greer et al., 2008; Centres for Disease Control and Prevention, 2011).

During floods, people may be exposed to health hazards, such as freshwater pollution (particularly the contamination of the sources of drinking water by pathogens and waste), lack of household hygiene, and reduction of food safety. Water supply and sanitation utilities are also key health determinants during heat and cold waves.

The safety of the water supply and sanitation sector clearly relies on close inter-sectoral cooperation; however, it was not until the end of the 1990s before Governments in the region undertook concerted international action to prevent, control and reduce water-related diseases, including response systems to counteract health hazards due to incidents and outbreaks of water-related diseases. These international efforts culminated in the Protocol on Water and Health to the UNECE Water Convention. It is the first international agreement, which – by linking water management and health issues – aims to ensure the adequate supply of safe drinking water and adequate sanitation for everyone. It complements the UNECE Water Convention with further measures to strengthen the protection of public health, particularly at the national level, for example, by establishing or maintaining comprehensive national and/or local surveillance and early warning systems to prevent and respond to water-related diseases. From its entry into force in 2005 until now, it has already yielded positive results: the parties to the Protocol not only strengthened their measures to achieve the water-related and health-related MDGs, but also initiated measures to achieve water supply and sanitation for everyone beyond 2015 (UNECE, 2010; UNECE, 2011a). International assistance through *inter alia* providing access to sources of finance for infrastructure projects is also part of this instrument, and is already being rendered for the Republic of Moldova and Ukraine.

30.3 Uncertainties and risks

Water management adapts continuously to uncertainties and responds to risks that are posed by external driving forces and/or political, economic and technical responses. This requires new kinds of action from all stakeholders, including national and local governments and, for transboundary waters, from the parties to agreements.

30.3.1 Non-climatic drivers

The fact that many water bodies cross boundaries between two or more states means that challenges and risks are shared and that solutions need to be coordinated. Since the 1970s and early 1980s, countries have been engaging in a growing number of multilateral and bilateral agreements to regulate the use and protection of transboundary waters, and since the 1990s, the countries that evolved after the dissolution of the former Soviet Union have been taking measures to establish transboundary water cooperation. Many have joined international conventions and agreements and/or have entered into new bilateral and multilateral agreements and established joint bodies (e.g. river or lake commissions, meetings of plenipotentiaries) to facilitate transboundary water cooperation. As a result, the status of many watercourses in the region has been considerably improved and there are far fewer disputes over shared waters compared to the earlier 1990s (UNECE, 2009b; 2011b). The UNECE Convention on the Protection and Use of Transboundary Watercourses and International Lakes (UNECE Water Convention) adopted in 1992 and entered into force in 1996 (UNECE, 1992) has played an important role in this process.

However, a few first- and second-order transboundary rivers and many transboundary aquifers (UNECE, 2011b) in Eastern Europe, the Caucasus and Central Asia, as well as in South-Eastern Europe are not yet covered by agreements, and in some cases existing agreements and joint bodies do not effectively address such current challenges as economic development. In addition, some states – either inside the region or bordering it – resist participating in agreements on transboundary watercourses, whether framework agreements or those for specific watercourses. This leads to uncertainties and risks in transboundary water management where there are no formal channels for joint action.

While a prerequisite for effective cooperation is political will, joint bodies must also have, from the onset, the right structures and mechanisms to effectively address their tasks. To cope with uncertainties and risks in transboundary cooperation, the many existing joint bodies in countries in transition improve their activities by strengthening institutional mechanisms. This implies achieving better representation of national authorities in the joint body and improving coordination at the national level, and eliciting greater financial commitments by riparian states to cover implementation of joint programmes and expenses of organizational structure.

Insufficient access to, and cumbersome conditions for, the exchange of water quality and water quantity data and information in a transboundary context as well as information about drivers and their impact on water management also pose uncertainties and risks. In some cases, official communication lines go through the ministries of foreign affairs, although the environment ministries or state water committees are increasingly empowered with transboundary data exchange. In recent years, joint bodies established by countries in Eastern Europe and Central Asia have taken some steps towards improving access to information and stakeholder participation. Participation of non-governmental organizations and other stakeholders in the activities of joint bodies exists for many joint bodies in North America and Western Europe (e.g. the International Joint Commission (Great Lakes, North America) and the Rhine, Meuse and Scheldt river commissions). At the end of 2007, the plenipotentiaries of the Republic of Moldova and Ukraine adopted a Regulation on Stakeholder Participation. This is the first example of formalized procedure for the dissemination of information and promotion of public participation in the activities of the joint bodies in Eastern Europe, the Caucasus and Central Asia. Lack of finances is often one of the barriers to broadening access to information and public participation.

Coping with the increasing water demands of different sectors of economy poses particular challenges and has led or may lead to uncertainties about proper response measures. An example is water allocation among riparian countries, as disagreement remains over use quotas for the upstream and downstream users belonging to different states, as it is the case for some rivers in the discharge area of the Caspian Sea. A similar issue arose in water allocation between different sectors of economy, such as the 'classical conflict' between hydropower production (high releases of water during winter to produce energy often associated with man-made flooding of downstream areas) and irrigated agriculture (with high water demands in the growing season when the upstream reservoirs are being filled up), which is particularly obvious in Central Asia (Amu Darya and Syr Darya basins). This has not yet been solved satisfactorily; however, the existing joint bodies, under the umbrella of International Fund for Saving the Aral Sea (IFAS) (Box 30.3), are now approaching the problem as the water demand from other sectors is also growing (including an expected growth of water demand in Afghanistan – an upstream

country outside the UNECE region) over the next two decades, and in the Aral Sea basin a reduction from around 2,500 m^3 per capita and year to 1,800 m^3 or even 1,300 m^3 depending on development scenarios.

Other examples of uncertainties and risks refer to the conflict between water use for economic activities and water for the maintenance of aquatic ecosystems. Lake Balqash, located in Kazakhstan and mainly fed by the transboundary river Ili with its source in China, may suffer the same fate of the Aral Sea if Kazakhstan and China fail to agree on sustainable water use and pollution control. The joint Kazakhstan–China Commission has recognized this issue and is approaching a solution to the problem with extreme caution owing to the many (scientific) uncertainties involved about the impact of response measures on the aquatic ecosystem of the Lake.

Growing abstraction pressures, including from groundwater aquifers, is another concern of transboundary cooperation. The work of many joint bodies in the area of transboundary groundwaters is still insufficient; this applies across the region, perhaps with some exemptions in Western Europe and North America. The staffs of joint bodies, often trained in the management of surface waters rather than groundwaters, do not supervise water supply from groundwaters and the licensing of groundwater abstraction.

In some countries, the aftermath of the political changes of the 1990s and the 2008–2009 global economic crisis continues to impact the stability and security situation, even today, with adverse effects on water and the environment as well as international cooperation on transboundary waters (Box 30.5).

In areas that witnessed armed conflicts, infrastructure was destroyed, causing pollution, and internally displaced people and refugees have put additional pressure on water supply and sanitation. Examples include the armed conflicts in the Balkans (1990s) and in the Caucasus (Armenia and Azerbaijan in the 1990s; Georgia and the Russian Federation in 2009). The internal political conflicts and ethnic tensions in Kyrgyzstan in the summer of 2010, causing death among its own population and large numbers of refugees, poses uncertainties and risks: it may not only have negative effects on transboundary water management in the Ferghana Valley (Aral Sea basin) as it was the case with the country's rural water supply and sanitation systems, but also negatively impact the solution of transboundary issues in the entire basin.

30.3.2 Climate change

The need to address climate change is a major concern as the entire UNECE region accounts for approximately one-half of the global greenhouse gas emissions. Climate change impact will vary considerably from region to region and even from basin to basin. These will include increased risk of inland flash floods, and more frequent coastal flooding, intensified erosion and extensive species losses (EEA, 2008; UNECE, 2009a, UNECE, 2011b); it may also affect hydropower, shipping, tourism and recreation, shoreline structures and human health (Greer et al., 2008; USEPA, 2007).

Governments in Europe (EEA, 2010a) are at different stages of preparing, developing and implementing national adaptation strategies, and the United States Environmental Protection Agency released in 2008 the National Water Programme Strategy with specific actions to adapt programme implementation in light of climate change (USEPA, 2009b). The adaptation

BOX 30.5

Impact of the 2008–2009 global economic crisis

The Emerging Europe and Central Asia region[3] was the most affected by the global financial and economic crisis beginning in mid-2008, with declines in economic output in 2009 averaging about 6%. The economic declines had major socio-economic implications, for example, the number of unemployed during the first six months of 2009 grew by almost half in Russia and Turkey compared to the same period in 2008. As most countries can expect at best a mild growth in the coming years, the crisis will continue to hinder the achievement of the Millennium Development Goals (MDGs) and human development in the region. In particular, there are limited prospects for increasing social protection because of the expected weakness of the economic recovery and the accumulation of public debt (UNECE, 2010). The financial crisis presents risks to further developing the water sector; however, it also provides opportunities to reinforce commitments to invest in water services and infrastructure as part of fiscal stimulus packages. The European Union and United Nations Economic Commission for Europe (UNECE) Member States play a crucial role in these policy areas, using public spending and grants to create and maintain necessary infrastructure, promote technological innovation, support behavioural change and render further assistance to countries in transition (OECD, 2009).

strategies depend on the magnitude and nature of the observed and predicted impacts, assessments of current and future vulnerability and the countries' capacity to adapt. In addition, some actions and measures are increasingly being taken at regional and local levels. However, the strategies are long-term programmes whose immediate effects are difficult to assess.

Ensuring adequate financial means to implement adaptation measures is an important precondition for success; however, there are still many uncertainties about the ability of a number of countries to adapt water management to climate change. For example, in Eastern Europe, the Caucasus and Central Asia, uncertainties remain as to investment and funding for adaptation measures and there is a lack of capacity (including human resources) for adaptation. Widespread poverty in these countries also limits their adaptive capacity. Moreover, policy makers are not used to uncertainty and risk considerations when taking decisions related to water management, water supply and sanitation.

There is another challenge for water managers (UNECE, 2009a): climate mitigation measures may produce adverse side-effects for water management. One example is 'water for food production versus water for bio-energy crops'. Large-scale biofuel production may increase water demand and may contaminate freshwater from enhanced leaching of pesticides and nutrients, and in conflicts with food production. Hydroelectric power plants adversely affect the existing river ecosystems and fisheries, for example, due to changes in flow regime, water temperature regime, and oxygen concentrations. Conversely, they help to regulate flow and are needed for irrigation.

Another example is inland waterway transport, which plays an important role in the transport of goods in Central Europe and is generally seen as more environmentally friendly than road transport. However, navigation activities and infrastructure works are typically associated with a range of hydromorphological changes with potentially adverse ecological consequences. Thus, despite the advantage of mitigation policies for society and for reducing greenhouse gas emissions, there is a need to strike a balance between the benefits and the impacts on the ecological status of water bodies, adjacent land ecosystems and wetlands.

Many river basins that are already stressed due to non-climatic drivers are likely to become more stressed because of their vulnerability to climate change. Of particular relevance is the vulnerability to climate change of costly water infrastructures (e.g. flood defence structures, water supply and sanitation infrastructure), which have to serve for decades but were designed on the assumption of stationary climatic conditions. Moreover, policy tools such as land planning are based on stable 'old' climate scenarios, which did not take into account variability and change. Other uncertainties related to climate change include the still insufficient knowledge base.

Uncertainties of climate predictions and predictions of precipitation patterns at the river-basin scale make scenario development particularly difficult for smaller river basins (UNECE, 2011b). Pilot projects were recently initiated, with finance from donor countries from Western Europe, in the Chu-Talas basin (Kazakhstan/Kyrgyzstan) and the Sava basin (Bosnia and Herzegovina, Croatia, Serbia, Slovenia). Other joint bodies, such as those for the Rhine, Meuse, Scheldt and Danube, also challenge the basin countries to develop a more coordinated approach and address the effects that pose the highest risk and uncertainties to human health and water management, and to develop appropriate adaptation measures to new risks as they become better understood.

30.4 Water governance

Water governance is well recognized in the UNECE region as a means for effective water management at the local, national and transboundary levels. Strategies, policies, legislation and assistance initiatives – designed as response measures – are at the same time 'political drivers' to achieve water governance.

Problems remain: in many countries in Eastern Europe, the Caucasus and Central Asia, capacities of institutions tend to be weak due to the institutional collapse and economic dislocation that marked the early years of the transition. While many of these countries have made great strides in reforming public administration and developing a dynamic civil society, the new institutions are not yet stable or well-rooted, nor have they completely moved away from the old mode of functioning. The political will to finance environmental protection is also weak; regular cuts in budgetary funding indicate that environmental protection receives little attention, and sometimes, the allocated funds are not even enough to ensure the normal functioning of state agencies. Moreover, it is difficult to recruit highly

qualified staff because salaries are low and public authorities are not held in high esteem (UNECE, 2007c; Mott MacDonald, 2010).

The new EU Member States have accomplished greater progress in building new institutional structures. They were assisted on multiple fronts by the acceptance of the European model offered by EU membership as a powerful incentive for collective action, and by massive financial and knowledge assistance (UNECE, 2010). Notwithstanding the focus of UNECE and the European Commission on water governance in countries in transition, there are also challenges in governance in other countries, particularly those with a federal structure (e.g. Germany, USA) with multiple actors within each jurisdiction (Rogers and Hall, 2003; Moss, 2004; Norman and Bakker, 2009; and Cohen, 2010).

30.4.1 Legislation and assistance initiatives

The EU legislation is an important response measure to the external drivers and addresses inter alia water problems in the EU area and beyond. A comprehensive range of legislation has been established for this purpose, including Directives related to urban wastewater treatment (1991), to control and limit nitrate pollution from agriculture (1991), to regulate the quality of drinking water (1998) other areas related to water-and-health issues. The most important piece of legislation is the Water Framework Directive (WFD), concluded in 2000 (European Commission, 2000). This Directive expands the scope of water protection to all waters, and requires the achievement of a 'good status' for all waters in EU countries by 2015. The WFD is a direct response of the European Communities and the Member States to fulfill their obligations under international conventions on water protection and management, particularly the UNECE Water Convention (UNECE, 1992). The WFD includes a strong economic component: it requires that EU Member States implement full recovery of the environmental and resource costs of water services; and water pricing policies are to be established that provide adequate incentives for the efficient use of water resources. More recently, 'daughter' directives, such as those on environmental quality standards, floods and groundwaters, supplement the WFD.

Apart from its effect to improve water management in EU countries, the application of principles of the WFD is of immense importance to improving water management and cutting down pollution in countries at the Eastern border of the EU (Belarus, the Republic of

Moldova, Ukraine, Armenia, Azerbaijan and Georgia). This is the reason for the EU (European Commission, 2007) to support these countries under the European Neighbourhood and Partnership Instrument (ENPI).

UNECE Environmental Conventions and Protocols are another response to the external drivers to resolve national and transboundary issues of water management, air pollution, industrial accidents, impact assessment and public participation. For what concerns water management, the central aim of the 1992 UNECE Water Convention is to strengthen local, national and regional measures to protect and ensure the quantity, quality and sustainable use of transboundary waters. It stipulates managing shared waters in a reasonable and equitable manner and calls for action guided by the precautionary principle and based on the polluter-pays principle. The Convention requires parties to enter into specific bilateral or multilateral agreements and to create institutions – joint bodies such as river and lake commissions – to meet these responsibilities.

The Environment for Europe process, including its ministerial conferences, became another prominent response measure to the external drivers in the region. UNECE Member States, UN system organizations and other intergovernmental organizations represented in the region, regional environment centres, non-governmental organizations, the private sector and other major groups act in partnership to help countries in transition to raise their environmental standards towards a common regional benchmark, provide access to sources of finance, and share experience and good practice.

30.4.2 National Policy Dialogues

International support to strengthen water governance should be a process that involves and supports two distinct levels of decision-making: decision-making on technical and managerial issues and decision-making on policy issues. This gave rise to the National Policy Dialogues on integrated water resources management, water supply and sanitation as part of the EU Water Initiative, launched at the World Summit on Sustainable Development in Johannesburg in 2002, which covers nine of the 12 countries in Eastern Europe, the Caucasus and Central Asia.

On the one hand, technical assistance programmes by the EU and Western European Countries enhance the expertise of staff in the water–environment ministries and improve legislation, institutions and management practices. On the other, National Policy Dialogues – led by the ministers for environment – enhance the political support of water management by key ministries such as economy, finance, justice, emergency situations, and foreign affairs, and involve additional stakeholders (e.g. academia, non-governmental organizations, parliamentary bodies responsible for environment, and international organizations and financial institutions). The production of highly policy-relevant outputs, such as new pieces of legislation (Box 30.6) in line with the principles of the UNECE Water Convention, the Protocol on Water and Health, the EU Water Framework Directive and other UNECE and EU instruments, the strong country commitment and the cooperation with other international organizations are among the strengths of the National Policy Dialogues in the region, and a means to strengthen water governance.

BOX 30.6

Wastewater treatment infrastructure in the Republic of Moldova

Of the 623 municipal wastewater treatment plants constructed in major cities and other settlements in The Republic of Moldova, only 24% were operational in 2010. This has led to a growing amount of untreated wastewater being discharged into the river system and only 4% of plants treat wastewater according to existing legal requirements. In addition, sanitation is unsatisfactorily in rural areas, where 70% of houses are not connected to the sewerage system.

An assistance programme is being developed, supported by European Union (EU) funds, and funds provided by other West European countries, to rehabilitate infrastructure in municipalities and improve sanitation in rural areas. New wastewater treatment legislation, modeled on the basis of EU legislation, was drawn up under the National Policy Dialogue process and entered into force in October 2008. This new legislation provides a sound basis for the rehabilitation of existing and the construction of new municipal wastewater treatment plants, as it no longer relies on the outdated Soviet-style requirements. Thus, the treatment performance of the state-of-the-art Western treatment technology no longer clashes with former Soviet-style Moldovan standards and no longer forces the Minister for Environment to apply to the Government for exceptions from the law to install these technologies (UNECE, 2011a).

Notes

1   Eight hundred and seventy million people live in the 'pan-European region', a term which does not include North America and Israel. The USA has a total resident population of about 310 million; Canada 34 million and Israel 7 million (UNECE Statistical Division Database at http://www.unece.org and UNECE, 2010).

2   North America is not included in these figures, which were compiled by the Regional Office for Europe of the World Health Organization (WHO/EURO)

3   Countries in Eastern Europe, the Caucasus and Central Asia and South-Eastern Europe, including Turkey, and the new EU Member States (Table 30.1).

References

Centres for Disease Control and Prevention. 2011. Water-related data and statistics. http://www.waterandhealth.org/newsletter/new/spring_2003/waterborne.html (Accessed 12 October 2011.)

Cohen, K. and Bakker, K. 2010. Groundwater governance: explaining regulatory non-compliance. *International Journal of Water.* Vol. 5, No. 3, pp. 246–66.

EEA (European Environment Agency). 2007. *Europe's Environment – The Fourth Assessment. State of the Environment Report No. 1/2007.* Copenhagen, EEA.

––––. 2010a. *National Adaptation Strategies.* http://www.eea.europa.eu/themes/climate/national-adaptation-strategies (Accessed 12 October 2011.)

––––. 2010b. *The European Environment – State and Outlook 2010: synthesis.* Copenhagen, EEA.

EEA (European Environment Agency), JRC (Joint Research Centre of the European Union) and WHO (World Health Organization). 2008. *Impacts of Europe's Changing Climate – 2008 Indicator-based Assessment.* EEA Report No. 4/2008, JRC Reference Report No. JRC47756. EEA (European Environment Agency), Copenhagen, Denmark. http://www.eea.europa.eu/publications/eea_report_2008_4

European Commission. 2000. Directive 2000/60/EC of the European Parliament and of the Council of 23 October 2000 Establishing a Framework for the Community Action in the Field Of Water. policy. *Official Journal of the European Communities.* http://eurlex.europa.eu/LexUriServ/LexUriServ.do?uri=OJ:L:2000:327:0001:0072:EN:PDF

––––. 2007. *Development and Cooperation – EuropeAid.* http://ec.europa.eu/europeaid/where/neighbourhood/index_en.htm (Accessed 12 October 2011.)

––––. 2009. *The 1st River Basin Management Plans for 2009–2015.* http://ec.europa.eu/environment/water/index_en.htm (Accessed 12 October 2011.)

Greer, A., Ng, V. and Fisman, D. 2008. Climate change and infectious diseases in North America: the road ahead. *Canadian Medical Association Journal,* Vol. 178, No. 6, pp. 715–22. http://www.cmaj.ca/content/178/6/715.full

GWP/CACENA (Global Water Partnership in Caucasus and Central Asia). 2006. *Implementing the UN Millennium Development Goals in Central Asia and the South.* Tashkent, Uzbekistan, GWP-CACENA.

ICPDR (International Commission for the Protection of the Danube River). 2007. *Issue Paper on Hydromorphological Alterations in the Danube River Basin.* ICPDR, Vienna, Austria. (http://www.icpdr.org/icpdr-pages/dams_structures.htm). (Accessed 12 October 2011.)

Moss, T. 2004. The governance of land use in river basins: prospects for overcoming problems of institutional interplay with the EU Water Framework Directive. *Land Use Policy,* Vol. 21, No. 1, pp. 85–94.

Mott MacDonald. 2010. *Project Completion Report: Water Governance in the Western EECCA Countries.* TACIS/2008/137-153 (EC), Brussels, European Commission.

Norman, E. S. and Bakker, K. 2009. Governing water across the Canada–U.S. borderland. Gattinger, M. and Hale, G. (eds), *Borders and Bridges: Navigating Canada's International Policy Relations in a North American Context.* Oxford, UK, Oxford University Press, Oxford, pp. 194–212. http://www.oup.com/us/catalog/general/subject/Politics/AmericanPolitics/ForeignDefensePolicy/~~/dmIldz11c2EmY2k9OTc4MDE5NTQzMjAwOA==?view=usa&sf=toc&ci=9780195432008

OECD (Organisation for Economic Co-operation and Development). 2009. *Managing Water for All: An OECD Perspective on Pricing and Financing – Key Messages for Policy Makers.* Paris, France, OECD. http://www.oecd.org/dataoecd/53/34/42350563.pdf

Perry, C. A. 2000. *Significant Floods in the United States During the 20th Century – USGS Measures a Century of Floods.* USGS Fact Sheet 024-00, March 2000. http://ks.water.usgs.gov/pubs/fact-sheets/fs.024-00.html (Accessed 12 October 2011.)

Rogers, P. and Hall, A. W. 2003. *Effective Water Governance.* TEC Background Papers No. 7. Sweden, Global Water Partnership, Sweden. http://eagri.cz/public/web/file/30598/Effective_Water_Governance_1_.pdf

Stulina, G. 2009: *Climate change and adaptation to it in the water and land management of Central Asia.* G Tashkent, Uzbekistan, Global Water Partnership in Caucasus and Central Asia.

UNECE (United Nations Economic Commission for Europe). 1992. *UNECE Convention on the Protection and Use of Transboundary Watercourses and International Lakes, 17th March 1992, Helsinki.* New York and Geneva, United Nations.. http://live.unece.org/fileadmin/DAM/env/water/pdf/watercon.pdf

----. 1998. *UNECE Convention on Access to Information, Public Participation in Decision-Making and Access to Justice in Environmental Matters, 25th June 1998, Aarhus.* New York and Geneva. http://www.unece.org/env/pp/welcome.html

----. *2005. Seminar on Environmental Services and Financing for the Protection and Sustainable Use of Ecosystems, 10–11 October 2005.* http://www.unece.org/env/water/meetings/payment_ecosystems/seminar.htm (Accessed 12 October 2011.)

----. 2007*a*: *First Assessment of Transboundary Rivers, Lakes and Groundwaters.* United Nations, New York and Geneva. http://www.unece.org/env/water/publications/pub76.htm (Accessed 12 October 2011.)

----. 2007*b*: *Recommendations on Payments for Ecosystem Services in Integrated Water Resources Management.* United Nations, New York and Geneva. http://unece.org/env/water/publications/documents/PES_Recommendations_web.pdf (Accessed 12 October 2011.)

----. 2007*c*. *From Intentions to Actions: Overcoming Bottlenecks – Critical Issues in Implementation of Environmental Policies Highlighted by the UNECE Environmental Performance Review Programme.* United Nations, New York and Geneva. http://unece.org/env/epr/publications/Critical%20issues%20implementation%20EPR.pdf

----. 2009*a*. *Guidance on Water and Adaptation to Climate Change.* United Nations, Geneva, Switzerland. http://www.unece.org/env/water/publications/documents/Guidance_water_climate.pdf

----. 2009*b*. *River Basin Commissions and other Institutions for Transboundary Water Cooperation: Capacity for Water Cooperation in Eastern Europe, Caucasus and Central Asia.* United Nations, New York and Geneva. http://unece.org/env/water/documents/CWC_publication_joint_bodies.pdf

----. 2009*c*. *Progress Report on National Policy Dialogues in Countries in Eastern Europe, Caucasus and Central Asia. New York and Geneva, United Nations.* ECE/MP.WAT/2009/6, Geneva, Switzerland. http://unece.org/env/documents/2009/Wat/mp_wat/ECE_MP.WAT_2009_6_e.pdf

----. 2009*d*. *Transboundary Flood Risk Management: Experiences from the UNECE Region. New York and Geneva, United Nations.* http://www.unece.org/env/water/mop5/Transboundary_Flood_Risk_Managment.pdf

----. 2010. *The MDGs in Europe and Central Asia: Achievements, Challenges and the Way Forward.* Prepared by UNECE in collaboration with UNDP, ILO, FAO, WFP, UNESCO, UNIFEM, WHO/Euro, UNICEF, UNPFA, UNAIDS, UNEP, UNIDO, UNCTAD, and the International Trade Centre. UNew York and Geneva, United Nations, 126 pp.

----. 2011*a*. *Setting Targets and Target Dates under the Protocol on Water and Health in the Republic of Moldova.* In collaboration with the Swiss Agency for Development and Cooperation and the Government of the Republic of Moldova. Chisinau, Moldavia, Eco-TIRAS, Elan INC SRL. http://www.eco-tiras.org/books/W&H-book-MD-En-2011.pdf

----. 2011*b*. *Second Assessment of Transboundary Rivers, Lakes and Groundwaters.* New York and Geneva, United Nations. ECE/MP.WAT/33. http://www.unece.org/env/water/publications/pub/second_assessment.html (Accessed 12 October 2011.)

----. UNECE Statistical Division Database. New York and Geneva, United Nations. n.d. http://www.unece.org (select Statistical Database) or http://w3.unece.org/pxweb/ (Accessed 12 October 2011.)

USEPA (US Environmental Protection Agency). 2007. *Possible Water Resource Impacts in North America* http://www.epa.gov/climatechange/effects/water/northamerica.html (Accessed 12 October 2011.)

----. 2009*a*: *National Water Quality Inventory Report to Congress.* USEPA Office of Water, EPA 841-F-08-003, January 2009. http://water.epa.gov/lawsregs/guidance/cwa/305b/upload/2009_01_22_305b_2004report_factsheet2004305b.pdf (Accessed 12 October 2011.)

----. 2009*b*: *National Water Program Strategy: Response to Climate Change. National Water Program Climate Change Strategy: Key Action Update for 2010–2011.* Washington DC, USEPA. http://www.epa.gov/ow/climatechange/strategy.html

WHO (World Health Organization). 2010. *Guidance on Water Supply and Sanitation in Extreme Weather Events.* Geneva, UNECE and WHO/EURO.

Wunder, S. 2005. *Payments for Environmental Services: Some Nuts and Bolts.* Occasional Paper No. 42. Jakarta, Indonesia, Center for International Forestry Research. http://www.cifor.cgiar.org/publications/pdf_files/OccPapers/OP-42.pdf

CHAPTER 31
Asia and the Pacific

UNESCAP (Energy Security and Water Resources Section, Environment and Development Division)
—

Authors Ti Le-Huu and Ermina Sokou[1]
Contributors Felix Seebacher, Salmah Zakaria and Marina Korzenevica

Acknowledgements Inputs were provided from Felix Seebacher on wastewater management, Salmah Zakaria on climate change adaptation and Marina Korzenevica on country-specific policies.

III

Trends and major challenges

Millions of people in the Asia-Pacific region are still not connected to improved water infrastructure for personal and productive uses, placing them in a state of human insecurity. In 2008, about 480 million people lacked access to improved water resources, while 1.9 billion had no access to improved sanitation facilities.

Population size, rapid urbanization, industrialization and economic development put pressure on freshwater resources. The region's water resources are also increasingly vulnerable to and threatened by natural disasters and pollution.

Natural water-related disasters such as floods and droughts undermine economic development. Coastal and flood-prone areas, where much economic growth is generated, are often struck by typhoons and rainstorms.

Of all wastewater generated, only 15–20% receives some level of treatment before discharge into water resources. The total volume of domestic wastewater currently produced in urban areas is a particular concern, estimated to be between 150 and 250 million cubic metres per day. This wastewater either is discharged directly into open water bodies or leaches into the ground.

Richer, urban households are in a better position to secure safe water and adequate sanitation. Inequalities in access to water between rich and poor households are evident all over Asia, but for sanitation, the inequality is more striking.

Emerging needs

Providing water and sanitation services to all requires sizeable financial resources – US$59 billion to meet the Millennium Development Goal of access to water and $71 billion to provide access to sanitation. If investment needs for all water services are included, the total annual investment costs for water infrastructure could reach $180 billion, of which $100 billion is needed in developing countries.

Extremes of flood and drought are expected to increase in both magnitude and frequency as a result of climate change.

Policies and solutions

To address the lack of adequate financing, time horizons of investment assessment need to be expanded. Environmental costs should be factored into prices charged for water and sanitation services. Governments need to create the market conditions for the development of sustainable and eco-efficient infrastructure.

Integrated stormwater management can prove invaluable during floods, as clean water bodies minimize spreading of polluted water and disease. Integrated rainwater harvesting, thanks to advances in technology, is also viewed as an integral part of water cycle management.

Central sewage treatment plants require a very large space, and are costly and difficult to maintain. Technology for compact small wastewater treatment plants has improved and offers many advantages.

Certain water-related challenges, such as stagnant access to sanitation, deteriorating water quality, and climate-related risks, are common in Asia-Pacific countries. Targeted, urgent action is needed to break the developmental deadlock that many countries find themselves in due to poor water resources management. Promoting household water security, recognizing the need to adapt to climate change threats and initiating a 'Wastewater Revolution' are proposed priorities for regional cooperation.

31.1 Introduction

'Asia and the Pacific' and 'ESCAP region' refer to the group of members and associate members of the Economic and Social Commission for Asia and the Pacific (ESCAP) that fall within the region. The geographical description of the region used in this chapter includes 55 member states of ESCAP in the five subregions: Central Asia, North-East Asia, the Pacific, South Asia and South-East Asia, as shown in Table 31.1.

31.1.1 General trends in the Asia-Pacific

The Asia-Pacific region has the largest share of renewable freshwater resources in the world, at 21,135 billion m². This endowment is coupled with high water utilization rates. On average, the region withdraws 11% of its total renewable resources, second in the world after the water-scarce Middle East and on par with European utilization rates (ESCAP, 2009a).

Despite some progress, millions in the Asia-Pacific remain disconnected from improved water infrastructure for personal and productive uses, forcing them into insecurity. In 2008, about 480 million people lacked access to improved water resources, while 1.9 billion had no access to improved sanitation facilities (WHO and UNICEF, 2010b).

The future is also uncertain. Population size, rapid urbanization, industrialization and economic development are placing pressure on freshwater resources. Water resources are also increasingly vulnerable and threatened by natural disasters and pollution. The Asia-Pacific is the world's most vulnerable region with respect to natural disasters. Pollution from industries, agriculture and households further jeopardize future water availability.

31.2 Issues

31.2.1 Meeting or missing the MDG target on drinking water and sanitation

Between 1990 and 2008, significant achievements were made towards meeting the Millennium Development Goals (MDG) target on access to safe drinking water. Asia, and the Pacific as a whole, is an early achiever for halving the proportion of people without access to safe drinking water, but not sanitation (ESCAP, ADB and UNDP, 2010). Between 1990 and 2008, the proportion of the region's population with

TABLE 31.1

Member states of the Economic and Social Commission for Asia and the Pacific (ESCAP) in the five subregions

Subregion	ESCAP member states
North-East Asia	China, Democratic People's Republic of Korea, Japan, Mongolia, Republic of Korea, Russian Federation
Central Asia and the Caucasus	Armenia, Azerbaijan, Georgia, Kazakhstan, Kyrgyzstan, Tajikistan, Turkmenistan, Uzbekistan
South-East Asia	Brunei Darussalam, Cambodia, Indonesia, Lao People's Democratic Republic, Malaysia, Myanmar, Philippines, Singapore, Thailand, Timor-Leste, Viet Nam
South and South-West Asia	Afghanistan, Bangladesh, Bhutan, India, Iran (Islamic Republic of), Maldives, Nepal, Pakistan
Subregion	**ESCAP member states**
	Sri Lanka, Turkey
Pacific	American Samoa, Australia, Cook Islands, Fiji, French Polynesia, Guam, Kiribati, Marshall Islands, Micronesia (Federated States of), Nauru, New Caledonia, New Zealand, Niue, Northern Mariana Islands, Palau, Papua New Guinea, Samoa, Solomon Islands, Tonga, Tuvalu, Vanuatu

Source: CARE (2009).

access to improved drinking water sources increased from 73 to 88 %, a 1.2-billion people increase (including population size increase). The access rate increased in all Asia-Pacific subregions, except for Central Asia and the Pacific region, where it stayed the same.

Compared with water supply, sanitation coverage is in a dire state. Only around 53% of the region's population has access to improved sanitation. Access to sanitation also varies considerably between subregions. The most rapid progress has been in South-East Asia where the increase was 22 percentage points, and in North-East Asia which between 1990 and 2008 increased access by 12 percentage points. The progress in South and South-West Asia was even weaker. Although the number of people with access doubled since 1990, by 2008 the average coverage was only 38% and the number of people without access was higher than it was in 2005.

Poor drinking water quality and inadequate sanitation threaten human health and productivity. According to the World Health Organization (WHO), 88% of diarrhoea incidents are attributed to poor sanitation and dirty water (WHO and UNICEF, 2010a). In South and South-East Asia, diarrhoea is responsible for up to 8.5% of all deaths, which is the highest rate in the world, followed by Africa, where it is responsible for 7.7% of deaths (WHO, 2010c). These numbers reveal a grim reality, which because of lack of access to basic infrastructure perpetuates poverty and poor health, and conceals the region's vast hidden potential for development.

32.2.2 Stretched carrying capacity
Water availability
In the ESCAP region, high total and internal renewable resources stand in sharp contrast with the per capita availability, which is the second lowest in the world at 5,224 m² per capita and far below the world average of 8,349 m² per capita – a result of the population size (Figure 31.1).

Physical water scarcity is only one part of the equation. Water allocation is another matter. The share of domestic water withdrawal over total withdrawal in Asia and the Pacific, the most populated region in the world, is the lowest at 7.7%, compared with Africa at 10%. Agriculture is the principal user of water, claiming around 70% of all withdrawals. The region's main staple food, rice, requires two or three times more

water for cultivation than other cereals. In many countries, agricultural practices are characterized by free-of-charge water abstraction, poorly managed irrigation schemes, outdated and damaged technological infrastructure, and production of water-intensive crops in dry regions. Many examples of over-abstraction of ground and surface water exist. The threat of disappearance of the Aral Sea, mainly from intensive irrigation upstream, demonstrates that even the biggest lakes of the world can be seriously affected (ESCAP, 2008).

Overall water availability for development across the region is on a steep decline. Some countries, like Uzbekistan and Tajikistan, withdraw very close to, or even more than, their total surface and groundwater combined (116 and 99.6% of the total renewable water respectively) (ESCAP, 2009a). Although critical conditions of freshwater availability appear localized in a number of countries, analysing existing data from a new, development angle reveals wider critical trends.

Water quality
The ecological carrying capacity of the region is further affected by the deteriorating water quality of water bodies. Of all wastewater generated worldwide, and in the region, only 15–20% receives some level of treatment before discharge into water resources; the remainder is discharged with its full load of pollution and toxic compounds (UNEP, 2002).

Domestic sewerage is of concern, as it affects ecosystems close to densely populated areas. The total volume of wastewater produced in urban areas is estimated at 150–250 million m² per day (UNEP, 2002). This wastewater is either discharged directly into open water bodies or leaches into the subsoil. In addition, most industries in the region continue to generate water pollution, as enforcement of relevant regulations lags behind.

Even relatively water-rich countries, such as Malaysia, Indonesia, Bhutan and Papua New Guinea, now face water supply and quality constraints in their major cities because of population growth, growing water consumption, environmental damage, harmful agricultural activities, poor management of water catchment areas, industrialization, and groundwater overuse.

Countries that are relatively less well-endowed with water, in Central Asia and in South and South-West Asia, are even more severely affected when water quality deteriorates. Countries with the least available water per person also tend to have poor water quality. Kazakhstan, Uzbekistan, Kyrgyzstan, Georgia, Myanmar, the Islamic Republic of Iran, the Maldives, Nepal, Tajikistan, Azerbaijan, Turkmenistan, Democratic People's Republic of Korea, Bhutan, Papua New Guinea and Mongolia are countries in which water quality pressures are strong.

31.2.3 Natural disasters

Asia-Pacific is a diverse region covering almost all of the different types of climatic regions, from tropical rain forest to more temperate areas; and from land-locked, mountain regions of the Himalayas to island states in the Pacific and Indian Oceans. Precipitation in many countries in the region is heavily influenced by the monsoon climate.[2] Some subregions, like South-East Asia, suffer from both floods and droughts at the same location, but at different times of the year.

Natural water-related disasters, such as floods and droughts undermine economic development. Coastal and flood-prone areas, where much economic growth is generated, are often struck by typhoons and rain-storms. Striking and sustaining an optimal balance between the developmental needs of many Asian developing economies (especially influenced by population growth, food and energy security issues) and the risks associated with the use of flood-prone land is a challenge, given uncertainties concerning the future state of the water regime.

Between 2000 and 2009, an average of 20,451 people were killed each year by water-related disasters, excluding tsunami disasters, in the region. World's annual average was 23,651 deaths for the same period (Center for Research on the Epidemidiology of Disasters, 2009). Unprecedented floods in Pakistan killed 1,974 people, damaged 1.65 million houses, and destroyed 2.24 million hectares of crop land in 2010 (ESCAP, 2010b).

Extreme weather conditions also jeopardize gains in access to water and sanitation. Droughts reduce drinking water availability and floods and storms can damage basic water infrastructure and spread disease.

31.3 Emerging drivers

Asia-Pacific is an incredibly dynamic region. Rapid urbanization, economic growth, industrialization, extensive and intensive agriculture development, as well as climate change, have resulted in increasing and exponential demand for water. Emanating from these trends are the following drivers shaping the region's capacity to meet its water needs.

31.3.1 Economic and social drivers
Inequality in access to drinking water and sanitation
Despite impressive growth in gross domestic product (GDP) rates and substantial improvements in access to drinking water and sanitation, income and gender inequalities persist. A basic typology analysis undertaken by ESCAP showed that richer, urban households are in a better position to secure safe water

FIGURE 31.1

Total renewable water per capita (total renewable/population), global regions (2007)

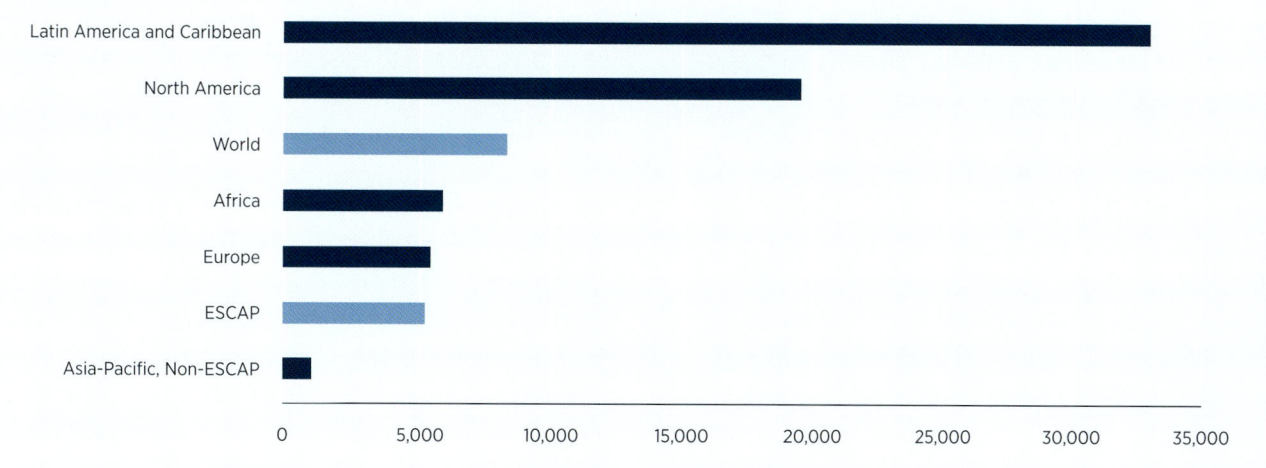

Source: ESCAP (2009a, fig. 28.4, p. 206).

supply and adequate sanitation. Inequalities in access to water between rich and poor households are evident all over Asia, but for sanitation, the gap is even bigger. The largest discrepancies between access of rich and poor people are in urban environments, particularly in smaller cities (MEASURE DHS, 2004–2008; UNICEF, 2004–2008).

Sex-disaggregated data on access to water and sanitation is not available at the international level. However, the Convention on the Elimination of All Forms of Discrimination Against Women (CEDAW) Committee has underlined that the health of rural women often depends on adequate and non-discriminatory access to water (UN Women, 2010). Provision of segregated toilets in schools is a necessity to increase school attendance by girls because gender inequalities in access to water and sanitation affect women disproportionally (Burrows et al., 2004).

The unfulfilled potential of women hampers progress. ESCAP research reveals that women invest more of their money in the health of their family, including water and sanitation, than men. The argument can also be made that women value access to water more than men. In national surveys from countries as diverse as Armenia, India, Indonesia, Lao People's Democratic Republic, Kazakhstan, Mongolia, Tajikistan and Viet Nam, female-headed households consistently had better access to improved water and sanitation than male-headed households (Table 31.2) (MEASURE DHS, 2004–2008; UNICEF, 2004–2008). However, in male-dominated environments, women's role in household decisions on water and sanitation remains marginal.

Infrastructure development and investment
Providing water and sanitation services to everyone requires sizeable financial resources. For all of Asia and the Pacific, it is estimated that US$59 billion is needed to meet the target of access to drinking water and a total of US$71 billion is needed to provide access to sanitation according to the MDG target (ESCAP, 2010a). If investment needs for all water services are included, the total annual investment cost for water infrastructure could reach US$180 billion, including about US$100 billion for all developing countries in the region (ESCAP, 2006b). Poor water quality requires vast investments, and increases in water treatment and distribution costs.

The coordinated drive to achieve the MDGs by governments, civil society and donors has boosted performance in related indicators over the past few years. In response to international calls for increased financing for water, the Asian Development Bank (ADB) launched the Water Financing Program (WFP) to double investments in the sector between 2006 and 2010 and established the Water Financing Partnership Facility (WFPF) to mobilize co-financing and investments from development partners, with some US$65 million reached as of December 2008 (Asian Development Bank, 2011).

Data from seven South-East Asian countries (Cambodia, Indonesia, Lao People's Democratic Republic, the Philippines, Thailand, Timor-Leste, Viet Nam), one country from Central Asia (Kazakhstan), one country from North-East Asia (Mongolia) and two countries from South Asia (Bangladesh, Nepal) indicated a diverse level of institutional engagement in water and sanitation planning. Countries like Cambodia, Lao People's Democratic Republic, Nepal and Thailand have adequate policies and institutions, while Cambodia and Lao People's Democratic Republic lack human resources and financial planning for implementation.[3] The Philippines, Cambodia, Timor-Leste, and Viet Nam also lagged behind in financial planning and resources, with Viet Nam indicating the best future potential for scale-up of resource allocation in meeting water and sanitation goals (UN-Water, 2010).

However, even if access to adequate water and sanitation systems is established, it is important to ensure that the built systems are financially sustainable, functional, reliable, affordable, responsive to needs, socially acceptable for both genders, and appropriate for children and adults. Often sanitation facilities are incompatible with women's needs, while the size of basic facilities is improper and even dangerous for children.

Wastewater treatment facilities in the region are also generally lacking. In cities, many small waterways are covered to allow more space for roads or commercial areas, put into concrete beds, used mostly to facilitate storm runoff or simply used as open sewers. Irrigation facilities in the region are often old and in poor condition, partly because of extremely low water prices and poor management of the facilities. Many governments have subsidized the construction of inefficient irrigation systems, along with fuel and electricity supplies. This has weakened price signals, tempting farmers to withdraw too much water from rivers, over-pump groundwater and waste freshwater resources (ESCAP, 2008).

Water for food
The changing economic, demographic and climatic backdrop is exacerbating difficult conditions for food production. Producing each calorie of food requires approximately 1 L of water. To provide each consumer with 1,800 calories per day, by 2050 Asia and the Pacific would need an additional 2.4 billion m² of water per day. Food security concerns aggravate the harm inflicted on those who lack basic water access, whether small-scale or large-scale producers.

31.3.2 Policies, law and financing drivers
Water management capacity
Countries that withdraw water very close to their internal renewable sources may face difficulties in supporting development trends in the long-term. Over-exploitation can modify water distribution and cause water crises in parts of the region. Many countries in the region have moved, with various levels of

TABLE 31.2
Percentage of male and female-headed households with access to safe drinking water

Country	Year	Male-headed (%)	Female-headed (%)	How much more women value access to water (% points)
Armenia	2000	93.8	95.4	2
	2005	95.8	96.4	1
Bangladesh	2007	97.0	97.6	1
India	1999	80.4	78.8	-2
	2006	87.7	89.2	2
Indonesia	1997	73.9	77.5	4
	2003	71.8	72.1	0
Kazakhstan	1999	92.5	96.2	4
	2006	94.0	95.9	2
Kyrgyzstan	2006	88.9	93.3	4
Lao PDR	2005	58.6	70.4	12
Mongolia	2005	65.3	76.3	11
Nepal	1996	76.9	78.5	2
	2006	82.3	80.3	-2
Philippines	1998	85.4	87.4	2
	2003	83.2	85.4	2
Tajikistan	2000	56.1	65.8	10
	2005	70.0	78.3	8
Thailand	2005	96.0	96.1	0
Uzbekistan	2006	89.5	95.9	6
Viet Nam	1997	71.5	78.6	7
	2000	76.1	83.1	7
	2002	77.1	84.4	7
	2006	87.7	92.2	4

Source: ESCAP analysis based on Demographic and Health Surveys (DHS) and Multiple Indicator Cluster Survey (MICS) from the period 1999–2008.

on-the-ground-success, to adopt Integrated Water Resources Management (IWRM). Tables 31.3 and 31.4 provide some examples of regional and country-level initiatives.

Water disputes and conflicts

Despite increased awareness and implementation of IWRM principles, the rapid economic growth of the region's developing countries, accompanied by high intensity of the use of natural resources, especially water, has led to a rapid increase in conflicts over water. This poses a threat to stability and development.

Over the past two decades, the number of reported water-related incidents has risen. Conflicts within countries are dominating the picture, particularly since 1990 (Table 31.5). In China alone, the number of disputes related to water reached over 120,000 during the 1990s, according to official sources.[4] In India, efforts and resources in water management are often focused on conflict management between different states. Allocation of increasingly scarce water resources has become the principal cause for water conflicts. Direct conflicts are most likely to occur at the local level over an ill-thought dam, ambiguous withdrawal rights or deterioration of water quality. Against the context of development, the biggest challenges are balancing the different uses of water and managing their economic, social and environmental impacts.

31.3.3 Technological drivers

Advances in technology are also changing the landscape of options for the region on water resources management to meet its needs for water supply and wastewater treatment coverage and socio-economic development.

TABLE 31.3

Regional Integrated Water Resources Management (IWRM) initiatives

Region	IWRM initiative
Central Asia	Aral Sea Basin: framework for subregional dialogue (October 2008)
	Aral Sea Basin: Executive Committee of the International Fund for Saving the Aral Sea (EC-IFAS)
	Global Water Partnership Central Asia and Caucasus (GWP CACENA): support for IWRM
South and South-West Asia	South Asian Association for Regional Cooperation (SAARC): Disaster Management Center
	SAARC: Comprehensive Framework on Disaster Management
	Global Water Partnership (GWP) – South Asia: support for IWRM
	South Asia Water Forum (SAWAF): directions for transboundary water management
	National Adaptation Plan of Action (NAPA) in all countries
	Political commitment for sanitation (SACOSAN)
	Water Utility Network –South Asia (SAWUN)
South-East Asia	Mekong River Commission establishment (1995)
	Mekong River Commission: IWRM-based Basin Development Strategy
	ASEAN: Working Group on Water Resources Management and IWRM
	GWP-SEA: support for IWRM
Pacific Islands	Pacific Wastewater Policy Statement
	Pacific Wastewater Framework for Action (2001)
	Pacific Regional Action Plan on Sustainable Water Management (2002)
	Drinking Water Quality and Health Framework for Action (2005)
	Pacific Islands Applied Geoscience Commission (SOPAC)

Source: Jin Lee, Ti LeHuu and Salmah Zakaria, Energy Security and Water Resources Section, Environment and Development Division, ESCAP, Status of IWRM Implementation in the Asia-Pacific Region (unpublished report), December 2009, in cooperation with Torkil Clausen, GWP.

Modular structures for water supply and wastewater
The advent of efficient modular design of water treatment using recent advances in technologies, such as membrane technology, allows effective decentralized water supply and wastewater management.

Technology for compact, small wastewater treatment plants (or units) has improved significantly and the requirement for space has been reduced, allowing introduction of these units even in crowded urban areas.

TABLE 31.4

Country-specific Integrated Water Resources Management (IWRM) initiatives

Country	IWRM initiative
Armenia	New Water Code with IWRM principles
Bangladesh	IWRM and Water Efficiency Plan, water codes
Cambodia	Law on Water Resources Management (2007)
	National Water Resources Strategy (2004)
China	District management guided by IWRM
	GWP and provincial GWP partnerships supporting IWRM
	Water Law integrating river basin management
Indonesia	Government Regulation on Groundwater (2008)
	Government Regulation on Water Supply System Development (2006)
	National Water Resources Council (2008)
	Revision of Government Regulation on Irrigation (2006)
	Revision of Government Regulation on Water Resources Management (2008)
Japan	Revised Basic Environment Plan (2000)
	Water management includes environmental sustainability
Kazakhstan	New Water Code with IWRM principles
Kyrgyzstan	New Water Code with IWRM principles
Lao PDR	Water Resources and Environment Administration
Malaysia	National Water Services Commission (2007)
	Water Services Industry Act (2006)
Mongolia	Water Authority supports IWRM through river basin councils
Myanmar	Conservation of Water Resources and Rivers Law (2006)
	National Commission for Environmental Affairs (2008): effluent standards for factories
Nepal	IWRM and Water Efficiency Plan, water codes
Pakistan	IWRM and Water Efficiency Plan, water codes
Philippines	Water Resources Commission to act as economic regulatory body
Republic of Korea	Comprehensive River Basin Plan revitalizes 12 rivers
Sri Lanka	IWRM and Water Efficiency Plan, water codes
Tajikistan	New Water Code with IWRM principles
Viet Nam	River basin management by Ministry of Natural Resources and Environment (2007)
	Water sector reform (2006–2008) separates water resources from water use management

Source: Jin Lee, Ti LeHuu and Salmah Zakaria, Energy Security and Water Resources Section, Environment and Development Division, ESCAP, Status of IWRM Implementation in the Asia-Pacific Region (unpublished report), December 2009, in cooperation with Torkil Clausen, GWP.

Water-sensitive urban design

Water-sensitive urban design is the cumulative process of designing urban environments to accommodate human and environmental needs for water, while respecting and supporting the natural water cycle. The design incorporates the basic water supply access and security; public health protection (e.g. through sewers); flood protection through drainage systems; environmental protection by rehabilitating waterways; protection of natural resources through the water cycle, paying specific attention to intergenerational equity and resilience to climate change (Brown et al., 2008).

Storm water management

Extremes of floods and droughts are expected to increase in magnitude and frequency as a result of climate change. Natural water bodies can turn into water supply sources during droughts, if rehabilitated. Integrated storm water management (ISWM), already implemented in the more developed countries of the region, can prove invaluable during floods, as clean water bodies minimize spreading of polluted water and disease.

Rainwater harvesting

TABLE 31.5

Chronology of major recent water conflicts in Asia, 2000–2008

Date	Countries involved	Description of conflicts or potential conflicts
2000	Central Asia: Kyrgyzstan, Kazakhstan, Uzbekistan	Kyrgyzstan cuts off water to Kazakhstan until coal was delivered. Uzbekistan cuts off water to Kazakhstan for nonpayment of debt. (Pannier, 2000)
2000	Afghanistan: Hazarajat	Violent conflicts broke out over water resources in the villages of Burna Legan and Taina Legan, and in other parts of the region, as drought depleted local resources. (Cooperation Center for Afghanistan, 2000)
2000	India: Gujarat	Water riots were reported in some areas of Gujarat to protest against failure of the authority to arrange adequate supply of tanker water. Police shot into a crowd at the village of Falla near Jamnagar, killing three people and injuring 20 others following protests against the diversion of water from Kankavati Dam to the town of Jamnagar. (FTGWR, 2000)
2001	China	In protest to the destruction of fisheries from uncontrolled water pollution, fishermen in northern Jiaxing City, Zhejiang Province, dammed for 23 days the canal that carries 90 million tonnes of industrial wastewater per year. The wastewater discharge into neighbouring Shengze, Jiangsu Province, killed fish and threatened people's health. (China Ministry of Water Resources, 2001)
2002	India: Kashmir	Two people were killed and 25 others injured in Kashmir when police fired at a group of villagers in Garend in a dispute over sharing water from an irrigation stream. (The Japan Times, 2002)
2002	India: Karnataka, Tamil Nadu	Continued violence over the allocation of Cauvery River between Karnataka and Tamil Nadu. Riots, property destruction, more than 30 injuries, and arrests occurred through September and October. (The Hindu 2002a,b, The Times of India 2002a)
2004	China	Tens of thousands of farmers staged a sit-in against the construction of Pubugou Dam on Dadu River in Sichuan Province. Riot police were deployed to quell the unrest and one person was killed. Some residents were killed. (See China 2006 for follow-up) (BBC, 2004b; VOA, 2004)
2007	India	Thousands of farmers breached security and stormed the area of Hirakud Dam to protest allocation of water to industry. Minor injuries resulted from the conflict between the farmers and police. (News Service, 2007)

Source: Gleick (2008).

Due to advances in rainwater harvesting technology, integrated rainwater harvesting is increasingly viewed as an integral part of water cycle management. Rainwater can be captured at the city level. In Singapore little rainwater is wasted. Rainwater is collected wherever it can - in streets and ponds, even on tall buildings and bridges - before being taken by drains to reservoirs, and then to treatment plants where it is cleaned to drinking water standards. The catchment area is being increased by the creation of a pair of reservoirs. The first of these reservoirs, will expand the rainfall-catchment acreage to two-thirds of the island's total land area (*The Economist,* 2010).

Domestic rainwater harvesting systems are also simple to install and operate. Their decentralized nature allows owners to benefit from direct management of demand and supply. With support technologies (modern and indigenous), rainwater harvesting is cost-effective, and can release capital in times of disaster. (Stockholm Environment Institute and UNEP, 2009).

31.4 Principal risks and uncertainties

31.4.1 Climate change

Hydrological extremes have increased in the Asia-Pacific as well as around the globe. Countries in the region are expected to be severely affected by increased climate variability. For example, in the Mekong River, the maximum flow is projected to increase by 35–42% in the basin and by 16–19% in the delta. In contrast the minimum flow is estimated to decline by 17–24% in the basin and by 26–29% in the delta, suggesting possible water shortages in the dry season. Heavily populated mega deltas in South-West, East and South-East Asia are expected to be at greatest risk of increased river and coastal floods. The interaction of climate change impacts with rapid development is expected to affect growth, including MDG gains (IPCC, 2007).

In addition to floods and droughts, saltwater intrusion in estuaries is expected to move further inwards. Snow melt and glaciers, as well as rising snow lines, could also be unfavourable for downstream agriculture in South and Central Asia. North-western China is projected to experience a 27% decline in glacier areas. Changes in runoff could impact power output from hydropower generating countries such as Tajikistan and increase demand for agriculture water in arid and semi-arid regions of Asia.

31.4.2 Hotspots

The many threats to water resources paint a complex picture. To better focus and prioritize regional action, ESCAP has identified hotspots of multiple challenges. Hotspots are countries, areas or ecosystems with overlapping challenges of poor access to water and sanitation, deteriorating water quality, limited water availability and increased exposure to climate change and water-related disasters. All or some of these challenges may be of concern (Table 31.6).

As shown in Figure 31.2, countries in South-East Asia are at a crossroads of development. High growth rates provide financing for better water resources management, but development priorities ignore the risks from disaster, climate change and poor household water and sanitation access. Uzbekistan and India are also facing exceptional circumstances because of little preparedness for natural disasters and climate change (India), and unsustainable patter of water use (Uzbekistan). Basic access to sanitation remains a determining concern for Bangladesh.

31.5 Achievements through policy-making

After decades of high economic growth, the region is now facing severe environmental risks. Water insecurity is one manifestation of the unfolding environmental damage. Informed policy-making is the only tool to enhance resilience while sustaining growth.

31.5.1 Policy options

Pricing in costs to the environment

The Asia-Pacific development pattern has relied primarily on cheap natural and human resources. This, however, has created economies that run in two speeds: one of rapid advances in economic performance, and another of persisting poverty and environmental degradation. To promote more balanced growth, prices of production factors need to reflect the real cost, including costs to the environment and ecosystem services. This shift has important implications for water resources management, including expanding time horizons of investment assessment to more adequately incorporate benefits of access to water, sanitation, and wastewater treatment; and factoring environmental costs into water and sanitation service charges. Payments for Ecosystem Services (PES) is one way of determining the value and paying a price for these services (Box 31.1).

Eco-efficient water infrastructure development

Eco-efficient water infrastructure aims to harmonize water infrastructure within the environment and can be envisaged in urban and rural contexts. Eco-efficient urban solutions include river rehabilitation, storm water management, decentralized wastewater treatment, and water re-use and recycling while rural options include modern irrigation practices, decentralized water and sanitation systems, water reuse and re-cycling, as well as rainwater harvesting.

Many countries such as Cambodia, China, Malaysia, and the Republic of Korea have already been pursuing eco-efficient water infrastructure development. Although specific examples of large-scale eco-efficient water infrastructure are difficult to find, some governments are already discussing and integrating these terms in their national planning. Indonesia integrated the eco-efficiency concept into its five-year National Development Plan for 2010–2014, and the Philippines adopted the eco-efficiency dimensions into its Mid-Term National Development Plan.

To support this process, ESCAP has developed eco-efficiency water infrastructure guidelines and completed capacity-building initiatives in several developing countries, including support to the development of guidelines for Eco-efficiency in Water Infrastructure for Buildings in Malaysia, recommended to be implemented in all public sector buildings; the implementation of a pilot project on an ISWM system in the Philippines; and a river rehabilitation programme for a tributary of the Brantas River in Indonesia.

Sustainable consumption and production

Water resources management is shifting from supply-side to demand-side management and this is increasingly recognized in the region. Non-revenue water averages 30% of production in Asian cities, but ranges from 4 to 65% (McIntosh, 2003). Approximately half of this loss is from leaking distribution networks. There are many examples of implementation of demand-side management measures across the region and interest

TABLE 31.6

Basic framework for defining water hotspots

Challenge	Measures available*	Countries at risk
Water availability	Water utilization level (Threat* 1) Index of Water Available for Development (IWAD**) (Threat 2) Water quality (Threats 3 and 4)	Afghanistan, Azerbaijan, Bhutan, Democratic People's Republic of Korea, Georgia, India, Indonesia, Kazakhstan, Kyrgyzstan, Malaysia, Maldives†, Mongolia, Myanmar, Nepal, Pakistan‡, Papua New Guinea, Philippines, Tajikistan, Thailand, Turkmenistan, Uzbekistan‡
Vulnerability and risk	Frequency of floods (Threat 5) Frequency of cyclones (Threat 6) Frequency of droughts (Threat 7) Climate change pattern (Threat 8)	Australia, Bangladesh‡, Cambodia‡, China‡, DPRK, India‡, Indonesia‡, Iran, Kazakhstan‡, Kyrgyzstan, Lao PDR‡, Myanmar, ‡ Malaysia‡, Maldives†, Nepal, Pacific Islands†, Pakistan, Papua New Guinea‡, Philippines‡, Republic of Korea, Sri Lanka, Thailand‡, Timor-Leste‡, Turkmenistan, Uzbekistan‡, Viet Nam‡
Household water adequacy	Access to water (Threat 9) Access to sanitation (Threat 10) Disability adjusted life-years (DALY) from diarrhoea	Afghanistan†, Bangladesh, Cambodia†, China, India, Indonesia, Lao PDR†, Mongolia, Nepal, Pacific Islands, Papua New Guinea†, Timor-Leste
Human development	Life expectancy at birth Inequalities in access People living in poverty	Cambodia, Democratic People's Republic of Korea, Indonesia, Lao PDR, Myanmar, Pacific Islands, Papua New Guinea, Philippines

*. The 'Threat' numbers refer to columns in Figure 31.2 and measures that were actually used to estimate water hotspots.
**. The Index of Water Available for Development (IWAD) examines the current trends of rapidly increasing water withdrawal in relation to the limited amount of renewable freshwater resources.
†. Challenges exist in two of the indicated measures. IWAD is defined as an index measuring the balance between the total internal renewable water resources and total water withdrawals in a particular year against the base line of 1980 of this balance.
‡. Challenges exist in more than two of the indicated measures.
Note: Data not used for hotspot identification.
Sources: Compiled from Dilley et al. (2005); ESCAP (2009a).

in improving water use efficiency is growing. Bangkok and Manila leak detection programmes have lowered estimated Uncounted-for-Water (UFW), thus postponing the development of new infrastructure (Molle et al., 2009). Since 2008 Sydney Water in Australia has provided homes in the Hoxton Park area with two water supplies: recycled water and drinking water (dual reticulation) (Sydney Water, 2011).

Singapore has reduced urban domestic water demand from 176 L per person a day in 1994 to 157 L in 2007 through the comprehensive policy, based on three principles: voluntary, pricing and mandatory (Kiang, 2008). To apply these principles, several actions were taken: water tariffs and water conservation tax were restructured, maximum allowable flow rates were set, public education and awareness campaigns were launched, and water audits to large customers were implemented as a part of the market-oriented programme to obtain industry feedback. As a result, Singapore now has one of the lowest UFW rates in the world (below 5%) (Kiang, 2008).

In Hamirpur district of India, the Department of Rural Development and the Department of Agriculture have embarked on a programme of Soil and Water Conservation to reduce runoff, create 'high efficiency life-saving irrigation' and promote groundwater

FIGURE 31.2

Asia-Pacific water hotspots

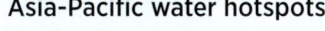

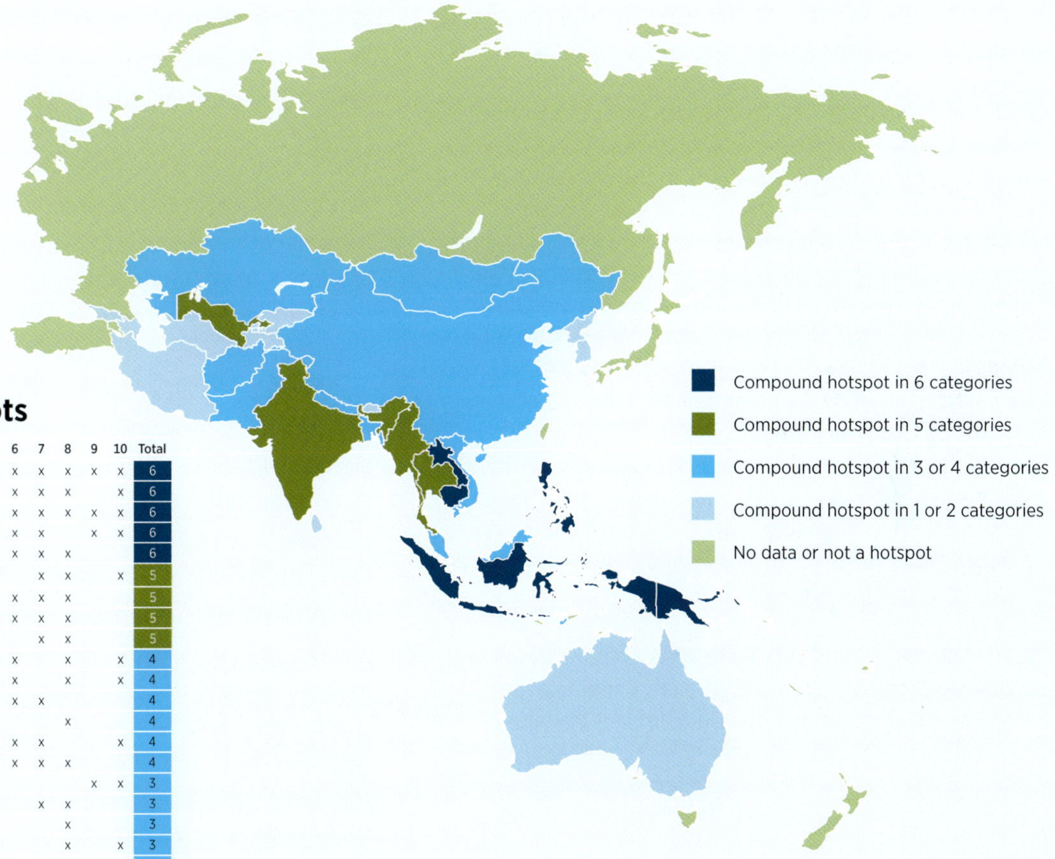

Compound hotspots

	1	2	3	4	5	6	7	8	9	10	Total
Cambodia					x	x	x	x	x	x	6
Indonesia		x			x	x	x	x		x	6
Lao PDR				x	x		x	x	x	x	6
Papua New Guinea				x	x	x		x	x	x	6
Philippines	x		x		x	x	x	x			6
India	x				x		x	x		x	5
Myanmar			x		x	x	x	x			5
Thailand			x		x	x	x	x			5
Uzbekistan	x	x		x			x	x			5
Bangladesh					x	x		x		x	4
China					x	x		x		x	4
Malaysia			x		x	x	x				4
Pakistan	x		x				x	x			4
Timor-Leste					x	x	x	x			4
Viet Nam					x	x		x		x	4
Afghanistan	x								x	x	3
Kazakhstan				x			x	x			3
Maldives	x				x			x			3
Mongolia				x			x			x	3
Nepal				x			x			x	3
Pacific Islands						x		x		x	3
DPRK				x	x						2
Kyrgyzstan				x			x				2
Tajikistan				x			x				2
Turkmenistan				x			x				2
Australia						x					1
Azerbaijan				x							1
Bhutan				x							1
Georgia				x							1
Iran								x			1
Republic of Korea				x							1
Sri Lanka								x			1
Prevalence (countries affected)	6	2	5	14	15	13	17	19	4	12	

Legend — map

- Compound hotspot in 6 categories
- Compound hotspot in 5 categories
- Compound hotspot in 3 or 4 categories
- Compound hotspot in 1 or 2 categories
- No data or not a hotspot

Legend

1 Increasing water scarcity threat
2 High water utilization
3 Deteriorating water quality
4 Poor water quality and low water endowment
5 Flood-prone countries
6 Cyclone-prone countries
7 Drought-prone countries
8 Elevated ecosystem/Climate change risk
9 Poor access to drinking water
10 Poor access to sanitation

Sources: Compiled from Dilley et al. (2005); ESCAP (2009a); FAO (2010) (AQUASTAT).

recharge. The goal of the Himachal Pradesh Mid-Himalayan Watershed Development Project is to combine protection of natural resources with rural household income increase. The project also intends to harmonize watershed development projects and policies across the state in accordance with best practices (Asian Development Bank, 2010b).

31.5.2 Country responses

BOX 31.1

Payments for Ecosystem Services (PES) in Asia and the Pacific

Innovative policies to support payment for ecosystem services have been established, or are under consideration, in some countries in the region, including Viet Nam, Indonesia, the Philippines and Sri Lanka.

An example of an innovative policy to support payment for ecosystem services is the ecosystem service fee collected from water users by the district water utility on the island of Lombok, Indonesia, as prescribed by local government regulations. A water utility in the water catchment in which the provincial capital of Aceh is located has agreed to pay two local communities for securing the watershed. The fee is paid to targeted communities that can impact water quality and supply and who then have a contractual obligation to sustainably manage their land. Five million Rp will be paid every year, for three years and will be managed by a community forum. The agreement will be expanded if both sides fulfil their commitments and improvements in water quality and quantity are achieved. The result is that water users enjoy cleaner water and more sustainable supply. The payment for ecosystem services mechanism was seen as a way to address escalating conflicts over water use.

ESCAP and the World Wide Fund (WWF) have been supporting action by BAPEDAL (Badan Pengendalian Dampak Lingkungan [Environmental Impact Management Agency]), Aceh to lead a Payments for Ecosystem Services project in Aceh, Indonesia for Nature Aceh programme and other partners. Under this project, a PES arrangement has been agreed to in the Krueng Aceh watershed area and is being implemented. A community forum (FORSAKA) has been established to develop and implement an agreement between the water utility and three communities, under which the water utility will pay for enhanced protection against illegal logging. Sustainable management arrangements will follow in subsequent phases of the project, as trust is built and implementation arrangements are refined. A pilot project in the Krueng Peusangan watershed area is also being developed by WWF (ESCAP, 2009b).

Integrated planning approach

Water resources management traditionally has been compartmentalized in government policy-making, with different water users – agriculture, industry, domestic water supply and sanitation, environment – falling in the jurisdiction of different line ministries and institutions. Over the past few decades, the momentum has picked up across the region for introducing and implementing IWRM policies.

An indicative profile report on the current status of IWRM implementation in the region was presented at the 5th World Water Forum held in March 2009. A proposed framework to facilitate IWRM implementation and monitoring at the country level has also been developed (Lee, 2009).

There are many country-specific examples that showcase the importance of IWRM. To address the problem of poor management of water resources and high withdrawal for agricultural needs, Kazakhstan launched a water resources management project in 2008 aiming to strengthen water management organization and institute the practice of IWRM. Stakeholders forums with experts and the public took place to draw feedback from major water users and providers. As a result, River Basin Councils were established in all the eight river basins of the country to implement national water policy (GWP, 2010).

Decentralization and inclusiveness

Decentralization of the planning and decision-making process for water resources management, together with enhancement of public participation is essential for introducing sustainable solutions.

Inclusiveness in decision-making is also a prerequisite for buy-in on water-related policy and investment decision-making. For example, in the state of Victoria, Australia, the Department of Sustainability and Environment in partnership with rural and urban water corporations, catchment management authorities, key regional stakeholders, interest groups and communities has developed long-term sustainable water strategies in the Our Water Our Future action plan. Every strategy aims to secure water for local growth, as well as regulate water systems and protect rivers and other water sources; therefore in each case, water-related risks are evaluated and analysed, and appropriate action is taken (Government of Australia, Department of Sustainability and Environment, 2010).

31.6 Sectoral priorities and regional initiatives

The identification of hotspots revealed that certain water-related challenges are common in Asia-Pacific countries. Among the most prominent challenges are stagnant access to sanitation and sometimes drinking water, deteriorating water quality, and climate-related risks. These sectoral priorities require targeted, urgent action to unblock the developmental deadlock that many countries find themselves in, due to poor water resources management.

31.6.1 Household water security

Meeting the MDG targets remains a priority for the region, but the benefits of access to water and sanitation expand beyond the basic need for life. Adequate water and sanitation are linked to various desirable developmental outcomes, such as healthy ecosystems and productive livelihoods and also linked to GDP growth through increase in tourism, foreign direct investment, labour productivity and agricultural outputs. A study of four South-East Asian countries estimated the total economic benefits of achieving universal access to sanitation at between US$5.4 billion and US$27 billion (Hutton et al., 2008). The narrow definition of access to drinking water and sanitation facilities is thus expanded to accommodate a broader concept of household water security linked to socio-economic development.

Better monitoring and assessment of achievements is required to inform policy-making. The question remains whether recent progress, particularly with respect to water targets, represents a one-time event or a real take-off for the Asia-Pacific.

To improve water and sanitation services in the second largest city in the country, Chittagong, the Government of Bangladesh recently initiated the Chittagong Water Supply Improvement and Sanitation Project with the support from the International Development Association. The project supports institutional development by enhancing the services provided by Chittagong Water Supply and Sewerage Authority and will focus on formulating a sewerage and drainage master plan for Chittagong. The project targets the poor, particularly those in urban slums, where piped distribution networks are not available (WaterWorld, 2010).

Cambodia's Phnom Penh Water Supply Authority (PPWSA) is unlike typical water utilities in Asia. It has an efficient service and an increasing consumer base. With the assistance of external funding agencies, particularly the Asian Development Bank, and through internal reforms, PPWSA transformed itself into an efficient, self-financed, autonomous organization in a city still recovering from many years of war and civil strife. Today, PPWSA is a model public sector water utility that provides drinking water to Phnom Penh 24 hours a day. The main factors behind the Authority's success are streamlining the organization's workforce; improving collection levels (e.g. installing meters for all connections, computerizing the billing system, updating the consumer base, and confronting high-ranking nonpayers and cutting off their water if they refuse to pay); rehabilitating the whole distribution network and the treatment plants; minimizing illegal connections and unaccounted-for water (e.g. setting up inspection teams to stop illegal connections, penalizing those with illegal connections, and giving the public incentives to report illegal connections); and increasing water tariffs to cover maintenance and operating costs by proposing a three-step increase in tariffs over seven years, although the third step was ultimately not required because revenues began to cover costs (Asian Development Bank, 2007).

Sanitation is also increasingly understood as expanding beyond toilets. There is a need for behavioural change and for institutional reforms to address sanitation in its broader interpretation, which includes hygienic disposal of human excreta and grey water management. The momentum of the International Year for Sanitation (2008), for example, urged regional leaders to assert that sanitation improves not just human health (access to toilets), but also environmental health, as domestic wastewater is a major contributor of bacterial contamination to groundwater supplies and rivers across the region (Asian Development Bank, 2010c).

Dhaka Water Supply and Sewerage Authority has been implementing the Dhaka Water Supply and Sanitation Project for Bangladesh through rehabilitating and strengthening sewerage systems and stormwater drainage, as well as implementing environmental and social safeguards. It has been also planned to provide local communities with services after strengthening institutional capacity and extending mainstream services (World Bank, 2011a).

Governments and international organizations need to work together to generate demand and ultimately willingness to pay for these services. For the poorest, governments need to step in and subsidize a transition to sustainable, adequate, eco-efficient infrastructure. An example of potential demand generation initiative can be found in Cambodia. The Ministry of Rural Development and the Government of Cambodia have acknowledged that the market can play an important role in sanitation improvements. In the new Sanitation Marketing Project (launched in 2009), market forces and demand creation activities have been widely used to install 10,000 toilets in rural village households. Unlike previous projects, the focus is on changing behaviour within communities to create demand for sanitation facilities. As part of the market-based solutions, an affordable and simple latrine core was designed and branded as Easy Latrine, and introduced to the market through local producers. The innovative pour-flush latrine sells for as low as US$25, and producers are receiving training in sanitation and hygiene education, latrine production, and basic business and sales management (Water and Sanitation Program, 2011). An additional example of market creation for water and sanitation activities is the WaterSHED programme (Box 31.2).

31.6.2 Green growth and wastewater revolution in the Asia-Pacific

Water quality in the region is at a critical stage as more wastewater is continuously being released into the natural environment. The wastewater revolution initiative, which was begun and promoted by the UN Secretary-General's Advisory Board on Water and Sanitation's (UNSGAB) with the launching of Hashimoto Action Plan II (HAPII) in late January 2010 looks at the rapidly deteriorating water environment in the Asia-Pacific and the need to revolutionize the way wastewater is being handled and treated.

Recognizing the critical stage of water pollution challenges, ESCAP convened the Regional Dialogue on Wastewater Management in Kuala Lumpur, held on 15–16 June 2010, within the context of eco-efficient water infrastructure development of the Green Growth approach in the region. The Regional Dialogue reviewed regional experiences and issues related to wastewater management and various initiatives and recent developments, including decentralization efforts and advances in technologies.

In Malaysia, the Government has introduced new wastewater regulations. Taking into account shortcomings in the 1979 Regulations, a comprehensive review was initiated and culminated in the enforcement of three new sets of regulations on 10 December 2009: Environmental Quality (Industrial Effluents, Sewage, Control of Pollution from Solid Waste Transfer Station and Landfill) Regulations 2009 (Lee, 2010).

The National Ganga River Basin Authority in India, with the financial support of the World Bank, launched a programme in 2009 to clean the Ganges, to ensure that 'no untreated municipal sewage or industrial effluents would be discharged into the river by 2020'. Previous action plans did not improve the health of the river, in which almost 95% of the pollution is caused by sewers and open drains (World Bank, 2011b). This time the governmental approach has moved from a town-centric approach to a broader river basin approach, focussing on strengthening the newly formed National Ganga River Basin Authority, and financing the estimated US$4 billion needed to stop all discharge of untreated sewage and effluent into the Ganges by 2020 (World Bank, 2009).

Finally, the Regional Dialogue recommended support for the Wastewater Revolution in Asia of UNSGAB, to be implemented in collaboration with the Green Growth initiative of ESCAP. The regional initiative was subsequently presented at the Sixth Ministerial Conference on Environment and Development (MCED-6) in 2010, and included the Regional Implementation Plan of the MCED-6 as part of the Astana Green Bridge Initiative of Kazakhstan.

31.6.3 Adapting to climate change

The Asia-Pacific region is home to two-thirds of the world's poor, and as the poor are generally the least resilient to and least prepared for climate change impacts, the region faces challenges in achieving its MDG targets, as well as the potential for some erosion of its past MDG achievements. Despite efforts to understand the extent of climate change impacts, effective adaptation and adaptive capacity in developing Asian countries will continue to be limited by various ecological, social and economic, technical, institutional and political constraints.

To address this multitude of problems, a knowledge hub on climate change was recently established within the framework of the Asia-Pacific Water Forum (APWF) to promote more effective regional cooperation, including more targeted research to identify types of vulnerability, appropriate policies, strategies, and action plans on adaptation. It is expected that the knowledge hub would promote the mainstreaming of these policies and strategies into national development agendas and enhance the needed capacity building.

Bhutan has been developing mitigation and adaptation policies, while incorporating them in strategies for economic growth and national plans. For many years the main tool for mitigation of climate change has been hydropower, which is also the largest driving factor of the country's pro-poor economic growth, as it accounts for 25% of GDP and more than 40% for national revenues. Adaptation strategies have been included in the government's 10th Five-Year Plan (2008–2013) with the special note for potential adverse impacts on hydrological flows for power plants and irrigation, which may affect national energy and food security, and flood hazards, such as glacial lake outburst floods (GLOF). Climate change risks are additionally addressed in the Disaster Risk Management Framework (Asian Development Bank, 2010a). Formulation of the Water Act following principles of IWRM has been at the core of these strategies. Despite this effort to address climate change-related risks, Bhutan does not have a comprehensive climate change policy (National Environment Commission Royal Government of Bhutan, UNEP, 2009).

Several globally sponsored adaptation projects were recently initiated in Bhutan. The GLOF Risk Reduction Project focused on the development of a regional GLOF database and risk management strategies in the Himalayan region for climatic and meteorological risk reduction and mitigation (UNDP, 2010). International partners are helping Bhutan reduce GLOF risks arising from climate change in the Punakha-Wangdi and Chamkhar valleys including plans for an early warning system for the Punakha-Wangdi Valley (UNDP, 2011). A midpoint assessment in 2010 showed that mitigation action so far focused on lowering the water levels of the Thorthormi Lake, to reduce the risk of glacial floods in the valley resulting in lowering the water level by 67 cm while the aim is to lower it by 5 m (Meenawat and Sovacool, 2010). Early warning systems have also improved: while previously only one warning station was operated manually by two employees, in 2010 representatives of 21 vulnerable communities were

BOX 31.2

WaterSHED: Using markets to bring water, sanitation, and hygiene to Asia's poor

Water, Sanitation, and Hygiene Enterprise Development (WaterSHED) is a USAID-funded project implemented in Cambodia, Lao People's Democratic republic and Viet Nam as a public–private partnership led by the University of North Carolina at Chapel Hill in the United States. The programme is designed to bring effective, affordable water and sanitation to poor and disadvantaged consumers in Asia. Providing affordable and desirable water and sanitation products increases consumer demand and encourages adequate use among the poor. Using proven market-based principles, WaterSHED leverages the power of private enterprise to bring water, health, and wealth to the poor.

An enterprise development programme supports the market creation initiative. The enterprise development programme focuses on manufacturing, marketing, and distributing household water treatment and storage products, as well as hygiene and sanitation products, such as latrines. This 'business incubator' approach aims to create private, for-profit companies and develop a well-functioning supply chain to ensure programme sustainability long after the development dollars are gone.

The success behind such programmes relies on two main business principles: (a) offering products consumers want at prices based on full cost and (b) selling to local retailers and consumers at full cost, instead of providing free or subsidized products, which can distort the natural business environment.

A second factor of success is building on the existing efforts of nongovernment organizations to develop transformational technologies, provide training and education, and drive demand for clean water solutions. The for-profit business model needs to be driven by sustainability and efficiency rather than being based on permanent donor funding. By creating new distribution channels for clean water products, such as microfranchises, the overall supply chain is strengthened and local entrepreneurs are empowered to determine community-specific needs. Engaging local microfinance institutions is also crucial, as these provide finance options for consumers, allowing for monthly payments (over 12–24 months) on the part of creditworthy borrowers whose cash flow patterns do not allow them to incur a single lump expense.

Through this programme, WaterSHED has provided water filters to over 100,000 people and new latrines to over 25,000. In addition, design innovations include a low-cost aspirational water filter and a low-cost, build-it-yourself latrine costing less than US$100.

Source: Adapted from USAID (2010).

provided with mobile phones to contact national authorities in case of flood events. The replacement of the manual system by gauges and sensors for monitoring glacial lake depth and rivers is planned.

In 2009, India embarked on the National Water Mission as a part of the National Action Plan on Climate Change (2008), identifying several strategies to tackle climate change and achieve water-related goals. The main goals are to create a comprehensive water database and proper public awareness and education campaigns, shift focus on overexploited areas, increase water use efficiency by 20% and promote IWRM on a basin level. Key strategies include regulatory mechanisms with differential entitlements and pricing, promotion of environmentally friendly solutions and behavioural change, efficiency improvement of existing facilities, and implementation of programmes for groundwater recharge (Box 31.3) (Government of India, Ministry of Water Resources, 2011).

||||||||||||||||||||||||||||||||||||||||||||||||||||||||||||||||||||||||

Notes

1   The views expressed herein are those of the authors and do not necessarily reflect the views of the United Nations.

2   Affected by the oceanic air current in summer and controlled by the continental air current in winter, resulting in dry winter and wet summer.

3   Kazakhstan is a very low performer in all categories, possibly because of the scarce and limited data provided through the survey.

4   For the purpose of this analysis, conflict is not limited to armed conflict, but includes all water-related disputes that have necessitated mediation. Whether violent or not, these disputes have threatened the stability of the socio-economic development process.

||||||||||||||||||||||||||||||||||||||||||||||||||||||||||||||||||||||||

References

Asian Development Bank. 2007. *Phnom Penh Water Supply Authority: An Exemplary Water Utility in Asia.* http://www.adb.org/water/actions/CAM/PPWSA.asp (Accessed 10 October 2011.)

----. 2010a. *Capacity Building of the National Environment Commission in Climate Change: Bhutan.* http://pid.adb. org/pid/TaView.htm?projNo=43021&seqNo=01&typeCd=2 (Accessed 10 October 2011.)

----. 2010b. *Climate Change Adaptation in Himachal Pradesh: Sustainable Strategies for Water Resource.* Asian Development Bank, India. (Accessed 10 October 2011.) http://www.adb.org/documents/books/cca-himachal-pradesh/cca-himachal-pradesh-3.pdf#page=12

----. 2010c. *Follow-up Conference of the International Year for Sanitation, Tokyo, January 2010.* http://beta.adb.org/news/events/follow-conference-international-year-sanitation (Accessed 10 October 2011.)

----. 2011. *Water Financing Programme 2006–2010.* http://www.adb.org/water/wfp/default.asp (Accessed 10 October 2011.)

Brown, R., Keith, N., and Wong, T. (2008). *Transitioning to Water Sensitive Cities: Historical, Current and Future Transition States*, 11th International Conference on Urban Drainage, Edinburgh, Scotland, UK, p. 5.

Burrows, G., Acton, J., and Maunder, T. 2004. *Water and Sanitation: The Education Drain.* Education Media Report 3. WaterAid, London, UK. http://www.wateraid.org/documents/education20report.pdf (Accessed 10 October 2011.)

Center for Research on the Epidemiology of Disasters. 2009. *EM-DAT: The OFDA/CRED International Disaster Database.* Université Catholique de Louvain, Belgium. http://www.em-dat.net (Accessed 10 October 2011.)

Dilley, M., Chen., R. S., Deichmann, U., Lerner-Lam, A. L., Arnold, M. and Agwe J. et al. 2005. *Natural Disaster Hotspots: Global Risk Analysis. Synthesis Report.* The World Bank and Columbia University.

The Economist. 2010. Every drop counts: and in Singapore every drop is counted. Special report: Water. (20 May 2010). Bangkok, ESCAP. http://www.economist.com/node/16136324

ESCAP (Economic and Social Commission for Asia and the Pacific). 2006a. *State of Environment in Asia and the Pacific 2005 Synthesis.* Bangkok, ESCAP. http://www.unescap.org/esd/environment/soe/2005/download/SOE%202005%20Synthesis.pdf (Accessed 10 October 2011.)

----. 2006b. *Enhancing Regional Cooperation in Infrastructure Development Including That Related to Disaster Management.* Bangkok, ESCAP. http://www.unescap.org/pdd/publications/themestudy2006/themestudy_2006_full.pdf (Accessed 10 October 2011.)

----. 2008. *Sustainable Agriculture and Food Security in Asia and the Pacific.* Bangkok, ESCAP. http://www.unescap.org/65/documents/Theme-Study/st-escap-2535.pdf (Accessed 10 October 2011.)

----. 2009a. *Statistical Yearbook for Asia and the Pacific 2009.* Bangkok, ESCAP. http://www.unescap.org/stat/data/syb2009/index.asp (Accessed 10 October 2011.)

----. 2009b. *Turning Crisis into Opportunity: Greening Economic Recovery Strategies.* Bangkok, ESCAP. http://www.unescap.org/EDC/English/Commissions/E65/E65_6E.pdf (Accessed 10 October 2011.)

ESCAP, ADB and UNDP (Economic and Social Commission for Asia and the Pacific; Asian Development Bank; and

United Nations Development Programme) 2010. *Achieving the Millennium Development Goals in an Era of Global Uncertainty, Asia-Pacific Regional Report 2009/10.* Bangkok, ESCAP. Available at http://content.undp.org/go/cms-service/stream/asset/?asset_id=2269033 (Accessed 10 October 2011).

————. 2010*a. Financing an Inclusive and Green Future.* Bangkok, ESCAP.

————. 2010*b. UN and Government of Pakistan Working Together to Protect Against Future Flood Damage*, UN Press Release No: G/58/2010. Bangkok, ESCAP.

FAO (Food and Agriculture Organization). 2010. Global Information System on Water and Agriculture (AQUASTAT) database. http://www.fao.org/nr/water/aquastat/main/index.stm (Accessed 10 October 2010). Rome, FAO.

Gleick, P. H. 2008. *Water Conflict Chronology,* database updated on 11/10/08. Oakland, USA, Pacific Institute for Studies in Development, Environment, and Security. http://www.worldwater.org/conflictchronology.pdf

Government of Australia, Department of Sustainability and Environment. Our Water: Government programs: *Sustainable Water Strategies.* http://www.ourwater.vic.gov.au/programs/sws (Accessed 11 November 2010).

Government of India. Ministry of Water Resources. 2009. *National Water Mission under National Action Plan on Climate Change.* Comprehensive Mission Document. Vol. I. New Delhi, India. http://www.india.gov.in/allimpfrms/alldocs/15658.pdf

Global Water Partnership. 2010. *Kazakhstan: Institutional Reform in Water Sector to Implement IWRM Plan.* http://www.gwptoolbox.org/index.php?option=com_case&id=238&Itemid=44 (Accessed 10 November 2010).

Hutton G, Rodriguez UE, Napitupulu L, Thang P, Kov P. 2008. *Economic Impacts of Sanitation in Southeast Asia.* Water and Sanitation Program (WSP). Jakarta, Indonesia.

IPCC (Intergovernmental Panel on Climate Change). 2007. *Climate Change 2007: Impacts, Adaptation and Vulnerability.*

Kiang, Tay Teck. 2008. *Singapore's Experience in Water Demand Management.* Paper presented at the 13th International Water Resources Association World Water Congress, 1–4 September 2008, Montpellier, France.

Lee, Heng Keng. 2010. New wastewater regulations. *MyWP,* Malaysian Water Partnership Newsletter, Department of Environment Management, Government of Malaysia. Issue No.7, September 2010.

Lee J., LeHuu T. and Zakaria S . 2009. *Status of IWRM Implementation in the Asia Pacific Region.* ESCAP, unpublished report.

MEASURE DHS (Monitoring and Evaluation to Assess and Use Results Demographic and Health Surveys). 2004–2008. http://www.measuredhs.com (Accessed 10 October 2009).

McIntosh, Arthur C. 2003. *Asian Water Supplies: Reaching the Urban Poor.* Manila, Asian Development Bank and International Water Association. http://www.adb.org/documents/books/asian_water_supplies/asian_water_supplies.pdf (Accessed 10 October 2011.)

Meenawat H., Sovacool B. 2010. Improving adaptive capacity and resilience in Bhutan. *Mitigation and Adaptation Strategies for Global Change.* Vol. 16, No. 5. pp. 515–533. Climate Adaptation to Protect Human Health. Bhutan. http://www.adaptationlearning.net/sites/default/files/Bhutan%20Country%20Profile%20_10.2.11.pdf (Accessed 10 October 2011.)

Molle, F. and Valle D. 2009. Managing competition for water and the pressure on ecosystems. WWAP (World Water Assessment Programme), *World Water Development Report 3: Water in a Changing World.* Paris/London, UNESCO/Earthscan.

National Environment Commission Royal Government of Bhutan and UNEP (United Nations Environment Programme). 2009. *Strategizing Climate Change for Bhutan.* http://www.rrcap.unep.org/nsds/uploadedfiles/file/bhutan.pdf

Stockholm Environment Institute and UNEP (United Nations Environment Programme). 2009. *Rainwater Harvesting: A Lifeline for Human Well-being.* Nairobi, Kenya , UNEP.. http://www.unep.org/Themes/Freshwater/PDF/Rainwater_Harvesting_090310b.pdf

Sydney Water. 2011. *Hoxton Park Recycled Water Scheme.* www.sydneywater.com.au/Majorprojects/SouthWest/HoxtonPark/(Accessed 10 October 2011.)

UNDP (United Nations Development Programme). 2010. *Project Facts – Himalayas: Glacial Outburst Flood (GLOF) Risk Reduction in the Himalayas.* Disaster Risk Reduction and Recovery. http://www.undp.org/cpr/documents/disaster/asia_pacific/Regional_Glacial%20Lake%20Outburst%20Flood%20(GLOF)%20Risk%20Reduction%20Himalayas.pdf (Accessed 10 October 2011.)

————. 2011. *Project Database – Bhutan: Reducing Climate Change-induced Risks and Vulnerabilities from Glacial Lake Outburst Floods in the Punakha-Wangdi and Chamkhar Valleys.* http://www.undp.org.bt/150.htm (Accessed 10 October 2011.)

UNEP (United Nations Environment Programme). 2002. *Environmentally Sound Technologies in Wastewater Treatment for the Implementation of the UNEP Global Programme of Action (GPA).* Guidance on Municipal Wastewater.

————. 2010. Environmentally Sound Technologies in Wastewater Treatment for the Implementation of the UNEP Global Programme of Action (GPA). *Guidance on Municipal Wastewater.* http://www.unep.or.jp/ietc/Publications/Freshwater/SB_summary/index.asp (Accessed 10 October 2011.)

UNICEF. 2004-2008. Multiple Indicator Cluster Survey (MICS). http://www.unicef.org/statistics/index_24302.html (Accessed 15 November 2009.)

UN-Water and WHO (World Health Organization). 2010. UN-Water *Global Annual Assessment of Sanitation and Drinking-Water (GLAAS): Targeting Resources for Better Results.* WHO, Geneva, Switzerland.

UN Women. 2010. *At a Glance – Women and Water.* UNIFEM Fact Sheet. http://www.unifem.org/materials/fact_sheets.php?StoryID=289 (Accessed 10 October 2011.)

USAID (United States Agency for International Development). 2010. WaterSHED programme. hhtp://www.watershedasia.org (Accessed 10 October 2011.)

Water and Sanitation Program. 2011. *Sanitation Marketing Takes Off in Cambodia.* http://www.wsp.org/wsp/node/230 (Accessed 10 October 2011.)

WaterWorld. 2010. *Water, Sanitation Improvements in Bangladesh get World Bank Funding.* http://www.waterworld.com/index/display/article-display/5090805031/articles/waterworld/world-regions/india-central_asia/2010/07/Water-sanitation-improvements-in-Bangladesh.html (Accessed 10 October 2011.)

World Bank. 2009. *World Bank Support to Ganga River Basin Authority.* Washington DC, World Bank. hhtp://www.worldbank.org.in/WBSITE/EXTERNAL/COUNTRIES/ SOUTHASIAEXT/INDIAEXTN/0,,contentMDK:22405084~pagePK:1497618~piPK:217854~theSitePK:295584,00.html (Accessed 10 October 2011.)

----. 2011a. *Dhaka Water Supply and Sanitation Project.* http://web.worldbank.org/external/projects/main?pagePK=64312881&piPK=64302848&theSitePK=40941&Projectid=P093988 (Accessed 10 October 2011.)

----. 2011b. World Bank Press Release No: 2011/518/SAR: *US$1 Billion Support from World Bank for Ganga Clean-up.* http://web.worldbank.org/WBSITE/EXTERNAL/NEWS/0,,contentMDK:22928173~pagePK:34370~piPK:34424~theSitePK:4607,00.html (Accessed 10 October 2011.)

WHO (World Health Organization). 2010. *Water-related Diseases.* www.who.int/water_sanitation_health/diseases/diarrhoea/en/ (Accessed 15 June 2010).

WHO and UNICEF (World Health Organization and United Nations Children's Fund. 2010a. *Diarrhoea: Why Children Are Still Dying and What Can Be Done.* New York/Geneva, WHO/UNICEF. http://www.who.int/child_adolescent_health/documents/9789241598415/en/index.html

----. 2010b. *Progress on Sanitation and Drinking Water 2010 Update.* New York/Geneva, WHO/UNICEF. http://www.wssinfo.org/data-estimates/introduction/

UNECLAC
—

Author Terence Lee
Contributors Andrei Jouravlev (Coordinator), Caridad Canales, Jean Aquatella,
Andrian Cashman, Colin Herron, Enrique Aguilar, Jorge Ducci, Michael Hankte-Domas,
Fernando Miralles-Wilhelm and Humberto Peña

|||||||||||||||||||||||||||||||||||||||||||||||||||||||||||||||||||||||||||||||||||||||||||||||||||||||||||||||||||||||||||||||||||

till taught by pain, Men really know not what good Water's worth
— *Don Juan*, Lord Byron

There is a long tradition of water management in Latin America and the Caribbean, and it has gone through many changes. In the 1960s and 1970s, water resources development was among the leading development priorities with projects such as dams for hydroelectricity generation and irrigation.[1] These developments slowed with the serious economic crisis that affected most countries in the 1980s. More recently the emphasis in water management has changed as the priorities of governments have changed. The focus of the governments of the countries of the region is now primarily on fulfilling the Millennium Development Goals (MDGs) for the reduction of poverty, which for water management translates to a concentration on improvements in drinking water supply and sanitation, as exemplified by such major projects as the Water for All Programme in Peru. Water supply and sanitation are not, however, the only concern: there is a growing preoccupation with improving water governance as well with strengthening the role of water management in environmental protection. The concern for governance, in particular, is based on the perception that water management remains fragmented and inadequate and this could jeopardize progress in the reduction of poverty and in the achievement of sustainable development.

As in almost every other area of economic activity and social conditions, there are both marked contrasts as well as many commonalities in the water sectors of the countries of the region. Commonality can be seen in the advances that have occurred in water management in all countries, and in the fact that these advances have not yet translated into universal increases in water use efficiency, any overall change in the levels of water quality, or region-wide sustained increases in the contribution of water to social and economic development. Local advances can be observed in many aspects of water management. A few countries have undertaken large-scale reforms of their water management institutions, notably Mexico and Brazil, but these efforts have so far had only partial success.[2]

The main issues facing the countries of the region in water management have not changed significantly over the last two decades. There has been a widespread inability to establish institutions that are able to deal with water allocation issues under conditions of scarcity and conflict. Various segments of the water sector still exhibit many examples of poor management, and there is a general absence of self-financing and a consequent dependence on fluctuating political support. In general, there is an inability to respond to crises. Despite much improvement, reliable information is often missing, including on the resource itself, on the infrastructure, on institutional responsibilities, and especially on water uses and users and on future needs.

Contrasts also abound in the region, however, and are not just due to variations in climate and hydrology or to the scale at which water management must operate – Brazil is 10,000 times the area of Dominica, for example. Equally or more so the contrasts are due to differences in the nature, stability and potency of institutional systems, dissimilarities in the distribution and demographic structure of the population, and sizeable variations in levels of income. Some impressive advances in specific water management activities – such as the substantial, sustainable and nationwide development of urban water supply, sewerage and wastewater treatment in Chile – have also contributed to the differences among the countries.

The issues that water management in Latin America and the Caribbean has had to confront do not all come from within the 'water box'. There have always been strong external drivers or forces affecting both the water resource and its management. The more significant of these come from general social change, but they also include macroeconomic policies, often a negative influence, stemming from abrupt changes in domestic policies and from outside (such as the global financial crisis of 2008–2009), but they are sometimes positive: macroeconomic administration has improved domestically and globally, as with the recent expansion of participation in world markets and adoption of countercyclical macroeconomic policies. Political instability – for example the turmoil in Honduras in 2009 – can hamper the sustainability of water management policies. There are also important, if subtle, pressures on the sector produced by gradual economic and social change that can produce issues difficult for water managers to resolve. Extreme climatic events, especially hurricanes in the Caribbean, have long had a negative influence on water management, particularly the destruction of infrastructure. Recently, the complex of uncertainties related to and derived from climate change has become a looming challenge.

This chapter will examine the risks, uncertainties and opportunities offered by the most important contemporary external drivers, as well as focus on a number of areas of particular concern within water management itself. The examination will be illustrated by references to both positive and negative experiences in the region.

32.1 External drivers and their effects

Only those external influences or drivers with the most significant influence on water management are discussed here. Naturally, there are others that may have influence on occasion – particularly events stemming from the endemic political instability in many countries. A more permanent negative driver is the inefficiency and weakness in the wider public sector, which can hamper seriously even well-planned and well-managed water management policies and projects. The influence of the state of the wider public sector can be seen in many of the examples of innovative policies and programmes cited here.

32.1.1 The changing economic and social environment

Obviously, there are consequences for water use and the demand placed on the water resource as the economic and social environment, in which water management is immersed, changes. The influence of economic and social change goes beyond the short-term effect of global financial crises, such as that of 2008–2009, and national crises, such as the Mexican peso crisis of 1994 or the collapse of the Argentinean economy in 2001 (Klein and Coutiño, 1996). Crises can and do interrupt ongoing programmes, but they rarely have more than short-term consequences. Of more far-reaching influence has been the historical volatility in the rates of economic growth in the region (Figure 32.1).

Fortunately, volatility has markedly lessened recently and the trend in rates of growth has been positive. The greater stability in the general economy has permitted more sustainable water management, but also has resulted in the emergence of new demands for water-related services as growth has wrought notable changes in the economic and social structure of Latin American and Caribbean societies. The growth and greater stability in the economies of the countries of the region has caused many apparently disparate changes in demand for water services, such as that for tourism in the Caribbean and for energy almost everywhere, both of which tend to be closely related to per capita income within the countries themselves and in the rest of the world.

Poverty and the related unequal distribution of income remain unresolved issues in all countries of Latin America and in most of those of the English-speaking Caribbean. Although one-third of the population is estimated to still be living in poverty – some 180 million people – the average rates of poverty have fallen steadily over the past 20 years (ECLAC, 2009c). Less progress has been made in reducing income inequality. The water resource sector has a major role to play in poverty reduction programmes through the provision of drinking water supply and sanitation services, which governments have increasingly recognized. Demands for improved services can be expected to continue to increase between now and 2015 as the countries of the region attempt to meet the MDGs for poverty reduction.

As levels of poverty have declined there has been a large increase in that part of the population that can be considered to be middle class due to increasing

FIGURE 32.1

Latin America and the Caribbean: GDP at constant 2005 prices, 1951–2010 (variation rates)

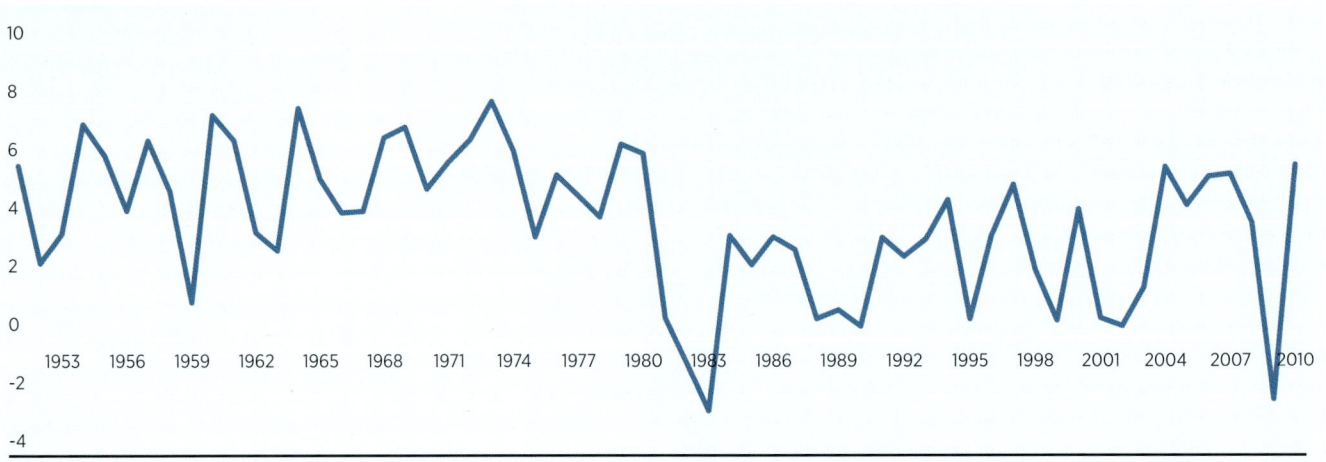

Source: From ECLAC CEPALSTAT ((http://www.eclac.cl/estadisticas, accessed in 2011).

levels of income and some improvement in the very unequal income distribution characteristic of the region.[3] One consequence of this emergence of a larger middle class has been the increasing demands to give more emphasis to the resolution of environmental issues, illustrated by the controversies arising from dam construction or over the construction of pulp mills on the River Uruguay. There are a number of examples in the region related to the increasing concern for the social and environmental repercussions of water projects, particularly the construction of large hydro-electricity generation plants, such as the controversies surrounding the decision of the Brazilian government to approve the building of the Belo Monte Dam on the Xingu tributary of the Amazon and over the proposed construction of hydroelectricity generation plants in the Río Baker basin in Chile.[4] Overall, there has been an abandonment of reservoir-based hydroelectricity generation plants in favour of run-of-the-river plants.

A subtler example of the influence of rising expectations among the new middle class can be deduced from the popular acceptance in Chile of a very significant increase in water supply and sewerage tariffs. Tariffs were increased substantially following the decision of the government to place greater emphasis on health and environmental concerns as well as to protect the export of agricultural products through the development of an ambitious programme for the treatment of domestic sewage discharges. By 2010, almost 90% of urban sewage was receiving treatment (SISS, 2011).

32.1.2 External demands for natural resources

With the exceptions of Mexico and some of the small countries of Central America, the countries of Latin America base their economies on the export of natural resources. The global demand for these products, whether minerals, food crops or other agricultural products, timber, fish or tourism, has increased notably in recent years. Moreover, much of the production of these goods and services is financed by external capital and many of the facilities are foreign owned. The result is that the major engine of economic growth in the region, with heavy demands on the water resource, is subject to factors outside the direct control of the governments of the countries of the region. This is so even when the producing companies are locally owned, as it is the world markets that determine demand.

For water management, the dependence on natural resources is complicated by the physical location of many of the activities to obtain them. For example, the expansion of copper and gold mining in Chile and Peru has mainly occurred in arid areas and has led to competition for scarce water resources both with export agriculture dependent on irrigation, and with the needs of the indigenous population. Tourism demand has increased water stress on many Caribbean islands as tourists consume far more water than local residents. Coffee production uses large quantities of water and can seriously affect water quality. One potential future demand for irrigation could come from the production of biofuels. However, in Brazil, the only current significant producer in the region,[5] sugar cane production is rain fed and only 3.5% of irrigation demand at present is used for biofuel production (de Fraiture et al., 2008).

The uncertainty in the level of demands of the global market and the changing nature of these demands have always considerably complicated water management decision-making in the region as local economies expand and contract according to the demands of the global economy.

32.1.3 Macroeconomic policies

'Macroeconomic policy has a pervasive influence on the structure of incentives and performance in the entire water sector' (Donoso and Melo, 2004, p. 4): this has been very evident in the countries of Latin America and the Caribbean. For example, high rates of inflation can destroy any attempts to develop effective charging systems for water use or to protect water quality.

Successful macroeconomic policies leading to high rates of growth, as in Chile in the 1990s and in Argentina and Peru more recently, also impose challenges on water managers as new demands can emerge more rapidly than water management policies can be adapted.

At the same time, rapid economic growth offers many opportunities. Strong water institutions can attract investment not just for expansion of and improvement in water-related infrastructure, but also for water management itself. There are examples of this in Brazil, Mexico and Chile where, as the respective economies have grown, the political decision has been taken to strengthen water management institutions.

What is required most of all, however, is not just periods of economic growth, but stability in policies over time. Many water management programmes can take decades to mature. For example, the current urban drinking water supply and sanitation system in Chile grew out of decisions taken in the mid-1970s, and the regional environmental authorities (CARs) in Colombia were first created in 1961.

32.1.4 Social policies

In recent years most governments in Latin America and the Caribbean have placed great stress on improving the social conditions of their populations. The programmes and projects carried out under their policies are of the most diverse nature, but many have direct bearing on water management and on decisions made within the water sector. This is obvious with the recent stress on policies to increase the provision of drinking water supply and sanitation services. However, it is not always obvious what the impact of any set of social polices might be. For example, efforts to extend coverage of drinking water supply and sanitation may raise issues related to water quality at both ends of the pipe. The need can arise to protect all water sources – whether streams and lakes or groundwater – while at the same time there is the need to protect drinking water sources from pollution caused by the disposal of untreated wastewaters. This is, perhaps, a fairly obvious external driver on water management. An example of a less obvious driver is the results of the improvement in living standards. In resort areas close to major population centres, this has generated both increased wastewater flows and demands for greater pollution control. Protecting popular beaches from pollution has driven a number of decisions to develop sewage treatment, including the Clean Beaches programme in Mexico (CONAGUA, 2009). In Uruguay, protecting beaches of the La Plata estuary was a major driver of the decision to build sewage treatment plants in Montevideo (IDB, 2010).

Housing policies too can provide a different kind of boost for the water sector. Improving housing means not only providing drinking water and sanitation, but can also lead to the adoption of programmes to control urban flooding in the new residential areas. Urban flooding remains a perennial problem in all large urban areas in Latin America, often worsened by the building of informal residential developments in flood-prone areas sometimes in areas set aside for flood mitigation.

32.1.5 Extreme events and climate change

Any impact of climate change on the water resources will be conditioned by their abundance in Latin America and the Caribbean. About 35% of the world's continental waters (freshwater) are found in the region, but the distribution within and across countries is highly variable. Many areas (e.g. northern Mexico, North eastern Brazil, coastal Peru, northern Chile) have great difficulty meeting their water needs. Moreover, large portions of Argentina, Bolivia, Chile, Peru, north eastern Brazil, Ecuador, Colombia, and central and northern Mexico are semi-arid and subject to wide variations in rainfall. Often, as in Peru, much of the population and economic activity is concentrated in water-scarce areas. For the region as a whole it is estimated that 30% of the population live in arid or semiarid areas.

Water managers in Latin America and the Caribbean have long faced the challenges posed by increased climate variability and change and related extreme events, such as the extreme events recurrent in Haiti and the annual havoc caused by hurricanes in the Caribbean, Central America and Mexico.

Examples include tackling the problems associated with El Niño/La Niña-Southern Oscillation (ENSO) events in Peru and with the cycle of dry and wet years in the drought polygon of North Eastern Brazil, dominated by a large semi-arid expanse, the *sertão*, which encompasses about 900,000 km². The *sertão* is subject to recurrent droughts, which are often followed by floods. These events may not affect the entire semi-arid region at any one time, but have been of sufficient recurrence, intensity and magnitude to warrant permanent protective policies and programmes, not just emergency measures.

32.1.6 Demographic change

The countries of Latin America and the Caribbean are going through a new period of rapid demographic change. Following the great migration to the cities in the 1960s and 1970s, the last major demographic event, the main characteristic of the current demographic situation in the region is a rapid decline in birth rates resulting in a rapidly slowing rate of population growth: 1.3% in the 1980s and expected to fall to a rate, for Latin America as a whole, of less than 0.5% by 2050 (Figure 32.2). The region has a relatively clean energy matrix due to its high share of hydroelectricity, which at 11% of total primary energy supply almost doubles the world average. In terms of carbon dioxide emissions from fossil fuel combustion per capita, Latin America and the Caribbean is still four times bellow the OECD average and less than half that of China although slightly above the level of India. The decline is so great that if current trends continue, the population will begin to fall absolutely in some countries, notably in Cuba and Uruguay (CELADE, 2007).

The decline in birth rates also means that, even if the total national population remains stable, many regions will lose population, especially rural and isolated ones. Maintaining services for smaller populations raises new issues. In the case of water supply and sewerage it can also mean that facilities may end up over-designed, hampering their operations and undermining financial stability.

The fall in birth rates has been accompanied recently by an even faster increase in longevity. It is estimated that the number of people over the age of

FIGURE 32.2

Annual average rate of population growth for Latin America and selected single countries (1950–2050)

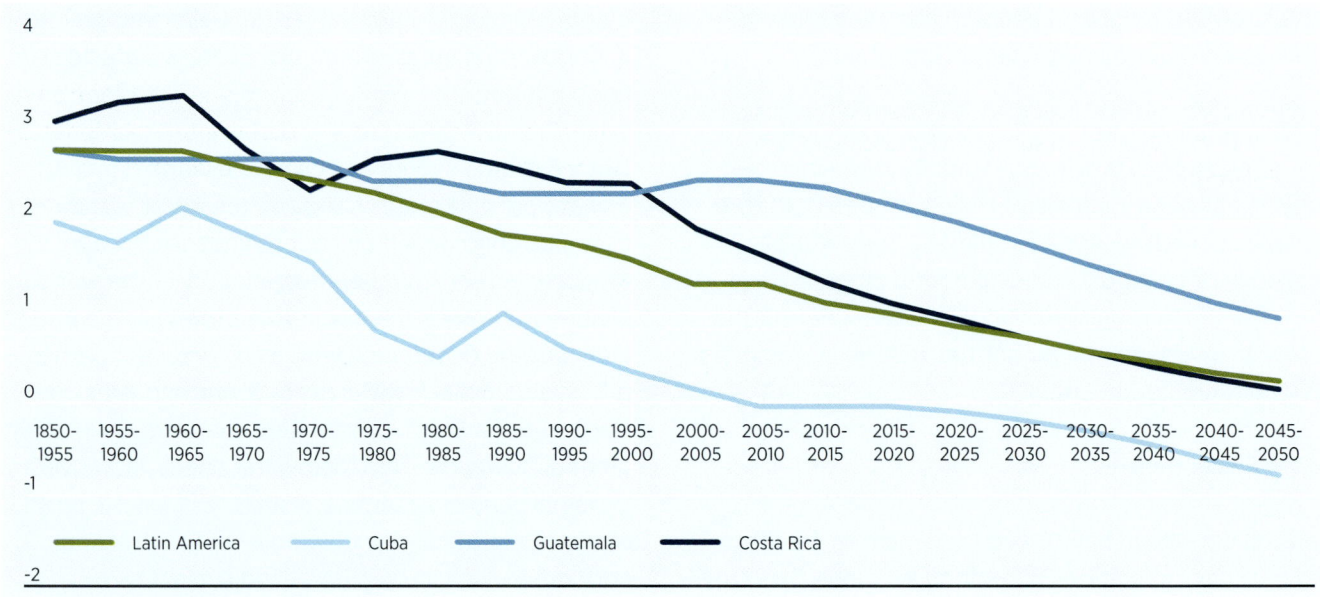

Source: CELADE (2009).

65 in Latin America and the Caribbean will triple by 2050 (CELADE, 2007); again, this can be expected to change the nature of the demand for many services related to water, such as increased recreational demands and lower water supply demands as a higher proportion of the population live in apartment complexes.

Latin America is already the world's most urbanized developing region, with more than 80% of the population living in towns and cities (ECLAC, 2010). There

BOX 32.1

Latin America and the Caribbean and the global financial crisis

Given the magnitude of the global financial crisis, the Latin American and Caribbean region has not been spared its impacts. Yet this crisis has differed from those the region has experienced in the past, not only because the epicentre lay in developed countries, although this played no small part in accounting for recent economic trends, but, above all, because of the juncture at which the crisis broke out in the region and how the region was affected. The combination of highly favourable external conditions and more prudent management of macroeconomic policy have enabled the region to reduce its outstanding debt and to renegotiate it on advantageous terms, while also building up international reserves. The Latin American economies thus went into the crisis with unprecedented liquidity and solvency. The countries' financial systems have not deteriorated and there has been no flight from local currencies, which has helped to maintain calm in the region's currency markets. However, a number of Caribbean countries are carrying hefty external debts and facing rather more complex exchange rate situations. Also unlike the situation during previous crises, the broadened macroeconomic policy space in many of the region's countries has given them substantial capacity for anti-crisis policy-making.

Although poverty levels in the region have remained high, and the impact of the crisis on social variables was predictably negative, the deterioration was not as great as had initially been projected. The rise in social spending in the past few years and the increase in the number and effectiveness of social programmes played an important role in containing the social costs of the crisis. Learning the lessons from previous crises, the countries in the region have sought to maintain – and expand – the coverage of these programmes, even in the context of a gradually tightening fiscal space.

Source: ECLAC (2009b).

has been a massive shift of population from rural to urban areas and increasingly large inter-city migratory flows, resulting in the establishment of an urban system characterized by a high percentage of large cities (with more than one million inhabitants) and by a high concentration of the population in some countries living in the largest (or two largest) cities. However, urbanization is not the only significant characteristic of changes in the spatial distribution of the population. There has also been the progressive – and sometimes aggressive – settlement of what has historically been sparsely populated land in the heart of the region, particularly in the Amazon and Orinoco river basins. These changes have played their part in the new priorities of the governments of the region. The emphasis on urban water problems has arisen from the heavy weight of the urban populations in the political process and, in general, their more active role in politics. In Brazil, the growing economic importance of settlements in the Amazon basin is playing and expected to continue to play a crucial role in the policies adopted towards the development of the basin. In fact, the die has probably been already cast in the decision between development and conservation to the advantage of the former, as the rate of growth of population in the basin accelerates.

32.2 Risks, uncertainties and opportunities

The most significant risks and uncertainties facing water management in Latin America and the Caribbean appear likely to stem from global economic events, climate change and domestic demands for continuing improvement in the provision of water services – all three will provide significant challenges for water managers and decision makers in the broader frames alike. Moreover, there is a complex inter-relationship among them. One obvious example: global economic events will play a large part in guiding development and associated domestic prosperity (or not) in the countries of the region which, in turn, through changes in income, will influence the demands for water-related goods and services, and consequently water management. Another example: climate change will introduce a basket of unexpected factors – directly through its impact on the water resource and indirectly through its influence on many aspects of the economy.

32.2.1 Global economic events

The recent global financial crisis noticeably affected the economies of the countries in the region, but compared with similar occurrences in the recent past, the countries withstood the problems well (Box 32.1). Moreover, the economies are now recuperating fairly rapidly and seem set to resume the period of rapid expansion that the crisis interrupted. This will provide a positive environment for investment in the region. This investment, given the structure of the economies of the countries of Latin America and the Caribbean, will increase water demands. In continental Latin America, however, overall demand on the regions' water resources remains low and spatially very concentrated. It is estimated that water abstractions amount to only about 1% of available water; in contrast, in the Caribbean, 14% of the available water is abstracted. This compares with a world average of some 9% (United Nations, 2010). However, there are significant restrictions on access to this abundance, as the location of the population and economic activities in the region does not coincide with plentiful water sources: approximately one-third of the population live in arid and semi-arid areas.

The Copiapo valley in northern Chile provides an example of the potential conflicts that can arise from large-scale investments related to serving global markets in areas of water scarcity. This is a region that produces large volumes of export crops, particularly table grapes, but at the same time the valley is the site of an increasing number of copper and other mines. The surface waters of the valley have long been committed and increasing reliance is placed on groundwater. The result has been the drilling of increasingly deeper wells by the fruit farmers and consequently the mining of the groundwater as rates of extraction have exceeded any capacity for recharge (*El Mercurio*, 2010). This problem has arisen despite the generally high level of governance in Chile and the existence of water markets. Deficiencies in the definition of water rights and weakness of water management institutions, have contributed to the current over-exploitation of water resources in the region.

32.2.2 Climate change

The region makes only a minor contribution to global greenhouse gas emissions (GHG): in 2008, Latin America and the Caribbean accounted for 8.6% of the world's population, 8.2% of global gross domestic product (GDP) and 7.6% of global GHG emissions,

excluding those from changes in land use (Figure 32.3). However, on a per capita basis and when emissions from land use changes are included, the region contributes more GHG emissions than do all other developing countries, including China and India. The main source of emissions comes from deforestation, accounting for almost half of total emissions (WRI, 2009). Vast forest areas, equivalent to 4 million hectares per year since 2000, are being lost in the region as the agricultural frontier expands, and many forest areas remain under threat despite the efforts that are being made to control deforestation (FAO, 2010). Efforts to address changes in land use and reduce the emissions from deforestation are a priority for the region as a contribution to the global effort to reduce greenhouse gases.

At the same time, many parts of the region are highly vulnerable to the adverse consequences of climate change, and climate change threatens the progress made in recent decades in development and in the achievement of the MDGs.

The countries estimated to be in areas of high or extreme risk from global climate change are often the poorest countries of the region – those in Central America, the Caribbean and the Andes. It is in these countries with relatively weak water management capacities that the greatest challenges will be faced.

The most serious challenges arising from climate change for the management of water resources in Latin America and the Caribbean can be expected to lie in the following areas:

- Significant deterioration in the quality, quantity and availability of water for all uses in many areas.
- Damage to coastal areas owing to a potential rise in sea levels, which in turn will affect river regimes.
- Increased economic damage from the greater intensity and frequency of hurricanes and tropical storms due to higher ocean surface and air temperatures (ECLAC/IDB, 2010).

Climate change will also bring significant opportunities for the wider application of imaginative innovations in many aspects of water management, particularly in hydrometeorology. There are already examples of successful innovation, such as the development of a national meteorological system providing local forecasts specifically directed at agriculture in Chile, and the use of weather forecasts in Peru to counteract the negative

FIGURE 32.3

Greenhouse gas emissions from Latin America and the Caribbean as a share of the global total (1990–2005)

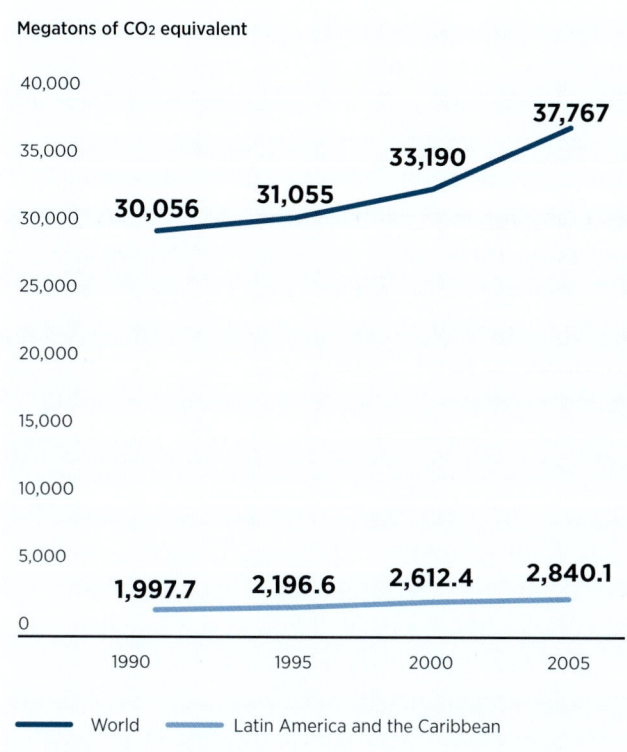

Megatons of CO₂ equivalent

Note: Emissions include CO_2, CH_4, SF_6, N_2O, PFCs and HFCs, but exclude those from land use changes.
Source: WRI (2009).

consequences of El Niño events (Box 32.2). While, as yet, there is little sign of major changes in water management policies in Latin America because of the perceived consequences of climate change, there is more realization of the potential negative effects among the governments of the islands of the Caribbean and Andean countries, as in Bolivia and Peru, particularly in relation to urban water supply.

32.2.3 The demand for better water management
It is very likely, given the economic and social environment in many countries of the region, that pressure to improve water management as a result of changing social priorities and alterations in patterns of water availability and use will increase. New demands and priorities can be expected to arise, including the need to protect the increased investment in urban infrastructure from flooding; improve the efficiency of water use in irrigation farming; address the greater use of water resources for recreation; respond to

awareness of environmental issues and conflicts over greener energy and construction of dams; and improve water pollution control. Many countries are discussing the reform of water laws, some have already changed them or adopted new ones (as for e.g. Brazil, Chile, Honduras, Mexico, Nicaragua, Peru and Paraguay), virtually all have reformed drinking water supply and sanitation sector legislation, and some are modifying it again. Only in few cases have these changes already produced extensive innovation in practice (Solanes and Jouravelev, 2006).

Rising expectations for better water management create risks and pose challenges, but also offer great opportunities. In many areas, there has been noticeable improvement in irrigation efficiency, as the area under irrigation has slowed its expansion, through the adoption of advanced irrigation techniques (drip irrigation, for example) and the use of new crop varieties that demand less water; however, more than 95% of the cultivated area remains under surface irrigation (FAO, 2009). There remains, therefore, much room for better, more efficient irrigation. This is especially so given the intention announced by a number of countries to play a major role in satisfying the increased global demands for food and biofuels.

Water issues are not well understood by the public at large. Prominent examples of improved water management, such as the construction of large dams in the 1960s and 1970s or the recent clean-up of the Mapocho River in Santiago, Chile, have not been sufficient to raise public awareness of the importance of water management over the long term.

Traditionally, there has been a widespread political interference in water management affecting even technical decisions. There are favourable signs of attempts to isolate water institutions from political interference as seen in the institutional design of the National Water Agency (ANA) in Brazil.

32.3 Areas of particular concern
Within Latin America and the Caribbean, there are major areas of concern that affect all countries in the region and touch on all issues likely to face the water sector in the near future, but there are also geographical areas with their own particular water management scenarios. Some of these follow.

Use of weather forecasts in Peru

In Peru, since 1983, forecasts of the upcoming rainy season have been issued each November based on observations of wind and water temperatures in the tropical Pacific region and the output of numerical prediction models.

Once the forecast is issued, farmer representatives and government officials meet to decide the appropriate combination of crops to sow to maximize the overall yield. Rice and cotton, two of the primary crops grown in northern Peru, are highly sensitive to the quantities and timing of rainfall. Rice thrives on wet conditions during the growing season followed by drier conditions during the ripening phase. Cotton, with its deeper root system, can tolerate drier weather. Hence, a forecast of El Niño weather might induce farmers to switch from rice to cotton or vice versa.

Source: NOAA (2010).

- Around 80% of the population of Latin America and the Caribbean lives in cities and almost half in cities of more than one million inhabitants. Many of these large urban conglomerations have precarious drinking water supply and sewerage networks and nearly all lack sewage treatment. There is also little regulation or control of industrial waste discharges and many urban areas are subject to episodic flooding.
- The poorer countries of Central America, many of the smaller islands of the Caribbean, and Bolivia and Paraguay face grave problems of water management and are among the most exposed to the negative consequences of climate change. They tend to have only a limited capacity to respond to challenges due to weak institutions and a lack of financial resources and trained personnel.
- Latin America and the Caribbean is the world's most humid region, but, as already mentioned, there are large arid and semi-arid areas in northern Mexico, Peru, Chile, Argentina and Northern Brazil that will likely be the most susceptible to any negative repercussions from climate change.
- The shrinking of glaciers and the reduction of available water resources represent a major concern for the Andean countries. This will have considerable effects on the region's water sources, hydroelectric

power and agriculture, as well as the conservation of natural ecosystems – in the Amazon in particular.

32.3.1 Improving water governance

The Economic Commission for Latin America and the Caribbean (ECLAC) has long maintained that any 'reference to a water shortage in our region in the absolute physical sense is not very appropriate ... There is no denying, however, that water management systems are often poorly organised if not non-existent' (ECLAC, 1997, p. 1), so that in Latin America and the Caribbean the 'water crisis' is more an institutional one than one of water scarcity (ECLAC, 2001). All the countries of the region will continue to face constant challenges in water management and, therefore, need to find legislative and institutional answers that can help prevent and resolve growing conflicts over water use, as well as mitigate extreme natural phenomena. Regional associations and the interaction of motivated and informed professional groups may prove decisive in improving sector governance problems and in giving technical viability to proposals for change. Fundamental is the dissemination and opening up of the debate to the public and a wide range of decision-makers. In Brazil, the discussion process leading to the National Water Act of 1997 was opened to different sectors of society. Organizations of water professionals played a key role in leading the discussion (Porto et al., 1999). For instance, the Brazilian Water Resources Association produced formal statements, approved by its members that helped introduce novel concepts into the discussion of the law. The Brazilian example shows the significance of the existence of a basic consensus if solid progress is to be made in governance.

It can be very difficult to implement reform even when it receives widespread political support and is legally enforced. For example, in Brazil, one of the central features of the 1997 water law was establishing user fees for water use, but these are not being collected on a regular basis (Benjamin et al., 2005); in Colombia, the collection of fees from polluters by CARs has been hampered by the reluctance of municipalities to pay; and in Mexico, few of the new river basin agencies created under the *National Water Law* of 2004 are fully functioning.

Poor governance in many countries of Latin America and the Caribbean runs from the top to the bottom of the sector. It is not restricted to the management of the water resource but is rife in the management of most water-based services (Solanes and Jouravlev, 2006).

A serious constraint on improving management stems from the absence of any large-scale formal education for water management at either the university or technical level. There is a plentiful supply of well-educated water professionals in most fields of a more technical nature and many courses in almost all countries to prepare them. However, there is little offered for the formation of professionals with a wider and integrated view of the water management process. The training of professionals with such skills remains largely a process of learning through experience. There have been a number of attempts by international agencies, including ECLAC, to establish water management training programmes, but these have tended to be short lived. A number of institutions, such as the Tropical Agricultural Research and Higher Education Center (CATIE) in Costa Rica, offer regular short courses to reinforce the work experience of water management professions, but these by their very nature can only offer a relatively general review of the knowledge available. A few universities do offer programmes, for example, the masters' degree in integrated river basin management at the University of Querétaro in Mexico and the similar degree programme at the Universidad de La Plata, Argentina. A growing number of Latin American professionals have studied the concepts and skills of integrated river basin management outside the region, but any regular and accessible means of obtaining the necessary knowledge within the countries of Latin America is still absent.

32.3.2 Water supply and sanitation

Over the past two decades there has been a slow but steady increase in most countries of Latin America and the Caribbean in the provision of both drinking water and sanitation. By 2008, piped water supply was available to more than 90% of the urban population and almost 60% of the rural population, exceeding the MDGs at the regional level (WHO/UNICEF, 2010). These aggregate statistics, however, do not show the variations in the quality of the services. In many countries, water supply and sanitation services are plagued by what has been defined as a vicious circle of low quality. Political interference, poor management and low tariffs all conspire to produce low levels of coverage, low quality services and poor maintenance leading to constant interruptions in supply, as well as periods of low pressure leading to

contamination within the drinking water supply system. A large number of wastewater treatment plants have been abandoned or function precariously. All produce a high level of dissatisfaction in the populations served (Corrales, 2004).

The overall national statistics also hide the large regional variations in access within countries. For example, in central and southern Mexico, Honduras and Nicaragua, there are many municipalities where less than 10% of the population has access to drinking water. In water supply and sanitation, the definition of what constitutes improved access, used in compiling international statistics, is very general and lax, so the published statistics provide little guidance to the real situation in many countries of the region (ECLAC, 1999; Jouravlev, 2009; United Nations, 2010).

Undeniably, there has been an expansion of water supply and sewerage networks in most countries, but this in turn has brought to the fore other issues.[6] It is estimated for the region as a whole that at most only 28% of sewage is treated before discharge - which constitutes very significant progress in comparison with the situation of only a decade or two ago - leading to serious contamination of watercourses, including the sea, from both sewage outfalls and industrial discharges from urban areas (Lentini, 2008). Too often the introduction of measures to control pollution has produced mixed results due to political and technical complexity. For example, it is not clear that the introduction of charges for wastewater discharges in Colombia has been the sole or the main determining factor in reducing water pollution (Box 32.3).

There remain many problems to be resolved in water supply and sanitation, including the recurring issue of the failure to ensure adequate and sustainable financing for utilities, so that any gains in provision are negated, or at least reduced, by lack of maintenance and through low levels of operating efficiency. Lack of maintenance leads to large losses in piped water systems; for example, in Cuba, losses in distribution are estimated to amount to at least half the water leaving the treatment plants (Business News Americas, 2010). Even in Chile, few systems have unaccounted for water under 30 % (SISS, 2011).

32.3.3 Climate change and natural hazards

According to a recent ECLAC study, between 1970 and 2008 extreme hydro-meteorological events likely to be exacerbated by climate change (storms, floods, drought, landslides, extreme temperatures and forest fires) cost the region over US$80 billion (Samaniego, 2009). If the region fails to take action to mitigate the impact of extreme events, many of which are water related, costs could rise to as high as US$250 billion in 2100 or 1% of the regional GDP (ECLAC/IDB, 2010).

Estimates of what repercussions climate change may have on economic activity vary widely and depend crucially on factors such as the discount rate applied to estimates of future costs, the sectors considered, and the methodology and assumptions used in developing climate scenarios. The Intergovernmental Panel on Climate Change (IPCC) estimates that freshwater

BOX 32.3

The Colombian experience with wastewater discharge fees

Various regional authorities in Colombia have used discharge fees for more than 30 years, but it was Law 99 of 1993 that established the present national discharge fee system. It mandated the 33 regional environmental authorities (CARs) to develop comprehensive inventories of all organic waste discharges and to estimate baseline quantities. Each CAR was to map major basins and set five-year targets for reduction in discharges and then charge each polluter a fee for each unit discharged.

Despite the efforts of the environmental ministry the implementation of the programme encountered a number of obstacles:
- Only nine of the CARs had fully implemented the programme by 2003 and eleven had not even begun to collect fees
- On average only half of the dischargers were being charged
- Fee collection rates were low: on average, only 27% were collected
- There was consistent non-compliance by municipal sewage agencies, which caused many basins to be unable to meet reduction targets

Even with these problems, between 1997 and 2003 discharges dropped significantly in many river basins. The reasons for this seem to have been the existing pollution controls based on a command and control approach; the need to catalogue dischargers; the fact that the programme demanded greater transparency and accountability; and the fact that the CARs kept the fees, which gave them an economic incentive to make the programme work.

Source: Blackman (2006).

systems in Latin America and the Caribbean are potentially very sensitive to climate change and vulnerable to inter-annual fluctuations in climate, such as those associated with the ENSO phenomenon.

Excess rainfall is already a common problem, particularly in Central America and the Caribbean, which are subject to tropical storm and hurricane events. One specific issue that plagues most large metropolitan areas is flooding due to the lack of storm sewers, except in the older central parts of cities. In Rio de Janeiro, Brazil, more than 200 people died as a result of a rainfall induced landslide in March 2010. But flooding is a severe problem even in relatively flat cities, such as Buenos Aires, Argentina. If climate change leads to higher rainfall or more concentrated storms, urban flooding can only become more common and more costly.

The ability of water management to react to the challenge of climate change will be hampered by the inadequate hydrological and meteorological observation networks of most countries in Latin America and the Caribbean. Large, sparsely or uninhabited areas have no surface observation systems, and the densities and operational practices of existing networks – which were very negatively affected following the 1980s economic crisis – generally do not meet the recommended international and regional standards.

32.3.4 Water pollution and water quality

The region has a major deficit in water pollution control and overcoming this involves implementing successful institutional arrangements for the setting of standards, creating control and inspection mechanisms, and mobilizing significant financial resources, which may have alternative social or economic destinations. The failure is evident in the case of pollution from urban wastewater discharges where only a minor portion of wastes are treated and where it is difficult to place emphasis on waste treatment when so many people lack connection to sewage systems. Similarly, it has proved difficult to impose controls on industrial pollution, especially on small or medium-sized industries with low levels of technological development. Other difficulties in building effective governance in water pollution control include administrative limitations for dealing with matters such as monitoring watercourses, controlling and supervising clandestine dumps (especially concerning discharge into aquifers) and controlling diffuse non-point source pollution.

The implementation of water pollution control and water quality policies is an expensive process, involving far more than the direct control and regulation of water pollution, and, if water quality is to be improved, the funding issue must be resolved (Box 32.4).

32.4 The challenge ahead

The greatest challenge for water management in Latin America and the Caribbean is without any doubt to continue to improve overall governance. The needs are many, including establishing a clear separation of policy and regulatory activities from day-to-day operations, improving incentives for efficiency, formalizing water institutions, strengthening their operational capacity, improving management training, adopting greater transparency in decision-making, and developing better systems for conflict resolution through a clear deliberative framework while increasing the participation of stakeholders in management decisions.

Among the major drivers or exogenous factors that will condition challenges in water management, the water sector can only hope to influence directly its weight in the definition and implementation of national development strategies. The others are likely to remain beyond any direct influence from water management institutions. The water sector must continually adjust to taking these major external drivers into account as it defines water strategies, and make a maximum contribution to more rational economic policies and to the improvement of institutional quality, governance and transparency while reducing corruption.

Challenges do not end with being prepared to tackle the most significant external drivers. There is a great deal to be done to improve management and governance within the 'water box' itself but there are no simple and universal ways to do this. One limitation that all water management systems seem to share is a notorious lack of operational capacity, due to a variety of factors, including the well-recognized limited financial, legal and human resources and, too often, the lack of importance given to the role of regulation and management in water resource policies. For example, a recent article on irrigation management in Latin America concluded that 'large amounts of water are inefficiently supplied to farmers because the right tools are not available for irrigation managers that allow them to schedule water deliveries and satisfy crop water requirements in an effective way' (de Oliveira et al, 2009, p. 13).

One emerging issue is the need for the management of transboundary water resources. Few of the river basins that are shared have formal agreements that regulate their use or active institutions to focus on issues arising from this situation. In the case of groundwater, the countries sharing the immense Guarani Aquifer (Argentina, Brazil, Paraguay, Uruguay), have recently entered into a binding agreement regulating some key aspects of management and protection of this resource, setting an unprecedented example at the global level.

The size of the challenges ahead, however, should not deter water managers from confronting them and making every effort to further strengthen management within the sector. There have been a number of interesting experiences in the region over the past few decades regarding the establishment of water institutions outside sector ministries. For example, in Mexico, water resources are managed by the National Water Commission (CONAGUA) and in Brazil, the National Water Agency (ANA) was set up in 2000 with the principal objective of achieving the sustainable use of water by overcoming traditional conflicts and limitations imposed by a system in which water had been under the responsibility of functional ministries. Other examples of institutions that are not linked to specific sectors of water use include the Ministry of Environment, Housing and Territorial Development in Colombia, the Water Resources Authority in Jamaica, the Ministry of Environment and Natural Resources in Venezuela, and the General Water Directorate of the Ministry of Public Works in Chile.

BOX 32.4

Investment in sanitation infrastructure in Chile

The total investment in sanitation infrastructure in Chile between 1999 and 2008 has been estimated at more than US$2.8 billion in the water supply and sanitation sector alone – in addition to huge investments in industrial pollution control and separated storm drainage networks. The investment can be estimated to equate to more than US$2,000 per capita. Yet even before 1999, the provision of sanitation in Chile was above the regional average.

Source: Yarur (2009).

These initiatives provide examples of attempts at reform in water management. However, it would be a mistake to think that complex problems can be resolved only by top-down initiatives, through the mere creation of new organizations, or by extrapolating from the experience of effective legislation and organizational structures that were achieved elsewhere only after a significant effort of coordination and capacity building. One of the most powerful is to introduce charges for water use or for waste disposal. The imposition of charges has been a part of reforms in a number of countries, including through the ANA in Brazil, the CARs in Colombia and CONAGUA in Mexico. One interesting new proposal is the trust fund established for water conservation and protection in Quito, Ecuador (FONAG). The idea behind FONAG is to create a system of payment for environmental services to be placed in a capital fund for water protection (ECLAC, 2009a).

If reform is to be placed on the political agenda it is not sufficient to have proposals that are supported only by experts – it is essential that any initiative have the widest public support. This means opening up decision-making processes to wide participation among stakeholders, but this has to be done in a meaningful manner so as not to drown the possibility of reaching decisions. Mechanisms, as proposed in much recent legislation, should be developed within the water sector to allow the creation of a consensus on the direction to be followed. If such a consensus does not exist, no true climate of confidence can be created for reform and any proposed reform, or even adopted legislation, will never produce results. The challenge is to open water management to society as a whole. In doing so the water sector can build on its previous achievements to continue to make a sustainable contribution to the betterment of society in all countries of Latin America and the Caribbean.

||||||||||||||||||||||||||||||||||||||||||||||||||||||||||||||||||||||||

Notes

1   The World Bank had no active loans for large dams in Latin America and the Caribbean in the first decade of the twenty-first century (Independent Evaluation Group, 2010).

2   The objective of the reforms in Brazil is to establish autonomous river basin agencies that will have both stakeholder representation and their own sources of revenues from charges

for bulk water abstraction. However, the restricted legal nature of the river basin agencies has hindered the introduction of charging in most states (Porto and Kelman, 2000).

3   ECLAC estimates that in Uruguay, Chile and Costa Rica 60% or more of the population is not vulnerable to poverty – that is, they have incomes 1.8 times the poverty level – and a number of other countries have over half their population with this level of income (ECLAC, 2009c, p.35).

4   There is strong opposition in Chile, with wide international support, to the building of hydroelectricity generation plants on the Río Baker and its tributaries in Chilean Patagonia, a popular area for adventure tourism (Chilean Patagonia Without Dams!, http://www.patagoniasinrepresas.cl/final/)

5   In 2007, 98.6% of biofuel production in Latin America and the Caribbean was in Brazil (OLADE, 2008).

||||||||||||||||||||||||||||||||||||||||||||||||||||||||||||||||||||||||||||||

References

Benjamin, A. H., Marques, C. L. and Tinker, C. 2005. The water giant awakes: an overview of. water law in Brazil. *Texas Law Review,* Vol. 83, October, 2005, pp. 2186-90.

Blackman, A. 2006. Economic incentives to control water pollution in developing countries. *Resources Magazine,* Issue 161 (Spring).

Business News Americas. 2010. INRH to repair water network over 10–15 years, Cuba, Business News Americas.. 12 January www.bnamericas.com.

CELADE (Latin American & Caribbean Demographic Centre). 2007. *Proyección de Población.* Observatorio Demográfico No. 3, LC7G.2348-P. Santiago, CELADE.

––––. 2009. *Population Projection.* Demographic Observatory. No. 7, LC/G.2414-P. Santiago, CELADE.

CONAGUA (National Water Commission, Mexico). 2009. *Playas Limpias.* Mexico City, CONAGUA. www.cna.gob.mx/Espaniol/TmpContenido.aspx?id=b78c2fbd-d1ee-47ec-87d7-0a5ff08ed386|%20%20%20%20Playas%20Limpias|0|25|0|0|0

Corrales, M. E. 2004. Gobernabilidad de los servicios de agua potable y saneamiento en América Latina. *Rega,* Vol. 1, No. 1, pp. 47–58.

Donoso, G. and Melo, O. 2004. *Water Institutional Reform: Its Relationship with the Institutional and Macroeconomic Environment.* Santiago, Pontificia Universidad Católica de Chile.

ECLAC (Economic Commission for Latin America and the Caribbean). 1997. Editorial remarks. *Circular of the Network for Cooperation in Integrated Water Resource Management for Sustainable Development in Latin America and the Caribbean,* No. 6, p. 1.

––––. 1999. *Tendencias actuales de la gestión del agua en América Latina y el Caribe (avances en la implementación de las recomendaciones contenidas en el capítulo 18 del Programa 21).* LC/L.1180. Santiago, ECLAC. http://www.cepal.org/publicaciones/xml/1/19751/lcl1180s.pdf

----. 2001. Editorial remarks. *Circular of the Network for Cooperation in Integrated Water Resource Management for Sustainable Development in Latin America and the Caribbean,* No. 12, January, pp.1.

----. 2009*a.* Water Protection Fund (FONAG). *Circular of the Network for Cooperation in Integrated Water Resource Management for Sustainable Development in Latin America and the Caribbean,* No. 29, pp. 5–6.

----. 2009*b. Preliminary Overview of the Economies of Latin America and the Caribbean.* Santiago, ECLAC.

----. 2009*c. Social Panorama of Latin America.* Santiago, ECLAC.

----. 2010. *Statistical Yearbook for Latin America and the Caribbean, 2009.* Santiago, ECLAC.

ECLAC (Economic Commission for Latin America and the Caribbean)/IDB (Inter-American Development Bank). 2010. *Climate Change: A Regional Perspective.* Document prepared for the Unity Summit of Latin America and the Caribbean, Riviera Maya, Mexico, 22–23 February 2010.

El Mercurio. 2010. Opciones para mejorar el accesso al agua: Revista del campo. *El Mercurio,* No. 1759, 29 March.

FAO (Food and Agriculture Organization of the United Nations). 2009. CLIMPAG: Climate Impact on Agriculture. Rome, FAO. http://www.fao.org/nr/climpag/index_en.asp

----. 2010. *The Global Forest Resources Assessment 2010.* Rome, FAO.

de Fraiture, C., Giordano, M. and Liao, Y. 2008. Biofuels and implications for agricultural water use: Blue impacts of green energy. *Water Policy,* Vol. 10, Supplement 1, pp. 67–81.

IDB (Inter-American Development Bank). 2010. *Montevideo: Etudio de caso.* Washington, DC, IDB. http://idbdocs.iadb.org/wsdocs/getdocument.aspx?docnum=35143635

Independent Evaluation Group. 2010. An Evaluation of World Bank Support, 1997–2007, *Water and Development.* Washington, DC, World Bank.

Jouravlev, A. 2009. Introducción. D. Fernández, A. Jouravlev, E. Lentini and A. Yurquina (eds), *Contabilidad regulatoria, sustentabilidad financiera y gestión mancomunada: temas relevantes en servicios de agua y saneamiento.* LC/L.3098-P. Santiago, Economic Commission for Latin America and the Caribbean (ECLAC). http://www.eclac.cl/publicaciones/xml/7/37447/lcl3098e.pdf

Klein, L. R. and Coutiño, A. 1996. The Mexican Financial Crisis of December 1994 and lessons to be learned. *Open Economics Review,* Vol. 7, pp. 501–10.

Lentini, E. 2008. *Servicios de agua potable y saneamiento: lecciones de experiencias relevantes.* Document presented at the regional conference on Políticas para servicios de agua potable y alcantarillado económicamente eficientes, ambientalmente sustentables y socialmente equitativos, Economic Commission for Latin America and the Caribbean (ECLAC), Santiago, Chile, 23–24 September 2008.

NOAA (National Oceanic and Atmospheric Administration, USA). 2010. *El Niño Theme Page.* Washington, DC, NOAA. www.pmel.noaa.gov/tao/elnino/impacts.html

OLADE (Latin American Energy Organization). 2008. *Informe de Estadísticas Energéticas,* 2007 [Energy Statistics Report, 2007]. Quito, OLADE.

de Oliveira, A. S., Trezza, R., Holzapfel, E. A. Lorite, I. and Paz, V. P. S Eds). 2009. Irrigation water management in Latin America. *Chilean Journal of Agricultural Research,* Vol. 69 (Suppl. 1) (special issue).

Porto, M., La Laina Porto, R. and Azevedo, L. G. T. 1999. A participatory approach to watershed management. *Journal of the American Water Resources Association,* Volume 35, Issue 3, pp. 675–83.

Porto, M. and Kelman, J. 2000. *Water Resources Policy in Brazil.* www.kelman.com.br/pdf/Water_Resources_Policy_In_Brazil

Samaniego, J. (coordinator). 2009. *Cambio climático y desarrollo en América Latina y el Caribe: una reseña.* LC/W.232. Santiago, Economic Commission for Latin America and the Caribbean (ECLAC). http://www.eclac.cl/publicaciones/xml/5/35435/28-W-232-Cambio_Climatico-WEB.pdf

SISS (Superintendencia de Servicios Sanitarios). 2011. *Informe de Gestión del Sector Sanitario 2010.* Santiago, SISS. http://www.siss.gob.cl/577/articles-8333_recurso_1.pdf

Solanes, M. and Jouravlev, A. 2006. *Water Governance for Development and Sustainability.* Santiago, ECLAC.

United Nations (under the coordination of A. Bárcena, A. Prado and A. León). 2010. *Achieving the Millennium Development Goals with Equality in Latin America and the Caribbean: Progress and Challenges.* LC/G.2460. Santiago, United Nations Publications. http://www.eclac.cl/publicaciones/xml/5/39995/portada-indice-intro-en.pdf

WHO (World Health Organization) and UNICEF (United Nations Children's Fund). 2010. *Progress on Sanitation and Drinking-Water: 2010 Update.* Geneva, WHO/UNICEF Joint Monitoring Programme for Water Supply and Sanitation.

WRI (World Resources Institute). 2009. *Climate Analysis Indicators Tool (CAIT) Version 6.0.* Washington, DC, WRI. http:// www.cait.wri.org.

Yarur, I. 2009. *The Financial Crisis and its Implication for Infrastructure in Water Production and Sanitation: The Case of Chile.* Presentation to the PECC General Assembly, Washington, DC, May 13 2009.

CHAPTER 33
Arab region and Western Asia

UNESCWA

—

Authors Carol Chouchani Cherfane and Sung Eun Kim
Contributors Julie Abouarab and Hanan Atallah

||||||||||||||||||||||||||||||||||||||||||||||||||||||||||||||||||||||||||||||||||||||||||||||||||||||||||||||||||||||||||||||||||||||||||||||||||||||||

The Arab region is facing multiple water challenges due to population growth, food security, overconsumption of water resources, climate change, extreme weather events, damage to water infrastructure caused by regional conflicts, and risks posed by the potential for conflict over shared water resources.

Arab countries have responded to these challenges by improving water resources management, increasing access to water supply and sanitation services, strengthening resilience and preparedness, and expanding the use of non-conventional water resources. However, these measures are insufficient to overcome water scarcity constraints facing most countries in the region.

33.1 Regional developments

The 22 countries of the Arab region,[1] which include the 14 member states of the United Nations Economic and Social Commission for Western Asia (ESCWA),[2] are among the most water-scarce countries in the world. At least 12 Arab countries suffer from acute water scarcity with less than 500 m³ of renewable water resources available per capita per year (FAO, 2011). Arab countries that are relatively better endowed with water resources are either least developed countries or countries in crisis.

While the Arab region has long suffered from water scarcity, several drivers and challenges have increased strains on freshwater resources over recent decades, including population growth, migration, changing consumption patterns, regional conflicts, climate change and governance. These pressures have increased risks and uncertainty associated with water quantity and quality, as well as the realization of policies seeking to promote rural development and food security objectives.

In recognition of these challenges, and the need to address them in a coordinated and regional manner, Arab governments established the Arab Ministerial Water Council (AMWC) under the auspices of the League of Arab States. At its first session in June 2009, the AMWC responded to the request of heads of state convened at the Arab Economic and Social Summit (Kuwait, January 2009) to prepare an Arab strategy to help confront current and future challenges needed to ensure water security and sustainable development in the region.

The resulting Arab Water Security Strategy (2010–2030) was adopted in June 2011 and proposes a series of measures to respond to these challenges, and is complemented by a set of implementation projects focused on water use efficiency, non-conventional water resources, climate change, integrated water resources management, and water security. Arab countries are also seeking to reduce risks at the national level by developing water sector strategies, incorporating water considerations into national development plans, pursuing institutional and legal reforms, and addressing uncertainties related to the management of shared water resources.

This chapter examines some of the drivers and challenges raised in the Arab Water Security Strategy in view of identifying the risks and uncertainties they pose for the management of water resources, and elaborates on selected response measures and approaches adopted to overcome these challenges in the Arab region.

33.2 Drivers

33.2.1 Demographics, migration and urbanization

The total population of the Arab region stood at 352 million in 2009, and it is expected to reach 461 million by 2025 (UNESCWA, 2009a). Rapid population growth for the last a few decades has increased the demand for freshwater as well as water stress in urban and rural areas. Over 55% of the region's population lives in cities, with rural-to-urban migration trends observed in Egypt, Lebanon, Morocco, the Syrian Arab Republic and Tunisia (UNDESA, 2007) largely due to reduced income and employment opportunities in the agricultural sector and the burgeoning youth demographic. To stem this tide, Arab governments have pursued rural livelihoods policies that link agricultural production to rural development, even though this has skewed the allocation of water resources to the agricultural sector in most of the region.

Demand for water services has also grown in urban centres from migration associated with economic development and the movement of displaced persons due to regional conflicts, while adequate water services are not provided in several countries facing intermittent water supplies (Box 33.1). Displaced Iraqis led to an unanticipated spike in new housing development in Jordan and the Syrian Arab Republic, and increased pressures on already strained water networks and freshwater resources. Interregional and intraregional labour migration to otherwise sparsely populated countries of the Gulf Cooperation Council (GCC) is influencing water supply and sanitation decision-making, particularly in view of the aggressive investments being made to stimulate economic growth.

Additionally, most urbanization in the Arab region is concentrated along the coastline, which is vulnerable to floods, sea level rise, and saltwater intrusion into coastal aquifers. Urbanization is fuelling settlement in reclaimed deserts, expanded coastlines and urban peripheries, with new satellite cities emerging around Cairo, Abu Dhabi and along the Red Sea. This has increased public and private sector investment in non-conventional water resources, particularly desalination, to ensure adequate access to water.

Access to Water Supply and Sanitation in the Arab Region

According to the World Health Organization and United Nations Children's Fund Joint Monitoring Programme (WHO/UNICEF JMP) for Water Supply and Sanitation, Arab countries are generally on track to meet the Millennium Development Goal (MDG) targets on water supply and sanitation, with the exception of the region's least developed countries and countries in conflict.

However, field assessments reveal that these figures do not adequately reflect that state of access to water services in the region. For instance, while access to an improved water source in Jordan and Lebanon is reported to be 100% and 96% respectively (WHO/UNICEF JMP for Water Supply and Sanitation, 2010), many consumers only receive water once or twice a week and rely heavily on bottled water and the delivery of water through tanker trucks to meet basic needs. Palestinian achievements towards the MDG targets are now mitigated by damage, destruction and the inability to install or maintain water infrastructure due to the ongoing conflict and Israeli security restrictions (World Bank, 2009).

The Arab Ministerial Water Council (AMWC) accordingly mandated the United Nations Economic and Social Commission for Western Asia (ESCWA) to establish a regional mechanism to identify and report on the two MDG 7 targets and an additional set of water supply and sanitation indicators to determine the actual quantity and quality of water services available in the Arab region. ESCWA is implementing this MDG+ initiative in collaboration with the Arab Countries Water Utilities Association (ACWUA), the Arab Water Council (AWC), the Center for Environment and Development in the Arab Region (CEDARE), the Arab Network for Environment and Development (RAED), and WHO, with support provided by the Swedish International Development Cooperation Agency (SIDA).

resulting from high economic growth rates, proliferation of real estate development projects, and availability of energy for desalination. Meanwhile, tourism growth is creating seasonal peaks in water demand in the Gulf and Arab Mediterranean countries. The Environmental Agency of Abu Dhabi reports that the United Arab Emirates water usage is 24 times greater than its total annual renewable water resource availability (Al Bowardi, 2010). While Dubai signalled in 2011 that there would be no changes to its water or electricity tariffs in the coming years, graduated water tariffs have been instituted in Jordan and Tunisia, and revisions to tariff schedules are under way in Egypt and Lebanon to stem excess consumption and generate revenue to improve water services.

Agricultural water consumption is characterized by low productivity in the region, while drought has plagued agricultural heartlands in recent years. Irrigated agriculture has led to the exploitation of deeper groundwater resources at a cost to sustainability and income. Small-scale farmers in South Lebanon pump groundwater from a depth of over 350 m to irrigate patches of land that have become parched from shifts and reductions in seasonal precipitation patterns; 4–6.5% of gross revenues are allocated to cover the cost of diesel to operate pumps, which has reduced net income in rural areas not connected to irrigation networks (UNESCWA, 2010a). Increased exploitation of non-renewable aquifer systems is also witnessed in the Disi Aquifer, shared by Jordan and Saudi Arabia, as well as in the North Western Sahara Aquifer System, shared by Algeria, Libya and Tunisia where 80% of withdrawals are used for agricultural purposes (Sahara and Sahel Observatory, 2011). This is raising concerns about the depletion of fossil aquifers, and the trade-offs to consider when balancing food security, food self-sufficiency, regional cooperation and rural development priorities.

33.2.2 Water consumption trends

Water consumption levels in ESCWA countries is largely tied to gross domestic product (GDP), as illustrated in Figure 33.1, although this is only possible due to the heavy reliance on desalination. In other parts of the Arab region, water consumption is largely tied to the agricultural sector, which only contributes marginally to GDP.

Domestic water demand in GCC countries is significant and increasing, largely due to changing lifestyles

33.2.3 Regional conflicts and the Arab Spring

Cycles of conflict manifested by instability, civil strife, war and occupation have characterized the Arab region for decades. This has generated large numbers of internally displaced persons and increased migration at national and regional levels. As a result, 36% of displaced persons in the world are now found in the ESCWA region (UNESCWA, 2009c), imposing additional demands on water networks and on already strained freshwater resources. For instance, most of

FIGURE 33.1

Domestic water consumption relative to gross domestic product (GDP) per capita

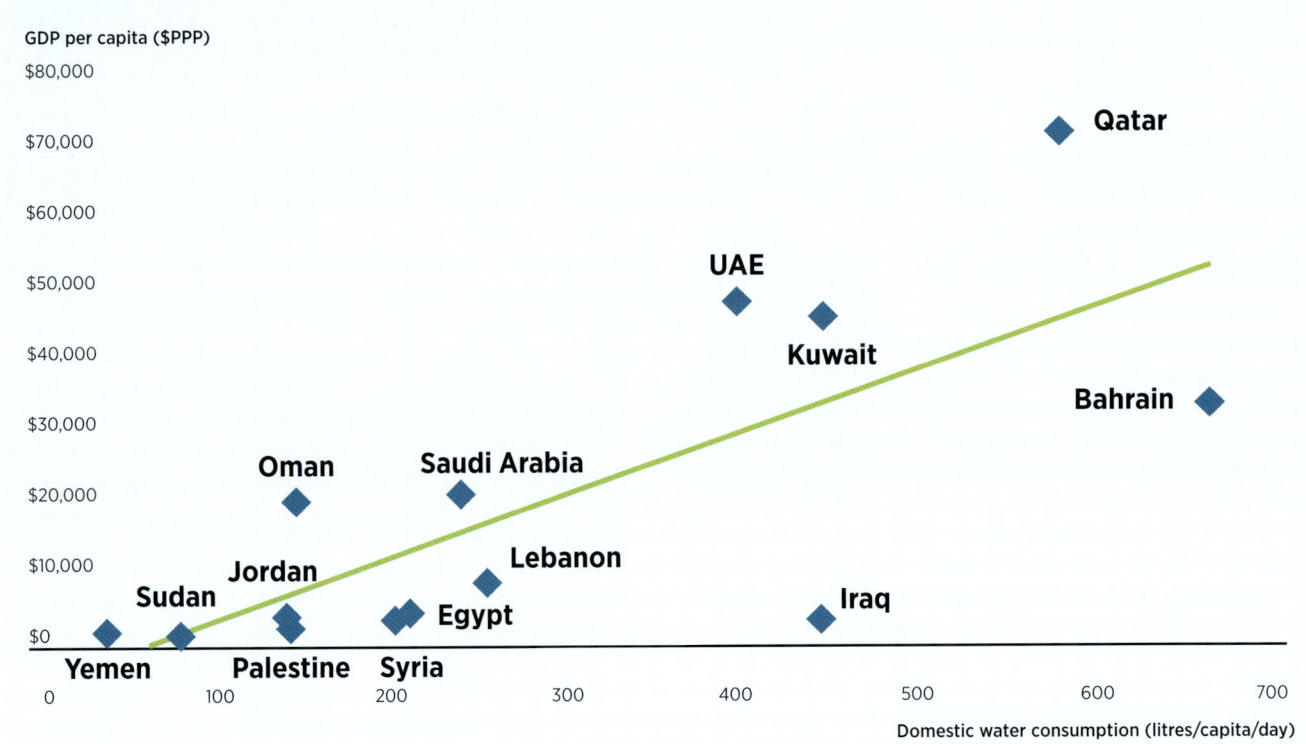

Source: UNESCWA (2009b, p. 7), based on data on domestic water consumption from FAO AQUASTAT and GDP per capita data from the United Nations Population Division.

Iraq's two million refugees found safe haven in Jordan and the Syrian Arab Republic, although Amman and Damascus already suffer from high rates of unaccounted-for water and intermittent water supplies. Crippling drought in Somalia led to a flood of refugees into neighbouring countries, including Djibouti and Yemen, despite civil strife in Yemen and projections that Sana'a will become the first capital city in the world to run dry. Women and children are among the most vulnerable in Sudan's internally displaced communities, and are not able to access clean water despite the wealth of freshwater resources in Sudan and its southern neighbours.

Ongoing conflicts and instability are also reversing progress towards water supply and sanitation targets. For instance, despite being once the most water- and oil-rich countries in the region, Iraq experienced water shortages in displacement camps (IRIN, 2007) and water services remain intermittent in urban centres and peripheries. Reduced surface water flows in the Tigris, Euphrates, Karoun and Karkeh rivers from growing demand and diversions upstream in Iraq, the Islamic Republic of Iran, the Syrian Arab Republic and

Turkey have increased saltwater intrusion through the Shatt al-Arab and reduced freshwater outflows to the Gulf (UNESCWA-BGR, 2012). This has affected water supply in Basra where water salinity – even after filtration – now exceeds drinking water standards. Increasing salinity in the Gulf also affects desalination operations and fisheries, and may contribute to renewed tensions between Iraq, Kuwait and nearby countries.

Water infrastructure is also damaged or destroyed by violent conflicts. Israel cut off water supplies to Beirut during the siege of 1982, while Iraq destroyed much of Kuwait's desalination capacity as it withdrew from Kuwait in 1991. A damage assessment after the 2006 Israeli offensive into Lebanon estimated US$80 million worth of damage to the water sector (Council for Development and Reconstruction, 2006). The ongoing blockade of the Gaza Strip has prevented the entry of materials and expertise needed to maintain water pumps and installations, and is affecting the ability of donors to invest in a new desalinization plant that is considered a strategic project for cooperation by the Union for the Mediterranean.

Meanwhile, Palestinian refugees are scattered in camps throughout the region with inadequate water supply and sanitation, and limited prospect for improvement.

Concurrently, the public uprisings that have swept through the Arab region since December 2010 offer opportunities to revisit water governance structures and foster greater consultation at the community level. While a relatively recent phenomenon driving change in the region, government officials in Tunisia and Egypt are already engaging with water user associations and local constituencies in renewed dialogue aimed at fostering greater public participation in planning and decision-making related to the water sector.

33.3 Challenges, risks and uncertainties

Four major challenges affect water resources management in the Arab region: water scarcity, dependency on shared water resources, climate change and food security. Financial and technical constraints, as well as poor access to and availability of reliable

data and information on water quality and quantity are cross-cutting factors that increase risks and uncertainty associated with managing these challenges.

33.3.1 Water scarcity

Nearly all Arab countries can be characterized as water-scarce, while those formally endowed with rich water resources have seen their total annual per capita share of renewable water resources drop by half over the past four decades (Figure 33.2). This declining trend presents the most significant challenge to the water sector in the Arab region.

Water quantity

As the availability of freshwater resources in the region has become scarcer relative to its population, efficient and integrated management of water resources has become more critical. Risks and uncertainties associated with the management of surface and groundwater resources must thus be considered jointly and based on local circumstances. For instance, countries with

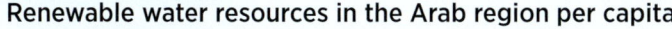

FIGURE 33.2

Renewable water resources in the Arab region per capita

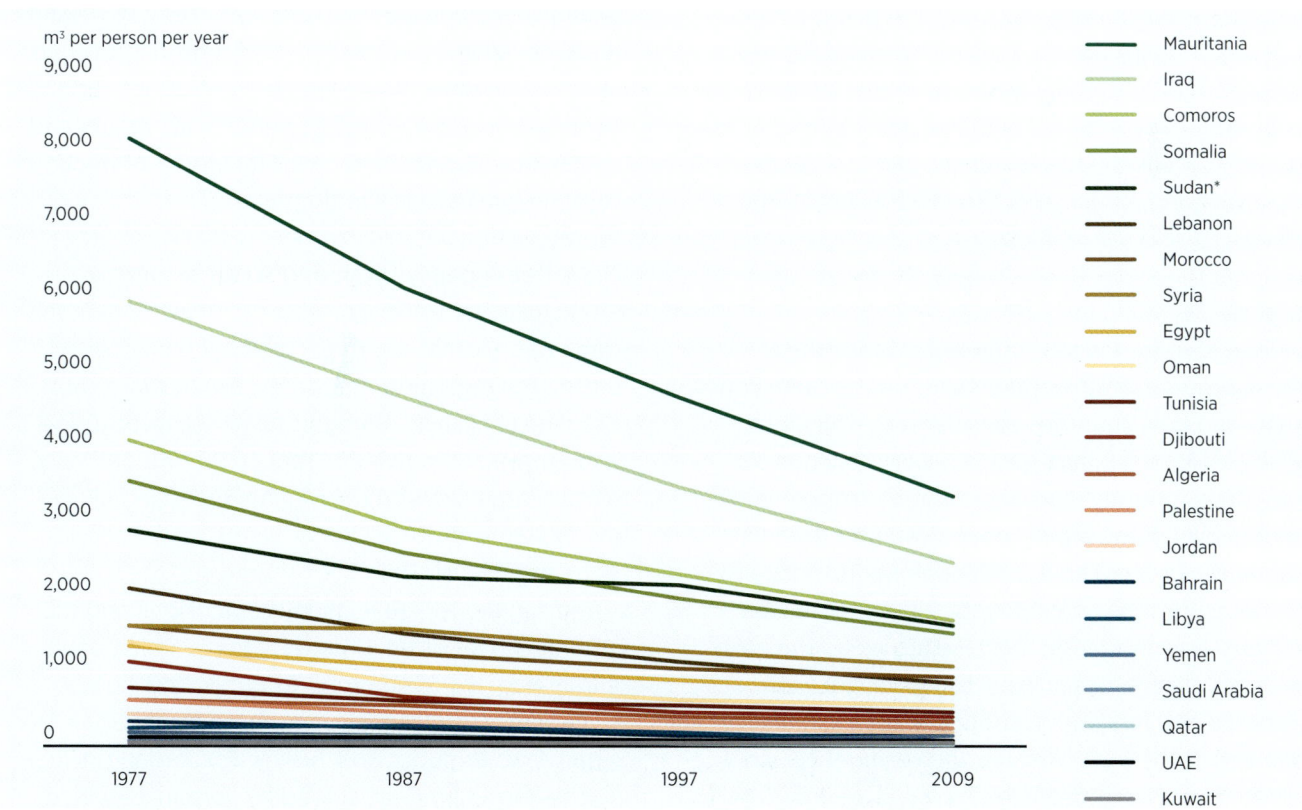

Note: *Area covering South Sudan and Sudan.
Source: Based on FAO AQUASTAT data (2011).

perennial rivers in which surface water constitutes the primary conventional source for freshwater and over 70% of the renewable water resources include Egypt, Iraq, Lebanon and Sudan (FAO, AQUASTAT, 2011). In other Arab countries, groundwater constitutes at least one-third of the total volume obtained from conventional sources, but surface water remains the primary source of freshwater, such as in Oman, Saudi Arabia, UAE and Yemen; ironically these four water-scarce countries are also characterized by intermittent rivers, or *wadi* systems, and are subject to seasonal flash floods. Some countries are thus considering ways to recharge aquifers with these floodwaters to increase the quantity of water available during dry periods.

As surface waters can no longer satisfy water needs in some parts of the region, the extraction of groundwater has increased and is threatening the sustainability of many national and shared aquifer systems and increasing the risk of conflict (UNESCWA, 2007*a*). However, as some groundwater resources are non-renewable, their very use challenges frameworks that seek their sustainable management. An integrated management framework is necessary where conventional and non-conventional approaches are applied to address water scarcity constraints in the region. Non-renewable shared aquifers that include fossil water include the Nubian Sandstone Aquifer shared by Chad, Egypt and Libya; the North Western Sahara Aquifer shared by Algeria, Libya and Tunisia; and the Basalt Aquifer underlying Jordan and Saudi Arabia. Additional deep non-renewable aquifers underlie Kuwait, Iraq and Saudi Arabia; Iraq and Jordan; and Iraq and the Syrian Arab Republic (UNESCWA, 2009*d*).

Water quality
Differences in freshwater regimes influence the response patterns of governments to water-scarce conditions and how countries consider water quality a priority. Coastal aquifers pose a major challenge for many Arab countries due to seawater intrusion resulting from over-pumping of groundwater for domestic or agricultural use. This is evident along the northern coast of Egypt, the Lebanese coastline, in the Gaza Strip and around several coastal cities along the eastern Gulf. Sea level rise is expected to increase stresses on coastal aquifers and river outlets, such as the Nile Delta and at the Shatt Al-Arab, increasing the salinity of these freshwater resources.

Pesticides and fertilizers mixed with agricultural runoff are contaminating surface and groundwater resources in rural and peri-urban areas, and have even become a source of contention in some shared surface water systems in the region, such as between Turkey and the Syrian Arab Republic. Post-harvest processes associated with agro-industries, garments production (leather tanneries and textiles) and domestic sewage pollute surface and groundwater resources throughout the region. For instance, river disposal of olive residues (Lebanon), sugar beet pulp (Morocco and the Syrian Arab Republic) and sugar cane (Egypt, Sudan) increases biological oxygen demand (BOD) levels and eutrophication of some inland water bodies causing fish kills. Nutrient pollution from sewage has reduced fish stocks in Lake Tunis in Northern Tunisia (Harbridge et al., 2007). Untreated effluents released in Cairo have affected aquaculture and agriculture in the Nile Delta. Oil production pollutes freshwater resources in the region, although marine ecosystems are more frequently affected by oil spills.

Watershed protection and management challenges are exacerbated by unregulated urban development, poor sanitation and sewage infrastructure, and the rapidity with which urban expansion is taking place. Inadequate urban planning and enforcement fuelled by bifurcated water governance structures and overlapping jurisdictional mandates between ministries and municipal bodies involved in permitting, testing and compliance contribute to the difficulty of protecting water resources in the region.

33.3.2 Dependency on shared water resources
A big challenge to water resources management in the Arab region is that the major international river systems in the region are shared by two or more countries. The challenge is magnified where institutional regimes are not in place to reduce the risk and uncertainty associated with the management and allocation of water resources under water-scarce conditions at the basin level. The major shared surface water systems in the region include the (a) Tigris and the Euphrates river basin, shared by the Islamic Republic of Iran, Iraq, the Syrian Arab Republic and Turkey; (b) Orontes (or *Al-Assi*) river, shared by Lebanon, the Syrian Arab Republic and Turkey; (c) Jordan (including the Yarmouk) river, shared by Jordan, Lebanon, the Occupied Palestinian Territory, the Syrian Arab Republic and Israel; (d) Nile river basin covering

11 countries, of which Egypt and Sudan are Arab States; (e) Senegal River with four riparian countries, including Guinea, Mali, Mauritania and Senegal; and (f) Lake Chad, with eight riparian countries namely Algeria, Cameroon, Central African Republic, Chad, Libya, Niger, Nigeria and Sudan.

The Arab Water Security Strategy estimates that 66% of surface water resources in the Arab region originates outside of the region and enters through the Euphrates, Nile, Senegal and Tigris rivers. This has become at times a source of political conflict with the upstream countries. There are also many smaller surface water resources (rivers, streams, seasonal spate flows) that cross into the region and between Arab countries on a regular and intermittent basis, which have sparked localized disputes regarding water resources and fuelled border tensions. For instance, reduced flows from intermittent rivers originating in the Islamic Republic of Iran affect border communities and agriculture in eastern Iraq. Many Arab countries have thus turned to groundwater to complement dwindling domestic freshwater supplies and increase water for irrigation and development. However, with shallow aquifers under threat of total exploitation, countries are exploring possibilities to develop deeper and farther aquifers, which, in many cases, are part of more extensive regional cross-boundary aquifer systems.

Additionally, water conflicts can also exist at the subnational level between administrative districts, communities and tribes. Tensions emerge in water-scarce environments and stakeholders with competing interests, which are then manifested through local level conflicts, such as in Yemen (Box 33.2).

In recognition of the importance of reducing conflict, countries in the region have tried to conclude international agreements and establish shared water resources institutions. However, despite efforts to establish formal agreements, those that exist require increased capacity and improved institutional and legal frameworks to support the integrated management of shared water resources, particularly when political will and commitments are absent or insufficient. Prevailing political tensions and ongoing conflicts also frustrate efforts to collaborate at the technical level. For instance, despite years of efforts to strengthen cooperation in the Nile River basin, countries have failed to reach agreement on a common management scheme. The establishment of the Republic of South Sudan in July 2011 increases to 11 the number of countries requiring agreement on this shared resource.

However, while water scarcity and ongoing conflicts are key drivers influencing shared water resources management, opportunities for collaboration can still emerge. For instance, the divergent interests of riparian countries in the Senegal River basin allowed for constructive compromise, mutual benefits and the prevention of a potential conflict. The resulting establishment of the Organization for the Development of the Senegal River in 1972, the adoption of the Senegal River Charter in 2002, and the tie-in to a financing mechanism for ensuring the generation of revenues and benefits among the four basin countries has reinforced confidence in cooperation and generated income and energy for development.

33.3.3 Climate change and climate variability

Although climate change is a global phenomenon, its impacts are felt differently throughout the world. The Arab region is particularly sensitive to climate change and variability as it already suffers from water scarcity; small changes in climate patterns can thus result in dramatic impacts on the ground. Climate scenarios predict an increase in temperature in the region, which several impact assessments expect to contribute to increased aridity, lower soil humidity, higher evaporation–transpiration rates and shifts in seasonal rainfall patterns. Reduced snowfall and snow melt is projected in the High Atlas Mountains and Anti-Lebanon Mountains. Reduced surface water runoff and sea level rise is expected to reduce groundwater recharge

BOX 33.2

Water conflicts in Yemen

With acute water scarcity in Sana'a and Taiz, access to water has become an issue of survival.

Stresses on the delivery of water service come from water scarcity, the dependent relationship between water and energy resources for service delivery, internal strife manifested in urban–rural divides, and tensions over scarce resources. Challenges in balancing socio-economic priorities with sustainable water allocation for the agricultural sector complicate decision-making in this least developed country under conflict.

Source: UNESCWA (2010b).

rates and increase the salinity of coastal aquifers, respectively.

Some climate scenarios also anticipate increased climate variability and more frequent extreme weather events, such as floods and droughts. As a transitional climate zone, precipitation has already been fluctuating significantly in Morocco and Tunisia to the west, and Lebanon and the Syrian Arab Republic to the east. Evidence that climate change is affecting freshwater quantity and quality in the region is becoming stronger, although the expected intensity of these changes remains uncertain.

Droughts and land degradation
The increasing frequency of drought in the Arab region is a very important challenge facing the Arab region. Algeria, Morocco, Somalia, the Syrian Arab Republic and Tunisia have experienced significant droughts over the last 20 years, and the frequency and intensity of these events seem to be increasing. In Morocco, the drought cycle changed from an average of one year of drought in every five-year period before 1990, to one year of drought for each two-year period in the following decade (Karrou, 2002). The Horn of Africa is experiencing one of the worst droughts in decades.

Despite repeat experience, Arab countries remain vulnerable to drought. Socio-economic vulnerability to drought in ESCWA countries has intensified due to demographic and economic growth, increasing water scarcity, unsustainable water consumption patterns and land use practices (UNESCWA, 2005). The vulnerability of some Arab countries to droughts comes from their high dependency on agriculture, and particularly rainfed agriculture, as a main contributor to GDP and employment. An extended hydrological drought in north-eastern Syria from 2006 to 2009 drove an estimated one million people to abandon their homes and seek refuge in larger cities. A former Syrian Deputy Prime Minister has attributed this mass migration to having set in motion the popular uprisings initiated in Syrian secondary cities in 2011 (A. Dardari, personal communication, November 2011). In Somalia, where large segments of the population are economically dependent on pastoral and subsistence farming, prolonged drought has decimated families and caused widespread famine displacing communities in a conflict-ridden country that has faced droughts of varying intensity every year for over a decade.

Drought also contributes to increased land degradation and desertification, which is a regional phenomenon poignantly witnessed in Mauritania when it faced repeated cycles of drought during the 1960s, 1970s and 1980s. Dams erected along the Senegal River helped mitigate the effects of drought and introduce more certainty in water availability for development. Nevertheless, drought in the Sahel region in 2009 and 2010 has reduced water availability for agriculture and again increased food insecurity levels in Mauritania (CILSS et al., 2010).

Floods and extreme events
Extreme weather events have increased in the region, including greater frequency and intensity of flooding. In January 2010, heavy rainfall caused flash floods in Egypt in the Sinai Peninsula, Hurghada, and Aswan along the Red Sea – resulting in 12 deaths, the evacuation of over 3,500 people and the destruction of electricity towers, telephone lines and roads (DREF operation, 2010). The same storm caused flooding in the area of Wadi Gaza in the Gaza Strip, where the floods cut off roads and the bridge connecting Gaza City with southern parts of the Gaza Strip, causing a state of emergency.

Cyclone activity is also intensifying in the region. The three strongest tropical cyclones recorded in the Arabian Sea have occurred since 2001 (*Gulfnews*, 2010). Super Cyclonic Storm Gonu was the strongest and hit Oman, Yemen and Somalia in August 2007. Storm surges caused coastal damage and *wadi* flooding as rainfall reached 610 mm; the high water mark peaked at Ras al Hadd at the eastern tip of Oman and exceeded 5 m in what is normally an arid area. The cyclone resulted in an estimated US$4 billion worth of damage and at least 49 deaths, and is considered the worst natural disaster in the history of Oman. Saudi Arabia suffered devastating floods in Jeddah in November 2009 which killed 100 people and caused mortalities in Rabigh and Mecca (BBC News, 2009). Yemen has been experiencing landslides and rock slides caused by increasingly intensive seasonal flash flood events through mountainous valleys.

These high-consequence flood events are not only due to the increasing intensity of rainfalls, but also to the rapid and often haphazard development of high-risk areas such as *wadis* which are natural drainage areas for flash floods. Lax building codes and infrastructure standards, as well as weak regulation and enforcement, also permit the construction of buildings and infrastructure that are ill-prepared to sustain damage during major floods, such as those in Jeddah in 2009 (Assaf, 2010). These extreme events, however, led to increased public investment in storm water systems and preparedness planning that reduced risks in subsequent years.

33.3.4 Food security

Agricultural cultivation consumes the largest share of water in the Arab region and is a primary source of water stress. While per capita arable land and permanent croplands account for a small share of land in most ESCWA member countries, agriculture accounts for over 70% of total water demand; in Somalia and Yemen, the share exceeds 90% of total water demand (FAO, AQUASTAT, 2011).

Despite high usage rates, Arab countries are not able to produce sufficient quantities of food to meet basic needs. Accordingly, ESCWA member countries import 40–50% of their total cereal consumption, and this rate reaches up to 70% in Iraq and Yemen, despite the significant size of their agricultural sectors (UNESCWA, 2010*b*). This situation is likely to worsen with climate change.

Agricultural export bans have also been instituted in response to the recent food crises in an effort to increase domestic food security, prevent hording for sale in international markets and reduce price inflation for basic foodstuffs at the national level, such as in Egypt with rice exports. The fluctuations in the global cereal market during the past few years, and the instability of supplies, witnessed when Russia banned the export of grains in August 2010, proved problematic for the region as Egypt and the Syrian Arab Republic imported approximately half of their total wheat imports from Russia in 2008 and 2009. However, wheat and barley imports have become a necessity as the region does not have enough water to meet growing demand. Globalization, trade dependency and the global food crisis have thus added new dimensions to the food security challenge in the Arab region.

Further, the Arab region has a vulnerable social structure. While there is a concentration of wealth in some countries, a large share of the population is clustered around the poverty line, with many people living well below the poverty line in the Comoros, Djibouti,

Mauritania, Somalia and Yemen. Increased drought frequency, complemented by dependency on food imports and population growth, leaves the Arab region highly vulnerable to food insecurity.

To address the challenge, Arab countries initially tried to increase domestic cereal production and encouraged cultivation in strategic commodities through subsidies and guaranteed price supports (Egypt, Jordan, Saudi Arabia). Investments in irrigation networks and reservoir capacity increased (Lebanon, Syrian Arab Republic), as well as the pumping of groundwater resources for the production of cereals (Morocco, Saudi Arabia). Intraregional agricultural trade was encouraged through the Greater Arab Free Trade Agreement. However, limited agricultural productivity, continued land degradation and water scarcity made food self-sufficiency goals unachievable at the national or regional level. As a result, Arab food self-sufficiency policies shifted towards a broader concept of food security. Governments with the financial resources have been able to pursue alternative measures within the global marketplace to achieve this goal, while others are re-examining their development and trade policies. Some have also turned to emergency relief to overcome food crises, such as those experienced in the Horn of Africa and Sahel due to drought.

Biofuels

Global research and development has demonstrated that biofuels provide opportunities for increased energy security and rural development through a reliable market for certain agricultural commodities. Investors encouraged by the emerging biofuel market have thus sought to cultivate jatropha in Egypt and Sudan, as it is a drought-resistant non-food crop that can be grown in saline soils. However, a range of stakeholders have expressed concern that Arab farmers might shift cultivation to more profitable commercial biofuel crops instead of food crops, despite growing water scarcity and food insecurity in the region.

Arab governments responded by encouraging the development of second-generation biofuel instead. The Arab Ministerial Declaration on Climate Change (CAMRE, 2007, p. 4) warns of the 'consequences of the encouragement of developed countries to developing countries to cultivate agricultural crops that produce bio-fuel instead of food; while encouraging its production from bio-waste'. Meanwhile, the Strategy for Sustainable Arab Agricultural Development for the Upcoming Two Decades (2005–2025) adopted through the Arab Organization for Agricultural Development recognizes the added value for farmers of using agricultural residues for biofuel production and the positive impact this will have on the environment and on securing fuel. Assessments have also found the potential for expanding second-generation biofuel production in Egypt, Lebanon, Morocco, the Syrian Arab Republic and Sudan from residues resulting from sugar cane, sugar beet and olive processing, as well as from the livestock and dairy sectors (UNESCWA, 2009e).

33.3.5 Data and information

The difficulty of collecting consistent and credible data and information on water resources in the Arab region impedes accurate analyses and well-informed decision-making processes. It also prevents the establishment of coherent and cooperative policy frameworks for shared water resources management as well as observing changes and assessing progress.

Several initiatives have been launched to increase the knowledge base of water resources in the region, including intergovernmental processes tied to statistical reporting at the global level, and others at the regional and national levels through regional reporting mechanisms or as academic initiatives.

However, the difficulty of reducing the gaps and uncertainty associated with the knowledge base rests with the political sensitivity and national security considerations that are sometimes tied to this information. This results in a patchwork of information from different sources that is used by the research and professional community, while official data remains a coveted resource that is sometimes reserved for use by certain governmental institutions.

33.4 Response measures

In view of these drivers and challenges, Arab countries are seeking to improve water resources management and capacity, strengthen resilience and preparedness, and expand the use of non-conventional water resources as a means to ensure a water-secure future.

33.4.1 Improving water resources management

At the regional level

Arab countries clearly recognize the need for a common approach towards water resources management to achieve sustainable development of the region.

This led to the adoption of the Arab Water Security Strategy by the AMWC in 2011. The strategy lays out key issues facing the Arab region and identifies various priorities for action focused on:

- *Socio-economic development priorities* – namely access to water supply and sanitation, water for agriculture, finance and investment, technology, non-conventional water resources and Integrated Water and Resources Management (IWRM);
- *Political priorities* – related to the management of shared water resources and the protection of Arab water rights, particularly those under occupation; and
- *Institutional priorities* – associated with capacity building, awareness raising, research, and participatory approaches involving civil society.

Regional institutions and initiatives launched in recent years respond to these priorities. For instance, the Arab Countries Water Utilities Association (ACWUA) established its secretariat in 2009 and provides a platform for dialogue and capacity building on water supply and sanitation for public and private sector operators on various topics, including unaccounted-for water, tariffs and benchmarking. The Center for Water Studies and Arab Water Security, affiliated with the League of Arab States, convenes intergovernmental meetings on agreements and resolutions on shared water resources and Arab water rights. This includes deliberations on a legal framework on shared waters in the Arab Region, which the Center, and UNESCWA drafted at the request of the AMWC (2010) in consultation with Arab governments and with support provided by the Bundesanstalt für Geowissenschaften und Rohstoffe (Federal Institute for Geosciences and Natural Resources, BGR, Germany). The legal framework seeks to foster consensus on a core set of principles that can support bilateral and basin-level agreements on water resources shared by Arab countries (UNESCWA, 2011). The framework draws upon a vision that fosters cooperation and participation; equitable, reasonable, and sustainable use; and conflict prevention and resolution through peaceful means (UNESCWA and BGR, 2010). Regional capacity-building programmes have also been conducted in response to the strategy, such as training on negotiations by the Arab Water Academy and workshops on water governance by the AWC and CEDARE.

At the national level

At the national level, different ministries and authorities are responsible for managing water resources and delivering water services in Arab region. Only a handful of joint committees or units have been established to support shared water resources. However, efforts to improve institutional and legal frameworks in the water sector have been enacted or are under way, and are increasingly incorporating issues previously limited to IWRM planning.

For example, Law 10-95 in Morocco sets forth an institutional framework for managing water resources, with a view towards environmental protection as well as monitoring and responding to extreme events, such as droughts (Makboul, 2009). Egypt prepared a 2005 National Water Resources Plan, which includes many institutional procedures aimed at decentralization, public–private partnerships and engaging water users in water system management. A new draft water law seeks to empower the Egyptian Water Regulatory Agency (EWRA), differentiate between social and economic tariffs, and establish a set of performance indicators for utilities. Yemen devised a national strategy and investment programme for the water sector (2005–2009), which addresses water resource management, water and sanitation in urban areas, water and sanitation in rural areas, irrigation management, and the environment. Palestine is working to integrate water resource management into development planning, and examined the implications of climate change for groundwater resources as a means to inform the process. Jordan developed a national strategy that includes policies on groundwater management, irrigation, infrastructure, sanitation, water resource management and investment (UNESCWA, 2007b). Lebanon prepared a new National Water Sector Strategy focused on water supply and sanitation that is supported through a Water Sector Coordination Group that contributed social impact analysis, health assessments and climate change impact scenarios to the preparatory process. Nevertheless, there remains a need to strengthen legal and institutional frameworks and inter-ministerial coordination for IWRM to push forward progress in this area throughout the region.

33.4.2 Strengthening resilience and preparedness
Improving food security
As with most countries in the world, Arab countries seek to ensure their food security through trade, investment and contractual arrangements with other countries. Long-term leasing of agricultural land in other countries has emerged as another tool for overcoming shortcomings and shortfalls in domestic agricultural production due to water, land, energy or technological constraints. These investments are designed to ensure access to staple commodities and reduce exposure to global food price fluctuations and export bans, which often occur during food crises. Through these arrangements, investors reduce risk by leasing land to grow needed primary commodities in countries with suitable land and water resources, while host countries secure investments over an agreed time horizon that can allow for the development of transport, water and energy infrastructure in the targeted area. Employment and income generation is also fostered through primary and secondary agro-industries (fertilizers, packaging, shipping) given that these investments tend to be large in size. However, while these contracts offer the opportunity for mutual benefits, the operationalization of these investments has been controversial where indigenous communities and pastoralists have traditionally used the lands that are being opened to joint ventures or leased to investors by central governments or absentee landowners.

Several Arab countries are engaged in agricultural investments and land deals with other Arab countries and in neighbouring regions, and their numbers have increased in recent years as water scarcity and land degradation have become more evident. Jordan engaged in land deal talks with Sudan for livestock and crop cultivation (Hazaimeh, 2008), and the Abu Dhabi Fund for Development invested in the cultivation of 28,000 ha of farmland in Sudan (Rice, 2008). The King Abdullah Initiative for Saudi Agricultural Investment Abroad was established to maintain food security in the Kingdom given the Government's decision to reduce price supports for domestic wheat production and other commodities because of water constraints. The initiative encourages the private sector to invest in agriculture abroad and received its first rice imports in 2009. Staple goods are targeted, particularly wheat, barley, corn, sorghum, soybeans, rice, sugar, oil seeds, green fodder, livestock and fishery goods, which are all water-intensive products (Al-Obaid, 2010); Egypt, Sudan, Turkey, Ethiopia, the Philippines, and Brazil among other countries are targeted for investments. One study reports that five African countries (Ethiopia, Ghana, Madagascar, Mali and Sudan) approved a total of 2,492,684 ha of land for foreign investments in agriculture since 2004, excluding allocations below 1,000 ha and pending land applications, and that Arab countries contribute significantly to this total (Cotula et al., 2009).

Sovereign wealth funds, like the Qatar Investment Authority and Kuwait Investment Authority are engaged in these types of investments directly or through state-owned enterprises in Arab and South East Asian countries (Reuters, 2008*a*). The private sector is also engaged. Jenat, a consortium of Saudi agricultural companies, produces wheat, barley and livestock feed in Egypt, and announced plans to invest in Sudan and Ethiopia (Reuters, 2008*b;* 2009). Private investment funds, such as the Abu Dhabi-based Al Qudra Holding are also active in this sector (Blas, 2008). This demonstrates the market's recognition that investments abroad will help satisfy growing food demand given the lack of opportunity to invest in this sector at home because of increased natural resource constraints.

Nevertheless, the rapid rise of foreign land acquisitions in developing and least developed countries has raised concern that they may further reduce food security in these countries in face of global food crises, particularly among the least privileged and marginalized communities. As a consequence some Arab countries such as Qatar are now targeting more developed countries with significant food surplus for their agricultural investments (Reuters, 2010), while others are also supporting food programmes in countries under stress, such as Saudi Arabia through its donations to Somalia, Sudan and Mauritania.

Pursuing climate change adaptation and disaster preparedness

The Arab Ministerial Declaration on Climate Change (2007) expresses Arab commitment to move towards climate change adaptation and mitigation, and was followed by the preparation of the Arab Framework Action Plan on Climate Change for 2010–2020. Arab countries have concurrently sought to assess the impact of climate change on national water resources to inform their national adaptation plans and communications to the Intergovernmental Panel on Climate Change (IPCC). In view of providing a unified assessment for informing regional policies on climate change adaptation, the Regional Initiative for the Assessment of the Impact of Climate Change on Water Resources and Socio-Economic Vulnerability in the Arab Region was launched as coordinated UN-LAS effort under the umbrella of the AMWC and the UN Regional Coordination Mechanism.

Risks and uncertainty associated with climate change and extreme weather events have pushed forward national and regional efforts in the area of disaster risk reduction, planning and preparedness. The Arab Strategy for Disaster Risk Reduction 2020 was adopted in 2010 and is being supported by the United Nations International Strategy for Disaster Reduction (UNISDR) and partners through the preparation of national disaster inventories, regional platforms, and capacity-building programmes aimed at improving land use planning, regulatory frameworks, financing and access to user-friendly information and communication tools.

Arab countries are also responding to climate change nationally. For example, a drought insurance programme based on rainfall contracts in Morocco is an important climate change adaptation measure that has the potential to reduce the effect of drought hazards and has helped to safeguard the production of cereals (Medany, 2008). Programmes to implement no-regret measures are also proliferating in water use efficiency and non-conventional water resource management.

Management strategies focused on dam construction and aquifer recharge are increasingly visible in the region as a way to respond to flood risk and store water for future use. During the flash floods that hit Egypt in January 2010, the Government reported that the dams established in Sinai and Aswan played a positive role in protecting Na'ama Bay, Nuweiba'a and Dahab, while also allowing for the storage of storm water in aquifers; this raised the groundwater table along the coastline and has helped prevent saltwater intrusion and contributed to improving water quality in those areas (Government of Egypt, 2010). Dams built around Jeddah helped minimize damage caused by the floods and associated landslides in the city in 2009 (Saud, 2010).

While dams can have both positive and negative impacts on natural and urban ecosystems, some Arab countries have increased their total dam capacity. Egypt stands at the forefront with a capacity of at least 169 km^3 since 2003. However, total dam capacity in Iraq almost tripled from 50.2 km^3 to 139.7 km^3 between 1990 and 2000. Syrian dam capacity increased from 15.85 km^3 in 1994 to 19.65 km^3 in 2007, with new dams under development along the Al-Assi River to help regulate river flow and reduce flood risk. Lebanon is proposing a series of new dams in its National Water Sector Strategy.

Managed aquifer recharge is also being considered more closely, for two reasons: (a) to stave off saltwater intrusion into coastal aquifers from over-pumping and sea level rise, which affects Mediterranean and Arabian Gulf coastlines; and (b) to store excess production of desalinated water as a risk buffer to prepare for future peaks in demand or desalination plant failures in GCC countries.

33.4.3 Expanding use of non-conventional water resources

Non-conventional water resources have become a mainstream response to water scarcity in the Arab region. Desaliniation is the primary source of water in GCC countries, while the reuse of wastewater is common practice in Jordan and the UAE. Nevertheless, the sustainability of these measures requires further action by Arab Governments as they pursue research and investment in new non-conventional water resources under development.

Desalination
Growing water demand has increased investment in desalination throughout the Arab region. Saudi Arabia has the greatest desalination capacity in the world and produces over 10 MCM per day, while the UAE is the second largest producer; jointly their desalination capacity accounts for over 30% of global freshwater production (UNESCWA, 2009*b*). Outside of the GCC, desalination represents a growing share of water supply in Algeria, Egypt, Iraq and Jordan, with efforts to expand capacity in Palestine underway. Tourism growth along the Egyptian coastline is dependent upon desalination, as pipelines transferring Nile River water to the Red Sea coast are no longer sufficient to satisfy needs.

Co-generation is also expanding in the Gulf, where power and desalinated water are produced at a joint facility. For instance, in 2011, the Power and Water Utility Company for Jubail and Yanbu (Marafiq) in Saudi Arabia started construction on Yanbu 2, which aims to produce 850 MW of electricity and 60,000 m³ of desalinated water per day (Zawya, 2011). However, desalination and co-generation are not cost-effective solutions in energy-poor countries and poses a problem for climate change due to their energy intensity. Universities and research centres in the region are thus piloting renewable energy desalination facilities based on solar or wind energy (UNESCWA, 2009*b*), which are gaining currency in Algeria, Morocco, Tunisia, Saudi Arabia and the UAE. Prospects for nuclear desalination are also being advanced in Jordan, Morocco, Saudi Arabia and the UAE.

Desalination also emerged as a local response and community-based resilience scheme in the the Occupied Palestinian Territory, where access to water is limited and groundwater has become increasingly saline. Driven by the private sector, small reverse osmosis desalination units can now be found in about 100,000 households in the Gaza Strip, as a secondary source of drinking water when municipal supplies are not delivered (World Bank, 2009). However, a new challenge has been the false sense of security that these small household desalination units provide as the units continue to be used despite the difficulty of securing replacement filters, which has resulted in associated health risks and challenges caused by continued use of systems that require maintenance.

Reuse of wastewater
The reuse of domestic wastewater for urban landscaping and greenbelts to combat land degradation and desertification has been practiced in Arab countries for decades. Some Arab countries adopted quality standards to regulate wastewater reuse for certain purposes (WHO-EM/CEH, 2006). However, increasing water scarcity and development pressures have increased interest in the use of treated sewage. As a result, treated wastewater is now used in the urban, agricultural, industrial and environmental sectors.

Jordan, Kuwait, Saudi Arabia and the UAE produce a relatively large amount of treated wastewater, with direct use of treated wastewater representing nearly 1% and 3% of total water withdrawal in Saudi Arabia and Oman respectively in 2006, and nearly 9% and 10% of total water withdrawal in Jordan and Qatar respectively in 2005 (FAO, 2011). Jordan and the UAE have established classification systems for regulating the reuse of treated wastewater for different purposes, including the cultivation of food and non-food products. Bahrain Airport uses treated grey water for cooling and landscaping. Abu Dhabi contracted Veolia Water to tertiary treat sewage from its capital city at a desert location, where the treated wastewater will be used to green the desert and support the establishment of a new community and biodiversity reserve. The use of treated wastewater is also being considered as part of managed aquifer recharge schemes in some Gulf countries. However, increased investment in sanitation, sufficient access to energy to fuel tertiary treatment facilities, and the adoption of harmonized quality standards and classification systems are needed to generate further benefits from treated wastewater re-use in the region.

Water harvesting and fog collection

Water harvesting has been up-scaled and expanded in the Arab region based on traditional practices. Household and farm level rainwater collection is already common practice in the Occupied Palestinian Territory, Tunisia and Yemen, and is usually captured in storage tanks and reservoirs for watering residential gardens or meeting domestic water needs. Water harvesting through condensation by forests has been piloted to facilitate groundwater recharge in Oman, while other methods are in place to recharge aquifers along the northern coast of Egypt. Fog collection is another option. In Yemen, 25 large fog collectors were constructed in 2004 with an area of 40 m² each, estimated to provide 4500 L of drinking water per day during the dry winter season (Schemenauer et al, 2004). In 2006, three standard fog collectors spanning 1 m² each were installed in the south-western region of Saudi Arabia. During the winter season, the best average daily water production of 11.5 L/m² was obtained, which encourages the development of further application of this technology in the region (Al-Hassan, 2009). However, fog collection facilities need to be carefully introduced based on comprehensive feasibility studies as they only work where certain weather conditions are met.

Pilots and prospects for new non-conventional water resources

While cloud seeding became popular after its successful demonstration by China prior to the 2008 Beijing Olympic Games, several Arab countries, including Algeria, Libya, Morocco, Jordan, Iraq, Saudi Arabia, the Syrian Arab Republic and UAE have been piloting cloud seeding programmes since its introduction (Al-Fenadi, n.d.). Between 2001 and 2002, the UAE conducted cloud seeding field programmes and found that the characteristics of clouds differ from season to season; new cloud seeding experiments were successfully conducted by meteorological authorities in the UAE in 2008 (*Gulfnews*, 2008). However, cloud seeding has fostered debate in the region regarding who owns the clouds, particularly when they cross between countries (Majzoub et al., 2009).

Capturing freshwater from newly identified underwater springs in the region offers another way to overcome water deficits thanks to the introduction of advanced remote sensing techniques (Shaban, 2009). However, this may introduce new territorial conflicts regarding sea and submarine resources shared by countries, and may potentially affect salinity levels needed to maintain coastal marine ecosystems.

Conclusion

Despite the risks and uncertainties discussed in this chapter, water flows at the core of Arab culture and consciousness. A national Egyptian holiday commemorates the flooding of the River Nile every spring, even though seasonal flooding has stopped since the Aswan Dam was built in the 1950s. Most Arabs live in cities situated along the coastline or a riverbed. Islamic cleansing with water is practiced by millions of Arabs every day prior to prayer, while threats to Arab water rights remain a touchstone for solidarity throughout the region.

Nonetheless, water scarcity, population growth, food security, climate change, extreme weather events, regional conflicts and the potential for new conflict over shared resources influence the ability to manage surface water and groundwater resources in the Arab region. The future will show how assessing these risks and engaging stakeholders in constructive and participatory processes will stimulate action at the national and regional levels to overcome these challenges despite continuing conditions of uncertainty.

||||||||||||||||||||||||||||||||||||||||||||||||||||||||||||||||||||||||

Notes

1   The 22 countries of the Arab region are identified as those that are members of the League of Arab States, namely Algeria, Bahrain, the Comoros, Djibouti, Egypt, Iraq, Jordan, Kuwait, Lebanon, Libya, Mauritania, Morocco, Oman, the Occupied Palestinian Territory, Qatar, Saudi Arabia, Somalia, Sudan, Syrian Arab Republic, Tunisia, the United Arab Emirates and Yemen.

2   The 14 ESCWA member countries are Bahrain, Egypt, Iraq, Jordan, Kuwait, Lebanon, Oman, the Occupied Palestinian Territory, Qatar, Saudi Arabia, Sudan, Syrian Arab Republic, United Arab Emirates and Yemen.

||||||||||||||||||||||||||||||||||||||||||||||||||||||||||||||||||||||||

References

Al Bowardi. 2010. *Statement of H.E. Mohammed Al Bowardi, Secretary General, Abu Dhabi Executive Council and Managing Director, Environment Agency Abu Dhabi to the Arab Water Academy Water Leaders Forum.* Abu Dhabi, UAE, 11 July 2010.

Al-Fenadi, Y. n.d. *Cloud Seeding Experiments in Arab countries: History and Results.* Tripoli , Libya, Libyan National Meteorological Centre (LNMC). http://www.wmo.int/pages/prog/arep/wmp/documents/Cloud%20seeding%20experiments%20in%20Arab%20countries.pdf (Accessed 6 September 2011.)

Al-Hassan, G. 2009. Fog Water collection evaluation in Asir Region – Saudi Arabia, *Water Resources Management,* 23(13), pp. 2805–13.

Al-Obaid, A.A. 2010. *King Abdullah's Initiative for Saudi Agricultural Investment Abroad: A Way of Enhancing Saudi Food Security,* delivered by Mr Al-Obaid, Deputy Minister for Agricultural Research and Development Affairs, to Expert Group Meeting on Achieving Food Security in Member Countries in Post-crisis World, Islamic Development Bank, Jeddah, Saudi Arabia, 2–3 May 2010. http://www.isdb.org/irj/go/km/docs/documents/IDBDevelopments/Internet/English/IDB/CM/Publications/IDB_AnnualSymposium/20thSymposium/8-AbdullaAlobaid.pdf (Accessed 3 October 2011).

AMWC (Arab Ministerial Water Council). 2010. Session 2, Resolution 4, Item 3. Cairo, Egypt, League of Arab States, 01 July 2010.

Assaf, H. 2010. Water resources and climate change (Ch. 2), M. , El-Ashry, N. Saab, and B. Zeitoon (eds.), Arab Forum for Environment and Development (AFED), *Water: Sustainable Management of a Scarce Resource.* Beirut, Lebanon, pp. 25–38.

BBC News. 2009. Flood deaths in Saudi Arabia rise to around 100. 28 November 2009. http://news.bbc.co.uk/2/hi/8384832.stm (Accessed 6 September 2011.)

Blas, J. 2008. Land leased to secure crops for South Korea, *Financial Times,* 18 November, http://www.ft.com/cms/s/0/98a81b9c-b59f-11dd-ab71-0000779fd18c.html (Accessed 6 September 2011.)

CAMRE (Council of Arab Ministers Responsible for the Environment). 2007. *Arab Ministerial Declaration on Climate Change.* Adopted at 19th Session of CAMRE. LAS, Cairo, Egypt, 5–6 December 2007.

CILSS (Comité Permanent Inter-Etats de Lutte contre la Sécheresse dans le Sahel), FAO, Famine Early Warning Systems Network, World Food Program. 2010. *Commerce Transfrontalier et Sécurité Alimentaire en Afrique de l'Ouest: Cas du Bassin Ouest: Gambie, Guinée-Bissau, Guinée, Mali, Mauritanie, Sénégal.* Report funded by USAID. http://documents.wfp.org/stellent/groups/public/documents/ena/wfp219290.pdf (Accessed 3 October 2011.)

Cotula, L., Vermeulen, S., Leonard, R., and Keeley, J. 2009. *Land Grab or Development Opportunity? Agricultural Investment and International Land Deals in Africa.* London/Rome, IIED/FAO/IFAD.

Council for Development and Reconstruction. 2006. *Impact of the July Offensive on the Public Finances in 2006: Brief Preliminary Report.* Government of Lebanon, Ministry of Finance, p. 22.

DREF Operation, 2010. *Egypt: Flash Floods,* 21 January. International Federation of Red Cross and Red Crescent Societies. http://www.ifrc.org/docs/appeals/10/MDREG009do.pdf

FAO (Food and Agriculture Organization). 2011. AQUASTAT Online Database. http://www.fao.org/nr/water/aquastat/dbase/index.stm (Accessed 9 November 2011.)

Government of Egypt. 2010. Mubarak receives report on facing floods in future. Press Release. 13 February 2010. http://reliefweb.int/node/345133 (Accessed 6 September 2011.)

Gulfnews. 2008. Cloud seeding experiment has thundering success. 8 May, http://gulfnews.com/news/gulf/uae/environment/cloud-seeding-experiment-has-thundering-success-1.104086 (Accessed 6 September 2011.)

––––. 2010. Facts about Tropical Cyclone Phet. 6 June. http://gulfnews.com/news/gulf/oman/facts-about-tropical-cyclone-phet-1.636372 (Accessed 6 September 2011.)

Harbridge, W., Pilkey, O.H., Whaling, P. and Swetland, P. 2007. Sedimentation in the Lake of Tunis: A lagoon strongly influenced by man. *Environmental Geology,* 1(4), pp. 215–225. http://www.springerlink.com/content/452745427631420p/

Hazaimeh, H. 2008. Private company to run Sudan venture, *Jordan Times,* 13 July, http://www.zawya.com/printstory.cfm?storyid=ZAWYA20080713031509&l=031500080713 (Accessed 6 September 2011.)

IRIN. 2007. *IRAQ: Water Shortage Leads People to Drink from Rivers,* 18 February. http://www.irinnews.org/report.aspx?reportid=70243 (Accessed 6 September 2011.)

Karrou, M. 2002. *Climatic Change and Drought Mitigation: Case of Morocco. INRA, Rabat, Morocco.* Presented to the First CLIMAGRImed Workshop, Session 3, FAO, Rome, 25–27 September 2002. http://www.fao.org/sd/climagrimed/c_1_01_01.html

Majzoub T., Quilleré-Majzoub, F., Abdel Raouf, M., El-Majzoub, M., 2009. 'Cloud busters': Reflections on the right to water in clouds and a search for international law rules." Vol. 20, No. 3, *Colorado Journal of International Environmental Law and Policy,* p. 321-54..

Makboul, M. 2009. Loi 10-95 sur l'eau: acquis et perspectives. UNESCO Country Office in Rabat/Cluster Office for the Maghreb, *L'Etat des Resources en Eau au Maghreb en 2009,* Morocco, pp. 47–59.

Medany, M. 2008. Impact of climate change on Arab countries, Chapter 9. M.K. Tolba and N.W. Saab (eds). *2008 Report of the Arab Forum for Environment and Development: Arab Environment Future Challenges.* http://www.afedonline.org/afedreport (Accessed 6 September 2011.)

Reuters. 2008a. Kuwait signed $27bln of deals in asian tour, 17 August, http://uk.reuters.com/article/2008/08/17/kuwait-asia-idUKLH49515120080817 (Accessed 6 September 2011.)

----. 2008*b*. GEM BioFuels Plc – Offtake agreement signed. Press Release. 14 February, http://www.reuters.com/article/pressRelease/idUS80349+14-Feb-2008+RNS20080214 (Accessed 6 September 2011.)

----. 2009. Saudi firm in $400 million farm investment in Africa. 15 April, http://af.reuters.com/article/investingNews/idAFJOE53E02F20090415 [Accessed 6 September 2011]

----. 2010. Interview – Qatar in talks to buy Argentina, Ukraine farmland. 1 October, http://af.reuters.com/article/sudanNews/idAFLDE69C1P420101013 (Accessed 6 September 2011.)

Rice, X. 2008. Abu Dhabi Develops Food Farms in Sudan. *The Guardian,* 2 July, http://www.guardian.co.uk/environment/2008/jul/02/food.sudan (Accessed 6 September 2011.)

Sahara and Sahel Observatory. 2011. *The North-Western Sahara Aquifer System,* Tunis, Tunisia. http://www.oss-online.org/index.php?option=com_content&task=view&id=33&Itemid=443&lang=en. (Accessed 13 September 2011.)

Saud, M.A. 2010. *Use of Space Techniques and GIS for Mapping Transported Sediments: The Case of Jeddah Flood 2009,* King Abdel Aziz City for Science and Technology, Saudi Arabia, Posters for Workshop 6.

Schemenauer, R., Osses, P., and Leibbrand, M. 2004. *Fog Collection Evaluation and Operational Projects in the Hajja Governorate, Yemen.* http://www.geo.puc.cl/observatorio/cereceda/C38.pdf (Accessed 6 September 2011.)

Shaban, A. 2009. *Monitoring Groundwater Discharge in the Coastal Zone of Lebanon Using Remotely Sensed Data.* Remote Sensing Center, National Council for Scientific Research, Beirut, Lebanon, Poster 4 presented to Stockholm World Water Week 2009.

UNDESA (United Nations Department of Economic and Social Affairs). 2007. *World Population Prospects: The 2006 Revision – Highlights.* ESA/P/WP.202. New York, United Nations.

UNESCWA (United Nations Economic and Social Commission for Western Asia). 2005. *ESCWA Water Development Report 1: Vulnerability of the Region to Socio-Economic Drought.* E/ESCWA/SDPD/2005/9. New York, United Nations.

----. 2007*a*. *ESCWA Water Development Report 2: State of Water Resources in the ESCWA Region.* E/ESCWA/SDPD/2007/6. New York, United Nations.

----. 2007*b*. *Guidelines with Regard to Developing Legislative and Institutional Frameworks Needed to Implement IWRM at the National Level in the ESCWA Region.* (Arabic). E/ESCWA/SDPD/2007/1 New York, United Nations, 9 June 2007.

----. 2009*a*. *The Demographic Profile of the Arab Countries.* E/ESCWA/SDD/2009/Technical Paper.9. New York, United Nations, 26 November 2009. http://www.escwa.un.org/information/publications/edit/upload/sdd-09-TP9.pdf

----. 2009*b*. *ESCWA Water Development Report 3: Role of Desalination in Addressing Water Scarcity.* E/ESCWA/SDPD/2009/4. New York, United Nations.

----. 2009*c*. *Trends and Impacts in Conflict Settings: The Socio-Economic Impact of Conflict-Driven Displacement in the ESCWA Region.* Issue No. 1, E/ESCWA/ECRI/2009/2. New York, United Nations.

----. 2009*d*. *Knowledge Mapping and Analysis of ESCWA Member Countries Capacities in Managing Shared Water Resources.* E/ESCWA/SDPD/2009/7. New York, United Nations.

----. 2009*e*. *Increasing the Competitiveness of Small and Medium-sized Enterprises through the Use of Environmentally Sound Technologies: Assessing the Potential for the Development of Second-generation Biofuels in the ESCWA Region,* E/ESCWA/SDPD/2009/5, New York, United Nations.

----. 2010*a*. *Best Practices and Tools for Increasing Productivity and Competitiveness in the Production Sectors: Assessment of Zaatar Productivity and Competitiveness in Lebanon.* E/ESCWA/SDPD/2010/Technical Paper 3. New York, United Nations.

----. 2010*b*. *Food Security and Conflict in the ESCWA Region.* E/ESCWA/ECRI/2010/1, 13 September 2010. New York, United Nations.

----. 2011. *ESCWA Water Development Report 4: National Capacities for the Management of Shared Water Resources in ESCWA Member Countries.* E/ESCWA/SDPD/2011/4. New York, United Nations.

UNESCWA and BGR (United Nations Economic and Social Commission for Western Asia and the Federal Institute for Geosciences and Natural Resources, Germany). 2010. *Report of the Expert Group Meeting on Applying IWRM Principles in Managing Shared Water Resources: Towards A Regional Vision,* Beirut, Lebanon 1-3 December 2009; E/ESCWA/SDPD/2009/WG.5/1/Report issued 11 June 2010 (English).

----. 2012. *Inventory of Shared Water Resources in Western Asia.* Beirut, Lebanon, UNESCWA-BGR Cooperation, 2012 (*forthcoming*).

WHO/EMRO/CEHA (World Health Organization Regional Office for the Eastern Mediterranean Regional Center for Environmental Health Activities). 2006. *A Compendium of Standards for Wastewater Reuse in the Eastern Mediterranean Region.* Document. WHO-EM/CEH/142/E.

WHO/UNICEF JMP (World Health Organization/United Nations Children's Fund Joint Monitoring Programme) for Water Supply and Sanitation. 2010. *Progress on Sanitation and Drinking-water: 2010 Update.* New York, UNICEF.

World Bank. 2009. *West Bank and Gaza: Assessment of Restrictions on Palestinian Water Sector Development.* Sector Note, April 2009. Report No. 47657-GZ, Washington, World Bank.

Zawya, 2011. MARAFIQ - Yanbu Power and Desalination Plant - Phase 2. *Projects Monitor,* 29 April 2011. http://www.zawya.com/projects/project.cfm?pid150710103455/MARAFIQ--Yanbu-Power-and-Desalination-Plant--Phase-2?cc (Accessed 9 November 2011.)

WHO and UNICEF
—
Authors Jennifer Gentry-Shields and Jamie Bartram
Contributors Robert Bos, Claire-Lise Chaignat, Bruce Allan Gordon, Dominique Maison, Yves Chartier, Chee Keong Chew and Margaret Montgomery (WHO) and Peter Harvey (UNICEF)

© Taco Anema

||||||||||||||||||||||||||||||||||||||||||||||||||||||||||||||||||||||||||||||||||||||||||||||||||||||||||||||||||||||||||||||||||||||||||||||||||||||||||||||||

The global drivers predicted to have the greatest effect on disease rates via the water environment are population growth and urbanization, agriculture, infrastructure, and global climate change. Trends in these drivers directly and indirectly affect the global burden of disease, largely adversely, and increase the overall uncertainty in future human health.

There are numerous non-water-related environmental determinants of health, as well as non-environmental determinants of health, that make the identification of trends and hotspots in water and health challenging.

By outlining the environment–health nexus for each of the major water-related disease groups, five key solutions were identified: access to safe drinking water and sanitation, improved hygiene, environmental management and the use of health impact assessments. Implementation of these actions serves to reduce the burden of multiple diseases and improve quality of life for billions of individuals.

In-depth studies are required to more accurately identify the risks and opportunities related to water and health, such as The 2030 Vision Study which determined the major risks, uncertainties and opportunities related to the resilience of water supply and sanitation in the face of climate change.

Protection of human health requires collaboration among multiple sectors, including those in non-water and non-health sectors.

34.1 Introduction

Improving water resource management, drinking water supply, sanitation and hygiene has the potential to prevent 9.1% of the global disease burden or 6.3% of all deaths (Prüss-Üstün et al., 2008). Understanding the nature and magnitude of the burden of water-associated diseases provides the basis for effective interventions.

This report examines the diseases that contribute significantly to this global burden (in disability-adjusted life years, or DALYs, a weighted measure of deaths and disability; see Figure 34.1) and that are realistically preventable using available technologies, policies and public health measures.

Mapping the environment–health causal pathway provides insights that inform effective public health interventions. The driver, pressure, state, exposure, effect and action (DPSEEA) model, developed by the World Health Organization (WHO) provides a simple illustration of the way in which the environment influences health and how the environmental state is influenced by higher causes (Kjellström and Corvalán, 1995). The model allows for a clear understanding of the factors contributing to the burden of disease and supports the development of effective intervention strategies. Yet this process is complicated by the fact that each disease is associated with a variety of economic, societal and natural driving forces. We have used the DPSEEA model to determine the linkages for the disease groups, defined by Bradley (2008) as waterborne diseases, water-washed diseases, water-based diseases and water-related insect vector diseases.

34.2 Water-related disease groups, environment–health pathway and promising interventions

34.2.1 Waterborne diseases

Waterborne diseases are contracted by drinking contaminated water. The most predominant include diarrhoeal disease, from which over 2 million people die every year (WHO and UNICEF, 2010), and arsenic and fluoride poisoning, for which the global impacts are unknown. These diseases are driven by fluctuations in extreme weather events (e.g. inland flooding), climate change, deforestation, population growth and agriculture, as shown in Figure 34.2 which outlines the environment–health pathway for waterborne diseases. Promising interventions for waterborne diseases include the provision of safe drinking water (Box 34.1), improved sanitation (Box 34.2) and health impact assessments (Box 34.3).

Access to safe drinking water can prevent waterborne diseases by avoiding consumption of unsafe drinking water. Some strategies for providing access to safe drinking water are given in Box 34.1.

Access to water via a piped infrastructure can lead to substantive reductions in mortality due to diarrhoeal disease and arsenic and fluoride poisoning. Studies from the United States (Cutler and Miller, 2005; Watson, 2006) and India (Jalan and Ravallion, 2003) have shown that combined improvements in water access and quality can have enormous health returns. As the proportion of the global population that relies on improved sources of drinking water (including piped systems) increases, the quality of water received from these sources will become increasingly significant for health. Piped water is not necessarily safe – for example,

FIGURE 34.1

Diseases with the largest water, sanitation and hygiene contribution in 2000

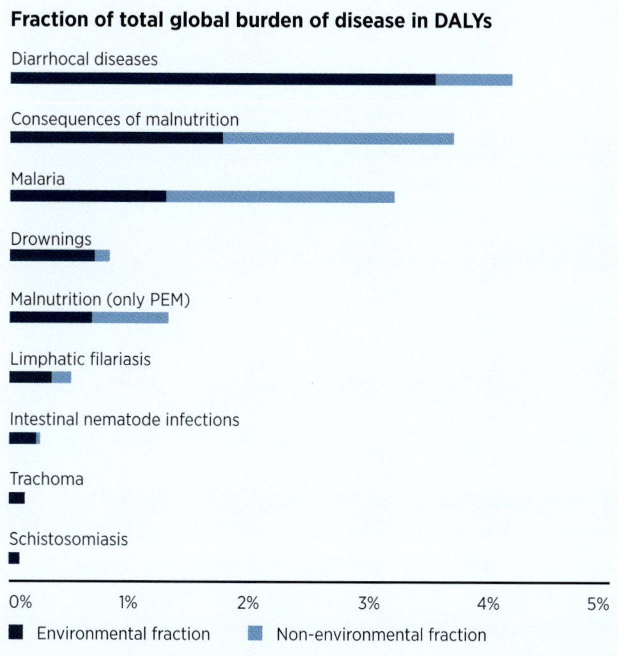

Fraction of total global burden of disease in DALYs

(Diarrhocal diseases; Consequences of malnutrition; Malaria; Drownings; Malnutrition (only PEM); Limphatic filariasis; Intestinal nematode infections; Trachoma; Schistosomiasis)

0%   1%   2%   3%   4%   5%

■ Environmental fraction   ■ Non-environmental fraction

Note: DALY, disability-adjusted life year (which measures the years of life lost to premature mortality and the years lost to disability); PEM, protein-energy malnutrition (which is malnutrition that develops in adults and children whose consumption of protein and energy is insufficient to satisfy the body's nutritional needs). Source: Prüss-Üstün et al. (2008).

FIGURE 34.2

Driver, pressure, state, exposure, effect and action (DPSEEA) model for waterborne diseases

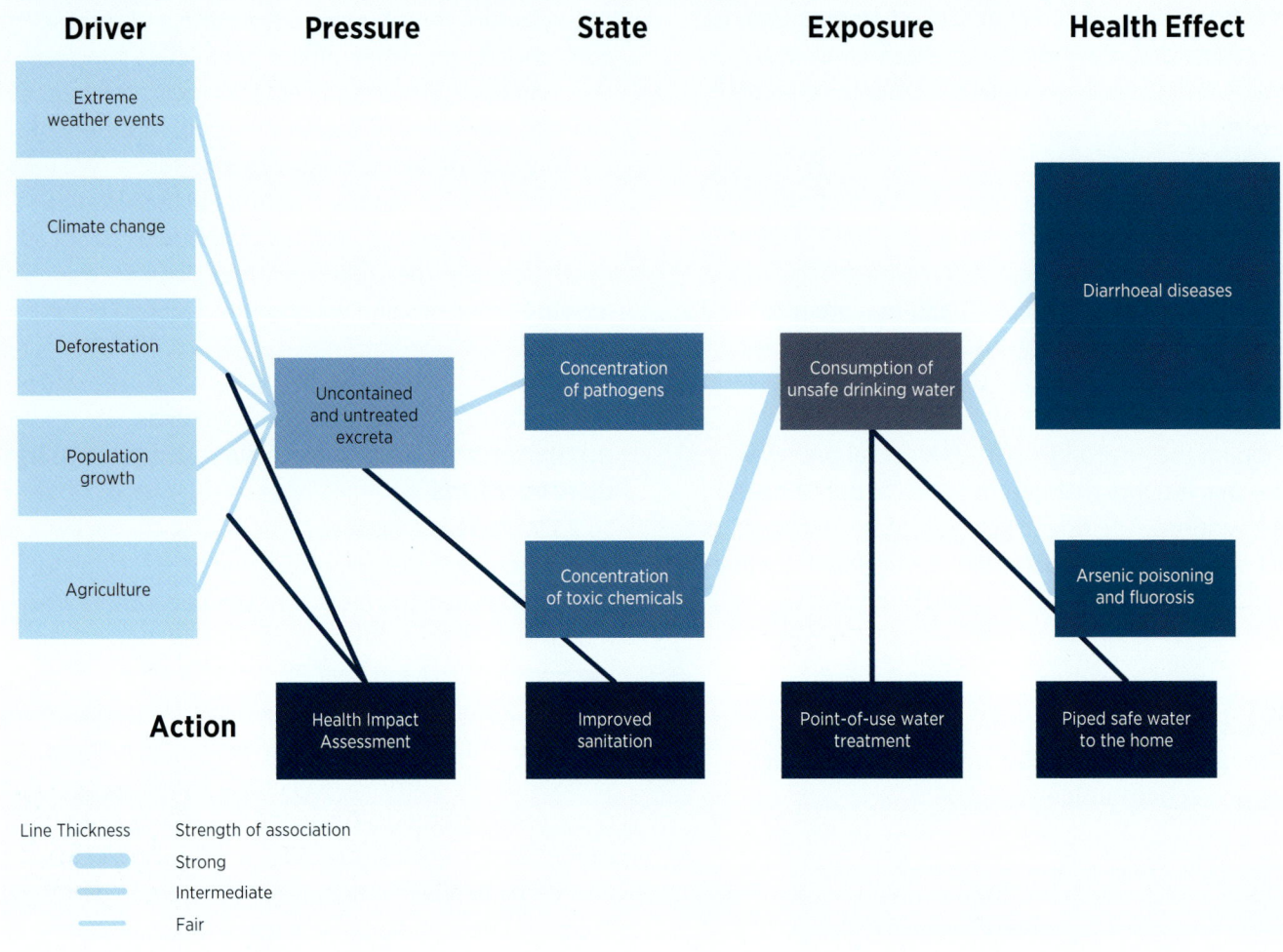

Note: The size of the health effect boxes varies with the corresponding global burden of disease in disability-adjusted life years: diarrhoeal diseases, 52,460,000 (including waterborne and water-washed diarrhoeal disease); arsenic poisoning and fluorosis, unknown (disease burden estimates from Prüss-Üstün et al., 2008).

BOX 34.1

Safe drinking water strategies for reducing waterborne disease

Safe drinking water, as defined in the third edition of the WHO guidelines for drinking-water quality, does not represent 'any significant risk to health over a lifetime of consumption, including different sensitivities that may occur between life stages' (WHO, 2008b). Solutions for providing safe drinking water include piped water infrastructure (through standpipes and household connections), wells and point-of-use (PoU) water treatment. Piped water supply has been shown to drastically reduce child mortality (Cutler and Miller, 2005; Watson, 2006). However, piped water services to some, especially dispersed rural, populations may not be readily achievable. The majority (84%) of the global population who do not have an improved drinking water source resides in rural areas (WHO and UNICEF, 2010), despite an increased rural coverage from 64% in 1990 to 78% in 2008. In rural regions, drinking water access is often outside the home, such as communal taps, wells and protected springs. Such protected sources may make water available closer to the home, but quantities transported are moderate, and water is readily and frequently contaminated. PoU water treatment and improved water storage practices can reduce pathogen contamination. Numerous PoU technologies are available, including chlorination, the use of flocculants, adsorption, filtration, boiling or solar disinfection.

insufficient treatment and interruptions to treatment and service can result in the consumption of unsafe water (Hunter et al., 2005). In aging systems, failure will likely become a principal risk related to water and health issues (USEPA, 2007) (see Chapter 24 for infrastructure tools and options).

Conversely, studies report little evidence for substantial health effects from rural water infrastructures (Esrey, 1996; Fewtrell et al., 2005). Small, especially rural, systems are frequently contaminated and improperly maintained. Water carried into the home frequently becomes contaminated in transport and storage (Wang and Hunter, 2010). Countless anecdotes exist about infrastructures that are poorly constructed, improperly maintained and eventually abandoned.

Point-of-use (PoU) water treatment is a promising way to counter contamination of water during transport and storage. Some evaluations of PoU water treatment systems found reductions of 20–30% in diarrhoeal incidence at the household level (Quick et al., 1999; Reller et al., 2003). Some PoUs remove arsenic and fluoride. Nevertheless, health benefits of PoU treatment depend on individual decisions to adopt and consistently adhere to certain behaviours. The introduction of water treatment technology without consideration for the sociocultural aspects of the community and without behavioural, motivational, educational and participatory activities within the community is unlikely to be successful or sustainable (as reviewed in Sobsey, 2006). Determining effective promotion strategies and

FIGURE 34.3

Driver, pressure, state, exposure, effect and action (DPSEEA) model for water-washed diseases

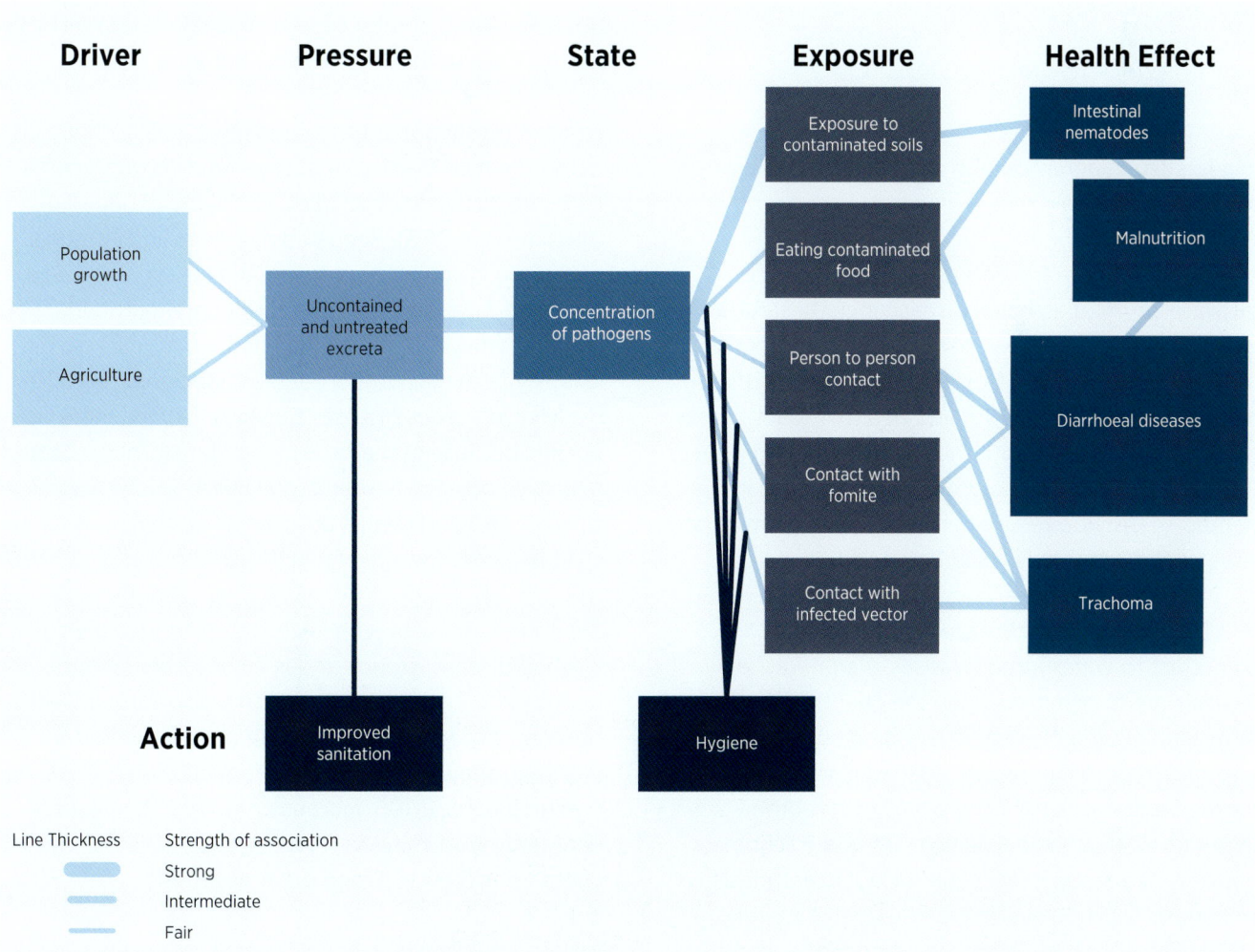

Note: The size of the health effect boxes varies with the burden of disease in disability-adjusted life years: diarrhoeal diseases, 52,460,000 (including waterborne and water-washed diarrhoeal disease); intestinal nematodes, 2,948,000; malnutrition, 35,849,000; trachoma, 2,320,000 (disease burden estimates from Prüss-Üstün et al., 2008).

BOX 34.2
Sanitation strategies for disease prevention

Sanitation is the safe disposal of human excreta (WHO and UNICEF, 2010), where 'safe disposal' means that excreta is contained or treated to avoid adversely affecting the health of the individual or that of other people (Mara et al., 2010). Improved sanitation can prevent disease by eliminating the source of contamination, by preventing pathogen spread by flies, and by preventing exposure to pathogens in contaminated fields. Most (99%) people in developed countries have access to improved sanitation, while only 53% have access in developing countries (WHO and UNICEF, 2010). Two-thirds of the approximately 2.6 billion people who lack access to improved sanitation live in Asia and sub-Saharan Africa, and approximately 1.2 billion people, over half of whom live in India, defecate in the open (WHO and UNICEF, 2010). Most of those lacking improved sanitation in developing countries are located in rural areas: urban sanitation coverage is 71% in developing countries, while rural coverage is only 39% (WHO and UNICEF, 2010). Sewerage systems, septic tanks with drainage beds, pour-flush latrines and pit latrines can effectively prevent disease if maintained and used consistently (WHO and UNICEF, 2000).

how to sustain behavioural changes should be a priority in PoU initiatives.

In addition to safe drinking water, actions to combat waterborne diarrhoeal disease include sanitation (eliminating the source of pathogen contamination of drinking water – see Box 34.2); hygiene improvements (see Section 34.2.2); and health impact assessments (HIAs) (to evaluate the potential health effects of projects or policies before they are built or implemented to provide recommendations to minimize adverse health outcomes – see Box 34.4).

34.2.2 Water-washed diseases

In contrast to waterborne diseases, water-washed diseases are transmitted when the quantity of water available is insufficient for washing and personal hygiene. Predominant water-washed diseases include diarrhoeal diseases (which are also waterborne – see Section 34.2.1), intestinal nematodes and trachoma. Intestinal nematode infections – including ascariasis, trichuriasis and hookworm – cause approximately 2 billion infections and affect one third of the world's population (de Silva et al., 2003). Approximately 40 million people are infected with *Chlamydia trachomatis*, the etiologic agent of trachoma, and 8.2 million have

BOX 34.3
Hygiene promotion

Hygiene refers to practices that prevent the spread of disease-causing organisms. Means to achieve hygiene include cleaning, such as hand washing, which removes infectious microbes in addition to dirt and soil. Along with improved sanitation and storing and using safe drinking water, washing hands correctly and at the right times is a key behaviour for reducing the spread of pathogens (EHP, 2004).

Hygiene promotion is 'a planned approach to preventing ... diseases through the widespread adoption of safe hygiene practices. It begins with, and is built on what local people know, do and want' (UNICEF, 1999, p. 10).

blinding trachomatous trichiasis (Mariotti et al., 2009). Figure 34.3 outlines the environment–health pathway for water-washed diseases. The dominant drivers are population growth and agriculture. Improved sanitation (Box 34.2) and hygiene (Box 34.3) would serve to significantly reduce the disease burdens.

These interventions contribute to reducing childhood undernutrition, as diarrhoeal diseases and intestinal nematode infections are closely tied to childhood undernutrition (Figure 34.3). Repeated diarrhoea and intestinal nematode infections are responsible for approximately half of all childhood underweight or undernutrition. Approximately 70,000 children under five years old die annually from malnutrition, and an additional 790,000 die from infectious diseases to which they are more vulnerable because of their nutritional status. Thus repeated diarrhoea or intestinal nematode infections are responsible for 860,000 deaths due to malnutrition per year in children under the age of five (Prüss-Üstün et al., 2008).

Sanitation interacts with both waterborne and water-washed disease groups and is a necessary component of effective prevention of the associated disease burdens, especially diarrhoea. Improved sanitation has been shown to reduce diarrhoeal disease rates (Fewtrell et al., 2005; Moraes et al., 2003), intestinal nematode transmission (Moraes et al., 2004) and trachoma prevalence (Emerson et al., 2004).

Hygiene reduces diarrhoeal disease (e.g. Luby et al., 2004) and trachoma (West et al., 1995), and is promoted as a public health intervention (Box 34.3).

BOX 34.4

Health impact assessments promote health across diverse sectors

A health impact assessment (HIA) 'is a combination of procedures, methods and tools by which a policy, program or projects may be judged as to its potential effects on the health of a population, and the distribution of those effects within the population (WHO, 1999, p. 4).

An HIA objectively evaluates the potential health effects of a project or policy before it is built or implemented and can identify means to increase positive health outcomes and minimize adverse health outcomes. The HIA framework brings potential public health impacts and considerations to the decision-making process for plans, projects and policies that fall outside traditional public health arenas, such as transportation, agriculture, land use and construction. These activities can greatly affect disease transmission, but are often planned without public health consequences in mind. Cooperation between health, agricultural and development sectors can lead to reduced pathogen transmission.

The major steps in conducting an HIA include:
1. Screen – identify projects or policies for which an HIA would be useful
2. Scope – identify which health effects to consider
3. Assess risks and benefits – identify which people may be affected and how they may be affected
4. Develop recommendations – suggest changes to proposals to promote positive or mitigate adverse health effects
5. Report – present the results to decision-makers
6. Evaluate – determine the effect of the HIA

FIGURE 34.4

Driver, pressure, state, exposure, effect and action (DPSEEA) model of water-based diseases

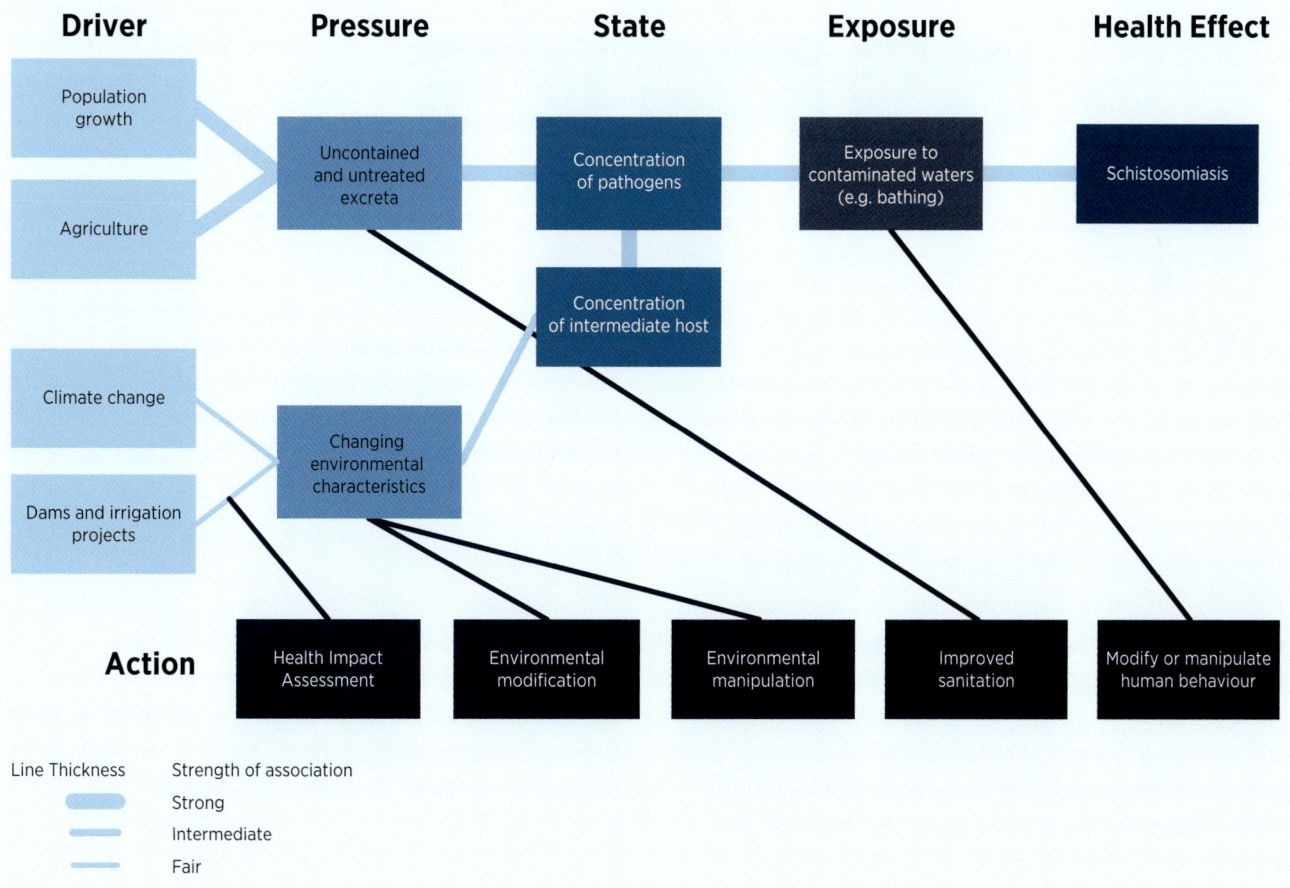

Note: The size of the health effect box varies with the corresponding global burden of disease in disability-adjusted life years: schistosomiasis, 1,698,000 (disease burden estimates from Prüss-Üstün et al., 2008).

FIGURE 34.5

Driver, pressure, state, exposure, effect and action (DPSEEA) model of the water-related insect vector diseases malaria, onchocerciasis, Japanese encephalitis and lymphatic filariasis in Africa

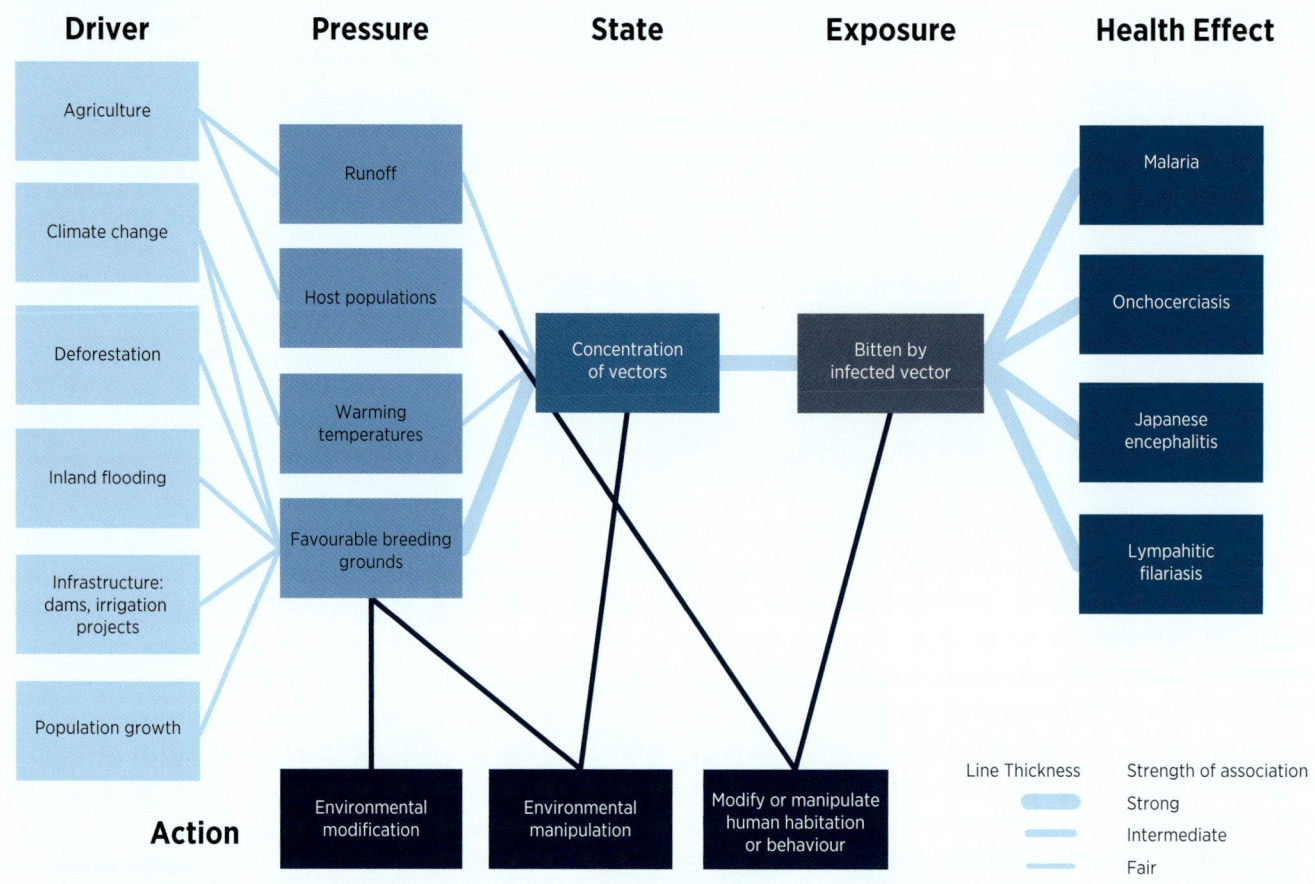

Note: The size of the health effect boxes varies with the corresponding global burden of disease in disability-adjusted life years: malaria, 19,241,000; onchocerciasis, 51,000; Japanese encephalitis, 671,000; lymphatic filariasis, 3,784,000 (disease burden estimates from Prüss-Üstün et al., 2008).

34.2.3 Water-based diseases

Water-based diseases are transmitted by hosts that live in water or require water for part of their life cycle. Schistosomiasis has the largest disease burden of these diseases; at any one given time, approximately 200 million people are infected with the trematodes of the species *Schistosoma*, which cause schistosomiasis. Schistosomiasis is principally driven by population growth, agriculture, climate change, deforestation and infrastructure such as dams and irrigation projects (Figure 34.4).

Effective interventions include sanitation (Box 34.2), environmental management (Box 34.5) and the use of HIAs (Box 34.4). Sanitation can reduce schistosomiasis prevalence by 57–87% (Esrey et al., 1991). Environmental management reduces transmission by eradicating host snail populations (e.g. by eliminating

marshes and ponds, draining irrigation areas, cleaning and removing vegetation from canals, introducing predators and pathogens, or using molluscicides) and by limiting human contact with infested waters. HIA applied to the design and planning of irrigation or dam projects enables incorporation of preventative safeguards rather than retrofitting responses.

34.2.4 Water-related insect vector diseases

Water-related insect vector-borne diseases (VBDs) are spread by insects that breed or feed near water. The major water-related insect VBDs (malaria, onchocerciasis, Japanese encephalitis, lymphatic filariasis and dengue) are responsible for more than 1.5 million deaths per year. Drivers of these diseases include agriculture, climate change, deforestation, inland flooding, infrastructure projects such as dams and irrigation projects, and population growth (Figures 34.5 and 34.6).

Historically, some of the most effective public health measures against water-related insect VBDs have been targeted at the vector (to interrupt transmission), particularly for diseases lacking vaccines such as malaria and dengue (Gubler, 1998). Such programmes are regaining favour due to environmental problems with chemical insecticide programmes and insecticide resistance. Environmental management of water-related insect VBDs is promoted by the WHO (Box 34.5).

Environmental management has been used to successfully control the transmission of malaria (Baer et al., 1999; Dua et al., 1997; Heierli and Lengeler, 2008),

Environmental management strategies to reduce and prevent vector-borne diseases

Environmental management for vector control is 'the planning, organization, carrying out and monitoring of activities for the modification and/or manipulation of environmental factors or their interaction with man with a view to preventing or minimizing vector propagation and reducing man-vector-pathogen contact' (WHO, 1980, p. 9). The three strategies are:

1. Modification of the environment: permanently changing land, water or vegetation conditions to reduce vector habitats, often using infrastructure. Examples include draining or filling-in water bodies or depressions; modifying river boundaries; lining canals; designing small dams as cascading systems; and covering overhead tanks and other water storage structures (Fewtrell et al., 2007).
2. Manipulation of the environment: recurrent activities, often with community involvement, to create temporarily unfavourable conditions for vector propagation. Examples include removal of aquatic plants from water bodies where mosquito larvae may find shelter (de-weeding); alternate wetting and drying of irrigated fields (intermittent irrigation); periodic flushing of waterways where mosquito breeding occurs in standing pools; screening or fitting household water storage containers with proper lids to exclude mosquitoes; and introduction of predators such as larvivorous fish (Fewtrell et al., 2007).
3. Modification or manipulation of human habitation or behaviour: reduce contact between humans and vectors. Examples include vaccination; zooprophylaxis; vector trapping and collection; bednets; door and window screens; and better housing construction.

FIGURE 34.6

Drivers, pressure, state, exposure, effect and action (DPSEEA) model of the water-related insect vector diseases lymphatic filariasis (Asia and the Americas) and dengue

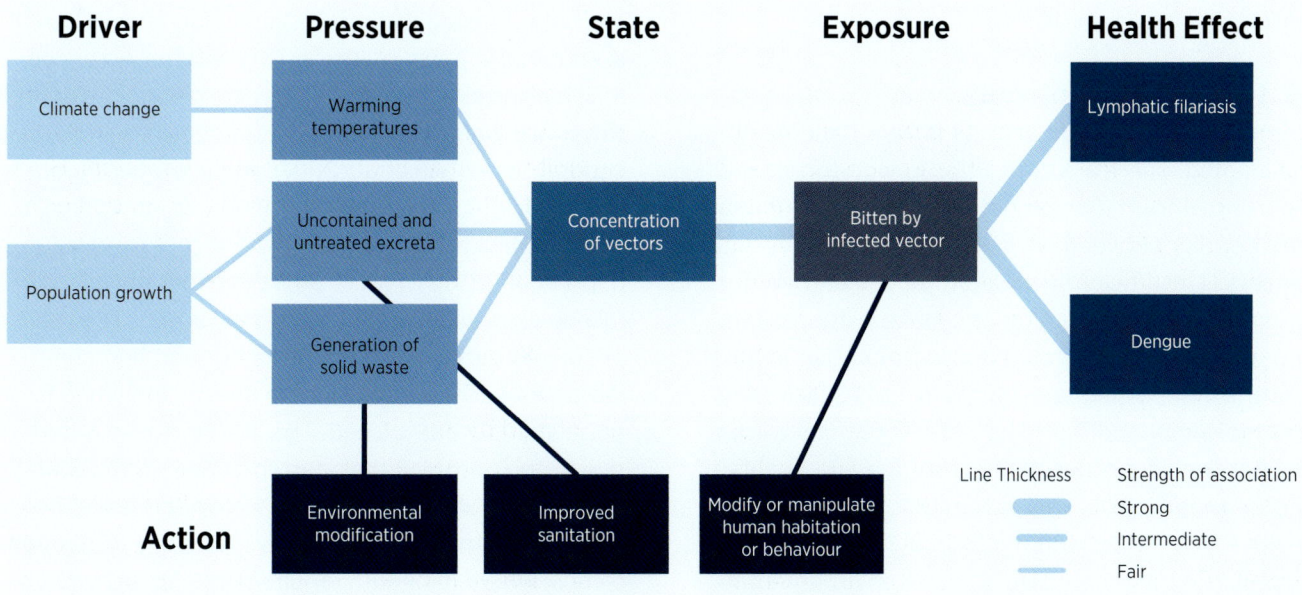

Note: The size of the health effect boxes varies with the corresponding global burden of disease in disability-adjusted life years: lymphatic filariasis, 3,784,000; dengue, 586,000 (disease burden estimates from Prüss-Üstün et al., 2008).

FIGURE 34.7

Cholera cases reported to the World Health Organization between 2000 and 2010

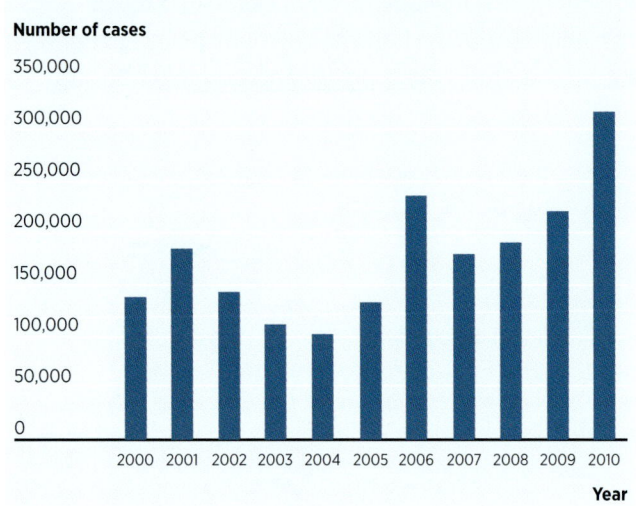

Source: Adapted from WHO (2011a).

onchocerciasis (Walsh, 1970), Japanese encephalitis (Keiser et al., 2005), dengue and lymphatic filariasis. Sanitation and drinking water also contribute to water-related insect VBD control. In urban areas of south and South-East Asia and the Americas, the mosquito vector of lymphatic filariasis breeds in organically-polluted water, including open sewerage drains and wastewater treatment ponds (Erlanger et al., 2005; Meyrowitsch et al., 1998). Piped water supplies contribute to dengue control by eliminating the need for water storage containers in which the mosquito vector breeds.

34.3 Trends and hotspots

Identifying trends and hotspots in water and health is challenging. There are difficulties in monitoring and reporting; information on determinants is lacking; and the interplay between environmental and other determinants is insufficiently understood. Current monitoring and reporting limitations make it impossible to quantify the water-related disease burden in most countries. Reporting constraints include a lack of reliable morbidity and mortality data; variations within and between countries in the coverage and quality of case reporting; as well as variations in access to health care services and the thoroughness of disease surveillance. There are also multiple environmental determinants concurrently affecting human health within the social, economic and physical environment. These include access to and quality of health care,

nutrition, education, governance, socio-economic status and resource availability. Non-environmental determinants of health – a person's individual characteristics and behaviours – also determine disease trends. Some characteristics, including age and sex, can be easily obtained. Others, such as health status and genetic make-up, are not readily available.

The inability to identify trends and hotspots impairs our ability to make well-informed policy and resource management decisions. Nevertheless, available insights give a basis for action. Some disease risks are rising (e.g. see Figure 34.7), and reasons for these increases can be addressed. Three examples are provided below that illustrate the complex nature of disease risk and highlight how prevention, control and mitigation are being investigated and implemented.

34.3.1 Cholera

Cholera is an acute diarrhoeal disease caused by the ingestion of food or water contaminated with the bacterium *Vibrio cholerae*. There are an estimated 3–5 million cholera cases and 100,000–120,000 deaths due to cholera each year (the WHO estimates that 5–10% of cases are reported). The number of cases reported to the WHO increased by 43% in 2010 compared to 2009, and this number has increased by 130% over the last decade (Figure 34.7) (WHO, 2010a). Cholera occurs in regions with poor socio-economic conditions, rudimentary sanitary systems, and where public hygiene and safe drinking water is lacking (Huq et al., 1996). It is endemic in parts of Africa, Asia and the Americas. Risk factors in endemic regions can include proximity to surface waters, high population densities and educational levels (Ali et al., 2001), while temperature, salinity, sunlight, pH levels, iron, as well as phytoplankton and zooplankton growth factors affect *V. cholerae* itself (Lipp et al., 2002). Figure 34.8 describes environmental cholera transmission (Lipp et al., 2002). The risk of cholera outbreaks is intensified during humanitarian crises, such as conflicts and floods, and when large populations are displaced. The 2010 increase is largely due to the outbreak that started in Haiti in October 2010. At-risk areas include peri-urban slums without basic water and sanitation infrastructure, and refugee camps, where minimum requirements for safe water and sanitation are not met. The re-emergence of cholera has coincided with increasing populations living in unsanitary conditions (Barrett et al., 1998).

FIGURE 34.8

Hierarchical model for environmental cholera transmission

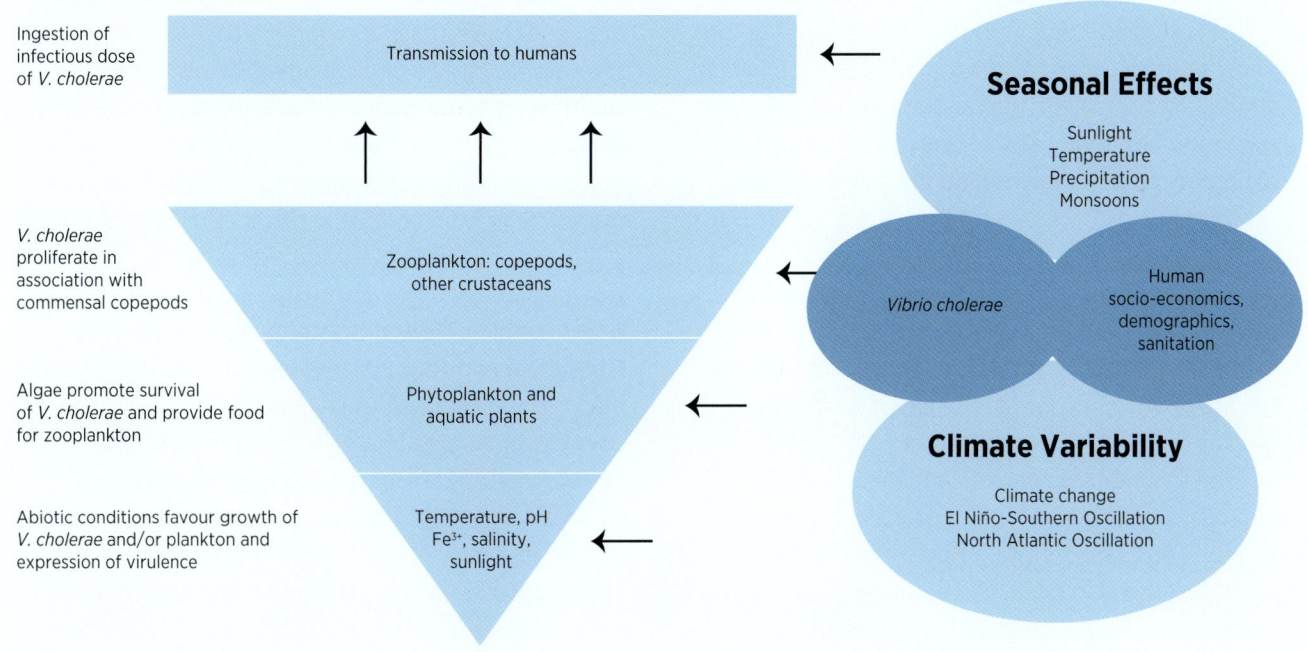

Source: Lipp et al. (2002, fig. 1, p. 763, reproduced with permission from The American Society for Microbiology).

Up to 80% of cholera cases can be effectively *treated* using oral rehydration salts. However *prevention* relies on availability and use of safe water and improved sanitation and hygiene. Prevention strategies are critical to averting or mitigating cholera outbreaks. In the case of the Haiti outbreak, the country's health response – led by the Ministry of Public Health and Population and supported by the WHO and other partners – incorporates multiple public health solutions: delivery of soap for hand washing; delivery of chlorine and other products or devices for household water treatment; construction of latrines; improved hygiene in public places (markets, schools, health care facilities and prisons); and health education through various media including community mobilizers (WHO, 2010b). In fact, the availability of safe water supplies may prove to be more important for combating cholera than antibiotics or vaccines. A recent study showed that provision of safe water may avert 105,000 cases of cholera (95% confidence interval [CI] 88,000–116,000) and 1,500 deaths (95% CI 1,100–2,300) in Haiti between March 2011 and November 2011, more than the estimated individual effects of antibiotics or vaccines (Andrews and Basu, 2011).

With increasing populations living in peri-urban slums and refugee camps, as well as increasing numbers of people exposed to the impacts of humanitarian crises, the risk from cholera will likely increase worldwide, reinforcing the need for safe drinking water, adequate sanitation and improved hygiene behaviour under these conditions.

34.3.2 Harmful algal blooms

Harmful algal blooms (HABs) comprise algae that are harmful to humans, plants or animals (most algal species are non-toxic natural components of marine and freshwater ecosystems). While HABs do not represent a major global disease burden, bloom detection is increasing and it is likely that disease incidence will similarly increase. The causes of increased bloom detection include natural and anthropogenic species dispersal, nutrient pollution, climate change, as well as increased surveillance (Granéli and Turner, 2006). Approximately 60,000 cases and clusters of human intoxication occur annually (Van Dolah et al., 2001). Although is not fully understood how HABs affect human health, authorities monitor HABs and develop guidelines to mitigate their impacts. For example, the United States Environmental Protection Agency has added specific HAB-related algae to its Drinking Water Contaminant Candidate List, which identifies priority organisms and toxins for investigation. Direct control (biological, chemical, genetic and environmental manipulation) of HABs is more difficult and controversial than mitigation, and HAB prevention is hampered by a lack of understanding of the causes of HAB blooms and an inability to modify or control determinants. For example, nutrients (from agriculture, households and industry) contribute to the growth of HABs, and much of the nutrient input comes from non-point sources (Anderson et al., 2002), which are difficult to control. Effective strategies include land use management, maintaining landscape integrity and reducing non-point source pollution (Piehler, 2008).

34.3.3 Dengue

In 2004, approximately 9 million people contracted the febrile illness dengue (WHO, 2008a), the global incidence of which is rising. Approximately 2.5 billion people are now at risk. Because there is no drug or vaccine for the virus, prevention is key. Dengue is transmitted by the *Aedes aegypti* and *Aedes albopictus* mosquitoes, which breed in temporary water storage containers. Thus safe storage of household water supplies is critical for dengue prevention, especially where rainwater harvesting is practised and where large household storage vessels are used (e.g. Mariappan, 2008). Household water containers can be fitted with screens or lids to exclude mosquitoes, but scrupulous maintenance and consistent use is hard to achieve. Covers treated with insecticide can reduce vector density and potentially impact dengue transmission (Kroeger et al., 2006; Seng et al., 2008). Water containers can also be eliminated with piped water supplies; however, extension of piped water supplies to villages has expanded the range of dengue, where unreliable piped water has forced people to store water in their homes for longer periods of time than when they relied on well water (e.g. Nguyen et al., 2011). An integrated approach, incorporating household water treatment and safe storage for reduction of diarrhoeal as well as other water-associated diseases (e.g. dengue and malaria) is needed.

34.4 Solution options

Modelling the environment–health pathway for each of the major threats associated with water and health (Section 34.2) assists in determining the effectiveness of public health solutions for combating water-related disease risks. However, further determination of the populations at greatest risk for each of these threats would allow resources to be targeted more effectively. In this section, regions susceptible to five of the diseases described above are used to illustrate how governments, communities and organizations apply public health solutions to these challenges.

34.4.1 Diarrhoeal diseases in India

Diarrhoeal diseases are a global problem. They are especially prevalent in low income countries, where they are the third leading cause of death, and among children under five years, for who diarrhoeal diseases are responsible for 17% of all deaths (Mathers et al., 2008). Diarrhoeal diseases cause 454,000 deaths annually in India alone (NCMH, 2005), despite the fact that the population using improved water sources has risen from 72% in 1990 to 88% in 2008 (WHO and UNICEF, 2010). Urban dwellers have more access to improved water sources (WHO and UNICEF, 2010) and piped water supplies 69% of households in large cities (McKenzie and Ray, 2009). Nevertheless, water supply in most Indian cities is available for a few hours per day and water quality is questionable (McKenzie and Ray, 2009). Problems with access and quality are mainly attributed to poor management and inadequate regulation (Planning Commission, 2002). Water supply is a state responsibility, but various ministries share responsibility at central and state levels. Institutional arrangements for water supply vary within cities: a state-level agency is responsible for planning and investment, and local government is responsible for operation and maintenance. Local governments are increasingly turning operating and maintenance responsibilities to private companies. This fragmentation results in duplication and ambiguity of functions; poor coordination between the water supply programme and health and education programmes; and a water system that does not aim to reduce disease and poverty, nor to improve hygiene and education (Planning Commission, 2002).

34.4.2 Intestinal nematode infections in Brazil

Intestinal nematode infections are frequent in low income countries, especially in children under 15 years, with high intensity infections common in Africa, South-East Asia and the western Pacific (WHO, 2008a). Salvador is the largest city on the north-east coast of Brazil and the capital of the north-eastern state of Bahia. In 1997, 26% of households were connected to an improved sanitation system, and most of these were in upper and middle socio-economic areas (Barreto et al., 2007). Other areas used septic tanks or insanitary methods such as discharging sewage into the street (Barreto et al., 2007). Intestinal nematode prevalence was 43% for *Trichuris trichuria*, 33% for *Ascaris lumbricoides* and 10% for hookworms (Mascarini-Serra et al., 2010). A large sanitation project (Bahia Azul or Blue Bay), mainly financed by a loan from the

Inter-American Development Bank, was initiated to increase the number of households with adequate sewerage systems from 26% to 80% and hence control the pollution of marine waters by domestic wastewater. Approximately half the total budget of US$440 million was allocated for constructing 2,000 km of sewer pipes, 86 pumping stations and over 300,000 household connections between 1996 and 2004 (Barreto et al., 2010). The prevalence of *A. lumbricoides, T. trichuria* and hookworm in schoolchildren was reduced by 25%, 33% and 82%, respectively (Barreto et al., 2010).

34.4.3 Trachoma and trichiasis in Morocco

The highest prevalence of active trachoma and trichiasis is in Africa, predominantly in the savannah regions of East and Central Africa and the Sahel of West Africa (Polack et al., 2005). Morocco was the first country to eliminate trachoma in the 'Alliance for the Global Elimination of Blinding Trachoma by the year 2020' (GET 2020) campaign. Trachoma was largely eradicated from urban areas in the 1970s and 1980s by increased standards of living and antibiotic treatment of schoolchildren, but the disease persisted in poorer rural regions. Incorporation of the SAFE (surgery, antibiotics, facial cleanliness and environmental improvement) strategy into the National Blindness Control Program enabled Morocco to eradicate trachoma (Montgomery and Bartram, 2010). Poor facial cleanliness is consistently associated with trachoma (Taylor et al., 1989; West et al., 1991; West et al., 1996) and is likely the most important modifiable risk factor (Wright et al., 2008). Key to the success of Morocco's programme was its aggressive approach to provide safe drinking water and improved sanitation for at-risk populations (Kumaresan and Mecaskey, 2003).

34.4.4 Malaria in Africa

Malaria is widespread in tropical and subtropical regions, including most of sub-Saharan Africa, Asia and the Americas. Approximately 3.3 billion people are at risk. In Africa, malaria is responsible for 27% of deaths in children under five (Black et al., 2010). The 'Roll Back Malaria' campaign focuses on controlling malaria in sub-Saharan Africa with prevention and case management. The principal interventions are long lasting insecticide treated mosquito nets (LLINs) and indoor residual spraying (IRS) (WHO, 2010c). Environmental management is rarely applied. Nevertheless, environmental management can be efficacious and cost-effective. Utzinger and others (2001) reviewed a malaria control programme at copper mines in the former

Northern Rhodesia (now Zambia), a hyperendemic area, between 1929 and 1949. The programme implemented multiple control methods, many of which were environmental management methods, including vegetation clearance, modification of river boundaries, draining swamps, oil application to open water bodies, house screening, as well as quinine administration and bednet provision (Watson, 1953). Utzinger and others determined efficacy and cost-effectiveness compared to current malaria control. Within the first three to five years of the programme it was observed that malaria-related mortality, morbidity and incidence rates reduced by 70–95%, and between 1929 and 1949 the programme averted 4,173 deaths and 161,205 malaria attacks (Utzinger et al., 2001). The cost per death averted (US$858) is similar to that for insecticide treated nets in Gambia, Ghana, Kenya and South Africa (US$219–US$2,958) (Goodman and Mills, 1999; Goodman et al., 2001), and the cost per malaria attack averted (US$22.20) is slightly higher than the cost for insecticide treated nets in Gambia (US$15.75) (Graves, 1998). Currently, environmental management is viewed as complementary to other malaria control methods in a minority of settings – where mosquito breeding sites are few, fixed, and easy to identify, map and treat (WHO, 2010c) – but it may be beneficial to further integrate environmental management with pharmacological, insecticidal and bednet interventions to decrease adverse ecological effects from chemical spraying and increase sustainability of malaria programmes.

34.4.5 Schistosomiasis in Lao PDR

Schistosomiasis is predominant in tropical and subtropical areas, especially in poor communities without access to safe drinking water and adequate sanitation. It is most prevalent in Africa (88% of all cases) (WHO, 2008a). A significant risk factor for schistosomiasis is proximity to irrigation schemes or dams. Of the estimated 779 million people at risk for schistosomiasis, 13.6% live in irrigation schemes or close to large dam reservoirs (Steinmann et al., 2006). The health impacts of development projects such as these were rarely addressed because health was considered the responsibility of the health sector. The spread and intensification of diseases such as schistosomiasis and malaria were unintended consequences of hydropower and irrigation projects (Jobin, 1999; Scudder, 2005; Southgate, 1997; Steinmann et al., 2006). There is an opportunity to improve public health by incorporating HIAs into non-health sector policies (Fewtrell et al., 2008). Use of HIAs for development projects has been increasing, but their influence on decision-making is limited by various challenges. One challenge is the availability of data for quantitative HIAs, especially for projects, programmes and policies within developing countries (Fewtrell et al., 2008). Nevertheless, an HIA was used in drafting the public health management plan for the Nam Theun 2 hydroelectric project in Lao PDR (Krieger et al., 2008). Through site visits, discussions with stakeholders, and gathering and analysis of (mainly qualitative) health and economic data, groups most at risk for specific adverse health effects were identified and mitigation strategies suggested (Krieger et al., 2008). Schistosomiasis was not considered to pose a great risk, and now that the dam is operating, the HIA's ability to predict and avert this disease (and others) can be evaluated. HIAs should be part of the planning, implementation and operation of development projects to efficiently avert adverse health effects.

Protection of public health requires practitioners to act outside the narrowly defined 'health sector' (Rehfuess et al., 2009). Public health professionals must collaborate widely to change the way energy is generated, land is managed, food is produced and transportation is managed in order to improve the health of both the population and the environment (Bartram and Platt, 2010). Policy-makers and project managers in diverse sectors must incorporate health concerns into decision-making. The benefits and disadvantages of development projects could be more thoroughly assessed if decision-making were better coordinated across agencies.

Conclusions

This report examines the water-related diseases that contribute the greatest burden of disease globally and that are realistically amenable to change: diarrhoeal diseases, arsenic and fluoride poisoning, intestinal nematodes, trachoma, schistosomiasis, malaria, onchocerciasis, Japanese encephalitis, lymphatic filariasis and dengue. Using an environment–health pathway and the DPSEEA framework, the drivers predicted to have the greatest effect on disease via the water environment are identified as population growth, agriculture, infrastructure development and climate change. These affect disease rates both directly and indirectly, and increase uncertainty for human health.

There are numerous other environmental and non-environmental determinants of health. The interplay of these with the drivers investigated here may drastically alter predicted morbidity and mortality rates. These determinants will not be proportional between geographic areas or between various populations, making the identification of trends and hotspots in water and health nearly impossible.

While this knowledge gap somewhat impairs our ability to make well-informed policy and resource management decisions, it cannot be used as an excuse for complacency. By outlining the environment–health pathway for each of the major water-related disease groups, five key public health interventions were identified: access to safe drinking water and sanitation, improved hygiene, environmental management and the use of HIAs. Implementation of these actions would contribute to reducing the burdens of diverse diseases and improve the quality of life for billions of people.

This was reaffirmed in May 2011, when resolutions on 'drinking-water, sanitation and health' and on 'Cholera: mechanism for prevention and control' were unanimously adopted at the sixty-fourth World Health Assembly (WHO, 2011c). These resolutions fix the policy framework for the WHO, its sister United Nations agencies, in particular UNICEF, and the ministries of health in its 193 Member States to take determined action to promote access to safe and clean drinking water, and to promote basic sanitation and hygiene practices. Member States were urged to re-affirm a strong role for drinking water, sanitation and hygiene in their public health strategies.

Actions for combating the major water-related disease burdens can be pursued at different levels:
- The formulation of policies and the creation of institutional arrangements resulting in an enabling environment (e.g. HIAs).
- Networking to bring together professionals – as promoted by WHO-hosted international networks (drinking water regulators network; small community water supplies management network), the WHO/UNICEF network on household water treatment and safe storage, and the WHO/International Water Association network on operation and maintenance.
- Strengthening normative capacities – such as the fourth edition of the WHO guidelines for drinking water quality (WHO, 2011b) and the water safety planning approach as the instrument to implement them (Bartram et al., 2009).

- Monitoring and surveillance – including global monitoring by the WHO/UNICEF Joint Monitoring Programme on Water Supply and Sanitation and by the UN-Water/WHO Global Analysis and Assessment of Sanitation and Drinking-water to guide policies, resource allocation, and actions to achieve the millennium development goals target and provide a platform for the development of indicators and targets for post-2015 monitoring linked to criteria for the human right to water and sanitation (WHO and UNICEF, 2011).

In addition to reinforcing these public health solutions, outlining the environment–health pathway for each disease also enabled the identification of major risks, uncertainties and opportunities. These include the risk of increasing failures of ageing water infrastructure and, conversely, the opportunity to increase the overall impact of water resource, water supply and sanitation infrastructure through improved management. The impact of such actions improves use of limited financial resources thereby enhancing both access to water and sanitation and associated service quality, and leads indirectly to improvements in wider health indicators such as malnutrition. In-depth studies are required to more accurately identify the risks and opportunities related to water and health. The 2030 Vision Study, commissioned by the United Kingdom Department for International Development (DFID) and the WHO, performed such an analysis of the major risks, uncertainties and opportunities related to the resilience of water supply and sanitation in the face of climate change (WHO and DFID, 2009). The study brought together evidence from projections on climate change, trends in technology application, and developing knowledge about drinking water and sanitation adaptability and resilience to identify key policy, planning and operational changes that will be required to adapt to climate change, particularly in low and middle income countries where access to water supply and sanitation services are more limited. Five key conclusions resulted from this study:

1. Climate change is widely perceived as a threat rather than an opportunity. There may be significant overall benefits to health and development in adapting to climate change.
2. Major changes in policy and planning are needed if ongoing and future investments are not to be wasted.
3. Potential adaptive capacity is high but rarely achieved. Resilience needs to be integrated into

drinking water and sanitation management to cope with present climate variability. It will be critical in controlling adverse effects of future variability.
4. Although some of the climate trends at regional levels are uncertain, there is sufficient knowledge to inform urgent and prudent changes in policy and planning in most regions.
5. There are important gaps in our knowledge that already or soon will impede effective action. Targeted research is urgently needed to fill gaps in technology and basic information, to develop simple tools, and to provide regional information on climate change.

The relationship between the drivers of water-related diseases and human health is complex. Protection of human health cannot be accomplished without intersectoral collaboration. Policies and projects in non-water or non-health sectors must incorporate health into decision-making to avoid unintended public health consequences and to increase overall benefits. In the case of drinking water quality, addressing the root causes of water contamination is more effective and sustainable then reacting to problems. The guidelines for drinking water quality (WHO, 2011b) emphasize collaboration between stakeholders, including land users or householders who may discharge industrial, agricultural or domestic waste; policy-makers from various ministries overseeing the implementation and enforcement of environmental regulations; practitioners delivering water; and consumers. This preventive and collaborative approach towards water safety planning yields cost-savings and sustainable improvements. Experience has also shown, most recently from south and east Asia, that while progress is being made, it remains a challenge to implement such a rigorous 'no short-cut' approach – each risk management solution needs to be tailor-made to the water supply in question, and demands that key stakeholders become engaged and committed to a common goal.

||||||||||||||||||||||||||||||||||||||||||||||||||||||||||||||||||||||||||||||||

References

Ali, M., Emch, M., Donnay, J. P., Yunus, M. and Sack, R. B. 2001. Identifying environmental risk factors for endemic cholera: a raster GIS approach. *Health & Place,* Vol. 8, pp. 201–10.

Anderson, D. M., Gilbert, P. M. and Burkholder, J. M. 2002. Harmful Algal blooms and eutrophication: nutrient sources, composition, and consequences. *Estuaries*, Vol. 25, pp. 704–26.

Andrews, J. R. and Basu, S. 2011. Transmission dynamics and control of cholera in Haiti: an epidemic model. *Lancet,* Vol. 377, pp. 1248–55.

Baer, F., McGahey, C and Wijeyaratne, P. 1999. *Summary of EHP Activities in Kitwe, Zambia 1997–1999.* Arlington, Va., USAID Environmental Health Project.

Barreto, M. L, Genser, B., Strina, A., Teixeira, M. G., Assis, A. M. O., Rego, R. F., Teles, C.A., Prado, M. S., Matos, S. M. A., Alcântara-Neves, N. M. and Cairncross, S. 2010. Impact of a citywide sanitation program in northeast Brazil on intestinal parasites infection in young children. *Environmental Health Perspectives,* Vol. 118, No. 11, pp. 1637–42.

Barreto, M. L, Genser, B., Strina, A., Teixeira, M. G., Assis, A. M. O., Rego, R. F., Teles, C.A., Prado, M. S., Matos, S. M. A., Santos, D. N., dos Santos L. A. and Cairncross, S. 2007. Effect of city-wide sanitation programme on reduction in rate of childhood diarrhoea in northeast Brazil: assessment by two cohort studies. *Lancet,* Vol. 370, No. 9599, pp. 1622–28.

Barrett, R., Kuzawa, C. W., McDade, T. and Armelagos, G. J. 1998. Emerging and re-emerging infectious diseases: the third epidemiologic transition. *Annual Review of Anthropology,* Vol. 27, pp. 247–71.

Bartram, J., Corrales, L., Davison, A., Deere, D., Drury, D., Gordon, B., Howard, G., Rinehold, A., Stevens, M. 2009. *Water Safety Plan Manual: Step-By-Step Risk Management for Drinking-Water Suppliers.* Geneva, World Health Organization. http://whqlibdoc.who.int/publications/2009/9789241562638_eng.pdf

Bartram, J. K. and Platt, J. L. How health professionals can leverage health gains from improved water, sanitation and hygiene practices. 2010. *Perspectives in Public Health,* Vol. 130, No. 5, pp. 215–21.

Black, R. E., Cousens, S., Johnson, H. L, Lawn, J. E., Rudan, I., Bassani, D. G., Jha, P., Campbell, H., Walker, C. F., Cibulskis, R., Eisele, T., Liu, L., Mathers, C. and the Child Health Epidemiology Reference Group of WMO and UNICEF. 2010. Global, regional, and national causes of child mortality in 2008: a systematic analysis. *Lancet,* Vol. 375, No. 9730, pp. 1969–87.

Bradley, D. J. 2008. Water supplies: the consequences of change. C. Elliott and J. Knight (eds), *Ciba Foundation Symposium 23 – Human Rights in Health.* Chichester, UK, John Wiley & Sons, pp. 81–98.

Cutler, D. M. and Miller, G. 2005. The Role of public health improvements in health advances: the 20th century United States. *Demography,* Vol. 42, No. 1, pp. 1–22.

Dua, V. K., Sharma, S. K., Srivastava, A. and Sharma, V. P. 1997. Bioenvironmental control of industrial malaria at Bharat Heavy Electricals Ltd., Hardwar, India – results of a nine-year study (1987–95). *Journal of the American Mosquito Control Association,* Vol. 13, No. 3, pp. 278–85.

EHP (Environmental Health Project). 2004. *The Hygiene Improvement Framework – A Comprehensive Approach for Preventing Childhood Diarrhea.* Joint Publication 8. Prepared by EHP, UNICEF/WES, USAID, World Bank/WSP, WSSCC. Washington, DC, EHP.

Emerson, P. M., Lindsay, S.W., Alexander, N., Bah, M., Dibba, S. M., Faal, H. B., Lowe, K. O., McAdam, K. P., Ratcliffe, A. A., Walraven, G. E. and Bailey, R. L. 2004. Role of flies and provision of latrines in trachoma control: cluster-randomised controlled trial. *Lancet,* Vol. 363, No. 9415, pp. 1093–98.

Erlanger, T. E., Keiser, J., Caldas de Castro, M., Bos, R., Singer, B. H., Tanner, M. and Utzinger J. 2005. Effect of water resource development and management on lymphatic filariasis, and estimates of populations at risk. *American Journal of Tropical Medicine and Hygiene,* Vol. 73, No. 3, pp. 523–33.

Esrey, S. A. 1996. Waster, water, and well-being: a multicountry study. *American Journal of Epidemiology,* Vol. 143, No. 6, pp. 608–23.

Esrey, S. A., Potash, J. B., Roberts, L. and Shiff, C. 1991. Effects of improved water supply and sanitation on ascariasis, diarrhea, dracunculiasis, hookworm infection, schistosomiasis, and trachoma. *Bulletin of the World Health Organization,* Vol. 69, No. 5, pp. 609–21.

Fewtrell, L, Kay, D., Matthews, I., Utzinger, J., Singer, B. H. and Bos, R. 2008. Health impact assessment for sustainable water management: the lay of the land. L. Fewtrell and D. Kay (eds), *Health Impact Assessment.* London, IWA Publishing, pp. 1–28.

Fewtrell, L., Kaufmann, R. B., Kay, D., Enanoria, W., Haller, L. and Colford, J. M. Jr. 2005. Water, sanitation, and hygiene interventions to reduce diarrhoea in less developed countries: a systematic review and meta-analysis. *Lancet Infectious Diseases,* Vol. 5, pp. 42–52.

Fewtrell, L., Prüss-Üstün, A., Bos, R., Gore, F. and Bartram, J. 2007. *Water, Sanitation and Hygiene: Quantifying the Health Impact at National and Local Levels in Countries with Incomplete Water Supply and Sanitation Coverage.* Geneva, World Health Organization. (WMO Environmental Burden of Disease Series, No. 15.)

Goodman, C. A. and Mills, A. J. 1999. The evidence base on the cost-effectiveness of malaria control measures in Africa. *Health Policy and Planning,* Vol. 14, pp. 301–12.

Goodman, C. A., Mnzava, A. E. P., Dlamini, S. S., Sharp, B. L., Mthembu, D. J. and Gumede, J. K. 2001. Comparison of the cost and cost-effectiveness of insecticide-treated bednets and residual house-spraying in KwaZulu-Natal, South Africa. *Tropical Medicine & International Health,* Vol. 6, pp. 280–95.

Granéli, E. and Turner, J. T. (eds). 2006. *Ecology of Harmful Algae.* Berlin, Springer. (Ecological Studies, Vol. 189.)

Graves, P. M. 1998. Comparison of the cost-effectiveness of vaccines and insecticide impregnation of mosquito nets for the prevention of malaria. *Annals of Tropical Medicine and Parasitology,* Vol. 92 pp. 399–410.

Gubler, D. J. 1998. Resurgent vector-borne diseases as a global health problem. *Emerging Infectious Diseases,* Vol. 4, No. 3, pp. 442–50.

Heierli, U. and Lengeler, C. 2008. *Should Bednets Be Sold, or Given Free? The Role of the Private Sector in Malaria Control.* Berne, Switzerland, Swiss Agency for Development and Cooperation.

Hunter, P. R, Chalmers, R. M., Hughes, S. and Syed, Q. 2005. Self-reported diarrhea in a control group: a strong association with reporting of low-pressure events in tap water. *Clinical Infectious Diseases,* Vol. 40, No. 4, pp. e32–e34.

Huq, A., Xu, B., Chowdhury, A. R., Islam, M. S., Montilla, R. and Colwell, R.R. 1996. A simple filtration method to remove plankton-associated Vibrio cholerae in raw water supplies in developing countries. *Applied and Environmental Microbiology,* Vol. 62, No. 7, pp. 2508–12.

Jalan, J. and Ravallion , M. 2003. Does piped water reduce diarrhea for children in rural India? *Journal of Econometrics,* Vol. 112, No. 1, pp. 153–73.

Jobin, W R. 1999. *Dams and Disease: Ecological Design and Health Impacts of Large Dams, Canals and Irrigation Systems.* London, E & F N Spon.

Keiser, J., Maltese, M. F., Erlanger, T. E., Bos, R., Tanner, M., Singer, B. H. and Utzinger, J. 2005. Effect of irrigated rice agriculture on Japanese encephalitis, including challenges and opportunities for integrated vector management. *Acta Tropica,* Vol. 95, pp. 40–57.

Kjellström, T. and Corvalán, C. 1995. Framework for the development of environmental health indicators. *World Health Statistics Quarterly,* Vol. 48, No. 2, pp. 144–54.

Krieger, G. R., Balge, M. Z., Chanthaphone, S., Tanner, M., Singer, B. H., Fewtrell, L. Kaul, S., Sananikhom, P., Odermatt, P. and Utzinger, J. 2008. Nam Theun 2 Hydroelectric Project, Lao PDR. L. Fewtrell and D. Kay (eds). *Health Impact Assessment for Sustainable Water Management.* London, IWA Publishing, pp. 199–232.

Kroeger, A., Lenhart, A., Ochoa, M., Villegas, E., Levy, M., Alexander, N. and McCall, P. J. 2006. Effective control of dengue vectors with curtains and water container covers treated with insecticide in Mexico and Venezuela: cluster randomised trials. *British Medical Journal,* Vol. 332, pp. 1247–52.

Kumaresan, J. and Mecaskey, J. 2003. The global elimination of blinding trachoma: progress and promise. *American Journal of Tropical Medicine and Hygiene,* Vol. 69, Suppl. 5, pp. 24–8.

Lipp, E. K., Huq, A. and Colwell, R. R. 2002. Effects of Global climate on infectious disease: the cholera model. *Clinical Microbiology Reviews,* doi: 10.1128/CMR.15.4.757-770.2002.

Luby, S., Agboatwalla, M., Painter, J., Altaf, A., Billhimer, W. and Hoekstra, R. 2004. Effect of intensive hand washing promotion on childhood diarrhea in high-risk communities in Pakistan: a randomized controlled trial. *Journal of the American Medical Association,* Vol. 291, No. 21, pp. 2547–54.

Mara, D., Lane, J., Scott, B. and Trouba, D. 2010. Sanitation and health. *PLoS Medicine,* Vol. 7, No. 11, e1000363.

Mariappan, T. A. 2008. *Comprehensive Plan for Controlling Dengue Vectors in Jeddah, Kingdom of Saudi Arabia.* Pondicherry, India: Vector Control Research Centre.

Mariotti, S. P., Pascolini, D., and Rose-Nussbaumer, J. 2009. Trachoma: global magnitude of a preventable cause of blindness. *British Journal of Ophthalmology,* Vol. 93, pp. 563–68

Mascarini-Serra, L. M., Telles, C.A., Prado, M.S., Mattos, S.A., Strina, A., Alcantara-Neves, N. M. and Barreto, M. L. 2010. Reductions in the prevalence and incidence of geohelminth infections following a city-wide sanitation program in a Brazilian urban centre. *PLoS Neglected Tropical Diseases,* Vol. 4, No. 2, e588.

Mathers, C. D., Boerma. T. and Fat, D. M. 2008. *The Global Burden of Disease: 2004 Update.* Geneva, World Health Organization.

McKenzie, D. and Ray, I. 2009. Urban Water supply in India: status, reform options and possible lessons. *Water Policy,* Vol. 11, No. 4, pp. 442–60.

Meyrowitsch, D. W., Nguyen, D. T., Hoang, T. H., Nguyen, T. D. and Michael, E. 1998. A review of the present status of lymphatic filariasis in Vietnam. *Acta Tropica,* Vol. 70, No. 3, pp. 335–47.

Montgomery, M. A. and Bartram, J. 2010. Short-sightedness in sight-saving: half a strategy will not eliminate blinding trachoma. *Bulletin of the World Health Organization,* Vol. 88, No. 2, pp. 82.

Moraes, L. R. S., Cancio, J. A. and Cairncross, S. 2004. Impact of drainage and sewerage on intestinal nematodes infections in poor urban areas in Salvador, Brazil. *Transactions of the Royal Society of Tropical Medicine and Hygiene,* Vol. 98, pp. 197–204.

Moraes, L. R. S., Cancio, J. A., Cairncross, S. and Huttly, S. 2003. Impact of drainage and sewerage on diarrhoea in poor urban areas in Salvador, Brazil. *Transactions of the Royal Society of Tropical Medicine and Hygiene,* Vol. 97, pp. 153–58.

NCMH (National Commission on Macroeconomics and Health). 2005. *National Commission on Macroeconomics and Health Background Papers: Burden of Disease in India.* New Delhi, NCMH, Ministry of Health & Family Welfare, Government of India.

Nguyen, L. A. P., Clements, A. C. A., Jeffrey, J. A. L., Yen, N. T., Nam, V. S., Vaughan, G. V., Shinkfield, R., Kutcher, S. C., Gatton, M. L., Kay, B. H. and Ryan, P.A. 2011. Abundance and prevalence of *Aedes aegypti* immatures and relationships with household water storage in rural areas of southern Viet Nam. *International Health,* Vol. 3, No. 2, pp. 115–25.

Piehler, M. F. 2008. Watershed management strategies to prevent and control cyanobacterial harmful algal blooms. H. K. Hudnell (ed.), *Cyanobacterial Harmful Algal Blooms: State of the Science and Research Needs.* New York, Springer, pp. 259–73. (Advances in Experimental Medicine and Biology, Vol. 619.)

Planning Commission. 2002. *India Assessment 2002: Water Supply and Sanitation.* New Delhi, Planning Commission, Government of India.

Polack, S., Brooker, S., Kuper, H., Mariotti, S., Mabey, D. and Foster, A. 2005. Mapping the global distribution of trachoma. *Bulletin of the World Health Organization,* Vol. 83, pp. 913–19.

Prüss-Üstün, A., Bos, R., Gore, F. and Bartram, J. 2008. *Safer Water, Better Health: Costs, Benefits and Sustainability of Interventions to Protect and Promote Health.* Geneva, World Health Organization.

Quick, R. E., Venczel, L., Mintz, E., Soleto, L., Aparicio, J., Gironaz, M., Hutwagner, L., Greene, K., Bopp, C., Maloney, K., Chavez, D., Sobsey, M. and Tauxe, R.V. 1999. Diarrhea prevention in Bolivia through point-of-use disinfection and safe storage: a promising new strategy. *Epidemiology and Infection,* Vol. 122, No. 1, pp. 83–90.

Rehfuess, E. A., Bruce, N. and Bartram, J. K. 2009. More health for your buck: health sector functions to secure environmental health. *Bulletin of the World Health Organization,* Vol. 87, pp. 880–82.

Reller, E., Mendoza, C., Lopez, M., Alvarez, M., Hoekstra, R., Olson, C., Baier, K., Keswick, B. and Luby, S. 2003. A randomized controlled trial of household-based flocculant-disinfectant drinking water treatment for diarrhea prevention in rural Guatemala. *American Journal of Tropical Medicine and Hygiene,* Vol. 69, No. 4, pp. 411–19.

de Silva, N., Brooker, S., Hotez, P., Montresor, A., Engels, D. and Savioli, L. 2003. Soil-transmitted helminthic infections: updating the global picture. Disease Control Priorities Project. *Trends in Parasitology,* Vol. 19, No. 12, pp. 547–51.

Scudder, T. 2005. *The Future of Large Dams.* London, Earthscan.

Seng, C. M., Setha, T., Nealon, J., Chantha, N., Socheat, D. and Nathan, M. B. 2008. The effect of long-lasting insecticidal water container covers on field populations of *Aedes aegypti* (L.) mosquitoes in Cambodia. *Journal of Vector Ecology,* Vol. 33, No. 2, pp. 333–41.

Sobsey, M. D. 2006. Drinking water and health research: a look to the future in the United States and globally. *Journal of Water and Health,* Suppl. 4, pp. 17–21.

Southgate, V. R. 1997. Schistosomiasis in the Senegal River Basin: before and after the construction of the dams at Diama, Senegal and Manantali, Mali and future prospects. *Journal of Helminthology,* Vol. 71, pp. 125–32.

Steinmann, P., Keiser, J., Bos, R., Tanner, M. and Utzinger, J. 2006. Schistosomiasis and water resources development: systematic review, meta-analysis, and estimates of people at risk. *Lancet Infectious Diseases,* Vol. 6, pp. 411–25.

Taylor, H. R, West, S. K., Mmbaga, B. B., Katala, S. J., Turner, V., Lynch, M., Muñoz, B. and Rapoza, P. A. 1989. Hygiene factors and increased risk of trachoma in central Tanzania. *Archives of Ophthalmology,* Vol. 107, pp. 1821–25.

UNICEF (United Nations Children's Fund). 1999. *Towards Better Programming: A Manual on Hygiene Promotion.* New York, UNICEF. (Water, Environment and Sanitation Technical Guidelines Series, No. 6.)

USEPA (National Service Center for Environmental Publications). 2007. *Addressing the Challenge Through Innovation.* Aging Water Infrastructure Research Program. Cincinnati, Ohio, Office of Research and Development, National Risk Management Research Laboratory.

Utzinger, J., Tozan, Y. and Singer, B. H. 2001. Efficacy and cost-effectiveness of environmental management for malaria control. *Tropical Medicine & International Health,* Vol. 6, No. 9, pp. 677–87.

Van Dolah, F. M., Roelke, D. L. and Greene, R. M. 2001. Health and ecological impacts of harmful algal blooms: risk assessment needs. *Human and Ecological Risk Assessment,* Vol. 7, pp. 1329–45.

Walsh, J. F. 1970. Evidence of reduced susceptibility to DDT in controlling Simulium damnosum (Diptera: Simuliidae) on the River Niger. *Bulletin of the World Health Organization,* Vol. 43, No. 2, pp. 316–18.

Wang, X., and Hunter, P. R. 2010. A systematic review and meta-analysis of the association between self-reported diarrheal disease and distance from home to water source. *American Journal of Tropical Medicine and Hygiene,* Vol. 83, No. 3, pp. 582–4.

Watson, M. 1953. *African Highway: The Battle for Health in Central Africa.* London, J. Murray.

Watson, T. 2006. Public health investments and the infant mortality gap: evidence from federal sanitation interventions and hospitals on U.S. Indian Reservations. *Journal of Public Economics,* Vol. 90, No. 8–9, pp. 1537–60.

West, S., Muñoz, B., Lynch, M., Kayongoya, A., Chilangwa, Z., Mmbaga, B. B. O. and Taylor, H. R. 1995. Impact of face-washing on trachoma in Kongwa, Tanzania. *Lancet,* Vol. 345, No. 8943, pp. 155–58.

West, S. K., Congdon, N., Katala, S. and Mele, L. 1991. Facial cleanliness and risk of trachoma in families. *Archives of Ophthalmology,* Vol. 190, pp. 855–57.

West, S. K., Munoz, B., Lynch, M., Kayongoya, A., Mmbaga, B. B. and Taylor, H.R. 1996. Risk factors for constant, severe trachoma among preschool children in Kongwa, Tanzania. *American Journal of Epidemiology,* Vol. 143, pp. 73–8.

WHO (World Health Organization). 1980. *Environmental Management for Vector Control. Fourth Report of the WHO Expert Committee on Vector Biology and Control.* Geneva, World Health Organization (WHO) Technical Report Series, No. 649. http://whqlibdoc.who.int/trs/WHO_TRS_649.pdf

----. 1999. *Health Impact Assessment: Main Concepts and Suggested Approach.* Gothenburg consensus paper, December 1999. (ed.). Copenhagen/Brussels, WHO Regional Office for Europe/European Centre for Health Policy. http://www.apho.org.uk/resource/view.aspx?RID=44163

----. 2008a. *The Global Burden of Disease: 2004 Update.* Geneva, WHO. http://www.who.int/healthinfo/global_burden_disease/GBD_report_2004update_full.pdf

----. 2008b. *Guidelines for Drinking-Water Quality,* 3rd edn, incorporating first and second addenda. Geneva, WHO. http://www.who.int/water_sanitation_health/dwq/GDWPRecomdrev1and2.pdf

----. 2010a. Cholera, 2009. *Weekly Epidemiological Record,* Vol. 85, pp. 293–308.

----. 2010b. *Haiti: Cholera Response Update. 13 December 2010.* Geneva, WHO. http://www.who.int/hac/donorinfo/haiti_donor_alert_cholera_response_13dec10.pdf

----. 2010c. *World Malaria Report: 2010.* WHO Global Malaria Programme. Geneva, WHO. http://www.who.int/malaria/world_malaria_report_2010/worldmalariareport2010.pdf

----. 2011a. Cholera, 2010. *Weekly Epidemiological Record,* Vol. 86, pp. 325–40.

----. 2011b. *Guidelines for Drinking-Water Quality,* 4th edn. Geneva, WHO. http://www.who.int/water_sanitation_health/publications/2011/9789241548151_toc.pdf

----. 2011c. *Drinking-Water, Sanitation and Health.* Resolution WHA64.2. Sixty-fourth World Health Assembly, 24 May

2011, Geneva. http://apps.who.int/gb/ebwha/pdf_files/ WHA64/A64_R24-en.pdf

WHO and DFID (World Health Organization/UK Department for International Development). 2009. *Vision 2030: The Resilience of Water Supply and Sanitation in the Face of Climate Change.* Geneva, WHO. http://www.who.int/water_sanitation_health/vision_2030_9789241598422.pdf

WHO and UNICEF (World Health Organization/United Nations Children's Fund). 2000. *Global Water Supply and Sanitation Assessment 2000 Report.* WHO/UNICEF Joint Monitoring Programme for Water Supply and Sanitation. Geneva, WHO/UNICEF. http://www.who.int/water_sanitation_health/monitoring/jmp2000.pdf

––––. 2010. *Progress on Sanitation and Drinking-Water: 2010 Update.* Geneva, WHO/UNICEF Joint Monitoring Programme for Water Supply and Sanitation.

––––. 2011. *Post-2015 Monitoring of Water and Sanitation: Report of a First WHO/UNICEF Consultation.* Geneva/New York, WHO/UNICEF.

Wright, H. R., Turner, V. and Taylor, H. R. 2008. Seminar: trachoma. *Lancet,* Vol. 371, No. 9628, pp. 1945–54.

CHAPTER 35
Water and gender

WWAP, with special thanks to the WWAP Gender Advisory Group
—
Author Vasudha Pangare
Acknowledgements Feedback received from the WWAP Advisory Group on Gender Equality was useful in finalizing the chapter. The author would like to acknowledge Gülser Corat, Kusum Athukorala and Marcia Brewster.

|||||||||||||||||||||||||||||||||||||||||||||||||||||||||||||||||||||||||||||||||||||||||||||||||||||||||||||||||||||||||||||||||||

Improving women's access to safe water for productive and consumptive uses will not only help increase food production globally, but also improve food, health and livelihood security at community and household levels.

35.1 Introduction

The gender gap in water arises from gender divisions in society, which allocate many water responsibilities to women but vest most water-related powers and rights in men. To improve the balance between responsibilities and powers and rights, changes need to be made in water policy, planning and management. The gender gap will be reduced when both men and women are able to challenge gender-based unequal water roles and allocations, and participate in decision-making at different levels.

Among the many challenges in water faced across the world, scarcity, deteriorating water quality, the linkages between water and food security and the need for improved governance are most significant in the context of gender differences in the access to and control over water resources. These challenges are expected to become more intense due to the growing uncertainty and risk associated with the availability and quality of freshwater resources arising from increasing demand for various uses, climate variability and natural disasters.

Water is used for a wide range of social and economic activities, including public health, agriculture, energy and industry. Water has different values for different uses and purposes, and the same source of water can be used for social as well as economic purposes. Social and environmental valuation is more prevalent at the local level, where water sources may be designated for different uses, such as for drinking, or for common use, such as bathing and washing, depending on the quality of water, or regarded as sacred for religious purposes. In fact, water that has been valued as an economic good, such as irrigation water supplied through an irrigation scheme, also has a social value for local communities, especially for women, who may use the same irrigation water source for both domestic and farming purposes. Opportunities for improving access to water for women and improving their water security can be found by analysing water values through the gender lens.

Water policies based on broad, generalized perspectives are more likely to miss out local knowledge, and social and gender dimensions and their implications. Recognizing the various purposes for which these local water resources are used by different groups of men and women in the community would help successfully integrate gender considerations not only in water resource management, but also in sectors such as urban water supply, agriculture, industry and energy that depend upon water resources, and which are often in conflict over water allocations and their demand for freshwater resources. By working together in partnership with these sectors, synergies and trade-offs in providing access to different groups of men and women in local communities can be understood and addressed by decision-makers in government bodies, private sectors and civil society. This would help in anticipating risks and uncertainties and planning for safe-guards to be put in place for the most vulnerable groups in the community.

35.2 Challenges and opportunities

35.2.1 Gender dimensions of water scarcity

About a third of the world's population is experiencing some kind of physical or economic water scarcity (IFAD, 2007). Among the many causes of scarcity, the growing competition for water from different sectors, including industry, agriculture, power generation, domestic use and the environment, is creating an acute crisis for poor people, making it difficult for them to access water for consumptive, productive and social uses. The scarcity created at the local level from this crisis is increasing inequity within local communities with regard to access and control over local water resources, affecting poor people, and poor women the most. Physical scarcity, especially in arid and semi-arid regions is increasing due to climate variability, droughts and population pressures. The drudgery and health consequences for women in these regions, especially for poor women, and their increased work

BOX 35.1

Women carry the water burden

There are 884 million people in the world who still do not get their water from improved sources, almost all of them in developing regions. For families without a drinking water source on the premises, it is usually women who go to the source to collect drinking water. Surveys from 45 developing countries show that this is the case in almost two thirds of households, while in almost a quarter of households it is men who usually collect the water. In 12% of households, children carry the main responsibility for collecting water, with girls under 15 years of age being twice as likely to carry this responsibility as boys under the age of 15 years.

Source: WHO and UNICEF (2010).

burden in acquiring water for home consumption is very well-documented.

Water scarcity can occur or be experienced due to 'social and gender constructs' or social and economic differences within the society, and customary behaviour that discriminates against women and the socially disadvantaged. When access to local water sources is denied to a section of the population, those people experience scarcity. Access can be denied due to caste (as in India) and class differences or because of conflict between ethnic communities. Women may also be denied access to water where the community water supply is located on the property of the village headman or a local official.

Scarcity can also be caused by the deteriorating quality of freshwater resources. When water sources are polluted, the quantity of clean water or safe drinking water in a particular location is reduced. Although there are accepted minimum standards for water quality, there are also concerns and cultural beliefs that determine and influence the use of different sources of water for different purposes, such as drinking, cooking and bathing. These cultural beliefs, which are often more significant for women, need to be kept in mind when water sources are being exploited for different purposes. If women need to travel long distances to fetch safe and clean water, then the time and energy costs of fetching water are likely to govern their perceptions of hygiene in disease prevention, resulting in lower hygiene levels in the home.

While scarcity affects the lives of all people in the community, these effects manifest themselves differently for men and women of different ages and socio-economic status. Scarcity aggravates the water poverty of women and of young girls who are expected to help their mothers to collect water, often missing school when the water shortage is acute. Research indicates that girls under the age of 15 are twice as likely to carry this responsibility than boys under the age of 15 (WHO/UNICEF, 2010) (Box 35.1). Women from economically well-off or 'upper class' families experience scarcity less intensely than women from poor and socially disadvantaged families.

35.2.2 Gender dimensions of water governance
'Water governance encompasses the political, economic and social processes and institutions by which government, civil society and the private sectors make decisions about how best to use, develop and manage water resources' (UNDP, 2004, p. 10). Water governance is more than national-level legislations, regulations and institutions, and refers to the processes that exist to promote stakeholder participation and mechanisms for decision-making.

Accessibility and availability of safe and sufficient water is therefore often determined by governance, which in turn is affected by social structures and gender relations. There is a close link between water governance, gender and power divides in society. Who takes decisions and at what levels, and the types of decisions taken are greatly influenced by the culture of social relations. Gender relations and social structures will determine at what level women, and which group of women, can participate in decision-making and what that mechanism will be. To make water governance more effective, existing formal and informal mechanisms for decision-making, including power structures within the society which are governed by class, gender and ethnicity need to be challenged. When traditional roles are challenged, power relations are likely to change therefore reducing the gender gap is a process that is accompanied by women's empowerment.[1]

Debates around gender dimensions of water governance tend to delegate gender considerations to the realm of the 'grassroots'. Keeping the focus of discussion on women's physical burden of fetching water for household purposes is politically comfortable and does not challenge the larger and broader access and power issues that increase women's water burden in the first place. It is easier to bring the drinking water pipeline to the community than to challenge the gender divide that places the responsibility of fetching water for the household on the woman. Although it may be true that gender concerns become more pronounced closer to the grassroots, where people interact directly with water and natural resources, it is important to understand that national and international policy affects access and control over local water resources as well.

Decisions about water sharing, allocation and distribution between different uses and across regions are most often made at higher levels where economic and political considerations play a more important role than social concerns. These decisions impact water resources locally available to communities that are likely to lose access to the very resources that sustained their livelihoods and fulfilled their needs. Rural women often rely upon common water resources, such as small water bodies, ponds and streams to meet their water needs, but in many regions these sources have either been eroded or have disappeared due to changes in land use or have been appropriated for development by the state or industry.

Water policies based on broad, generalized perspectives are more likely to miss out local knowledge, and social and gender dimensions and their implications. Social and gender analysis conducted at the lowest possible level to capture the local context, such as the community water source, the sub-basin level, or micro-watershed level can help in understanding the problems and potential impact of the policy on different groups of women. Community water sources, whether natural or man-made lakes, ponds and irrigation schemes, serve many purposes, including fishing, agriculture, kitchen gardens, washing and bathing. Women use water for many different purposes, including domestic, agriculture, health and sanitation, whereas men are generally concerned only with water use for agriculture and livestock. Recognizing the various purposes for which these local water resources are used by different groups of men and women in the community would help successfully integrate gender considerations in water management.

This analysis can inform broad national, regional and international policies, not only related to water management, but also to other sectors, such as agriculture, energy and industry. An evaluation of the Food and Agricultural Organization's (FAO) work and role in water found that irrigation and agriculture policy statements with the clearest description of local farmer typologies and the challenges faced by them succeeded best in developing strategies responsive to circumstances in the country (FAO, 2010a). By identifying different farmer groups, the policies were able to develop action plans for addressing the concerns of men and women farmers in Zambia, Malawi and Swaziland and to a lesser degree in Mozambique, Kenya and the United Republic of Tanzania (FAO, 2010a) (Box 35.2).

Climate change impacts, increasing population pressures on water resources, and competition from different uses are likely to increase women's water poverty in the future. Women depend upon and use water to sustain the food security, health and economic stability of their families and communities. To reduce women's water poverty, changes would need to be made at

many different levels. The decision-making and policy processes would need to be opened up to include consultation with or active participation of the appropriate group of women in the given context and to support their right to water. Recent trends in governance in various aspects of water management which use multi-stakeholder platforms for increasing participation and transparency can provide a space for women to express their views and opinions, and encourage a gender perspective in policy making and implementation.

At the field level, appropriate groups of women need to be consulted during the design and implementation of water projects to maximize the benefit of these projects. Wives of rich farmers, for example, are less likely to be interested in community irrigation or drinking water schemes than poorer women, but may participate for political reasons. Therefore it would be necessary to identify and involve women whose interests are directly affected by the project or intervention; if this is not done the project could have a negative impact on those women who need the intervention the most. Women are generally not recognized as decision-makers or as contributors to the household economy; in

BOX 35.2

Gender mainstreaming through effective policy formulation

An evaluation of the Food and Agricultural Organization's role and work in water in 2010 highlighted that for effective policy development, it was important to clearly identify the relevant target populations for whom the policy was meant. An analysis of irrigation and agriculture policies in seven countries from a gender and social inclusion perspective found that policy statements with the clearest description of local farmer typologies and the challenges faced by them in the context of the country's food security and poverty goals generally succeeded best in developing strategies responsive to circumstances in the country and took into account and addressed the issues and concerns of smallholder farmers and socially disadvantaged groups. Agriculture and irrigation policies in Zambia, Malawi and Swaziland identified gender disparities among farmers and developed strategies to address them, whereas although gender disparities were identified in Mozambique, Kenya and the United Republic of Tanzania, the strategies for addressing these were still being developed.

Source: FAO (2010a).

many aspects they are still viewed as family labourers or unpaid labour, especially in agricultural households. On one hand these cultural constraints usually hinder women's participation in water management organizations and decision-making, and on the other, women's engagement in domestic household chores usually prevents them from active participation in local water management organizations.

However, gender sensitization for men and women in the community, and capacity development for women could make their participation more effective. Women's groups, such as self-help groups, could also provide a collective voice for participation. Other interventions could include creating greater gender awareness among water managers, including gender expertise in water projects, providing technical training to women to enable them to participate in technical discussions, and developing and disseminating tools for gender mainstreaming in water management and governance.

35.2.3 Agriculture, food security and gender dimensions

According to latest estimates by FAO, 925 million people are undernourished, of which 62% live in Asia and the Pacific, the world's most populous region, followed by sub-Saharan Africa, which is home to 26% of the world's undernourished population. The rise in global undernourishment is a combined result of declining investments in agriculture, increased production costs and rising food prices, in particular the continued increase in prices of staple cereals and oil crops (FAO, 2010b).

Food production would have to increase by 70% to feed a population of 9 billion people by 2050. Of the 1.5 billion hectares (ha) of cropland worldwide, only 277 million ha (or 18%) is irrigated land; the remaining 82% is rainfed land. Recent research indicates that to meet the demand for food, water productivity needs to be improved, not only in irrigated, but also in rainfed areas (FAO, 2010b). This is because, due to the high investment costs and the growing competition for water, the scope for further expansion in irrigation is limited in many countries.

Women play an important role in irrigated as well as non-irrigated agriculture, and a larger number of women than men is engaged in rainfed agriculture, producing 'two-thirds of the food in most developing countries' (World Bank, 2006). It is important to note that 'the vast majority of the world's farms are small; 85% of them are less than 2 hectares, and 97% less than 10. In Africa, 80% of farmed land is cultivated by smallholder farmers, the majority of whom are women' (UN, 2009, p. 8). According to the *World Development Report 2008* (World Bank, 2007, p. 7), 'where women are the majority of smallholder farmers, failure to realize their full potential in agriculture is a contributing factor to low growth and food insecurity'.

Women comprise an average of 43% of the agricultural labour force in developing countries (FAO, 2011). Eighty% of the basic food in sub-Saharan Africa is produced by women (FAO, 2006). In Africa, Europe and Central Asia, and some East Asian countries, men and women work equally in agricultural self-employment (World Bank, 2007). 'In Mozambique, Rwanda, Uganda, and Egypt, women are even more likely to participate in agricultural self-employment, whereas in Latin America and South Asia, women reportedly work less in agricultural self-employment.' (World Bank, 2007, p. 79). In all these regions, as well as in Africa, women have broadened and deepened their involvement in agricultural production in recent decades (World Bank, 2007). In spite of this, agriculture and water policies continue to wrongly assume that farmers are men, reinforcing many of the constraints faced by women in agricultural production.

Gender inequalities exist all along the food production chain, beginning with asymmetries in ownership of, access to, and control of livelihood assets, such as land, water, energy, credit, knowledge and labour. Women in general have less access to productive resources than men.

Across the regions, less than 5% to about 15% women own agricultural land (FAO, 2011). In nearly all regions of the world, water rights and access to water are tied to land ownership. Land ownership is also associated with recognition as farmers. When women lack this recognition they cannot access other services important for food production, such as extension services, credit and subsidies, and are denied participation in decision-making processes. As membership to water users associations (WUAs) in formal and informal irrigation schemes is restricted to landowners, most women do not have access to irrigation.

In the developing world, men tend to focus on market-oriented or cash crop production, whereas women work with subsistence agriculture, minor crops and vegetable gardens, and often grow a wider diversity of crops (World Bank et al., 2009). Consequently, the use and management of irrigation water is likely to be different for men and women farmers (World Bank et al., 2009). For example, in gender-based farming systems in sub-Saharan Africa, where men and women often cultivate separate fields (Van Koppen, 2002), this reality has often been ignored in irrigation projects. As a result, while men could irrigate their cash crops, women did not have access to irrigation systems for vegetable gardens and subsistence crops.

The lack of recognition of the different needs of men and women has often resulted in the partial or total failure of irrigation schemes. As key decisions in site selection, beneficiaries, land (re)allocation and water rights are made during the planning phase of water-related investment projects, the lack of recognition of women's irrigation needs at the planning stage itself forms the basis of gender inclusion or exclusion in the projects (Van Koppen, 2002). As more men out-migrate, leaving women in charge of managing the farms, it becomes even more important to involve women in managing irrigation. It is also important to acknowledge and plan for the fact that women use 'irrigation' water for productive and domestic purposes. Multiple use systems therefore provide better opportunities for women to participate in irrigation management and decision-making, thereby improving the sustainability of the systems (Box 35. 3).

Technical interventions for improving rainfed agriculture, such as rainwater harvesting, which are also good climate change adaptation measures, access to small-scale irrigation technologies, and developing the capacity of women farmers for conserving water and soil moisture, would provide an opportunity for women to play an important role in increasing food production, securing livelihoods and improving food security. By improving the agricultural yields of women farmers, the number of undernourished people could be reduced by as much as 100–150 million (FAO, 2011).

Improving women's agricultural productivity would not only make more food available to their families, but also provide much-needed cash income for securing the health, education and food security of their households. Food and nutrition security varies within the household as family members have differential access to food. In many cultures women and girls eat last and therefore in poorer households women may be deprived of adequate food and nutrition. Improved incomes and economic empowerment may help women improve their own food and nutrition security, as well as that of their children.

35.2.4 Gender dimensions of biofuel production

As water rights are closely linked to land rights, and both land and water are required for crop production, any debate on the production of bio-fuels for energy would need to address the impacts of diverting land and water resources from food production to the production of bio-fuel, and the gender dimensions of food security.

BOX 35.3

Making participatory irrigation development beneficial for women in the United Republic of Tanzania

In an International Fund for Agricultural Development (IFAD)-supported Participatory Irrigation Development Programme (1997–2007) in the United Republic of Tanzania, farmers are encouraged to take responsibility for irrigation development so that schemes reflect their needs and not those of planners.

Water supply schemes are built for multiple uses besides irrigation, to address women's concerns about water availability for domestic uses. Thus, shallow tubewell schemes have been constructed to provide water for horticultural crops, rice seedling nurseries and domestic use. This is particularly aimed at reducing workloads by reducing the time women spend in fetching water for domestic use.

Women are actively involved in the water users associations (WUAs), sometimes even more than the male members. The responsibilities of the WUA committees are shared equally by male and female members. Although most plot owners are men, the proportion of women with plots and membership in WUAs is over 30%. Women manage shallow wells and have access to irrigation for growing vegetables for both food and income. As a result of gender training and sensitization, women have also taken up leadership roles in WUAs and district councils, and participate in savings groups and credit associations.

Source: IFAD (2005).

'FAO estimates that, in sub-Saharan Africa and the Caribbean, women produce as much as 80% of basic foods, while in South and Southeast Asia, 60% of cultivation work and other food production is done by women.' (FAO, 2006, p. 2). 'Furthermore, although FAO projections to 2010 indicate a continued reduction in the overall female participation in agriculture globally, the percentage of economically active women working in agriculture in LDCs (least developed countries) is projected to remain above 70%.' (FAO, 2006, p. 5).

The potential depletion (or degradation) of natural resources associated with biofuel production, such as increased soil and water pollution, soil erosion and water runoff, with subsequent loss of biodiversity and reduced production of food crops is therefore more likely to impact women's agricultural and rural livelihoods. In addition to decreasing food security, competition for land and water resources between food and energy crop production could displace farming communities from traditional farmlands and reduce access to common lands which provided fuel and fodder for rural households and their animals. This in turn would mean that women would have to spend longer hours in accessing fodder and firewood as it is traditionally their responsibility to do so. Further, 'the replacement of local crops with energy crop plantations could also threaten the extensive knowledge and the traditional set of skills of smallholder farmers in the management of local crops. It would also threaten the knowledge related to the selection and storage of seeds and crops, all activities traditionally performed mainly by women.' (FAO, 1999).

A growing concern about the possible impacts of biofuel production has initiated efforts to understand how biofuel production can be pro-poor, and pro-women, helping to not only safeguard women's livelihoods but also to alleviate their work burden. Research by the International Food Policy Research Institute (Arndt et al., 2009) shows that positive technological spillover effects from the cultivation of biofuel, particularly when key staple crops are cultivated, could benefit subsistence, smallholder agriculture. To address potential conflict between the goals of poverty reduction and agro-business,[2] industry type of biofuel production, some countries have begun to adopt strategies that integrate subsistence crop systems with energy crop production to 'avoid complete domination by mono-crop plantation systems and allow for a more varied agricultural landscape and the ability to capture pro-poor benefits.' (Arndt et al., 2009).

A review of local biofuel projects in Africa and Asia conducted by the International Network on Gender and Sustainable Energy (ENERGIA)[3] found that 'village level projects have great potential in terms of sustainable fuel production and increased access to energy in rural areas of developing countries – if participatory processes are employed in the development and implementation of the projects. On a small scale, locally produced plant oils and biodiesel can successfully be

BOX 35.4

Extraction and use of Jatropha oil by a village women's group to power shea butter processing equipment in Ghana

A women's group in Gbimsi, Ghana is producing biofuel to run shea butter processing equipment and to use it as a kerosene substitute in lanterns. The women grow Jatropha plants, extract oil from the seeds and mix it with diesel (70% plant oil/30% diesel) to produce fuel. The project serves as a model for village level biofuel production linked to the empowerment of women, and efforts are being made to finance similar projects in other villages.

For the members of the women's group, much of the drudgery involved in the shea butter processing has been eliminated, resulting in increased production and improved access to credit from the local bank. The processing time is reduced by six hours, making more time available for household interaction; more relaxation for improved health, entertainment, community peace and harmony; and increased attention to other income generating activities.

'Regular group interaction and participation in meetings and workshops has broadened the outlook of the women. … Over all, they have more ability to make their own choices, and have gained in terms of improved self-esteem, better negotiating skills, more time for volunteering, and greater opportunities for contributing to the household budget.'

Note: This project has been undertaken by a women's group in Gbimsi, a town about 2 km from Walewale in the West Mamprusi District of the northern region of Ghana, with support from the United Nations Development Fund for Women (UNIFEM), the GRATIS Foundation in Ghana, and the United Nations Development Programme – Global Environment Facility (UNDP-GEF) Small Grants Programme.
Source: Karlsson and Banda (2009, p. 15).

used to power diesel engines and generators in rural villages – for agricultural processing, enterprises, and income generation' (Box 35.4), and contribute to reducing the work burden of women. Women could then engage in new income-generating activities that could enable them to 'send their children to school, feed their families nutritious food, provide better health care and living conditions, and have more power to make decisions within their households and communities' (Karlsson and Banda, 2009, pp. 4–5).

It was also found that unlike the threats related to biofuel production which come from the operation of big plantations run on an agro-business model, in village-based models, it is possible to protect the interests of small landowners and engage them as producers and processors of biofuel as part of a larger value production and supply chain without compromising food and water security. By utilizing land and water resources effectively, production and use of biofuel locally can improve the livelihoods of women.

35.2.5 Gender dimensions of urban water security

It is expected that by 2020, the developing countries of Africa, Asia and Latin America will have the largest number of people living in urban areas. Seventy-five% (FAO, 2008) of all urban dwellers worldwide will be in these regions, and 85% of the poor in Latin America, and about 40–45% of the poor in Africa and Asia will be concentrated in towns and cities (FAO, 2008). Providing safe and secure water for this fast growing urban population is one of the greatest challenges for the present and the future. An even bigger challenge is to provide safe, secure and affordable water to the poor communities that live within these urban conglomerates.

An estimated 40% of people living in Asian cities with a population of over 1 million, most of whom are poor, do not have access to piped water (Das et al., 2010). Access to piped water within the household averages about 85% for the wealthiest 20% of the population, compared with 25% for the poorest 20% (UNDP, 2006). In most developing countries, the poorest people not only have access to less water, and to less clean water, but they also pay some of the world's highest prices. Poor people living in slums often pay 5–10 times more per litre of water than wealthy people living in the same city (UNDP, 2006). For example, 'people living in the slums of Jakarta, Indonesia; Manila, the Philippines; and Nairobi, Kenya, pay 5–10 times more for water per

unit than those in high-income areas of their own cities—and more than consumers pay in London or New York; and the poorest 20% of households in El Salvador, Jamaica and Nicaragua spend on average more than 10% of their household income on water. In the United Kingdom a 3% threshold is seen as an indicator of hardship.' (UNDP, 2006, p. 7).

Being able to access piped water supply depends upon the household's financial ability to connect to the pipeline. Connection fees are generally high and can exceed $100 even in the poorest countries (UNDP, 2006), making it difficult for poor people to have access to piped water supply. For example, in Manila the cost of connecting to the utility 'represents about three months' income for the poorest 20% of households', and 'about six months' income for the poorest in urban Kenya'. (UNDP, 2006, p. 10). In addition, utilities in many cities refuse to connect households that lack formal property titles, which again are often the poorest. (UNDP, 2006). Location is another barrier to connecting to the water utility. Slums or informal settlements are often situated in difficult-to-connect locations in terms of distance and topography (Pangare and Pangare, 2008).

As water passes through intermediaries and each adds transport and marketing costs, prices increase. The rising block tariff system being implemented by most utilities aims to combine equity with efficiency by raising the price with the volume of water used. However, distance from utilities tends to inflate prices, and in practice, the poorest households are often locked into the higher tariff bands as the intermediaries serving poor households are buying water in bulk at the highest rate. In Dakar, poor households using standpipes pay more than three times the price paid by households connected to the utility (UNDP, 2006).

Efforts to improve urban water supply through private sector participation have not been as successful as expected in improving access for poor households and women. The Cochabamba experience (in Bolivia) showed that social differences, inequities and vulnerabilities can increase if the approach is not pro-poor (Ledo, 2004). However the success of the reform process undertaken in Cambodia by the Phnom Penh Water Supply Authority (PPWSA) showed that the poor can gain access to piped water supply if the efficiency and effectiveness of public water utilities is improved (Box 35.5). Not only did the water supply in

Phnom Penh improve as a result of these reforms, but cost recovery measures were also successful because stratified subsidies were made available to the poor (Das et al., 2010).

When poor households or communities living in slums or informal settlements do not have access to piped water networks, they tend to meet their water needs through a combination of different sources and means. They (most likely women and girls) either collect water freely from public or private protected or unprotected sources and/or purchase water from formal or informal vendors, depending upon the quantity and quality of water available (Pangare and Pangare, 2008). As a result, the poorest, especially the women, often pay the most for water, particularly taking into account the smaller quantities of water they are able to purchase (such as paying for each bucket of water) and the additional indirect cost of poor quality water in terms of waterborne diseases and health care.

A recent study on urban water vending in Uganda found that water vendors by re-selling piped water to the poor who are unable to invest in obtaining a private or yard tap connection for their households, are

BOX 35.5

Improving access for the poor: Phnom Penh Water Supply Authority, Phnom Penh, Cambodia

Soy Najy, whose household consists of seven members, received her Phnom Penh Water Supply Authority (PPWSA) connection in 2005. She used it to purchase three drums (20 L per drum) of water from vendors every day at a price of 2000 Riel per drum, amounting to Riel 150,000 or US$37.5 per month. She has a sewing and tailoring shop, and requires more water than is normally used for domestic consumption. In 2005, residents from the squatter colony in which she lives urged PPWSA to extend their network to their locality. Now that Soy Najy has access to the water supplied by the public utility, she pays 15,000 Riel or US$4 per month for water – that is, one-tenth of what she paid before. It has helped her reduce expenses to a great extent.

Prior to the PPWSA connection, the locality received water only at night because the slum was located at a higher elevation. Now residents have 24-hour water supply and at a much lower cost.

Source: Das et al. (2010).

actually extending the National Water and Sewerage Corporation (NWSC) coverage to the urban poor (Pangare and Pangare, 2008). A majority of the water vendors in Uganda had employed young children or women to manage the taps or water-selling points, because they could be employed at very low salaries (Pangare and Pangare, 2008).

35.2.6 Gender concerns in health and sanitation

Access to water for life is a basic human need and a fundamental human right. Yet 884 million people are denied the right to clean water and 2.6 billion people lack access to adequate sanitation (WHO and UNICEF, 2010). Every day, almost 5,000 children, (about 1.8 million children per year), die as a result of diarrhoea and other diseases caused by unclean water and lack of sanitation, making it the second largest cause of child mortality. Easier access to clean water and sanitation improves hygiene behaviour and can reduce the risk of a child dying by as much as 50% (UNDP, 2006).

'Every day millions of women and young girls collect water for their families, a ritual that reinforces gender inequalities in employment and education.' (UNDP, 2006). Women often spend up to six hours every day fetching water, the time calculated includes walking to the source of water, waiting in queues and then carrying back the heavy containers filled with water (UNDP, 2006). In addition, carrying water in large containers on their heads is more likely to have severe health implications for women and girls, such as backache and headaches, and other problems, such as anxiety, stress, light-headedness, vomiting and vertigo after walking many hours with a huge gallon of water (UN-HABITAT/GWA, 2006).

With increasing contamination of surface water and groundwater sources, women, as primary collectors of water, are the first to be exposed to waterborne diseases. This not only affects their own health and reproductive health but also often results in birth defects and high infant mortality. Also the stigma attached to waterborne diseases, such as urinary schistosomiasis in women affects their own health-seeking behaviour and access to health care.

Both men and women suffer indignity and ill health from inadequate sanitation. However, men, women and children have different sanitation needs, and these need to be kept in mind when designing sanitation facilities. It is also important to facilitate privacy and security in common facilities for young children and women.

Lack of water and sanitation perpetuates gender inequality and disempowers women in different ways. Particularly in water-scarce regions, millions of girls are unable to attend school because they must fetch water for their households. In addition, lack of sanitation facilities in schools keeps young girls out of school, especially during puberty, limiting their opportunity for continuing their education, consequently limiting their life and livelihood choices. The time spent fetching and collecting water and caring for children and family members made ill by waterborne diseases and their own associated health problems reduces women's opportunities to engage in productive work.

In general, not having access to clean water and adequate sanitation is a major cause of poverty and malnutrition; the associated ill health traps vulnerable households in cycles of poverty, undermining the productivity of the poor people and reinforcing economic inequalities.

35.2.7 Gender dimensions of water-related disasters

Thousands of women and men die worldwide every year as a result of water-related disasters. It is predicted that climate change will further increase the number of human deaths from heat waves, floods, storms and droughts, as these extreme weather events will increase in frequency and intensity. Although there is not enough sex-disaggregated data available on how these disasters affect men and women, there are indications that mortality differences by sex may vary from one country to another and by type of hazard.

Recent information on the impact of the tsunami in December 2004 suggests that women and girls may be more vulnerable to some natural disasters as a result of less access to information and life skills development, and culturally constrained mobility of women outside of their homes. Many more women than men died in several locations hit by the tsunami, and a large number of them were between 19–29 years of age, suggesting a combination of increased vulnerability of women staying home with children at the time of the sea level rise and the more fortunate situation of some of the young men who were far away from the coastline, fishing at sea or out in the agricultural fields (Oxfam International, 2005).

Strategies and responses developed to mitigate the impacts of water-related disasters are usually designed for the entire population of the vulnerable area, and use existing social structures for decision-making and communicating information. Responses would be more effective if the different needs, constraints and strengths of different groups of men and women in the local community were identified and this information was used while preparing mitigation and response strategies and plans.

As the Pan American Health Organization (PAHO) points out on the basis of its experience, natural disasters often offer women the opportunity to challenge their gendered status in society. Not only do women take up traditionally male tasks outside their domestic spheres, but often do so against the wishes of the men in the community, thus challenging their perceived roles in society. Women are 'most effective at mobilizing the community to respond to disasters', and as a result of their response efforts, women are developing new skills, such as natural resource and agricultural management, which in the presence of appropriate enabling frameworks, could represent opportunities for income generation (PAHO, 2001).

35.3 The way forward

Over many decades, the UN has made significant progress in advancing gender equality, including through landmark agreements, such as the Beijing Declaration and Platform for Action, and the Convention on the Elimination of All Forms of Discrimination against Women (CEDAW), and setting up of UN Women to accelerate progress in achieving gender equality and women's empowerment. Water and Gender is listed as one of UN-Water's Thematic Priority Areas in its 2010–2011 Work Programme and promoting gender equality and the empowerment of women worldwide is one of UNESCO's two global priorities for 2008–2013 (UNESCO, 2009).

There is enough evidence to show that integrating a gender-sensitive approach to development can have a positive impact on the effectiveness and sustainability of water interventions and on the conservation of water resources. Involving both men and women in the design and implementation of interventions leads to effective new solutions to water problems; helps governments avoid poor investments and expensive mistakes; makes projects more sustainable; ensures that infrastructure development yields the maximum social and economic returns; and furthers development goals, such as reducing hunger, child mortality, and improving gender equality (Oxfam International, 2005 and 2007).

Although it is true that many socially constructed barriers need to be overcome to facilitate the involvement of both men and women in decision-making and management of water resources, it is also true that traditional gender roles have often been challenged successfully by developing women's capacities to manage water interventions and providing them with opportunities to play leadership roles and improve their economic conditions. However, these successes are more often limited to the local context as the larger issues, such as providing water rights to women, are governed by externalities which are not only outside the purview of these interventions, but involve traditional, cultural and political realities that are difficult to change in the short-term, and require long-term commitment from policy-makers, governments, politicians and advocacy groups.

It is clear that to meet future challenges in water in all its uses it is necessary to decrease the gender gap in water. Opportunities for addressing these challenges call for greater participation by women for which new methods of water governance would be required, actions would need to be taken to improve women's access to productive resources and capacities would need to be built to facilitate these changes and make them effective. Suggested below are action points in three areas.

35.3.1 Mainstreaming gender considerations in water governance

- Recognize women as important decision-makers in water governance.
- Recognize the diversity of women, and social and gender constructs in society. Identify the specific groups of women who form the relevant stakeholder group in a given context and enable them to participate in decision-making. Some of these specific groups include, but are not limited to, poor women, rural women, women in peri-urban areas, women farmers, and women who have been denied access to a water source due to social constructs, such as class, ethnicity and cultural constraints in the community.
- Enable women to become members of water management institutions, such as water user organizations through by detaching water rights from land rights, reducing membership fees and broadening

the mandate of irrigation schemes to acknowledge and include multiple water use.
- Enable women to participate in the decision-making process by organizing meetings and forums, keeping in mind the convenience of time and space for women to attend.
- Facilitate the development of the capacity of men and women to participate in joint meetings at different levels and to listen to each other's views.
- Facilitate the development of the capacity of women to express their views in multi-stakeholder meetings
- Establish accountability measures and indicators to ensure that the participation of women is encouraged and facilitated.
- Establish gender indicators and conduct gender audits to strengthen women's participation in governance processes. Collection and analysis of gender disaggregated data would need to be made mandatory for developing effective gender indicators and conducting gender audits.
- Ensure that the budgets provide for gender mainstreaming.

35.3.2 Improving women's access to water and other productive resources

- Recognize women as independent users of water.
- Enable women to access water rights, regardless of land ownership.
- Recognize women as farmers and irrigators.
- Ensure women have access to extension services, credit and other resources for improving livelihoods.
- Identify constraints that prevent different groups of women from accessing water resources, such as social and gender constructs, and power relations in the community, and facilitate the removal of these constraints.
- Provide technical training to women on water management, irrigation, rainwater harvesting, other small holder irrigation technologies and rainfed agriculture.
- Improve water supply services to cover the needs of the poorer sections of the population by initiating reforms that make water affordable to the poor families in urban and peri-urban areas, such as instalment schemes for connection charges and subsidies.
- Introduce new targets for improving gender sensitive sanitation: put gender equity in water and sanitation at the centre of national poverty reduction strategies.

35.3.3 Enhancing capacities of men and women to understand and address gender differences and concerns in water management

- Gender sensitization for different levels of government, project and civil society staff.
- Gender sensitization for men and women in the community.
- Improve, adapt and use existing tools for gender mainstreaming in water management and governance, and provide training in how these can be used effectively.

||||||||||||||||||||||||||||||||||||||||||||||||||||||||||||||||||||||

Notes

1   While women's access to education and employment has improved in recent decades, the transformative potential of those changes has been curtailed by persisting inequalities in the gender distribution of resources. There is an implicit assumption that as economic opportunities for women expand, households will adjust the gender division of unpaid labour in ways that allow women to respond to changing market incentives on an equal basis with men. Experience has not borne this assumption out. Women's increasing participation in paid work has not been accompanied by a commensurate increase in men's share of unpaid work within the home. The gender division of unpaid domestic work has displayed a remarkable resilience and continues to shape the terms on which women are able to take up paid work. It limits the transformative potential of employment for the position of women within the home and in the wider society (UNDESA, 2009).

2   Agro-business refers to modern economic activities devoted to the production, processing and distribution of food and fibre products and by-products (as opposed to family farms). In highly industrialized countries, many activities essential to agriculture are carried out separately from the farm. Many of these farms use extensive mechanization and computer technology to increase production (*Encyclopaedia Britannica,* 2011).

3   The International Network on Gender and Sustainable Energy (ENERGIA) has recommended that environmental and social impact assessments of proposed biofuel projects or programs should include an evaluation of gender-differentiated impacts – through consultative processes designed to ensure substantial participation of women – and that gender equity should be one of the principles considered in those assessments.

||||||||||||||||||||||||||||||||||||||||||||||||||||||||||||||||||||||

References

Arndt, C., Benfica, R., Tarp, F., Thurlow, J., Uaiene, R. 2009. Biofuels, poverty, and growth: a computable general equilibrium analysis of Mozambique. IOP Conference Series: *Earth and Environmental Science,* Vol. 6 (2009) 102008. doi:10.1088/1755-1307/6/0/102008

Das, B., Chan E. K., Visoth C., Pangare G., Simpson, R. 2010. *Sharing the Reform Process: Learning from the Phnom Penh Water Supply Authority.* Gland, Switzerland/Bangkok/Phnom Penh, IUCN/PPWSA.

Encyclopaedia Britannica. 2011. http://www.britannica.com/EBchecked/topic/9513/agribusiness (Accessed 14 November 2011.)

FAO (Food and Agricultural Organization). 1999. *Women – Users, Preservers and Managers of Agrobiodiversity.* Rome, FAO.

––––. 2006. *Agriculture, Trade Negotiations and Gender.* Prepared by Zoraida García with contributions from Jennifer Nyberg and Shayma Owaise Saadat, FAO Gender and Population Division, Food and Agriculture Organization of the United Nations, Rome.

––––. 2008. *Urban Agriculture for Sustainable Poverty Alleviation and Food Security.* Rome, FAO. http://www.fao.org/fileadmin/templates/FCIT/PDF/UPA_-WBpaper-Final_Draft-3_October_2008-FG-WOB.pdf (Accessed 14 November 2011.)

––––. 2010a. *Evaluation of FAO's Role and Work Related to Water,* Final Report. Rome, FAO Office of Evaluation. http://typo3.fao.org/fileadmin/user_upload/oed/docs/FAO_Role_Related_to_Water_2010_ER_.zip

––––. 2010b. *FAO at Work 2009–2010: Growing Food for Nine Billion.* Rome, FAO.

––––. 2011. *The State of Food and Agriculture: Women in Agriculture, Closing the Gender Gap for Development.* Rome, FAO.

IFAD (International Fund for Agricultural Development). 2005. *Participatory Irrigation Development Programme (PIDP) in the United Republic of Tanzania: Supervision Report.* Rome, IFAD.

––––. 2007. *Gender and Water: Securing Water for Improved Rural Livelihoods: The Multiple-uses Systems Approach.* Rome, IFAD, p. 2.

Karlsson, G., and Banda, K. (eds.). 2009. *Biofuels for Sustainable Rural Development and Empowerment of Women: Case Studies from Africa and Asia.* The Netherlands, ENERGIA Secretariat.

Lambrou, Y., and Laub, R. 2006. *Gender, Local Knowledge, and Lessons Learnt in Documenting and Conserving Agrobiodiversity.* Research Paper 2006/69. United Nations University, Helsinki, UNU-WIDER (World Institute for Development Economics Research).

Ledo, C. 2004. *Inequality and Access to Water in the Cities of Cochabamba and La Paz-El Alto.* Case Study prepared for the research project on Commercialization, Privatization and Universal Access to Water. United Nations Research Institute for Sustainable Development. http://www.unrisd.org/unrisd/website/projects.nsf/(httpAuxPages)/3810D5F1B5474815C1256F41003D49D1?OpenDocument&category=Case+Studies (Accessed 14 November 2011.)

Oxfam International. 2005. *The Tsunami's Impact on Women.* Oxfam Briefing Note. UK, Oxfam. http://www.oxfam.org.uk/what_we_do/issues/conflict_disasters/downloads/bn_tsunami_women.pdf (Accessed 14 November 2011.)

Oxfam International. 2007. *Climate Alarm – Disasters Increase as Climate Change Bites.* Oxfam Briefing Paper 108. UK, Oxfam. http://www.oxfam.org.uk/resources/policy/climate_change/downloads/bp108_weather_alert.pdf. (Accessed 14 November 2011.)

PAHO (Pan-American Health Organization). 2001. Gender and Natural Disasters. Fact Sheet of the Program on Women, Health and Development. Washington DC, PAHO.

Pangare G., and Pangare, V. 2008. *Informal Water Vendors and Service Providers in Uganda: The Ground Reality.* Research Paper for The Water Dialogues, UK. http://www.waterdialogues.org/documents/InformalWaterVendorsandServiceProvidersinUganda.pdf

World Bank. 2006. *Reengaging in Agricultural Water Management: Challenges and Options.* Washington DC, World Bank.

––––. 2007. *World Development Report 2008: Agriculture for Development.* Washington DC, World Bank.

––––. 2010. *Rainfed Agriculture.* http://water.worldbank.org/water/topics/agricultural-water-management/rainfed-agriculture (Accessed 14 November 2011.)

World Bank, FAO and IFAD (World Bank; Food and Agriculture Organization; International Fund for Agricultural Development). 2009. *Gender and Agriculture Sourcebook.* Washington DC, World Bank.

UN (United Nations). 2009. *Agriculture Development and Food Security.* Report of the Secretary-General, 64th Session, Item 62 of the provisional agenda, 3 August 2009. http://daccess-dds-ny.un.org/doc/UNDOC/GEN/N09/439/03/PDF/N0943903.pdf?OpenElement (Accessed 14 November 2011.)

UNDESA (United Nations Department of Economic and Social Affairs). 2009. *World Survey on the Role of Women in Development.* Report of the Secretary General, Women's Control over Economic Resources and Access to Financial Resources, Including Microfinance. New York, UN, Chapter III.

UNDP (United Nations Development Programme). 2004. *Water Governance for Poverty Reduction: Key Issues and the UNDP Response to the Millennium Development Goals.* New York, UNDP, p. 10.

––––. 2006. *Beyond Scarcity: Power, Poverty and the Global Water Crisis. Human Development Report 2006.* New York, UNDP. http://hdr.undp.org/en/media/HDR06-complete.pdf

UNESCO (United Nations Educational, Scientific and Cultural Organization). 2009. *Priority Gender Equality Action Plan 2008–2013.* Paris, France, UNESCO Division for Gender Equality, Bureau of Strategic Planning. http://www.unesco.org/genderequality

UN-HABITAT/GWA (United Nations Settlement Programme/Gender Water Alliance). 2006. *Navigating Gender in African Cities: Synthesis Report on Rapid Gender and Pro-Poor Assessment in 17 African Cities.* Nairobi, UN-HABITAT.

Van Koppen, B. 2002. *A Gender Performance Indicator for Irrigation: Concepts, Tools, and Applications.* International Water Management Institute (IWMI) Research Report 59. Colombo, Sri Lanka, IWMI.

Van Koppen, B., Moriarty, P. and Boelee, E. 2006. *Multiple-Use Water Services to Advance the Millennium Development Goals.* International Water Management Institute (IWMI) Research Report 98. Colombo, Sri Lanka, IWMI.

WHO and UNICEF (World Health Organization and United Nations Children's Fund). 2010. *Progress on Sanitation and Drinking-Water: 2010 Update.* Geneva, WHO/UNICEF Joint Monitoring Programme for Water Supply and Sanitation.

CHAPTER 36
Groundwater

WWAP, in collaboration with UNESCO-IHP

—

Author Jac van der Gun
Contributors Frank van Weert (UNESCO IGRAC) and Cheryl van Kempen (UNESCO IGRAC)
Acknowledgements Comments on successive drafts: Michela Miletto (WWAP), Alice Aureli (UNESCO-IHP), Olcay Ünver (WWAP), Richard Connor (WWAP), Holger Treidel (UNESCO-IHP), Alexandros Makarigakis (UNESCO-IHP) and Lucilla Minelli (UNESCO-IHP)

||||||||||||||||||||||||||||||||||||||||||||||||||||||||||||||||||||||||||||||||||||||||||||||||||||||||||||||||||||||||||||||||||||||||||||||||||

Knowledge on the world's groundwater resources, their functions and their use is quickly increasing and views on groundwater and its interlinkages are changing accordingly.

Groundwater is globally a resource in transition: during the twentieth century, groundwater exploitation started booming (the 'silent revolution'), resulting in much higher benefits from groundwater than ever before, but triggering unprecedented changes in the state of groundwater as well.

The key issues to be addressed to ensure the sustainability of groundwater resources are groundwater storage depletion (declining water levels) and groundwater pollution.

Climate change will affect groundwater, but groundwater is more resilient than surface water, due to its characteristic buffer capacity. Therefore, in areas where climate change will cause water resources to become scarcer, the relative role of groundwater may become more prominent.

Groundwater governance is complex and needs to be tailored to local conditions. In transboundary aquifer systems, the international dimension adds complexity.

36.1 Groundwater in a web of interdependencies

Addressing groundwater in a separate chapter of WWDR4 underlines the importance of groundwater in relation to coping with risks and uncertainties in a changing world, but should not suggest that groundwater systems can be understood and properly managed on the basis of hydrogeological information only, nor in isolation from surface water. On the contrary, groundwater is a component of the hydrological cycle and interacts closely with other components of this cycle, at various temporal and spatial scales. It is also involved in various other cycles, such as chemical cycles (solute transport) and biochemical cycles (biosphere), and is affected by climate change resulting from changes in the carbon cycle. In addition, groundwater interactions and interdependencies are not limited to physical systems, such as surface waters, soils, ecosystems, oceans, lithosphere and atmosphere, but are related as well to socio-economic, legal, institutional and political systems. Hence, groundwater is entrenched in a web of interdependencies. Changes in the state of groundwater systems are taking place due to these interdependencies, and causal chains link these changes to the drivers of change (root causes).

Different categories of drivers are behind the processes of change in groundwater systems. Demographic drivers and socio-economic drivers explain to a large extent water demands, pollution loads and people's behaviour with respect to groundwater. Science and technological innovation have put their footmarks as well on the use and state of many groundwater systems around the world (e.g. by systematic aquifer exploration and improved drilling and pumping technologies). Policy, law and finance form an important category of drivers behind planned change, in the context of groundwater resources development and management. Climate variability and change affect in particular aquifers in arid and semi-arid regions (changes in groundwater recharge, water demands and availability of alternative sources of fresh water) and in coastal zones (sea level rise). Finally, natural and anthropogenic hazards may cause sudden rather than gradual changes in the state of groundwater systems.

36.2 Panorama of change

36.2.1 Increasing knowledge of the world's groundwater

Significant advances in the knowledge of the world's groundwater have been witnessed in recent years. While they are observed at all scale levels, the focus in this *World Water Development Report* is on the global and regional scales. Important achievements are the consolidated version of the Groundwater Resources Map of the World (WHYMAP, 2008; Figure 36.1); the outcomes of global-scale hydrological modelling, such as on worldwide groundwater recharge with the WaterGAP Global Hydrological Model (Döll and Fiedler, 2008) and on groundwater depletion with PCR-GLOBWB (Wada et al., 2010); a global assessment of current groundwater use for irrigation (Siebert et al., 2010) and a comprehensive monograph on the geography of the world's groundwater (Margat, 2008). Special attention for transboundary aquifers has resulted in rapidly increasing documentation and tools on transboundary aquifers (Section 36.4).

The total volume of fresh groundwater stored on Earth is believed to be 8–10 million km^3 (Margat, 2008), which is more than two thousand times the current annual withdrawal of surface water and groundwater combined. This is a huge volume, but where are these freshwater buffers located and what fraction of their stock is available for depletion? Figure 36.1 answers the first question by showing the geographic distribution of the world's major groundwater basins (blue map units – covering 36% of the area of the continents). This is where the main groundwater buffers are located. Additional ones, but less continuous and smaller, are present in the areas with complex hydrogeological structure (green map units – 18%) and to a lesser extent even in the remaining 46% of the area of the continents. The groundwater buffers allow the convenient bridging of periodic, seasonal or multi-annual dry periods, without the risk of sudden unexpected water shortages. In large parts of the globe, sustainable groundwater development is possible by the alternation of storage depletion during dry periods and storage recovery during wet periods. The groundwater reservoirs are rather insensitive for variations in the length of the dry periods and therefore resilient to this aspect of climate variation and climate change. In principle it is possible to ignore the sustainability criterion and exploit a large part of the stored groundwater volumes, but in practice it is unattractive and difficult to do so, because depletion comes at a cost, as explained in Section 36.3.

Recent outcomes of the Gravity Recovery and Climate Experiment (GRACE) mark a major step forward in assessing groundwater storage variations in some of the world's major aquifer systems (Famiglietti et al., 2009;

FIGURE 36.1

Groundwater resources of the world

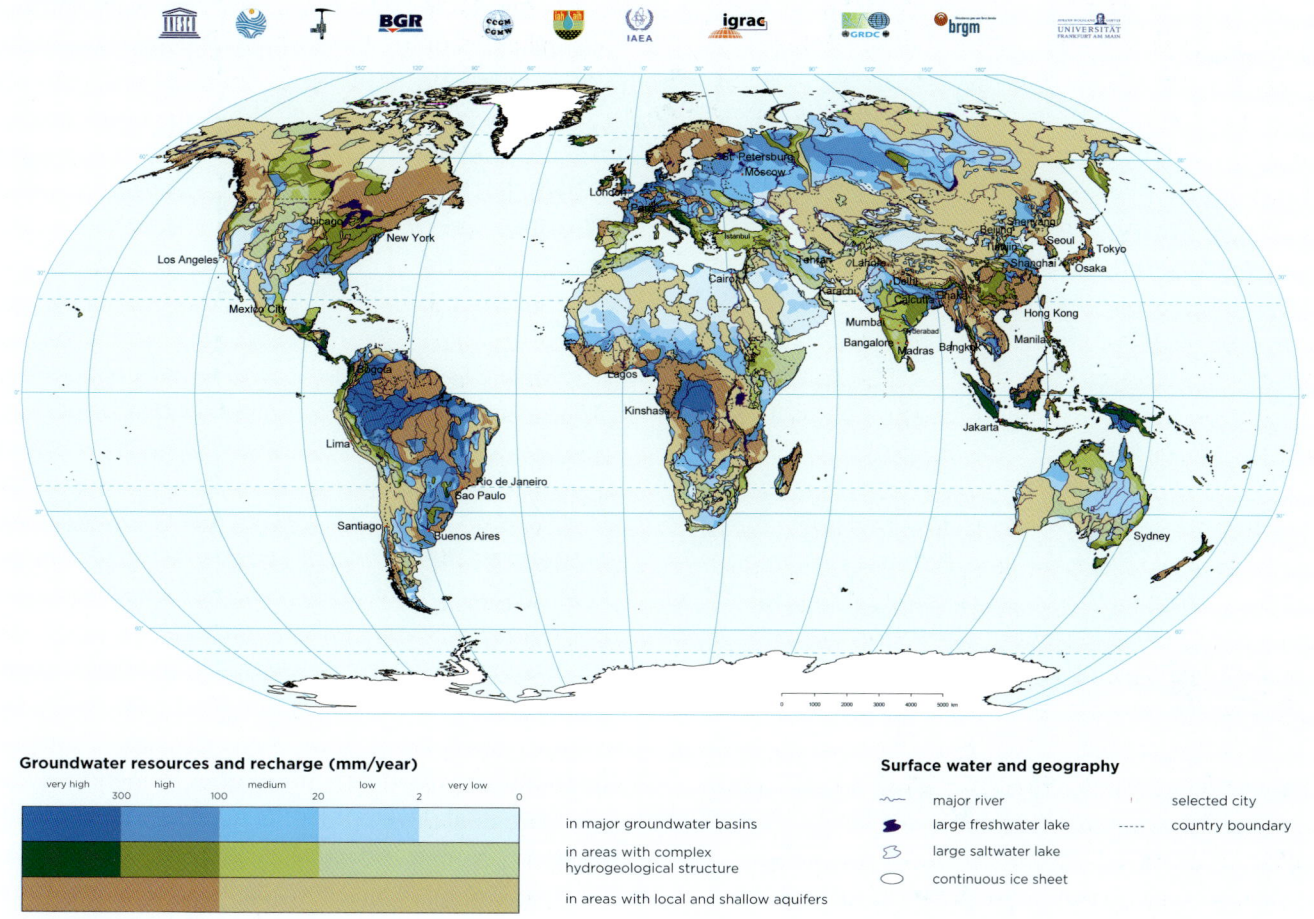

Groundwater resources and recharge (mm/year)

very high	high	medium	low	very low	
	300	100	20	2	0

in major groundwater basins

in areas with complex hydrogeological structure

in areas with local and shallow aquifers

Surface water and geography

major river — selected city
large freshwater lake — ----- country boundary
large saltwater lake
continuous ice sheet

Source: BGR and UNESCO, from WHYMAP (2008).

Rodell et al., 2009; Tiwari et al., 2009; Muskett and Romanovsky, 2009; Moiwo et al., 2009; Bonsor et al., 2010; Chen et al., 2009). The results of the experiment suggest that satellite mapping of the Earth's gravity field (satellite gravimetry) is a promising innovative technique for hydrogeological investigations in the near future[1], for monitoring long-term trends, seasonal variations and variations during droughts. Global simulation models linking the terrestrial and atmospheric components of the hydrological cycle are likely to become another important tool to enhance the knowledge of groundwater regimes, in particular for exploring how they may respond to climate change (Döll, 2009).

36.2.2 The 'silent revolution'

Driven by population growth, technological and scientific progress, economic development and the need for food and income, groundwater abstraction across the world has explosively increased during the twentieth century. By far the largest share of the additional abstracted volumes has been allocated to irrigated agriculture. The boom in groundwater development for irrigation started in Italy, Mexico, Spain and the United States during the early part of the twentieth century (Shah et al., 2007). A second wave began in South Asia, the North China Plain, and parts of the Middle East and North Africa during the 1970s, and still continues. The authors perceive a likely third wave of increasing abstractions in many regions of Africa and in some South and Southeast Asian countries such as Sri Lanka and Viet Nam. This worldwide boom in groundwater abstraction has resulted largely from numerous individual decisions by farmers, without centralized planning or coordination, and has been named the 'silent revolution' (Llamas and Martínez-Santos, 2005).

Based on recent estimates at country level (IGRAC, 2010; Margat; 2008; Siebert et al., 2010, AQUASTAT, 2011; EUROSTAT, 2011), the world's aggregated

FIGURE 36.2

Groundwater abstraction trends in selected countries (in cubic kilometres per year)

km³ per year

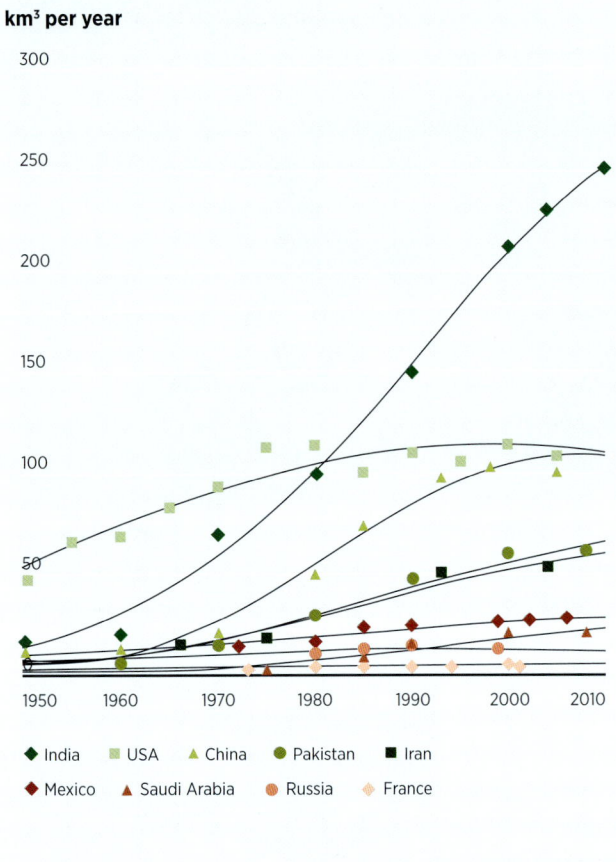

1950 1960 1970 1980 1990 2000 2010

◆ India   ◻ USA   ▲ China   ● Pakistan   ■ Iran

◆ Mexico   ▲ Saudi Arabia   ● Russia   ◆ France

Source: Adapted from Margat (2008, fig. 4.6, p. 107).

TABLE 36.1

Top 10 groundwater abstracting countries (as at 2010)

Country	Abstraction (km³/year)
1 India	251
2 China	112
3 USA	112
4 Pakistan	64
5 Iran	60
6 Bangladesh	35
7 Mexico	29
8 Saudi Arabia	23
9 Indonesia	14
10 Italy	14

Note: Around 72% of the global groundwater abstraction takes place in these ten countries only.

groundwater abstraction as at 2010 is estimated to be approximately 1000 km³ per year, of which about 67% is used for irrigation, 22% for domestic and 11% for industrial purposes (IGRAC, 2010)[2]. The lion's share of the total quantity (two-thirds) is abstracted in Asia, with India, China, Pakistan, Iran and Bangladesh as major consumers (Tables 36.1 and 36.2). The global groundwater abstraction rate has at least tripled over the last 50 years and is increasing at an annual rate between 1 and 2%. Nevertheless, in some countries where intensive groundwater development started early, abstraction rates have peaked and now are stable or even decreasing (Shah et al., 2007), as is illustrated in Figure 36.2. Although the global estimates are not accurate, they suggest that the current global abstraction of groundwater represents approximately 26% of total fresh water withdrawal on Earth (Table 36.2) and that its rate corresponds to some 8% of the mean globally aggregated rate of groundwater recharge. Groundwater is supplying almost half of all drinking water in the world (WWAP, 2009) and 43% of the global consumptive use of water in irrigation[3] (Siebert et al., 2010).

The silent revolution has contributed tremendously to economic development and welfare in many countries of the world, especially in the rural areas. Nevertheless, it has also introduced unprecedented problems that are in some areas difficult to control (Section 36.3).

36.2.3 Changing views on groundwater

Groundwater has become an interdisciplinary subject, no longer the exclusive domain of hydrogeologists and engineers, but also addressed by economists, sociologists, ecologists, climatologists, lawyers, institutional experts and communication specialists. Analysing groundwater from different angles puts it in a wider context, resulting in changing views on this natural resource.

There are changing views regarding the value and functions of groundwater. Measuring the importance of groundwater by comparing its recharge rate, withdrawal or stored volume to those of surface water is gradually being replaced by more economically oriented approaches, focused on the 'added value' produced by groundwater. Groundwater often produces higher economic returns per unit of water used in irrigation than surface water (Llamas and Garrido, 2007; Shah, 2007), because its stored volume reduces risk. Awareness is growing that functions and services of a

TABLE 36.2

Key estimates on global groundwater abstraction (2010)

Continent	Groundwater abstraction[1]					Compared to total water abstraction	
	Irrigation (km³/year)	Domestic (km³/year)	Industrial (km³/year)	Total (km³/year)	%	Total water abstraction[2] (km³/year)	Share of groundwater (%)
North America	99	26	18	143	15	524	27
Central America and the Caribbean	5	7	2	14	1	149	9
South America	12	8	6	26	3	182	14
Europe (including Russian Federation)	23	37	16	76	8	497	15
Africa	27	15	2	44	4	196	23
Asia	497	116	63	676	68	2 257	30
Oceania	4	2	1	7	1	26	25
World	666	212	108	986	100	3 831	26

[1] Estimated on the basis of IGRAC (2010), AQUASTAT (2011), EUROSTAT (2011), Margat (2008) and Siebert et al. (2010).
[2] Average of the 1995 and 2025 'business as usual scenario' estimates presented by Alcamo et al. (2003).

groundwater system go beyond water withdrawal and include a number of *in situ* services as well, such as the support of ecosystems, phreatophytic agriculture, spring flow and base flow; the prevention of land subsidence and seawater intrusion; and the potential for exploiting geothermal energy or storing heat.

A second category of changing views refers to the role of people. Not long ago, diagnostic analysis and management of groundwater resources was based almost exclusively on the analysis of the physical components (groundwater systems and related ecosystems). There is wide consensus now that socio-economic aspects deserve ample attention as well and that groundwater resources management is likely to be successful only if stakeholders are involved and if adequate groundwater institutions, legislation and related regulatory frameworks exist.

Further, the debate on climate change has made clear that hydrogeologists and hydrologists have to abandon their traditional implicit assumption of stochastic stationarity of natural hydrological fluxes. The assumption that groundwater recharge rates assessed in the past would provide an unbiased estimate for future conditions is no longer appropriate.

36.2.4 Conjunctive management, Integrated Water Resources Management and beyond

Groundwater is no longer explored and exploited as an isolated resource. After the advantages of *conjunctive use* of groundwater and surface water were recognized, already long ago (Todd, 1959), the notion of *conjunctive management* has been embraced. Under this paradigm the water resources are not only used but also managed, whereby surface water and groundwater are managed jointly as components of a single system. It may include Managed Aquifer Recharge (MAR), the intentional storage of water in aquifers for subsequent recovery or environmental benefit, applied in countless small and large schemes around the world (Dillon, 2009). MAR includes groundwater level control in flat areas by manipulating surface water levels, such as widely practiced in The Netherlands.

A next step is integration across water use sectors, as advocated by Integrated Water Resources Management (IWRM): the coordinated development and management of water, land and related resources, aiming for maximum economic and social welfare without compromising the sustainability of ecosystems and the environment (GWP, 2011). This cross-sectoral approach to water has replaced in many countries the previous traditional, fragmented sectoral approaches that ignored the interconnection between the different water uses and services. There are tendencies towards a higher level of integration of area-specific strategic planning, in search of better coherence between policy domains, such as water resources management, land use planning, nature conservation, environmental management and economic development.

36.2.5 Increasing international focus on groundwater

Groundwater, a local natural resource producing mainly local benefits, is progressively subject to initiatives at the international level. Initiatives such as the World-wide Hydrogeological Mapping and Assessment Programme (WHYMAP), International Groundwater Resources Assessment Centre (IGRAC), Groundwater Management Advisory Team (GWMATE), International Waters Learning Exchange and Resource Network (IW:LEARN), Internationally Shared Aquifers Resources Management Programme (ISARM) and global hydrological modelling are based on the idea that exchanging, sharing, compiling and analysing area-specific information on groundwater contribute to dissemination of knowledge and produce added value by providing views at a higher level of spatial aggregation. Several international initiatives are triggering or guiding action in the field of groundwater assessment, monitoring or management. Examples not specific for groundwater are the Millennium Development Goals and the European Water Framework Directive (WFD). Recent groundwater-specific initiatives in this category are transboundary aquifer projects in the Global Environment Facility (GEF) International Waters (IW) portfolio, the new European Groundwater Directive ('daughter directive' of the WFD), the Draft Articles on the Law of Transboundary Aquifers and the establishment of the African Groundwater Commission. Several recent international declarations, including the Alicante Declaration (IGME, 2006) and the African Groundwater Declaration demonstrate growing awareness on the relevance of groundwater and the willingness to address it.

36.3 Key issues on groundwater

36.3.1 Declining groundwater levels and storage depletion

The silent revolution caused an unprecedented increase in groundwater withdrawal across the globe. It has produced enormous socio-economic benefits around the world, but not without modifying drastically the hydrogeological regimes of many aquifers, in particular poorly recharged aquifers. The stress placed on groundwater systems by groundwater abstraction builds up when the ratio of abstraction to mean recharge increases. Figure 36.3 shows the geographical variation of the corresponding groundwater development stress indicator. The highest stresses occur in the more arid parts of the world. As the groundwater development stress indicator is averaged over entire countries, it cannot reveal stressed aquifer systems much smaller in size. As a result of intensive groundwater development, steady depletion of groundwater storage, accompanied by continuously declining groundwater levels, has spread over significant parts of the arid and semi-arid zones. This produces a wide range of problems (Van der Gun and Lipponen, 2010) and in many areas a lack of control threatens to result in a complete loss of the groundwater resource as an affordable source of irrigation and domestic water supply. In the more seriously affected aquifer zones, multi-annual groundwater level declines are typically in the range of one to several metres per year (Margat, 2008).

Prominent aquifers characterized by very significant long-term groundwater level declines are almost all located in the world's arid and semi-arid zones. In North America they include the Californian Central Valley (Famiglietti, 2009) and the High Plains aquifer (McGuire, 2009; Sophocleus, 2010) in the USA, as well as aquifers scattered over Mexico, including the Basin of Mexico aquifer (Carrera-Hernández and Gaskin, 2007). In Europe, the aquifers of the Upper Guadiana basin, the Segura basin and the volcanics of Gran Canaria and Tenerife can be mentioned, all belonging to Spain (Custodio, 2002; Llamas and Custodio, 2003; Molinero et al., 2008). Various zones of the huge non-renewable North-Western Sahara Aquifer System (Mamou et al., 2006; OSS, 2008) and the Nubian Sandstone Aquifer System in North Africa (Bakhbakhi, 2006) are affected by significant groundwater level declines. On the Arabian Peninsula, there are unprecedented trends of strongly declining groundwater levels in the Tertiary aquifer system of the Arabian Platform (mainly in Saudi Arabia; Brown, 2011) and in the Yemen Highland basins (Van der Gun et al., 1995). More eastward, the Varamin, Zarand and many other mountain basins of Iran suffer from steadily declining groundwater levels (Vali-Khodjeini, 1995; Motagh et al., 2008) as do parts of the extensive aquifer systems of the Indus basin, especially in the Indian states of Rajasthan,

Gujarat, Punjab, Haryana and Delhi (Rodell et al., 2009; Centre for Water Policy, 2005). The North China Plain aquifer has become notorious for severe groundwater level declines (Jia and You, 2010; Kendy et al., 2004; Sakura et al., 2003; Liu et al., 2001; Endersbee, 2006). Finally, continuous groundwater outflow through numerous artesian wells has produced groundwater level declines in excess of 100 m in parts of the Australian Great Artesian Basin (Habermehl, 2006). There are numerous other aquifers around the world where levels have declined or are still declining, with variable impacts on society and the environment.

New, useful information on the magnitude of groundwater storage depletion has become available in recent years. Konikow and Kendy (2005) estimate that about 700–800 km³ of groundwater has been depleted from aquifers in the USA during the twentieth century. Recent assessments by GRACE of the massive groundwater storage depletion observed in California's Central Valley and in north-western India have produced groundwater storage depletion estimates for some large groundwater systems (Rodell et al., 2009; Famiglietti et al., 2009; Tiwari et al., 2009). These estimates are shown in Table 36.3, together with estimated depletion rates for other large aquifer systems around the world. A model study by Wada et al. (2010) provides a global picture. The model estimates that by the year 2000 the world's groundwater was being depleted at a rate of 283 km³ per year, corresponding with 39% of the global abstraction rate as estimated by the authors[4]. The global pattern of groundwater depletion produced by this model matches existing knowledge on areas notorious for large and persistent groundwater level declines, such as in western North America, the Middle East, South and Central Asia and North China.

Depleting groundwater storage comes at a cost. This cost is not limited to a permanently higher unit cost of pumped groundwater, but may also include negative impacts on environmental and other *in situ* functions of the groundwater system, water quality degradation and even, in the long run, physical exhaustion of the aquifer. In some cases, however, there may be good reasons for planned groundwater depletion during a finite period and for accepting the associated negative impacts. This may be so in case of sudden disasters or if there is a need to buy time for a smooth transition to sustainable groundwater development after dynamic equilibrium conditions have been disturbed by exploding pumping intensities or by climate change.

FIGURE 36.3

Groundwater development stress indicator at country level (based on groundwater abstraction estimates for 2010)

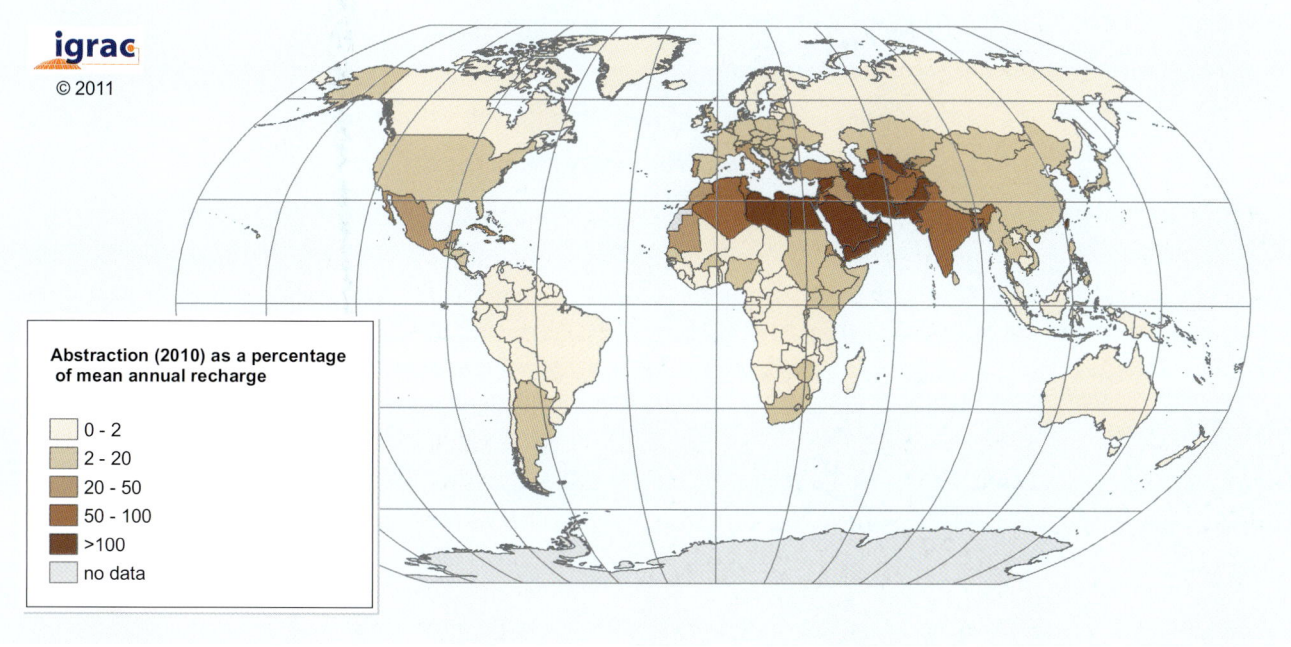

Source: Prepared by IGRAC for this chapter.

The risks and problems resulting from declining water levels vary from aquifer to aquifer, as do options and current practices for control. The situation on the High Plains is typical for numerous intensively exploited aquifers in the world, large and small. On the one hand there is a growing awareness of the need to stop depleting the resource; on the other hand, reducing groundwater abstraction to a sustainable level seems disastrous for the local economy and is not readily accepted by many individual stakeholders who risk to lose part of their income if groundwater abstractions are curtailed (Peck, 2007; McGuire, 2009; Sophocleous, 2010). A similar dilemma is present in the much smaller Sana'a basin in Yemen: effective partnerships with water users seem the only way to prevent catastrophic water shortages in the near future (Hydrosult et al., 2010). In the Umatilla basin (Oregon) a community-based approach is attempted to manage conflicts resulting from aquifer depletion (Jarvis, 2010). The Great Artesian Basin (Australia) is completely different: massive waste of water freely flowing from artesian wells can be eliminated by technical solutions. Although their implementation is expensive, these measures are less controversial because there is no explicit conflict of interests (Habermehl, 2006; Herczeg and Love, 2007; SKM, 2008; GABCC, 2009).

Shallow alluvial aquifers in arid and semi-arid zones form a special category. Due to their limited storage capacity, they are affected by seasonal rather than long-term depletion problems. Increasing abstraction rates shorten the period between the recharge season and the moment that wells run seasonally dry. Awareness of this phenomenon motivates people to conserve, even more so if springs and qanats[5] are linked to the system. Although groundwater depletion risks tend to be insignificant for groundwater systems in humid climates, control of groundwater levels may still be important, especially to prevent undesired environmental impacts, such as sea water intrusion, land subsidence and wetland degradation.

Fundamental options for controlling declining groundwater levels and storage are augmenting the groundwater resource and restricting its discharge. Resource augmentation measures are of a technical nature and include MAR techniques (artificial recharge) and land use management. Once decided upon, their implementation is relatively straightforward. Different types of measures are available for restricting pumping from aquifers (demand management). Enforcement of regulations (e.g. licensing well drilling and abstractions) based on groundwater legislation forms the first type. Alternatively, groundwater abstraction is discouraged selectively by financial disincentives, restricting energy supply or enhancing people's awareness on sustainability problems. A third type of measures for restricting groundwater outflow is the reduction of water losses at the well head and in transport (as in the Great Artesian Basin), or where it is used (e.g. by

TABLE 36.3

Groundwater depletion rates in large aquifer systems

Aquifer or region	Lateral extent km²	Rate of depletion (in recent years)		Period or year	Reference
		km³ per year	mm water per year[1]		
Renewable groundwater					
High Plains, USA	483 844	12.4	26	2000–2007	McGuire (2003, 2009)
Central Valley, California, USA	58 000	3.7	64	2003–2009	Famiglietti et al. (2009)
NW India	438 000	17.7	40	2003–2009	Rodell et al. (2009)
Northern India and surroundings	2 700 000	54	20	2003–2009	Tiwari et al. (2009)
North China Plain	131 000	6.12	47	2004	Jia and You (2010)
Non-renewable groundwater					
NW Sahara Aquifer System	1 019 000	1.5	1.5	2000	Margat (2008)
Great Artesian basin	1 700 000	0.311	0.2	1965–2000	Welsh (2006)

[1] Expressed as depth of an equivalent layer of water over the total horizontal extent of the aquifer system (scale-independent depletion indicator).

enhancing irrigation efficiency or recycling used water). Worldwide experiences show that successfully implementing measures is difficult, especially if existing withdrawals need to be reduced and alternative sources of water are not available. A common understanding of the problem among stakeholders and their firm commitment to support a chosen solution are crucial.

36.3.2 Groundwater quality and pollution

Although most groundwater around the globe at conventional well drilling depths is of good quality, it remains a major concern to protect this water against quality degradation and prevent poor quality groundwater from entering active freshwater cycles.

Trivial but important is the occurrence of brackish and saline groundwater, unfit for most intended groundwater uses. Most groundwater at great depths is saline. According to a recent global inventory (Van Weert et al., 2009), at shallow and intermediate depths (upper 500 m below surface, approximately) bodies of brackish or saline groundwater are found under 13% of the area of the continents. Only 8% of the identified brackish or saline bodies has an anthropogenic origin, with mineralization by irrigation return flows as the predominant mechanism. Risks of adding 'new' saline or brackish water to fresh groundwater domains are present near the coast (sea water intrusion), in zones of irrigated lands and at locations where liquid waste is dumped. As most of the saline or brackish groundwater bodies are immobile, it is a good strategy to keep them in that state. The same is true for bodies of groundwater with excessive concentrations of other natural constituents, such as fluoride or arsenic (Appelo, 2008).

Anthropogenic groundwater pollution and its control has been a major issue already for many decennia. It is a complex field due to the many sources of pollution, the myriad of substances that may be involved, large variations in vulnerability of aquifers, lack of monitoring data and uncertainties on impacts of excessive concentrations of pollutants, in addition to the usual dilemmas and problems in designing and effectively implementing programmes for protection and control (Morris et al., 2003; Schmoll et al., 2006). As groundwater usually is moving very slowly, groundwater pollution is almost irreversible or at least very persistent and, therefore, preventing and monitoring pollution influxes are basic components of any control strategy. In Europe, an important step forward is the new Groundwater Directive (GWD), introduced in 2006

as an integral part of the Water Framework Directive (WFD). GWD obliges European Union member states to take steps leading towards compliance with good chemical status criteria by the end of 2015. Reporting until 2010 reveals that 30% of all groundwater bodies is unlikely to achieve the envisaged 'good quality status' by 2015. However, GWD is flexible and offers the member states two options: adjusting the targets to more feasible values and delaying the compliance until 2021 or 2027 (European Commission, 2006 and 2008; European Environmental Agency, 2010).

Groundwater quality is also an important aspect in managed aquifer recharge. This management tool is in some cases even purposely used to improve or control water quality, making use of the aquifer's capacity for attenuation and decomposition of substances, or using the injected water to prevent excessive shrinking of exploited freshwater lenses overlaying saline groundwater. In all cases, however, there should be an awareness that managed aquifer recharge may also introduce risks, including groundwater pollution risks. Page et al. (2010) present an approach for assessing such risks.

In recent years there is growing attention for micro-pollutants, in particular for *pharmaceuticals and personal care products (PPCPs)* and for *endocrine disruptive compounds (EDCs)* (Schmoll et al., 2006; Musolff, 2009; SIWI, 2010). Disseminated by sewage, landfills and manure, these substances occur in natural waters in very low concentrations only (pg per L to ng per L range) and are not removed by conventional wastewater treatment plants. There is still much uncertainty on their possible impacts. Pharmaceuticals are designed to be bioactive and although in groundwater they are too diluted to provide therapeutic doses to humans and animals on the short-term, it is unknown what their effects may be after long-term exposure. EDCs – present in steroid-based food supplements, drugs, fungicides, herbicides and a range of household and industrial products – have the capacity to interfere with the functions of hormones that control growth and reproduction in humans and animals. PPCPs and EDCs are ubiquitous in surface water and shallow groundwater, and progress in analytical methods is likely to reveal them more widely in future years.

36.3.3 Climate change, climate variability and sea level rise

Climate change modifies groundwater recharge. Global hydrological models recently have produced estimates of mean annual global groundwater recharge, rang-ing from 12,700 km^3 per year (Döll and Fiedler, 2008) to 15,200 km^3 per year (Wada et al., 2010), which is at least three orders of magnitude smaller than the estimated total groundwater storage. These estimates and the corresponding spatial patterns, however, are based on mean climatic conditions prevailing during the second half of the twentieth century. For periods ahead, new estimates have to be produced, taking into account the possible influence of climate change. The latter has been subject of model investigations by Döll (2009), using four Intergovernmental Panel on Climate Change (IPCC) climate change scenarios and compar-ing the model outcomes with those of the reference period 1961–1990. She concludes that by the 2050s groundwater recharge is likely to have increased in the northern latitudes, but strongly decreased (by 30–70% or even more) in some currently semi-arid zones, in-cluding the Mediterranean, north-eastern Brazil and south-western Africa (Figure 36.4). Simulations for ten other climate scenarios produced different trends for some regions, except for the Mediterranean region and the high northern latitudes. The four simulated sce-narios in Figure 36.4 suggest a decrease of the long-term mean global groundwater recharge by more than 10%. Climate change is difficult to predict and at the scale of tens of years it is hard to distinguish it from the climate variability as produced by El Niño Southern Oscillation (ENSO), Pacific Decadal Oscillation (PDO), Atlantic Multidecadal Oscillation (AMO) and oth-er inter-annual to multi-decadal climate oscillations (Gurdak et al., 2009).

Climate change will not only change mean annual groundwater recharge and surface water flow, it is expected to also affect their distribution in time. Wet episodes may become more concentrated in time in many regions, while dry periods tend to become long-er. However, this will not significantly affect the water supply capacity of most groundwater systems, due to their buffer capacity. The buffers cannot prevent long-term groundwater availability to decrease if climate change reduces the mean recharge rates, but they fa-cilitate a gradual adaptation to new conditions.

Climate change will also modify water demands and water use. As the patterns of change in mean ground-water recharge shown in Figure 36.4 show positive correlation with patterns of change in mean precipi-tation and mean runoff as predicted by IPCC (Bates et al., 2008), it may be concluded that higher water demands will particularly affect areas where mean groundwater recharge is expected to decrease. This will produce severe problems, in the numerous small and shallow wadi aquifer systems scattered over arid and semi-arid regions probably more than anywhere else (Van der Gun, 2009). Nevertheless, it is expected that in many increasingly water-scarce areas around the world, dependency on groundwater will increase as the storage buffer renders groundwater more resil-ient than surface water sources. This is one more rea-son to manage groundwater carefully in such regions.

Ongoing and predicted sea level rise is largely caused by climate change, but progressive groundwater de-pletion contributes to it as well. Konikow and Kendy (2005) argue that the ultimate sink for groundwater removed from the aquifers by depletion is the oceans. They calculate that the total volume depleted from the High Plains aquifer in the USA during the twentieth century contributed 0.75 mm to sea level rise, which is 0.5% of the total sea level rise observed during the twentieth century. For all USA aquifers combined, the corresponding estimates are 2.03 mm and 1.3%, re-spectively (Konikow, 2009). Wada et al. (2010) esti-mated that global groundwater storage depletion by the year 2000 would have contributed 0.8 mm a year to sea level rise, which is 25% of the current rate of sea level rise according to the latest IPCC data. Assuming this estimated depletion to be reasonably reliable, thus a significant part of observed sea level rise is likely to be produced by causes other than climate change. In relation to groundwater, the main impact of sea level rise is intrusion of saline water into coastal aquifers. Worldwide, sea water intrusion is a real threat to coast-al aquifers and may have huge repercussions as a large percentage of the world's population lives in coast-al zones. A series of papers in a recent issue of the *Hydrogeology Journal* provides a geographic overview of saltwater–freshwater interactions in coastal aquifers (Barlow, 2010; Bocanegra et al., 2010; Custodio, 2010; Steyl and Dennis, 2010; White and Falkland, 2010). A recent study on the impact of sea level rise on coastal groundwater in the Netherlands (Oude Essink et al., 2010) concluded that expected sea level rise will affect the Dutch coastal groundwater systems and trigger saline water intrusion, but only in a narrow zone within 10 km from the coastline and the main lowland rivers.

36.3.4 Transboundary groundwater resources
Behaviour and functions of transboundary aqui-fers do not differ from those of other aquifers, but

FIGURE 36.4

Global pattern of estimated mean groundwater recharge in 1961–1990 and percentage change from 1961–1990 to 2041–2070 for four Intergovernmental Panel on Climate Change (IPCC) scenarios

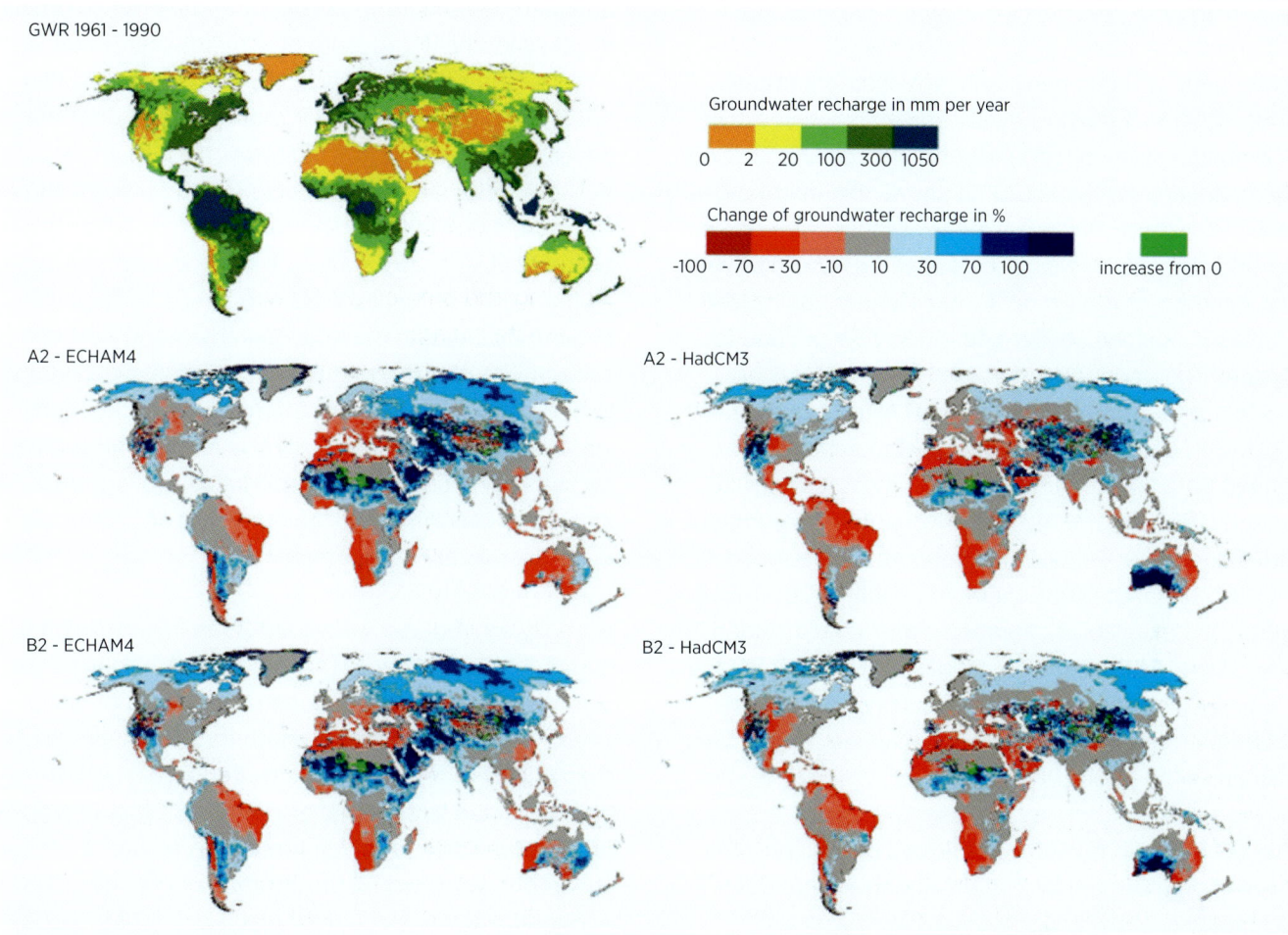

Note: Climate scenarios were computed using climate models ECHAM4 (Röckner et al., 1996) and HadCM3 (Gordon et al., 2000) on the basis of IPCC greenhouse gas emission scenarios A2 (emissions increase during 1990–2050 from 11 to 25 Gt C per year) and B2 (from 11 to 16 Gt C per year), respectively.
Source: Döll (2009, fig. 1, p. 6).

administrative borders that cross them render coordinated development and management of their groundwater resources more complex. Borders complicate the acquisition of consistent information on the entire aquifer, while allocating aquifer segments to different jurisdictions is at odds with the transboundary effects of pressures within each of these segments. Information gaps, conflicting interests and lack of coordination across the boundaries easily lead to problems that are avoidable if transboundary aquifer management approaches are adopted.

Enormous progress has been made since transboundary aquifers were put on the international agenda at the end of the twentieth century. Regional inventories and characterization of transboundary aquifer systems

have been conducted under the umbrella of the United Nations Economic Commission for Europe (UNECE) in Europe (UNECE, 1999) as well as in the Caucasus, Central Asia and South-East Europe (UNECE, 2007); and under the ISARM programme in the Americas (UNESCO, 2007 and 2008), Africa (UNESCO, 2010a) and Asia (UNESCO, 2010b). The map Transboundary Aquifers of the World (IGRAC, 2009), showing the locations and selected properties of 318 identified transboundary aquifers in the world, and ISARM's Atlas of Transboundary Aquifers (Puri and Aureli, 2009) are both largely based on the outcomes of these regional activities.

At the level of individual aquifers, important projects have been carried out or are ongoing in the framework of GEF's IW focal area. As an example, the

Guaraní Aquifer project (Argentina, Brazil, Paraguay and Uruguay) developed agreed transboundary aquifer management instruments and the four countries involved signed in August 2010 an agreement on this aquifer system.

Institutional arrangements and legal instruments are integral parts of transboundary aquifer resources management. A study on groundwater in international law by Burchi and Mechlem (2005) shows that international law until recently has rarely taken account of groundwater and that only few legal instruments exist exclusively designed for groundwater: for the Geneva aquifer, the Nubian Sandstone aquifer and the NW Sahara aquifer system. The development of such instruments is expected to be catalysed by the Draft Articles on the Law of Transboundary Aquifers, jointly elaborated by the United Nations International Law Commission (UNILC) and the UNESCO International Hydrological Programme (IHP) during 2002–2008 and adopted by resolution A/RES/63/124 of the UN General Assembly in December 2008 (Stephan, 2009). Important principles included in these Draft Articles are the obligation to cooperate and exchange information, the no-harm principle and the intention to protect, preserve and manage the aquifer resources.

The UN General Assembly reaffirmed in its sixty-sixth session on 9 December 2011 the importance of transboundary aquifers and the related Draft Articles. It adopted a resolution in which States are encouraged to make proper arrangements for transboundary aquifer management and UNESCO-IHP to continue its related scientific and technical support to the States. In addition, the General Assembly decided to put 'The Law of Transboundary Aquifers' on the provisional agenda of its sixty-eight session, in order to examine - among others - the final form to be given to the Draft Articles. The momentum produced by all ongoing transboundary aquifer activities are transforming transboundary aquifers from potential problems into opportunities for international cooperation.

Conclusions

Groundwater – by far the largest volume of unfrozen fresh water on Earth – is a natural resource of enormous importance, but it is hidden to the eye and poorly known and understood among the general public. Hydrogeologists and other scientists have made significant progress over the last few decades in collecting information on the world's groundwater systems, understanding their role and functions, observing changes over time, and identifying options for enhancing benefits from groundwater as well as threats that need to be addressed to safeguard the resource's sustainability. Gradually it has become clear how strongly the development and state of groundwater systems are interrelated with other systems and external drivers. It has also become clear that the value of groundwater is not limited to its abstraction for multiple uses, but includes a range of valuable in situ services, such as support of wetlands, springs, baseflows and stability of the land surface. As a result, groundwater resources management has evolved into a multi-disciplinary activity, addressing multiple objectives and not only focusing on physical systems and technical measures, but also paying significant attention to demography, socio-economics and governance. Modern groundwater resources management approaches incorporate the principles of conjunctive management and integrated water resources management.

Globally aggregated values and shares in total water supply are indicators of the relevance of groundwater, but it is worth looking beyond the volumes of water used. Without groundwater with its storage buffer, many parts of the dryer regions on Earth would be inhabitable due to seasonal or permanent lack of fresh water, and water supply in rural areas distant from permanent streams would be extremely expensive. The economic returns per unit of water used for irrigation and in other economic water use sectors tend to be higher for groundwater than for other sources of water because of groundwater's higher reliability.

Groundwater is in transition throughout the world. Current stresses on groundwater systems are in many parts of the world without precedent in history, as a result of the silent revolution and of progressive pollution inherent to modern lifestyles. These stresses are increasing and produce considerable risk and uncertainty. Will there be enough groundwater in the future, and will its quality meet the requirements of intended uses? After defining how to strike a balance between using and conserving groundwater, how should a corresponding behaviour of people be established in relation to this open-access resource that often is considered as common property? How should the inflow of anthropogenic pollutants into aquifers be reduced? Such questions pose enormous challenges to the groundwater community, water managers and local stakeholders. Solutions have to be tailored to the specific conditions of each area. Basic to the success of these solutions are a good understanding of the trade-offs between groundwater abstraction and other services of the aquifer, and the selection of measures compatible with the socio-political setting. The risks are in principle manageable, but their control is not easy and requires significant management efforts.

The buffer capacity of groundwater systems, on the other hand, offers unique opportunities for the overall reduction of risk and uncertainty regarding water availability, now and in the future. Changes over time of the availability and quality of groundwater proceed very slowly compared to those of the components of the water cycle with smaller mean residence times, and the predictability of these changes is much better for groundwater. This enables groundwater to bridge prolonged dry periods and allows time to smoothly adjust overall water use in areas where reduced levels of sustainable water availability are expected to result from intensification of water use upflow or from climate change.

||||||||||||||||||||||||||||||||||||||||||||||||||||||||||||||||||||||||||||||||

Notes

1   In June 2010 NASA and DLR signed an agreement to continue the current GRACE mission through 2015 (NASA, 2010).

2   Most values mentioned in this paragraph are globally aggregated or averaged and therefore cannot be used to draw conclusions on conditions at a local or regional scale.

3   Siebert et al. (2010) estimate global consumptive irrigation water use to be 1277 km^3 per year, being 48% of the global agricultural water withdrawals. Their estimate for the share of groundwater in this figure (545 km^3 per year), is fairly consistent with the estimated global groundwater abstraction for irrigation, taking into account irrigation water losses.

4   The accuracy of this global depletion figure obtained by modelling is significantly lower than most of the estimates shown in Table 36.3. While the latter are based on observation, the global figure is affected by groundwater abstraction data of variable quality, highly simplifying model assumptions and averaging over large spatial units.

5   A qanat is a slightly sloping tunnel, designed for tapping groundwater and conveying it under gravity, often over a large distance, into an open section, from where it can be diverted for use.

||||||||||||||||||||||||||||||||||||||||||||||||||||||||||||||||||||||||||||||||

References

Alcamo, J., Döll, P., Henrichs, T., Kaspar, F., Lehner, B., Rösch, T. and Siebert, S. 2003. Global estimates of water withdrawals and availability under current and future 'business-as-usual' conditions. *Hydrological Sciences Journal*, Vol. 48, No. 3, pp 339–48.

Appelo, T. (ed),   2008. *Arsenic in Groundwater: A World Problem.* Proceeding Seminar Utrecht, 29 November 2006. Netherlands National Committee of the IAH (NNC-IAH), Utrecht, The Netherlands.

AQUASTAT. On-line database of FAO. http://www.fao.org/nr/water/aquastat/data/query/index.html (Accessed 28 August 2011.)

Bakhbahki, M. 2006. Nubian Sandstone Aquifer System. In: Foster, S., and Loucks, D. P. 2006. *Non-Renewable Groundwater Resources. A Guidebook on Socially-sustainable Management for Water-policy Makers.* UNESCO-IHP, IHPVI, Series on Groundwater No. 10. UNESCO, Paris, France, pp 75–81.

Barlow, P. M. and Reichard, E. G. 2010. Saltwater intrusion in coastal regions of North America. *Hydrogeology Journal,* Vol. 18, No. 1, pp 247–60.

Bates, B., Kundzewicz, Z., Wu, S. and Palutikof, J. (ed.) 2008. *Climate Change and Water.* IPCC Technical Paper VI, IPCC Secretariat, Geneva.

Bocanegra, E., Cardoso da Silva, G., Custodio, E., Manzano, M. and Montenegro, S. 2010. State of knowledge of coastal aquifer management in South America. *Hydrogeology Journal,* Vol. 18, No. 1, pp 261–68.

Bonsor, H. C., Mansour, M. M., MacDonald, A. M., Hughes, A. G., Hipkin, R. G. and Bedada, T. 2010. Interpretation of GRACE data of the Nile Basin using a groundwater recharge model. *Hydrology and Earth System Sciences,* 7, pp. 4501–33.

Brown, L. R. 2011. Falling water tables and shrinking harvests. *World on the Edge: How to Prevent Environmental and Economic Collapse,* Earth Policy Institute, Washington DC, USA, pp. 21–33.

Burchi, S. and Mechlem, K. 2005. *Groundwater in International Law. Compilation of Treaties and Other Legal Instruments.* FAO Legislative Study 86. FAO, Rome, Italy, and UNESCO, Paris, France.

Carrera-Hernández, J. J. and Gaskin, S.J. 2007. The Basin of Mexico aquifer system: regional groundwater level dynamics and database development. *Hydrogeology Journal,* Vol. 15, No.8, pp. 1577–90.

Centre for Water Policy. 2005. *Some Critical Issues on Groundwater in India.* CWP, Delhi, India.

Chen, J. L., Wilson, C. R., Tapley, B. D., Yang, Z. L. and Niu, G. Y. 2009. 2005 drought event in the Amazon River basin as measured by GRACE and estimated by climate models. *Journal of Geophysical Research,* Vol. 114, B05404, pp 9.

Custodio, E. 2002. Aquifer overexploitation: what does it mean? *Hydrogeology Journal,* Vol. 10, No. 2, pp. 254–77.

----. 2010. Coastal aquifers of Europe: an overview. *Hydrogeology Journal,* Vol. 18, No. 1, pp. 269–80.

Dillon, P., Pavelic, P., Page, D., Beringen, H, and Ward, J. 2009. *Managed Aquifer Recharge: An Introduction.* Waterlines Report Series No. 13, Australian Government, National Water Commission, Canberra, Australia.

Döll, P. 2009. Vulnerability to the impact of climate change on renewable groundwater resources: a global-scale assessment. *Environmental Research Letters doi:10.1088/1748-9326/4/3/035006.*

Döll, P. and Fiedler, K. 2008. Global-scale modelling of groundwater recharge. *Hydrology and Earth System Sciences,* 12, pp 863–885.

Endersbee, L. 2006. World's water wells are drying up! EIR, Vol. 33, No. 10, 10 March 2006, pp. 22–29. http://www.larouchepub.com/other/2006/3310endersbee_water.html

European Commission. 2006. Directive 2006/118/EC of the European Parliament of the Council of 12 December 2006 on the protection of groundwater against pollution and deterioration. *Official Journal of the European Union,* 27 December 2006.

––––. 2008. *Groundwater Protection in Europe. The new Groundwater Directive – Consolidating the EU Regulatory Framework.* European Commission, Brussels, Belgium.

European Environmental Agency. 2010. *The European Environment, State and Outlook 2010 – Freshwater quality.* EEA, Copenhagen, Denmark.

EUROSTAT. On-line database of the European Commission. http://epp.eurostat.ec.europa.eu/portal/page/portal/eurostat/home/ (Accessed 28 August 2011.)

Famiglietti, J., Swenson, S. and Rodell, M. 2009. *Water Storage Changes in California's Sacramento and San Joaquin River Basins, Including Groundwater Depletion in the Central Valley.* PowerPoint presentation, American Geophysical Union Press Conference, 14 December 2009, CSR, GFZ, DLR and JPL.

GABCC (Great Artesian Basin Coordinating Committee). 2008. *Great Artesian Basin Strategic Management Plan: Progress and Achievements to 2008.* GABCC Secretariat, Manuka, Australia.

Gordon, C., Cooper, C., Senior, C. A., Banks, H., Gregory, J. M., Johns, T. C., Mitchel, J. F. B. and Wood, R. A. 2000. The simulation of SST, sea ice extents and ocean heat transports in a version of the Hadley Centre coupled model without flux adjustments. *Climate Dynamics* Vol. 16, No. 2–3, pp. 147–168.

Gurdak, J. J., Hanson, R. T. and Green, T. R. 2009. *Effects of Climate Variability and Change on Groundwater Resources in the United States.* U. S. Geological Survey Factsheet 2009–3074. USGS, Office of Global Change, Idaho Falls, Idaho, USA.

GWP (Global Water Partnership). 2011. *What is IWRM?* http://www.gwp.org/en/The-Challenge/What-is-IWRM/ (Accessed 28 February 2011.)

Habermehl, M., 2006. The Great Artesian Basin, Australia. In: Foster, S. and D. Loucks, 2006. Non-renewable Groundwater Resources. *A Guidebook on Socially Sustainable Management for Water-policy Makers.* UNESCO-IHP, IHPVI, Series on Groundwater No. 10, pp. 82–88(103). UNESCO, Paris, France.

Herczeg, A. L. and Love, A. J. 2007. *Review of Recharge Mechanisms for the Great Artesian Basin.* Report to the Great Artesian Basin Coordinating Committee, CSIRO, Australia.

Hydrosult, TNO and WEC. 2010. *Hydro-geological and Water Resources Monitoring and Investigations.* Project report, Sana'a, Republic of Yemen.

IGME (Instituto Geológico y Minero de España). 2006. *The Alicante Declaration.* International Symposium on Groundwater Sustainability. Alicante, Spain, 23–27 January 2006. http://aguas.igme.es/igme/isgwas/ing/The%20Alicante%20Declaration%20-%20Final%20Document.pdf

IGRAC (International Groundwater Resources Assessment Centre). 2009. *Transboundary Aquifers of the World.* Map at scale 1: 50 M. Special edition for the 5th World Water Forum, Istanbul, March 2009.

IGRAC (International Groundwater Resources Assessment Centre). 2010. Global *Groundwater Information System (GGIS).* http://www.igrac.net (Accessed 23 November 2010.)

Jarvis, T. 2010. Community-based approaches to conflict management: Umatilla County critical groundwater areas, Umatilla County, Oregon, USA: NEGOTIATE Toolkit: case studies. In *NEGOTIATE – Reaching Fairer and More Effective Water Agreements.* International Union for Conservation of Nature (IUCN), Gland, Switzerland. http://cmsdata.iucn.org/downloads/northwestern.pdf

Jia, Y., and J. You. 2010. *Sustainable Groundwater Management in the North China Plain: Main Issues, Practices and Foresights.* Extended abstracts XXXVIIIrd IAH Congress, Krakow, Poland, 12–17 Sept 2010, no 517, pp 855–862.

Kendy, L., Zhang, Y., Liu, C., Wang, J. and Steenhuis, T. 2004. Groundwater recharge from irrigated cropland in the North China Plain: case study of Luancheng County, Hebei Province, 1949–2000. *Hydrological Processes* 18, pp. 2289–302.

Konikow, L., 2009. *Groundwater Depletion: A National Assessment and Global Perspective.* The Californian Colloquium on Water, 5 May 2009. http://youtube.com/watch?v=Q5s0Uit8V6s

Konikow L. and Kendy, E. 2005. Groundwater depletion: a global problem. *Hydrogeology Journal,* Vol. 13, pp. 317–20.

Liu, Ch., Yu, J. and Kendy, E. 2001. Groundwater exploitation and its impact on the environment in the North China Plain. International Water Resource Association. *Water International,* Vol. 26, No. 2, pp. 265–72.

Llamas, M. R. and Custodio, E. 2003. Intensive use of groundwater: a new situation which demands proactive action. Llamas, M.R. and Custodio, E. (eds) *Intensive Use of Groundwater: Challenges and Opportunities.* Balkema Publishers, Dordrecht.

Llamas, M. R. and Garrido, A. 2007. Lessons from intensive groundwater use in Spain: Economic and social benefits and conflicts. Giordano, M. and Vilholth, K. G. (eds). 2007. *The Agricultural Groundwater Revolution: Comprehensive Assessment of Water Management in Agriculture.* CABI, Wallingford, UK, pp. 266–95.

Llamas, M. and Martínez-Santos, P. 2005. Intensive groundwater use: a silent revolution that cannot be ignored. *Water Science and Technology Series,* Vol. 51, No. 8, pp. 167–74.

Mamou, A., Besbes, M., Abdous, B., Latrech, D. and Fezzani, C. 2006. North Western Sahara Aquifer System. Foster, S. and D. Loucks. 2006. *Non-renewable Groundwater Resources. A Guidebook on Socially Sustainable Management for Water-policy Makers.* UNESCO-IHP, IHPVI, Series on Groundwater No. 10, UNESCO, Paris, France, pp. 68–74.

Margat, J. 2008. *Les eaux souterraines dans le monde.* Paris, BGRM Editions/UNESCO.

McGuire, V. L. 2003. *Water-level Changes in the High Plains Aquifer, Predevelopment to 2001, 1999 to 2000, and 2000 to 2001.* USGS Fact Sheet FS-078-03, 4p, USGS, Reston, Virginia, USA.

––––. 2009. *Water-level Changes in the High Plains Aquifer, Predevelopment to 2007, 2005–06 and 2006-07.* Scientific Investigations Report 2009-5019, USGS, Reston, Virginia.

Moiwo, J. P., Yang, Y., Li, H., Han, S. and Hu, Y. 2009. Comparison if GRACE with in siu hydrological measurement data shows storage depletion in Hai River basin, Northern China. *Water SA,* Vo. 35, No. 5, pp. 663–70.

Molinero, J., Custodio, E., Sahuquillo, A. and Llamas, M. R. 2008. *Groundwater in Spain: Overview and Management Practices.* IAHR International Groundwater Symposium, Istanbul, June 18-20, 2008. CD of proceedings.

Morris, B. L., Lawrence, A. R., Chilton, J., Adams, B., Calow, R. and Klinck, B. A. 2003. *Groundwater and its Susceptibility to Degradation: A Global Assessment of the Problem and Options for Management.* Early Warning and Assessment Report Series, RS 03-03, UNEP, Nairobi, Kenya.

Motagh, M., Walter, T. R., Sahrifi, M., Fielding, E., Schenk, A., Anderssohn, J. and Zschau, J. 2008. Land subsidence in Iran caused by widespread water reservoir overexploitation. *Geophysical Research Letters,* Vol. 35, L16403.

Muskett, R. D. and Romanovsky, V. E. 2009. Groundwater storage changes in arctic permafrost watersheds from GRACE and in situ measurements. *Environmenal Research Letters,* 4 (2009) 045009, pp. 1–8.

Musolff, A. 2009. Micropollutants: challenges in hydrogeology. *Hydrogeology Journal,* Vol. 17, No. 4, pp 763–66.

NASA (National Aeronautics and Space Administration). 2010. *NASA and DLR Sign Agreement to Continue Grace Mission Through 2015.* News and Features. Jet Propulsion Laboratory, California Institute of Technology, NASA. 10 June 2010. http://www.jpl.nasa.gov/news/news.cfm?release=2010-195

Oude Essink, G.H.P., van Baaren, E. S. and de Louw, P.G.B. 2010. Effects of climate change on coastal groundwater systems: A modelling study in the Netherlands. *Water Resources Research,* Vol. 46, W00F04, pp. 1–16.

Page, D., Dillon, P., Vanderzalm, J., Toze, S., Sidhu, J., Barry, K., Levett, K., Kremer, S., and Regel, R. 2010. Risk Assessment of aquifer storage transfer and recovery with urban stormwater for producing water of a potable quality. *Journal of Environmental Quality,* Vol. 39 (6), pp. 2029–39.

Peck, J. 2007. Groundwater management in the High Plains aquifer in the USA: Legal Problems and Innovations. *The Agricultural Groundwater Revolution: Opportunities and Threats to Development.* M. Giordano and K.G. Villholth, IWMI, (eds), Colombo, Sri Lanka. CABI, Wallingford, UK, 2007, pp 296–319.

Puri, S. and Aureli, A. 2010. *Atlas of Transboundary Aquifers,* UNESCO-IHP ISARM Programme, Paris, France.

Röckner, E., Arpe, K., Bengtsson, L., Chistoph, M., Claussen, M., Dümenil, L., Esch, M., Giogetta, M., Schlese, U. and Schulzweida, U. 1996. *The Atmospheric General Circulation Model ECHAM-4: Model Description and Simulation of Present Day Climate.* MPI-Report No 218. MPI für Meteorologie, Hamburg, Germany.

Rodell, M., Velicogna, I. and Famiglietti, J. S. 2009. Satellite-based estimates of groundwater depletion in India. *Nature,* Vol. 460, pp. 999–1002.

Sahara and Sahel Observatory (OSS). 2008. *The North-Western Sahara Aquifer System: Concerted Management of a Transboundary Water Basin.* Synthesis Collection, No. 1. OSS, Tunis, Tunisia.

Sakura, Y., Tang, C., Yokishioka, R., Ishibashi, H. 2003. Intensive use of groundwater in some areas of China and Japan. Llamas, M.R. and Custodio, E. (eds) *Intensive Use of Groundwater: Challenges and Opportunities.* Balkema Publishers. Dordrecht, pp. 337–53.

Schmoll, O., Howard, G., Chilton, J. and Chorus, I. 2006. *Protecting Groundwater for Health – Managing the Quality of Drinking-water Sources.* WHO Drinking-water Quality Series. WHO, Geneva, Switzerland, and IWA, London, UK.

Siebert, S., Burke, J., Faures, J., Frenken, K., Hoogeveen, J., Döll, P. and Portmann, T. 2010. Groundwater use for irrigation – a global inventory. *Hydrology and Earth System Sciences,* 14, pp. 1863–80

Sinclair Knight Merz (SKM). 2008. *Great Artesian Basin Sustainability Initiative. Mid-term Review of Phase 2.* Report prepared for Australian Government, Department of the Environment and Water Resources. SKM, Brisbane, Australia.

Shah, T. 2007. The Groundwater Economy of South Asia: An Assessment of Size, Significance and Socio-ecological Impacts. *The agricultural groundwater revolution: opportunities and threats to development.* M. Giordano and K.G. Villholth (eds). IWMI, Colombo, Sri Lanka. CABI, Wallingford, UK, 2007, pp 7–36.

Shah, T., Burke, J. and Villholth, K. 2007. Groundwater: A global assessment of scale and significance. Comprehensive Assessment of Water Management in Agriculture, *Water for Food, Water for Life: A Comprehensive Assessment of Water Management in Agriculture.* London/Colombo, Earthscan/International Water Management Institute, pp. 395–423.

SIWI (Stockholm International Water Institute). 2010. *The Malin Falkenmark Seminar: Emerging Pollutants in Water Resources – A New Challenge to Water Quality. World Water Week 2010.* http://www.worldwaterweek.org/sa/node.asp?node=750&sa_content_url=%2Fplugins%2FEventFinder%2Fevent%2Easp&id=3&event=239 (Accessed 4 March 2011)

Sophocleous, M. 2010. Review: groundwater management practices, challenges and innovations in the High Plains aquifer, USA – lessons and recommended actions. *Hydrogeology Journal,* Vol. 18, No. 3, pp. 559–75.

Stephan, R. M. 2009. Transboundary aquifers: Managing a vital resource. *The UNILC Draft Articles on the Law of Transboundary Aquifers.* UNESCO-IHP, Paris, France.

Steyl, G., and Dennis, I. 2010. Review of coastal-area aquifers in Africa. *Hydrogeology Journal,* Vol. 18, No. 1, pp 217–26.

Tiwari, V., Wahr, J. and Swenson, S. 2009. Dwindling groundwater resources in northern India, from satellite gravity observations. *Geophysical Research Letters,* Vol. 36, L18401.

Todd, D.K. 1959. *Ground Water Hydrology.* New York and London. John Wiley & Sons.

UNECE (United Nations Economic Commission for Europe). 1999. *Inventory of Transboundary Groundwater.* UN-ECE Task Force on Monitoring and Assessment, Vol. 1, RIZA, Lelystad, The Netherlands, ISBN: 9036953154.

––––. 2007. *Our Waters: Joining Hands Across Borders. First Assessment of Transboundary Rivers, Lakes and groundwaters.* United Nations, New York and Geneva.

UNESCO (United Nations Educational, Scientific and Cultural Organization). 2007. *Sistemas acuíferos transfronterizos en las Américas.* UNESCO-PHI and OEA, Series ISARM Americas no.1, Montevideo/Washington.

––––. 2008. *Marco legal e institucional en la gestión de los sistemas acuíferos transfronterizos en las Américas.* UNESCO-PHI and OEA, Series ISARM Americas no.2, Montevideo/Washington.

––––. 2010a. *Managing Shared Aquifer Resources in Africa.* Proceedings of theThird International ISARM Conference, Tripoli, 25–27 May 2008. IHP-VII Series on Groundwater No. 1, UNESCO, Paris, France.

––––. 2010b. *Transboundary Aquifer in Asia.* IHP-VII Technical Document in Hydrology, UNESCO, Beijing and Jakarta.

Vali-Khodjeini, A. 1995. Human impacts on groundwater resources in Iran. *Man's Influence on Freshwater Ecosystems and Water Use.* Proceedings of a Boulder Symposium. IAHS Publ. No. 230.

Van der Gun, J. A.M. 2009. Climate change and alluvial aquifers in arid regions: Examples from Yemen. *Climate Change and Adaptation in the Water Sector.* CPWC, Earthscan, London, UK, pp 143–58.

Van der Gun, J.A.M. and Abdul Aziz Ahmed. 1995. *The Water Resources of Yemen. A Summary and Digest of Available Information.* WRAY project, Delft and Sana'a.

Van der Gun, J. and Lipponen, A. 2010. Reconciling storage depletion due to groundwater pumping with sustainability. *Sustainability, Special Issue Sustainability of Groundwater,* 2(11).

Van Weert, F., van der Gun, J. and Reckman, J. 2009. *Global Overview of Saline Groundwater Occurrence and Genesis.* IGRAC, Report nr GP-2009-1, Utrecht, The Netherlands.

Wada, Y., Van Beek, L. P. H., Van Kempen, C. M., Reckman, G. W., Vasak, S. and Bierkens, M. F. P. 2010. Global depletion of groundwater resources. *Geophysical Research Letters,* Vol. 37, L20402.

Welsh, W. D. 2006. *Great Artesian Basin Transient Groundwater Model.* Australian Government, Bureau of Rural Sciences, Canberra, Australia.

White, I. and Falkland, T. 2010. Management of fresh-water lenses on small Pacific Islands. *Hydrogeology Journal,* Vol. 18, No. 1, pp. 227–46.

WHYMAP (World-wide Hydrogeological Mapping and Assessment Programme). 2008. *Groundwater Resources of the World,* Map 1: 25 M. UNESCO, IAH, BGR, CGMW, IAEA. http://www.whymap.org/whymap/EN/Downloads/Global_maps/gwrm_2008_pdf.pdf?__blob=publicationFile&v=2

WWAP (World Water Assessment Programme). 2009. *World Water Development Report 3: Water in a Changing World.* Paris/London, UNESCO/Earthscan.

BOXES, TABLES AND FIGURES

TABLES

FIGURES